The Essential Guide
to Pricing Businesses
and Franchises

2016
BUSINESS
REFERENCE GUIDE

Copyright © 2016 Business Brokerage Press
businessbrokeragepress.com
800.239.5085

Introduction

Important Note to the Reader
"This publication is designed to provide accurate and authoritative information with regard to the subject matter covered. It is sold with the understanding that the authors, editors and publisher are not engaged in rendering legal, accounting or other professional advice. If legal advice or other expert assistance is required, the services of a competent professional should be sought."

Copyright © 2016 Business Brokerage Press
All rights reserved. No part of this publication may be reproduced or transmitted in any form or by any means, electronic or mechanical, including photocopy, recording or any information storage and retrieval system, without permission in writing from the publisher.

Introduction

Notes to the *2016 Business Reference Guide* and the *Business Reference Guide Online*

Just a few explanations concerning the information in this year's *Guide*:

- Some quotes in the sections may be grammatically incorrect or some words improperly capitalized. We attempt to remain true to the original source and make changes only to improve readability.

- Due to space requirements, some information, such as General Information and Advantages and Disadvantages, is not included in the hard copy *Guide*, but is available in the online edition.

Pricing Methods

Pricing methods such as multiples of SDE, EBIT and EBITDA all have two things in common: each requires that the actual earnings be calculated and then a multiple based on many factors relating to the business must also be calculated. Multiplying the two should then produce the price for that business. Unfortunately, these methods are based on the figures being calculated by the person doing the pricing.

The other method used in the *Guide* is the rule of thumb that calls for a multiple of sales. The big advantage to this method is that it doesn't call for calculating the figures as the methods above require. One simply takes the total annual sales (less sales taxes) and multiplies it by a percentage that "people in the know" are comfortable with, based on their knowledge and experience. In many cases there is a universal rule of thumb for the multiple based on many transactions. And, the annual sales of a business are usually a provable figure.

An argument could be made, especially in very small businesses, that the owner could be "taking money off the top," thus reducing sales. However, unless the owner is really "stealing" from the business, small amounts shouldn't influence the price dramatically.

The purpose of the above information is to show that, although multipliers may stay about the same, the final result is based on figures that do reflect the impact of the economy. Sales are down and costs go up, especially in relation to sales. Therefore, we are comfortable with the final pricing results. As we keep saying, rules of thumb are just that. The purpose in supplying Benchmark and other data is so the user can adjust the rule of thumb up or down based on such information.

Introduction

The pricing of businesses is based on the sales and earnings, for the most part. However, another major factor in pricing a business is whether the seller will finance a portion of the selling price. If the seller won't finance a portion of the selling price, the price will generally be lower than if the seller will finance a portion of the selling price. The rule is usually the lower the down payment, the higher the full price. And, the seller who demands an all cash transaction will receive, in most cases, a lower full case.

The price of a business is ultimately what someone will pay for it—it is market driven. Or, as the old saying goes, the price is what a buyer will pay and that the seller will accept.

Using the Rules of Thumb

Despite all of the caveats about using rules of thumb in pricing businesses, they are commonly used to do just that. The answer is quite simple—the rules are very easy to use and almost seem too simplistic. But how accurate are they? A lot more accurate than many people think. They may supply a quick fix, but if used properly, rules of thumb can come pretty close to what the business will ultimately sell for.

Rules of thumb in the *Guide* usually come in two formats. The most commonly used rule of thumb is simply a percentage of the annual sales, or, better yet, the last 12 months of sales/revenues. For example, if the total sales were $100,000 for last year, and the multiple for the particular business is 40 percent of annual sales, then the price based on the rule of thumb would be $40,000.

Quite a few experts have said that revenue multiples are likely to be more reliable than earnings multiples. The reason is that most multiples of earnings are based on add-backs to the earnings, which can be a judgment call, as can the multiple. Sales or revenues are essentially a fixed figure. One might want to subtract sales taxes if they have not been deducted, but the sales are the sales. The only judgment then is the percentage. When it is supplied by an expert, the percentage multiplier becomes much more reliable.

The second rule of thumb used in the *Guide* is a multiple of earnings. In small businesses, the multiple is used against what is termed Seller's Discretionary Earnings (SDE). SDE is also called Seller's or Owner's Cash Flow and similar names. It is usually based on a multiple (generally between 1 and 5), and this number is then used as a multiple against the earnings of the business. Many of the entries also contain a multiple of EBIT and/or EBITDA.

Introduction

The terms used to express earnings are as follows:

EBDIT (EBITDA)—Earnings before depreciation (and other noncash charges), interest, and taxes

EBDT—Earnings before depreciation (and other noncash charges), and taxes

EBIT—Earnings before interest and taxes

SDE—Seller's Discretionary Earnings

Source: Pratt et al., *Valuing a Business*

Seller's Discretionary Earnings (SDE): "The earnings of a business enterprise prior to the following items:
- income taxes
- non-recurring income and expenses
- non-operating income and expenses
- depreciation and amortization
- interest expense or income
- owner's total compensation for one owner/operator, after adjusting the total compensation of all owners to market value."

Source: The International Business Brokers Association (IBBA)

The above definition of Seller's Discretionary Earnings, although completely accurate, is a bit confusing. If you change the words "prior to the" and substitute the word "plus" it may be easier to understand. We would also suggest that the highest salary be used in the calculation of SDE. The reason is that we must assume that the buyer will replace the highest compensated employee or owner—at least for the SDE calculation. We should also add that this is our definition and not necessarily that of the IBBA.

Keep in mind that the multiples for the different earnings acronyms mentioned above will be different than the multiple of SDE, which, as mentioned, generally is a number between 0 and 5. The rules contained in the *Guide* are specific about what is being used. It will say 2.5 times SDE or 4 times EBIT, etc.

The Basics

The businesses are arranged alphabetically. In some cases, the business may go by two name descriptions, for example, gas stations and service stations. We use the one that we feel is the most common, and we try to cross-reference them. If you can't find what you are looking for, see if it is listed under another name. If there is a particular franchise you are working on and it's not in the rules,

Introduction

check the type of business for more information. For example, if the franchise is an ice cream store, check the name of the franchise; if it's not there, go to ice cream stores and other ice cream franchises. If the business is not listed, find a similar business and start there.

Name/Type of Business

The information just below the type of business is the approximate number of businesses of that type in the U.S. Where there was an IBISWorld report, we generally use that number. In the top section where the type of business is located, in some cases we have rounded the number of businesses for ease of use.

IBISWorld provides excellent reports on many, many different businesses: www.ibisworld.com. Most of these reports are well over 20 pages and are not only extensive, but most informative. They are well worth the price.

We have also provided the Standard Industrial (SIC) Classification code and the North American Industry Classification System (NAICS). For NAICS and SIC codes, go to www.naics.com.

The Rules of Thumb

The price, based on the rule of thumb, does not include inventory (unless it specifically states that it does), or real estate, and other balance-sheet items such as cash and accounts receivable. We have noticed an increase in Industry Experts telling us that inventory is included in the multiples. The price derived from the rule of thumb is for the operating assets of the business plus goodwill. It also assumes that the business will be delivered free and clear of any short- and long-term debt. If any debt is to be assumed by a purchaser, it is subtracted from the price based on the rule of thumb method.

In other words, the rules, unless mentioned otherwise, create a price that includes goodwill, FF&E (furniture, fixtures & equipment), and leasehold improvements, less outstanding debt, including, accounts payable, loans on FF&E, bank loans, etc. The business, unless otherwise mentioned, is assumed delivered to a purchaser free and clear of any debt or encumbrances.

Accounts receivable are not included as they are generally handled outside of any transaction and also almost always belong to the seller. Work in progress, prepaid memberships, etc. also normally belong to the seller. Items such as these may be divided between buyer and seller. For example, in a dry cleaning business, the seller may have taken in a customer's clothing for dry cleaning, but the buyer may take over the business before the work has been completed and

Introduction

delivered back to the customer. This is generally handled outside the transaction and does not usually figure in a pricing or valuation.

Pricing Tips

After the rules of thumb are the Pricing Tips. These provide information from industry experts and other sources. They are intended to amplify the rules themselves. We include lots of new information every year, while maintaining important information from prior years.

Industry Experts' Comments

This section allows our Industry Experts to add their own personal comments about this type of business. These comments may amplify a particular area or provide additional pricing information. Many times these Industry Experts provide information or data that can't be found anywhere else. We should add that some Industry Experts, who own or manage an office with associates, list themselves under more than one business. It may just mean that one or more agents in that office are experts in that industry.

Benchmark Data

This is a valuable section. We feel it is very important, in analyzing and pricing a business, that you compare it to similar businesses, or benchmarks, that are unique to this type of business. One common benchmark unique to each business is the expenses. We have included as many of these as we could find. Many have been contributed by Industry Experts. If no source is mentioned, then you can assume that an Industry Expert(s) has supplied them. In many cases we have used a breakdown of expenses from IBISWorld.

The figures in "Expenses as a Percentage of Annual Sales" may not always add up to 100 percent. We provide only the major categories, and there may be other expense items not included which would make up any difference. Also, in many cases, we have to meld the figures from several different Industry Experts or sources. This may also cause some totals to slightly exceed 100 percent.

We recommend *Nation's Restaurant News*, an invaluable resource, and *Franchise Times*, also an excellent resource, for information on pricing businesses and lots of other information. Still other information is from Industry Experts, local newspapers, magazines, newsletters, etc. Some of the benchmark data is from IBISWorld, a subscription research service, which we use. It is an excellent resource.

26th Edition

Introduction

We mentioned, at the beginning of this section, that if the rule of thumb was used properly, the price derived could be more accurate than simply multiplying the sales by the percentage rule or the SDE multiple. Reviewing market-driven data, one can reasonably assume that a 10 percent swing (that's our number; yours may be higher or lower) on either side of the percentage multiple would allow for the additions or subtractions to arrive at a more accurate multiple of annual sales. Using our example above, the 40 percent figure, and then using available benchmark data could lower or raise that percentage by 10 percent. The multiple then might be more accurate.

Critics of rules of thumb claim that a rule is simply an average and doesn't allow for the variables of each individual business. Comparing the business under review with industry standards—benchmarks—can allow one to raise or lower the percentage accordingly. A 40 percent figure then could be as low as 30 percent, or as high as 50 percent.

The Benchmark section can help you look at the vital signs of the business and compare them to similar businesses. Looking at the expenses as a percentage of annual sales can be a good start. For example, if the business under review has an occupancy percentage of 12 percent against an average 8 percent benchmark, perhaps the price then should be reduced to compensate for the higher rent. The rent is pretty much a fixed expense; but the higher the rent, the lower the profit. Certainly a new owner could lower some of the expenses, but a trained labor force, for example, is hard to replace. Obviously, reducing the percentage multiple is a judgment call; but let's face it, even business valuation is not a science, but an art—and judgment plays a large part in it.

Resources

Included in Resources are trade associations related to the particular types of businesses. For most of the associations, we have included their Website if available. Some are very informative; others are really only for members or consumers. However, many of the associations offer books or pamphlets or studies that can be informative. Every year we find that more and more associations are offering research materials to members only and offer them to non-members at a much higher price. Don't forget that IBISWorld has great reports on many, many different businesses including franchises and many "mom and pop" type businesses.

Franchises

This edition of the *Guide* contains more franchise data than any previous one. For a quick rule for many franchises, go to the Franchise entry. Additional information can be found under the entries for the specific businesses.

Introduction

If you can't find the one you are looking for, see if there is a similar type of franchise that has one. If that fails, go to the particular type of business that the franchise represents. You may add or subtract from that rule of thumb based on your assessment of the value of the franchise—is it a plus or a minus? Even if there is a rule of thumb, it is always wise to refer to the type of business for more information.

Some Final Notes

Some associations conduct their studies and surveys only every other year or even further apart. In some cases, we have done a particular section prior to the new data becoming available; however, we attempt to keep the *Guide* as current as possible.

We know that some of the information may be contradictory, but since we get it from those whom we believe to be experts, we still include it. The more information you have to sort through, the better your final conclusion. We think the information and data are reliable, but occasionally we find an error after the book has been printed.

Also, keep in mind that rules of thumb can vary by area and even by location. For example, businesses on the West Coast tend to sell for a higher price than the East Coast business which sell for a higher price than the Midwest ones.

Thanks to our Industry Experts

We want to thank all of those who contributed rules of thumb, industry data, and information to the *Guide*. It is a tribute to them that they are willing to contribute not only a rule of thumb, but also their knowledge on pricing.

We are focusing on the Industry Experts and are offering to put them on our Website, provide BBP Industry logos and anything else we can do to set them apart, in gratitude for their contribution to the *Guide*—and the profession. We also give them a complimentary copy of the current copy of the *Business Reference Guide*. If you're interested and feel that you are qualified, go to www.bbpinc.com and click on Industry Experts. Or, just pick up the phone and call me, Tom West, at 978-692-0323 or email me at tom@bbpinc.com.

And When All Else Fails

Keep in mind that if it's not in the *Guide*, we really don't have a rule of thumb for that business. We get calls from people asking for a rule of thumb for some

Introduction

oddball type of business like Elephant Training Schools (not really). Honestly, if we knew of one, it would be in the *Guide*. We're always happy to help if we can, but unless there is sufficient sales data, there generally isn't a rule of thumb available. Here are some suggestions if you can't find what you need in the *Guide*:

Call a similar business in your area and see if they are aware of one. Check with a vendor, distributor, or equipment manufacturer and see if someone there can help. Call a trade association for that particular industry and see if they can direct you to someone who can help. Don't do it by email or fax, but call and speak to someone. Trade associations really don't want to get involved, but an individual might get you to the next step.

If none of the above helps, then we're afraid you just have to accept the fact that there isn't one for the business you are checking on.

Thanks to our Sponsors

(For more information on any of the below resources, please see the blue pages in the center of the Guide.)

AICPA
Alliance for a Better Business Brokering Experience
BizComps
Business Valuation Resources
Businessbroker.net
Business Transaction Academy
Capital Business Solutions
Deal Studio
Diamond Financial
GCF Valuation
IndustryExpert.net
International Business Brokers Association
International Franchise Professionals Group
Murphy Business and Financial Corporation
Nationwide Valuations
PeerComps
Selling Middle Market Businesses
Transworld Business Advisors
ValuTrax

Introduction

Businesses in the 2016 Guide

A&W Restaurants 1
AAMCO Transmission 1–3
accounting firms/CPAs 3–8
accounting firms/practices 8–11
accounting/tax practices 11–15
Ace Cash Express 15
Ace Hardware... 15–16
Adam & Eve stores 16
adult clubs/nightclubs .... See bars—adult only
advertising agencies... 16–17
Aero Colours.. 17–18
air conditioning contractors .... See HVAC
aircraft cleaning 18
aircraft manufacturing—parts, supplies, engines, etc.................................. 19–20
airport operations.. 20–23
alarm companies .... See security services/systems
All Tune and Lube... 23
Allegra Marketing—Print—Mail 23
AlphaGraphics.. 24
aluminum smelting machinery 24
ambulance services... 25–29
American Poolplayers Association (APA) 29
amusement routes... See route distribution businesses
Andy OnCall 29–30
antique malls 30
antique shops/dealers 31
Anytime Fitness... 31
apartment locators... 32
appliance stores 33
appraisal/valuation services 33–34
arcade, food & entertainment complexes 35–37
architectural firms 37–38
art galleries and dealers 38–40
arts and crafts/retail stores 40–42
art supplies 42
assisted living facilities 42–44
Atlanta Bread Company 45
audio and film companies.. 45–46
audio/video conferencing... 46–47
auto
       body repair 47–50
       brake services 50

Introduction

dealers—new cars	50–54
dealers—used cars	54–56
detailing	56–57
glass repair/replacement	57–58
lube/oil change	58–60
mufflers	60
parts and accessories—retail stores	60–61
rental	61–63
repair (auto service centers)	64–69
service stations	See gas stations
tire stores	See tire stores
towing	See towing companies
transmission centers	70–72
auto/wrecking/recyclers/dismantlers/scrap/salvage yards	72–74
aviation and aerospace	74–75
awning installation	See sunroom and awning installation
bagel shops	75–76
bait and tackle shops	76
bakeries	76–78
bakeries—commercial	78–80
bakery and restaurant	See bakeries, restaurants
banks—commercial	80–82
barbecue restaurants	See restaurants—barbecue
barber shops	82
bars	82–86
bars—adult only (adult clubs/nightclubs)	86–88
bars—nightclubs	89–91
bars with slot machines	91
baseball teams (professional)	91–92
basketball teams (professional)	92
Baskin-Robbins Ice Cream	93
Batteries Plus Bulbs	93
beauty salons	93–96
bed and breakfasts	96–99
bedding and mattress shops (retail)	99–101
Beef 'O' Brady's Family Sports Pubs	101
beer distributorships/wholesalers	101–103
beer taverns—beer and wine	103–104
beer & wine stores—retail	104
Ben & Jerry's Homemade, Inc.	105
Between Rounds Bakery Sandwich Café	105
bicycle shops	105–109
Big Apple Bagels	109
Big City Burrito	110
Big O Tires	110

Introduction

billboard advertising companies (outdoor advertising)	110–112
billiards	112–113
Blackjack Pizza	113
Blimpie—America's Sub Shop	113
boat dealers	114–115
Boba Loca Specialty Drinks	115
book and stationery stores	115–116
book stores—adult	116
book stores—Christian	116
book stores—new	117–119
book stores—rare and used	119–120
bookkeeping services	See accounting
bottled gas	See liquefied petroleum gas
bowling centers	120–123
brew pubs	124–125
bridal shops	125–127
Bruster's Real Ice Cream	127
Budget Blinds	127
building inspection	See home inspection
Burger King	128
bus companies (charter, school, & scheduled)	128–130
business brokerage offices	130–132
business service centers	See mail and parcel centers
butcher markets	See meat markets
call centers	132–135
camera stores	135–136
campgrounds	137–141
camps	141–142
candy stores	143–144
card shops	144–145
Carl's Jr. Restaurants	145
carpet cleaning	145–146
carpet/floor coverings	146–147
Cartridge World	147
Carvel Ice Cream	147–148
car washes—coin operated/self service	148–150
car washes—full service/exterior	150–153
Car X Auto Service	153–154
casinos/casino hotels	154–156
caterers/catering	156–157
catering trucks	157–158
cellular telephone stores	158
cemeteries	158–160
CertaPro painters	160
check cashing services	160–161

26th Edition

Introduction

Cheeburger Cheeburger restaurants 161
chemical product & preparations mfg. .... See manufacturing—chemical
Chick-fil-A 161
child care centers .... See day care centers
children's and infants' clothing stores 161–162
children's educational franchises 162–163
Chinese restaurants .... See restaurants—Chinese
chiropractic practices 163–169
cigar stores .... See tobacco stores
Closet Factory 170
Closets by Design 170
clothing stores—used 170
cocktail lounges 170–171
coffee shops 171–173
coffee shops (specialty) 173–174
coin laundries 175–181
Cold Stone Creamery 181–182
collectibles stores 182
collection agencies 183–184
comic book stores 184–185
community newspapers .... See publishers—community papers
computer
    consulting 185–186
    programming services—custom 186
    services 187
    stores 187–188
    systems design 188–189
concrete bulk plants 189–190
consignment shops 190
construction
    buildings 190–192
    electrical 192–193
    excavation (site preparation) 193–194
    heating & AC .... See HVAC
    in general 194–198
    specialty trades 198–199
consulting .... See sales consulting
contract manufacturing 199–200
contractors—masonry 200–201
convenience stores 201–207
convenience stores with gas 207–213
Cost Cutters Family Hair Care 213
country inns .... See bed & breakfasts
country/general stores 213
coupon books 214

Introduction

courier services	See delivery services
court reporting services	214–215
Coverall Health-Based Cleaning Systems	215
Culligan International—Franchise/Dealership	216
Curves for Women	216–217
dairy drive-thru	217
Dairy Queen	217–218
data processing services	218–220
dating services	220–222
day care centers/adult	222–225
day care centers/children	225–230
Deck the Walls	230–231
delicatessens	231
delivery services	231–233
Del Taco	233
dental laboratories	233–234
dental practices	234–239
detective agencies	See investigative services
diagnostic imaging centers	239–240
dialysis centers	241–242
Dick's Wings & Grill	242–243
diners	243
direct mail—advertising	243–244
direct selling businesses	244–245
display advertising	See billboard advertising companies
distribution/wholesale	
durable goods	246–247
electrical products	247–248
grocery products/full line	248–249
industrial supplies	249–250
in general	250–252
janitorial	252–253
medical equipment & supplies	253–254
paper	254–255
tools	255–256
document destruction	257–258
dog kennels	258–260
dollar stores	260–263
Domino's Pizza	263
donut shops	263–264
Dream Dinners	264
drive-in restaurants	265
drive-in theaters	265
driving schools (instruction)	See schools—tutoring and driving schools
drug stores	See pharmacies

26th Edition

Introduction

Dr. Vinyl	266
dry cleaners	266–272
dry cleaning pickup outlets/stores	272
dry cleaning routes	272
Dry Clean USA	272
Dunkin' Donuts	272–275
Eagle Transmission Shop	275
e-commerce (electronic shopping)	275–278
electric motor repair	278–279
electrical contracting	See construction—electrical
embroidery services/shops	279
employment agencies	See recruiting agencies
engineering services	279–280
environmental testing	280–281
Environment Control (commercial cleaning services)	281
event companies	282–283
fabric stores	283–284
family clothing stores	284–285
family entertainment centers	286
Fantastic Sam's	286
fast food	See restaurants—limited service
Fast-Fix jewelry and watch repairs	286
FastFrame	286
FasTrac Kids	287
Fast Signs	287
film companies	See audio and film companies
fine dining	See restaurants—full service
fire suppression systems sales & services	287–288
fish and seafood markets	289
fitness centers	290–295
floor coverings	See carpet stores
flower shops (florists)	295–298
food processing and distribution	298
food service—contractor	298–300
food service equipment and supplies	300–302
food stores	See supermarkets/grocery stores
food stores—specialty	302–304
food trucks	304–307
football teams (professional)	307–308
Foot Solutions	308
Framing and Art Centre	308
franchise food businesses	309–310
franchises	310–319
freight forwarding	320
Friendly Computers	320–321

Introduction

Friendly's Restaurant	321
fruits and vegetables (wholesale)	321–322
fruit & vegetable markets (produce)	323
fuel dealers (wholesale)	323–324
funeral homes/services	324–329
furniture and appliance stores	330
furniture refinishing	330
furniture stores	331–332
garage door sales and service	332–333
garbage/trash collection	333–334
garden centers/nurseries	334–337
gas stations—full and/or self-serve	337–342
gas stations w/convenience stores/mini marts	343–352
Gatti's Pizza	352
Geeks on Call	352
General Nutrition Centers	353
gift shops	353–355
Godfather's Pizza	355
Goin' Postal	355
golf carts—sales & service	356
golf courses	356–359
golf driving ranges & family fun centers	359–360
golf shops	360
Goodyear Tire Stores	361
gourmet shops	361
Grease Monkey	361
Great Clips	361
Great Harvest Bread Company	362
Great Steak	362
green businesses	362
grocery stores	See supermarkets/grocery stores
ground transportation companies	363–364
Grout Doctor	365
guard services	365–366
gun shops and supplies	366–368
hardware stores	368–371
Harley-Davidson motorcycle dealerships	372
health clubs	See fitness centers
health food stores	373–374
hearing aid sales	374–377
heating contractors	See HVAC
heating oil dealers	377–379
heavy equipment sales & service	379
hobby shops	380–381
home-based businesses	381–382

26th Edition   xvii

Introduction

home centers	382–383
home health care—care-giving	384–387
home health care—equipment and supplies)	388–389
home health care rental	389–390
Home Helpers	390
home inspection	391–392
Homeland Security	392–393
home nursing agencies	393–394
homes—retirement	See retirement homes
Home Team Inspection Service	394
Honest-1 Auto Care	395
hospital laundry—supply	395–396
hotels & motels	396–401
House Doctors	401
Hungry Howie's Pizza & Subs	402
Huntington Learning Center	402
HVAC—heating, ventilating, and air conditioning	402–405
i9 Sports	406
Iceberg Drive Inn	406
ice cream trucks	406–407
ice cream/yogurt shops	407–409
ice hockey teams (professional)	409
incentive companies	410
industrial safety and health	410
information & document management service industries	410
information technology companies	410–412
injection molding	412
inns	413–414
instant print	See print shops
insurance agencies/brokerages	414–423
insurance companies (in general)	424
insurance companies—life	424–425
insurance companies—property & casualty	425–426
Internet hosting—colocation	426
Internet publishing	See publishing—Internet
Internet sales	See e-commerce
Internet related businesses	427
investigative services	427
investment advice	427–428
Jani-King	428
janitorial services	429–431
Jersey Mike's Subs	431
jewelry stores	431–433
Jiffy Lube International	433
Jimmy John's Gourmet Sandwiches	433–434

Introduction

job shops/contract manufacturing	434–435
John Deere dealerships	436
Johnny Rockets	436
Jon Smith Subs	436
Juice It Up	437
junk yards	See auto wrecking
KFC (Kentucky Fried Chicken)	437
kosher food stores	See food stores—specialty
Kumon Math & Reading Centers	437–438
Kwik Kopy Business Center	438
Lady of America	438
landscaping services	438–441
land surveying services	441–442
language translation	See translation and interpretation services
Laptop Xchange	442
Laundromats	See coin laundries
law firms	442–444
lawn maintenance & service	444–447
Lenny's Subs	447
Li'l Dino Subs	448
Liberty Tax Service	447
limousine services	448–450
linen services—supply	See uniform rental
liquefied petroleum gas	450–452
liquor stores/package stores	452–457
Little Caesar's Pizza	458
lock & key shops	458–459
Logan Farms Honey Glazed Hams	459
lumberyards	459–461
MAACO Auto Painting and Bodyworks	461
machine shops	462–465
MaggieMoo's Ice Cream and Treatery	466
Maid Brigade	466
maid services	466–467
mail and parcel centers	467–470
mail order	470–472
Mama Fu's Asian House	472
management consulting	472–473
manufacturing	
aluminum extruded products	473
chemical	474–475
contract	See contract manufacturing, job shops, machine shops
custom architectural woodwork and millwork	476
electrical	476–477
electrical connectors	477–478

Introduction

food 478–479
furniture/household 479–480
general 480–485
general-purpose machinery 485
guided missile and space vehicle 485–487
machinery 487–488
marine products 489–490
metal fabrication 490–492
metal stamping 492–493
metal valve and pipe fitting 493
miscellaneous electrical and components 494
office products 494–495
ornamental and architectural metal 495–496
personal health products 496
pharmaceutical preparation and medicine 496–499
plastic and rubber machinery 499
plastic products 500–503
powder metallurgy processing 503–504
prefabricated wood buildings 504–506
products from purchased steel 506
scientific instruments 507
showcase, partition, shelving, and lockers 507
signs 507–509
small 509
specialty vehicle 509–510
sporting goods and outdoor products 510–511
stainless steel food service fabrication 511
turbine and turbine generator set units 511
valves 512–513
wood kitchen cabinets and countertops 513
wood office furniture 513–514
Marble Slab Creamery 514
marinas 514–517
marine/yacht services (boat repair) 517–518
markets .... See supermarkets/grocery stores
Martinizing Dry Cleaning 518
masonry contractors .... See contractors—masonry
massage parlors .... See tanning salons, medical spas
McGruff's Safe Kids ID System 519
meat markets 519–520
medical and diagnostic laboratories 520–522
medical billing 523–524
medical practices 524–533
medical spas 533–535
medical transcription 536–539

Introduction

medical transportation	See ambulance services
Meineke Car Care Centers	539
Merry Maids	539
microbreweries	See brew pubs
Midas International	540
middle market businesses (in general)	540–541
Minuteman Press	541
mobile home parks	541
modeling agencies	542
Molly Maid	543
Money Mailer	543
Montessori schools	543–545
motels	See hotels and motels
MotoPhoto	545
motorcycle dealerships	545–547
Mountain Mike's Pizza	547
movie theaters	548–549
moving and storage	549–551
Mr. Jim's Pizza	551
Mr. Payroll	551
Mr. Rooter Plumbing	551
Mrs. Fields Original Cookies	552
Murphy's Deli	552
Music Go Round	552
music stores (record stores, musical instruments)	552–555
My Favorite Muffin	555
mystery shopping companies	555–556
nail salons	556–558
Nathan's Famous	558
Natural Chicken Grill	558
Nature's Way Café	559
needlepoint shops	See fabric stores
newspaper routes	559
newsstands	559
nurseries	See garden centers
nursing homes	559–561
office staffing and temporary agencies	561–562
office supplies and stationery stores	562–564
oil and gas related businesses	564–566
Once Upon a Child	566
online sales	See e-commerce
optical practices	See optical stores, optometry practices
optical stores	566–568
optometry practices	568–572
Orange Julius	572

26th Edition

Introduction

Original Italian Pie	573
outdoor advertising	See billboard advertising companies
OXXO Care Cleaners	573
packaging and shipping services	See mail & parcel centers
packaging (industrial)	573–575
paint and decorating (wallpaper) retailers	575–576
Pak Mail	576
Panera Bread	576
Papa John's Pizza	577
Papa Murphy's Take 'n' Bake Pizza	577
Parcel Plus	577
parking lots and garages	578–580
parking lot sweeping	580–581
pawn shops	582–586
payday loans	586–589
pest control	589–593
pet boarding	See dog kennels, pet grooming
pet grooming	593–594
Petland	594
pet stores	594–597
pet supply (wholesale)	597
pharmacies & drug stores	597–600
photographers & photographic studios	600–601
physical therapy	601–605
physicians	See medical practices
picture framing	605–606
Pillar to Post—home inspection	606
Pizza Factory	606
Pizza Inn	607
pizza shops	607–612
Planet Beach	612
Play It Again Sports	612
plumbing and heating contractors	See HVAC
podiatrists	612–617
pool service (swimming)	617–621
portable toilet companies	621–622
power/pressure washing	623
Precision Tune Auto Care	623
printing/flexographic	623–624
printing/silk screen	624–625
print shops/commercial printers	625–628
print shops (general)	628–631
print shops/quick print	631–634
process serving	634–635
produce markets	See fruit and vegetable markets

Introduction

propane companies .... See liquefied petroleum gas
property management companies 635–638
publishers
    books 638–639
    in general 639–641
    Internet (and broadcasting) 641–642
    magazines/periodicals 643–644
    newsletters 644–645
    newspapers—dailies 645–647
    newspapers—weeklies/community papers 647–649
    software 649–650
publishing—monthly community magazines 650–651
publishing—newspapers (in general) 651–654
Pump It Up 654
Purrfect Auto 654
Quaker Steak & Lube 655
quick print .... See print shops/quick print
Quiznos Classic Subs 655
racquet sports clubs .... See fitness centers
radio communications, equipment, and systems 655–656
radio stations 656–659
real estate offices 659–661
records management 661–662
recruiting agencies 661
recruiting agencies (online) 663
recycling 663–665
Red Robin Gourmet Burgers 665
registered investment advisors 665–666
remediation services 666–668
Renaissance Executive Forums 668
rental centers 668–671
rent-to-own stores 671–673
repair services 673
repossession services 673–674
resale shops 674–675
resort businesses .... See ski shops
restaurants
    an introduction 675–678
    Asian 678–679
    barbecue 679
    Chinese 679
    full service 679–695
    limited service 696–701
    Mexican 701–702
retail businesses (in general) 702–704

26th Edition   **xxiii**

Introduction

retail stores (small specialty) 705
retirement homes 706
Rita's Italian Ice 706
Rocky Mountain Chocolate Factory 706
Roly Poly Sandwiches 707
route distribution businesses 707–710
routes—newspaper ..... See newspaper routes
RV dealerships 710–711
RV parks 711–712
Safe Ship 713
sales businesses (in general) 713
sales consulting 713
Samurai Sam's Teriyaki Grill 714
sand and gravel mining 714–715
sandwich shops 715–716
Sarpino's Pizzeria 716
schools—educational & non-vocational 716–719
schools—tutoring & driving schools 719–720
schools—vocational & training 720–722
Sears Carpet and Upholstery Care & Home Services 722
secretarial services 722
security services/systems 722–726
self-storage (mini storage) 726–731
Senior Helpers 731
service businesses (in general) 731–732
service stations ..... See gas stations
ServiceMaster Clean 732
Servpro 732–733
shoe stores 733–734
short line railroads 734–735
shuttle services & special needs transportation 735
Signarama 735
sign companies 736–738
silk screen printing ..... See printing—silk screen
Sir Speedy Printing 738
ski shops 739–741
Smartbox Portable Self-Storage 741
Smoothie King 741
snack bars ..... See sandwich shops, restaurants—limited-service
Snap Fitness 742
soft drink bottlers 742–743
software companies 743–748
sound contractors 748–749
Soup Man (The Original) 749
souvenir & novelty stores ..... See retail stores—small specialty

Introduction

sporting goods stores 749–750
staffing services 751–754
staffing services (health care) 754
Subway 754–756
sun room and awning installation 756–757
SuperCoups 757
supermarkets/grocery stores 758–762
sustainable businesses .... See green businesses
Swisher (restroom hygiene service) 762
Sylvan Learning Center 762–763
Synergy Home Care 763
Taco John's 763
tanning salons 764–768
tattoo parlors 768–769
taverns .... See bars, cocktail lounges, restaurants
taxicab businesses 769–771
tax practices .... See accounting/tax practices
TCBY 771
technology companies—information 771
technology companies—manufacturing 772
technology companies—service 772–773
tee shirt shops 773
telecommunication carriers (wired) 773–774
telecommunications 774
telemarketing .... See call centers
telephone companies/independent 775
television sales and service 775
television stations 775
temporary agencies 775–776
The Maids 776
thrift shops .... See consignment shops, used goods
ticket services 777
tire stores 777–780
title abstract and settlement offices 780–781
tobacco stores 781
Togo's Eatery 782
tour operators 782–783
towing companies 783–785
toy stores 785–786
translation and interpretation services 786–787
travel agencies 787–791
travel wholesalers/consolidators 791–792
trophy studios 792
Tropical Smoothie Café 792
trucking companies 792–795

26th Edition

Introduction

truck stops	795–798
Two Men and a Truck	799
uniform rental	799–800
UPS Store	800
U Save Car & Truck Rental	800–801
used goods	801
Valpak Direct Marketing Systems	802
Valvoline Instant Oil Change	802
vending machine industry	802–809
veterinary hospitals	809
veterinary practices	809–815
video stores	815–816
visa/passport companies	816–817
waste collection	817–819
water companies	819
Web-based companies	819
wedding stores	See bridal shops
weight loss services/centers	819–820
wholesale distribution	See distribution/wholesale
Wienerschnitzel	820
wild bird shops	820
Wild Birds Unlimited	821
wind farms (energy)	821–822
window cleaning	822
window treatment/draperies	822
Wine Kitz	823
wineries	823–824
Wingstop restaurants	825
wireless communications	825–826
Wireless Toyz	827
women's clothing	827–828
World Wide Express	828
yardage shops	See fabric shops
Your Office USA	828
You've Got Maids	828
Ziebart International (auto services)	829
Zoo Health Club	829

Rules of Thumb - **A**

	Franchise
A&W Restaurants (A&W Root Beer) (See also Franchises)	
Estimated Annual Sales/Unit	$290,000
SIC 5812-06 NAICS 722513	Number of Businesses/Units 1,000 +

Rules of Thumb
➢ 45 percent of annual sales plus inventory

Benchmark Data
- "Recommended square footage is between 1,500 and 2,000 square feet ..."

Resources

Websites
- www.awrestaurants.com

	Franchise
AAMCO Transmission (See also Auto Transmission Centers, Franchises)	
Approx. Total Investment	$227,000 to $333,000
Estimated Annual Sales/Unit	$645,000
SIC 7537-01 NAICS 811113	Number of Businesses/Units 700+

Rules of Thumb
➢ 40 to 42 percent of annual sales plus inventory
➢ 2 to 3 times EBITDA
➢ An industry rule of thumb for AAMCO is 20 times average weekly sales for the past 16–26 weeks for a shop that has average weekly sales of less than $20,000 per week, and up to 27 times average weekly sales for shops above $20,000 per week.

Pricing Tips
- "One observation is that franchised shops who are following the model with a good manager are successful. The typical shop has three technicians, a rebuilder and two mechanics, and a manager. Most of the franchised shops have an owner who oversees but might be considered absentee.
"The better way to analyze a business is from a well-defined proforma as opposed to tax returns and financial statements. Looking at the top line on the tax return, I sell from a proforma using market values for parts, cost and labor."
"Detailed weekly reports provided to the franchisor are more important documents for analyzing historical performance than financial statements and tax returns, as these reports will reveal the prices charged ratio of major/minor repairs and warranty repairs."
- "Established shops with a manager in the expenses:
Small Shops—Less than $20,000 per week

A - Rules of Thumb

- ✓ Sixteen to twenty (16–20) times weekly sales for the last 26 weeks—and/or one and one half (1.5) to three (3) times adjusted earnings (EBITDA). If the seller is the manager or builder—assets plus one year's SDE.
- ✓ "Minimum sale price for an established, poorly performing, franchised transmission shop that is in a proven location which historically has been profitable but has recent sales which at least are 'breakeven' ($8,000 to $10,000 per week) is no less than the total cost it would take to put in a new franchise and reach breakeven—typically $195,000 to $225,000."

"Large Shops—$20,000 per week and higher

- ✓ Twenty to Thirty (20–30) times average weekly sales for the last 26 weeks—and/or two (2) to three (3) times adjusted earnings (EBITDA).

Expert Comments

"Typically a buyer assumes responsibility for warranty repairs. In my analysis I look at this very carefully and at the compensation to the rebuilder to see if it is too low."

"The Internet has changed the marketing and advertising model—lowering cost but making it more difficult for the small independent to compete with the franchises in the major market areas."

Benchmark Data

Expenses as a percentage of annual sales

Production labor costs	20%
Sales/Labor	08% to 10%
Occupancy	06% to 10%
Profit (estimated pretax)	10% to 20%

Percentage of Gross Sales: (where they should be):

Sales	100%

Cost of Sales:

Parts & Fluids	22%
Production Labor (All Technical Employees)	20%
Towing	1%
Misc. Production Supplies	3%
Total Cost of Sales	46%

Sales & Administration Expenses:

Salaries (Center Mgr. & Office)	10%
Rent	8%
Insurance	3%
Utilities	1%
Advertising-Yellow Pages	8%
Telephone	1%
Legal/Accounting	1%
Bank Fees/Bad Debt	1%
Training	1%
Total Sales & Administration Expenses	34%
Net Profit	20%

Seller Financing

- "50 percent down—five (5) years"

Rules of Thumb - A

Resources

Websites
- AAMCO Franchises:www.aamcofranchises.com

Accounting Firms/CPAs (See also Accounting Firms)

SIC 8721-01	NAICS 541211	Number of Businesses/Units 121,125

Rules of Thumb
- ➢ 100 to 125 percent of annual revenues plus inventory
- ➢ 1.8 to 3 times SDE plus inventory
- ➢ 2 times EBIT
- ➢ 2.2 times EBITDA

Pricing Tips
- "Most practices will sell for a minimum of 1 x earnings. Anywhere from 1.0 to 1.5 x sales. Profitability and location are some of the most important variables when determining asking price."
- "In Florida I find the multiples of SDE to be slightly lower than 2. Important to understand that generally speaking CPA and accounting practice sales will require the seller to stay on for at least one tax season and that there typically will include an earnout structure. It is important that purchaser has a similar style to seller to maximize client retention."
- "Premiums paid above 100% of gross revenues for above average net income (of 45%), location (major metro area), special expertise (tax, etc.), established clientele with above average fees."
- "Even distribution of revenue from tax return preparation and accounting fees is better."
- "CPAs commonly use 1 times gross although we have frequently exceeded that amount."
- "Product mix and any special areas of practice can affect selling price to the right buyer. There is always the possibility to split up a practice among two or more buyers if specialty work is involved."
- "Revenue composition is important; retail tax, write-up, monthly accounting, review work, audit, consulting, types of revenue streams—all have an effect on sale's price."
- "Generally sold based on an annual multiple of gross revenue."
- "Biggest factor is the terms and whether seller will guarantee part or all of the income."
- "SDE should be between 40% and 60% of revenue."
- "CPA buyers always want to pay 1 times gross . . . sellers tend to want more . . . terms drive price."
- "1 to 1.25 times revenue, with SDE of 30% to 60% of gross revenue."
- "Employees on non-compete will increase; composition of services, accounts receivable, pricing of client work, recovery percentages. These last few will swing price in both directions."
- "Accounting, tax, bookkeeping, EA and/or CPA firms typically sell for 100% to 135% of annual gross revenue. They tend to sell for 2–4 times SDE."

A - Rules of Thumb

- "Sale price should yield an SDE range of 40% to 60%."
- "Location is paramount. Same practice will sell for 1.3 times gross revenue in one location and 1 times gross revenue in another."
- "The composition of billings is important. The split between recurring/one time. The split among taxes/accounting/audit/consulting/other is important in determining staff composition. Labor costs are extremely important in bottom line. Accounts receivable levels may indicate problems with billings and/or clients."
- "The commonly accepted rule of thumb is one times annual gross sales. The biggest cause for variation from this (50% more or less) is location. Prices in big metro areas are seldom that low. Prices in rural areas are often not that high. Also, it is VERY important to consider the wide variation in definition of 'one times annual gross.' One definition is a total 'work out' situation paying seller 20% of collection each year for five years. On the other end of the scale is a check for all cash at closing with no seller risk regarding retention of clients. These differences in definition of 'price' can mean that actual present value can vary by as much as 100% depending on definition used. Owners (sellers) and buyers are often very confused and misled regarding these issues."
- "Sales price will be the lesser of 1.3 times gross revenues or 3 times SDE—and will include FF&E."
- "CPA firms typically sell for 100% to 130% of Annual Gross Sales. Larger firms typically demand a higher percentage. Small single CPA offices may only warrant 100%. The size, training, and qualifications of the firm's staff have an impact on pricing."
- "Earnouts are used for most do-it-yourselfers."

Expert Comments

"Buyer will need to be a CPA or have an accounting background in order to buy the business. It is a specialized and niche field. Buyers will need this education and background in order to retain the existing client base. Not everyone who wants to buy a business will be able to buy an accounting or tax practice."

"Although I don't think ease of replication is that difficult, I've found that the personality types that are drawn to CPA/accounting practices are not strong in sales, and as a result they usually need to purchase rather than start a practice. I have many CPA/accounting buyers so I would say marketability is high."

"Great buyer demand....difficult industry to grow organically."

"Most smaller CPA firms either specialize in a type of industry audit or avoid all audits. The special industry audit firm may be more difficult to sell due to small demand."

"Competition is aging and the regulating agencies are making an impact on various areas of practice, in particular taxation. Accountants are usually not very good at generating new business so acquisitions are a key growth strategy."

"The profit trend and industry trend is upward due to increased tax and government regulations on businesses and individuals. Location and facilities are located in office or upscale retail locations. A profitable, well-

Rules of Thumb - A

balanced CPA practice is highly marketable to those entering the profession from corporate and established firms to expand their client base. Replication or opening a practice is not difficult. Establishing a client base is the challenge for a new CPA practice."

"Although a very stable industry, current government regulations and the changes of such have put increasing demand on service. There is also a decline in numbers of people entering and staying in public accounting."

"Risk of client loss is the biggest factor in a purchase."

"The marketability of accounting firms is much greater in major metro areas but still fairly marketable even in rural areas."

"People don't leave their CPA often—so there's competition but it doesn't affect established firms much. Very low risk—very few CPAs go out of business. Profits are up although firms can be adversely affected by local trends—i.e., Silicon Valley fallout where CPAs have a concentration in a particular industry. Facilities are often Class A buildings. There's definitely a market for CPA firms but finding the right buyer is difficult. The industry is increasing while fewer people enter the profession. Replicating an existing practice is often very difficult and the reason we sell 400+ practices a year."

"The accounting/tax industry as it pertains to small privately owned locations has been steady for some years. Profitability has always been high and replication difficult, especially in the CPA field. As for risk, CPAs are the second best rated business loans to make—their default rate is very low."

Benchmark Data

Statistics (Accounting Services)
Number of Establishments	123,984
Average Profit Margin	17.8%
Revenue per Employee	$186,600
Average Number of Employees	4.5
Average Wages per Employee	$67,511

Products and Services Segmentation
Financial auditing services	34.1%
Other services	19.1%
Corporate tax preparation and representative services	13.5%
Individual tax preparation and representative services	11.1%
Tax planning and consulting services	10.4%
General accounting services	5.6%
Financial statement review services	3.4%
Other financial assurance services	2.8%

Major Market Segmentation
Other businesses	23.5%
Finance sector	20.7%
Individuals	18.0%
Manufacturing sector	12.7%
Retail sector	10.7%
Utilities and mining sector	6.6%
Nonprofit organizations	4.7%
Federal, state and local government	3.1%

A - Rules of Thumb

Industry Costs

Profit	17.8%
Wages	36.3%
Purchases	4.9%
Depreciation	1.4%
Marketing	1.5%
Rent & Utilities	5.3%
Other	32.8%

Market Share

PricewaterhouseCoopers	8.8%
Ernst & Young	8.5%
Deloitte Touche Tohmatsu	8.1%
KPMG International	4.8%

Source: IBISWorld, February 2015

- "Owners and/or staff should be able to bill out around $100,000 per year. No inventory, so generally no COGS."
- "Every CPA/accounting practice seller already knows that 100% of billable sales is a good benchmark. Depth of staff and systems in place, especially technology, help increase this multiple slightly. Conversely sole practitioners that are absent of technology will sell for lower multiples."
- "Generally practice may generate $100,000+ in billings per staff person."
- "Staff wages no more than 33% of revenue. Professional staff should annually bill 3 to 5 times their salary."
- "SDE as a percentage of sales should be, as a minimum, 35%."
- "Payroll should be less than 30% of gross receipts. Net earnings to the owner, including salary, can easily range from 30% to 50% of gross revenue."
- "Adjusted net income of SDE can have a big impact. Industry average tends to be 33% of sales but can be much higher in a very good office."
- "Solid accounting firms with gross revenues of $100K to $2 million tend to have SDE of 35% to 50% and even more in some cases."
- "Hard to benchmark due to high fluctuations of billable rates. CPAs in the same community may bill from $75 per hour to $250 per hour or more depending upon size of firm and expertise. Professional staff should be able to bill 3 times their base salary."
- "A successful CPA practice will value employees as well as clients. Finding and keeping good employees for work in public accounting is a distinguishing feature of a successful firm. Flex hours, on-premises nursery, and production bonuses are a few of the successful firm employee benefits."

Expenses as a percentage of annual sales

Cost of goods	0% to 05%
Payroll/labor Costs	25% to 35%
Occupancy	10% to 20%
Profit (estimated pretax)	35% to 45%

Industry Trend

- "Growing. Baby boomers are getting older and more and more are retiring."
- "The merger wave among CPA firms is expected to continue its strong pace in 2014, particularly among small to midsized regional firms, according to the

Rules of Thumb - A

authors of a new American Institute of CPAs-published book on acquisition strategies.

"Drivers for this trend include succession planning, cross-selling opportunities and market share expansion, say Joel L. Sinkin and Terrence E. Putney, CPA, co-authors of "CPA Firm Mergers & Acquisitions: How to Buy a Firm, How to Sell a Firm, and How to Make the Best Deal."

- "Another overlooked factor: the search for talent, they say. Unemployment remains low in the accounting profession, and many smaller firms find themselves in an increasingly competitive market for the next generation of leaders. As recruiting battles heat up, buying or selling a firm makes sense as a growth strategy or exit plan."

Source:"Book Offers Advice on When to Buy, Sell or Merge an Accounting Practice,"
CPA Practice Advisor, Jan 14, 2014

- "Employee costs as a percentage of sales is an important number. 40% or less is considered good. Above this leaves little room for profits."
- "As the CPA population is aging, more opportunity will exist to purchase or absorb this clientele. It appears that fewer graduates are heading in this direction, so the opportunity will continue to increase for established firms or those entering this profession."
- "Industry trend is upward due to increased tax and government regulations on businesses and individuals."
- "Still a seller's market"
- "Industry regulation makes entry difficult yet demand for services continually increase."
- "An increase in the number of small single-owner firms billing $100K or less as laid-off industry CPAs open their own firms."
- "More consolidations. More minority and foreign ownership."
- "Although the marketplace of accountants is aging, there are excellent opportunities for the future entrants into the industry. Future government legislation will result in fewer competitors in taxation. The audit market has slowed with legal difficulties, but other sectors have expanded with government legislation."

Seller Financing

- "The transactions I've participated in were based on notes based on client retention, or earnouts over a 1–3 year period. Most commonly through 2 tax seasons. Heaviest weight of earnout based on first tax season."
- "Four years earnout method with 25% to 50% down"
- "Seller financing is usually only a last resort."
- "3 to 5 years"

Questions

- "What type of services do you perform? Who is on staff that has primary contact with customers?"
- "What period of time will they guarantee the billings."
- "Any client concentrations, risks of client losses."
- "Why are you selling? Is any individual client fee over 10% of the Gross Revenue? Is any single industry over 10% of Gross Revenue? How much of Revenue is earned from tax return preparation and how much from accounting or auditing? What percent are corporate returns or individual returns? What

A - Rules of Thumb

type of client audits? What type of work does your staff do? What tax and accounting software do you use? What is the billing rate per hour? Do you bill by hour or project? How long have your clients been with this firm? How long have the employees been with this firm?"
- "What are the strengths of your firm? What areas can be improved? Have you attempted to sell on your own?"
- "Client mix, services mix, average billings for services, accounts receivable and status of employees"
- "Info relating to clientele, fee structure, employee information, pending litigation, office lease, type of services performed, need for licenses/certifications"
- "Do you do any audit work? Are your licenses current? How many hours do you personally bill per year?"
- "The quality of the fees should be investigated both by looking at the cash flow percentages and investigating the billing rates of the personnel and the owner. Post-sale competition is a major risk factor so this possibility should be investigated carefully."

Resources
Associations
- American Institute of CPAs: www.aicpa.org

Accounting Firms/Practices	(See also Accounting Firms/CPAs/Tax Practices)	
SIC 8721-01	NAICS 541219	Number of Businesses/Units 140,000

Rules of Thumb

➢ There are three Rules of Thumb generally cited: #1—.75 to 1.25 annual revenues, depending on characteristics of practice; #2—9 to 15 times monthly net sales, depending on characteristics of practice; and #3—2 to 5 times the seller's SDE. Rules of Thumb normally include FF&E, Lease and Intangibles. Current assets, real estate, and all related liabilities must be considered separately.

➢ 2.5 to 3.5 times SDE plus inventory (if any)

➢ One to 1.25 times annual revenues (non-CPA) plus inventory

➢ Generally sold for a multiple of 1 to 1.5 times gross revenues depending upon net earnings. Rarely sell below one times gross.

➢ One times gross for low-level billings, up to 1.5 times gross for high-level billings

➢ 100 percent to 115 percent of one-year's revenue + FF&E with one-year guarantee of gross

➢ 90 to 110 percent of anticipated annual revenues under new ownership, subject to seller guarantee and earnout provisions

➢ 100 to 115 percent of annual revenues, plus fixtures & equipment; seller keeps accounts payable & accounts receivable

➢ Sales price generally 100 to 125 percent of annual revenue; higher in some metropolitan areas such as New York City, Dallas, Atlanta, etc.

➢ 45 percent times EBIT

Rules of Thumb - A

Pricing Tips
- "Almost all of the deals will be subject to attrition and retention clauses. But it is equally important for the deal to also include a clause for the growth within the portfolio."
- "Fee structure, client complexity, location and overall staffing requirements affect practice desirability."
- "Typically, accounting firms are sold on a percentage of collections and based on a client retention clause. This number can range from 1.0 times to 1.50 times revenues depending on location, average rates, etc."
- "Priced based on a multiple of annual gross revenue."
- "Good ones should sell for more than 1 times gross."
- "Accounting and tax practices' purchase price is typically based on a multiple of the gross billings anywhere from 1.0 to 1.5 times. There is also usually a discount for an all-cash deal or no-retention clause (fixed price) deal."
- "Sales of accounting practices range from .5 to 1.6 times gross revenues, with a very high concentration at 1.0 times annual gross revenue. However, in the majority of cases, the price was contingent on retaining the clients for some period of time, most typically one year, with the final price reduced by the amounts for any clients not retained. The median ratio of price/SDE was 1.64."
- "Metro areas on the high side (New York City maybe 200 percent of annual billings). High fee structure adds to price unless highly specialized. Compliance work (recurring type) increases price. All tax work reduces price."

Expert Comments

"As taxes get more complicated the need for good accountants keeps increasing. There is lots of consolidation in this industry as the older accountants start to retire and the newer ones know that to grow their practice faster, they need to acquire."

"There seem to be plenty of buyers for a good accounting practice."

"With technology today, accountants can process the client's work from anywhere. Office location is not as important unless it is an all-1040 tax practice."

Benchmark Data
- "Labor at less than 33% is best."
- "Each employee should generate around $100k–$150k in annual billings. Owners/Partners—$200k–$250k."
- "Net income should be at least 40%. Owners expected to bring in around $200k in annual billings."
- "Generally revenue based on employee costs."
- "Not moving the office will help retain the client base."
- "Number of repeat clients on the book; it usually takes at least 250–350 to break even and above that to be profitable."

Expenses as a percentage of annual sales	
Cost of goods	n/a
Payroll/labor Costs	30% to 35%
Occupancy	08% to 12%
Profit (estimated pretax) 30% to 45%	

26th Edition

A - Rules of Thumb

Industry Trend
- "More people preparing own returns with 'off-the-shelf' software."
- "Any new tax laws that would take effect that could decrease people's needs for accountants (i.e., Fair Tax)."
- "Steady to upward"
- "Generally an upward trend"
- "Consolidation and firms sending work offshore"

Seller Financing
- "5 year financing period"
- "Typical seller financed over 2 to 3 years and it is tied to the retention of the clients."
- "Earnouts are very typically between one and two years."
- "30 percent down payment, 70 percent seller carry back, five years, 8 to 10 percent"
- "20 to 40 percent down, financing three to five years for small practices; seven to 10 years for larger ones"
- "Three years average"
- "Three to five years"
- "30 to 35 percent down, balance financed over three to five years with one-year client retention guaranteed by the seller to the buyer"
- "Usually seller financed—25 percent to 40 percent down. From three to 10 years, depending on size of the practice"

Questions
- "1) What do you plan to do after you sell the practice 2) How often do clients come in to the office to meet with you? 3) How many personal taxes do you do a year vs corporate tax returns? 4) What percentage of your work includes 'specialty' consulting work? 5) Does your practice also provide bookkeeping services?"
- "Demographic of the client base. Number of years average client has been with the firm."
- "Gross revenue, revenue type, number of clients, fees generated from each client, employee compensation and experience, lease on facilities, type of software used, net income."
- "Will clients likely stay with new owner?"
- "Break down the composition of fees on an annual basis (percent from tax, bookkeeping, payroll, accounting, auditing, technology, consulting, etc.). Also ask if fee structure is based on hourly or fixed-fee arrangements. What is the effective percent of production hours (total firm hours billed/total firm hours spent)? What are the rate realizations (total fees billed/standard rates x hours billed)? Clients making up over 10% of annual fees? Any major clients coming to end of service agreements, and details? Answers indicating poor production and rate realizations have a negative impact on pricing, while positive statistics have positive impacts on pricing."

Resources

Websites
- Buying a Practice by Leon Faris and Vance Wingo: www.cpasales.com

Rules of Thumb - **A**

Associations
- American Institute of Certified Public Accountants (AICPA): www.aicpa.org
- National Society of Accountants: www.nsacct.org

Accounting/Tax Practices (See also Accounting Firms/Practices/CPAs)		
SIC 7291-01	NAICS 541213	Number of Businesses/Units 120,120
Rules of Thumb		
➢ 1 to 1.35 times annual revenues plus inventory		
➢ 2 to 3 times SDE plus inventory		
➢ 5 to 7 times EBIT		
➢ 4 to 6 times EBITDA		

Pricing Tips
- "Many factors may add a premium or discount to the 'rule of thumb' multiple: years established, billing rates, net earnings, reputations, location, type of work performed, established clientele, trained staff, etc."
- "Diversification of client industry and no client over 20% of the practice gross revenue. Should have a good mix of accounting and tax."
- "Practices in urban areas are priced higher. Practice prices do not include equipment or inventory."
- "Most practices are sold on a multiple of the gross billings. This is typically anywhere from 1.0 to 1.30."
- "Even distribution of revenue from tax return preparation and accounting fees is better."
- "Buyers generally want earnouts, sellers want cash."
- "Repeat clients, accounting vs. tax preparation work."
- "Tax related revenues are priced at 1 to 1.25 times annual revenues. Monthly write-up revenues are priced at 1.25 to 1.5 times annual revenues. Other revenues priced at one times annual revenue."
- "National franchises can hurt sale price due to franchise, royalty, and advertising fees charged."
- "Higher average price per return results in higher asking price."
- "Higher end practices will net 40%"
- "Dependent on type of clients; 1040 clients result in lower pricing; monthly and retainer clients result in higher pricing. Audit only preferred by a minority of firms."
- "Typically practices sell for multiples of revenue from 1x to 1.75x based on location and demand in area and type of practice."

Expert Comments
"While there are lots of accountants and tax preparers, satisfied clients are very loyal. Small businesses need help and often look for help from their accountant."

"Accounting work growing due to outsourcing"

A - Rules of Thumb

"The profit trend and industry trend is upward due to increased tax and government regulations on businesses and individuals. There is a greater need of business bookkeeping and records for proof of compliance with government regulations. Location and facilities are located in office or retail locations. A profitable, well balanced practice is highly marketable to those entering the profession from corporate and established firms to expand their client base. Replication or opening a practice is not difficult. Establishing a client base is the challenge for a new accounting practice."

"Historically profitable practices will sell for a higher price."

"Lots of competition. Marketing for new clients is difficult, so building a large client base takes time."

"The major concern for any buyer should be retaining the clients they are purchasing. An owner willing to stay on after the sale to help with the transition should help the buyer feel more comfortable. Practices where owners do not stay on should be sold at a discount and less than market price."

"Tax preparation has become a commodity. Anyone with $5,000, a PC, and software can easily open a tax prep office. A number of recent national franchises have over-saturated the market. "

"Fair amount of competition in the industry. Very profitable businesses when compared to many others. Accounting practices in major metro areas are highly marketable."

"Industry is in need of personnel and has no lack of new regulations which necessitate new audit or forensic work."

"Not a location-dependent business...service usually at the client's business address. Tough business to grow organically but many with financial wherewithal to purchase firms or accounts."

"High risk, as it is easy to duplicate this type of business. Customer loyalty is not as strong in this business as in a CPA practice."

"Easily transferable. High visibility of offices necessary to attract large number of walk-in clients. Majority of clients are seen only once a year for tax preparation and filing of tax returns. Office location is critical."

Benchmark Data

Statistics (Tax Preparation Services)

Number of Establishments	127,314
Average Profit Margin	27.2%
Revenue per Employee	$28,600
Average Number of Employees	2.6
Average Wages per Employee	$11,095

Products and Services Segmentation

Standard tax preparation services	57%
Basic tax preparation services	23%
Full-service tax preparation services	14%
Tax-related financial products	6%

Rules of Thumb - A

Industry Costs

Profit	27.2%
Wages	38.7%
Purchases	5.0%
Depreciation	2.3%
Marketing	12.0%
Rent & Utilities	7.5%
Other	7.3%

Market Share

H&R Block Inc.	31.8%
Jackson Hewitt Inc.	2.0%

Source: IBISWorld, April 2015

- "Tax Return Preparation Fee Averages $246
  National Society of Accountants survey finds average cost for an itemized return is reasonable
  - ✓ $205 for a Form 1040 Schedule C (business)
  - ✓ $556 for a Form 1065 (partnership)
  - ✓ $759 for a Form 1120 (corporation)
  - ✓ $717 for a Form 1120S (S corporation)
  - ✓ $468 for a Form 1041 (fiduciary)
  - ✓ $628 for a Form 990 (tax exempt)
  - ✓ $59 for a Form 940 (Federal unemployment)
  - ✓ $134 for Schedule D (gains and losses)
  - ✓ $155 for Schedule E (rental)
  - ✓ $185 for Schedule F (farm)"

Source: National Society of Accountants (NSA)

- "$100,000 billings per staff person"
- "A successful accounting practice should have Seller's Discretionary Earnings of 45% to 60% of revenue. The larger firm will earn 40% to 50% of revenue and the smaller firm should be 50% to 60% of revenue."
- "Well-run practices have profits of 30% to 45% of revenues."
- "SDE should be 45% to 60% of Revenue"
- "Write-up work and monthly payroll preparation should provide approximately 75% of total revenues. Taxes should provide the remaining 25%."
- "Taxpayers may also benefit by obtaining tax preparation estimates from more than one preparer from different size companies. For example, the survey found that tax preparation fees for an itemized Form 1040 with Schedule A and a state tax return averaged only $217 at one-person firms, and rose to an average of $245 for firms with three or more staff."
- "Most net approx. 45+ percent."
- "Employee cost should be under 25%. Occupancy cost may be high for newer offices as they move into newer strip centers with higher rents."

Expenses as a percentage of annual sales

Cost of goods	02%
Payroll/labor Costs	25% to 30%
Occupancy	05% to 10%
Profit (estimated pretax)	30% to 45%

26th Edition

A - Rules of Thumb

Industry Trend
- "Up and possibly up sharply depending on the IRS Tax Code changes and effects of the Affordable Care Act"
- "Computers are making it easier and easier for businesses and individuals to prepare their own taxes, but people will always need professionals to help with audits, the tax code, etc."
- "More industry regulation from IRS"
- "Any new tax laws would greatly affect the accounting and tax industry."
- "I see the trend to remain about the same as it has been the past 10 years."
- "Growth...consistent growth due to regulations"
- "Continued demand for acquisitions and continued exiting by aging population of CPAs."
- "IRS free e-file along with PC software continues to pull customers away from paid preparers. More tax preparation franchises opening will take business away from established firms."

Seller Financing
- "Generally seeing more outside financing, with a combination of owner and bank financing in place."
- "Usually, an accounting practice is sold for 1 to 1½ times annual gross revenue, with 25% to 50% down payment. The balance is paid to the seller as a percent of revenue received from a purchased client list over a negotiated period of time (may be 2 to 6 years). The payments may be paid monthly or quarterly or annually as a percent of revenue received from the previous period. EXAMPLE: Annual Revenue $100,000, Purchase Price $ 125,000, 30% down payment $37,500, Balance due $87,500, Annual Revenue $100,000 = 87.5 %/4 years = 21.875% per year. For each dollar of revenue received from a purchased client list, the buyer would pay 21.875% to the seller for four years. Balance check: Annual revenue received $100,000, 21.875% = $21,875 for 4 years = $ 87,500 Balance due"
- "Almost always has some seller financing which is usually 5 years for moderate or larger practices and 2 to 4 years for smaller practices."

Questions
- "Why are you selling? Is any individual client fee over 10% of the Gross Revenue? Is any single industry over 10% of Gross Revenue? How much of Revenue is earned from tax return preparation and how much from accounting or bookkeeping? What type of work does your staff do? What tax and accounting software do you use? What is the billing rate per hour? Do you bill by hour or project? How long have your clients been with this firm? How long have the employees been with this firm?"
- "Why do you want to sell your business? What will you do after closing. Are you willing to sign a broad Non-Competition Agreement?"
- "Repeat clients, accounting vs. tax preparation work"
- "Strengths and weaknesses of the firm. Information about the area."
- "What is the breakdown between tax, write-up, consulting and audit revenues? Also, who else in the firm can do the tax and write-up work? Who reviews the work?"
- "How long has the firm been in business? List of clients that have left within the

Rules of Thumb - **A**

past 3 years. List of new clients within the last 3 years. Does the owner plan on being available after the sale? Review sample returns and work papers to get a feel for the amount of work that is done for each client."
- "Why are you selling? Are the clients leaving because of location or other reason? What type of software is used now? If the clients are not walk-in, how long have they been tax clients? What industry are most of the clients? What % of clients are personal returns or business returns? Are bookkeeping services included with any client?"
- "What are the seller's goals in the sale of the practice? They are not the same for all sellers."
- "Fee structure, number of clients, services performed, employee costs, franchise fees paid, licenses required."
- "Any clients not in the local service area?"

Resources

Associations
- American Institute of CPA's: www.aicpa.org
- National Association of Enrolled Agents: www.naea.org
- National Association of Tax Professionals: http://www.natptax.com/Pages/default.aspx

Ace Cash Express (See also Check Cashing Services, Franchises)		
SIC 6099-03	NAICS 522390	Number of Businesses/Units 1,750

Rules of Thumb
➢ 1.25 times annual sales plus inventory

Resources

Websites
- Ace Cash Express—this company is publicly held, and their annual report is available online and is an excellent resource.: www.acecashexpress.com

		Franchise
Ace Hardware (See also Hardware Stores, Franchises)		
Approx. Total Investment		$400,000 to $1,100,000
SIC 5251-04	NAICS 444130	Number of Businesses/Units 4,100

Rules of Thumb
➢ 45 percent of annual sales plus inventory

Pricing Tips
- Sales seem to indicate that smaller sales bring a higher multiple (50%+) than stores with sales over $1 million, which seem to bring lower multiples. Price is plus inventory, and that may be the reason for lower multiples for larger stores.

26th Edition

A - Rules of Thumb

Resources

Websites
- www.myace.com

Adam & Eve Stores (See also Franchises) — Franchise

Approx. Total Investment	$100,000–$300,000
NAICS 451120	Number of Businesses/Units 55

Rules of Thumb
> 35 percent of annual sales plus inventory

Resources

Websites
- Adam & Eve stores: www.adamevestores.com

Advertising Agencies

SIC 7311-01	NAICS 541810	Number of Businesses/Units 14,077

Rules of Thumb
> 50 percent of annual revenues (billings) plus inventory. May require an earnout.

Benchmark Data

Statistics (Advertising Agencies)

Number of Establishments	68,691
Average Profit Margin	7.8%
Revenue per Employee	$207,700
Average Number of Employees	3.8
Average Wages per Employee	$70,657

Products and Services Segmentation

Advertising services	69.5%
Other	9.9%
Creative services	9.0%
Media planning and buying	6.4%
Media representation services	2.6%
Public relations services	2.6%

Major Market Segmentation

Other	41%
Automotive sector	24%
Food sector	9%
Retail sector	9%
Telecommunications and financial services sectors	6%
Travel and tourism	4%
Medicine and pharmaceutical sectors	4%
Hygiene and beauty care sectors	3%

Rules of Thumb - **A**

Industry Costs
Profit	7.8%
Wages	34.5%
Purchases	36.3%
Depreciation	1.1%
Marketing	3.1%
Rent & Utilities	4.7%
Other	12.5%

Market Share
Omnicom Group Inc.	7.7%
Interpublic Group of Companies Inc.	6.5%
WPP PLC	4.8%

Source: IBISWorld, April 2015

Industry Trend
- "There are three trends in particular that marketers need to get ahead of:
  1) Social media increasingly means paid media. The rules are changing. Facebook has now decreed that brands need to pay to get visibility, even when it comes to reaching people who opt in to follow those brands. With Twitter, Instagram, and other social platforms, the only way to ensure wide reach is to support strong creative with paid media.
  2) Default social activity shifts from public to private. Social media usage keeps skyrocketing. Yet much of the growth is coming from private social activity, where people are sending messages and multimedia directly to select individuals or groups of friends, rather than sharing everything publicly.
  3) People are buying from each other instead of from brands. What if it doesn't matter how big your brand is, how many locations you have, how great your products are or how good your service is? What if, instead, people would rather buy products and services from each other?"

  Source: "Three Seismic Threats to Marketers Hitting in 2015" by David Berkowitz, http://adage.com/article/digitalnext/seismic-threats-marketers-hitting-2015/296406/
  12/31/14

- "The Internet is still the fastest growing medium for advertising, an international survey found, showing an upsurge of 16.3% in 2012 and forecasts of an average of 15% annual growth for 2013 to 2015."

  Source: "World Magazine Trends 2013/14 Show Online Ad Upsurge," www.huffingtonpost.com
  January 12, 2014

Resources
Websites
- American Association of Advertising Agencies: www.aaaa.org

	Franchise
Aero Colours, Inc. (See also Franchises)	
Approx. Total Investment	$49,000 to $174,000
SIC 7532-02 NAICS 811121	Number of Businesses/Units 200+
Rules of Thumb	
➢ 70 percent of annual sales	

26th Edition 17

A - Rules of Thumb

Resources

Websites
- www.aerocolours.com

Aircraft Cleaning (See also Airport Operations)		
SIC 4581-04	NAICS 561720	Number of Businesses/Units 3,807

Rules of Thumb
➢ 100 percent of annual sales plus inventory
➢ 3 times SDE plus inventory

Pricing Tips
- "Minimum 3 yrs. in business, 2.5x net if owner operated, as much as 4x net if work is performed by a crew or crews."

Expert Comments
"Strong barrier to entry; quality equipment is a must; high profit; labor intense; and a current downturn in general aviation"

"Aviation is a very difficult industry as a startup business."

Benchmark Data
- "Labor should run approximately 25% of sales."
- "Corporate aircraft cleaning is a very specialized service; if it survived the first 18 months, chances are it will do well."
- "All services are mobile."

Expenses as a percentage of annual sales
Cost of goods	05% to 10%
Payroll/labor Costs	25% to 35%
Occupancy	10%
Profit (estimated pretax)	55% to 60%

Industry Trend
- "The industry will bounce back, as always."
- "Increase in demand"
- "Private aviation is a rapidly growing industry."

Questions
- "Number of accounts, how long servicing those accounts, percentage of sales from which accounts"
- "How many aircraft do you service per week, per month? Number of employees? The buyer is going to need to keep the employees."
- "Transition period is very important."

Resources

Associations
- National Business Aviation Association: www.nbaa.org

Rules of Thumb - A

Aircraft Manufacturing—Parts, Supplies, Engines, etc. (Kit-built & Ultralight aircraft industry)

| SIC 3724 | NAICS 336412 | |

Rules of Thumb
➢ 40 to 70 percent of annual sales includes value of equipment
➢ 4 times EBIT

Pricing Tips
- "Add for any FAA approvals and for high-value equipment."
- "FAA approvals and/or contracts with major OEM's very important."
- "Each business varies so greatly from the next. It takes someone who knows the industry to know the exact business being described before a price can be established."
- "When very specialized equipment is needed, add some if a good business. Add value of real estate."

Expert Comments
"Sales and profits declining due to technological factors such as increased time between overhauls"

"Low competition based on high barriers to entry."

Benchmark Data
- "Revenue per employee should be at least $100,000 per annum."

Expenses as a percentage of annual sales
Cost of goods	35%
Payroll/labor Costs	35%
Occupancy	20%
Profit (estimated pretax)	10%

Industry Trend
- "Highly cyclical with the economy and military spending"

Seller Financing
- "3 years max, 1 year least"
- "We've never sold a 'seller-financed' ultralight aircraft business. It is always a cash deal."

Questions
- "Approvals and contracts"
- "What is the reputation of the aircraft or related product being sold? What is the reputation of the company? Is business up or down? What about accidents—any deaths? A company with a great reputation may be worth little because of their product—or, vice versa."
- "Where are sales today in comparison to one, two . . . years ago? Why are

A - Rules of Thumb

they up or down?" [We don't know if the pun was intended or not.] Have there been any structural failures or successful liability suits against them? Is it movable or must buyer move?"

Airport Operations (See also Aircraft Cleaning)		
SIC 4581-06	NAICS 488119	Number of Businesses/Units 2,235

Rules of Thumb
- 90 to 100 percent of annual sales includes inventory
- 4 times SDE includes inventory
- 4 times EBIT
- 5 times EBITDA

Pricing Tips

- "Pricing would be highly dependent on the sector. In certain segments there is lot of personal goodwill. A prospective buyer should separate the personal goodwill from the business goodwill in calculating a purchase price. Many smaller businesses are highly dependent upon the owner's talent or specialty. These businesses should be valued with consideration to an earnout or employment contact to ensure ongoing stability."
- "FBOs and MROs are about real estate. Revenues per square foot can be a good metric, but most transactions above $3MM use a multiple of EBITDA plus inventory"
- "The FBO business is really a real-estate play. Take a careful look at the city leasehold agreements and the fuel farm, as EPA regulations can be costly to implement. Most fuel farms now must be built above ground. For air charter companies, take a close look at the age/condition of the aircraft used and existing contracts."
- "Multiples are dependent on market. Large market FBOs will generally be in the 4–5 x EBITDA range with second and third tier market FBOs valued at 3–4 x EBITDA. There are, however, several important factors affecting value including lease terms, services offered, and airport as well as area competition. The shorter the leasing terms and more restrictive the lease, the lower the multiple will be. If new facilities or improvements must be made, a 20-year lease is often needed for financial feasibility. FBOs with a monopoly on local operations will be valued higher than those facing competition. Buyers tend to value the diversity of income streams differently: Larger chains tend to shy away from maintenance and hangar rentals due to the added complexity while owner/operators tend to appreciate the more stable income these additional sources provide. Fueling rights are also an important factor in pricing. Airports often restrict who is able to install fuel tanks and for what purpose. An entity which has the exclusive right to sell fuel on the airfield carries significant value; however, if co-op fuel arrangements are common place on the field, this may drastically reduce local demand."
- "First, if a fixed base operator, perform due diligence on EPA regulation adherence (e.g., fuel farm) and hangar leases with city or county."

Expert Comments

"EPA guidelines/inspections can ruin risk, or promote you against your competition. The 14x EBITDA multiple of the Trajan FBO days (sold to

Rules of Thumb - A

Macquarie) are long gone. Multiples have improved from the bottom level of 3X seen during the Recession."

"A major source of income is from fuel sales. Margins vary greatly depending on competition. Location is a key factor that affects the amount of traffic at an airport and thus the volume of business. Smaller FBOs are harder to market because most require owner operators with a passion for aviation. After a long down period the industry is tending up. FBOs are difficult to duplicate as the property is generally owned and controlled by some government entity. The number of operators allowed at any given airfield in limited."

"The private jet industry has taken an economic hit the past few years, as a luxury brand. Industry growth rate is under 2%. The political climate has not helped. The high growth areas now are in southeast Asia and in Brazil."

Benchmark Data

Statistics (Airport Operations)

Number of Establishments	2,242
Average Profit Margin	3.5%
Revenue per Employee	$294,100
Average Number of Employees	36.3
Average Wages per Employee	$67,805

Products and Services Segmentation

Fixed base operations	64.2%
Airport administration and operation services	13.2%
Handling services for goods	11.2%
Other services	7.9%
Repair and maintenance services for aircraft	3.5%

Major Market Segmentation

Commercial flights	64.4%
Business and private flights	30.5%
Freight and other flights	5.1%

Industry Costs

Profit	3.5%
Wages	22.6%
Purchases	18.8%
Depreciation	27.3%
Marketing	2.1%
Rent & Utilities	6.2%
Other	19.5%

Market Share

The Port Authority of New York and New Jersey	10.6%

Source: IBISWorld, June 2015

- "For FBO labor costs should be 20–35%. Occupancy could be variable depending on the airport and real estate costs. Rent+utilities, 14%"

26th Edition

A - Rules of Thumb

- "Variable cost for pumping fuel is about 40 cents per gallon. Thinking of the eventual exit strategy, the FBO should be pumping 80,000 gallons a month to attract a global buyer. Such an FBO would have about 30 employees and generate from $8 million to $15 million in annual sales, depending on location."
- "Standard & Poor's benchmarks are a good starting place. Premiums placed on location, e.g., Van Nuys, CA or major cities."
- "High private-jet-traffic airports. Jet fuel sales a plus. General aviation service only and/or airports with less than 5,000-foot runways sell at a discount."

Expenses as a percentage of annual sales

Cost of goods	30% to 40%
Payroll/labor Costs	25% to 35%
Occupancy	05% to 10%
Profit (estimated pretax)	05% to 15%

Industry Trend

- "Governmental regulation is putting pressure on smaller companies. Consolidation is expected to be the norm as smaller entities are absorbed by larger entities such as Nation Fixed Based Operators, local governments (city/county) or private equity investors."
- "Although the slow growth of the U.S. economy and the European recession has dampened the near term prospects for general aviation, the long-term outlook remains favorable. We see growth in business aviation demand over the long term driven by a growing U.S. and world economy especially in the turbo jet, turboprop and turbine rotorcraft markets. As the fleet grows, the number of general aviation hours flown is projected to increase an average of 1.5 percent a year through 2033."

  Source: FAA Aerospace Forecast Fiscal Years 2013-2033
- "Private jet aviation is the main driver of many of these airport businesses; how the business jet industry goes is how these services will go."
- "Major research firms are showing a delivery of over 10,000 private jets in the next 10 years, implying a need for more airport service providers, including FBOs. City governments are now taking ownership of some FBOs, which is a threat to entrepreneurship. The inability of FBO owners to get more than a 25-year lease from a city is also a threat to profitability."

Seller Financing

- "Outside and partial seller financing. Depends on the particular sale"
- "Partial seller financing is sometimes available and the term is generally 5 years."
- 3–5 years

Questions

- "Why sell? How long is lease with city? Any renewable lease clauses? If so, at what rate?"
- "Insurance can be a major cost component. What is the company's safety record? Does the business operate under any FAA certificates (IE 135 charter or 141 flight school)? Is maintenance involved with the FBO? How many IAs and A&Ps are employed? Are they contract workers? Is it an FAA certified repair station? Is it an authorized repair station for an OEM? What is the hangar occupancy rate? Is there a waiting list? How long? What are the

Rules of Thumb - A

average rates per square foot?"
- "Why sell now? Any trouble with city/local governments? Status of existing leases/agreements? Trouble with EPA? Labor issues?"

Resources

Websites
- FAA Aviation Forecasts: http://www.faa.gov/about/office_org/headquarters_offices/apl/aviation_forecasts/

Trade Publications
- Aviation International News: http://ainonline.com

Associations
- Aeronautical Repair Station Association (ARSA): www.arsa.org
- Aircraft Electronics Association (AEA): www.aea.net
- Aviation Suppliers Association (ASA): www.aviationsuppliers.org
- National Air Transportation Association (NATA): www.nata.aero
- Aircraft Owner's and Pilot's Association (AOPA): www.aopa.org
- Professional Aviation Maintenance Association (PAMA): www.pama.org
- General Aviation Manufacturers Association: http://www.gama.aero/
- International Air Transport Association (IATA): www.iata.org

	Franchise
Allegra Marketing-Print-Mail (See also Franchises, Printing)	
Approx. Total Investment	$167,352 to $589,654
NAICS 323114	Number of Businesses/Units 304

Rules of Thumb
➢ 60% to 65% of annual sales plus inventory

Resources

Websites
- www.allegranetwork.com

		Franchise
All Tune and Lube		
(See also Auto Lube, Franchises, Grease Monkey, Jiffy Lube)		
Approx. Total Investment		$150,000
SIC 7549-03	NAICS 81191	Number of Businesses/Units 358

Rules of Thumb
➢ 20 to 25 percent of annual sales

Resources

Websites
- www.alltuneandlube.com

26th Edition 23

A - Rules of Thumb

AlphaGraphics (See also Franchises)	Franchise
Approx. Total Investment	$258,300 to $395,900
Estimated Annual Sales/Unit	$1,125,700
SIC 7336-02 NAICS 541430	Number of Businesses/Units 245

Rules of Thumb
➤ 60 to 65 percent of annual sales plus inventory

Aluminum Smelting Machinery	
	NAICS 331316

Rules of Thumb
➤ 70 percent of annual sales plus inventory
➤ 5 times EBITDA

Pricing Tips
- "If balance sheet is sound, business is worth an average between twice net assets and 5 times EBITDA."

Expert Comments
"Highly specialized market. Vendor must establish himself on short list of major EPCMs through references. Spare parts market captive and profitable."

Benchmark Data
- "$250,000 per employee"

Expenses as a percentage of annual sales
Cost of goods... 70%
Payroll/labor Costs.. 25%
Occupancy... 05%
Profit (estimated pretax) 10%

Industry Trend
- "The aluminum market is growing fast. New smelters are being built. Older are being extended or revamped. Market for machinery will be excellent for next 5 years at least."

Questions
- "Indebtedness? Officers' loan or debt? Backlog and list of references."

Rules of Thumb - A

Ambulance Services

| SIC 4119-02 | NAICS 62191 | Number of Businesses/Units 47,665 |

Rules of Thumb
- 40 percent of annual revenues plus inventory
- 2 to 4.0 times SDE includes inventory
- 2.75 to 5.2 times EBITDA

Pricing Tips
- "There are fourteen (14) different business characteristics which all affect the value of these companies. As such the EBITDA multiplier can be as low as 2.0 and as high as 6.5 in the current market, depending on these characteristics within each company."
- "Prices and Multiples paid by buyers can vary greatly... They can vary by 30–40% on the same exact size company, with the same amount of earnings/EBITDA. There are 14 specific characteristics which all affect a company's value to buyers."
- "Owner's level of involvement is definitely a major contributor to a multiplier. Revenue per vehicle is a very top level gauge of company's performance. Revenue per vehicle varies with geography. For example, in No. California revenue per vehicle is 20% higher than in So. California. Two major expenses to watch after are payroll and cost of fuel."
- "Large pricing range due to a larger number of key variables that affect valuation. Transition period with seller is critical (should be at least 6 months to a year, even on smaller businesses)."
- "Payer mix & breakdowns very important; breakdowns on advanced life support (ALS) vs. basic chair transports diminish profitability."

Expert Comments

"Very few companies consistently provide a high level of service and generate solid EBITDA margins in the 18–25% range. The industry is very fragmented, with companies over $10 MM in Net Cash Sales and solid earnings securing premium pricing."

"Amount of competition varies by region. Some areas in California are very densely populated and the density is connected to a number of medical facilities in the area. Location of the office is irrelevant to the business, however parking availability for the fleet is definitely a benefit. Government cut rates several times, therefore profits suffered and owners had to streamline their businesses and cut expenses in order to maintain profit margins. Threshold of entry in the industry is pretty high, especially if company wants to get paid by the government. The approval process is quite lengthy."

"Aging baby boomers will drive increased transport volume. Regional and statewide Medicaid brokerage contracts are becoming more common, but only account for a small percentage of transports and are low-profit runs. Implementing appropriate technologies is becoming a requirement for operators in order to maintain profit levels. It is very hard for startups to steal customers away from high-level providers."

A - Rules of Thumb

"Growing number of transports, but tougher for the smaller provider (all under $5–$7 million in sales) to compete effectively against the mid-sized players; trend is to sell, merge or acquire; knowledge of ambulance billing is very important."

Benchmark Data

Statistics (Ambulance Services)
Number of Establishments	47,665
Average Profit Margin	8.4%
Revenue per Employee	$73,400
Average Number of Employees	4.7
Average Wages per Employee	$32,484

Products and Services Segmentation
BLS nonemergency care	41.9%
ALS emergency care	35.9%
BLS emergency care	19.0%
ALS nonemergency care	2.5%
Other	0.7%

Major Market Segmentation
Sprains or strains of neck and back	21.9%
Contusion with intact skin surface	21.5%
Open wounds	16.5%
Fractures	13.4%
Sprains or strains excluding neck and back	13.2%
Spinal disorders	8.8%
Other	4.7%

Industry Costs
Profit	8.4%
Wages	44.3%
Purchases	20.4%
Depreciation	4.4%
Marketing	1.0%
Rent & Utilities	3.6%
Other	17.9%

Market Share
Envision Healthcare	11.2%
Air Methods	5.8%

Source: IBISWorld, April 2015

Establishments by Employment Size
Number of Employees	Share of total
1 to 4	15.3%
5 to 9	7.7%
10 to 19	15.1%
20 to 99	28.3%
100 to 499	11.9%
More than 500	21.7%

Source: IBISWorld, May 2014

Rules of Thumb - A

- "Industry avg EBITDA is 7–8% of Net Cash Sales per year; well-run operations generate 18–25% EBITDA margins and these companies sell for a premium compared to equally sized companies in the market. Keeping total payroll costs down and having a good billing process/dept. are keys to drive profitability."
- **"The Study**
  In October, as required by the Middle Class Tax Relief Act of 2012, the GAO undertook compiling the results of the study in an attempt to provide Congress with an update to the 2007 study which also looked at ambulance costs across the U.S.A. The methodology came from the end-product of an April 2012 web-based survey of a sample invitation size of 294 ambulance providers of which 154 responses were accepted and considered valid as representative of the industry by the GAO.
  "Big Variation
  The GAO reported finding that ambulance transport costs varied greatly across the country, ranging from $224 on the low end to $2,204 per run on the high end of the scale. The study ultimately focused on medians (not averages, as the 2007 study did.) It was determined that the median per transport cost to provide EMS services in America is $429 per run with a projected overall median cost range coming in at between $401 to $475 across the board.
  "Urban/Rural/Super Rural
  The sample showed a wide range of costs for urban ambulance providers versus rural ambulance providers versus super rural ambulance providers, as would reasonably be expected.
  "The urban providers who responded to the survey reported a median per trip cost of $397 per run with an estimated range of $374 to $410. Rural providers checked in with a range of $404 to $550 per trip and a median cost amount of $469."
  Source: http://www.ambulancebillingservices.com/2013/03/american-ambulance-industry-cost.html
- "In No. California sales per vehicle is $100,000; in So. Cal. it is around $85,000."
- "Over 55% Medicare payer mix; wheelchair runs lower profits, so fewer the better. Companies with over 25% of their cash being collected via runs being from hospitals typically show stronger profits and collect more cash per run."
- "UHU rating .35 or higher"
- "4–6 transports per day, per ambulance; logistics are critical and impact profitability, as does scheduling."

Expenses as a percentage of annual sales
Cost of goods	08%
Payroll/labor Costs	45% to 57%
Occupancy	01.5% to 03.0%
Profit (estimated pretax)	07% to 22%

Industry Trend
- "'Ambulances are transporting patients that are healthy enough to travel by other means. It is a very lucrative business because each patient that is transported three times a week—[for example,] a typical dialysis patient—is worth, bills Medicare $60,000 per patient,' said Ron Kerr, assistant special agent in charge in the Office of Inspector General, U.S. Department of Health and Human Services.

26th Edition

A - Rules of Thumb

"One undercover video showed patients—Medicare beneficiaries—riding in the front seat of an ambulance as they were taken to a doctor's appointment. What should have been a $20 cab ride now skyrocketing to more than $400 roundtrip, all paid for by Medicare."

Source:"Millions Lost Yearly to Ambulance Companies Acting Like a 'Taxi Service,'" by David Kerley, http://abcnews.go.com/blogs/politics/2015/01/millions-lost-yearly-to-ambulance-companies-acting-like-a-taxi-service 1/16/15

- "Smaller companies doing $2 MM or less in cash sales are having a tough time competing. Expect continued growth due to aging baby boomer population, but fewer smaller companies will be able to compete long term."
- "Increased technology & efficiencies improvements will become a requirement to survive."
- "I believe any industry related to servicing aging and ill population will grow over the next 20–30 years. People live longer and get sick and need transportation to get to medical offices. Therefore demand for medical transportation will only grow."
- "GIA announces the release of a comprehensive global report on Ambulance Services markets. Global market for Ambulance Services is projected to reach US $59 billion by 2018, driven by aging population, increasing occurrences of road accidents and natural calamities and rising prevalence of critical health conditions."

Source: "Aging Population Drives the Global Ambulance Services Market, According to New Report by Global Industry Analysts, Inc.," PR Web, June 19, 2013

- "Increased volume, more technology being utilized to maximize profits"
- "Higher CAPEX cost due to need to implement technology for both logistics management and patient record management"
- "Ambulance providers face unique financial challenges due to inadequate Medicare payments and barriers to receiving federal homeland security funds."

Source: American Ambulance Association

Seller Financing
- "On deals under $3 MM in price, seller financing is a requirement on all deals; larger deals are 70–80% cash including bank financing (includes 5–8% Rep & Warranty Escrows for 12–24 months)"
- "Although we use both (Outside Financing and Seller Financing), seller financing is more typical lately."
- 3–5 years

Questions
- "Knowledge of medical billing; logistics management; attention to details."
- "Except regular financial due diligence, buyers should be watching for lawsuits against the company and traffic tickets. High level of lawsuits and traffic tickets indicates that the business doesn't have good driver education and discipline in place."
- "Lots—There are a lot of fraudulent practices and brokers need to understand the industry and billing guidelines or they should avoid taking a listing/representing the owner; need to know the quantity of dialysis patients; businesses with a high percentage of dialysis runs get discounted in valuation/pricing"
- "Who does billing: in-house or sub out to 3rd party? What software is used? What systems do you have in place & utilize for billing and for logistics? Do you prescreen your transports/patients?"

Rules of Thumb - **A**

- "Medicare & Medicaid audits & status of these? Billing processes & procedures; qualifying transports."

Resources

Associations
- California Medical Transportation Association (CMTA): cmtasite.com
- American Ambulance Association- primarily for members: www.the-aaa.org

	Franchise
American Poolplayers Association (APA)	
(See also Billiards, Franchises)	

Approx. Total Investment		$16,695 to $19,865
SIC 7999-12	NAICS 713990	Number of Businesses/Units 300

Rules of Thumb
- ➢ 1.4 times annual sales
- ➢ $1,000 to $1,800 per team in sales: selling price—$2,000 to $2,500 per team

Pricing Tips
- "These franchises are purchased by areas. Pricing is normally based on the number of teams in the area. The general rule of thumb is $2,000 per team in a well-managed area."

Expenses as a percentage of annual sales
Cost of goods	n/a
Payroll/labor Costs	n/a
Occupancy	n/a
Profit (estimated pretax)	35%

Industry Trend
- "Increase in popularity and participation in recreational billiards"

Resources

Websites
- www.poolplayers.com

	Franchise
Andy OnCall (See also Franchises)	

Approx. Total Investment		$35,650 to $62,050
	NAICS 236118	Number of Businesses/Units 50

Rules of Thumb
- ➢ 25 percent of annual sales
- ➢ Andy OnCall connects unemployed craftsmen with homeowners who need home repairs.

26th Edition

A - Rules of Thumb

Benchmark Data

Statistics (Handyman Service Franchises)
Number of Establishments	1,042
Average Profit Margin	4.7%
Revenue per Employee	$146,900
Average Number of Employees	9.2
Average Wages per Employee	$36,385

Products and Services Segmentation
Maintenance services	63.1%
Plumbing	8.6%
Electrical	7.5%
Others	7.3%
Decks and Fences	5.1%
Painting	5.1%
Flooring	3.3%

Major Market Segmentation
Households	68.2%
Property owners and managers	14.8%
Commercial clients	10.0%
Other	7.0%

Industry Costs
Profit	4.7%
Wages	24.9%
Purchases	46.3%
Depreciation	1.5%
Marketing	2.5%
Rent & Utilities	2.9%
Other	17.2%

Source: IBISWorld, September 2014

Resources

Websites
- www.andyoncall.com

Antique Malls

		Number of Businesses/Units 10,000

Rules of Thumb
> 2 to 4 times EBITDA with a minimum of $100,000 EBITDA not including real estate

Resources

Associations
- National Association of Antique Malls (NAAM): www.antiqueandcollectible.com

Rules of Thumb - A

Antique Shops/Dealers

SIC 5932-02	NAICS 453310	Number of Businesses/Units 1,258

Rules of Thumb
> 20 percent of annual sales plus inventory

Resources

Websites
- Art and Antique Dealers League of America: www.artantiquedealersleague.com

Anytime Fitness (See also Fitness Centers, Franchises)

Franchise

Approx. Total Investment		$61,599 to $215,299
	NAICS 713940	Number of Businesses/Units 2,400

Rules of Thumb
> 2.5 times SDE plus inventory

Pricing Tips
- "Multiples of SDE vary based on size of the owner benefit. SDE less than $75k, typically we see multiples in the 1 range. $75–$150k, we see multiples in the 1.8 to 2.5 range. Greater than $150k multiples may be higher."

Expert Comments

"'We've never had any major incidents in our 12 years. I think people love getting their own key and going anytime they want. I should mention that we're not completely unstaffed; a franchise owner will likely work 30 to 50 hours a week, depending on the time of year. In January they're going to work longer, and in the summer months less.'

"'When we came up with the concept, it was a new category in the fitness industry. There was no such thing as a nonstaffed club. By using technology we dramatically minimized overhead—taxes, utilities, rent, payroll. So-called industry experts said it would never work. They felt there was no way people would join if they didn't get hands-on service with every single visit.'"

Source: "Anytime Fitness," quotes from Chuck Runyon and Dave Mortensen, edited by Cristina Lindblad & Dimitra Kessenides, *Businessweek*

Seller Financing
- 2 years

Questions
- "How much in prepaid memberships?"

A - Rules of Thumb

Apartment Locators

| SIC 6531-11 | NAICS 531110 | Number of Businesses/Units 666,656 |

Rules of Thumb
➢ 80 percent of annual revenues

Pricing Tips
- "This is generally a secondary revenue source to real estate sales."
- Note: A real estate license may be required for the operation of this business.

Benchmark Data

Statistics (Apartment Rental)
Number of Establishments	666,656
Average Profit Margin	33.9%
Revenue per Employee	$177,800
Average Number of Employees	1.4
Average Wages per Employee	$21,781

Products and Services Segmentation
Rental of one-unit structures	35.4%
Rental of two- to four-unit structures	19.2%
Rental of five- to nine-unit structures	12.5%
Rental of 10- to 19-unit structures	11.9%
Rental of 50- or more unit structures	8.7%
Rental of 20- to 49-unit structures	8.4%
Rental of manufactured homes, mobile homes or trailers	3.9%

Major Market Segmentation
1 person	36.2%
2 persons	27.2%
4 or more persons	21.2%
3 persons	15.4%

Industry Costs
Profit	33.9%
Wages	12.3%
Purchases	9.4%
Depreciation	20.1%
Marketing	1.4%
Rent & Utilities	3.5%
Other	19.4%

Source: IBISWorld, May 2015

- "Fees are most often paid by the apartment owner, usually about 10% to 15% or one month's rent."

Questions
- "How long have they been in business? How do they locate apartments? Do they have an online database? How many apartment communities do they work with?"

Source: www.austinapartmentfinder.com

Rules of Thumb - **A**

Appliance Stores (See also Furniture and Appliance Stores)		
SIC 5064	NAICS 443111	Number of Businesses/Units 33,760

Rules of Thumb
➢ 2 times monthly sales plus inventory

Benchmark Data
- "Markup is about 27 percent with some discounters working on a 25 percent markup."

Resources

Associations
- Association of Home Appliance Manufacturers: www.aham.org
- North American Retail Dealers Association: www.narda.com

Appraisal (Valuation Services)		
SIC 7389	NAICS 541990	

Pricing Tips
- "For a firm with less than 10 professionals—1.25 to 1.5 times EBITDA. This would include all FF&E and related software and exclude Accounts Receivable and Accounts Payable. Most of the deals are where there is a merger of firms or a buyout by a CPA firm wanting to get into the appraisal business. They usually want the seller to manage the operation for several years."

Benchmark Data

Statistics (Real Estate Appraisal)
Number of Establishments	74,233
Average Profit Margin	14.3%
Revenue per Employee	$79,800
Average Number of Employees	1.3
Average Wages per Employee	$29,176

Products and Services Segmentation
Real estate appraisal - commercial	50.2%
Real estate appraisal - residential	26.5%
Real estate consulting	10.9%
Appraisal management	6.6%
Real estate brokerage and other services	5.8%

Major Market Segmentation
Financial institutions &brokers	58.0%
Law offices	15.0%
Private owners	13.0%
Government and other	8.0%
Accountants	6.0%

26th Edition

A - Rules of Thumb

Industry Costs

Profit	14.3%
Wages	36.7%
Purchases	9.3%
Depreciation	1.3%
Marketing	2.6%
Rent & Utilities	7.8%
Other	28.0%

Market Share

CBRE Group Inc.	7.0%

Source: IBISWorld, March 2015

Statistics (Business Valuation Firms)

Number of Establishments	84,924
Average Profit Margin	8.8%
Revenue per Employee	$63,800
Average Number of Employees	1.1
Average Wages per Employee	$25,840

Products and Services Segmentation

Comprehensive appraisals	55.2%
Preliminary value studies	23.4%
Limited partnership appraisals	17.0%
Other	4.4%

Major Market Segmentation

Service sector	30.1%
Retail trade	25.7%
Manufacturing	19.8%
Other industries	12.7%
Finance, insurance and real estate	6.1%
Wholesale trade	5.6%

Industry Costs

Profit	8.8%
Wages	40.7%
Purchases	12.1%
Depreciation	1.5%
Marketing	1.7%
Rent & Utilities	4.3%
Other	30.9%

Source: IBISWorld, February 2015

Resources

Associations

- American Society of Appraisers: www.appraisers.org
- Institute of Business Appraisers (IBA): instbusapp.org
- National Association of Certified Valuation Analysts (NACVA): www.nacva.com

Rules of Thumb - **A**

Arcade, Food & Entertainment Complexes

SIC 7993-03	NAICS 713120	Number of Businesses/Units 7,609

Rules of Thumb

> ➤ 25 percent of annual sales includes inventory
> ➤ 3 times SDE includes inventory
> ➤ 3 to 3.5 EBITDA

Pricing Tips

- "Make sure the equipment is either owned and is in current, 'fashionable' condition, or make sure there is an attractive lease arrangement that enables simple trade-in for more current gaming. These games are only as valuable as the current trend. There are 'stability' games such as air hockey, certain pinball games and redemption games where you can win toy prizes straight from the machine. The store must have a mix of current trend equipment and the stability games. Stability games are the work horses but the trendy games are very expensive to stay on top of."

- "This industry is not for everyone! Although, if you are an experienced retailer and have a stomach for high rent-to-gross sales percentages, this could be a great opportunity for you to enter into a fun and rewarding industry! It is a simple business model and can be improved significantly by introducing customer promotions combining game tokens with redemption prize incentives and local food retailers."

Expert Comments

"Games must also be attractive/specific to area demographics. Interestingly, my clients that owned a chain of stores in and around New York City found that the Asian neighborhoods demand more high-tech, challenging games and they will correspondingly pay a higher price per use. This is not a business that a client should jump into ill-informed or insufficiently researched. Only buy tried and true locations. Don't build new locations unless on a massive scale like Dave & Busters. They are a one-stop entertainment supercenter including food, bowling and usually booze. The smaller locations in malls and plazas are way too risky given the fact that kids don't need to leave the home anymore to get the most current and challenging gaming. So, if there is a location that has withstood the transition to home-based gaming through the 80s, 90s and up to now, it is likely a winner. These arcade formats only now work in certain neighborhoods, need high volume given the price of commercial real estate, etc. Get a long lease."

"Location is KEY. This is a capital-intensive industry but a proven location is a very valuable semi-absentee opportunity. If you are buying existing units, you can use the assets in the purchase to back part of the financing."

Benchmark Data

Statistics (Arcade, Food & Entertainment Complexes)

Number of Establishments	6,697
Average Profit Margin	14.1%
Revenue per Employee	$54,900
Average Number of Employees	5.5
Average Wages per Employee	$12,255

A - Rules of Thumb

Products and Services Segmentation

Debit-card and coin-operated games and rides	45.1%
Food and beverages	35.9%
Admissions	14.2%
Corporate and party event services	4.2%
Other	0.6%

Industry Costs

Profit	14.1%
Wages	22.3%
Purchases	25.1%
Depreciation	7.8%
Marketing	2.6%
Rent & Utilities	8.4%
Other	19.7%

Market Share

CEC Entertainment Inc.	40.7%
Dave & Buster's Entertainment Inc.	34.4%

Source: IBISWorld, November 2014

Statistics (Golf Driving Ranges and Family Fun Centers)

Number of Establishments	54,151
Average Profit Margin	4.1%
Revenue per Employee	$74,200
Average Number of Employees	2.6
Average Wages per Employee	$19,422

Products and Services Segmentation

Other	31.6%
Amusement and recreation services	30.5%
Coin operated games and rides	14.0%
Amateur sports teams and club services	6.7%
Meals and beverages	5.5%
Fitness and recreational sport center services	5.1%
Registration for sports tournaments and matches	3.8%
Golf course and country club services and memberships	2.8%

Industry Costs

Profit	4.1%
Wages	26.2%
Purchases	27.5%
Depreciation	1.3%
Marketing	1.0%
Rent & Utilities	16.0%
Other	23.9%

Source: IBISWorld, May 2015

- "Game costs range from $2,500 to $15,000 per new machine. You do not have to buy new machinery! Sell older technology online and buy new circuitry for new games and put them in your existing game machines. It will save tremendous operating capital and the customer will not know the difference."

Rules of Thumb - A

Expenses as a percentage of annual sales

Cost of goods .... 05% to 10%
Payroll/labor Costs 15%
Occupancy .... 40% to 50%
Profit (estimated pretax) .... 15% to 20%

Industry Trend

- "This industry has seen a significant decline since the advent of in-home video gaming. However, it is my estimation that the business has seen its bottom and consistent sales should continue indefinitely, given good gaming technology for your clients."

Questions

- "Asset values?"

Resources

Websites

- Coaster Grotto: http://www.coastergrotto.com/theme-park-attendance.jsp

Architectural Firms		
SIC 8712-02	NAICS 541310	Number of Businesses/Units 74,595

Rules of Thumb

➤ 40 percent of annual sales plus inventory

Pricing Tips

- "Consulting firms that specialize in ownership transitions develop a fair-market value based on a handful of factors including adjusted net worth (book value), weighted net income, weighted net fees, projected fees, and backlog of unearned fees.

  "These factors produce a range of a firm's value. For example, some consultants value a firm at between 1 and 1.5 times adjusted net worth for an internal transition or between 2 and 3 times for an external sale. Other consultants value a firm at between 3 and 5 times weighted net income or apply a percentage of their average earnings to their backlog of unearned fees."

  Source: "How Much Is Your Firm Really Worth?" excerpted and adapted from an AIA Architect article by Michael Strogoff

- "Goodwill is at a minimum due to the non-repetitiveness of the clients. It is also a personal service business. The stature, reputation and contacts of the principal(s) are generally not transferable, especially in a smaller firm."

Expert Comments

"Tools for Small Firms: Simple Business Practices that Reduce Risk
- ✓ Not documenting advice given or decisions made during conversations with the client.
- ✓ Not using a written agreement.

A - Rules of Thumb

- ✓ Beginning work before having a signed written agreement.
- ✓ Not following the written agreement once it is in place.
- ✓ Taking any job that walks through the door."

Source: Rena M. Klein, FAIA, principal of R.M. Klein Consulting, in Seattle, Washington, is a member of the Soloso Editorial Content Review Board and serves as the Subject Matter Expert for Practice.

Benchmark Data

Statistics (Architects)

Number of Establishments	74,595
Average Profit Margin	12.7%
Revenue per Employee	$173,700
Average Number of Employees	2.9
Average Wages per Employee	$63,915

Products and Services Segmentation

New project architectural services	58.0%
Renovation and rehabilitation architectural service	42.0%

Major Market Segmentation

Institutional construction	53.0%
Commercial and industrial construction	27.0%
Residential construction	16.0%
Other	4.0%

Industry Costs

Profit	12.7%
Wages	37.1%
Purchases	10.3%
Depreciation	1.4%
Marketing	1.2%
Rent & Utilities	4.5%
Other	32.8%

Source: IBISWorld, May 2015

Resources

Websites
- The American Institute of Architects, an excellent site: www.aia.org

Art Galleries and Dealers		
SIC 5999-69	NAICS 453920	Number of Businesses/Units 24,398

Rules of Thumb
- ➢ 30 percent of annual revenues plus inventory

Pricing Tips
- "In some galleries, much of the art work may be on consignment."

Rules of Thumb - A

- "A surprising number of people search for answers to these and similar questions in attempts to quantify the art market. The art market, however, is not quantifiable, and the answers to these questions don't exist. To begin with, art is not a commodity that can be regulated. Anyone can call him or herself an artist, anyone can call anything that they create 'art,' and anyone can be an art dealer. Anyone can sell art wherever, whenever and under whatever circumstances they please, and price or sell whatever they call 'art' for whatever amounts of money they feel like selling it for, as long as that art is offered without fraud or misrepresentation."

Source: www.artbusiness.com

Expert Comments

"5 tips to building your own art business:
- ✓ Find your niche
- ✓ Know and understand basic business principles and essentials
- ✓ Build and maintain a network of professionals already running their own successful art business
- ✓ Learn to brand yourself, and start with social media and a functioning Website
- ✓ Don't get down on yourself and don't give up"

Source: http://theartcareerproject.com

Benchmark Data

Statistics (Art Dealers)

Number of Establishments	24,398
Average Profit Margin	7.0%
Revenue per Employee	$320,000
Average Number of Employees	1.5
Average Wages per Employee	$60,479

Products and Services Segmentation

Paintings	54%
Drawings	33%
Sculptures	8%
Photography and other media	3%
Prints	2%

Major Market Segmentation

Art collectors	65.7%
Companies	23.9%
Other art buyers	10.4%

Industry Costs

Profit	7.0%
Wages	18.8%
Purchases	49.0%
Depreciation	0.7%
Marketing	4.0%
Rent & Utilities	9.8%
Other	10.7%

A - Rules of Thumb

Market Share
Christie's International	3.7%
Sotheby's Holdings Inc.	3.6%

Source: IBISWorld, May 2015

Resources

Associations
- Art Dealers Association of America: www.artdealers.org

Arts & Crafts/Retail Stores (See also Hobby Shops)

SIC 5085	NAICS 45113	Number of Businesses/Units 21,674

Rules of Thumb
- 35 percent of annual sales plus inventory
- 2 times SDE plus inventory

Pricing Tips
- "Inventory should be priced separately and should include any costs associated with shipping the inventory to the place of business. Also, any needed labor required to re-package product should be part of COGS and not part of labor. As with most other business valuations, look hard at attractors and detractors to the 36% rule of thumb."
- "You should be able to tell if a 'crafter' is operating the business as opposed to a 'business person,' by their financials."
- Note: The people who actually create the finished arts and crafts (craftspeople) are unique and their business might be difficult to sell because of the very nature of what they produce. Their skill is usually not transferable.

Benchmark Data

Statistics (Fabric, Craft & Sewing Supplies Stores)
Number of Establishments	21,674
Average Profit Margin	5.0%
Revenue per Employee	$77,900
Average Number of Employees	2.8
Average Wages per Employee	$11,344

Products and Services Segmentation
Fabrics	40.0%
Sewing and craft supplies	33.0%
Other	12.0%
Seasonal decorations	8.0%
Fabric home decor	7.0%

Industry Costs
Profit	5.0%
Wages	14.6%
Purchases	60.2%
Depreciation	0.9%
Marketing	2.1%
Rent & Utilities	5.5%
Other	11.7%

Rules of Thumb - A

Market Share

Michaels Stores Inc.	47.7%
Jo-Ann Stores Inc.	26.5%
Hobby Lobby Stores Inc.	19.1%
Hancock Fabrics Inc.	6.0%

Source: IBISWorld, July 2015

- "A benchmarking study on the business practices of private store front and home-based businesses that sell crafts directly to the public was recently released by Craft & Hobby Association (CHA). The purpose of the study was to explore best practices that make an independent craft retailer successful and to share the data with CHA members and industry suppliers.

Business practices that were common among the top 15% of the independent retailers were:
- ✓ 86% were store front businesses
- ✓ 46% were paper related businesses
- ✓ 47% had a strong customer database and did outbound marketing
- ✓ More than half use social media to market their business; with Facebook as the most active
- ✓ More than half invested time in continuing education and professional development"

Source: Craft and Hobby Association, May 2015

- "Rent at 10% of GAS (Gross Annual Sales). Sales per square foot at $150–$175. Sales per employee at $75,000–$125,000. Advertising at 3%–4% of GAS."

Expenses as a percentage of annual sales

Cost of goods	50%
Payroll/labor Costs	15%
Occupancy	15%
Profit (estimated pretax)	20%

Industry Trend

- "Last year's hot item, rubber band jewelry-making kits from Rainbow Loom, has transitioned into an ongoing children's department item after significantly boosting the retailer's sales in the second half of 2013, CEO Chuck Rubin said. Rubin was upbeat about the company's prospects during a conference call with analysts Wednesday morning. 'I feel good about where we are and where we are going. And while we are realistic about the sales comparisons in the back half of fiscal 2014, we are confident in our overall business, our outlook and our strategies,' Rubin said.

"Michaels.com, which launched earlier this year, has had good traffic that continues to grow, Rubin said. But he said the company believes its e-commerce business won't be as big as it is for other retailers given the large number of items and low-cost items the retailer sells. Michaels added WiFi to all its stores in the quarter so shoppers can look up project ideas from Pinterest or michaels.com on their mobile devices.

"The retailer is going after the 'novice customer' who sees projects she likes in social media but doesn't know how long it will take or how to get started. They can also be overwhelmed by all the items in a craft store, Rubin said. As part of that program, the company has new exclusive yarn assortments with 40 product ideas and simplified instructions, he said."

Source: "Arts and crafts retailer Michaels is upbeat" by Maria Halkias, http://www.dallasnews.com/business/retail/20140827-arts-and-crafts-retailer-michaels-is-upbeat.ece 8/27/14

26th Edition

A - Rules of Thumb

Resources

Websites
- Craft and Hobby Association (CHA): www.craftandhobby.org

Trade Publications
- The Crafts Report—excellent publication: www.craftsreport.com

Art Supplies (See also Arts & Crafts, Hobby Shops)

SIC 5999-65	NAICS 453998	Number of Businesses/Units 21,778

Rules of Thumb
➢ 25 to 30 percent of annual sales plus inventory

Pricing Tips
- "Many hobby stores and related businesses may carry a line of art supplies. A store specializing in just art supplies requires an owner with the appropriate knowledge."

Benchmark Data
- For Benchmark Information see Retail Stores—Small Specialty

Assisted Living Facilities (See also Nursing Homes)

SIC 8361-05	NAICS 623311	Number of Businesses/Units 17,932

Rules of Thumb
➢ 75 percent of annual sales

➢ $30,000–$60,000 per bed. Pricing above this range typically raises a red flag for individual buyers.

➢ This business is based on net operating income divided by a capitalization rate of 10 to 14 percent.

Pricing Tips
- "Real-estate-intensive business. SBA pays extra attention to this industry to ensure that the buyers are not acting as 'passive real-estate investors,' but rather as small-business owners."
- "Capitalization of income for going concern value including real estate"
- "Occupancy in market area. Going cap rates at that specific time. Whether Medicaid or private pay?"

Benchmark Data

Statistics (Nursing Care)

Number of Establishments	17,932
Average Profit Margin	8.0%
Revenue per Employee	$73,900
Average Number of Employees	104.1
Average Wages per Employee	$30,754

Rules of Thumb - **A**

Products and Services Segmentation

For-profit nursing homes	39%
For-profit skilled nursing facilities	25%
Nonprofit nursing homes	14%
Nonprofit skilled nursing facilities	10%
Hospice centers	7%
Government nursing homes and skilled nursing facilities	5%

Industry Costs

Profit	8.0%
Wages	41.9%
Purchases	17.0%
Depreciation	2.6%
Marketing	0.4%
Rent & Utilities	7.0%
Other	23.1%

Source: IBISWorld, June 2015

- "More than 8 million people in the United States, most of whom are women and older than 65, used the services of a long-term care provider in 2012, according to federal data compiled for the first time focusing on provider types and the people who use them.

"The new data comes from the National Study of Long-Term Care Providers, a National Center for Health Statistics project with the aim of better understanding long-term care support services. The data covers five areas of paid, regulated providers – assisted living and related residential care communities, adult day service centers, home health agencies, hospices and nursing homes.

"The study noted that the long-term care services delivery system in the United States has changed substantially over the last 30 years. For example, although nursing homes are still a major provider of long-term care services, there are now a variety of home- and community-based alternatives, including residential care communities. For example, each day in 2012, there were approximately 713,300 residents in residential care communities and 1.38 million in nursing homes. About 58,500 paid, regulated long-term care services providers served the 8 million people in 2012, and that 58,500 breaks down into 22,200 assisted living and residential care communities, 3,700 hospices, 15,700 nursing homes, 12,200 home health agencies and 4,800 adult day services centers.

"The data also reflect trends in various regions of the United States. For example, in the western United States, the supply of residential care and nursing home communities was comparable but nursing homes far outnumbered residential care communities in all other regions. Residential care communities were more prevalent in the Midwest and West than in the Northeast and South.

"The report also touches on financing related to long-term care services. Most residents pay out-of-pocket for assisted living with a small percentage using Medicaid to pay for services. In contrast, the largest single payer for long-term nursing home is Medicaid while Medicare finances hospice costs and a major portion of the costs for short-stay, post-acute care in skilled nursing facilities for Medicare beneficiaries, it said."

Source: Harris-Kojetin L, Sengupta M, Park-Lee E, Valverde R. "Long-term care services in the United States: 2013 overview." Hyattsville, MD: National Center for Health Statistics. (the latest data available)

26th Edition

A - Rules of Thumb

Long-Term Care Spending by Payer:

Medicaid	42%
Medicare	25%
Out of Pocket	22%
Private Insurance and Other Sources	11%

Source: www.leadingage.org/facts

- "The average assisted living center resident is an 85-year-old female who pays close to $3,000 a month—though many needing greater care pay closer to $4,000 or $5,000. While the assisted living industry is currently strong, experts said a major shift in demographics and the looming threat of federal regulation could transform the industry over the next two decades."

    Source: "Assisted Living Centers Are Costing the Elderly a Pretty Penny" www.foxbusiness.com

- "Total expenses excluding debt service should average 68 percent."
- "Operating expense ratio—65 to 70 percent"

Industry Trend

- "In 2012, about 58,500 paid, regulated long-term care services providers served about 8 million people in the United States. Long-term care services were provided by 4,800 adult day services centers, 12,200 home health agencies, 3,700 hospices, 15,700 nursing homes, and 22,200 assisted living and similar residential care communities. Each day in 2012, there were 273,200 participants enrolled in adult day services centers, 1,383,700 residents in nursing homes, and 713,300 residents in residential care communities; in 2011, about 4,742,500 patients received services from home health agencies, and 1,244,500 patients received services from hospices."

    Source: "Long-Term Care Services in the United States: 2013 overview" by U.S. Department of Health and Human Services http://www.cdc.gov/nchs/data/nsltcp/long_term_care_services_2013.pdf

- "Between 2007 and 2015, the number of Americans ages 85 and older is expected to increase by 40 percent. By 2020, 12 million older Americans will need long-term health care."

    Source: HIAA, "A Guide to Long-Term Care Insurance"

Seller Financing

- 5 to 10 years

Resources

Websites
- National Center for Assisted Living: www.ncal.org
- A Place for Mom: www.aplaceformom.com

Associations
- Leading Age: www.leadingage.org
- Assisted Living Federation of America: www.alfa.org

Rules of Thumb - A

Franchise
Atlanta Bread Company (See Bakeries, Franchises)

Approx. Total Investment	$650,000 to $1,000,000
Estimated Annual Sales/Unit	$1 million
SIC 5812-08	NAICS 722211	Number of Businesses/Units 169

Rules of Thumb
➢ 25 to 30 percent of annual sales plus inventory

Audio and Film Companies	
NAICS 512120	Number of Businesses/Units 11,451

Rules of Thumb
➢ 4 to 6 times EBITDA

Pricing Tips
- "Ownership of the intellectual property is key to value. Companies that provide work-for-hire services are not as valuable as those that own the final production. Since this medium ages quickly, the economic life span of the films/videos is critical."

Benchmark Data

Statistics (Audio Production Studios)
Number of Establishments	5,106
Average Profit Margin	12.4%
Revenue per Employee	$121,300
Average Number of Employees	2.0
Average Wages per Employee	$41,737

Products and Services Segmentation
Postproduction sound editing & design (audio works)	24.7%
Music recording services	23.8%
Other sound editing & design	18.1%
Postproduction sound editing & design (video works)	13.2%
Radio recording services	12.8%
Spoken word recording services	7.4%

Major Market Segmentation
Music industry	50.0%
Film producers	17.0%
Advertising agencies	16.0%
TV and video producers	12.0%
Multimedia developers	5.0%

26th Edition

A - Rules of Thumb

Industry Costs
Profit	12.4%
Wages	34.5%
Purchases	20.3%
Depreciation	3.6%
Marketing	2.1%
Rent & Utilities	10.0%
Other	17.1%

Source: IBISWorld, September 2015

Statistics (Movie & Video Production)
Number of Establishments	6,410
Average Profit Margin	14.8%
Revenue per Employee	$510,600
Average Number of Employees	9.0
Average Wages per Employee	$81,555

Products and Services Segmentation
Action and adventure films	46.7%
Comedy films	21.9%
Thriller/suspense films	14.5%
Dramas	9.2%
Other films	7.7%

Major Market Segmentation
Domestic distributors of feature films, short films and other	56.2%
International distributors of feature films, short films and others	43.8%

Industry Costs
Profit	14.8%
Wages	15.8%
Purchases	52.1%
Depreciation	3.4%
Marketing	7.9%
Rent & Utilities	4.0%
Other	2.0%

Market Share
The Walt Disney Company	21.3%
21st Century Fox	18.9%
NBCUniversal Media LLC	14.9%
Time Warner Inc.	14.3%
Viacom Inc.	11.6%

Source: IBISWorld, March 2015

Seller Financing
- 3 to 7 years

Audio/Video Conferencing

SIC 4822-06	NAICS 518210

Rules of Thumb
➢ 3 to 4 times EBITDA

Rules of Thumb - A

Expert Comments
"Cost of setting up public centers is substantial. Industry is upgrading services and equipment."

Industry Trend
- "New technology is outdating old. Tele-presence is the new upgrade name."

Questions
- "How long are the contracts? What services are being provided?"

Auto Body Repair		
SIC 7532-01	NAICS 811121	Number of Businesses/Units 127,012

Rules of Thumb
➢ 25 to 35 percent of annual sales plus inventory

➢ 1.5 to 2.3 times SDE plus inventory

➢ 3 times EBIT

➢ 2 to 4 times EBITDA

Pricing Tips
- "Annual volume is critical. Low volume (below $600K) shops are difficult to sell. The higher the volume the higher the multiple. Franchises sell for lower multiples. Lease terms are very important."
- "Shops doing a volume of $500,000 are worth $125,000 or less."
- "Number of DRPs and length of time active a critical item."
- "Pricing usually 2.5 x owner benefit [SDE] plus fair market value of FF&E."
- "Shops doing less than $100,000 monthly sales are worth $125,000 or less, regardless of any other rule of thumb. Shops doing less than $40,000 in monthly sales are worth $75,000 or less."
- "Market value of FF&E is critical to accurate price development. Also—number of years in business, diversity of supplier base; with auto body shops the number & quality of DRP contracts, stability of labor pool, ease of replacing skilled employees & diversity/ stability of supplier base."

Expert Comments
"The industry is dominated by insurance companies. Contracts are not assumable by buyers. Without a contract, your volume is going to be very small. Regardless of how well the current owner is doing, when the business is transferred, the contracts are cancelled."

"Insurance referrals can go away very easily with ownership changes."

"Volume continues for a good quality shop even in a flat to declining economy."

"Body shops should only be purchased by experienced buyers in this industry. Shops doing less than $100,000 a month in sales all make around the same profit, which is $60,000 to $100,000 for a working owner. Working owner means one who physically works on cars some of the time. Only shops with a multiple of insurance contracts are easy to market. Shops without insurance contracts are very difficult to sell."

A - Rules of Thumb
Benchmark Data

Statistics (Car Body Shops)
Number of Establishments	127,012
Average Profit Margin	2.9%
Revenue per Employee	$121,400
Average Number of Employees	2.6
Average Wages per Employee	$35,063

Products and Services Segmentation
Body repair services	59.7%
Painting services	20.7%
Glass replacement and repair	11.6%
Merchandise sales	3.0%
Upholstery and interior repair	3.0%
Detailing services and body conversions	1.7%
Upholstery and interior repair	1.7%
Other services	1.6%

Industry Costs
Profit	2.9%
Wages	28.9%
Purchases	41.7%
Depreciation	0.7%
Marketing	1.4%
Rent & Utilities	6.7%
Other	17.7%

Source: IBISWorld, April 2015

Estimated Gross Annual Sales for 2014 (single repair facility)
Under $100K	2.8%
$100K-$250K	7.0%
$250K-$500K	18.6%
$500K-$750K	20.2%
$750K-$1M	21.5%
$1M-$1.5M	16.9%
$1.5M-$2M	8.3%
Over $2M	4.5%

Average Ticket (Top 4 Responses)
$200-$250	15.2%
$250-$300	21.0%
$300-$350	14.8%
$350-$400	12.8%

Ownership Status
Independent	83%
Dealership	7%
Network/Franchise	4%
Multi-Shop Operator	6%
Consolidator	1.2%

Rules of Thumb - A

Average Repair Order

$1–$1,500	7%
$1,501–$2,500	55%
$2,501–$3,500	35%
More than $3,500	3%

- "90% are family-owned businesses."
- "The higher the revenue and net, the higher the multiple. Less than $600K in revenues are difficult to sell. Number of DRP's and length of time active is very important."
- "The successful shop generates $150K per bay."
- "Rent can't be over 10% of gross income."
- "Shops doing over $100,000 per month in sales have a wide variation in profit, depending on the quality of the general manager and his ability to keep costs under control."

Expenses as a percentage of annual sales

Cost of goods	35% to 40%%
Payroll/labor Costs	20%
Occupancy	05% to 10%
Profit (estimated pretax)	15% to 20%

Industry Trend
- "Upward for established, quality-oriented operations with DRP relationships with clients, mainly insurance companies."

Seller Financing
- 3 to 5 years
- 5 years
- "Sellers carry for three to five years with SBA requiring the seller not to receive payments for the first two years."

Questions
- "How much of their time does the owner work on cars? When does your paint supplier contract expire? Lease terms. Employee census. Worker's comp mode rate. Reason for selling. Upside potential."
- "Percentage of volume that is DRP Contracts? (Insurance Contracts) Percentage of rent to gross sales? How much space is there indoors for car storage?"
- "Do you supply loan cars? If so, do you get rebates from rental companies for the loaners? When will a job be booked as a sale? Do you have steady referrals from dealerships? When are initial assessments made? Is any charge made for them? After the initial estimate is made, how are contacts made with the insurance company?"
- "What is your real sales volume? How many DRP contracts do you have? Which insurance companies are your DRP contracts with? What is the labor rate paid by the insurance companies? How many employees do you have? Are your employees paid a salary or a percentage of the production they produce? How many frame machines do you have? is your spray booth heated?"

A - Rules of Thumb

- "Show me your profit & loss statements, tax returns, environmental compliance & OSHA documents."

Resources

Trade Publications
- AutoInc.org—great, great site: autoinc.org
- Body Shop Business is an excellent publication and Web site; it also offers back issues: www.bodyshopbusiness.com

Associations
- Automotive Service Association, (ASA)—Great site with lots of information: www.asashop.org

Auto Brake Services (See also Auto Repair)

SIC 7539-14	NAICS 811118	

Rules of Thumb
- 30 percent of annual sales plus inventory
- 4 times monthly sales plus inventory

Auto Dealers—New Cars

SIC 5511-02	NAICS 441110	Number of Businesses/Units 23,805

Rules of Thumb
- Depending on the franchise, it's three to six times EBITDA plus real estate and hard assets
- Blue Sky—two to four times EBIT Earnings
- Total transaction value in the industry currently ranges from two to four times pretax earnings
- Blue Sky—two to three times net profit or new unit sales (most recent year) times average front-end gross profit per unit
- Hard assets at cost—new parts, FF&E– Book + 50 percent depreciation,
- Blue Sky—3 times recast earnings
- The goodwill component of the sale price of an auto dealership (franchised only) normally falls within the range of two to six percent of gross revenues. Where added to the assets or book value of the business, this is a reliable method of determining price.
- Goodwill = 1 to 3 times pretax earnings (recast)
- Parts = current returnable parts
- FF&E = book value + one-half depreciation
- New Vehicles = net dealer cost
- Used Cars = as agreed

Rules of Thumb - A
Pricing Tips
- "Be aware of rental cost paid to owners of dealerships. Be aware of compensation to owners, family members, and general managers."
- "Automobile dealerships should have net income of around 2% of total revenue if domestic and higher if import. Service department customer pay labor, gross profit should be between 65% and 70%, parts GP between 35% and 40%. A multiple of 4 to 6 times net income is typical. Imports bring a higher multiple than domestics. Larger stores in a mid-size or large market bring a higher multiple than smaller, rural stores."
- "In valuing auto dealerships, a common method is to look at pretax earnings for the total dealership and then adjust for the two key variables—compensation and rents—for any amounts that are either above or below market, according to Poonam Vaidya, who led the recent NACVA/CTI webinar New Developments & Trends in Dealership Valuation. 'Then we apply a blue sky multiple,' she explained.

"Until recently, however, new vehicles have not been contributing much to an auto dealership's overall operating profits. Do these circumstances change the methodology? 'For example,' Vaidya said, 'if we are valuing a Toyota dealership and [new sales] didn't contribute a single dollar to the profits, should we apply some multiple to adjusted earnings before tax to develop blue sky?' Or should the blue sky multiple apply only to the new vehicle department's adjusted pretax earnings?

"The answer: In most cases, BV appraisers should not have to change their valuation methodology to reflect new industry dynamics, Vaidya said. 'We continue to apply our blue sky multiples to total profits,' particularly where the facts support doing so. For instance, in her example of the Toyota dealership, the parts and services department and used car departments continued to drive customer traffic—and profit—due to the franchisee's continuing relationship with the manufacturer."

> Source: "New trends in auto sales may affect blue sky multiples but not methodology for valuing dealerships," BVWire Issue #127-1, April 3, 2013

- Note: If you do any business valuation work, you need to receive the resources of Business Valuation Resources: www.BVResources.com
- "The brand is the key factor when buying or selling a dealership; Toyota and Honda are about the most difficult to buy and make the highest profits."
- "New auto dealerships usually have 4 profit centers, parts, used cars, F&I, and service. New car sales typically have very little margin. Ask the dealer about their absorption ratio (an industry term that indicates how much of their back-end is absorbing their overhead). Any new buyer would have to be approved by the manufacturer (Ford, GM, Toyota, etc.) Key people: used car manager, parts manager, service manager."
- "The health of the brand is vital."
- "The current value is two to four times net profit of the most recent year. However, the new car franchises that are bringing up to five times net profit are Honda, Toyota and Mercedes Benz."
- "Other pricing methods include: (1) application of industry averages for gross profit as percentage of sales to the total revenues of the dealership being evaluated; (2) assessing financial data and applying appropriate multiples to recast net profit; (3) projection of potential based on industry average penetration statistics times appropriate multiples."
- "The goodwill of an auto dealership can generally be valued at one year's

A - Rules of Thumb

pretax profit plus the dealer's salary and benefits, plus any adjustments from normalizing the financial statement against standard industry operating data."

Expert Comments

"All dealerships are governed by state franchise laws and controlled by the various manufacturers and/or distributors. Transfer of ownership is very difficult and restricted. Capitalization demands are high."

"New-car profits are weak. In fact, the used cars they generate (trades) are the lifeblood of a new-car dealership."

Benchmark Data

Statistics (New Car Dealers)

Number of Establishments	23,805
Average Profit Margin	0.5%
Revenue per Employee	$821,800
Average Number of Employees	44.8
Average Wages per Employee	$56,986

Products and Services Segmentation

New vehicles	57.6%
Used vehicles	31.0%
Parts and repair services	8.2%
Finance and insurance	3.2%

Industry Costs

Profit	0.5%
Wages	7.0%
Purchases	86.0%
Depreciation	0.2%
Marketing	1.1%
Rent & Utilities	1.1%
Other	4.1%

Market Share

AutoNation Inc.	2.5%
Penske Automotive Group Inc.	1.1%

Source: IBISWorld, April 2015

Profile of dealerships' service and parts operations, 2014 (average dealership)

Total service and parts sales	$5,594,388
Total gross profit as percent of service and parts sales	46.14%
Total net profit as percent of service and parts sales	6.39%
Total number of repair orders written	17,070
Total service and parts sales per customer repair order	$255
Total service and parts sales per warranty repair order	$230
Number of technicians (including body)	17
Total parts inventory	$328,114
Average customer mechanical labor rate	$135

Source: NADA Industry Analysis Division, 2014

Rules of Thumb - **A**

Average Dealership Profile—2014

Total Dealership Sales	$49,165,223
Total Dealership Gross	$6,459,256
Total Dealership Expense	$5,365,451
Net Profit before Taxes	$1,093,805
Average Net worth	$3,749,838
Net profit as % of net worth	29.2%

Share of total dealership sales dollars in 2014

New Vehicle	57.6%
Used Vehicle	31.0
Service and Parts	11.4%

Source: 2014 National Auto Dealers Association (NADA) Data, We can't say enough about how valuable this site is for anyone doing their homework on the retail auto sales industry. It is one of the very best sites we have seen.

Expenses as a percentage of annual sales

Cost of goods	75% to 80%
Payroll/labor Costs	08% to 10% of gross profit
Occupancy	10% of gross profit
Profit (estimated pretax)	01.5% to 03%

Industry Trend

- "Highlights from the 2014 National Auto Dealers Association (NADA) Data:
    - ✓ "Competition among dealers also remains strong. Despite rising wages, downloading costs from the OEMs to retailers and increased regulation, this business continues to attract new entrants. The total number of dealers increased by over 200 from 2013 levels. Net profit margins have remained flat for the third year in a row at 2.2 percent.
    - ✓ "The outlook for 2015 is just as robust. Expect total light- and heavy-duty sales to top 17.3 million. NADA does see some challenges ahead, including rising interest rates and continued lackluster wage growth. But these factors shouldn't derail the growing automobile market."

Source: 2014 National Auto Dealers Association (NADA) Data

Seller Financing

- "Can be a mixture of both seller and outside financing."
- "3 years—very small percentage of selling price is carried."
- "5 years—only goodwill is seller-financed."

Questions

- "How many cars per month do they sell? How is their CSI rating? Is the manufacturer requiring upgrades to the facility? If so when?"
- "What is your motivation for selling? Any family members part of your succession plan? Are you retiring or moving to a different location/life structure? What is your ideal 'deal'? Are you interested in holding the real property—or selling with a carry back note? What tax attributes are associated with your business (LIFO, Goodwill, etc.)?"
- "What is your parts obsolescence percentage? CSI Scores?"
- "Staff that will stay on? Building lease if not owned. Franchise ratings and CSI ratings."

A - Rules of Thumb

- "Are you ready to sell for market value?"
- "Is financing in place for new and used sales? Do you have a floor plan? Does the factory have any future plans for your facility—new or larger?"
- "Employee retention is key at this time with the downturn in the economy and sales."
- "Age of key personnel? What is the absorption ratio? Can I see your claims history? Who finances the new and used inventory? If this is a multiple-franchise operation under one roof, discover if the manufacturers are pushing for the dealership to split the franchise out into separate facilities."
- "Sales trends; consumer satisfaction survey results; recent market studies commissioned by manufacturer; facility standards adopted by manufacturer"
- "How many family members on the payroll? What dollar amount of personal items is being deducted from the financial statement?"

Resources

Websites
- Ward's Auto: www.wardsauto.com

Trade Publications
- AutomotiveNews: www.autonews.com

Associations
- National Automobile Dealers Association: www.nada.org
- American International Automobile Dealers: www.aiada.org
- Business Valuation Resources: www.BVResources.com

Auto Dealers—Used Cars

SIC 5511-03	NAICS 441120	Number of Businesses/Units 133,801

Rules of Thumb

➢ Wholesale book value of cars; no goodwill; add parts, fixtures & equipment

Benchmark Data

Statistics (Used Car Dealers)
Number of Establishments	133,801
Average Profit Margin	2.5%
Revenue per Employee	$472,900
Average Number of Employees	1.7
Average Wages per Employee	$25,615

Products and Services Segmentation
Used vehicles	37.5%
Parts and services	29.4%
Financing and insurance	27.8%
Other	5.3%

Rules of Thumb - A

Industry Costs

Profit	2.5%
Wages	5.4%
Purchases	82.3%
Depreciation	0.3%
Marketing	1.0%
Rent & Utilities	2.6%
Other	5.9%

Market Share

CarMax Inc.	12.7%

Source: IBISWorld, January 2015

- "The retail price for the average used vehicle was $18,111, up 3.2% from $18,846. Franchised new-car dealers obtained 66 percent of these used units from trade-ins, 25 percent from auctions, and 8 percent from street purchases and other sources. Share of total dealership sales dollars: Used vehicles 31%."

Source: National Automobile Dealers Association (NADA), 2014 NADA Data

- "Dealer Operating Information:

Average units sold per dealer (BHPH deals only)	610
Average cash in deal per vehicle sold	$4,926
Average ACV per vehicle sold (includes recon)	$5,487
Average reconditioning cost per vehicle sold	$1.026
Average gross profit per vehicle sold	$4.509
Average cash down payment	$1,134
Average amount financed	$9.664
Average term of loan (in weeks)	143"

Source: http://usedcarnews.com 3/1/15

- "Sources of used vehicles retailed by dealerships, 2014

Trade-in on new vehicle	42%
Auction purchase	26%
Trade-in on used vehicle	24%
Street purchase	4%
Other	4%"

Source: National Automobile Dealers Association (NADA), 2014 NADA Data

Questions

- General Questions
  What types of sales transactions did you have for the year under examination?
  a. Any sales at auctions? If yes, which?
  b. Any sales to wholesalers? If yes, which?
  c. Any sales to other dealers? If yes, which?
  d. Any consignment sales? If yes, describe.
  e. Any scrap sales? If yes, describe.
  f. Any in-house dealer financing sales?
  g. Any third-party financing sales?
  h. Did you have any other types of sales transactions?
  i. Did you have any sales that resulted in a loss on the sale? If yes, describe the nature of these sales.
  j. What sales did you have to relatives or family friends during the year? Identify.

A - Rules of Thumb

Resources

Trade Publications
- Used Car News: www.usedcarnews.com

Associations
- National Independent Automobile Dealers Association (ADA): www.niada.com

Auto Detailing (See also Car Washes/Coin Operated, Full Service)

SIC 7542-03	NAICS 811192	Number of Businesses/Units 14,000

Rules of Thumb
➢ 40 to 45 percent of annual sales plus inventory

Benchmark Data

Detailer Type	% of Total
Freestanding Detail Shop	44%
Car Wash Combo	37%
Mobile Services	13%
Other Combo	6%

Operating Costs as Percentage of Revenue

Rent	16.1%
Equipment/Supplies/Maintenance	7.1%
Chemicals (incl. soap, wax, compound, etc.)	7.8%
Labor	34.4%
Utilities (incl. water/sewer)	6.3%
Advertising & Promotion	1.7%
Insurance	4.6%
Customer Claims	0.4%

Average Number of Cars Detailed Annually

Freestanding	1,137
Car Wash Combo	1,232
Mobile Service	1,050

Retail (Free-standing)

Complete Interior/Exterior Detail	$243.11
Interior Detail Only	$129.25
Exterior Detail Only	$139.25
Average Gross Revenue Per Car (Car Wash Sales Only)	$16.25
Average Number of Cars Washed Per Month	4,456

Source for the above 5 charts: "Detailing Survey 2015—Results from AutoLaundry News," www.carwashmag.com. This is a very informative site—and publication—for Car Washes and Auto Detail—all sites should be this good.

Rules of Thumb - A

- "A skilled detailer, who is working hard but not rushing, can probably complete a car in about 4 to 4.5 hours and make it look great. The average car would be only a few years old, be a mid-size, and be in average cosmetic condition with no major scratches or blemishes, and no major stains or excessive dirt on the interior."

Source: www.dealermarkclicks.com

Resources

Websites
- Auto Detailing: www.autodetailingnetwork.com

Publications
- AutoLaundry News: www.carwashmag.com

Auto Glass Repair/Replacement

SIC 5231-10	NAICS 811122	Number of Businesses/Units 2,025

Rules of Thumb

➢ 45 to 50 percent of annual sales plus inventory

➢ 1.8 times SDE plus inventory

Benchmark Data

Statistics (Auto Glass Repair & Replacement Franchises)

Number of Establishments:	1,896
Average Profit Margin	5.1%
Revenue per Employee	$123,600
Average Number of Employees	3.8
Average Wages per Employee	$34,938

Products and Services Segmentation

Windshield repair	65%
Windshield replacement	24%
Window repair	7%
Window replacement	4%

Major Market Segmentation

Households	45%
Commercial clients	25%
Insurance companies	18%
Other	12%

Industry Costs

Profit	5.1%
Wages	28.1%
Purchases	41.0%
Depreciation	1.9%
Marketing	2.9%
Rent & Utilities	4.7%
Other	16.3%

26th Edition

A - Rules of Thumb

Market Share
Glass Doctor	19.9%
Novus Glass	16.7%
Super Glass	5.9%

Source: IBISWorld, September 2014

Industry Trend

- "Smart glass in the automotive industry is expected to become a $2.1 billion market by 2019, compared with $1 billion in 2014, according to Smart Glass Opportunities in the Automotive Industry–2014, a recent report from NanoMarkets. The report defines smart auto glass as any kind of glass used in the automotive sector that is made 'intelligent' with the addition of layers of smart materials or the embedding of sensors and other kinds of electronic and electrical functionality into the glass."

  Source: "Market Trends: Smart Auto Glass Continues Growth"
  http://www.ceramicindustry.com/articles/93976-market-trends-smart-auto-glass-continues-growth 6/2/14

- "A number of factors are impairing the ability of independent auto-glass-replacement shops to compete with large chains. Johnson Auto Glass and Trim Shop Vice President Dan Johnson said those factors include rising prices for replacement auto glass, lower reimbursements from insurance companies and efforts to steer insured parties away from independent auto-glass-replacement companies."

  Source: "Business Tougher for Independent Auto-Glass-Replacement Companies"
  by Dan Heath, www.pressrepublican.com

Resources

Trade Publications
- Glass Magazine—an informative site with archived articles of past issues: www.glassmagazine.com

Associations
- National Windshield Repair Association: www.nwrassn.org/
- National Glass Association (NGA): www.glass.org

Auto Lube/Oil Change (See also All Tune & Lube, Grease Monkey, Jiffy Lube)

SIC 7549-03	NAICS 811191	Number of Businesses/Units 8,865

Rules of Thumb
➢ 40 percent of annual sales (tune-up) plus inventory
➢ 3 times EBIT (tune-up)
➢ 45 percent of annual sales (only auto lube businesses) plus inventory
➢ 1.5 to 2.25 times SDE plus inventory

Pricing Tips
- "There are two different service and working environments applicable to this business. The first being an oil and lube facility only, no service work is performed. The second being a tune-up business, performs oil and lube, in addition to service work, brakes, tune-ups, smog inspection, etc.

Rules of Thumb - A

"The first auto lube business generally shows a greater multiple, 2.5 SDE, while the auto tune-up business described above normally shows a 2.0 SDE.

"The reasoning for the difference in the multiples above is the first business described is generally in a low-tech environment, with non-specialized training and employee wages are lower in comparison to specialized standards in this industry. In addition, most owners have multiple locations. The owner is mostly absentee in this operation and a manager is trained to perform all facets of operation and office functions as required. Demand is also higher.

"The second business described above requires a higher skilled employee (usually certified) and in most states the employees need to be tested. In addition the owner needs to be involved in the everyday functions of the operation, if only as an administrator. Most have a manager in place as well.

"Critical factors affecting business value are as follows: franchise vs. independent, manager and staff, customer base and vehicle count per day, average ticket per day, lease terms, equipment leased, owner's participation and location."

Above figures are plus inventory.

Benchmark Data

Statistics (Oil Change Services)
Number of Establishments	8,865
Average Profit Margin	11.5%
Revenue per Employee	$110,400
Average Number of Employees	7.3
Average Wages per Employee	$22,692

Products and Services Segmentation
Oil changes	58.4%
Tire rotations	17.5%
Cabin air filter services	10.5%
Transmission flush services	8.5%
Other	5.1%

Major Market Segmentation
Consumers aged 26 to 40	49.0%
Consumers aged 41 to 50	23.0%
Consumers aged 51 to 59	12.0%
Consumers aged 18 to 25	8.0%
Consumers aged 60 and older	8.0%

Industry Costs
Profit	11.5%
Wages	20.6%
Purchases	40.3%
Depreciation	2.0%
Marketing	3.0%
Rent & Utilities	8.0%
Other	14.6%

A - Rules of Thumb

Market Share
Royal Dutch/Shell Group 18.9%
Source: IBISWorld, October 2014

Expenses as a percentage of annual sales (Auto Lube - Repair Services)
Cost of Goods .... 24% to 30% (average 27%)
Payroll Costs .... 22% to 26% (with manager 26%)
Occupancy .... 10% to 16%
Royalty Fees (franchise) .... 4% to 8%
Profit (estimated) .... 14% to 23%
Source: Auto Laundry News Fast-Lube Survey

Seller Financing
- 4 years

Resources

Trade Publications
- AutoInc.: www.autoinc.org
- National Oil & Lube News: www.noln.net

Associations
- Automotive Service Association: www.asashop.org

Auto Mufflers (See Meineke, Midas)

SIC 7533-01	NAICS 811112	Number of Businesses/Units 15,200

Rules of Thumb
➢ 35 to 40 percent of annual sales plus inventory
➢ 1 to 1.5 times SDE plus inventory

Auto Parts and Accessories—Retail Stores

SIC 5531-11	NAICS 441310	Number of Businesses/Units 36,451

Rules of Thumb
➢ 40 percent of annual sales plus inventory

Pricing Tips
- "New cost of fixtures and equipment plus inventory at wholesale cost, nothing for goodwill. The inventory should turn over 4–6 times per year."

Benchmark Data

Statistics (Auto Parts Stores)
Number of Establishments 36,451
Average Profit Margin 3.2%
Revenue per Employee $160,700
Average Number of Employees 8.8
Average Wages per Employee $25,098

Rules of Thumb - A

Products and Services Segmentation

Accessories	4.8%
Maintenance parts	9.8%
Critical parts (used)	10.4%
Critical parts (new)	68.0%
Performance parts	7.0%

Major Market Segmentation

Household and individuals	56.3%
Repair shops	22.7%
Retailers and Wholesalers for resale	12.8%
Other	8.2%

Industry Costs

Profit	4.1%
Wages	15.6%
Purchases	60.5%
Depreciation	1.0%
Marketing	1.3%
Rent & Utilities	4.6%
Other	12.9%

Market Share

Advance Auto Parts Inc.	18.8%
AutoZone Inc.	18.2%
O'Reilly Automotive Inc.	15.3%
Genuine Parts Company	10.1%

Source: IBISWorld, July 2015

Miscellaneous Sales Information

Average store size	6,350 sq. ft.
Average per store sales	$1,573,000
Inventory turnover	1.81
Average net sales per store sq. ft.	$248

Expenses as a percentage of annual sales

Cost of goods	61.3%
Payroll/labor Costs	19.9%
Occupancy	03.4%
Profit (estimated pretax)	05.3%

Resources

Associations
- Automotive Aftermarket Industry Association: www.aftermarket.org

---

Auto Rental (See also U Save Car and Truck Rental)

SIC 7514-01	NAICS 532111	Number of Businesses/Units 13,482

Rules of Thumb

➢ 45 percent of annual sales plus inventory

➢ Number of cars times $1,000

A - Rules of Thumb

Pricing Tips

- "Reservation system and national sales efforts are critical. Many airport locations receive 70% or more of their business from this source. Off-airport locations are different; they can survive on local advertising as well as national."

Benchmark Data

Statistics (Car Rental)

Number of Establishments	13,482
Average Profit Margin	11.4%
Revenue per Employee	$358,000
Average Number of Employees	8.1
Average Wages per Employee	$42,485

Products and Services Segmentation

Leisure car rental	50.5%
Business car rental	27.3%
Car leasing	20.2%
Car sharing	2.0%

Major Market Segmentation

Off-airport market	40.9%
Airport leisure customers	38.4%
Airport business customers	20.7%

Industry Costs

Profit	11.4%
Wages	12.0%
Purchases	28.1%
Depreciation	28.0%
Marketing	3.3%
Rent & Utilities	7.0%
Other	10.2%

Market Share

Enterprise Rent-A-Car Company	35.8%
Hertz Global Holdings Inc.	17.9%
Avis Budget Group Inc.	15.5%

Source: IBISWorld, February 2015

2013 U.S. Car Rental Market

Company	U.S. Cars in Service	#U.S. Locations
Enterprise Holdings	979,370	6,045
(Includes Alamo Rent A Car, Enterprise Rent-A-Car, National Car Rental)		
Hertz *(Includes Advantage Rent-A-Car)*	488,000	5,900
Avis Budget Group	344,000	3,100
Fox Rent A Car'	18,000	18
U-Save Auto Rental System Inc.	11,500	125
ACE Rent A Car	10,000	92

Source: Auto Rental News (ARN), Fact Book 2014

Rules of Thumb - A

- "Income comes from two sources: operating income from rental and add-on services (such as CDW); and resale of vehicles (if the risk has not been assumed by the OEM in the fleet agreement). Accounting treatment (depreciation schedules for vehicles) can distort these sources."

Expenses as a percentage of annual sales
Cost of goods	82%
Payroll/labor Costs	08% to 10%
Occupancy	04%
Profit (estimated pretax)	06%

Industry Trend

- "Though aspects of carsharing have existed since 1948 in Switzerland, it was only in the last 15 years that the concept has evolved into a mobility solution in the United States. In that time, the carsharing market has grown from a largely subsidized, university research-driven experiment into a full-fledged for-profit enterprise, owned primarily by traditional car rental companies and auto manufacturers. Today, Zipcar (owned by Avis Budget Group), car2go (owned by Daimler), Enterprise CarShare and Hertz 24/7 control about 95% of the carsharing market in the U.S.

  "Compared to car rental, total fleet size and revenues for carsharing remain relatively small. The Fall 2014 Carsharing Outlook, produced by the Transportation Sustainability Research Center at the University of California, Berkeley, reports 19,115 carsharing cars in the U.S., shared by about 996,000 members. Total annual revenue for carsharing in the U.S. is about $400 million, compared to the $24 billion in revenue for the traditional car rental market."

  Source:"CarSharing: State of the Market and Growth Potential" by Chris Brown, http://www.autorentalnews.com/channel/rental-operations/article/story/2015/03/carsharing-state-of-the-market-and-growth-potential.aspx

- "When it comes to employment in U.S. franchises, the rental car industry had a negative year-over-year growth rate. According to the recent ADP National Franchise Report, the rental industry's year-over-year growth rate decreased 1.1%.In addition, the rental industry's franchises experienced a negative average growth rate (-0.1%) over a 12-month period, according to the report.

  "For employment numbers, the rental industry's average monthly employment is 100 with a monthly growth rate of 0.3%.As a whole, U.S. private-sector franchise jobs increased by 16,520 during the month of January, according to the report.

  "'During the month of January, franchises created 16,520 new jobs, less than half the number created in December 2013,' said Ahu Yildirmaz, senior director of the ADP Research Institute.Distributed to the public each month free of charge, the ADP National Franchise Report measures monthly changes in franchise employment derived from ADP's actual transactional payroll data."

  Source: ADP, a global provider, from ADP's transactional payroll data

- "Increasing transparency of pricing with Internet travel sites. Increasing use of 'yield management' in pricing. Regulatory scrutiny of merged entities."

Questions
- "Relationships with franchisor; license agreement and royalty rate"

Resources

Trade Publications
- Auto Rental News: www.autorentalnews.com

A - Rules of Thumb

Auto Repair (Auto Service Centers)		
SIC 7514-01	NAICS 811111	Number of Businesses/Units 271,176

Rules of Thumb

- 25% to 30% of annual sales plus inventory
- 1 to 2.5 times SDE plus inventory, ($75,000 to $100,000 SDE)
- 3 times SDE plus inventory ($150,000 + SDE)
- 3 to 3.5 times EBITDA
- 1.25 to 1.75 owner's provable net income includes inventory

Pricing Tips

- "Inventory on hand is usually small. Most parts can be delivered in a few hours. Must be a great mechanic. Small shops make a small return. Need a busy shop to make any real money."
- "Lack of owner dependence is very important. Auto repair is a customer service oriented business with many owners working the front counter. Buyers often ask themselves what will happen to the customer base if the owner is not there to greet them. Advise sellers to distance themselves from the front desk and hire a service writer. One-man shows almost never sell. Tire stores grossing over $1 million are very desirable, despite low margins, and are fetching a 3–3.5 multiple. Employee costs should be around 25%; oftentimes an owner can trim some fat to boost SDE to justify a higher asking price."
- "A business with fleet and commercial customers is worth a higher multiple than a full retail business. Having more than one bay and one lift per technician is important, since many times a vehicle is waiting on parts after being torn down so it's important for the technicians to have more than one work space to move from job to job. Shops that do heavy line work, such as power train and transmission repairs, also are worth a higher multiple than shops that just do light duty work only."
- "Typically when pricing a shop location is a large part of the valuation and marketability of the business. If a shop has $1 million plus in revenues the multiplier can be higher vs. a shop that does a few hundred thousand in revenues. If a shop has too much equipment the owner may believe his business is worth more, but we let them know that is just 'stuff' that helps you generate your revenues. For example if a shop's value is $200,000 based on SDE and they have $400,000 in assets I may have the client not include every tool they own in the deal. I let them know to sell that equipment another way because they will never get paid for it on the transaction."
- "Large volume shops tend to get a larger multiple percentage. If inventory is valued at less than 15% of selling price, it is often included. Shops with a high tire volume may have larger inventories and these inventories would not be included."
- "If the business is an independent service repair shop the % to SDE will normally be higher than if the business were a franchise. A franchise has a royalty fee as an added expense; this lowers the % of gross profit to SDE. That being said, a franchise center, such as Meineke, Honest 1, or Midas, etc. will also bring forth a higher value to the owner when it comes time to sell the business. The market continues to shift towards the preference of a well-known

Rules of Thumb - **A**

franchise brand name for buyers. The key for an auto repair center is to obtain revenues of $700k or higher on an annual basis. This brings a strong SDE to the bottom line."

- "1. Distinguish between Personal Goodwill that goes home with the owner at night and might not transfer versus Business Goodwill that will transfer to any Buyer. Personal Goodwill needs to be addressed through adjustment in Sales Price or with an Earnout. 2. Are any customers tied to a key employee? If so address with an employee contract or discount Sales Price. 3. Determine ratio of commercial accounts to retail. If the Seller has multiple shops the commercial accounts might leave."
- "Most auto service businesses will sell for between 3 and 3.5 times SDE."
- "Length of lease is very important. Percentage of tire sales if significant can reduce SDE and sales ratio and affect price. Condition of equipment, cleanliness of shop and brand or banner will affect local desirability and price. Reputation is also very important."
- "Lower if owner is main technician and fewer employees. Higher if owner runs business and has techs that do the work."
- "Many auto centers with sales revenues under $500k per year have closed their doors due to little or no profit. Consumers are driving less due to the high price of gas and this directly affects sales revenues. Rents continue to escalate and it becomes increasingly more difficult to find good managers or top-line techs. Major auto dealerships are also becoming more aggressive in their service departments and have taken some of the sales revenues away from the independent auto centers. Conversely the auto centers with sales exceeding $1 million per year continue to show good profits and will benefit from the smaller auto centers who close their doors. The above multiples do not include inventory, at cost; the multiples do include equipment, FF&E."
- "Rent can be added to the SDE if the seller also owns the building and is selling the building with the business. If the seller hires too many employees, it is sometimes possible to show the buyer why the business can be run with fewer employees, and add the soon-to-be-terminated employee's salary to the SDE."
- "It is a labor-intensive business, the labor being specialized mechanics who have to be managed well, as mechanics can be lured away by car dealerships for a better wage."

Expert Comments

"Any mechanic with a tool box can open a shop. Many closed gas stations available for rent. Auto repair shops on every corner in most towns."

"Auto repair is one of the few industries that thrive during recessions (cash for clunkers being an anomaly). Buyers without a target industry in mind can be made aware of this and are often swayed to enter the business. Competition is high, but as technology advances, older generations leave the industry to be replaced by owners who are willing to invest in the technology and training to repair today's and tomorrow's vehicles."

"Although competition is extremely high, most customers will be loyal to an auto repair center that provides reliable service in a reasonable amount of time. People like knowing who they're trusting their vehicle to, and repair shops that can provide that personal touch should always be in demand."

A - Rules of Thumb

"There are always going to be many shops and car dealers that work on vehicles as competition, but the good thing is there are millions of vehicles on the road and they always break or need regular service. Vehicles seem to last longer these days, but that just means people are waiting for service and repairs. The end results being higher ticket values per job.

"The risk in getting into this industry usually has to do with location. If the location is hidden away it may be harder to build the business. If the location is in a prime spot the rent may become too expensive. A good technician is hard to come by and that makes it difficult, but with a good shop and location the good techs are always available. Buyers are always intrigued by this industry and see the potential in a sound investment by purchasing a shop. An owner does not need to be a mechanic, which drives the demand."

"Multiple shops can be started or purchased, but it comes with a whole new set of challenges. It may be easier than some industries, but is still not simple. Personnel and location will be your main factor that makes it difficult."

"In this marketplace there is competition, however you will see a good number of auto centers come and go if they fail to provide honesty and quality service to their customers. Many smaller auto centers have gone out of business; those shops that are underachievers normally have sales under $300k annually and are not profitable. If you list a shop with sales over $500k annually you'll have a good chance of selling that business; the key is to have a good staff in place with mgt. that will stay."

"In general the industry is recession resistant."

"Extremely competitive but when the economy is bad, people keep their cars longer and they need to be repaired and maintained. When the weather is bad or the temperature is high cars break down and need to be repaired and maintained."

"The level of repair needed in today's cars is reduced. However, the number of vehicles on the road is growing and the number of bays available to service those vehicles is declining as real estate values outstrip the capacity to pay market rent. Many shops on good corners are being torn down. Zoning is hard to get for new shops. So ease of replication is difficult."

"Cars are becoming increasingly complex. Qualified mechanics can be tough to find. Owner needs to have knowledge base or be able to retain quality techs to survive."

"Location is a prime factor that can dictate how successful a shop is and also dictates how much you can push the limits on valuation. The industry trend is going towards fewer cars being worked on, but higher average ROs [repair orders]."

Benchmark Data

Statistics (Auto Repair - Auto Mechanics)

Number of Establishments	271,176
Average Profit Margin	7.7%
Revenue per Employee	$109,900
Average Number of Employees	2.1
Average Wages per Employee	$29,519

Products and Services Segmentation

Powertrain repair services	21.4%
Brake repair services	17.4%
Other repair and maintenance services	17.4%
Scheduled and preventive repair and maintenance services	16.1%
Electrical system repair services	9.2%
Heating repair services	6.8%
Muffler and exhaust repair services	6.6%
Wheel alignment and repair services	5.1%

Industry Costs

Profit	7.7%
Wages	26.7%
Purchases	45.5%
Depreciation	1.8%
Marketing	1.2%
Rent & Utilities	5.8%
Other	11.3%

Source: IBISWorld, March 2015

- "Mechanics must generate revenue of at least $1500 to $2000 per week to cover their own salary. Many mechanics learn the business then leave and open their own shop. Customers are easy to find, but hard to keep."
- "Average ticket should be between $400 and $550 per car. A very busy and well-staffed shop can produce on a regular basis $35K per month per technician. Cost of parts and labor should not exceed 20% of total revenues."
- "$100,000 to $150,000 in annual sales per bay is typical. Any shop that is on the high side of this scale is likely to be significantly more profitable if costs are controlled. I like to see gross rent under $1500 per month per bay."
- "Higher multiples for higher SDE's."
- "Benchmarks in this business, cost of goods is critical to maintain a certain %. Wages need to be kept in check; good mechanics need to be able to generate a min. of $20k in sales per bay per month. Most new auto repair centers are scaling down the size of their facility to approx. 3500 sf on average; this includes owner's office, waiting area, customer service counter and the service bays. The average work order ticket varies from $250 to $400 per vehicle, this does not include tires."
- "Estimated average annual sales is $475,000."
- "I'm finding that an average repair order of $500 to $550 is common for areas with higher incomes. In the lower income areas, average RO ranges from $300 to $350."
- "Gross sales per year $300K–$400K is needed to at least survive and break even."

Expenses as a percentage of annual sales

Cost of goods	30% to 40%
Payroll/labor Costs	20% to 30%
Occupancy	08% to 12%
Profit (estimated pretax)	10% to 18%

Industry Trend

- "Trend is more volume for shops with good employees. Population keeping cars longer and having them repaired instead of replaced."

A - Rules of Thumb

- "The trend that we are seeing is that shops are having to invest in original equipment manufacturers diagnostic equipment and tools. This leads to additional costs for an independent or franchised auto repair shop. The upside is that those shops that are willing to make that investment are taking customers and jobs from other shops. Technician wages and ongoing training requirements are on the rise."
- "Trending toward more computer technology and higher equipment costs for the business."
- "Less cars entering a shop because of the quality of newer cars and the high cost of used cars. Newer cars on the road, but when they do come in the average ticket seems to be increasing"
- "Small shops are being bulldozed. Consolidation of larger shops and banners. Harder to find trained staff."
- "Severe cold and icy conditions in much of the U.S. recently may generate some much-needed business for privately held auto repair and maintenance shops, which saw minimal sales growth in 2013 as U.S. auto sales hit a six-year high.

  "A new estimate from Sageworks, a financial information company, shows that privately held auto repair and maintenance shops on average posted 1.7 percent sales growth last year. That makes the industry one of the slowest-growing of all, and it is the industry's smallest sales growth since 2009, when sales actually decreased, according to Sageworks' financial statement analysis. The exact cause of the slowdown isn't clear, but Sageworks analyst Peter Brown noted automobile dealers in Sageworks' database of privately held companies increased sales an average of 11.9 percent last year.

  "'As we've seen record growth in sales in the auto industry—both at the retail and wholesale levels – it's likely that people who've been buying cars in the last year or two have not needed repair work done,' Brown said. 'Also, when you look at the data for public auto repair shops, they had stronger sales growth than the private shops, so it may be that the bigger repair shops gobbled up some market share.' Specialized repair shops posted generally weaker sales growth than general auto repair and maintenance firms, though the reason behind the difference isn't clear, Brown said.

  "Reuters recently reported that U.S. auto industry sales in 2013 increased nearly 8 percent, to 15.6 million vehicles, from 2012, and sales were the strongest since 2007. Despite slower sales growth, or perhaps because of it, profitability improved for the average auto repair shop. In fact, net profit margin nearly doubled, to 9.1 percent from 4.7 percent in 2012, according to Sageworks' data. 'It appears that some operating expenses have gone down by a fairly substantial amount,' Brown said. Indeed, net profit margin for auto repair shops has been steadily improving since 2009, when the average auto repair and maintenance shop took home about 2 cents for every dollar brought in.

  "Through its cooperative data model, Sageworks collects financial statements for private companies from accounting firms, banks and credit unions, and aggregates the data at an approximate rate of 1,000 statements a day. Net profit margin has been adjusted to exclude taxes and include owner compensation in excess of their market-rate salaries. These adjustments are commonly made to private company financials in order to provide a more accurate picture of the companies' operational performance."

  Source: "Auto Repair Shops' Growth Stalls" by Mary Ellen Biery 1/26/14 http://www.forbes.com/sites/sageworks/2014/01/26/auto-repair-shops-financial-analysis/

- "Increasing in mid-income demographics. Holding steady in high income."

Rules of Thumb - A

Seller Financing
- "Mostly sold at a discounted level for heavy cash down. It is impossible to find bank financing for business only shops without Real Estate as collateral."
- "Bank financing is very easy to obtain, if the books are clean and the numbers work, as with any business."
- "Seller financing is a must for an automotive repair business."
- "Banks will fund these deals with 25% down. The banks do like to see the seller carry minimum of 10% of the purchase price."
- 5 years
- "Financing for this business is usually easy to obtain with the seller showing good books and records for at least three years, seller carry note is normally for three to five years at 6% interest."

Questions
- "Are customers in a computer base? Amount of advertising needed to keep customers. Promotions used to generate new business."
- "How many technicians, how many bays, how many lifts do you have? What are your hours per RO, dollars per RO? Do you do fleet or commercial repairs? How many repair orders per month do you average?"
- "Price your business according to these terms or it will just sit on the market and not sell. If you are buying a business in this market try and buy one that has at least $500,000 in revenues and has a location with drive by traffic. Ask how many cars per week do they work on (should be minimum 25). What is the average RO (should be minimum $450). What is your mark up on parts (should be 60% but if it's not, don't be too concerned; you will have room for better profits)."
- "Ask the seller if he is an active mechanic in the business. If not what are his daily functions? Are there any family members in the business? Is there a good mgr. in place who will stay on after the sale? Will the key mechanics stay after the sale? Does the owner have a good software program in place and does the owner have all his customers in the database? Any hazardous waste issues in the last five years? Does the owner pay all his employees on a W-2 ? Are any employees paid under the table?"
- "Hours per repair order, dollars per repair order, how many bays, how many lifts, do you do transmission and power train work, average hours flagged per week per tech, do you pay techs by the hour or on salary?"
- "What is your average repair order (RO) and average weekly car count? A good mechanical repair shop generally has an average weekly car count of 50 or more. A lube shop would have much higher car counts."
- "Profit margins on parts should be 55% to 60% average."

Resources

Websites
- AutoInc: www.autoinc.org

Associations
- Automotive Service Association—an excellent site for both auto services/collision businesses: www.asashop.org
- The Automotive Maintenance & Repair Association (AMRA) : www.amra.org
- National Institute for Automotive Service Excellence: www.ase.com

A - Rules of Thumb

Auto Transmission Centers (See also AAMCO Transmission)

SIC 7537-01	NAICS 811113	Number of Businesses/Units 17,000

Rules of Thumb

> 35 to 45 percent of annual sales includes inventory

> 1.5 to 2 times SDE includes inventory (as the SDE increases so will the multiple, i.e., SDE $50,000 the multiple will be 1.5 times, SDE $200,000 the multiple will be 2 times—all include inventory)

> 3 times EBITDA

> Auto Transmission Centers: e.g., Franchise, Cottman, Sparky's, AAMCO
> Index Owner's Cash Flow (SDE)
> 1.0 x   to $50K + SDE
> 1.5-2.0 x   to $100K + SDE
> 2.0-2.25 x   to $150K + SDE
>   (sales normally exceed $800K)

> Rule of thumb—deduct 20 percent for independent centers.

Pricing Tips

- "Parts Cost
    - ✓ 18–22% for classic shop without general auto repair.
    - ✓ Lower than 18% it is a red flag indicating significant used parts which trigger high warranty(comeback)costs
    - ✓ Higher than 30% indicates that there might be some green cash not reported

  Labor Cost
    - ✓ A traditional shop has four employees three technical employees—a builder and two mechanics, paid weekly/hourly, representing about 20% of the booked sales, and a manager paid on commissions, typically 10% of sales with oversight by the owner.
    - ✓ A progressive shop has labor related to general auto repair paid a flat rate percentage of shop rate, or 'flag rate'.
    - ✓ General Information
    - ✓ Ratio of commercial accounts to retail is a topic that can affect pricing if the account is tied to the owner or will not transfer to a buyer.
    - ✓ Adding back the manager's compensation to inflate discretionary earnings is a red flag, as most buyers do not have industry experience."
- "Shops with a manager in place where the owner oversees with EBITDA at minimum of $100,000 are in demand and sell for about 3 times EBITDA. Ratio of retail to commercial-parts cost, and warranty repairs need be checked."
- "2 X discretionary earnings; 20 X average of last 16 weeks' sales; 16 X average of last 16 weeks plus equipment"
- "The industry is changing because of the improved reliability of transmissions, increased incorporation of electronics that make it difficult to determine if there is a transmission or an engine problem. The slowdown in new car sales has resulted in special deals from the manufacturers through dealers to provide extended warranty and incentives to trade in old and fuel inefficient cars. Many shops including AAMCO are reacting by adding full auto repair. This has disrupted the 'model' of the classic shop's proforma by having to address

added specialty labor. Competition from auto repair and even 'lube/tunes' are adding transmission repair; and rather than refer to specialty transmission shops, buy finished transmissions from third party and dealers. Pricing for a franchised shop, which in the recent past has shown sign of breakeven (typically $8,000 to $10,000/week), I try not to go below what it would cost to start a new franchise and reach breakeven ($200,000); but without profits to support debt service, the buyer pool is difficult."

Expert Comments

"People keeping cars longer is a positive. Parts distributors are consolidating and fixing prices. Technology and the economy are encouraging total car repair which destroys classic parts and labor models."

"Reliability of transmissions, longer warranties, technology, competition from auto repair & dealers selling remanufactured transmissions."

Benchmark Data

- "Rent above 8–10% is a flag. Parts costing less than 15% indicates use of used parts. Part costs above 30% indicates skimming or high concentration general auto service. High concentration of fleet business versus retail may indicate the goodwill is tied to one owner or a key employee and might not transfer."
- "Parts cost not to exceed 22%, and if less than 14%, a flag."
- "$3,500 to $4,000 per shop employee. Parts cost lower than 15% indicates used parts being used. High parts cost indicates high warranty costs, and/or skimming. High ratio of commercial sales to retail sales indicates a personal relationship that may not be transferable. Average invoice less than $1,000 on transmission repairs is an indication of a poor manager. Ratio of major to minor repairs should be high."
- "Estimated Average Annual Sales/Unit—$600,000"

Expenses as a percentage of annual sales	
Cost of goods	18% to 24%
Payroll/labor Costs	20% to 25%
Occupancy	08% to 12%
Profit (estimated pretax)	10% to 20%

Industry Trend

- "Will end up merged into general auto repair because of improved transmissions, longer warranties, technology, and cost to replace versus repair."
- "Changing from specialty shop to general auto repair"
- "Better but trending toward franchises and large independents in major market—full-service auto repair with emphasis on diagnostics."

Seller Financing

- "Seller financing unless real estate is included"
- Five years
- 3 to 6.5 years
- "50% down, 5 years; better if 10-year amortized with a 3–5 year balloon."

A - Rules of Thumb

Questions
- "Who is your competition?"
- "Why are you selling? What are your plans after selling? Ratio of retail to commercial sales. Ratio of general auto repair to transmission. How many employees and pay? How much is the rent?"
- "Reason for sale? Reason for sale again? Get specifics on employee function, pay rate and longevity. Get details on manager. What about warranty repairs? Ratio—retail to commercial concentration of sales? Rent and terms of lease?"
- "Why are you selling? What are the sales trends for last few years? How stable is the manager if ownership changes? What is the percentage of transmission service to general auto repair? How are your employees compensated? What is the ratio of retail/walk-in versus commercial? What is ratio of major to minor repairs? What is the average invoice for a major? What is percentage of warranty returns (comebacks)? Do your expenses include Workman's comp or alternative insurance?"

Resources

Trade Publications
- Gears Magazine: www.gearsmagazine.com
- Transmission Digest: www.transmissiondigest.com

Associations
- Automatic Transmission Rebuilders Association (ATRA): www.atra.com

Auto Wrecking/Recyclers/Dismantlers/Scrap/Salvage Yards (Auto parts -- used & rebuilt)

SIC 5015-02	NAICS 441310	Number of Businesses/Units 2,953

Rules of Thumb
- "Auto Wrecking yards sell for 2 to 2.5 times the owner's provable net income. Parts inventory is included, but cars for sale inventory is not included."
- "Values are based on the following: 3-5 times earnings, land and improvements, vehicle and parts inventory discounted based, anticipated time to liquidate. Goodwill such as customers, strategic location, and permitting can be fairly significant."
- 100% of Annual Gross Sales including inventory
- 25% times EBITDA

Expert Comments
"Sellers should expose their opportunity to several potential buyers."

"Self-service auto recycling is the trend, due to lower personnel costs."

Rules of Thumb - **A**

Benchmark Data

Statistics (Used Car Parts Wholesaling)
Number of Establishments	2,953
Average Profit Margin	3.5%
Revenue per Employee	$248,500
Average Number of Employees	6.2
Average Wages per Employee	$31,106

Products and Services Segmentation
General auto recycling	55.0%
Specialized motor vehicle dismantling and parts sales	45.0%

Major Market Segmentation
General auto parts wholesalers	30.3%
Automotive mechanics and repair shops	27.4%
Other	13.0%
Do-it-yourself customers	11.9%
Auto parts retailers	9.9%
Auto parts rebuilders and remanufacturers	7.5%

Industry Costs
Profit	3.5%
Wages	12.7%
Purchases	55.0%
Depreciation	0.8%
Marketing	1.2%
Rent & Utilities	4.6%
Other	22.2%

Market Share
LKQ Corporation Inc.	13.0%
Schnitzer Steel Industries Inc.	7.5%

Source: IBISWorld, July 2015

- "Low rent"
- "For self-service yards, 50% of all customers entering the yard typically make a purchase, and that purchase averages approximately $25–$30 nationally."

Expenses as a percentage of annual sales
Cost of goods	40% to 50%
Payroll/labor Costs	10%
Occupancy	14%
Profit (estimated pretax)	25%

Industry Trend

- "Consolidation is a trend that will continue. Smart operators will have to manage their businesses better every year."
- "Wrecking yards do well in good and bad economies."
- "The recycling facilities industry, or businesses selling recycled commodities and finished goods, has grown at an annual rate of 3.3 percent in the past five

A - Rules of Thumb

years, according to a new study. Because of that, the report states, recycled product makers have demanded more recycled commodities from wholesalers, aiding demand for recycling facilities in turn."

Source: "Recycling Facilities Industry Sees Steady Growth—Study" by Allan Gerlat,
Waste Age, May 29, 2013

- "The average age of the 247 million cars and trucks on U.S. roads hit a record of 11.4 years in January—the latest figures available. The Polk research firm gathered state registration data to conclude that.
- "The average was up from 11.2 years in 2012, and was nearly two full years older than in 2007, before the start of the Great Recession, Polk said.
- "People are keeping their cars because the quality is so much better and they are trying to avoid monthly payments, said Mark Seng, a Polk vice president. The annual percentage of vehicles sent to the scrap yard has dropped 50 percent since the recession, he said."

Source: "Americans keeping their vehicles a record 11.4 years" by Tom Krisher,
Associated Press, Boston Globe, August 7, 2013

Seller Financing
- "Quality buyers pay in cash, or lease facilities long term. Some seller financing takes place, usually when involving a first time buyer."
- "6 years for self-service yards, and 12 years for full-service yards."

Questions
- "Are they able to pitch the sale of their yard to at least ten potential buyers?"

Resources

Associations
- Automotive Recyclers Association of New York: www.arany.com
- Automotive Recyclers Association: www.a-r-a.org
- Institute of Scrap Recycling Industries: www.isri.org

Aviation and Aerospace

Rules of Thumb
- 80 percent of annual sales
- 3.8 to 6.0 times SDE
- 4 times EBIT
- 5 times EBITDA

Pricing Tips
- "Type of aircraft, market served, age of aircraft, revenue per flight hour and asset utilization."
- "Must use both inventory and sales."

Expert Comments
"Aviation has always been a 'darling' industry. Buyers aren't hard to find if you're making money."

Rules of Thumb - **B**

Benchmark Data
- "Revenue per flight hour"

Expenses as a percentage of annual sales
Cost of goods	20%
Payroll/labor Costs	50%
Occupancy	10%
Profit (estimated pretax)	20%

Industry Trend
- "Very high growth"

Seller Financing
- "Outside financing"

Questions
- "Age of aircraft, maintenance costs, revenue flights per hour, % of utilization of assets, marketing and sales"

Resources

Associations
- www.rotor.com: Helicopter Association International

Bagel Shops (See also Bagel Franchises, Bakeries)
SIC 546101	NAICS 722513	Number of Businesses/Units 7,800

Rules of Thumb
- ➢ 30 to 35 percent of annual sales plus inventory
- ➢ 2.5 SDE plus inventory

Pricing Tips
- "Generally worth 1/3 of gross sales volume, with a decent rent. Higher rent or upcoming increase will lower price."
- "Rent a large factor; hand-rolled or frozen product?"

Expert Comments

"As the team from Always Bagels in Lebanon, PA, put it, a bagel is a bagel, which means carbs and calories. Even whole grain, fiber-packed attempts at added nutrition carry a calorie count that scares off consumers today. While items such as cake and cookies can enjoy their treat status, and loaf bread can benefit from whole grains, bagels still must contend with their rotund size and everyday breakfast positioning."
Source: "Walking the bagel line," by Charlotte Atchley, www.foodbusinessnews.net 6/25/2014

"Easy to duplicate. Setup cost expensive. Most shopping centers already have a bagel shop."

B - Rules of Thumb

Benchmark Data
- For additional Benchmark Information see also Restaurants—Limited Service
- "Rent and payroll the most important factors"
- Estimated annual 2013 unit sales for Bruegger's Bagel Bakery: $700,000. Estimated 2014 annual sales for Einstein Brothers: $670,000.

Expenses as a percentage of annual sales
Cost of goods	10%
Payroll/labor Costs	25%
Occupancy	20%
Profit (estimated pretax)	20%

Industry Trend
- "This precarious position has the bagel field staring down flat sales, and bagel bakers looking for new ways to jump-start sales momentum. According to data from IRI, a market research firm based in Chicago, for the 52-week period ending Jan. 26, the entire bagel category only grew 2% in dollar sales and 2.8% in unit sales, with private label seeing the biggest boost at 9.1% growth in dollar sales. Shrinking the bagel's size to reduce calorie and carb counts, cleaning up ingredient labels and reenergizing old channels with new promotions and creative uses for these rolls all provide opportunities to bring new life to the breakfast product."

Source: "Walking the bagel line," by Charlotte Atchley, www.foodbusinessnews.net 6/25/2014

Resources

Associations
- Independent Bakers Association: www.bakingnetwork.com

Bait and Tackle Shops (See also Sporting Goods Stores)		
SIC 594-33	NAICS 451110	Number of Businesses/Units 9,000

Rules of Thumb
- 30 percent of annual sales plus inventory

Benchmark Data
- For Benchmark Information see Sporting Goods Stores

Bakeries (See also Bakeries—Commercial, Food Stores/Specialty)		
SIC 5461-02	NAICS 445291	Number of Businesses/Units 29,000

Rules of Thumb
- 40 to 45 percent of annual sales plus inventory
- 2 times SDE plus inventory

Pricing Tips
- "Receivables; years in business; scope of market; new 'state-of-art' equipment vs. old."

Rules of Thumb - B

Benchmark Data

Expenses as a percentage of annual sales
Cost of goods sold (Food)	05% to 10%
Payroll/Labor Costs	30% to 35%
Occupancy Cost	06% to 08%
Other Overhead	10% to 15%
Profit (estimated)	20%+

- "About one-third of bakers reported no change in customer counts, and only 14 percent claimed fewer customers, with an average decrease of 13 percent. The average number of customers visiting a retail bakery on a given day is also up. On the busiest days, an average of 258 customers are served, up from 225 in 2009. Even slow days have seen an uptick in customers coming through the door—105 in 2011 compared to 86 in 2009.The median sale per customer rose 50 cents in the last two years, to $13."

Percentage of average full-line retail bakery's dollar sales 2011
Custom-decorated cakes	14%
Upscale dessert cakes/tortes	04%
Wedding cakes	09%
All-occasion decorated cakes	09%
Cookies	09%
Crusty bread/rolls	10%
Other bread/rolls	08%
Yeast-raised donuts	03%
Cake donuts	01%
Danish	02%
Muffins	04%
Puff pastry	03%
Pies	06%
Bagels	04%
Scones	02%
Cupcakes	05%
Other bakery items	06%

Source: "Retail Bakery Survey 2011: Optimism reigns supreme" by Katherine Martin, chief editor, modern-baking.com/bakery management

- "Percentage of full-line retail bakery operators offering the following items:
    1. Sodas, juices, teas 61%
    2. Conventional coffee service 56%
    3. Sandwiches 45%
    4. On-site dining 31%
    5. Espresso, other gourmet coffee 30%
    6. Other deli (salads, cheeses, etc.) 30%"
    Note: Figures above are approximate.
- For additional Benchmark Information see Food Stores—Specialty

Industry Trend
- "According to the report, the global bakery market is anticipated to grow at a Compound Annual Growth Rate (CAGR) of 7.04% between 2014 and 2019."
    Source: Global Bakery Market 2015–2019 report from Research and Markets

B - Rules of Thumb

- "Although market growth has slowed somewhat in relative terms, the appeal of gluten-free foods does not appear to be abating. Over the five-year period ended in 2014, sales of gluten-free products in traditionally grain-based categories posted a compound annual growth rate of 34%. The gluten-free segment demonstrated growth in several categories during the 2013-2014 period, including pasta, cold cereal, baking mixes, and frozen bread/dough, even though overall sales in those categories dropped slightly."

Source: http://www.packagedfacts.com/Gluten-Free-Foods-8108350/

Resources

Trade Publications
- Modern Baking: http://supermarketnews.com/product-categories/bakery

Associations
- Independent Bakers Association: http://www.independentbaker.com/

Bakeries—Commercial (See also Bakeries)

SIC 5149-02	NAICS 311812	Number of Businesses/Units 6,000

Rules of Thumb
- 65 percent of annual sales plus inventory
- 2 times SDE plus inventory
- 3 to 5 times EBITDA

Pricing Tips
- "Gross sales in retail & wholesale; operating hours; location."
- "The above price/earnings Rules of Thumb assume a 'minimal asset sale,' meaning fixed assets, inventory and intangibles only. Assumes the buyer replaces all other elements of working capital, and that the assets are transferred free of liabilities. Typical light manufacturing value drivers and risk factors apply (customer concentration, brand, product differentiation, growth prospects, distribution channel, longevity in the market, condition and capacity of equipment, management depth, etc.)"
- "Age & sophistication of equipment; convenience of bakery to major transportation hubs allowing for plentiful pool of employees."
- "Gross sales . . . what portion is from retail sales & how much from wholesale; inquire as to the amount of 'bags of flour' purchased weekly; loaves of bread sold weekly."
- "The SDE multiplier is subject to increase or decrease based on the age and type of equipment. Further, large commercial bakeries require specialized human resources which may be the seller(s) whose expertise will need to be replaced. Oftentimes sellers minimize the difficulty in replacing their expertise, but this should be carefully evaluated and valuation adjustments made accordingly."
- "Be careful to check if one or two customers comprise a high percentage of the bakery's revenues."
- "Don't be fooled by the owner's overstatement of the value of the equipment. Most bakery equipment is valued at between 10% and 25% of replacement cost new. The larger equipment requires riggers to move it. The dismantling and re-installation of ovens requires specialized skill and knowledge."
- "Price will vary greatly depending on the volume and types of labor-saving

Rules of Thumb - B

equipment. This is an industry where payroll can be significantly reduced by machinery. Commercial contracts with restaurants, hotels, etc. are also a source of value."

Expert Comments

"Fastest growing market segments are functional foods, organic, low calorie, all natural, gluten free."

"This industry over the past several years has been under a tremendous squeeze on profitability. Price of flour & other needed ingredients has been most volatile, yet the market place has been most resistant to price increases...thus profit margins (& profit) have been reduced!!!"

"The bakery business traditionally produces much of its product at night so it can be delivered fresh in the morning. This limits the human resources available to work in the industry. While 'mom & pop' bakeries continue to do well, mid-size (sales $750K–$2.5M) companies are experiencing shrinking margins due to increased health care costs and pressure from larger, highly automated competitors."

"Industry is declining due to eating habits of population. Cost of entry is very high due to equipment cost, unless used equipment is purchased. Marketability is limited by the size of the marketplace of professional bakers. In some parts of the U.S., facilities tend to be old. Competition is growing a bit due to the business education of young professional bakers."

"Receivables are very important since they determine the amount of start-up capital needed. It was the cause of the demise of many a big wholesaler in New York."

"Price will vary greatly depending on the volume and types of labor-saving equipment. This is an industry where payroll can be significantly reduced by machinery. Commercial contracts with restaurants, hotels, etc. are also a source of value."

Benchmark Data

- "Pounds of flour used; # of loaves of bread baked/sold."
- "Cost of goods should be no more than 20% tops . . . just as rent should be no more than 10% of sales."
- "22%–25% cost of goods"
- "Direct cost of goods varies significantly from product to product. There is no little commonality between a bread bakery and a cake and pastry bakery. A well-run facility with reasonable market share should result in an SDE of 15%–20% of Gross Revenues."
- "Difficult to measure since many of these businesses operate from facilities that are old and much larger than required with new highly automated equipment available."

Expenses as a percentage of annual sales	
Cost of goods	28% to 30%
Payroll/labor Costs	30% to 40%
Occupancy	15% to 19%
Profit (estimated pretax)	15% to 18%

B - Rules of Thumb

Industry Trend
- "Down . . . as the major bakers take over the industry."
- "As obesity becomes more of an issue, I anticipate a slight decline in the industry."
- "Fewer and fewer competitors . . . with a growing trend toward baking artisan products."
- "There will be less & less competition, with a few giants controlling the market!"

Seller Financing
- "Mostly seller financing...but if equipment is modern (which most are not) then outside financing can be arranged."
- "5 to 7 years, or the length of the lease if building is not owned"

Questions
- "Ask for flour and water bills, cost/price list of major items carried, aging of receivables & payables; see gas/electric bills; determine age and condition of equipment."
- "Is location of any importance to sales . . . if so how long is lease?"
- "Review and interview key customers—evaluate equipment carefully—check for expansion opportunity."

Banks—Commercial		
SIC 6021-01	NAICS 522110	Number of Businesses/Units 78,965

Rules of Thumb
➢ 1 to 2 times Book Value
➢ 350% of Annual Gross Sales includes inventory
➢ 15 times SDE includes inventory
➢ 15 times EBIT

Expert Comments
"The post-recession regulatory environment has burdened smaller community banks with compliance issues that are forcing many of them to consolidate in order to achieve the necessary economies of scale required to enable compliance."

Benchmark Data

Statistics (Commercial Banking)
Number of Establishments	78,965
Average Profit Margin	24.8%
Revenue per Employee	$482,900
Average Number of Employees	19.3
Average Wages per Employee	$75,491

Rules of Thumb - B

Products and Services Segmentation

Depository services and other noninterest-income generating products	34.5%
Real estate loans	29.3%
Commercial and industrial loans	13.1%
Loans to individuals	10.3%
Other	7.8%
Credit card loans	5.0%

Major Market Segmentation

Retail customers	49.9%
Corporate clients	47.1%
Other clients	3.0%

Industry Costs

Profit	24.8%
Wages	15.8%
Deprecation	3.6%
Marketing	2.1%
Rent & Utilities	9.7%
Other	44.0%

Market Share

Wells Fargo & Company	9.8%
JPMorgan Chase & Co.	8.0%
Bank of America Corporation	6.5%

Source: IBISWorld, March 2015

Expenses as a percentage of annual sales

Cost of goods	25%
Payroll/labor Costs	35%
Occupancy	05% to 10%
Profit (estimated pretax)	25%

Industry Trend

- "The Top 10 Retail Banking Trends and Predictions for 2015 are:
    - ✓ Using Customer Analytics to Drive Contextual Experiences
    - ✓ Expedited Deployment of Digital Delivery
    - ✓ Mobile-First Design
    - ✓ Increasing Digital and Social Selling
    - ✓ Mass Market Acceptance of Mobile Payments
    - ✓ Focus on Security and Authentication
    - ✓ Industry Consolidation
    - ✓ Enhanced Customer Incentivization
    - ✓ Investment in Innovation, Incubation and Uncommon Alliances
    - ✓ Increased Impact of Digital Disruptors"

    Source: "Top 10 Retail Banking Trends and Predictions for 2015," http://thefinancialbrand.com/46189/2015-top-banking-trends-predictions-forecast-digital-disruption/ 12/19/14

- "Consolidation of smaller banks, high scrutiny of risk in making loans, lower profit due to building up of capital and reserves."

26th Edition

B - Rules of Thumb

Questions
- "Are you now or have you ever been involved in banking? How much liquid capital do you have to invest? Have you spoken with any bank regulatory authorities about your plans to acquire a bank?"

Barber Shops (See also Beauty Salons, Hair Care, Franchises)		
SIC 7241-01	NAICS 812111	Number of Businesses/Units 50,000

Rules of Thumb
➤ 10 to 25 percent of SDE plus inventory; add $1500 per chair

Benchmark Data
- For Benchmark Data see Beauty Salons

Bars (See also Cocktail Lounges)		
SIC 5813-01	NAICS 722410	Number of Businesses/Units 70,791

Rules of Thumb
➤ 35% to 45% percent times annual sales—business only plus inventory
➤ 2 to 2.5 times SDE plus inventory
➤ 1.5 to 2.5 times EBIT
➤ 2 to 2.5 times EBITDA
➤ 4 times monthly sales + game revenue (net) plus inventory
➤ 4 times monthly sales + liquor license and inventory

Pricing Tips
- "High volume locations bring higher multiples. Value very location driven. Location often times more important than financials. Value of liquor license can also drive value dependent upon ease of obtaining liquor licenses in particular area where business is located. Prices have not recovered from 2009 economic woes. Good financial documentation also helps sale process and value."
- "Competition, number of available licenses in town, previous violations"
- "Top-line method is used due to the perception of a cash business. This is changing and it is much more difficult to sell bars without documented earnings."
- "Understand the value of liquor license and percentages of alcohol vs. food."
- "Main variable is the fair market value of the liquor permit, as some areas have a high number of available permits which results in the permit having no, or limited, additional value, while in other areas limited number of available permits may cause the permit to have a substantial value. One will need to research type of permit and its availability and if in fact a market exists for the permit itself. I have seen liquor permits being sold for as high as $150,000, which obviously impacts the value of the business."
- "The location, lease rate, and restrictions on the conditional use permit or

Rules of Thumb - B

liquor license will largely impact any given operation's value. As some licenses are valued at $75K plus, there is always some 'floor' value regardless of profitability."

- "Discretionary cash flow can be very different from deal to deal. There is one very important DCF item that should be identified: Does the bar or taproom have any vending? (Examples of this are video poker, tobacco, juke box, pool tables, etc;) If the answer is 'Yes,' then the next question should be, is there a vendor arrangement, or does the seller own the machines? A vendor arrangement means that the vendor owns the machines and collects a portion of the proceeds. If the seller owns the machines, the seller collects all of the proceeds, and can use these funds to reduce their COGS and labor considerably. In each case, (with the seller as owner or the vendor as owner of machines) OFF BALANCE SHEET seller financing or vendor financing can be a very powerful source of funds. There are a few little things that can alter the valuation in a bar or taproom. Generally, these types of establishments derive a lot of revenue from draft beer. (COGS for draft beer 25%–30%, gross profit 70%–75%). If the establishment is operating on an antiquated draft system, glasses may not appear clean, spouts look discolored, . . .this could warrant a discount. Most states require that draft system/draft lines are cleaned weekly. A potential buyer should ask for vendor beer invoices to determine the 'popular' products of the establishment. This is important if the buyer has a potential age group in mind as the primary patrons. This is a forward cash flow assumption that should be acknowledged. If vendor beer invoices are not made available, check the trash dumpster on a regular basis, it is an excellent source of information. If liquor is being served, the pouring routine should be observed. Measured shot or free pour can materially change COGS. 750ML bottle yields 26 ounces, which is 14 shots at a 1.75oz free pour, and 21 shots at a 1.25oz measured shot. This difference could be the cost of 1.5 bottles. (Generally these establishments sell mostly beer/draft beer, but this scenario should be included in forward cash flow assumptions.)"

- "Never trust the books. Check sales tax returns, bank statements, etc. Also, check the price points and compare to the actual COGS. Are the comps legitimate on the P&L? Are COGS high due to the owner skimming, or are they giving the house away? We never address a value to skimming and never represent it to buyers. Experienced buyers will recast the financials using their own labor percentage, etc."

Expert Comments

"All of the reality shows glamorizing the industry have popularized the business."

"Having practical work experience in the industry is a definite plus. Avoid a 'bad' lease situation. Be comfortable with customers. Sellers should make the place look presentable and not have a bunch of broken equipment around. Police runs and bad health department inspections drive down value. "

"True bars (without food) are becoming less profitable. Bars in good, dense, urban locations are still strong but suburban bars are struggling. Stronger drunk driving laws, smoking bans, etc. have contributed. Plus full-service restaurants with bars have cut into some of the business."

B - Rules of Thumb

"These businesses are highly marketable due to the public demand (and dream) of owning their own bar. The difficulty of obtaining new permits adds significant value to existing operations."

"Neighborhood bars seem to be popular despite a good or bad economy. Sometimes the closer to home the better, with tougher DUI laws."

"Competition may keep a bar from succeeding initially; and, conversely, a competitive environment indicates a good area for customers and traffic. The fact that bars and nightclubs are extremely trendy could lead to significant profit declines after the 'buzz' has worn off."

Benchmark Data

Statistics (Bars & Nightclubs)

Number of Establishments	70,791
Average Profit Margin	5.0%
Revenue per Employee	$66,000
Average Number of Employees	5.6
Average Wages per Employee	$15,974

Products and Services Segmentation

Sale of beer and ale	36.4%
Sale of distilled spirit drinks	32.5%
Sale of meals and nonalcoholic beverages	10.4%
Sale of wine drinks	6.9%
Admissions to special events and nightclubs, including cover charges	2.4%
Other	11.4%

Industry Costs

Profit	5.0%
Wages	24.2%
Purchases	44.0%
Depreciation	2.6%
Marketing	1.2%
Rent & Utilities	6.5%
Other	16.5%

Source: IBISWorld, August 2015

- "Food costs under 34% helpful."
- "High rents have been the cause of many failures."
- "Total occupancy costs of 10% or less."
- "There is no greater markup than that of liquor."
- "Annual sales of $1,000 per square foot is a great general benchmark for a successful bar!"
- "Small easily operated bars are the most desirable. Rent at 10%–12% (or less) of sales help."
- "Benchmarks vary widely with markets and types of establishments; food costs tend to be 25%–33%; however, productivity per square foot is a function of size and location (and subsequent lease rate)."
- "Hard to say. Still a very high percentage of 'bad books.' Any neighborhood bar (without food) that has an occupancy cost of ten percent or less is a great benchmark. Of course, skim or bad books skews the numbers."

Rules of Thumb - B

- "$327 sales per sq. ft. in a bar generating $850,000 in sales with a 5% net profit"

Expenses as a percentage of annual sales
Cost of goods	20% to 30%
Payroll/labor Costs	20% to 28%
Occupancy	06% to 10%
Profit (estimated pretax)	10% to 20%

Industry Trend
- "Having emerged from the recession relatively unharmed, the Bars and Nightclubs industry turned around in 2010 and has continued to make strides over the past five years. Revenue growth has been slow, however, hampered by shaky consumer confidence and stubbornly high unemployment, meaning people have been more content to drink at home rather than at bars or nightclubs. In the coming years, bar and nightclub owners will reap the rewards of increasing household incomes and consumer spending."

    Source: IBISWorld, January 2015
- "With the amount of new products emerging from the market with flavored wines, vodka, whisky...one has to stay up on what is in."
- "Increasing cost inflation and changing consumer tastes, e.g., craft beer, local foods, etc. Smoking blue collar 'sports' bars on the decline."
- "Most bars are improving on their food to drive more bar business."
- "Flavored vodkas, spirits, organic"
- "Increasing costs and increasing competition from chains"
- "More bars, more craft beers, wines from different regions. I think we will see more pub-type concepts."
- "Increased governmental regulation, e.g., smoking bans"
- "More wine bars, tapas bars; drinking is always popular. More pricey drinks."
- "Liquor licenses in certain areas where there are high concentrations of establishments within major cities have become extremely difficult to obtain, thus driving the value of those licenses very high."

Seller Financing
- "All cash or some element of owner financing is usually necessary to make a deal happen. Bank financing very difficult"
- "3 to 7 years"

Questions
- "Length of time employees have been at work, number of employees, tax audits? Recent violations?"
- "Violations, invoices for purchases, customer count and sales"
- "Unpaid taxes? Liquor license violations? Police runs?"
- "Please provide me with a copy of the permit or conditional use permit, as provided by the city and the state Alcohol Control Board."
- "The variance between the internal books and records versus the tax returns. Purchase invoice availability."
- "Liquor license violations, amount of revenue generated from games/amusements on a weekly basis, # of 'cash' employees"

B - Rules of Thumb

- "What conditions have been placed on the license restricting the hours, use, or entertainment associated with the license?"
- "Scrutinize happy hour, comps, etc. Many buyers think they can increase sales by eliminating giveaways which usually does not work. Ask to see all liquor invoices and cash receipts from liquor purchases."
- "For the tax returns, why they are selling? Cooperation is key in this business. Bars are difficult to sell when there are unreported sales, weak returns. Many of the sellers in our market will not hold notes."
- "Discretionary Cash Flow should be evaluated very carefully. There can be a huge difference from deal to deal."
- "How much cash revenue is not reported? Are there any conditions on the license or permits? What type of entertainment is specifically included in the permit for entertainment?"

Resources

Trade Publications
- "Bar Confidential: Running a Successful Bar" by Bob Johnson: www.barproducts.com

Bars—Adult Only (Adult Clubs/Nightclubs)		
SIC 5813-01	NAICS 722410	

Rules of Thumb

- ➢ 100 to 120 percent of annual sales includes inventory
- ➢ 3.5 times SDE includes inventory

Pricing Tips

- "Real estate typically will lease out at a 12%–20% premium to market. Alcohol licenses may have intrinsic value to be added to cost of purchase."
- "A recasted, SDC flow is the best starting point. Be sure to examine either property or rental costs to make sure they are in line with area...Typically rental cost show a premium of 10%–20% above comparable market rates. FFE is a consideration related to its age."
- "Additional income is available from dancers and door."
- "The industry has experienced a shake-out of weaker performing clubs being swallowed by larger operators as they become available. Although we have experienced recessionary forces, as the entire industry has, the Adult Club industry by and large has been more resilient than mainstream bars and nightclubs to the effects of discretionary dollar competition and distribution. The more troubling aspects are more related to legal issues of Independent Contractor Status and the efforts of the Citizens for Community Values (CCV)."
- "Adult clubs are of course cash heavy operations. Verifying internal ratios of cost can lead to a back-ended method of providing gross cash flow."
- "A true EBITDA + owner's compensation recast is a necessity . . ."
- "The best thumbnail is SDE. It stands up well to real-world numbers on the sales prices. Real estate, inventory, FFE all should be considered separately as add backs to total sale price. Some states allow the sale of inventory alcohol to the buyer, some do not. MAI appraisals do well for real estate. FFE is a 'swag' and over 3 years old stuff ought to write down to 10%–20% of initial cost."

Rules of Thumb - B

Expert Comments

"Industry is vital, and succeeding....the average club life can be measured almost in decades."

"Major risk is from legislative actions. Operator chooses location and level of sophistication and markets accordingly."

"The economy really hits discretionary earnings spending . . . "

"Clubs took a hit this year and last year that was, in essence, an acceleration of a downward trend for the last 2 years . . . I do see signs of stabilization and stronger sales, as well as better customer #'s in certain markets . . "

"Conservative nibblings at the edges of law have served to limit growth of the industry. There has been a generalized effort on the part of the larger chains and owners to absorb reasonably priced clubs in targeted areas. Past the big and midsized players, the single and small operators struggle to maintain a stable cash flow with controlled labor costs, dancers, and stable legal environments."

Benchmark Data

Statistics (Strip Clubs)

Number of Establishments	3,642
Average Profit Margin	19.1%
Revenue per Employee	$52,900
Average Number of Employees	32.4
Average Wages per Employee	$11,017

Products and Services Segmentation

Service revenue	44.5%
Alcohol	38.5%
Food and merchandise	10.9%
Other services	6.1%

Industry Costs

Profit	19.1%
Wages	20.8%
Purchases	19.4%
Depreciation	4.1%
Marketing	4.8%
Rent & Utilities	5.2%
Other	26.6%

Source: IBISWorld, August 2014

- "Liquor cost should be in the range of 18%–22%; Rent: optimally in the 8%–10% of gross sales."
- "SDE x 2.5–3.5 = possible sale price."
- "Should be reporting an SDE in neighborhood of 23%–26% or higher."
- "Rick's and its competitors benefit as well from what may well be a unique aspect of their business model. The entertainment that brings folks in the door is actually a moneymaker: Dancers pay to work there as independent

B - Rules of Thumb

contractors (how much depends on location and shifts, with some shifts costing several hundred dollars) and get paid from tips. That keeps overhead and salary and benefit expenses low.

"There are basically three revenue streams, in addition to the fees from dancers: cover charges, which can top $20; food and drinks; and services, which include the renting of private rooms. A customer may pay the club $400 to $500 for a spell in one of those rooms."

- "Rent: <10%; liquor cost: 15%"

Expenses as a percentage of annual sales
Cost of goods	20%
Payroll/labor Costs	n/a
Occupancy	<10%
Profit (estimated pretax)	25%

Industry Trend
- "Like so many other 'sin' categories, the business seems to be resistant to economic downturns, especially as the customer base keeps expanding."
- "This industry is facing a slight decrease in profit margins: a constriction of the industry growth rate due to local government interference."

Seller Financing
- "Usually 2–4 years"
- "Usually all cash"

Questions
- "What is the legal status of licenses and permits: alcohol, privilege, local?"
- "Detailed explanation of all income sources. Current political atmosphere. Security of license."
- "What violations have been charged? Is the owner aware of any pending litigation or legislation (either local or state) which will have a negative impact? There are others but the rest are more site specific."
- "How would he replace the cash flow of this business with something comparable?"
- "Why is he/she selling? What is wrong with this picture? I have yet to have an owner list a club with me because he woke up one morning, said, 'Gee, I think I'll let someone else make a bunch of money off my club, and I'll finance it to him on easy terms, too!' Inevitably, if someone wants to sell, there is usually a serious reason that is material! Caveat Emptor, and make sure that both buyer and seller have their own individual attorneys."

Resources

Trade Publications
- Exotic Dancer Magazine: www.edpublications.com

Associations
- Association of Club Executives: www.acenational.org

Rules of Thumb - **B**

Bars—Nightclubs (See also Bars)	
NAICS 722410	Number of Businesses/Units 71,560

Rules of Thumb
- 40 percent of annual sales
- 2.5 times SDE plus inventory
- 3 times EBIT
- 2 times EBITDA

Pricing Tips
- "The conditions or potential restrictions on the liquor license are paramount. Are there abbreviated hours, are happy hours or door fees allowed, what is the security guard-to-patron ratio, does a significant percentage of sales need to be derived by food sales, etc."
- "Buyers of nightclubs are generally going to implement their own concept and theme. Sellers rarely seek to sell when they are at the peak of their game, but when revenues begin to slide. The lifespan of a 'hot' club rarely lasts beyond 3 to 4 years, so at that point an owner may need to give the business a 'face lift' or sell it to a new owner who will implement a new theme. That in mind, value based on cash flow becomes less relevant since a new owner's investment will be the same regardless."

Expert Comments
"This industry is highly volatile as trends are constantly changing. Also, clubs on the Strip in Las Vegas, in Hollywood or in SouthBeach are significantly different from main street America."

Benchmark Data

Statistics (Bars & Nightclubs)
Number of Establishments	71,560
Average Profit Margin	5.0%
Revenue per Employee	$66,300
Average Number of Employees	5.6
Average Wages per Employee	$16,032

Products and Services Segmentation
Sale of beer and ale	36.4%
Sale of distilled spirits drinks	32.5%
Other (accommodation, cigarettes, rentals, and packaged liquor)	11.4%
Sale of meals and nonalcoholic beverages	10.4%
Sale of wine drinks	6.9%
Admissions to special events and nightclubs, including cover charges	2.4%

Industry Costs
Profit	5.0%
Wages	24.2%
Purchases	44.0%
Depreciation	2.6%
Marketing	1.2%
Rent & Utilities	6.5%
Other	16.5%

Source: IBISWorld, August 2015

B - Rules of Thumb

- "Of the top 100 survey participants, 42.8% identified their venues as nightclubs; 70.6% of them described their hotspots as dance clubs. Of those identifying their venue as bars, 31.7% are sports bars and 29.3% are traditional bar/taverns. DJs and live entertainment are featured by 88.3% and 73.6% of total respondents, respectively. Nearly 80% offer a dance floor, 70.1% provide VIP areas, and 65% offer bottle service.

  "Drinks generate the lion's share of venue revenues—56% of sales from alcohol is the mean among Top 100 survey participants. While in the venues, partyers favored spirits, which generate 44% of alcohol sales. Beer contributes 25% and wine 9%. A full food menu is offered by 68% of survey respondents' venues. Gaming, such as pool tables, video games systems and jukeboxes, are available at 42% of respondents' venues. Nearly three quarters (73%) have outdoor patio, terrace or rooftop space, which is an increase from 63% a year ago.

  "Small companies can compete effectively by serving a local market, offering unique products or entertainment, or providing superior customer service. The industry is extremely labor-intensive: average annual revenue per worker is $60.000.

  "Size varies greatly, from small corner taverns to warehouse-sized dance clubs. The majority of nightclubs range from 3,500 to 7,000 square feet, according to nightclubbiz.com. Experienced owners tend to run the largest nightclubs, which range from 10,000 to 30,000 square feet. A 3,000 square foot club can gross between $24,000 and $64,000 per month. A 15,000 square foot club can gross between $100,000 and $260,000 per month."

  Source: National Club Industry Association of America www.nciaa.com

- "Successful bars and nightclubs should sell at least $4,000 to $5,000 per well on weekends and busy nights."

Expenses as a percentage of annual sales

Cost of goods	25%
Payroll/labor Costs	30%
Occupancy	15%
Profit (estimated pretax)	20%

Industry Trend

- "Improving conditions across the economy, which will speed up starting in 2013, will bring the industry back to solid health in the near future. Through 2015, the industry is projected to continue experiencing competition from non-industry establishments such as restaurants as well as from people opting to drink at home."

  Source: National Club Industry of America www.nciaa.com

- "There will always be a market for such venues, and buyers willing to pay premiums to A+ locations for venues."

Questions

- "Original invoices for liquor sales, and, with your fingers crossed, door counts per night."

Resources

Websites

- Nightclub & Bar: http://www.nightclub.com/

Rules of Thumb - B

Associations
- National Club Industry Association of America, NCIAA: www.nciaa.com

Bars with Slot Machines (See also Casinos/Casino Hotels)		
	NAICS 722410	

Rules of Thumb
➢ 3 times SDE plus inventory

Pricing Tips
- "Drinks are free to slot players. Pay close attention to only the net, providing other operating costs are in line."

Expenses as a percentage of annual sales
Cost of goods 32%
Payroll/labor Costs 30%
Occupancy 10%
Profit (estimated pretax) 17%

Seller Financing
- "Where the debt service does not exceed 35 percent of the SDE."

Baseball Teams (professional)		
SIC 7997-08	NAICS 711211	

Pricing Tips
- "The Los Angeles Dodgers are currently valued by *Forbes* at $1.6 billion, second highest in baseball. The St Louis Cardinals are ranked 10th league-wide at $716 million."

  Source: "The St Louis Cardinals: Baseball's 'Little Engine That Could' Just Did Against Baseball's Highest Payroll" by Patrick Riche, *Forbes*, October 19, 2013

Benchmark Data

Statistics (Sports Franchises)
Number of Establishments 944
Average Profit Margin 6.3%
Revenue per Employee $399,500
Average Number of Employees 71.1
Average Wages per Employee $261,026

Products and Services Segmentation
Ticket sales 38.0%
Broadcasting and other media rights 31.0%
Advertising 12.5%
Other 11.5%
Concessions 3.5%
Licensing of rights to use property 2.0%
Merchandise sales 1.5%

26th Edition

B - Rules of Thumb

Industry Costs

Profit	6.3%
Wages	64.9%
Purchases	8.5%
Depreciation	3.3%
Marketing	7.7%
Rent & Utilities	8.3%
Other	1.0%

Source: IBISWorld, May 2015

Major US team sport revenue

League	Share of industry revenue (%)
NFL	37.4
MLB	28.7
NBA	18.7
NHL	13.9
Other	1.3

Source: Forbes.com

Industry Trend

- "Billionaires own 49% of the major professional sports teams in America. Long-tenured owners are becoming billionaires thanks to soaring team values, while the pool of prospective buyers is increasingly limited to the super-rich."

    Source: "Billionaires Own Nearly Half of All Major Professional Sports Teams," by Dan Alexander, *Forbes*, 3/7/15

Basketball Teams (professional)

SIC 7941-03	NAICS 711211	

Pricing Tips

- MBA revenues, which were $118 million for the 1982–83 season, hit $4.6 billion for the league's 30 teams last year. The Sacramento Kings—sold for $10.5 million in 1983—changed hands in May for $534 million. . .

  "The average NBA franchise is worth (equity plus debt) $634 million, up 25% over last year. Collectively the 30 teams are worth $19 billion versus $400 million in 1984 when there were 23 teams. Stern has served his owners well. Under his watch, every team built or completely renovated their home arena leading to total gate receipts of $1.3 billion last season.

  "The average NBA franchise is worth (equity plus debt) $634 million, up 25% over last year."

    Source: "As Stern Says Goodbye, Knicks, Lakers Set Records As NBA's Most Valuable Teams," by Kurt Badenhausen, *Forbes*, January 22, 2014

- Note: *Forbes Magazine* has some interesting articles on valuing companies, etc.

Benchmark Data

- Note: For more information see Benchmarks under Baseball Teams

Rules of Thumb - B

Franchise
Baskin-Robbins Ice Cream (See also Franchises, Ice Cream/Yogurt Shops)

Approx. Total Investment		$125,000 to $250,000
Estimated Annual Sales/Unit		$175,250
SIC 2024-98	NAICS 722515	Number of Businesses/Units 7,000

Rules of Thumb
➢ 46 to 56 percent of annual sales plus inventory

Resources
Websites
- Baskin Robbins: www.baskinrobbins.com

Franchise
Batteries Plus Bulbs (See also Franchises)

Approx. Total Investment		$208,450 to $385,750
	NAICS 441310	Number of Businesses/Units 600

Rules of Thumb
➢ 30 to 35 percent of annual sales plus inventory

Resources
Websites
- Batteries Plus: www.batteriesplus.com

Beauty Salons (See also Barber Shops, Hair Care, Nail Salons)		
SIC 7231-06	NAICS 812112	Number of Businesses/Units 1,258,854

Rules of Thumb
➢ 35 percent of annual revenues; add fixtures, equipment & inventory
➢ 2 times SDE plus inventory
➢ 4 times monthly sales plus inventory
➢ 2.5 times EBIT

Pricing Tips
- "25% to 35% of annual sales"
- "Whether the operators are W-2 or #1099—and also how the chemical product costs are debited."
- "What percentage of the gross sales is generated by a service generating owner and how may the change in ownership shift the owner's income? The most effective pricing point is utilizing the SDE."

26th Edition

B - Rules of Thumb

- "Check reason(s) for empty stations—turnover? Are stations rented?"
- "1. Check on chair rental versus commissioned stylist. 2. Check on staff turnover. It can be very high. 3. Reputation and location very important."
- ". . . installation of beauty shops in today's market costs from $2,000 to $2,200 per station (verify), but selling price is usually about $1,500 to $2,000 per station. The ultramodern shops usually have a considerable amount of tenant's improvements which should be taken into consideration . . . Rents are from $50 to $75 per station or the operators rent a station and retain a portion or all of the commissions earned . . . with resulting loss of goodwill value. Other approaches: (1) is to price the salon at 20 percent of gross sales, (2) 1–1.5 times recasted cash flow, or (3) 35 percent of gross sales plus equipment & inventory."

Expert Comments

- "The beauty industry is as old as mankind and essentially a replenishment industry; the resale possibilities are endless; rebranding is the next frontier."
- "Location and marketing are big factors in the success of a salon."
- "Highly competitive industry with a fair level of risk. Can be easily replicated. Location, location, location."
- "Market saturation has occurred likely due to the creative nature of the salon professional wanting to expand yet not completing the necessary business market research. The risks are considered low because of the small monetary initial investment. The beauty industry trends will always grow due to vanity and fashion."
- "Fair amount of turnover, but fair amount of buyers."

Benchmark Data

Statistics (Hair & Nail Salons)

Number of Establishments	1,258,854
Average Profit Margin	5.8%
Revenue per Employee	$30,000
Average Number of Employees	1.4
Average Wages per Employee	$13,221

Products and Services Segmentation

Haircutting services	45.5%
Hair coloring services	17.1%
Nail care services	15.9%
Merchandise sales	9.7%
Other hair care services	4.7%
Other beauty care services	3.6%
Skin care services	3.5%

Industry Costs

Profit	5.8%
Wages	43.0%
Purchases	16.3%
Depreciation	1.9%
Marketing	1.6%
Rent & Utilities	12.9%
Other	18.5%

Source: IBISWorld, July 2015

Rules of Thumb - B

- "Economic Trends: Percent of Gross Revenue by Category
  Hair Color Service Sales... 34%
  Hair Cutting Service Sales... 31%
  Retail Sales... 17%
  Skin Care, Body Care, Spa-type Service Sales.. 8%
  Nail Service Sales... 4%
  Chemical Service Sales... 3%
  Other... 3%"

  Source: "Salon Today"

- "If seller earns commission credits, do not include them in the owner's benefit—just what is earned as solely an owner."
- "A successful salon's gross sales should average $1000 per week per employee."
- "Full-time operators should produce a minimum of $50,000 annual gross revenue."

Expenses as a percentage of annual sales
Cost of goods...	12%
Payroll/labor Costs...	60%
Occupancy...	10% to 20%
Profit (estimated pretax)...	10% to 15%

Industry Trend

- "Haircutting services constitute the largest single service group for this industry at about 46.9% of total revenue. Services in this segment include cutting, trimming and layering hair for all demographic groups. Additionally, haircutting also extends to beards and mustaches, which is traditionally done by barbers. Services that accompany haircuts, such as shampooing, blow-drying and styling, are also included in this segment."

  Source: IBISWorld, February 2015

- "Color is king! Now, more than ever, it's important for salons to put an emphasis on their color services. Many salons have opted to become a full-service Spa-lon. Specializing in services that reach beyond the hair, and focus on overall health and wellness, spalons offer many unique treatments not found in typical salons or spas."

  Source: "Salon Industry Trends 2015," by Rosey,
http://hairnerd.hubpages.com/hub/Salon-Industry-Trends-2014

- "More and more foreign buyers and growth in chain operations."
- "Growing trend with the Baby Boomers being more concerned with aging and graying."
- "Mainstream beauty services will continue. Natural processes for beauty treatments. Minor cosmetic surgery/treatments will interchange with spa and salon services. Male client services are increasing."

Seller Financing

- 3 to 5 years

Questions

- "What percentage of the gross sales is generated by the seller?"

26th Edition

B - Rules of Thumb

Resources

Trade Publications
- Modern Salon: www.modernsalon.com

Bed & Breakfasts (See also Inns)		
SIC 7011-07	NAICS 721191	Number of Businesses/Units 4,633

Rules of Thumb

- ➢ 550 percent of annual sales includes inventory and real estate
- ➢ 4.2 times gross room sales for small B&Bs (less than eight rooms); a little higher for dinner-service inns, 4.5; these are for businesses as opposed to real-estate-driven small properties
- ➢ 8 to 9 times SDE includes inventory and real estate

Pricing Tips

- "The smaller the inn and lower the business income, the more the real value factor weighs heavy in the formula. The larger the inn and the higher the business income, the less weight this factor affects total value. Many of the larger inns have been selling in the 8 to 10 capitalization rate of net income, less any needed repairs and up to a 20% discount if seller financing is not involved."
- "Smaller B&Bs (fewer than 8 rooms) are usually real-estate driven."
- "5 times gross room income; gross room income minus the net operating expenses (no debt service or management costs) = NOI times 11 percent."

Expert Comments

"Many of the larger inns have been selling in the 8 to 10 capitalization rate of net income, less any needed repairs and up to a 20% discount if seller financing is not involved. In the middle part of U.S., B&Bs are selling for $80K-$100K/guestroom on avg. The popular East & West Coast locations could be up to twice that amt. The larger the inn, the less value/guestroom. Values & Expenses vary greatly due to the non-standardized structure of the bldgs. & locale."

"B&B buyers must make both a lifestyle & financial purchase decision. Innkeeping is one of the few businesses that you want to live where you work! For the past 5+ years, we have had smaller B&Bs sold/converted back to homes than we've had homes being converted to inns! Start-ups are more difficult to accomplish today versus the mid-1980's primarily due to rising real estate values, high conversion cost, zoning restrictions, tougher lending practices, & a lack of market demand for innkeeping (during a strong economy). Some of the smaller inns in less popular areas were converted to alternative uses and a minority of inns closed for avoidance of taxes from capital gains and depreciation recapture."

Rules of Thumb - **B**

Benchmark Data

Statistics (Bed & Breakfast & Hostel Accommodations)

Number of Establishments	4,633
Average Profit Margin	16.8%
Revenue per Employee	$87,400
Average Number of Employees	4.6
Average Wages per Employee	$22,075

Products and Services Segmentation

Bed & Breakfast	69%
Other - including Hostels	31%

Major Market Segmentation

Vacation travelers	58.2%
Family travelers	21.8%
Business travelers	12.0%
Other - including meetings	8.0%

Industry Costs

Profit	16.8%
Wages	25.3%
Purchases	21.5%
Depreciation	8.0%
Marketing	2.5%
Rent & Utilities	12.5%
Other	13.4%

Source: IBISWorld, October 2014

- "Many of the larger inns have been selling in the 8 to 10 capitalization rate of net income, less any needed repairs and up to a 20% discount if seller financing is not involved. In the middle part of U.S., B&Bs are selling for for $80K-$100K/guestroom on avgerage. The popular East & West Coast locations could be up to twice that amount. The larger the inn, the less value/guestroom. Values & Expenses vary greatly due to the non-standardized structure of the bldgs. & locale."
- "There are more small B&Bs becoming homes vs. homes becoming B&Bs. Most new innkeepers are replacing an income, and the supplemental income B&Bs tend to sell as homes. The larger, more profitable inns, that are within 3 hrs. driving of a metro area, are doing better than ever due to closer & quicker getaway travel patterns."
- "B&B buyers must make both a lifestyle & financial purchase decision. Innkeeping is one of the few businesses in which you want to live where you work! For the past 5+ years, we have had smaller B&Bs sold/converted back to homes than we've had homes being converted to inns! Start-ups are more difficult to accomplish today versus the mid-1980's primarily due to rising real estate values, high conversion cost, zoning restrictions, tougher lending practices, & a lack of market demand for innkeeping (during a strong economy). Some of the smaller inns in less popular areas were converted to alternative uses and a minority of inns closed for avoidance of taxes from capital gains & depreciation recapture."

B - Rules of Thumb

- "The larger inns are selling for 8 (w/o seller financing) to 10 times (w/seller financing) adjusted net operating income. The base real estate value of the smaller B&B contributes to a large part of the value. In small, supplemental income B&Bs, their value is typically $25,000 to $50,000 more than the base real estate value as a house or other real estate use. There are probably more supplemental income B&Bs than cash flow inns of the 20K+ U.S. B&Bs."
- "Profit (estimated) 40% to 45% of sales"
- "Many resort inns within three hours of a metro area can produce occupancy in the 40% to 50% range. Urban inns can produce 50% to 80% occupancy. Most non-urban inns below seven guestrooms provide to only supplemental income. It's kind of like owning a duplex; you can live in a better location & house than you could otherwise afford, but you don't give up your day job. About 50% of the U.S. B&Bs are this size."
- "Bed and Breakfast/Country Inn Statistics: The data below is from Studies and Surveys done by www.innkeeping.org—a very informative site."

Performance (in medians)
Occupancy Rate	43.7%
Average Daily Rate	$150
Revenue per Available Room	$58

About the Inns
- ✓ 72% of B&Bs are run by couples
- ✓ 79% of innkeepers live on premises
- ✓ The typical B&B has between 4 and 11 rooms, with 6 guest rooms or suites being the average
- ✓ The average B&B has been open for 15 years
- ✓ The average age of the oldest part of a B&B building is 107 years
- ✓ 29% of B&Bs were in rural locations, 23% were urban, 5% suburban, and 43% were village
- ✓ 94% of rooms have private baths
- ✓ 36% have achieved an "historical designation" by a local, state or national historic preservation organization
- ✓ 5,700 square feet is the average size for a B&B
- ✓ 93% offer free high speed wireless Internet
- ✓ Most B&Bs provide the following in common areas: Internet, magazines, hot/cold beverages, board games, fireplace, refrigerator, newspapers, telephone, cookies/cakes/candies/fruit, fresh flowers and televisions.
- ✓ Most B&Bs provide the following in guest rooms: Internet, television, luxury bed/linens, premium branded toiletries, robes, fireplaces, magazines and jetted tubs.

Expenses as a percentage of annual sales
Cost of goods	15%
Payroll/labor Costs	10%
Occupancy	10%
Profit (estimated pretax)	10%

Rules of Thumb - **B**

Industry Trend
- "The B&B room rates & occupancy have been growing steadily each year. Travelers are taking closer, quicker getaways instead of taking 2 wks. off& traveling abroad. B&Bs primarily cater to affluent, Baby Boomer & Millennial travelers. That market appears to be growing. This is also the market that the next generation of innkeepers is coming from."

Seller Financing
- "Inns that are < $700K, conventional commercial financing is available. Over $700K, the seller and the SBA is usually involved. Typically it's buyer 10%, seller 25% and lender 65%."
- "5 to 8 years; partial financing."

Questions
- "Ask the broker/seller how their B&B will work for you w/the buyer's downpayment."

Resources

Websites
- Inns for Sale—This site has Inns and B&Bs for sale and also offers educational programs: www.innsforsale.com
- Information for B & B owners: www.bedandbreakfast.com

Associations
- MichiganLake to Lake Bed & Breakfast Association: www.laketolake.com
- Professional Association of Innkeepers International—a wonderful site, lots of good information: www.innkeeping.org

---

Bedding and Mattress Shops (Retail) (See also Furniture Stores)		
SIC 5712-09	NAICS 442110	Number of Businesses/Units 9,227

Rules of Thumb
> ➢ 35 percent of annual sales plus inventory

Pricing Tips
- "More retail locations equal more favorable manufacturer pricing."

Expert Comments
"Bedding continues to be a needed product and the consumer now has a perceived need for enhanced comfort and a better night's rest."

26th Edition

B - Rules of Thumb

Benchmark Data

Statistics (Bed and Mattress Stores)

Number of Establishments	9,227
Average Profit Margin	1.5%
Revenue per Employee	$254,800
Average Number of Employees	5.0
Average Wages per Employee	$30,227

Products and Services Segmentation

Traditional mattresses	49.3%
Specialty mattresses	23.1%
Frames and box springs	19.0%
Other, including bedding and pillows	8.6%

Industry Costs

Profit	1.5%
Wages	12.1%
Purchases	60.3%
Depreciation	0.5%
Marketing	6.7%
Rent & Utilities	7.0%
Other	11.9%

Market Share

Mattress Firm	20.9%
Select Comfort Corporation	9.8%
Sleepy's	7.2%

Source: IBISWorld, March 2015

- "Increased ticket % for same store sales for the same month as opposed to previous year."

Expenses as a percentage of annual sales

Cost of goods	25%
Payroll/labor Costs	10%
Occupancy	20%
Profit (estimated pretax)	45%

Industry Trend

- "Something Extraordinary happened in the Specialty Sleep Arena last Year— For the first time since the International Sleep Products Association began breaking out innerspring and specialty mattress figures (in 2004), specialty sleep mattress units and dollars declined in a non-recession year. And for the first time ever, the innerspring category grew in units and dollars when the specialty category declined.

"Those figures show innerspring mattress units outperforming specialty mattress units by 10 percentage points, and innerspring mattress dollars outperforming specialty mattress dollars by 12.4 percentage points. Those are wide margins.

"Why the big wins for innersprings? Hybrid sleep sets are a big part of the story. Those beds combine innersprings and specialty foams. ISPA doesn't break out hybrid sleep sets as a separate category, something that would be impossible to do, as one man's hybrid is another man's traditional sleep set. So there is no telling exactly how much hybrids are responsible for the innerspring resurgence.

"On the negative side of the ledger, specialty sleep sets have clearly hit the wall. It should be noted that specialty beds are often premium products retailing at $1,000 and above, and some say the higher-end bedding market, in particular, is suffering of late. Other specialty sleep issues include reduced advertising and ineffective marketing, analysts say.

"Since history can be of no help to us in predicting future specialty sleep trends, we must let the sales trends this year tell the story. Specialty sleep appears poised for a rebound based on a slew of strong introductions. But the hybrid story is resonating with consumers."

Source:http://www.furnituretoday.com/blogpost/12892-specialty-sleep-sank-in-2013-but-can-bounce-back by David Perry, *Furniture Today*, February 16, 2014

Questions
- "What is the reason for selling? Where do you stand in terms of your relationships with the major bedding suppliers? What customer service issues might be pending?"

Resources

Trade Publications
- Bedding Today: www.furnituretoday.com/

		Franchise
Beef 'O' Brady's Family Sports Pubs (See also Franchises)		
Approx. Total Investment		$206,500 to $826,500
Estimated Annual Sales/Unit		$1,000,000
	NAICS 722410	Number of Businesses/Units 216

Rules of Thumb
➢ 25 percent of annual sales plus inventory

Resources

Websites
- www.beefobradys.com

Beer Distributorships/Wholesalers		
SIC 5181-01	NAICS 422810	Number of Businesses/Units 4,397

Rules of Thumb
➢ $5.00 to $15 per case sold over the last 12 months; add hard assets & inventory. Multiple per case is dependent on brands sold—the popular ones command the higher multiples.

➢ "These types of distributing businesses are usually sold for the price of inventory at cost, plus the rolling stock, plus the land and improvements, if these are part of the sale, plus $1.00 for each case delivered per year, plus $1.50 for each keg delivered per year."

26th Edition

B - Rules of Thumb

Pricing Tips
- "The two most important characteristics are (1) the brands carried, and (2) the territory. Brands vary considerably in market sales, and also vary regionally. Territories that are densely populated tend to be serviced more efficiently."
- 1 U.S. BBL (beer barrel) = 31 U.S. gallons = 13.778 = 24/12-oz. cases

Expert Comments
"Franchise restrictions are important constraints on resale."

Benchmark Data

Statistics (Beer Wholesaling)
Number of Establishments	4,397
Average Profit Margin	4.4%
Revenue per Employee	$578,300
Average Number of Employees	26.0
Average Wages per Employee	$52,985

Products and Services Segmentation
Cans of beer and ale (12 oz.)	45.8%
Cases of bottled beer and ale	38.3%
Cans of beer and ale (not 12 oz.)	9.1%
Beer and ale barrels and kegs	5.2%
Other malt beverages and brewing products	1.6%

Major Market Segmentation
Food and drink establishments	39.0%
Retail liquor stores	23.0%
Other (including casinos)	18.0%
Grocery stores	15.0%
Hotels and motels	5.0%

Industry Costs
Profit	4.4%
Wages	9.1%
Purchases	67.5%
Depreciation	1.0%
Marketing	2.3%
Rent & Utilities	1.5%
Other	14.2%

Enterprises by Employment Size
Number of Employees	Percentage
0 to 4	24.8%
5 to 9	9.1%
10 to 19	10.8%
20 to 99	35.0%
100 to 499	18.0%
500+	2.2%

Source: IBISWorld, July 2015

- "• 97% of U.S. breweries produce less than 60,000 barrels per year
  • 93% of U.S. breweries produce less than 15,000 barrels per year
  • 91% of U.S. breweries produce less than 7,143 barrels per year
  (Note: 7,143 barrels is a measurement the U.S. Alcohol and Tobacco Tax and Trade Bureau uses for a paperworkreduction rule for filing federal excise taxes.)"

  Source: "Data Show Craft Brewers with Double Digit Volume Share of U.S. Beer Market," http://www.nbwa.org/news/america%E2%80%99s-beer-distributors-applaud-continued-growth-craft-beer 3/19/15

- "Market values for beer distributors tend to be discussed as a multiple of cases sold in the past 12 months. These often vary from $5 to $15 per case sold, for well-established brands and successful operations. Struggling brands and operations can be priced less. There is no comparable metric for wine or spirits."

Industry Trend

- "Craft brewers now represent more than 10 percent of the beer volume sold in the U.S. marketplace—the first time the craft segment has reached double-digit volume."

  Source: "Data Show Craft Brewers with Double Digit Volume Share of U.S. Beer Market," http://www.nbwa.org/news/america%E2%80%99s-beer-distributors-applaud-continued-growth-craft-beer 3/19/15

- "The 'three-tier' system set up in most states after Prohibition is being challenged, at least on the edges, by interstate shipping of wine. Legal developments in this area will affect the value of wine distributors, although not beer distributors, over the next few years. Once you have a good operation in a decent area, this business will keep producing cash. Remember, the beer and wine business is over 2,000 years old."

Resources

Websites
- Beer Institute: www.beerinstitute.org

Trade Publications
- Beer Marketer's Insights: www.beerinsights.com

Associations
- The National Beer Wholesalers Association (NBWA)—an informative Website: www.nbwa.org

Beer Taverns—Beer & Wine (See also Bars, Brew Pubs)		
	NAICS 722410	

Rules of Thumb
- ➢ 6 times monthly sales plus inventory
- ➢ 1 to 1.5 times annual EBIT
- ➢ 55 percent of annual sales plus inventory

B - Rules of Thumb

Pricing Tips
- "There are 1,980 ounces in a keg, less 10 percent waste, about 1,700 net ounces per keg. If there are 12 ounces (net) in a glass of beer, divide 12 ounces into 1,700 net ounces per keg to determine cost and number of glasses that should be poured from that keg. Determine what a 12-ounce glass of beer is selling for, then multiply that times the number of glasses that is poured from the keg. This will give you the total gross per keg."

Resources

Websites
- Beer Institute—an excellent site: www.beerinstitute.org

Beer & Wine Stores—Retail (See also Liquor Stores/Package Stores)		
SIC 5921-04	NAICS 445310	
Rules of Thumb		
➢ 4 times monthly sales plus inventory		

Benchmark Data
- For Benchmark Data see Liquor Stores/Package Stores

Industry Trend
- "The Beer Institute research department continued to work closely with members to track the U.S. malt beverage industry on many levels. In addition to our standard reporting of production, imports-exports and state shipments, we also compiled data on total sales to retail volume and dollars. We are pleased to report that total sales to retail grew one percent to reach $105.5 billion dollars, despite experiencing a 1.2 percent decrease in volumes. This is a direct result of trading up by consumers, as 25 percent of industry volumes and 35 percent industry dollars are now attributed to the high-end beer segments.

"The data are divided up into two categories – on-premise sales (beer purchased and consumed away from home) and off-premise sales (beer purchased for consumption at home). Sales in restaurants led the on-premise category, earning $23.6 billion, representing 22.4 percent of the share of total dollars. This is a very important channel for brewers, as the National Restaurant Association reported its own membership is poised to add 20,000 new locations and 600,000 new employees in 2014. Overall, on-premise retailers earned $56.2 billion in beer sales in 2013. For the off-premise category, convenience stores led the way by earning $18.1 billion, accounting for 17.2 percent of sales. The convenience channel also enjoyed store growth with more than 2,000 new stores according to the National Association of Convenience Stores (NACS) Industry. Store count data: Overall, total off-premise sales to retail amounted to $49.3 billion in 2013. Once again, beer sales far outpaced our competitors in terms of total dollar and total volume sales within the alcohol beverage sector."

Source: "Beer Institute Annual Report 2013–2014"

Rules of Thumb - **B**

Franchise
Ben & Jerry's Homemade, Inc.
(See also Franchises, Ice Cream/Yogurt Shops)

Approx. Total Investment	$188,485 to $485,800
Estimated Annual Sales/Unit	$300,000
SIC 2024-98	NAICS 722515	Number of Businesses/Units 600

Rules of Thumb
- 35 to 40 percent of annual sales plus inventory

Benchmark Data

Estimated Annual Sales (2012–2013)

Cold Stone Creamery	$360,000
Baskin Robbins	$205,000
Ben & Jerry's	$300,000

Franchise
Between Rounds Bakery Sandwich Café
(See also Franchises, Sandwich Shops)

Approx. Total Investment	$313,000 to $416,000
Estimated Annual Sales/Unit	$600,000
SIC 5461-01	NAICS 722513	Number of Businesses/Units 4

Rules of Thumb
- 40 to 45 percent of annual sales plus inventory

Resources

Websites
- Between Rounds: www.betweenroundsbagels.com

Bicycle Shops
SIC 5941-41	NAICS 451110	Number of Businesses/Units 4,130

Rules of Thumb
- 20 percent of annual sales plus inventory
- 1.5 times SDE plus inventory

Pricing Tips
- "Gross profit should be at a minimum in the 40-45% range. Inventory turns should 2.4x-2.7x. Check whether the business is over-inventoried. This is a common problem with bike shops. Also check to see that the inventory is

26th Edition 105

B - Rules of Thumb

current and sale-able. How much inventory is left over from last year? Will the buyer be able to retain the relationships with the manufacturers, ensuring a steady stream of product. Single brand shops have difficulty surviving in our market."

- "If shops don't repair as well as sell, they could lose most of their income. Need to have mechanic in store!"

Expert Comments

"Success or failure of bicycle shops is directly tied to the owner/operator. While brands and location can be a factor, it is the dedication of the owner to the bicycling industry and his/her participation in community events, industry shows, and local business organizations that makes a difference. In many ways, owners are subject to the whims of manufacturers and the changing tastes of the public. Inventory control is key and owners have to be quick on their feet and be able to respond to a constantly changing environment in the cycling industry."

Benchmark Data

Statistics (Bicycle Dealership and Repair)

Number of Establishments	4,130
Average Profit Margin	4.2%
Revenue per Employee	$198,300
Average Number of Employees	4.7
Average Wages per Employee	$39,423

Products and Services Segmentation

Hybrid/cross bicycles	32%
Mountain bicycles	29%
Road bicycles	22%
Other bicycles	17%

Industry Costs

Profit	4.2%
Wages	20.2%
Purchases	62.3%
Depreciation	0.9%
Marketing	3.0%
Rent & Utilities	7.7%
Other	1.7%

Source: IBISWorld, October 2014

- "Average Expenses for Specialty Bicycle Retailers (expressed as a percentage of gross annual sales)

Payroll Expenses	20.5%
Occupancy Expenses	7.7%
Advertising/Promotion	3%
Auto and Delivery	0.5%
Depreciation	0.9%
Insurance	0.8%
Licenses/Other Taxes	0.5%
Professional Services	0.5%

Office Supplies/Postage 1.2%
Telephone 0.6%
Travel/Entertainment... 0.4%
Other operating expenses 1.3%
Total Operating Expenses... 37.7%
Net Income before Tax... 4.2%
Gross Margin on Bicycle Sales... 36%
Gross Margin on Clothing Sales 43%
Gross Margin Other Equpt... 48.1%

Source: "NBDA Cost of Doing Business Survey"

- "The Independent Bike Blog—Are bikes the black hole of bike shop profitability?
"A new financial study confirms a sad truth about bicycle retailing: most bike shops do not make a profit on the sale of new bicycles. The average retailer's operating expenses (expenses as a percent of gross sales) were 42.2% in 2011. In 2013, that number fell dramatically to 38.7%, mostly through payroll reduction.
"The lower expense number was still not enough to make new bicycle sales profitable as a category though. With an average margin of 35%, new bicycle sales yielded an average margin 3.7% below the break-even point for these businesses.
"The biggest expense factor for the average store was payroll. Payroll expenses dropped from 25.6% in 2011 to 23.5% in 2013. Occupancy expenses, rent, utilities and maintenance, were 8%. General and Administrative expenses were 7.2%, with advertising and promotion the largest expenditure at 1.7%. This category also included office expenses, phone, travel and insurance.
"The survey also illustrates that some things about bike shops have remained remarkably consistent in the last 20 years, based on a comparison with the 1993 survey. Some examples:
    - ✓ In 1993, bicycles represented 49% of the average store's sales. In 2013, the number was 46%.
    - ✓ In 1993, parts and accessories represented 33% of the average store's sales. In 2013, the number was 31%. In 1993, repair generated 11% of the dollars for the average store, compared with 13% in 2013. In 1993, the average store's net profit was 4.7% compared to 5.7% in 2013.The high profit firms (the top 25%) returned 8.6% in 1993, a much better 13.7% in 2013.

"Some other highlights from the study: While the operating margin of 44.4% (average margin for all products sold) was down from 2011, as was the net profit, the 5.7% net profit was in line with that of previous years. High profit stores (the top 25%) more than doubled that number, returning a 13.7% profit due to a combination of lower costs and higher margins. High profit stores reported operating margins of 49.8%, and operating expenses of 36%. High profit stores did manage to make a profit on bicycle sales, with an average margin of 37% versus their break-even of 36%. The higher margin areas include parts and accessories (46%), fitness equipment (40% and clothing (44%).
"Bicycle retailing has dramatically changed over the years, but the calculator shows that many of the financial basics have remained startlingly consistent. Also consistent are the reasons high profit stores make more money. They maintain higher margins and control their costs, same as they did 20 years ago."

Source: bikedealerblog.wordpress.com/July 29, 2014

B - Rules of Thumb

Expenses as a percentage of annual sales

Cost of goods	55%
Payroll/labor Costs	0
Occupancy	08%
Profit (estimated pretax)	08%

Industry Trend

- "An emerging trend is the web-based, direct sale to consumer business model that has emerged in the past five years. It's the trickle down of the Amazon style of online selling that is being adopted by specific industries, such as bicycling, and it is a direct threat to the retail model. Shop owners have to be alert to this threat and need to be prepared to challenge it with excellent customer service and customer engagement."
- "The number of independent bicycle dealers is dropping, from a high of about 8,000 in the early 1980s to about 5,000 in early 2004. The bicycle retail industry typically loses about 1,000 bicycle dealers each year, mostly start-ups, but gains that many back because of even more start-ups. However, the overall number of storefronts has been declining in the last few years. Many people have lost their lives' savings in the retail bicycle business because they loved bikes but didn't have a similar zest for the art of retailing. Bike shops run by people who are only bicycle hobbyists, and not business people, typically find the going tough in today's competitive market.

  "Add all that to the overall slim profitability in the bicycle industry, and you can really get depressed. NBDA studies show the typical bicycle dealer needs about a 36% profit margin to cover the costs of doing business and break even financially. Studies also show the average realized profit margin on bicycles to be around 36%, which is a break-even proposition devoid of profit. Fortunately accessories products generally carry a higher profit margin than bicycles. Still, the average bike dealer's profit is less than 5% at year's end—about $25,000 for an average size store of $500,000 in annual sales.

  "The level of innovation and diversity has never been higher in 'dealer-quality' bicycle products. The number of entrepreneurial companies designing and manufacturing appealing products for the public is high, both in bicycles and accessories items. There isn't any part on a bicycle which hasn't been improved in the last five or so years. The bicycle is tied to health, vitality, fun and exercise. The bicycle is one of the least expensive transportation choices available, as well as a wonderful tool for fitness and fun. The bicycle affects people's lives in very positive ways, and its use contributes to the betterment of the environment.

  "Cycling participation is solid. There are approximately 45 million adult 'cyclists' today, and cycling ranks fifth on the list of most popular outdoor recreational activities."

  Source: NBDA

- "Mobile bike repair, e-bike dealers, and private label bikes are industry trends worth watching, according to Scott Chapin, bicycle industry risk specialist with Marsh &McClennan Agency in Minneapolis. Here are some of the trends from Scott's position on the front lines of the bicycle insurance world:
    - ✓ Mobile bike shops
    - ✓ E-bike dealers
    - ✓ Spin-off bike rental business

Rules of Thumb - B

✓ Spin-off bicycle tour/guide services
✓ Online retailers
✓ Private labeling

"The Internet Challenge—Competition from large Internet companies was rated as the biggest challenge facing independent retailers, with 71% ranking Internet competition as a very or extremely significant challenge. Among bike dealers, an emphatic 97% agreed.

"Pricing and Terms—Another issue was supplier pricing and terms that favor big competitors 'to use their market power to pressure suppliers.' 63% said regulators should more vigorously enforce antitrust laws against large and dominant companies.

"Insurance and Rent—High costs for health insurance were cited by many as a problem, as well as growing expenses for effective marketing. Bike dealers added two other challenges to the mix: high occupancy cost relative to sales, and competition from large brick-and-mortar stores."

Source: "The Independent Bike Blog," March 26, 2015

Seller Financing
- "Outside financing via the SBA is common, with some seller financing involved. Most buyers have to finance the purchase, since the value of inventory can be very high."

Resources

Trade Publications
- Outspoken: Published by the NBDA
- Bicycle Retailer & Industry News—an informative site: www.bicycleretailer.com

Associations
- People For Bikes: www.peopleforbikes.org
- Bicycle Product Suppliers Association—excellent site, well worth visiting: www.bpsa.org
- National Bicycle Dealers Association (NBDA): www.nbda.com

			Franchise
Big Apple Bagels (See also Bagel Shops, Franchises)			
Approximate Total Investment			$276,700 to $396,800
Estimated Annual Sales/Unit			$350,000
	NAICS 722513	Number of Businesses/Units	100

Rules of Thumb
➢ 35 to 40 percent of annual sales plus inventory

Resources

Websites
- www.babcorp.com

26th Edition

B - Rules of Thumb

Big City Burrito (See also Franchises)	Franchise
NAICS 722513	Number of Businesses/Units 9

Rules of Thumb
➢ 50%–55% of annual sales plus inventory

Big O Tires (See also Auto Tire Stores, Franchises)		Franchise
Approx. Total Investment		$238,000 to $1,000,125
	NAICS 441320	Number of Businesses/Units 400

Rules of Thumb
➢ 35 percent of annual sales plus inventory

Resources

Websites
- Big O Tires: www.bigotires.com

Billboard Advertising Companies (Outdoor Advertising)		
SIC 7312-01	NAICS 541850	Number of Businesses/Units 13,121

Rules of Thumb
➢ 12 times EBITDA

➢ 500 percent of annual sales

Pricing Tips
- "Billboards are bought and sold based on multiples of Net Revenue and Cash Flow, so these are the most common methods of valuation."
- "Values of billboard companies tend to be higher in large metropolitan areas, and lower in rural areas. Prices tend to be between 3 x and 6 x annual revenue."
- "EBITDA is normally 45% to 50%. Cap rates tend to be very low, usually more like real estate than an operating business. Acquirers prefer long-term leases at low rates for existing billboard locations."
- "Billboard companies are usually worth surprisingly high prices in the market. Buyers and sellers rely almost exclusively on market multiples that are widely recognized as the best measures of fair market value. Discount rates and capitalization rates in this industry are more closely aligned with real estate yields than returns on operating businesses."

    Source: "Appraising Billboard Companies" by Jeffrey P. Wright, ASA, CFA, Business Valuation Review

Rules of Thumb - B

Expert Comments

"Industry growing, difficult to build new billboards"

"Revenue growth is up, while other advertising media are experiencing trouble. City, county and state rules controlling new billboard construction continue to tighten."

Benchmark Data

Statistics (Billboard & Outdoor Advertising)

Number of Establishments	13,121
Average Profit Margin	13.2%
Revenue per Employee	$259,000
Average Number of Employees	3.1
Average Wages per Employee	$39,993

Products and Services Segmentation

Billboards	64.0%
Transit displays	17.0%
Alternative and other leased displays	12.0%
Street furniture and other urban fixture displays	7.0%

Major Market Segmentation

Other	25.8%
Amusement and miscellaneous services	18.8%
Finance, insurance and real estate companies	13.8%
Media and advertising companies	10.5%
Miscellaneous retailers	8.8%
Public transportation, hotels and resorts	8.2%
Restaurants	7.6%
Communications	6.5%

Industry Costs

Profit	13.2%
Wages	15.5%
Purchases	9.2%
Depreciation	14.4%
Marketing	4.0%
Rent & Utilities	29.5%
Other	14.2%

Market Share

Outfront Media Inc.	15.0%
Lamar Advertising Company	13.0%
Clear Channel Outdoor Holdings	12.3%

Source: IBISWorld, May 2015

- "Achieving cash flow margins of 35% or higher"
- "Net revenue multiples range from 3 to 8 times, and cash flow multiples range from 7 to 18 times."
- "Occupancy cost = 20%. Profit (estimated pretax) = 20%"

26th Edition

B - Rules of Thumb

- "EBITDA margins are very high in this industry, usually around 45% to 50%. Fixed expenses normally represent a rather high percentage of fixed expenses, with 75% to 85% typical for larger companies. This includes site leases, taxes & licensing, lighting, vehicles, and to some degree labor. Workers must be employees to change advertising even if ad revenue is not strong. Variable expenses include a small number of items like printing and sales commissions."

Source: "Appraising Billboard Companies" by Jeffrey P. Wright, ASA, CFA, Business Valuation Review

Expenses as a percentage of annual sales

Cost of good	05%
Payroll/labor Costs	05%
Occupancy	10%
Profit (estimated pretax)	45%

Industry Trend
- "Stabilization, should weather the recession better than other media."

Seller Financing
- 5 years

Questions
- "Net revenue, cash flow, lease costs and occupancy levels"

Resources

Trade Publications
- BPS Outdoor: www.bpsoutdoor.com

Billiards (See also American Poolplayers Association)

SIC 7999-12	NAICS 339920	Number of Businesses/Units 5,225

Rules of Thumb
➢ 50 percent of annual sales plus inventory

Benchmark Data
- "According to the 2012 USA Sports Participation Survey—Billiards, conducted by the Sporting Goods Manufacturers Association (SGMA):
    - ✓ There are 36,831,000 Billiards/Pool participants in the U.S.
    - ✓ There are 12,132,000 core (13+/year) Billiards/Pool participants in the U.S.
    - ✓ 65% of all Billiards/Pool participants and 68% of core (13+/year) Billiards/Pool participants are male.
    - ✓ 59% of all Billiards/Pool participants and 55% of core (13+/year) Billiards/Pool participants are between ages 25 and 54.
    - ✓ 57% of all Billiards/Pool participants have a household income of under $75,000 per year.
    - ✓ 42% of all Billiards/Pool participants reside in a market size of 2,000,000+
    - ✓ 42% of all Billiards/Pool participants have a college degree or higher.

Source: Billiard Congress of America, www.home.bca-pool.com

Rules of Thumb - B

Industry Trend
- "Over the five years to 2014, revenue the Pool and Billiards Halls industry has steadily declined as a result of the recession and poor consumer sentiment. Because the industry is highly sensitive to changes in per capita disposable income, the subsequent decrease in the Consumer Confidence Index following the recession discouraged consumers from spending on leisurely activities such as pool and billiards. Furthermore, the industry faces fierce external competition from other bars and nightclubs that offer similar services to the casual pool player, as well as increasing alternative entertainment options such as video games and mobile technology."

Source: IBISWorld, May 2014

Resources
Associations
- Billiard Congress of America: http://home.bca-pool.com/

Blackjack Pizza (See also Franchises, Pizza Shops)
Franchise

| SIC 5812-22 | NAICS 722513 | Number of Businesses/Units 30 |

Rules of Thumb
- 40% percent of annual sales plus inventory
- 3 to 4 times SDE (15% discount for cash) plus inventory

Resources
Websites
- Blackjack Pizza: www.blackjackpizza.com

Blimpie—America's Sub Shop (See also Franchises, Sandwich Shops)
Franchise

Approx. Total Investment	$60,000 to $200,000
Estimated Annual Sales/Unit	$185,000

| SIC 5812-19 | NAICS 722513 | Number of Businesses/Units 560 |

Rules of Thumb
- 45 to 50 percent of annual sales plus inventory

Benchmark Data
- For Benchmark Data see Sandwich Shops

Resources
Websites
- Blimpie: www.kahalamgmt.com

26th Edition

B - Rules of Thumb

Boat Dealers (See also Marinas)

SIC 5551-04	NAICS 441222	Number of Businesses/Units 99,311

Rules of Thumb

> 2 to 3 times SDE includes used boat inventory, parts and FF&E

> "Most dealerships finance their new boat inventory with flooring companies which are now requiring some type of industry background and/or experience. In most cases the new owner will take over the financing arrangements with the flooring companies for all current and future new boat inventory. The multiple can vary depending."

Pricing Tips

- "Boat dealerships in the Pacific Northwest typically sell for 2–3 times SDE which includes used boat inventory, parts and FF&E."

Benchmark Data

Statistics (Boat Dealership and Repair)

Number of Establishments	99,311
Average Profit Margin	3.5%
Revenue per Employee	$122,200
Average Number of Employees	1.3
Average Wages per Employee	$11,726

Products and Services Segmentation

New boats	56.3%
Parts and repair services	19.0%
Other	14.0%
Used boats	10.7%

Industry Costs

Profit	3.5%
Wages	9.6%
Purchases	73.0%
Depreciation	0.6%
Marketing	1.3%
Rent & Utilities	4.7%
Other	7.3%

Market Share

MarineMax Inc.	4.4%

Source: IBISWorld, December 2014

Industry Trend

- "NMMA said sales of powerboats totaled 161,130 units nationwide in 2013, the most recent year for which full statistics are available. That was up 2.4 percent from the previous year. The association is projecting a 5 percent to 7 percent year-over-year increase in 2014, once all the numbers are tabulated.

"Powerboats are another ballgame. Mello (Sally Mello, co-owner of Mello

Marine in CA) said the age demographic for powerboat buyers is about 50 to 70. Mello Marine sells Centurion-brand powerboats, and the price range for a new boat is about $70,000 to $120,000. Even so, sales have boomed of late."
Source:"Underwater during the recession, boating/marine industry is riding a wave of sales gains," by Mark Glover, http://www.sacbee.com/news/business/article8801072.html 2/01/15

- "More than half (54.7%) of marine industry participants expect sales to increase 5% to 10% this year, according to survey results released today (Feb. 28) by GE Capital, Commercial Distribution Finance (CDF). That's up from the 43% who expected growth in that range last year.

"'Our theme for our annual industry conference this year is 'Riding a Wave of Optimism' and that really reflects our outlook,' said Bruce Van Wagoner, president of CDF's marine group, a leading provider of financing to marine dealers. 'We see a stronger industry that's poised for growth.'

"This comes in spite of lingering worries about consumer demand, which is the top concern of 64.6% of survey respondents, up from 42% in 2013. The second-greatest concern was product affordability at 12.5%. The industry has a positive outlook when it comes to product availability, according to 37.1% of survey respondents. It's excited about new model and product introductions, according to 34.7% of respondents, and more 'base' or lower-cost models, according to 31.6%."
Source: "GE Capital Poll: Boat Industry Optimistic for '14," by RVBusiness, February 28, 2014

Resources

Associations
- National Marine Manufacturers Association (NMMA): www.nmma.org

Boba Loca Specialty Drinks (See also Franchises)		Franchise
NAICS 722515		Number of Businesses/Units 22

Rules of Thumb
- ≥ 30 percent of annual sales plus inventory

Resources

Websites
- Boba Loca Specialty Drinks: www.bobaloca.com

Book & Stationery Stores (See also Book Stores)		
SIC 5942-01	NAICS 451211	

Rules of Thumb
- ≥ 15% of Annual Gross Sales
- ≥ 2.0 to 2.5 times Seller's Discretionary Earnings

B - Rules of Thumb

Pricing Tips
- "Fixtures and equipment value plus inventory at wholesale cost, plus one-half year's net profit"

Expenses as a percentage of annual sales
- Cost of goods .... 45% to 50%
- Payroll/labor Costs 0
- Occupancy .... 06% to 08%
- Profit (estimated pretax) .... 01% to 03%

Book Stores—Adult
| SIC 5942-01 | NAICS 451211 | |

Rules of Thumb
➢ 100 percent of annual sales includes inventory

Pricing Tips
- "Half down at closing; other half financed and used to prove gross sales (a kind of earnout schedule)"

Expert Comments
"Internet retail is driving down profits."

Benchmark Data
- "1,000 SF should equal $200k–$250k in gross sales."

Expenses as a percentage of annual sales
- Cost of goods 20%
- Payroll/labor Costs .... n/a
- Occupancy 12%
- Profit (estimated pretax) 40%

Industry Trend
- "Slight drop but steady in some markets."

Book Stores—Christian (See also Book Stores—New Books)
| SIC 5942-11 | NAICS 451211 | Number of Businesses/Units 3,600 |

Rules of Thumb
➢ 15 percent of annual sales plus inventory

Resources

Associations
- The Association for Christian Retail: www.cbaonline.org

Rules of Thumb - **B**

Book Stores—New Books

| SIC 5942-01 | NAICS 451211 | Number of Businesses/Units 26,005 |

Rules of Thumb
- 15 to 20 percent of annual sales plus inventory
- 1.5 to 2 SDE plus inventory

Pricing Tips
- "The underlying lease is very important. The inventory turns should be between 4 and 5 times. It is important that the store is diligently returning new book inventory as allowed."
- "We don't use EBIT or EBITDA because the owner pretty much always works in the business. Normalizing for an industry standard expense would drive EBIT or EBITDA towards zero, making the multiple unrealistic. One note is that gift certificates outstanding need to be accounted for and treated as a liability. Lots of negotiation around this point."
- "Management should have an ongoing program to return new, unsold books to publishers. This keeps inventory fresh. Occupancy costs and lease terms are critical, of course. A store with lots of community involvement (school book fairs, author events, book groups) will do better than average. Best prices can be derived by 'going public' with availability, assuring an emotionally connected buyer. For stores with good reputations, buyers will be eager to engage."

Expert Comments
"An independent bookstore doing over $2,000,000 in an affluent, highly educated community can be sold."

"Anyone can open a bookstore, but many cannot succeed as they don't attract buyers. One needs to attract buyers by becoming part of the community. Many landlords like having bookstores, as they attract foot traffic."

Benchmark Data

Statistics (Book Stores)
Number of Establishments	26,005
Average Profit Margin	3.1%
Revenue per Employee	$105,500
Average Number of Employees	5.8
Average Wages per Employee	$11,970

Products and Services Segmentation
Other merchandise	33.3%
Textbooks	27.1%
Trade books	26.9%
Magazines and newspapers	4.9%
Religious books	3.7%
Other books	2.3%
Paperback books	1.8%

26th Edition

B - Rules of Thumb

Industry Costs

Profit	3.1%
Wages	11.4%
Purchases	67.4%
Depreciation	1.4%
Marketing	2.7%
Rent & Utilities	8.1%
Other	5.9%

Market Share

Barnes & Noble Inc.	36.4%
Follett Higher Education Group	9.2%

Source: IBISWorld, December 2014

- "One would like to see sales over $200psf. Occupancy needs to be less than 10%. Cost of goods sold should approach 50%, unless it is a discounter, in which case it may be lower."
- "Sales per square foot need to be in excess of $200. Gross margin needs to approach 50% if not exceed this. Occupancy should be less than 8% of sales. A well-run café, even if outsourced, is a plus. A healthy sidelines business helps margins quite a bit."
- "Inventory turns of 3–4 times should be realized. Non-book sales should be at least 20% of overall sales. Store should be doing at least one event per week."

Expenses as a percentage of annual sales

Cost of goods	30% to 35%
Payroll/labor Costs	20% to 25%
Occupancy	06% to 10%
Profit (estimated pretax)	02% to 04%

Industry Trend

- "Gradual growth in the number of independent bookstores, but the ones coming in are small. Owners of larger bookstores are aging out, but being replaced with relatively old owners (70+ selling to 50+). Competition will continue to increase from online sources, so the store has to be a community gathering spot to be successful."
- "A new survey of U.S. book-buying behavior by Nielsen Books & Consumer shows that both hardcover and paperback print books significantly outsold e-books in the first half of 2014. A 2013 American Booksellers Association report confirmed sales at indie bookstores were on the rise."

  Source: *American Way* magazine, February 2015

- "With a growing number of independent sellers operating more than one store, the number of actual outlets topped 2,000 for the first time since 2005."

  Source: "Independent booksellers expand, stepping in as national chains struggle," *Boston Globe*, May 28, 2014

- "As both a bookseller and the president of the American Booksellers Association, I would heartily agree that the book industry has seen an astounding digital transformation. What shouldn't be overlooked is that it's also witnessing a vibrant renaissance in indie bookselling. Nationwide, sales in independent book stores are up over the past two years, new stores are opening nationwide and a whole new generation of booksellers is coming to the fore."

  Source: Letter to the Editor from Steve Bercu, *New York Times*, August 18, 2013

Seller Financing
- "Usually, these stores are sold to wealthy buyers for cash. If there is any financing, it is typically from the sellers. Due to the high risk in the industry, seller financing is limited."

Questions
- "Sales trends, community standing, online sales, Website condition, staffing quality"
- "Tenure of staff, number of events, social media exposure, program of inventory returns, seasonality and is there a frequent buyer program in place."

Resources

Trade Publications
- Independent Bookselling Today—This site offers good information on opening a bookstore.: www.pazbookbiz.com
- Publishers Weekly: www.publishersweekly.com

Associations
- American Booksellers Association: www.bookweb.org

Book Stores—Rare and Used (See also Book Stores)

SIC 5932-01	NAICS 453310	Number of Businesses/Units 5,000

Rules of Thumb
> 10 to 15 percent of annual sales plus inventory. In the case of rare books, the cost of the inventory would be based on some form of wholesale value or less the bookseller's standard markup.

Pricing Tips
- "Used book stores seem to be a vanishing business. Many owners of these stores have closed them and now offer their books online. Rare book stores would have the same multiple as used stores, perhaps a bit higher. The real value is the inventory."
- "In response to your question about a pricing rule of thumb [we had emailed our request for this to Susan Spiegel of Book Hunter Press, and perhaps the leading authority on used bookstores in the U.S.], I'm not aware of any, but I doubt that even if one existed it would be helpful. But then, I must confess that I haven't been involved in buying or selling a business.
"The reason for my skepticism: even among just-open shops, there is such a wide, wide range of inventory, that the same pricing mechanism could not automatically be used for all shops. Two shops may each have 10,000 books—but very, very different books in terms of wholesale or retail value.
"The inventory in new bookstores is pretty homogeneous; this is not the case in a used bookstore. Even within a given store, there could be a range of value in the inventory with mass market paperbacks selling at one price point and hard-to-find hardcovers selling for $25-50+.
"Stores with vastly different size inventories can have the same gross sales, depending on what types of books they are selling. In my humble judgment,

B - Rules of Thumb

one would have to arrive at a selling price based on the value of the inventory for that particular store, as well as that store's sales records.

"One problem is that most dealers have only a small portion of their inventory computerized. And I have no idea of what type of pencil and paper records they keep for tax purposes on the cost of what they've bought.

"Open shops that have gone out of business have disposed of their inventory in several different ways. Assuming that they can't sell the business to someone else who will continue it as a used bookstore (usually the first choice), some sell off their inventory to another, larger dealer. This may or may not involve donating the undesirable volumes to a library.

"Some dealers close their shops, sell off a portion of their inventory, and continue selling online with a smaller inventory, often, but not always, in a specialty area/s."

Source: Susan Spiegel, Book Hunter Press

Expert Comments

"They began perfecting the list of which books they absolutely had to have in stock, which today is a key piece of their strategy: no hodgepodge of books at estate-sale prices and in poor condition. Rather, they buy from a used-books warehouse armed with their list of must-haves."

Source: "The book is dead ... long live the book," *Franchise Times*, February 2013

Benchmark Data

- "Three quarters of the dealers [open shops] sold an average of more than 200 books per month with 23% selling 200–499 books, followed closely by 21% selling 500–999 books a month. Sixteen percent of the open shops sold 2,000 or more books per month.

"For shops in the most frequent open-shop size category (25,000–44,999 volumes), 31% of the dealers sold an average of 500–999 volumes per month, followed by 28% selling 200–499 volumes. Only 8% of the dealers within this size category sold fewer than 200 books per month and, at the other extreme, 16% sold 2,000 books or more."

Source: "A Portrait of the U.S. Used Book Market," published by Book Hunter Press.
Note: A bit dated, but still valuable information and probably still very accurate.

Bowling Centers		
SIC 7933-01	NAICS 713950	Number of Businesses/Units 3,925

Rules of Thumb

➢ 160 to 180 percent of annual sales plus inventory
➢ "Maybe 2 times annual sales in highly-exceptional situation"
➢ 5 to 6.5 times SDE plus inventory
➢ 5 to 6.5 times EBITDA

Pricing Tips

- "Location, age of equipment, physical condition of facility and additional amenities are important factors."
- "All multiples if real estate included. If leased, 4–5 times EBITDA after lease expense."

Rules of Thumb - B

- "Quality bowling centers today sell for 1.5 to 1.8 times total revenues including real estate, or 5 to 6 times EBITDA. Prices can be reduced if the facility or equipment need capital expenditures to bring them up to par."
- "$40,000 to $60,000 per lane for older centers. Newer centers up to $80,000 per lane (price must fit cash flow)."
- "Needed capital expenditures are a deduction."
- "Larger centers, metro markets and facilities in top physical condition each attract higher prices. Smaller centers, those in rural markets and/or those in need of capital get lower prices."
- "Maybe 2 times sales in highly exceptional situations"

Expert Comments

"Owner needs attention to detail, focus on superior customer service, cater to specific demographics in local market."

"As the economy improves, most bowling centers are doing much better than in recent prior years."

"Location is critical factor. Demographics, access, size of population base are important."

"Bowling generally does well in tough times; cheap recreation close to home."

"Bowling centers are expensive to build."

"Historical trend, i.e., stability of performance, very important. Competition is not very important."

Benchmark Data

Statistics (Bowling Alleys)

Number of Establishments	3,925
Average Profit Margin	2.1%
Revenue per Employee	$50,900
Average Number of Employees	17.8
Average Wages per Employee	$14,395

Products and Services Segmentation

Bowling - open play	17.8%
Bowling - league play	15.8%
Other	15.1%
Bar/lounge	14.8%
Restaurant	14.2%
Snack bar	11.1%
Laser tag	7.0%
Shoe rental	4.2%

Industry Costs

Profit	2.1%
Wages	28.4%
Purchases	18.8%
Depreciation	5.1%
Marketing	2.2%
Rent & Utilities	12.3%
Other	31.1%

26th Edition

B - Rules of Thumb

Market Share

Bowlmor AMFF	17.4%

Source: IBISWorld, April 2015

Gross Revenues per Lane per Year

Excellent	$40,000 or more
Good	$35,000 to $40,000
Average	$29,000 to $34,000
Inadequate	$28,000 or less

Target Costs vs. Cost of Goods

Target Costs	Cost of Goods
Bar	28%-30% of total bar revenues
	22%-25% of liquor revenues
	28%-30% or draft beer revenues
	30%-33% of cans, bottles revenues
Supplies	2%
Food/Beverage	30% of total food/beverage revenues
Supplies	3%
Pro-Shop	60%-65% of total pro shop revenues
Vending, Other	60% of total vending revenues

Controllable Expenses

Payroll- Bowling	30% of lineage revenues
Payroll-Bar	20% of bar revenues
Payroll-Food	25%-30% of snack bar revenues
Total Payroll	25%-28% of total revenues
Payroll Taxes	13% of total payroll
Employee Benefits	5%-7% of total payroll
Total Employee Costs	28%-33% of total revenues
Advertising & Promotion	3% of total revenues
Repair, Maintenance & Supplies	5%-6% of total revenues*
Utilities	5%-7% of total revenues

*Varies with age and condition of center, building and equipment

Operating Income** as % of Total Revenues

Above Average	Average	Below Average
30%-33%	25%–28%	20%–22%

**Operating Income is defined as the funds generated by an operation before interest, real estate rent, non-recurring expenses, principal payments, capital improvements, depreciation and owner's salaries (above normal limits) and fringe benefits.

Courtesy: Sandy Hansell & Associates, Bowling's Only Full-Service Brokers, Appraisers & Financial Advisors, (800) 222-9131, June 2015

- "The 2014 Experian Simmons National Consumer Survey found that the median income of a bowling household is over $76,000 per year. Over 28% of all bowlers have household incomes exceeding $100,000/year, and 64% of all bowlers are homeowners. The median age of all bowlers is 36. Almost 60% of bowlers earn their livings in professional fields (management, professional, sales, office, etc.) and the percentage of bowlers who have graduated college is significantly higher than in the population as a whole."

Source: "Overview of the Bowling Industry" by Sandy Hansell and Associates

Expenses as a percentage of annual sales

Cost of goods	25% to 35%
Payroll/labor Costs	28% to 30%
Occupancy	10% to 20%
Profit (estimated pretax)	20% to 30%

Rules of Thumb - **B**

Industry Trend
- "Trending up for FEC's."
- "As of December 2014, approximately 4,500 bowling centers with about 95,000 lanes were operating in the United States. Of that group, an estimated 4,100 facilities were commercial centers; the others were operated by the military, colleges, fraternal organizations and private clubs. Approximately 25% of the commercial centers are 32 lanes or larger in size. In addition, the industry also has about 170 duckpin and candlepin centers with approximately 2,400 lanes in the United States, mostly along the east coast.
  "During the past ten years, the makeup of the industry has changed. In general, as older and smaller centers closed, they were replaced by new, larger and more diversified operations. Indeed, between 30 and 50 new facilities featuring bowling have been built annually in this country over the past few years, many in vacant big-box store buildings."
  Source: "Overview of the Bowling Industry" by Sandy Hansell and Associates
- "Most centers will add additional amenities/profit centers to attract a broader clientele. Examples include upgraded food operation, larger arcade, redemption, perhaps volleyball, laser tag, go carts, etc."
- "Space conversion to more profit centers."
- "Well-run, well-promoted centers should do well—not much new competition"
- "Flat or declining revenues. Bowling is dependent upon customer's disposable income."

Seller Financing
- Typically financed outside, many sales financed by SBA.
- "In few cases with seller financing, loans are short-term (3 to 5 years) with balloon"
- "15 years with 5–10 year call; not done very often, mostly all-cash sales"

Questions
- "Time commitment, general business and management skills. Keep the facility in good shape, accurate accounting."
- "Makeup of local market, history of facility and equipment repairs and upgrades, league schedules."
- "Physical condition, necessary cap x, condition of equipment, life of lanes"
- "How much ready cash on hand? Experience in bowling?"
- "Why selling?"
- "Are you open 365 days/yr.?"

Resources

Trade Publications
- International Bowling Industry magazine: www.bowlingindustry.com
- BowlingCenter Management: www.bcmmag.com

Associations
- Bowling Proprietors Association of America: www.bpaa.com

B - Rules of Thumb

Brew Pubs

	NAICS 722410	Number of Businesses/Units 4,467

Rules of Thumb
➢ 40 percent of annual sales plus inventory

Benchmark Data

Note: The following report is for Micro-Breweries

Statistics (Craft Beer Production)
Number of Establishments	4,467
Average Profit Margin	8.2%
Revenue Per Employee	$$262,300
Average Number of Employees	4.6
Average Wages per Employee	$55,122

Products and Services Segmentation
IPA	25.2%
Seasonal	23.7%
Pale ale	17.3%
Amber ale	10.9%
Lager	8.6%
Wheat	6.9%
Bock	3.9%
Fruit beer	3.5%

Industry Costs
Profit	8.2%
Wages	20.8%
Purchases	40.0%
Depreciation	4.4%
Marketing	4.5%
Rent & Utilities	6.5%
Other	15.6%

Market Share
D.G. Yuengling & Son Inc.	19.3%
Boston Beer Company	18.3%

Source: IBISWorld, August 2015

- "In 2014, craft brewers produced 22.2 million barrels, and saw an 18 percent rise in volume and a 22 percent increase in retail dollar value. Retail dollar value was estimated at $19.6 billion representing 19.3 percent market share."
  Source: "Craft Brewer Volume Share of U.S. Beer Market Reaches Double Digits in 2014," Brewers Association, 3/16/15
- "According to Michelle Dorfman, writing in ID: The Voice of Foodservice Distribution, 'brew pubs, by definition, have an on-site brewery and more than 50 percent of the brew product is consumed on premise.'"
- "Under current law, brewers producing more than 2 million barrels pay the full, $18 tax on every barrel they make. Because Boston Beer sells in the vicinity of 2.7 million barrels a year, it finds itself in the large brewer category.

Rules of Thumb - **B**

"The legislation that Koch is pushing would not only expand who qualifies for the excise tax discount, it would also enlarge the break itself—which has helped draw legions of small-time brewers to the cause. Qualifying brewers would pay $3.50 per barrel on their first 60,000 barrels, or half of what they currently pay, and then $16 per every barrel after that, up to 2 million barrels."
Source: "Big seller Boston Beer argues for small-brewer tax break" by Noah Bierman, *Boston Globe*, May 13, 2013

Industry Trend

- "To see how a small business can transform a neighborhood, just follow the barrels.
  "About 30 years ago, beer lovers wanting to create their own drinks started talking over abandoned buildings in rundown city districts, refitted them with tanks, kettles, and casks, and started churning out beer. The byproduct was a boom in craft beer drinkers: Barrels shipped have more than doubled in the past decade, according to trade publication Beer Marketer's Insights. Craft beer now makes up nearly 7 percent of the slow-growing U.S. beer market."
  Source: "New business bubbles up with brewers" by TaliArbel, Associated Press, *Boston Sunday Globe*, July 7, 2013.

- "In Brewing, Size Matters
  - ✓ Nanobrewery—There is no agreed-upon definition yet within the industry, but New Hampshire law defines it as those who produce less than 2,000 barrels annually. Examples below:
  - ✓ Microbrewery—produces less than 15,000 barrels a year (One barrel equals 31.5 gallons). Example: Idle Hands Craft Ale.
  - ✓ Regional Brewery—A brewery with an annual beer production of between 15,000 and 6 million barrels. Example: Harpoon
  - ✓ Large Brewery—A beer maker with annual production over 6 million barrels. Example: Anheuser-Busch

  Seven breweries have opened in New Hampshire since it became the first state to recognize nanobreweries with a law differentiating them from larger-scale beverage manufacturers."
  Source: "A Class of Their Own" by Brandon Gee, *Boston Globe*, February 5, 2013

Bridal Shops		
SIC 5621-04	NAICS 448190	Number of Businesses/Units 44,949

Rules of Thumb

➢ 10 to 15 percent of annual sales plus inventory

Pricing Tips

- "Special-order gowns require deposits—many bridal stores don't put the deposits aside but co-mingle funds during the normal course of operations (a liability issue that could be deadly for a new buyer unless appropriate safeguards are in place). A bridal store's inventory is made of samples and the samples should be considered 'amortized over the ordering life of the gown style.'"

- "Bridal is not retail—to be successful in bridal, an owner has to treat it as a sales company and recruit and train salespeople. Traditional bridal is special-

B - Rules of Thumb

order and requires an excellent control system to monitor the progress of the customer's gown. Most bridal stores have 40 percent to 60 percent of their gown inventory tied up in 'one- of-a-kind' gowns. These are styles that are discontinued by the manufacturer and no additional orders can be placed. This severely curtails potential for a store. Some manufacturers are notorious for discontinuing their styles quickly. The bridal business is extremely sensitive to word-of-mouth; one horrendous experience and that bridal transaction will cost the company about $50,000 in sales over a period of 18 months, according to my estimations. Liquidation of our bridal inventory was 23 cents on the dollar—guaranteed."

Benchmark Data

Statistics (Lingerie, Swimwear & Bridal Stores)

Number of Establishments	44,949
Average Profit Margin	8.3%
Revenue per Employee	$119,000
Average Number of Employees	3.3
Average Wages per Employee	$14,440

Products and Services Segmentation

Lingerie	48.7%
Other	18.8%
Swimwear	13.7%
Bridal gowns	10.9%
Uniforms	7.9%

Industry Costs

Profit	8.3%
Wages	12.3%
Purchases	53.8%
Depreciation	0.7%
Marketing	4.4%
Rent & Utilities	8.2%
Other	12.3%

Market Share

L Brands Inc.	32.5%

Source: IBISWorld, August 2015

"The average wedding cost in the United States is $25,200. Couples typically spend between $18,900 and $31,500 but, most couples spend less than $10,000. This does not include cost for a honeymoon."

Source: www.costofwedding.com

Industry Trend

- "By offering an 'elevated experience,' the retailer hopes to encourage customers to spend more on their wedding dresses than at other stores in the chain.
"At the newest David's Bridal store, wedged in a Los Angeles strip mall with an auto parts merchant and a Subway sandwich shop, customers won't find the

chain's usual budget-conscious dresses, fluorescent lighting and wall-to-wall carpeting.

"Instead, there's glossy tile flooring. Chandeliers. Curated displays of shoes, glittering jewelry and pearl-encrusted clutches. Artfully draped curtains lead into a bright area lined with mirrored dressing rooms and plush chairs, evoking the boutique salons on Robertson Boulevard or Melrose Place. Women try on exclusive looks from couture designers Zac Posen and Vera Wang, some costing nearly $2,000.

"About a year after being bought by private equity firm Clayton, Dubilier& Rice for $1.05 billion, 65-year-old David's Bridal is trying to establish itself as a more upscale player."

Source: "David's Bridal believes new upscale store will be more engaging," by Tiffany Hsu, *LA Times*, January 23, 2014

	Franchise
Bruster's Real Ice Cream (See also Franchises, Ice Cream/Yogurt Shops)	
Approx. Total Investment	$180,000 to $1,200,000
NAICS 722515	Number of Businesses/Units 203

Rules of Thumb
- 40 to 45 percent of annual sales plus inventory

Resources
Websites
- Bruster's Ice Cream: www.brusters.com

	Franchise
Budget Blinds (See also Franchises, Window Treatment/Draperies) o	
Approx. Total Investment	$89,240 to $173,070
Estimated Annual Sales/Unit	$700,000
NAICS 442291	Number of Businesses/Units 850

Rules of Thumb
- 2 times annual EBIT plus inventory & equipment
- 50 to 55 percent of annual sales plus inventory

Resources
Websites
- www.budget-blinds-franchise.com

B - Rules of Thumb

Burger King (See also Franchises)

	Franchise
Estimated Annual Sales/Unit	$1,200,000
NAICS 722513	Number of Businesses/Units 13,615

Rules of Thumb
➢ 35 percent of annual sales plus inventory

Resources

Websites
- www.bk.com

Bus Companies (Charter, School & Scheduled)
(See also Ground Transportation Companies)

SIC 4142-01	NAICS 485510	Number of Businesses/Units 19,965

Rules of Thumb
➢ 35 percent of revenues plus asset value of buses plus inventory

Benchmark Data

Statistics (Scheduled and Charter Bus Services)
Number of Establishments	7,978
Average Profit Margin	8.9%
Revenue per Employee	$103,200
Average Number of Employees	7.0
Average Wages per Employee	$32,390

Products and Services Segmentation
Scheduled bus services-interurban transit	46.3%
Long-distance charter bus services	22.7%
Local charter bus services	21.0%
Scheduled bus services-rural transit	10.0%

Major Market Segmentation
Private consumers-local	65.0%
Private consumers-long-distance	30.0%
Business travel	5.0%

Industry Costs
Profit	8.9%
Wages	33.2%
Purchases	38.0%
Depreciation	10.6%
Marketing	1.0%
Rent & Utilities	5.2%
Other	3.1%

Market Share

FirstGroup PLC	14.3%
Stagecoach Group plc	9.8%

Source: IBISWorld, March 2015

Statistics (Public School Bus Services)

Number of Establishments	11,987
Average Profit Margin	6.9%
Revenue per Employee	$53,100
Average Number of Employees	20.2
Average Wages per Employee	$20,459

Products and Services Segmentation

Public school busing for elementary and middle school students	68.9%
Public school busing for high school students	20.7%
School busing for private schools	5.0%
Other transportation and services	2.8%
Employee bus services	2.6%

Major Market Segmentation

Public elementary and middle schools	65.7%
Public high schools	26.2%
Private schools	5.1%
Other	3.0%

Industry Costs

Profit	6.9%
Wages	38.4%
Purchases	18.2%
Depreciation	9.1%
Marketing	0.6%
Rent & Utilities	8.7%
Other	18.1%

Market Share

FirstGroup PLC	18.2%
National Express Group PLC	8.4%

Source: IBISWorld, October 2014

- "'The motorcoach industry continues to be a small-business success story, with small and medium-sized operators representing more than 98% of the total industry,' observed Peter Pantuso, President and CEO of the American Bus Association."

Source: American Bus Association Foundation's 2015 Motorcoach Census

Motorcoach Fleet Size	Carriers		Motorcoaches	
	Number	Percent	Number	Percent
100 or more	19	0.5%	8,904	24.1
50 to 99	50	1.3%	3,359	9.1%
25 to 49	155	4.1%	5,355	14.5%
10 to 24	462	12.2%	7,023	19.0%
1 to 9	3,115	82.0%	12,262	33.3%
Industry Total	3,801	100.0%	36,903	100.0%

B - Rules of Thumb

- Size and activity of the motorcoach travel industry in the United States and Canada for 2013

    Highlights
    U.S. Carriers 3,471
    U.S. Motorcoaches 32,811
    Passenger Trips 605,084,000
    Passenger Trips per Motorcoach 16,400
    Passenger Miles per Gallon of Fuel 207.8

    Demographics
    Students 21.0%
    Seniors 28.3%
    All Other 50.7%

    Source: American Bus Association Foundation's 2015 Motorcoach Census

- "It is important to note that the motorcoach industry provides an average of 745 million passenger trips annually which is comparable to the domestic airlines and 25 times more than Amtrak."

Industry Trend

- "According to a new study released by the American Bus Association Foundation, the U.S. and Canadian motorcoach industry continues to show steady, solid growth as one of the most flexible, cost-effective and environmentally efficient modes of transportation. Passenger trips by motorcoach grew by 1.7% in 2012, continuing a trend of nearly 6% growth in the last three years. Total passenger trips increased to nearly 640 million as compared to 736 million enplanements1 on domestic air carriers and 31 million passengers for Amtrak2."

    Source: ABA Foundation: 2013 Census Shows Motorcoach Industry is Healthy, Vibrant, and Growing, March 18, 2014, http://www.buses.org/News-Publications/Press-Releases

Seller Financing

- 3 years

Resources

Trade Publications
- Bus Ride Magazine—another interesting site: www.busride.com

Associations
- American Bus Association: www.buses.org—a very informative site and their magazine, *Destinations*, is also very informative
- United Motorcoach Association—also an informative site: www.uma.org

Business Brokerage Offices (See also Real Estate Offices)		
SIC 7389-22	NAICS 531210	Number of Businesses/Units 2,610

Rules of Thumb
> If you were to sell your business brokerage business, what multiple of SDE would you expect to sell it for?
> ✓ Average 2.4 for 2010

Rules of Thumb - B

- ✓ Average 2.1 for 2011
- ✓ Average 2.8 for 2012
- ✓ Average 2.8 for 2013
- ✓ Average 2.8 for 2014

Source: Business Brokerage Press Survey of the Business Brokerage Profession

> 50 percent of annual sales plus inventory
> 2 times SDE plus inventory
> 3 to 5 times EBITDA

Pricing Tips

- "Look at cash flow not annual gross sales. Bottom line is what the business is making; EBITDA."
- "There have been sales reported at 2 times SDE. If owner is active in production, then his or her production must be subtracted, unless they will be staying for a period of time. Even then, some discount must be applied to his or her sales, because after selling, their production will most likely drop off."
- "One school of thought on pricing a business brokerage office is to pay for fixed assets, and a certain amount for each year with the same phone number, as there is a goodwill factor for it. A ballpark figure might be $10,000 per year (area code change doesn't count). Then the 'house's' portion of the commissions received on the listings purchased by the new owner would be split between the new owner and the selling owner. For example: Take a $10,000 fee; the selling agent would receive $2,500, the listing agent would receive $2,500 and the remaining $5,000 would be split 50/50. This is one way to handle an earnout. This method would apply to all listings at the time of sale and one renewal period. Deals in progress would be handled as follows: Offers signed both ways would belong to the selling owner and sales signed one way would belong to the new owner."

Expert Comments

"There seems to be a 'falling out' of the part-time business broker, leaving the space open to full-time professionals."

"The average number of associates/agents per office was six; the average number of businesses sold annually was 21."

Benchmark Data

Statistics (Business Brokers)

Number of Establishments	2,610
Average Profit Margin	9.0%
Revenue per Employee	$262,500
Average Number of Employees	1.4
Average Wages per Employee	$109,002

Products and Services Segmentation

Valuation	45%
Due diligence	25%
Other services	20%
Advertising	10%

C - Rules of Thumb

Major Market Segmentation

Retail	34.9%
Service	27.3%
Restaurants	20.0%
Manufacturing	12.6%
Other	5.2%

Industry Costs

Profit	9.0%
Wages	41.7%
Purchases	3.5%
Depreciation	1.5%
Marketing	1.8%
Rent & Utilities	7.5%
Other	35.0%

Market Share

Murphy Business & Financial Corp.	6.6%
Sunbelt Network	5.6%
Transworld Business Advisors	3.0%
VR Business Brokers	2.4%
First Choice Business Brokers	0.5%

Source: IBISWorld, March 2014

- "Must understand owner's role and recast out personal production."
- What were your firm's approximate gross commissions for 2013 (Business brokerage activities only)?

Total Average	$447,628
Office Average for 201	$542,937
Sole Practitioner	$436,426
M & A Office	$1,473,074

Source: 2014 Business Brokerage Press Survey of the Business Brokerage Profession

Industry Trend

- "Increased business transactions with boomers nearing retirement or being laid off from corporate jobs."

Resources

Associations
- International Business Brokers Association (IBBA): www.ibba.org

Call Centers (Telemarketing)

SIC 7389-12	NAICS 561421	Number of Businesses/Units 27,793

Rules of Thumb

➢ 10 to 12 times current monthly billings for larger services; may require earnout

➢ 5 to 7 times current monthly billings for smaller services; may require earnout

Rules of Thumb - C

Pricing Tips

- "Annual rate increases are recommended. One of the most important formulas I use in evaluating a business is determining profitability, which comes down to your rate structure. I recently sold a medical service for over 14 times monthly billing, and the reason it sold for that multiple was the way the services were priced. It was very profitable, averaging $365 per client. The service had only 140 accounts but billed over $50K per month, producing a net profit margin of over 38%. Do not increase your rates just before selling your business to boost your monthly billing. A potential buyer will want to see a reasonable conversion history for the rate increase. I would also recommend going to a 28-day billing structure. This will give you an additional one month's billing per year, which should increase cash flow and your annual revenue.

"Buyers are interested in businesses with a good profit margin of at least 25% or better, that have advanced equipment with updated software, management in place and a history of growth. One of the first items buyers ask for after reviewing your listing information is a current financial statement along with at least one previous year's financials. Financials show historical growth as well as future potential.

"A telemessaging service with minimal profit and technology can sell for around 2.5 to 2.8 times annual net, whereas a highly profitable operation with the latest in technology, management in place, and located in a major market could sell for as high as four times annual net. If a hypothetical $30k per month business is averaging a 25% EBITDA, then it would most likely sell for between 3 and 3.5 times yearly net. For the sake of this particular example, let's assume that it is a 3.2 yearly net, which means the selling price would be $90,000 x 3.2, or $288,000 (which equals 9.6 times monthly billing)."

Source: Steve Michaels, TAS Marketing, tas@tasmarketing.com, an excellent site with lots of information on call centers. TAS Marketing is probably the nation's largest business brokerage firm specializing in answering services, call centers, etc.

Expert Comments

"Equipment—If you are six months away from selling your service then don't purchase new equipment or upgrade your software. You will not recoup your investment in that short period of time. If you sell, the buyer may also prefer a different brand of equipment or may buy only your accounts. You would then have to sell your equipment on the used market, which usually brings only pennies on the dollar. If you are two to three years from selling and have old equipment, then by all means consider either hosting or buying newer equipment. This enables you to keep up with technology and your competition by offering the same or more enhanced services.

"Automate—The biggest expense in the telephone answering service business is labor. Automating some of the functions required in the taking/delivering process can ultimately reduce your costs. Automating the messages delivery via email, fax, voice mail, text or cell phone will free up labor. You might also want to consider offering an automated attendant to increase call efficiency.

"Financial Record Keeping—Buyers are interested in businesses with a good profit margin of at least 25% or better, that have advanced equipment with updated software, management in place and a history of growth. One of the first items buyers ask for after reviewing your listing information is a current financial statement along with at least one previous year's financials. Financials show historical growth as well as future potential."

Source: Steve Michaels, TAS Marketing, tas@tasmarketing.com

C - Rules of Thumb

Benchmark Data

Statistics (Telemarketing & Call Centers)
Number of Establishments	27,793
Average Profit Margin	6.9%
Revenue per Employee	$49,100
Average Number of Employees	16.8
Average Wages per Employee	$29,069

Products and Services Segmentation
Telemarketing	61.6%
Customer service and technical support	26.1%
Other	6.8%
Debt collection	3.4%
Fundraising	2.1%

Major Market Segmentation
Telecommunications and IT	48.3%
Other	20.7%
Banking and finance	13.9%
Retail	8.7%
Technology	8.4%

Industry Costs
Profit	6.9%
Wages	59.3%
Purchases	16.0%
Depreciation	4.3%
Marketing	1.7%
Rent & Utilities	7.1%
Other	4.7%

Market Share
Convergys Corporation	9.9%

Source: IBISWorld, March 2015

Enterprises by Employment Size
Number of Employees	Number of Enterprises	Share
0 to 4	1,487	35.6%
5 to 9	543	14.4%
10 to 19	672	16.5%

Source: IBISWorld, February 2013

- "A well-run answering service can generate a 30% profit. Your labor should run you around 40%, with 10% going to phones and taxes, and 20% for administration. Utilizing a voice mail system along with faxing and email for message delivery should reduce your labor by at least 10% to 15%."
- "As of the beginning of 2014, there were 1,557 telephone answering services nationwide, billing $3.7 billion per year using 48,500 employees. Agents take approximately 41 calls per hour at 43 seconds each. The average revenue per minute is $1.09 and the revenue per call is $1.08."

Source: TAS Services, www.tasmarketing.com.

Rules of Thumb - **C**

Industry Trend

- "Telephone answering services are evolving into the contact centers of tomorrow by offering a multitude of services including: telephone answering, voice mail, fax-on-demand, text messaging, order taking, customer service and support, product fulfillment, appointment making, referral locator, credit processing, and more."

    Source: Steve Michaels, TAS Marketing, tas@tasmarketing.com

Resources

Websites
- TAS Marketing, Inc.—a telephone answering service brokerage firm: tasmarketing.com

Associations
- ContactCenterWorld: www.contactcenterworld.com
- International Customer Management Institute: www.icmi.com

Camera Stores		
SIC 5946-01	NAICS 443130	Number of Businesses/Units 2,123

Rules of Thumb

➢ 10 to 15 percent of annual revenues plus fixtures, equipment & inventory

Benchmark Data

Statistics (Camera Stores)

Number of Establishments	2,123
Average Profit Margin	1.6%
Revenue per Employee	$310,700
Average Number of Employees	4.0
Average Wages per Employee	$35,316

Products and Services Segmentation

Cameras	47.2%
Photographic equipment and supplies	26.0%
Audio equipment	8.3%
Computer hardware, software and supplies	7.7%
Other merchandise	7.3%
Video cameras and gaming consoles	1.7%
Repairs	1.8%

Industry Costs

Profit	1.6%
Wages	11.3%
Purchases	65.6%
Depreciation	1.1%
Marketing	1.3%
Rent & Utilities	7.3%
Other	11.8%

Source: IBISWorld, June 2015

26th Edition

C - Rules of Thumb

Establishments by Employment Size

Number of Employees	Share
0 to 4	43.6%
5 to 9	38.7%
10 to 19	13.9%
20 to 49	3.3%
50+	0.5%

Source: IBISWorld, April 2014

Industry Trend

- "The only remaining Cord Camera store, at 1132 W. 5th Ave., is scheduled to close on Wednesday. The once-thriving local chain fell victim to changing technology and the proliferation of digital cameras and smartphones. 'This is no longer a profitable industry,' said A.C. Strip, the attorney for Colfax Financial, owner of Cord Camera. 'Camera stores have gone the way of Kodak and Polaroid and manual typewriters.'

  "At its peak, Cord Camera had more than 30 shops in Ohio and Indiana. Cord closed six of its eight remaining stores in January. The Westerville store on Schrock Road closed last week. The company will not file for bankruptcy protection, Strip said. 'We hung on and hung on, but this is no longer an industry,' he said, adding that few people buy rolls of film or have them processed at stores such as Cord. 'We were competing with the big-box stores and Amazon (for equipment sales), and they sold the same cameras for the same price.'"

  Source: "Cord Camera closing last store on Wednesday," by Steve Wartenberg, *The Columbus Dispatch*, March 11, 2014, http://www.dispatch.com/content/stories/business/2014/03/10/cord-closing-last-store.html

- "As if smartphones hadn't already made the point-and-shoot camera, well, pointless, Nokia's NOK-0.25% new Lumia 1020—which has a full-featured camera jammed into its slim body—makes clear that soon few snapshots will be taken on devices that cannot also play Fruit Ninja.

  "But while those who carry an iPhone or Android handset have little reason to reach for a point-and-shoot, smartphones still can't replace higher-end cameras. In fact, sales of SLRs are actually rising as photo sharing drives more consumers to seek out professional-level cameras for their personal use, says Chris Chute, a technology analyst at IDC.

  "Consumers in the U.S. spent $1.9 billion on digital point-and-shoot cameras between June 2012 and May 2013—a 26% drop from the year before, according to The NPD Group's Retail Tracking Service. Yet Americans spent $2.1 billion on detachable lens cameras during the same period, up 5% from the previous year."

  Source: "Smartphones aren't killing these cameras" by Maria LaMagna, MarketWatch, www.marketwatch.com July 15, 2013

Resources

Associations

- Photo Marketing Association (PMA)—good site: www.pmai.org

Rules of Thumb - **C**

Campgrounds (See also RV Parks)		
SIC 7033-01	NAICS 721211	Number of Businesses/Units 14,534

Rules of Thumb
- 8.5 times EBITDA
- 8.5 to 8.9 times SDE; add store inventory

Pricing Tips
- "Typically 3–4 times SDE + value of Real Estate. 9–13% cap rates (depending on physical condition and location)."
- "'It's a relatively secure investment,' said Smith. 'When buying a house, you're really concerned about fluctuations in property values. But, when you buy a campground or RV park, the value of the property isn't as worrisome because much of the value of the business is based on the income it generates.'
"As a result, values for campgrounds and RV parks never really went down. But, buyers wouldn't pay as much for them because they were getting such good deals on houses for the past several years, he explained.
"The capitalization rate for a business is best described as the ratio between the net operating income produced by the asset and its capital cost, either the original price paid to buy the asset or its current market value. 'During the recession, buyers were paying an 8 to 12 cap rate,' said Smith. 'Now it's as low as 6. That means prices have gone up.' Interest rates on mobile home properties that also allow RVs, or permanent RV properties, is between 4.5 and 5 percent, he noted.
"'Never, in the 33 years I have been in the real estate business, have I seen interest rates this low,' he added. 'One client got 3.95 percent on a commercial property at a 5-year fixed rate.'
"There are also options, like seller financing, that help motivated buyers acquire properties. Some sellers have even agreed to accept a second mortgage on their properties, when working with the right buyers, Smith explained. 'Anyone who was close to retirement in 2007 and thinking about selling their campground or RV park, is really motivated to do so today,' he added. 'They've been waiting six or seven years.'"
Source: "Florida partnership aids campground buyers and sellers," March 27, 2014, http://rvdailyreport.com/campground/florida-partnership-aids-campground-buyers-and-sellers/
- "The above always includes real estate and, 65 percent of the time, owner financing and in good condition. In some areas, the real estate value may be much higher than the value as a campground. Rules of Thumb generally do not apply to the 'low end' or to large RV resorts. We have seen a lot of activity lately from investors who are trying to use cap rates and off-site management but this is primarily a business of owner managers."
- "Amenities sought after in both RV parks and campgrounds include large sites (nearly 50%), high ratings in a national camping directory, attractive landscaping and cooking areas, and quick check-in."
Source: National Association of RV Parks (ARVC)
- "First, campgrounds and RV parks are the same business. Some just prefer to call themselves RV parks if they are looking for the higher end of the business, and they might exclude tent campers from the park. A much more important aspect for valuation purposes would be if they are open all year or seasonal, if they rent sites on an overnight basis or weekly, monthly or for the whole season."

C - Rules of Thumb

- "Campgrounds that have a high percentage of seasonal sites have sometimes become more like a trailer park with lots of junk stored outside and they sometimes do not keep up with modern electrical, etc. for the newer RVs. Campers do not want to stay in parks like this."
- "The most value tends to be in overnight parks near destination areas like National Parks. They can charge a much higher rate for the site, the people tend to buy more items from the camp store, and there are usually extra people in the family who pay another $2 to $5 per night to stay on the site, and all want to go home with T-shirts and souvenirs from the gift shop. Some also do very well with breakfasts, etc. This type does not need to have much of an advertising budget either because they feed from the other activities in the area."
- "One perception that is often wrong is that the highest registration fees come from the huge motor homes on a 50-amp site with sewer hookups. They would have two people who brought all of their groceries with them, and they sit inside with the air conditioner running, using up electricity for $40 per night. On the other hand, you have a family of five who stays in a pop-up trailer on a water and electric site. They paid $35 for the site, $3 each for the extra three people and didn't have room to bring groceries. The kids spent $15 in the rec room, Mom spent $5 in the laundry, they each bought a $12 T-shirt and bought $16 worth of soda pop and groceries. And . . . the owners are only open for six months out of the year and spend their winters in Florida."
- "Another type with a high value is the resort park. They need to be looked at very differently because they are much more like a hotel. The income, amenities, land values, etc. are much more and they require more employees. Also, the type of buyer is not the same. The owner is not behind the counter checking in the campers, and their kids are not cleaning the restrooms. Seasonal operations are good in this business because the value is associated by the income whether it takes 6 months or 12 months. Most owners would prefer a break."
- "Another thing that has changed the business is camping cabins and park models. KOA did a great job of developing this into a substantial source of income for many campgrounds. The whole industry copied the concept too. They rent for much more than a campsite and are very popular with people who used to camp in a tent, the baby boomers. The addition of cabins and lodges has increased the potential pool of customers substantially because they no longer need to look to just RV owners as customers."
- "You also need to be very careful about zoning and how well accepted the park is with neighbors. If they are operating on agricultural land with a special use permit and the area is surrounded by residences . . . look out! If they are on leased land, it might be impossible to expand or continue to lease if it expires."
- "Some buyers are looking for a year-round facility so they can make more money. Actually, the value is set by the income produced over a year. I would rather work for six months for the same price! This is another lengthy subject.
  "Many campgrounds are sitting on land that is worth much more than the business and it is very difficult to obtain permits to build a new park. These two things will make it more attractive to purchase an outdated park with the right zoning and make it more modern.
  "When we look at Rules of Thumb, the following would apply to the 'typical campground' with a camp store and average amenities: registration income (site rental only) x 4.8; gross profit (after cost of goods for the store) x 4.2; adjusted net income (SDE) x 8.5.

Rules of Thumb - C

"Multiply each one out and see if they come out reasonably close. If they are within $50,000 or so, they really mean something. If they are way off, it can mean some of the following: If the GP multiple is much higher than the RI, it is positive because they have strong store sales. If the GP multiple is lower, they are probably doing a poor job in the store or they are eating too much inventory (literally)."

- "Obviously the net is very important, but I would tend to place a great deal of importance on the Gross Profit. This gives credit to strong store sales, good registration fees and the overall ability of the park to produce revenue. It also shows a picture before bad management. We know that a properly run park should net between 40 percent and 60 percent of the gross profit to the bottom line, or they are not good managers. (Could be a good opportunity for the new owner.)"
- "The net income multiple will float with interest rates. Since many are sold on a contract, the multiple goes up when interest rates are down. As in any business, you really need to understand how the adjustments were made. It is very normal for some owners to work very long hours with not enough employees. This is a pace that wore them out, and that is why they are selling."
- "When we look at the above multiples, I would qualify it with the following: 'This is assuming that the park has modern utilities (some 50-amp service, most 30-amp), a good source of water and sewer (city services best). The sites need to be large enough for newer modern RVs with wide roads and level sites, and many pull-thru sites. The buildings need to be in good repair and include a rec room, laundry and convenience store."

Expert Comments

"Start 3 years with planning before selling. The price is directly tied to cash flow."

"Difficult start-up business due to lake shore and PCA regulations. Typically seasonal businesses."

"Sellers: Buyers are more sophisticated now and want to see credible valuation information to support the asking price and a business plan that shows the future. Have documentation about repairs and maintenance, permits and zoning and other issues that could limit the future. If you have a bank loan now, talk with your banker to see what they will require for a new owner.

"Buyers: You will need to work hard for the first few years but at a realistic pace. If the current owner is completely worn out, you may want to watch their labor costs and deferred maintenance. Financing can take time and the bankers will need to see plenty of working capital in addition to the down payment. Take time up-front to understand valuation before you get caught up in negotiating based on feelings. Leased property has a far lower value. The great locations will cost more but will also provide a much better future. Different campgrounds will have a different type of customer too. Look for a location that caters to customers that you can relate to."

"We are seeing an increase in people wanting to own real estate based business that they can understand. It is very difficult and expensive to get permitting to build a new facility so replication is hard. The next 20 years should be good for the business as baby boomers retire and travel."

C - Rules of Thumb

"Campgrounds are no more risky than a main street business. The one thing that gives them stability is the difficulty in building a new one, both from a cost standpoint and a land use standpoint."

Benchmark Data

Statistics (Campgrounds & RV Parks)

Number of Establishments	14,534
Average Profit Margin	8.5%
Revenue per Employee	$116,500
Average Number of Employees	3.4
Average Wages per Employee	$29,404

Products and Services Segmentation

Campground membership, tuition and long term fees	43.2%
RV and tent sites for travelers and others	35.9%
Other unit accommodations and service fees	20.9%

Industry Costs

Profit	8.5%
Wages	25.3%
Purchases	16.1%
Depreciation	4.6%
Marketing	2.0%
Rent & Utilities	10.4%
Other	33.1%

Source: IBISWorld, February 2015

- "A successful business will have operating expenses at 30% of GOI."
- "It is difficult to provide percentages for expenses because of the tremendous variety of operations. Cost of Goods for store sales should run 65% if they have a mix of groceries and souvenirs. Some facilities are much more labor intensive due to extensive landscaping and cabin cleaning. Food service can be a great amenity and help to separate yourself from the competition."
- "I do not believe in sales per employee or square foot in this business. My experience shows that there is too much variety in operations to make it accurate."

Expenses as a percentage of annual sales

Cost of goods	10%
Payroll/labor Costs	10%
Occupancy	40%
Profit (estimated pretax)	40%

Industry Trend

- "When selecting which campgrounds to visit and stay, free Wi-Fi ranks as the third most important amenity, behind only clean bathrooms and a kid-friendly environment, and outpaces access to recreational activities such as a campground store, cabins and even safety lighting.

"According to campers, reconnecting with nature (55%), reducing stress (54%), and spending more time with family and friends (49%) are the key reasons they camp. Economic and practical values were only identified as reasons for camping by less than 35% of those surveyed. Campers are likely to say that camping improves family relationships—in fact, 41 percent 'completely agree' with this.

"Additionally, fully 4-in-10 campers (39%) suggest that camping has 'a great deal of impact' on allowing them to spend more time with family. Another third of campers say that camping has a positive impact on their relationships with family and friends (35%) and their emotional well-being (36%)."

Source: RV Business, March 2015

Seller Financing
- "The majority of campgrounds are sold with a combination of owner and bank financing. When the closing date is set as it relates to their season can complicate things. If the closing is in the fall and the campground is closed for the winter, it could mean several months of payments without income. We often see delayed closings to make it realistic."
- 20 years

Questions
- "Will you carry a contract? Do you have a data base of customers? Age and condition of all utilities. We always would ask about: roof, sewer, property lines and permits."

Resources

Associations
- National Association of RV Parks and Campgrounds (ARVC): www.arvc.org

Camps		
SIC 7032-03	NAICS 721214	Number of Businesses/Units 3,050
Rules of Thumb		
➢ 2 times annual sales plus inventory		
➢ 5 to 8 times SDE plus inventory		

Pricing Tips
- "Years in business. More years, the higher the multiple."

Expert Comments

"More and more moms and dads have to work today and that creates a need for child care in the summer months when the kids are out of school."

Benchmark Data

Statistics (Summer Camps)
Number of Establishments	3,050
Average Profit Margin	8.4%
Revenue per Employee	$124,600
Average Number of Employees	7.7
Average Wages per Employee	$35,593

C - Rules of Thumb

Products and Services Segmentation

Overnight recreational camp tuition or fees	85.2%
Other services	8.4%
Food items prepared for immediate consumption	2.8%
Room or unit accommodation for travelers and others	2.7%
Membership dues and fees	0.9%

Major Market Segmentation

Adolescents aged 10 to 17	63.4%
Children aged 9 years and younger	32.4%
Adults 18 and older	4.2%

Industry Costs

Profit	8.4%
Wages	28.7%
Purchases	34.0%
Depreciation	9.3%
Marketing	2.3%
Rent & Utilities	9.1%
Other	8.2%

Source: IBISWorld, August 2015

- "47% are primarily resident (overnight) camps, 28 percent are primarily day camps, 26% offer both day and resident camps. (2011 ACA Sites, Facilities, Programs Report)
"Camp Costs: Fees to attend camp vary: resident camp average = $690 week (can cost up to $2,000+ a week); Day camp average = $304 work (can cost up to $500+) as of 2012. There is a camp for every child and for every budget. (2012 ACA Business Operations Report)
"Programs: 87% of camps offer recreational swimming, 67% offer camping skills, 48% offer climbing/rappelling, 38% offer horseback riding, 78% teambuilding, 47% community service, 23% farming/ranching/gardening, and 28% wilderness trips. (2011 ACA Sites, Facilities, Programs Report)
"Activities: Top five camp activities - Recreational Swimming, Arts/Crafts, Challenge/Ropes, Archery, and Aquatic Activities (2011 ACA Sites, Facilities, Programs Report)"

Source: www.acacamps.org/media/aca-facts-trends

- "Weekly cost spread for the majority of Sleep Away Camps in New England: $500–$1,200; for the majority of Day Camps in New England: $250–$550.
Source: "Who's Ready for Summer Camp" by Melissa Schorr, *Boston Globe Magazine*, March 2, 2014

Resources

Associations

- American Camp Association: www.acacamps.org

Rules of Thumb - **C**

Candy Stores

| SIC 5441-01 | NAICS 445292 | Number of Businesses/Units 7,500 |

Rules of Thumb
- 30 to 35 percent of annual sales plus inventory
- 1.7 times SDE plus inventory

Benchmark Data
- See Food Stores—Specialty for additional Benchmark Information

Sales by Segment—2012
Chocolate	55.6%
Sugar	30.7%
Gum	13.7%
2012 Sales	$32.7 billion

2012 U.S. Chocolate Market
Hersey's	42%
Mars	20%
Nestle	06%
Russell Stover	05%
Lindt	05%

U.S. Non- Chocolate Sales
Chewing Candy	39.1%
Seasonal Candy	18.9%
Novelty Candy	12.8%
Hard Candy	10.1%
Licorice	9.1%
Other	10%
Total	100%

Source: above figures are the latest available from Candy Industry.com

- "Candy proved its resilience last year, even in challenging economic times, by increasing sales across the board by 5.8 percent industrywide. Average sales per store rose 4.5 percent to $40,786."
- "Convenience stores remain the No. 2 confectionery source for consumers, ranking only behind supermarkets. (3.21 percent of in-store sales; 4.95 percent of in-store gross margin dollars).

Source: "A Sweet year for Candy," Convenience Store News Market Research, June 2012

Industry Trend
- "Founded by candy veteran Jeff Rubin in 2006, this saccharine experience has become one of the largest and fastest growing specialty candy and gift retailers in the world. The IT'SUGAR Empire consists of over 70 retail locations in US hotspots such as New York, Las Vegas, Los Angeles, San Francisco, Miami, Scottsdale, Washington DC and Palm Beach, in addition to chic international destinations such as London, Dubai, and Grand Cayman.

"With aggressive growth plans, IT'SUGAR sees a future where we are all 'twenty-something' years old and have access to the pure joy that comes from

C - Rules of Thumb

indulging in a world where life has no rules and the answer is always YES! "With retail locations ranging in size from 2,000 to 7,500 square feet, IT'SUGAR is a trendy sweets shop that lives at the intersection of attitude and fun. It's a place about joy, taste, color and sound. Sweet and sour, rich and creamy – that's how life should be, and that's how it is at IT'SUGAR."

Source: http://www.itsugar.com/about-itsugar

- "A recent Nielson Report stated that consumers are calling for healthier choices from their food products. The question asked was would people really purchase their favorite candy, etc. if the manufacturers made them. The results as of September 2015 are that 67% of the respondents said Yes."

Source: www.candyindustry.com

Resources

Trade Publications
- Candy Industry magazine—an excellent and informative site: www.candyindustry.com

Associations
- National Confectioners Association: www.candyusa.com

Card Shops (See also Gift Shops)

SIC 5947-10	NAICS 453220	Number of Businesses/Units 69,945

Rules of Thumb

➢ [Note: We debated whether to leave card shops as a stand-alone business, but there are few, if any, pure card shops. However, card shops still have a SIC and a NAICS number, so someone feels that they are still a stand-alone business. On the other hand, we have seen few gift shops that didn't have cards. In either event, we suspect that the rule of thumb would be about the same.]

Benchmark Data

Statistics (Gift Shops & Card Stores)
Number of Establishments 69,945
Average Profit Margin 5.0%
Revenue per Employee $88,700
Average Number of Employees 3.2
Average Wages per Employee $11,520

Products and Services Segmentation
Souvenirs and novelty items 34.5%
Other 17.1%
Seasonal decorations 15.2%
Greeting Cards 11.9%
Kitchenware and home furnishings 10.8%
Clothes and jewelry 10.5%

Rules of Thumb - C

Industry Costs

Profit	5.0%
Wages	13.1%
Purchases	54.3%
Depreciation	1.0%
Marketing	1.6%
Rent & Utilities	16.5%
Other	8.5%

Market Share

Armsan Holdings Inc.	8.1%

Source: IBISWorld, February 2015

	Franchise
Carl's Jr. Restaurants (See also Franchises, Restaurants—Limited Service)	
Approx. Total Investment	$1,260,000 to $1,949,500
Estimated Annual Sales/Unit	$1,300,000
SIC 5812-06 / NAICS 722513	Number of Businesses/Units 1,462

Rules of Thumb

> 40 percent of annual sales plus inventory

Resources

Websites

- Carl's Jr. Restaurants: www.CKEfranchise.com

Carpet Cleaning	
SIC 7217-04 / NAICS 561740	Number of Businesses/Units 44,399

Rules of Thumb

> 60 percent of annual revenue plus inventory

> 1.5 times SDE plus inventory

Benchmark Data

Statistics (Carpet Cleaning)

Number of Establishments	44,399
Average Profit Margin	7.1%
Revenue per Employee	$59,800
Average Number of Employees	1.7
Average Wages per Employee	$20,838

Products and Services Segmentation

Residential carpet and upholstery cleaning	42.9%
Commercial carpet and upholstery cleaning	28.9%
Other	17.3%
Offsite cleaning services	10.9%

26th Edition

C - Rules of Thumb

Industry Costs

Profit	7.1%
Wages	34.8%
Purchases	23.3%
Depreciation	2.7%
Marketing	3.8%
Rent & Utilities	6.1%
Other	22.2%

Market Share

The ServiceMaster Company	8.0%
Chem-Dry Inc.	4.8%

Source: IBISWorld, February 2015

Resources

Websites
- Carpet and Rug Institute: www.carpet-rug.org

Associations
- Professional Association of Cleaning & Restoration (PACR): http://professionalassociationofcleaningandrestoration.org/
- Restoration Industry Association: www.restorationindustry.org

---

Carpet/Floor Coverings

SIC 5713-05	NAICS 442210	Number of Businesses/Units 22,301

Rules of Thumb
➤ 20 percent of annual sales plus inventory

Benchmark Data

Statistics (Floor Covering Stores)

Number of Establishments	22,301
Average Profit Margin	3.1%
Revenue per Employee	$276,300
Average Number of Employees	3.2
Average Wages per Employee	$35,488

Products and Services Segmentation

Soft-surface (textile) floor coverings	34.7%
Other hard-surface floor coverings	24.7%
Other services	14.9%
Hardwood flooring	14.5%
Carpets and rugs not requiring installation	11.2%

Major Market Segmentation

Household consumers	59.7%
Building contractors	25.7%
All other establishments for resale	8.8%
Businesses for end use in their own operation	5.8%

Rules of Thumb - C

Industry Costs

Profit	3.1%
Wages	12.9%
Purchases	61.5%
Depreciation	0.7%
Utilities	2.1%
Rent	5.0%
Other	14.7%

Source: IBISWorld, August 2015

Resources

Trade Publications
- Floor Covering Weekly: www.floorcoveringweekly.com
- Floor Covering News: www.fcnews.net/
- Floor Daily: www.floordaily.net

Cartridge World (See also Franchises) — Franchise

Approx. Total Investment		$61,800 to $135,300
	NAICS 424120	Number of Businesses/Units 1,400

Rules of Thumb
➢ 30 to 35 percent of annual sales plus inventory

Resources

Websites
- Cartridge World: www.cartridgeworld.com

Carvel Ice Cream (See also Franchises, Ice Cream/Yogurt Shops) — Franchise

Approx. Total Investment		$35,100 to $354,550
SIC 2024-98	NAICS 722515	Number of Businesses/Units 450

Rules of Thumb
➢ 55 percent of annual sales or 20 to 25 times the number of gallons of liquid ice cream mix purchased plus inventory
➢ 2.25 to 2.5 times SDE plus inventory

Pricing Tips
- "Typically [priced] at $30 per gallon of ice cream mix used. Therefore, a 5,000-gallon store, which grosses approximately $250,000 would sell for $150,000 to $160,000 with SDE at about $65,000. The $150,000–$175,000 equates to approximately 60% of gross. Stores with disproportionate rental expense would be closer to 50% of gross or 2 times SDE. The exception is for the very few higher volume stores, above 8,000. These would sell for closer to $40 per gallon with SDE of 2.5."

26th Edition

C - Rules of Thumb

- "Some franchised ice cream businesses with a positive history, updated facilities and verifiable sales numbers will move to 2.5 SDE. Conversely, a short lease and less than five years on franchise agreement will result in less than 2 times SDE."
- "Location drives price higher and typically has higher returns on product usage, therefore more profit. Free-standing buildings with volume in excess of 10,000 gallons, rule of thumb would be 60 percent of annual sales, with average lease of 7 years remaining."

Benchmark Data

- "Food cost percentage typically is equal to SDE unless rent is above $25 per sq. ft."

Expenses as a percentage of annual sales
Cost of goods	26%
Payroll/labor Costs	21%
Occupancy	11%
Profit (estimated pretax)	25%

Seller Financing
- 3 to 5 years

Resources

Websites
- www.carvelicecream.com

Car Washes—Coin Operated/Self-Service
(See also Car Washes—Full-Serve/Exterior)

SIC 7542-05	NAICS 811192	Number of Businesses/Units 14,616

Rules of Thumb
➤ Operations less than five years old generally sell for cost of original real estate, equipment, and improvement cost, plus negotiated figure 2 to 3 times EBIT.
➤ 4 times annual gross sales—"A good place to start"

Pricing Tips
- "Total cash business. Passive investment, almost labor free."
- "90 percent of self-service car washes will have combination of self-service and automatic bays."
- "98 percent of self-service/automatic car washes are sold with real estate, equipment and assets."
- "Nearly impossible to sell business only"
- "Takes 5 years to build new operation—gross annual sales volume to maturity."

Rules of Thumb - C
Benchmark Data

Exterior Only/Express Exterior Operating Costs (as a percentage of total revenues)

Rent	13.8%
Equipment & Bldg. Maintenance	5.2%
Chemicals	6.6%
Labor	
Exterior Only	23.3%
Express Exterior	17.6%
Utilities	9.8%
Insurance	2.5%
Advertising & Promotion	1.7%
Equipment on Lease	0%
Customer Claims	0.8%
Average gross revenue per car	$8.69
Average purchase price of the new property (land only)	$642,000
Average cost of improvements (bldg., landscaping etc.)	$1,417,000
Average cost of equipment	$550,000

Source: *Auto Laundry News* 2015 Exterior Conveyor Survey

Expenses (Operating Costs as Percentage of Total Monthly revenues) 2015 Report

Electricity	6.6%
Fuel (Gas, Oil, Etc.)	5.3%
Water	4.6%
Sewer	4.1%
Chemicals	6.5%
Vending Products	1.9%
Softener Salt	1.4%
Collection	1.7%
Lot Sweeping	3.3%
Attendant Labor	10.6%
Bookkeeping	2.2%
Replacement Parts (Normal Wear and Tear)	5.2%
Replacement Parts (Vandalism)	1.4%
Vehicle Damage	0.7%
Refunds	0.6%
Pit Pumping	1.8%
Advertising & Promo	1.5%

Source: *Auto Laundry News*, Self-Service Survey 2015

Self-Serve Statistics for a single operation (Wand or Coin-op Style)

Average monthly gross income per bay	$1,450
Average monthly gross income per vacuum	$245

Source: *Auto Laundry News*, Self-Service Survey 2015, CarWashMag.com—a wonderful site. Check it out if you have any dealings in the car wash or car detailing industries. It has reports on Auto Detailing and Car Washes; it is a must see.

- "Competition in this industry is high."
- "Volatility medium (revenue fluctuations between 3 and 10 points)"
- "The life cycle stage is growth."
- "There are no major players in this industry."

26th Edition

C - Rules of Thumb

	Low Side	High Side	Low Side	High Side
Operating Exp.	$26,850	$42,960	$44,870	$71,792
Gross Margin	$80,550	$64,440	$134,610	$107,688
Debt Service	$27,924	$27,924	$46,665	$46,665
Profit*	$52,626	$36,516	$87,945	$61,023
*before depreciation and tax	49%	34%	49%	34%"

Industry Trend
- "Consumers are increasingly turning to professional car washing, with those who wash their cars at home declining significantly over the last 10 years. Demographic and societal trends support a continuation, and likely an acceleration, in the use of professional car washing. It is estimated that total annual car wash sales revenue exceeds $24 billion."

Source: *Auto Laundry News* 2015 Exterior Conveyor Survey

Resources

Associations
- International Carwash Association: www.carwash.org

Car Washes—Full-Service/Exterior

(See also Auto Detailing, Car Washes—Coin Operated/Self-Service)

SIC 7542-01	NAICS 811192	Number of Businesses/Units 64,472

Rules of Thumb
- .80 to 1 times annual sales plus inventory
- 32 percent of annual sales includes inventory
- 3 times SDE includes inventory
- 23 times EBIT
- 3.75 to 4.75 times EBITDA
- 4 to 6 times owner's provable net income includes income

Pricing Tips
- "Car Wash Industry in a 'Free Fall' past few years, 90% of our sales are with real estate, and that is almost the value of the transaction. I have just closed on two washes: Self Service bought for $990,000./7SS—3 Automatic. Bought in 2006....Closing Price today $330,000. Full Service Conveyor bought for $850,000.00 now sold for $130,000. Both operations sold with real estate. Most car washes are 'under water' with their financing."
- "The value of a car wash varies greatly from the East Coast to the West Coast. Weather conditions dictate the value vs. sales and earnings, as the West Coast sees more sunshine and therefore more revenues on average."
- "Plus economic value of the land, plus inventory not attached to the carwash tunnel"
- "Mostly sold with real estate and is a cash business and not easy to verify income numbers."

Rules of Thumb - C

- "Tax returns are not easily available and estimating is generally the rule; therefore using water bills, etc. to figure out the sales is one common method."
- "Key factors include current market conditions, owner salary, benefits, condition of equipment... these are just some of the typical costs and items buyers and sellers negotiate over."
- "4 times SDE without land;2 times SDE + land & equipment"

Expert Comments

"A good high-volume car wash, $500k plus in annual sales with a good lease, brings forth a desirable business and good profit picture. The industry has slowed down some as the economy continues to struggle along with per household spending."

"Good weather brings forth more sales; summer is generally a better season than winter. There is some seasonality in this business; best time to purchase is early summer or late spring. Have working capital and cash flow in reserve for the winter months."

"Southern California market is saturated. Slow economy and increased labor costs are driving avg. performing full-service carwashes out of business. Express washes (fully automated, min. labor) are the new-trend car washes."

"Location, marketing, management, and visual appeal"

"In some areas replication is easy, and in others it's difficult due to the local restrictions on the usability of water and recycling it, plus the traffic problems."

"Expensive to build a new full-service facility."

Benchmark Data

Statistics (Car Wash & Auto Detailing)

Number of Establishments	64,472
Average Profit Margin	15.5%
Revenue per Employee	$47,000
Average Number of Employees	3.1
Average Wages per Employee	$16,657

Products and Services Segmentation

Conveyor car washes	49.7%
Detailing	17.7%
Self-service bays	17.7%
In-bay automatic car washes	11.4%
Hand washing	10.4%

Industry Costs

Profit	15.5%
Wages	35.4%
Purchases	21.3%
Depreciation	9.2%
Marketing	1.3%
Rent & Utilities	13.1%
Other	4.2%

Source: IBISWorld, July 2015

C - Rules of Thumb

Operating Costs (As a percentage of total revenues)

Rent	9.0%
Equipment & Bldg. Maintenance	4.5%
Chemicals	5.5%
Labor	34.4%
Utilities	7.1%
Insurance	3.8%
Advertising & Promotion	3.0%
Equipment on Lease	2.5%
Customer Claims	0.7%

Source: *Auto Laundry News* 2015 Full/Flex Survey

Car Wash Industry Statistics

Number of full-service carwashes	9,000
Number of exterior conveyor washes	10,500
Number of self-serve car washes	36,000
Number of in-bay automatics	58,000
Total number of carwashes	113,000
Total number of car wash employees	350,000
Number of cars washed annually	2.3 billion
Number of cars washed per day	8 million
Percent of car washes that also dispense gasoline	65%
Percent of car washes owned by small business persons	90%
Estimate number of gallons of water used on each car	38 gallons
Average annual number of gallons of water lost per car wash	48,000

In-Bay Automatic Statistics for a single operation

Average number of cars washed annually	19,947
Average sale per vehicle	$6.34
Average profit per vehicle	$4.35
Average annual profit	$86,531
Average annual revenue	$139,000

Self-Serve Statistics for a single operation (Wand or Coin-op Style)

Average monthly revenue per bay	$1,489
Average annual revenue for a 2 bay operation	$41,000

Tunnel Carwash Statistics for a single operation

Average number of cars washed per year	45,750
Average price per carwash	$15
Average annual revenue	$686,250

Source: http://www.statisticbrain.com/car-wash-car-detail-industry-stats/ 2/2/15

- "Car washes typically have lower numbers if tied in with a gas station and will do much higher numbers if it's a stand-alone drive-thru."
- "Majority are sold with real estate."
- "$300 per sq. ft. is very good."
- "Car washes usually run at 1/3 profit from gross. Example: $90,000 gross = $30,000 net."

Expenses as a percentage of annual sales

Cost of goods	05% to 10%
Payroll/labor Costs	42.5%
Occupancy	10% to 20%
Profit (estimated pretax)	25%

Industry Trend

- "Consumers are increasingly turning to professional car washing, with those who wash their cars at home declining significantly over the last 10 years. Demographic and societal trends support a continuation, and likely an acceleration, in the use of professional car washing. It is estimated that total annual car wash sales revenue exceeds $24 billion."

Source: *Auto Laundry News* 2015 Exterior Conveyor Survey

- "A further depletion of car wash locations due to going out of business, foreclosures, and closings.... New operations only to be built by major oil companies... I have 4 children that at one time were car wash owners, all sold in 2000 to 2005, and I would not recommend their return to the industry."

Seller Financing

- "Virtually no outside financing or SBA available because of figures, and lack of bookkeeping."
- "Seller will generally carry 30–35% over five to seven years at 6% interest per annum."

Questions

- "How many vehicles per month do they do, summer vs. winter and the average ticket on each vehicle. Any environmental issues? The length of the lease and the rent factor. Is there at least one mgr.?"
- "You need to ask the Seller the name of the equipment, the age of the equipment. Is the car wash brush or brushless, any problems with the system?"
- "Provable Gross and Net. Is all labor on the books. What percentage of gross income is cash. Average monthly car count and ticket price, all sources of income"
- "Water bills, proof of car counts and any other paperwork proving the stated numbers"
- "Are you clear with employees and are they all registered? Is there ground contamination? How are the tax records?"

Resources

Associations
- International Carwash Association: www.carwash.org

			Franchise
Car X Auto Service (See also Franchises)			
Approx. Total Investment			$214,000 to $326,000
Estimated Annual Sales/Unit			$750,000
	NAICS 811111		Number of Businesses/Units 170

Rules of Thumb
> 35 to 40 percent of annual sales plus inventory

C - Rules of Thumb

Resources

Websites
- www.carx.com

Casinos/Casino Hotels		
SIC 7993-02	NAICS 713210	Number of Businesses/Units 866

Rules of Thumb

➢ Las Vegas Strip average: 8.1 times EBITDA

➢ Indian Gaming management contracts: 30 to 40 percent net (this is pulled from the top in "Operating Income" and should be calculated before debt service). 5 to 7 percent of gross used to be standard for Indian Gaming contracts. The NIGC must approve all contracts and agreements between management and tribal nations. The NIGC (National Indian Gaming Commission) is an independent federal regulatory agency of the United States. Management cannot own any part of the Indian casino. Contracts are typically five years with options to renew. The tribe will be responsible for paying down the debt service.

Pricing Tips

- "Casinos Only: Annual Revenue less than $3,000,000: 2.25 to 2.75 times verifiable annual cash flow (I would use a weighted average of the past three time periods). If the 'casino' doesn't own the slot machines, then the multiple would be less."
- "Annual Revenue $3,000,000 to $10,000,000: 2.75 to 3.25 times verifiable annual cash flow (I would use a weighted average of the past three time periods). If the 'casino' doesn't own the slot machines, then the multiple would be less."
- "Annual revenue over $10,000,000 (but not over $25,000,000): 3.00 to 4.00 times verifiable annual cash flow (I would use a weighted average of the past three time periods). If the 'casino' doesn't own the slot machines, then the multiple would be less."
- "Remember the buyer must get a gaming license. In Nevada, that could run: 6–7 months and $5,000 in cost for a 'Restricted License.' This allows the licensee to operate not more than 15 slot machines, not table games, etc. This is common in what we call 'Tavern Licenses.'"

Benchmark Data

Statistics (Casino Hotels)

Number of Establishments	415
Average Profit Margin	17.7%
Revenue per Employee	$135,300
Average Number of Employees	1,044
Average Wages per Employee	$34,273

Products and Services Segmentation

Gambling machines	52.7%
Other	16.3%
Gaming tables	12.8%
Accommodations	11.9%
Alcoholic beverages	4.3%
Admissions to live performances	2.0%

Industry Costs

Profit	17.7%
Wages	25.2%
Purchases	8.0%
Depreciation	6.9%
Utilities	9.5%
Rent	4.0%
Other	28.7%

Market Share

Caesars Entertainment Corporation	13.6%
MGM Resorts International	11.2%

Source: IBISWorld, April 2015

Statistics (Non-Hotel Casinos)

Number of Establishments	451
Average Profit Margin	14.6%
Revenue per Employee	$145,200
Average Number of Employees	250
Average Wages per Employee	$33,692

Products and Services Segmentation

On-premises gaming (riverboat and barge casinos)	69.3%
Off-track betting (riverboat and barge casinos)	14.7%
Cruise casinos	7.0%
Food and non-alcoholic beverages (riverboat and barge casinos)	4.8%
Alcoholic beverages (riverboat and barge casinos)	2.2%
Arcades and video games (riverboat and barge casinos)	2.0%

Industry Costs

Profit	14.6%
Wages	23.4%
Purchases	5.0%
Depreciation	5.3%
Marketing	8.5%
Rent & Utilities	3.4%
Other	39.8%

Market Share

Caesars Entertainment Corporation	7.7%
Penn National Gaming Inc.	7.3%

Source: IBISWorld, November 2014

- The opening of a new casino in Philadelphia, along with the reclassification of properties in suburban Philadelphia and Pittsburgh, led to the inclusion of the two cities on the list of top earning casino markets for the first time.

C - Rules of Thumb

Industry Trend

- "Oxford's study found that the U.S. gaming industry:
    - ✓ Contributes $240 billion—nearly a quarter-trillion—to the U.S. economy, which is equivalent to the total state budgets of New York and Texas combined;
    - ✓ Supports more than 1.7 million jobs—more than double Washington, D.C.'s total employment—and nearly $74 billion in income;
    - ✓ Generates $38 billion in tax revenues to local, state and federal governments—enough to pay more than half-a-million teachers' salaries."

    Source: http://www.gettoknowgaming.org/news/groundbreaking-new-research-reveals-impressive-magnitude-us-casino-gaming-industry 9/30/14

- "Legalization of Internet betting in several U.S. states is turning the gaming industry on its head and turning some states, like New Jersey, into a case study for the promise and pitfalls inherent in Internet disruption of status quo businesses. New Jersey's gaming companies have emerged as pioneers in online gaming—Nevada and Delaware are the only competition—but the Garden State's big online bet is still stuck somewhere between cutting-edge technology and desperation in what has been a slowly dying market."

    Source: "For casinos, baby steps on a virtual Atlantic City boardwalk," by Nia Hamm, www.cnbc.com January 21, 2014

- "Northern Mississippi's largest casino will close in June. It won't be the last. There is evidence across the nation that overall gambling may be approaching saturation levels.

    "The closing could be a sign of things to come as the $38 billion U.S. gambling industry bumps up against two unlucky trends, a proliferation of casinos and still-skittish consumers in the wake of the financial crisis. Some 39 states have casino gambling of some kind, up from only two in 1988, and more Las Vegas-style resorts are on the way in New York, Pennsylvania, Massachusetts, and Maryland. 'They have saturation problems,' says William Thompson, a professor at the University of Nevada at Las Vegas who studies the industry. 'We have a wave of new casinos coming.'"

    Source: "Casinos Know When to Fold 'Em," *Bloomberg Businessweek*, April 7, 2014

Resources

Websites
- Interactive Gaming Council: www.igcouncil.org
- North American Association of State & Provincial Lotteries: www.naspl.org
- Indian Gaming: www.indiangaming.com

Associations
- National Indian Gaming Association: www.indiangaming.org
- American Gaming Association: www.americangaming.org

Caterers/Catering		
SIC 5812-12	NAICS 722320	Number of Businesses/Units 11,105
Rules of Thumb		
➢ 35 to 40 percent of annual sales plus inventory		

Rules of Thumb - **C**

Benchmark Data

Statistics (Caterers)

Number of Establishments	11,105
Average Profit Margin	7.8%
Revenue per Employee	$63,700
Average Number of Employees	12.7
Average Wages per Employee	$19,645

Products and Services Segmentation

Food served at events on customer's premises	37.3%
Food served at events on caterer's premises	31.4%
Other services	10.0%
Food dropped off at the customer's event	8.0%
Food prepared for immediate consumption	10.0%
Alcoholic and nonalcoholic beverages	2.6%
Food prepared for customer pick-up	2.1%

Industry Costs

Profit	7.8%
Wages	30.7%
Purchases	39.5%
Depreciation	2.0%
Marketing	1.5%
Rent & Utilities	9.1%
Other	9.4%

Source: IBISWorld, June 2015

Resources

Trade Publications
- Cater Source Journal: www.catersource.com

Associations
- The National Association of Catering Executives (NACE): www.nace.net
- International Caterers Association: www.internationalcaterers.org

Catering Trucks (See also Food Trucks, Ice Cream Trucks, Routes)

NAICS 722330	Number of Businesses/Units 33,290

Rules of Thumb

➢ 40 percent of annual sales plus inventory

Benchmark Data

Statistics (Street Vendors)

Number of Establishments	33,290
Average Profit Margin	6.8%
Revenue per Employee	$35,000
Average Number of Employees	1.1
Average Wages per Employee	$10,699

26th Edition

C - Rules of Thumb

Products and Services Segmentation
Traditional street vendors	45%
Mobile food preparation vehicles	37%
Industrial catering vehicles	18%

Major Market Segmentation
Street locations and corners	55%
Other locations, venues and events	18%
Industrial or construction worksites	15%
Shopping malls	12%

Industry Costs
Profit	6.8%
Wages	30.6%
Purchases	37.8%
Depreciation	5.0%
Marketing	1.0%
Rent & Utilities	7.1%
Other	11.7%

Source: IBISWorld, September 2014

- "This type of business will be largely cash intensive, since most individuals purchasing items from a mobile vendor pay in cash. Accordingly, gross receipts will be the main focus for the examination. The examiner will expect to see large cash deposits to the business bank account. To verify all cash is deposited or accounted for, the examiner must analyze the markup percentage. The examiner should expect to see a consistent markup percentage of about 100% on cold foods sold and about 200% on hot foods sold. For example, if an item is purchased for $0.50, it will generally sell for $1 or more."

Source: Internal Revenue Service Retail Industry Audit Technique Guide (ATG)

Cellular Telephone Stores   NAICS 443112
Rules of Thumb
➢ 40 percent of annual revenues plus inventory

➢ "Most cell-phone stores receive a small percentage of the usage fees based on the sale of the plan purchased by the customer with the telephone."

Resources
Associations
- Cellular Telecommunications & Internet Association (CTIA): www.ctia.org

Cemeteries
SIC 6553-02	NAICS 812220	Number of Businesses/Units 8,270

Rules of Thumb
➢ 6 times SDE includes real estate

➢ 8 times EBIT includes real estate

➢ 6 times EBITDA includes real estate

Rules of Thumb - C

Pricing Tips
- "Valuations will vary depending on the strategic fit of the buyer. A local funeral home is generally the best strategic fit and should, therefore, be willing to pay the most."

Benchmark Data

Statistics (Cemetery Services)
Number of Establishments	8,270
Average Profit Margin	9.9%
Revenue per Employee	$113,200
Average Number of Employees	3.9
Average Wages per Employee	$35,512

Products and Services Segmentation
Sale of graves, plots and other spaces	39.1%
Interment	21.7%
Merchandise sales	18.8%
Cremation	13.1%
Cemetery maintenance services	3.7%
Pre-burial services	3.3%
Other	0.3%

Industry Costs
Profit	9.9%
Wages	31.6%
Purchases	12.4%
Depreciation	3.6%
Marketing	2.3%
Rent & Utilities	5.7%
Other	34.5%

Market Share
Service Corporation International	28.6%
StoneMor Partners LP	5.3%

Source: IBISWorld, April 2015

Industry Trend
- "The cemetery's trustees celebrated the groundbreaking of their new columbarium, which will house cremated remains. It is a building that represents what is increasingly becoming the future of death. 'People are looking for alternatives to in-ground burials,' said Michael Lally, office manager of LowellCemetery. 'They can be any nationality, any religion.'

"In Massachusetts, 45 percent of all deceased persons will be cremated in 2015, according to the National Funeral Directors Association, and the rate has been steadily increasing for decades. The Bay State is closely following the nationwide trend, which saw just 3.5 percent of Americans choose cremation in 1960 but nearly 50 percent today. Maine and New Hampshire are near the top of the pack, with cremation rates higher than 70 percent."

Source: "With cremations on rise, LowellCemetery decides to build a home for all those ashes," by Todd Feathers, *Lowell Sun*, 05/04/2015

C - Rules of Thumb

Questions
- "Trust fund information is critical. What are the liabilities? Are they properly funded? Is there a successful sales organization/program in place?"

CertaPro Painters (See also Franchises)	Franchise
Approx. Total Investment	$129,000 to $161,000
Estimated Annual Sales/Unit	$741,000
SIC 1721-01 NAICS 238320	Number of Businesses/Units 452
Rules of Thumb	
➢ 45 percent of annual sales plus inventory	

Resources

Websites
- www.certapro-franchise.com

Check Cashing Services (See also Ace Cash Express, Payday Loans)	
SIC 6099-03 NAICS 522390	Number of Businesses/Units 61,500
Rules of Thumb	
➢ 75 percent of annual revenues ➢ 2 times SDE	

Pricing Tips
- "The check cashing business is growing; every state has its own rules and regulations. Lease terms and whether a franchise or independent will affect pricing."

Benchmark Data
- See Payday Loans for additional Benchmark Data.

    Services/Products Offerings & Volumes

Check Cashing	96%
Money Orders	96%
Money Transfers	96%
Bill Payments	96%
Prepaid Debit Cards	88%
Payday Advances	58%
Travelers Checks	4%
Installment Loans	25%
Other Financial Products	63%

    Source: Financial Service Centers of America, www.fisca.org

- "Check cashing should provide the owner with 1% of total gross sales as owner's discretionary income."

Rules of Thumb - C

Expenses as a percentage of annual sales

Cost of goods	99%
Payroll/labor Costs	01%
Occupancy	01%
Profit (estimated pretax)	01%

Resources

Websites
- Financial Service Centers of America—an excellent site with lots of information: www.fisca.org

	Franchise
CheeburgerCheeburger Restaurants	
(See also Franchises, Restaurants—Limited Service)	
Approx. Total Investment	$230,000 to $585,000
SIC 5812-19 NAICS 722513	Number of Businesses/Units 70

Rules of Thumb
- 35 to 40 percent plus inventory

Resources

Websites
- www.cheeburger.com

	Franchise
Chick-fil-A (See also Franchises, Restaurants—Limited Service)	
Estimated Annual Sales/Unit	$2,500,500
SIC 5812-06 NAICS 722513	Number of Businesses/Units 1,750

Rules of Thumb
- 60 to 70 percent of annual sales plus inventory

Resources

Websites
- www.chick-fil-a.com

Children's and Infants' Clothing Stores (See also Family Clothing Stores)	
NAICS 448130	Number of Businesses/Units 14,898

Rules of Thumb
- 25 to 30 percent of annual sales plus inventory

C - Rules of Thumb

Benchmark Data

Statistics (Children's & Infants' Clothing Stores)

Number of Establishments	14,898
Average Profit Margin	3.1%
Revenue per Employee	$107,500
Average Number of Employees	7.2
Average Wages per Employee	$13,298

Products and Services Segmentation

Girls' clothing	34.0%
Infants' and toddlers' clothing	33.7%
Boys' clothing	24.3%
Other	8.0%

Industry Costs

Profit	3.1%
Wages	12.0%
Purchases	60.1%
Depreciation	2.1%
Marketing	7.3%
Rent & Utilities	6.6%
Other	8.8%

Market Share

Toys"R"Us Inc.	28.2%
The Children's Place Retail Stores Inc.	13.7%
Carter's Inc.	13.5%
Ascena Retail Group Inc.	12.7%
The Gymboree Corp.	11.0%

Source: IBISWorld, February 2015

Children's Educational Franchises

(See also FasTracKids, Floppy's Mouse Club, Franchises, Huntington Learning Center, Kumon, Montessori Schools, Sylvan)

Rules of Thumb

- ➢ 2.5 times SDE
- ➢ 2 times EBIT
- ➢ 2 times EBITDA

Pricing Tips

- "The typical learning center with sales of up to $300k and EBITDA of $85k will sell at approximately a 2.5 multiple. While deals are done for more than that, it should not be the expectation of the seller."

Benchmark Data

- "$250/sq. ft."

Expenses as a percentage of annual sales
Cost of goods 20%
Payroll/labor Costs 25%
Occupancy 20%
Profit (estimated pretax) 25%

Industry Trend
- "Demand is increasing as schools are having a difficult time keeping up with the curriculum changes mandated by the states. As a result, the perception of parents is that they need to invest in their children's supplemental education in order to help them succeed in school."

Seller Financing
- "Seller financing is common but with the more recent loosening of the lending practices by banks outside financing is also becoming more prevalent."

Questions
- "Buyer needs to know the retention rate of the business, the demographics of the area, the average length of stay for the clients. How often has franchisor changed the royalty structure in the past."

Chiropractic Practices		
SIC 8041-01	NAICS 621310	Number of Businesses/Units 70,992

Rules of Thumb
- 55 to 60 percent of annual sales includes inventory
- 1 to 2.5 times SDE includes inventory
- 1.5 to 2 times EBITDA

Pricing Tips
- "A full educational video on healthcare practice valuation is available at MedicalPracticeAppraisal.com homepage."
- "Most appraisers favor the Income Approach in valuing small, privately held professional services businesses, as it best reflects the impact of profit or dividends rather than just gross collections. It is the income above what the buyer could earn in employment that creates value in chiropractic practices."
- "The value of chiropractic practices is at an all-time low. Decisions regarding what, where, when and how to practice are influenced by numerous factors, including: personal preferences, market forces, State and Federal policies and programs, and institutions that constitute the health care system and medical education infrastructure. Insurance reimbursement is a serious hassle factor. 'Percentage of annual gross sales' or 'SDE multiplier' as valuation Rules of Thumb are obsolete, if ever valid. Growth Rates are available through the Congressional Budget Office reports; rarely above 2% historically. Chiropractic practice is riskier—and demands higher Cap rates—than other professional practices like accounting, law, architecture and engineering which are not subject to clinical malpractice risks, or subject to Medicare or insurance company changing reimbursement limitations or denials. The impact of specialty and location is profound, as is the FTE work schedule and leverage of employed licensed providers. Medicare is continually

reducing reimbursement, which impacts other insurances which often base their payment on a percent of Medicare (i.e., 80–120% of Medicare), so dependence on insurance reimbursement is an important consideration in value. In addition, specific diagnosis and procedure ('ICD/CPT') billing-code reimbursement changes—like what has happened in other fields of medicine—have further reduced reimbursement and profits during the past decade. Cash and cosmetic practices are usually worth more since there is a higher profit for less work, and often provide a better lifestyle, but even those can be difficult to sell."

- "Increasing retirement, plus the trend toward shorter working hours, increases the supply of practices for sale, and decreases the available FTE workforce available as buyers. The increasing rate of Boomer retirement contributes to a reduction of value of practices for sale. Of particular concern when determining value of a chiropractic practice accepting Medicare payments is ensuring not only that the purchase price is Fair Market Value, but also that the valuation method does not take into account the volume or value of referrals that the selling chiropractor has made or may make to the purchaser, such that the purchase price could be challenged as a kickback or inducement. The OIG has provided guidance on the question of how to value practices. The ailing economy is leading many Americans to skip doctor visits, and put off X-rays. The results of the Income Approach of valuation identifying 'dividends' [(SDE minus market rate compensation of one working owner) x 1.5-2 (i.e., 50–65% Cap rate on dividends)] is becoming more important. You may hear from sellers or buyers that chiropractic practices sell—or sold—for lot more than that, which is true. There was a flurry of sale of practices in the 1990s–2000s wherein the buyers then later failed, and defaulted on their loans, because they paid more than the business-income could sustain. My practice-purchase lenders tell me that many banks have quit lending—or now require much bigger down payments—to chiropractors because of that."

- "Patient records are not a true 'asset' of the practice since they can't be put on the balance sheet as an asset using the Asset Approach valuation methodology. Patient record valuation is only used to specifically allocate intangibles, assuming they exist at the time of the valuation. The doctor has the physical record, but usually cannot legally sell or dispose of it without the patient's consent (per state statutes), only transfer 'custodianship.' So the doctor is basically a 'custodian' of the record rather than an owner of an asset with independent value. When paper charts are involved, I have come to the opinion that the value of the chart is zero because of the attendant custodianship liability costs. With EMR, a digital record may need to be converted from one digital platform to another either by custodianship transfer or technology succession, in which case a printout and re-entry may be required, probably exceeding in labor costs any physical value to the original digital chart."

- "The library in a smaller practice—as opposed to a university or a 'super-group'—is presumed to not include historical or rare publications, be organized with bibliographic cataloging, nor represent a complete or unique collection for the specialty. Materials are presumed to be of mixed currency and technological validity. No value is therefore assigned to the practice library."

- "Accounts Receivable represent past gross charges for services rendered and as yet uncollected or adjusted-off. These receivables must be discounted to reflect both insurance company reimbursement disallowances, plus the decreasing value over time due to difficulty in collections of past due accounts. In other words, the historic collection ratio of the practice does not yet include the 'standing wave' of uncollectable accounts at practice end, or at a particular point in time, as in a valuation at a particular date."

Rules of Thumb - C

- "On March 21, 2010, the Democratic Congress passed Health System Reform Legislation (H.R. 3590), fulfilling President Obama's promise made in 2008 for the largest social legislation since the formation of the Social Security and Medicare programs. We now have a federal law applicable to ERISA plans that makes it against the law for insurance companies to discriminate against Doctors of Chiropractic and other providers relative to their participation and coverage in health plans. The legislation establishes a National Health Care Workforce Commission to review needs in the healthcare workforce, and specifically includes doctors of chiropractic by defining them as part of the healthcare workforce, and includes them in the definition of health professionals. A number of states quickly filed lawsuits seeking to block it, the outcome of which will not be known for some time. The future of chiropractic economics is still unclear."
- "Don't try to use boilerplate broker contracts to sell chiropractic practices, as it is easy to violate State or Federal regulations; have all the paperwork and terms done by a medical practice transaction specialist attorney."
- "Historically there were higher values, pre-Obamacare. It's dividends that count, i.e., income above compensation for similar labor."
- "Most chiropractors take insurance and Medicare, and so are subject to the same equity valuation multiples as medical physicians."
- "In addition to a thorough statistical analysis, other factors to consider when determining fair market value of an established practice include a compilation and assessment of the following:
    - ✓ Office location, appearance, accessibility, visibility, equipment and layout; staff profile; gross and net income; accounts receivable; payor provider profile; HMO/PPO affiliations; referral alliances; active patient list; office procedures (overall practice philosophy, consultation, examinations, report of findings, adjusting techniques and ancillary care.)

    "Only after a comprehensive review and evaluation of all of these factors can we look beyond the practice finances and statistics and determine a fair market value."

    Source: www.chiroequity.com
- "Depends on hours worked. Value of equipment can vary considerably depending on techniques/technology. Equipment value for solo practice may range from $20k to $150k+ so this can affect value quite a bit. Price usually does not include A/R and sold as asset sale."
- "Cash practice is worth more than insured practice."
- "It is my personal belief that chiropractic market values are overheated, as practice sales are occurring that are difficult to support with earnings. Some lenders are leaving the market for the same reason, due to high & increasing rates of default on loans to buyers. I find that values of [3-4x (SDE minus one owner's market rate salary for work performed)] can be supported by earnings, the income approach to valuation, and the principle of substitution. On the other hand, there are demonstrated sales far above this level."
- "Are you and the doctor a compatible personality match? Is the personality of the selling doctor vivacious and outgoing, while the 'new' doctor is a little reserved? Is your chiropractic technique compatible with the seller's? Every instance of non-compatibility may mean one fewer patient will remain with you.

    "With compatibility being addressed, I value the practice and goodwill to be equal to one-year net income. This figure will be corrected based upon a few factors: blend of patient financial classes; percentage of actual overhead (high overhead lowers value). Purchasing a practice is a very smart thing to do. I would always look for a practice to buy rather than start fresh."

Source: From an article by Bruce A. Parker, D.C. in *Today's Chiropractic*.
For more information, go to www.bruceparkerconsulting.com.

C - Rules of Thumb

Expert Comments

"Don't do it without using an expert healthcare transactions specialist attorney, even if you are using an expert broker."

"It's easier to become a chiropractor than an MD or DO, so competition is often higher, and compensation lower."

"You usually have to be a chiropractor to buy. See all the same risks as medical practices, especially for chiropractic practices accepting Medicare, Obamacare, and insurance."

"Fairly easy to start a solo practice in many underserved communities. Many communities are over-served. Many chiropractors are located in small communities. However, the distribution of chiropractors is not geographically uniform. This occurs primarily because new chiropractors frequently establish their practices in close proximity to one of the few chiropractic educational institutions. Growth in this sector mirrors demand by the increasingly health-conscious consumer who seeks alternatives to prescription drugs and invasive surgical procedures. Benefit coverage of chiropractic care is an important trend and continues to increase. Currently, coverage is offered in Medicare, Medicaid, Federal Employees Health Care Benefits Programs, Federal Workers' Compensation, Departments of Defense and Veterans Affairs, approximately three quarters of employer health programs and all state workers' compensation programs. Job prospects for new chiropractors are expected to be good, especially for those who enter a multi-disciplined practice, consisting of, for example, a chiropractor, physical therapist, and medical doctor. Multi-disciplined practices are cost effective and allow patients to remain in-house. Should a patient be referred to a medical doctor, they may use the 'in-house' doctor or one of their own choosing. Chiropractors usually remain in the occupation until they retire and few transfer to other occupations, so replacement needs arise almost entirely from retirements."

"Practice income can be heavily influenced by state regulation of Personal Injury/Workers Comp laws. Many states have changed laws in last 10 years which drastically reduced practice incomes (by 50%–70%) as chiropractic stopped being reimbursed by insurance. Hard to finance. Most lenders shy away from chiro deals. Many buyers have less than ideal credit."

"Insured practices subject to more risk"

Benchmark Data

Statistics (Chiropractors)

Number of Establishments	70,992
Average Profit Margin	16.0%
Revenue per Employee	$89,000
Average Number of Employees	2.4
Average Wages per Employee	$29,581

Products and Services Segmentation

General chiropractic care	60.0%
Family chiropractic care	21.7%
Other	9.0%
Sports and rehabilitation chiropractic care	8.3%
Pediatric chiropractic care	1.0%

Major Market Segmentation

Private health insurance	35.9%
Patients paying out-of-pocket	34.2%
Medicare and Medicaid	13.2%
Auto insurance	9.8%
Workers' compensation	4.3%
Other	2.6%

Industry Costs

Profit	16.0%
Wages	33.2%
Purchases	5.8%
Depreciation	2.1%
Marketing	2.5%
Rent & Utilities	10.8%
Other	30.3%

Source: IBISWorld, February 2015

- "High variability in practice settings, from solo docs with no staff, to highly leveraged multi-specialty institutions."
- "There are many subspecialty modalities, often described by chiropractors as 'straights' versus 'mixers', i.e., straights do just spinal manipulation, mixed add other modalities; so benchmarks vary."
- "65%–75% overhead"

Components of Chiropractic Practice

Direct patient care	52.9%
Documentation	18.9%
Patient education	15.1%
Business management	13.2%

Source: National Board of Chiropractic Examiners

Reimbursement Categories, Managed Care, and Referral

Private Insurance	21.5%
Private pay/cash	21.2%
Managed care	19.4%
Personal injury	13.6%
Medicare	10.8%
Workers' Comp	07.8%
Pro Bono	03.9%
Medicaid	01.8%

Source: National Board of Chiropractic Examiners

Expenses as a percentage of annual sales

Cost of goods	05% to 10%
Payroll/labor Costs	05% to 15%
Occupancy	04% to 08%
Profit (estimated pretax)	25% to 50%

Industry Trend

- "*Fast Company*, *Forbes*, Career Cast, and other organizations repeatedly name chiropractic as a top job. Aside from the personal satisfaction of helping

C - Rules of Thumb

people, a chiropractic career is in demand; the Bureau of Labor Statistics has reported that the employment of chiropractors is expected to increase faster than the average for all occupations through the year 2022. Because chiropractors emphasize the importance of healthy lifestyles, chiropractic care is appealing to many health-conscious Americans. Projected job growth for the chiropractic profession stems from increasing consumer demand for a more natural approach to health care."

Source: "Chiropractic profession has the best job security, according to Market Watch, 4/3/15

- "High exit of boomers increases practices for sale. Lousy insurance reimbursement and control of patient referrals under PPACA ACOs is a big concern."
- "More insurance and Obamacare driving down profits"
- "A concerted advocacy effort by ACA will increase Medicare payments to DCs by an estimated $60 million in 2014. The Centers for Medicare and Medicaid Services (CMS) has announced that the value of Chiropractic Manipulative Treatment (CMT) CPT® codes will increase up to 10 percent in the 2014 Physician Fee Schedule for services rendered beginning January 1, 2014. The change in Medicare payment rates reflects a more appropriate and rigorous valuation of chiropractic services that should have a ripple effect in private insurance markets. As reported in the Washington Post, recent research shows that a one-dollar change in the price that Medicare pays yields a $1.30 change in what private insurers pay."

Source: ACA 2013 Annual Report

- "The projected job growth for chiropractors through 2020 is twice as high as the 14 percent average for all U.S. occupations combined. According to the U.S. Bureau of Labor Statistics, the number of jobs for chiropractors will climb by 28 percent."

Source: "Chiropractor Job Outlook & Growth" by Maria Christensen, Demand Media, www.work.chron.com

- "High provider saturation keeps values up due to difficulty getting patients from scratch"
- "Up as boomers' health deteriorates"
- "Ancillary product revenue is increasing trend (nutrition, pillows, ointments, orthotics, exercise, etc.)."

Seller Financing
- "75% SBA guaranteed financing is generally available."
- 2–5 years

Questions
- "Source of new patients, wait list, insurance impact, ancillary services or providers, ratio of established and returning patients ('once a back patient, always a back patient')"
- "Any regulation/law changes in recent years (or planned) that may significantly impact revenue? % income from professional services versus product sales. Hours worked, number of patient visits/week, payer mix/insurance reimbursement."
- "If the buyer is not a licensed chiropractor, the buyer should inquire of the state if a non-chiropractor is allowed to own a chiropractic practice or employ a chiropractor in that state."
- "Is the practice set up to support the way you want to work? If you want to

run a family practice, and most of the clientele are work-related injury or PI (personal injury) patients, you will have to start from scratch to attract families to your practice. If your technique is notably different from the previous doctor's, you will have a difficult time transitioning the patients.

"Is the practice located in the right place? If the practice is in a town you want to move to and live in for a long time, you can proceed knowing that you will be buying a business you can stay with for years. If the practice is not exactly where you want to be located, you will probably be better off finding a town you like and starting your own practice.

"Is the price reasonable? Many doctors will inflate the prices of their practices for two reasons: 1. They want to get paid for their years of work, and 2. They have been counting on using the proceeds of the practice sale to fund their retirement.

"A practice in which the doctor has only been working a few days a week might seem like a steal, but if the selling doctor won't come down in price, you could end up paying too much for the practice.

"Can you get a non-compete from the doctor? The last thing you want is to buy a practice and have the selling doctor open up down the street and take back all of his or her former patients. Some states (like California) do not uphold non-compete agreements, and you will have to pay a reasonable amount of money for a non-compete as part of the purchase price.

"If you don't think you can get a good non-compete, or you don't think it will be upheld in court, the practice may not be for you. Make sure that you know the actual reason the doctor is selling. If your instincts tell you that you're not getting the whole story, be cautious.

"How long will it take you to make a living from the practice? If the price is too high, if there is no strong patient base, or if you are going to have to start effectively from scratch, you might be better off going down the street and opening your own practice.

"Finally, trust your instincts. If the offer sounds too good to be true, it probably is. If everything looks great and you have a good feeling about the practice and the location, it could be a wonderful lifelong investment for you."

Source: Jean Murray, PhD, who has been counseling small business owners since 1974 and is currently helping chiropractic students and graduates who want to start their own practices.

Resources

Trade Publications
- Today's Chiropractic: www.todayschiropractic.com
- Chiropractic Economics: www.chiroeco.com

Associations
- American Chiropractic Association: www.acatoday.org
- National Board of Chiropractic Examiners—an excellent site: www.nbce.org
- National Society of Certified Healthcare Business Consultants: www.nschbc.org
- Medical Group Management Association: www.mgma.com

C - Rules of Thumb

Closet Factory (See also Closets by Design, Franchises) — Franchise

Approx. Total Investment	$162,500 to $310,000
NAICS 238390	Number of Businesses/Units 60

Rules of Thumb
- ➢ 45 to 50 percent of annual sales plus inventory

Resources

Websites
- Closet Factory: www.closetfactory.com

Closets by Design (See also Closet Factory, Franchises) — Franchise

Approx. Total Investment	$124,900 to $278,400
SIC 1521-20	NAICS 238390	Number of Businesses/Units 34

Rules of Thumb
- ➢ 45 percent of annual sales plus inventory

Resources

Websites
- Closets by Design: www.closetsbydesign.com

Clothing Stores—Used
(See also Consignment Shops, Resale Shops, Used Goods)

SIC 5932-05	NAICS 453310	Number of Businesses/Units 20,000

Rules of Thumb
- ➢ 20 percent of annual sales plus inventory unless it is on consignment

Benchmark Data
- For Benchmark Data see Used Goods

Resources

Associations
- The Association of Resale Professionals (NARTS)—a good site: www.narts.org

Cocktail Lounges (See also Bars)

SIC 5813-03	NAICS 722410	Number of Businesses/Units 10,000

Rules of Thumb

- ➢ 40 percent of annual sales plus inventory
- ➢ 3 to 4 times monthly sales; add license (where applicable) and plus inventory
- ➢ 1.5 to 2 times SDE; add fixtures, equipment and inventory
- ➢ $ for $ of gross sales if property is included, 40 percent of annual sales for business only plus inventory

Benchmark Data

- "Sales price 2½ to 3 times the annual liquor sales. Rent should never exceed 6 percent of the gross sales."
- "When buying liquor, only purchase what you can sell. Ignoring this simple rule has put many bars out of business...The only way to maintain a profitable operation is to establish a firm system of liquor control, and usage, that lets you know, to the penny, exactly how much each drink costs, and how much liquor is poured...Each dollar tied up in inventory is a dollar not working for you. And cash flow is the name of the game. So keep your inventory lean.... If you sell one-ounce drinks for $2 each, a quart bottle can generate 32 drinks, and $64 in revenues. If the quart bottle costs you $12, your gross profit will be $52. Subtract about $15 to cover labor and overhead, and you should clear $37.... However, if your bartender 'free pours' liquor, and his shots average 1 1/2 ounces, the number of drinks you get from a quart will be cut from 32 to 21. This will cut your revenue from $64 to $42. And your gross profit will fall from $52 to $30. And, if your bartender also gives away 4 free drinks out of the same bottle, your gross profit will drop to $22, minus your $15 in labor and overhead, which will leave you with just $7. That's why your liquor should be guarded like cash."

Source: "Eleven Tips to Owning a Profitable Bar," Specialty Group, Pittsburgh, PA

Expenses as a percentage of annual sales

Cost of goods	Food—30% to 40%; Beverages—18% to 22%
Payroll/labor Costs	25%
Occupancy	08%
Profit (estimated pretax)	10%

Industry Trend

- "Demand for this type of business seems to be declining."

Coffee Shops

(See also Coffee Shops (Specialty), Restaurants—Limited Service)

SIC 5812-28	NAICS 722515	Number of Businesses/Units 67,598

Rules of Thumb

- ➢ 3.5 to 4 times monthly sales plus inventory
- ➢ 35 to 40 percent of annual sales plus inventory
- ➢ 2 to 2.2 times SDE plus inventory

C - Rules of Thumb

Pricing Tips

- "It is rare in business to discover a product where consistently offering 100% quality is the best commercial decision you can make. . . Promote multiple sales. A coffee shop will never make enough money to pay the bills from coffee sales alone. . . Coffee may be the prime motivator for customers coming to the business, but they must leave with multiple sales if you are going to be successful. . . As a target, coffee should be no more than 40% of your weekly sales and two item sales per customer transaction means you are getting it about right."

  Source: "What's The Secret To A Successful Food Business" by Peter Baskerville, Founder of 20 Cafes and Food Businesses, www.forbes.com

- "Trend of sales; owner's compensation including benefits, net profit, lease terms"

Expert Comments

"Ease of entry; unsophisticated owner/operators; personal use of products"

Benchmark Data

Statistics (Coffee and Snack Shops)

Number of Establishments	67,598
Average Profit Margin	6.7%
Revenue per Employee	$69,800
Average Number of Employees	9.0
Average Wages per Employee	$15,100

Products and Services Segmentation

Coffee beverages	51%
Food	36%
Other beverages	9%
Other	4%

Industry Costs

Profit	6.7%
Wages	21.5%
Purchases	39.0%
Depreciation	3.8%
Marketing	3.5%
Rent & Utilities	11.9%
Other	13.6%

Market Share

Starbucks Corporation	35.0%
Dunkin' Brands Inc.	19.8%

Source: IBISWorld, April 2015

- "Food costs should not exceed 30%–33% of sales."

Expenses as a percentage of annual sales

Cost of goods	28% to 32%
Payroll/labor Costs	25%
Occupancy	08% to 12%
Profit (estimated pretax)	16% to 20%

Industry Trend

- "The NCA's 2015 National Coffee Drinking Trends© (NCDT) also finds that 59% of Americans say they drink coffee each day, while 71% reported partaking at least once per week. For 2015, total coffee consumption remained steady within the study's margin of error. Past-year consumption came in at 78% versus last year's 79%, past-week at 71% versus 73% and past-day at 59% versus 61%."

  Source: "Coffee is Americans' Favored Daily Beverage Next to Water," 3/13/15
http://www.ncausa.org/i4a/pages/index.cfm?pageID=1062

- "Frequent openings, frequent closings. Independents lose out to franchises."

Questions

- "Why are you selling? What problems have you had with employees, landlord, vendors, municipal officials, etc.? Do company records show all income? (unlikely)."

Coffee Shops (Specialty)

(See also Coffee Shops, Restaurants—Limited Service)

SIC 5812-28	NAICS 722515	Number of Businesses/Units 20,000

Rules of Thumb

➢ 40 percent of annual sales includes inventory

➢ 2.2 times SDE includes inventory

➢ 3 times EBIT

➢ 2.5 times EBITDA

Pricing Tips

- "The value of a coffee house is repeat business from a loyal customer base. Ensure that all vendor contracts will convey or transfer."
- "Recognize that profitability is key to determining overall value of the operation. A well-run, mature coffee house can net to the owner in excess of 20 percent of gross revenue."

Expert Comments

"While it is relatively easy to start a coffee house business, especially in relation to other types of food establishments, it can be a higher risk type of business due to the perceived simplicity of the business. Historically, specialty coffee establishments have participated in a high-growth industry segment and consequently have greater than average interest from potential buyers who are looking for a business."

"Opening a coffee house is relatively easy relative to other food and beverage businesses, however understanding the unique dynamics of the coffee house business can be a challenge. Is your location on the correct side of the road? Is your wholesale coffee pricing and quality up to par? How are you going to differentiate your location from the ubiquitous Starbucks?"

C - Rules of Thumb

Benchmark Data

- "Consumers appear to be shifting to gourmet coffee options, according to the NCA National Coffee Drinking Trends (NCDT) market research study. Daily consumption of gourmet coffee beverages is up to 34% of American adults over 2013's 31%, while daily non-gourmet coffee drinking is down to 35% from last year's 39%.
"Released during today's preview of research findings at the NCA annual convention, NCDT data also reveal that espresso-based beverages accounted for the increase in gourmet coffee beverage consumption. Daily consumption of espresso-based beverages came in at 18% of American adults versus last year's 13%, while gourmet coffee was flat at 19%. Gourmet coffee beverages consist of espresso-based beverages and regular coffee made with gourmet coffee beans."
Source: Consumers Shifting to Gourmet Coffee Options, Says New NCA Market Research
3/22/14, ncausa.org

- "Specialty coffees represent 37% of U.S. coffee cups and are considered the highest quality in the world. The retail value of the U.S. coffee market is estimated at $30–$32 billion, with specialty comprising approximately a 37% volume share but nearly 50% value share."
- "Drink COGS should not be higher than 28% inclusive of all paper-goods costs."

Expenses as a percentage of annual sales	
Cost of goods	28%
Payroll/labor Costs	25%
Occupancy	10%
Profit (estimated pretax)	20%

Industry Trend

- "Among demographic specific data, NCDT findings indicate that those 25–39 years of age are the strongest consumers of gourmet coffee beverages, with 42% who say they consume daily, as compared with about one-third among consumers aged 18–24 and those 40–59, and just one-quarter of those 60+.
"Daily consumption of gourmet coffee beverages is also strongest among Hispanic-Americans, 48% of whom said they drink gourmet coffee beverages daily, as compared with 42% of Asian-Americans, 32% of Caucasian-Americans and 23% of African-Americans."
Source: Consumers Shifting to Gourmet Coffee Options, Says New NCA Market Research,
3/22/14, ncausa.org

Seller Financing
- 3 years

Questions
- "What is your average ticket sale? What marketing efforts are currently in place? Have you measured customer loyalty? Are your employees cross trained?"

Resources

Associations
- National Coffee Association of USA: www.ncausa.org
- Specialty Coffee Association of America: www.scaa.org

Rules of Thumb - C

Coin Laundries

| SIC 7215-01 | NAICS 812310 | Number of Businesses/Units 23,297 |

Rules of Thumb

➤ 100% to 125% of annual sales plus inventory
➤ 1 to 1½ times annual sales plus inventory
➤ 3 to 5 times SDE includes inventory (higher multiple for newer equipment and long lease)
➤ 4 to 5 times SDE plus inventory—assumes long-term lease (10+ years) and newer equipment (3–5 years old).
➤ 3 to 6 times EBIT
➤ 3 to 6 times EBITDA
➤ "Generally 2.5 to 5.0 times annual SDE; depends on various parts of the U.S. California, for example, sells between 4 and 5 times SDE, whereas in Nebraska it's 1.5 to 2.5 times SDE."

Pricing Tips

- "Location, age of equipment, Clean and orderly, Lighting, State of the Art Equipment and services offered."
- "Most Laundromats in our market sell for 1 to 1.5X gross sales depending on the age and condition of the equipment. Their sales trend and lease also come in to play on the value."
- "Coin Laundry operations consist of three basic areas:
    ✓ Janitorial
    ✓ Maintenance
    ✓ Money Handling (Collecting & Loading Coin Changers)"

    Source: Laundry Industry Overview, Coin Laundry Association, www.coinlaundry.org
- "One ill-advised means of independent verification, which is commonly promoted by coin-laundry touts (both on-line and as half-learned authors of books on the subject), is the comparison of claimed revenue to water usage.
"I consider it ill-advised for several reasons. Firstly, it is a relatively inexpensive method by which a seller can perpetrate a fraud by simply running-off water. Secondly, issues such as leaking water and mineral deposits within water meter mechanisms (water meter maintenance tends to be neglected by water providers) can significantly affect the accuracy of an analysis. Thirdly, many commercial washers now offer surreptitious programming which can significantly impact water usage (e.g., Wascomat 'Generation 6' washer can be adjusted to utilize 1.2 to 1.9 gallons of water per lb. of laundry—a maximum differential of 58.3%!)."

    Source: An excellent article by Gary Ruff, an industry consultant who is also an attorney. Gary Ruff can be reached via his informative Web site: www.laundromatadvisor.com or at (212) 696-8502 or (631) 389-280. He maintains two offices; if you need advice or legal services in the coin laundry business—he knows his stuff.
- "Depending on the location, competition and most of all the lease, % of rent to sales and age of equipment."
- "Coin laundries normally sell for a multiple of their net earnings. The multiple may vary between three and five times the net cash flow, depending on several valuation factors. The following primary factors establish market value:

26th Edition

C - Rules of Thumb

- ✓ The net earnings before debt service, after adjustments for depreciation and any other nonstandard items including owner salary or payroll costs in services.
- ✓ The terms and conditions of the real estate interest (lease), particularly length; frequency and amount of increases; expense provisions; and overall ratio of rent to gross income.
- ✓ The age, condition and utilization of the equipment, and leasehold improvements; the physical attributes of the real property in which the coin laundry is located, particularly entrances/exits, street visibility and parking.
- ✓ Existing conditions, including vend price structure in the local marketplace.
- ✓ The demographic profile in the general area or region
- ✓ Replacement cost and land usage issues.

"This resale market standard assumes an owner/operator scenario, with no allocation for outside management fees. Marketing time for store sales averages 60 to 90 days, depending on price, financing terms and the quality and quantity of stores available at the time of sale. Coin laundry listings are generally offered by business brokers who charge a sales commission of 8 percent to 10 percent. Many coin laundry distributors also act as brokers. The accepted standard of useful life for commercial coin laundry equipment is as follows:

- ✓ Topload Washers (12 lbs. to 14 lbs.): 5–8 years
- ✓ Frontload Washers (18 lbs. to 50 lbs.): 10–15 years
- ✓ Dryers (30 lbs. to 60 lbs.):15–20 years
- ✓ Heating Systems: 10–15 years
- ✓ Coin Changers: 10–15 years"

Source: Laundry Industry Overview, Coin Laundry Association, www.coinlaundry.org, an excellent and informative site.

- One Industry Expert has reported that a review showed that several hundred sales were for 80 percent of the asset value of the laundry.
- "You must buy value; which means you need to understand exactly what you are buying, being very careful not to pay too much. One of several major keys to price is gross sales. In fact, it is fair to say that a 10% misrepresentation as to gross sales can impact the overall value of a coin-laundry business by some 20%, and maybe considerably more; therefore, you must ask the right questions, and be able to assess the accuracy of the answers.

  "Determine the age and condition of the equipment. Inspect the water heating systems, as this is many times the most expensive single component to replace. These two observations will go a far way in determining an asking price, or variance from the standard of 100% of gross revenue as an asking price. Another great metric is determining water usage. Quite often water companies will sell water in HCF or Hundred Cubic Feet Units. 7.48 gallons of water is equal to one cubic foot of water, so 748 gallons of water equals a Hundred Cubic Feet. A standard top loader uses 30 gallons of water, and the 30 and 50 pound units are multiples of the top loader. The dryer revenue should equal at least half of the washer revenue, up to 100% of the washer revenue."
- "Location is very important. Good locations are in densely populated areas with high percentage renters and low-to-mid income."

Rules of Thumb - C

- "Population demographics within 1-mile radius should show high percentage renters (50+%), low-to-mid income, limited competition, larger family size."
- "Coin laundry business is predictable. It does not jump up and down or respond to marketing as quickly as, say, a restaurant would. Having said that, the flat trend, old but functional equipment and slightly run-down interiors, get about 5 times the SDE; the newer equipment, crisp and clean interior with slight uptick in historical volume trend, tends to get high multiples. The annual sales number around $180,000 seems to be almost magical. Over that amount of annual sales, demand is huge, since they can be flowing around $100,000+ in profits."
- "The good news is that, although banks want buyers to meet the same requirements for existing laundries, they can purchase a lower risk opportunity that requires less cash, because existing laundries, in most all cases, cost far less for the investor.

    "Existing laundries often have leaseholds grandfathered in, so buyers end up paying three to four times the net cash flow for an up-and-running business and save tons of money. Let's say that a laundry has a net cash flow of $75,000. You'll likely pay $225,000 to $300,000, and the bank would need 30% of these numbers. This saves more than two-thirds of the cash out of pocket compared to the new laundry scenario.

    "Fortunately, the current state of our economy has not affected the fact that people need to cover the bare necessities such as eating and washing clothes. Many of my customers have maintained their margins, and others who aggressively execute their marketing plans are actually seeing increases in revenue."

    Source: "New vs. Existing Stores: Starting a Coin Laundry in a Tough Economy" by Robert J. Renteria, WashProUSA, www.american coinop.com

- "If you lose your lease, it is very expensive to set up in a new location: machine pad construction (far more expensive if there is a basement); sufficient gas supply for dryers; lawful wastewater egress; plumbing (including sufficient water supply); three-phase and single-phase electrical layouts; dryer venting system; flooring, ceiling, and counter space. Accordingly, laundromats need to have a long and easily assignable lease."

    Source: Gary Ruff, www.laundromatadvisor.com.

- "Location and demographics. It's important to study the surrounding area for city planned changes or housing changes that may affect business performance."
- "Larger multiplier number used for newer equipment & long-term lease"
- "Age of equipment a huge factor in price determining. Fold and wash service available?"
- "Typically laundries sell for between 55 and 65 times monthly net."
- "Net Income should = 1/3 of Gross Income. Sales price is 5+ x Net"
- "Try and achieve a 25% return on capital; not including owner's salary."
- "Higher multiplier for businesses with newer equipment (3–4 years) and long-term lease (10+ years) increase business value."
- "Here are the steps used to calculate how many times the washers would have to be used to use all the water reflected in the water bill: (1) Get the water bills for the last year, (2) Since water bills are usually in cu. ft., you will have to figure out how many gallons of water were used (there are approximately 7.5 gallons per cu. ft.), (3) Find out how many gallons of water the particular washer type uses, (4) Calculate how many times the washers have to be used to use all the water based on the bill. That should give you the number of washes. Multiply that by the cost per wash. The national average for 'turns' is (5)—the number of times the washer is used. Dryer income is generally half

26th Edition

C - Rules of Thumb

that used of washer income, and vending income can produce 10 percent of total. Historically, laundries have been priced to sell at some multiple of their annual gross. Primarily because of tradition, this multiple varies from one section of the country to another, but normally it's within the 90 percent to 150 percent range. Variations on the annual gross formula include such Rules of Thumb as 12 to 18 times monthly gross, or three to five times annual net income (before taxes)."

Expert Comments

"The establishment of a new facility to compete with an existing store is very expensive. An existing store is established and for the most part a better investment than building a new competing facility."

"Review the utility bills and match those up to the monthly sales. Review the lease rate and terms, especially future increases upcoming "

"Obtaining permits to build can be quite challenging"

"Larger, bigger stores 5-10,000 sq. ft. with more services and larger washers and dryers. More 'card' stores."

"Competition in this category is not a significant concern, as most of the establishments have found their population niche. Therefore the amount of risk is not significant relevant to new Laundromats opening. At the same time the amount of growth is limited by the same geographic and population element, and so while the business is consistent, the potential for growth is limited. Locations are usually in economic areas that would support this type of business, and the facilities for the most part are average. Marketability spreads quickly by word of mouth. So, if you have a clean store with working machines and good lighting, you can be assured to be in the game. The trend in the industry has been and will remain consistent. While card-operated and automated machines have made some inroads, basic coin operation still leads the pack. While not difficult to replicate, the cost of replication is significant. And therefore the calculated return on the investment is long term."

"Coin-op laundries typically are recession proof."

Benchmark Data

Statistics (Laundromats)

Number of Establishments	23,297
Average Profit Margin	11.8%
Revenue per Employee	$92,300
Average Number of Employees	2.2
Average Wages per Employee	$16,420

Products and Services Segmentation

Washer services	55.2%
Dryer services	33.0%
Self-service dry cleaning	5.3%
Other	5.2%
Commercial laundry services	1.3%

Major Market Segmentation

Renters using laundromats	38.6%
Renters using on-site laundry facilities	22.4%
Commercial, industrial, service industries and routes	16.9%
Colleges and universities	13.1%
Homeowners	9.0%

Industry Costs

Profit	11.8%
Wages	17.8%
Purchases	24.2%
Depreciation	10.5%
Marketing	0.9%
Rent & Utilities	23.8%
Other	11.0%

Market Share

CSC ServiceWorks	22.1%

Enterprises by Employment Size

Number of Employees	Share
0 to 4	90.4%
5 to 9	6.4%
10 to 19	2.0%
20 to 99	0.9%
100 to 499	0.1%
500+	0.03%

Source: IBISWorld, February 2015

- "A self service laundry that is well laid out and with equipment to handle most garments should create a gross revenue of $70 per square foot per year."
- "The amount of money you can make from a laundry varies tremendously. According to the Coin Laundry Association's Brian Wallace, the annual gross income from one store can range from $30,000 to $1 million. The expenses incurred while running a store range between 65 and 115 percent of the gross income. That means that for a store grossing $30,000 per year, at best it nets $10,500 and at worst it loses $4,500. For a store grossing $1 million per year, the profit could be as high as $350,000, or there could be a loss of up to $150,000, depending on expenses. Wallace says these profit margins have less to do with the size of the store than with its owner. An owner who runs his or her store well—who keeps it clean, repairs its equipment quickly, uses energy-efficient systems and offers good customer service—will see profit margins of about 35 percent."

Source: www.entrepreneur.com

- "Varies a lot depending if it's attended or unattended and what type of location it's in."
- "Cleanliness tops all; working equipment; neighborhood business (quarter to half mile needs 15,000–20,00 population, predominance of renters and incomes from $15,000–$49,000 per annum.)"
- "The term coin laundry is defined as commercial-grade, self-service laundry equipment placed into service in a retail space. Coin laundries generally occupy the retail space on long-term leases (10-25 years) and generate steady cash flow over the life of the lease. Coin laundries are unique small businesses

C - Rules of Thumb

- in that they have no inventory or receivables. A minority of coin laundries employ attendants."
- "Coin laundries can range in market value from $50,000 to more than $1 million, and can generate cash flow between $15,000 and $200,000 per year."
- "Coin laundries are perfect examples of passive income generators. Coin laundries are also referred to as coin-op laundries, coin-operated laundries or laundromats."

Source: Coin Laundry Association, coinlaundry.org, June 26, 2014

- "Average store 2500 sq. ft.; utilities 25–35%; payroll 10%; occupancy costs 25%; gross profit 40%"
- "Dryer income is usually expressed as a percentage of overall income. Generally, dryer income varies between forty and sixty percent of total washer income. Income and expense percentages may vary significantly for stores offering additional services such as drycleaning and fluff and fold."

Source: Laundry Industry Overview, Coin Laundry Association,
www.coinlaundry.org, An excellent and informative site.

- "Rent-to-gross ratio should be no more than 25%. Labor costs run a minimum of 10% of monthly gross."

Expenses as a percentage of annual sales

Cost of goods	0%
Payroll/labor Costs	09% to 12%
Occupancy	14% to 25% (40% to 55% including utilities)
Profit (estimated pretax)	25% to 35%

Industry Trend

- "The trend for housing is smaller as opposed to what we had experienced in the past. More and more families will enjoy the convenience of self service laundries."
- "I see these businesses becoming more in demand, as many people are retiring but still want something to do that makes a good income without a full-time work load."
- "As more and more people become renters, the industry should prosper."
- "The trend will continue to pace or follow history. The need or demand for the industry is not changing, so I would conclude a bright future."
- "Large facilities will drive out smaller facilities. Successful operations will provide a wide range of services and customer assistance including pickup and delivery."
- "Laundromats adding some other services: children's play areas, sales of ancillary items, video rentals and more."
- "Changing from cash operations to debit card operations"
- "Great potential for growing areas, especially in dense population areas with large numbers of renters"

Seller Financing

- "Most use seller financing, although we have financed 4 with SBA funding recently."
- "Seller, if any."
- 5 to 10 years
- Financing of new stores according to a survey conducted by the Coin Laundry Association:
    - ✓ 27% local bank

Rules of Thumb - **C**

✓ 17% equipment manufacturer
✓ 05% independent financing
✓ 12% SBA
✓ 41% family & friends

Questions
- "Books and records. Are they available?"
- "What is the percentage of utility cost to your represented income?"
- "Occupational license? Water and sewer impact (connection) fees? Organizational skills?"
- "#1—why are you selling? If you can find out the real reason, you have a clear shot at success!! What is the crime rate in the immediate area? Who does the maintenance, how old are the machines? Do you know of a new laundromat being build or planned? Water, sewer, electric and gas bills for 2 years. Can you work with the landlord? What other services could you provide: wash & fold, dry cleaning, vending machines, ATM, shoe repair, soaps and supplies, spot cleaning service, shoe shine, tanning beds, fax & Internet connection, more?"
- "Area crime rate. Review utility bills. New development in trade area. New competition in trade area."
- "I would request copies of utility bills for at least 12 months. Request model numbers and age of washers and dryers, and ask for maintenance records. Especially request information on water heating systems, as this is probably the one single point of failure that can easily be the most costly repair item."
- "Age & condition of equipment. Is equipment mix suitable for market area? Are they taking in wash & fold or dry cleaning? Is store attended? Easy loading and parking? Environmental compliance and local government fees and restrictions? Length of increase value of business. Typically, the lease should be at least 10 years or more."

Resources

Trade Publications
- American Laundry News: www.americanlaundrynews.com
- Coin-Op Magazine: www.americancoinop.com

Associations
- Drycleaning& Laundry Institute: www.dlionline.org
- Coin Laundry Association: www.coinlaundry.org

	Franchise
Cold Stone Creamery (See also Franchises, Ice Cream/Yogurt Shops)	
Approx. Total Investment	$294,250 to $438,850
Estimated Annual Sales/Unit	$285,000
SIC 2024-98 NAICS 722515	Number of Businesses/Units 970

Rules of Thumb
➢ 30 percent of annual sales plus inventory
➢ 1.5 to 2 times SDE plus inventory

C - Rules of Thumb

Expert Comments

"Product is unique, large machinery investment is required, thus difficult to duplicate without industry knowledge and sizeable investment ($250,000) in equipment."

Benchmark Data

- "Food cost is low at 20%, rent is typically above 10% since it is location dependent. Leases must be at least 15 years to provide value and time for ROI long term."

Expenses as a percentage of annual sales	
Cost of goods	20%
Payroll/labor Costs	22%
Occupancy	12%
Profit (estimated pretax)	22%

Questions

"Will you finance, how is the store managed, do you have a production staff, separate from your counter staff? Are there any wholesale or outside accounts?"

Resources

Websites
- www.kahalamgmt.com

Collectibles Stores (See also Used Goods)

SIC 5947-05	NAICS 453220	Number of Businesses/Units 13,562

Rules of Thumb

➢ 20 percent of annual sales plus inventory

➢ Note: Inventory of collectibles is difficult to price. It is normally the cost that the seller paid for it (wholesale price), not the current retail price. However, with collectible inventory, it is quite possible that the current "wholesale price" has increased (or even decreased). The offer or letter of intent should cover how the inventory is to be handled.

Benchmark Data

- For Benchmark Information see Retail Stores—Small Specialty

Industry Trend

- "The growth of Websites competing with retail shops has forced many retail shop owners to close their doors and offer their inventory just on the Web."
- "Although hard sales data have been difficult to come by, the general consensus in the industry is that after a down period, sales of collectibles are slowly on the upswing."

Source: "Crazy About Collectibles" by Randall G. Mielke, www.giftshopmag.com

Rules of Thumb - **C**

Collection Agencies

| SIC 7322-01 | NAICS 561440 | Number of Businesses/Unit 10,360 |

Rules of Thumb
- For agencies with revenues of $1 million +, 75 percent to 125 percent of annual revenues
- 100 percent of annual revenues includes inventory
- 4 to 6 times EBIDTA

Pricing Tips
- "Collection agencies are typically priced on a recast EBITDA income stream which includes earnings before interest, taxes, depreciation, and amortization and should add shareholders' salaries, perks and non-recurring expenses and then subtract a replacement salary for the shareholders. The valuation multiple typically ranges between 4 and 6 times EBITDA. The primary determinant of the multiple is the size of the company."
- "Adjustments are made for non-recurring expenses to arrive at adjusted EBITDA."
- "Debt collection agencies have contracts with clients that are usually only for 30 days or less. In addition, client concentration is a major force as well."

Expert Comments
"Sustainability of profits is important."

"Collection agencies typically have 30-day contracts with clients, whereby a client can pull back accounts in 30 days if performance is not meeting expectations."

Benchmark Data

Statistics (Debt Collection Agencies)
Number of Establishments	10,360
Average Profit Margin	11.7%
Revenue per Employee	$104,400
Average Number of Employees	12.9
Average Wages per Employee	$38,177

Products and Services Segmentation
Contingent-fee servicing	52.0%
Portfolio acquisition	32.0%
Fixed-fee servicing	10.0%
Collateral recovery and repossession services	3.5%
Credit rating services	2.5%

Major Market Segmentation
Financial services	34.5%
Telecommunications	22.1%
Other	14.0%
Healthcare	10.6%
Retail and commercial	10.2%
Government	8.6%

C - Rules of Thumb

Industry Costs

Profit	11.7%
Wages	37.3%
Purchases	8.3%
Depreciation	1.9%
Marketing	1.7%
Rent & Utilities	8.3%
Other	30.8%

Market Share

Expert Global Solutions	8.8%
Encore Capital Group	7.5%
Portfolio Recovery Associates Inc.	6.9%

Source: IBISWorld, April 2015

- Some Benchmarks from the ACA International
  - ✓ "The average collection 'recovery rate' was 17.6% and the median was 16.2%. The average commission rate was 28.9% and the median was 28.1%."
  - ✓ "$70k per employee"
  - ✓ "Sales per collector in successful collection agencies typically exceed 3–4X the collector's compensation on a monthly basis."
  - ✓ "EBITDA should equal 20% or more of revenues."
  - ✓ "50% of revenues are employee cost."

Expenses as a percentage of annual sales

Cost of goods	10%
Payroll/labor Costs	40% to 50%
Occupancy	05% to 10% (Varies by area)
Profit (estimated pretax)	15% to 20%

Industry Trend
- "Profitability should rise as unemployment improves."

Questions
- "Tenure of existing clients, percent of revenues from clients, any change in commission rates and placement volumes, tenure of the collection staff and management, pipeline of business opportunities."

Resources

Trade Publications
- Collection Advisor: www.collectionadvisor.com

Associations
- International Association of Commercial Collectors: www.commercialcollector.com

Comic Book Stores

SIC 5942-05	NAICS 451211	Number of Businesses/Units 2,000

Rules of Thumb
➢ 12 to 15 percent of annual sales plus inventory

Rules of Thumb - **C**

Benchmark Data
- "It's difficult to say what average sales are because very few stock only comics. We would guess that the average store turns $150,000 to $200,000 in comics, but again, that is not likely to be all that any of them sell."

Industry Trend
- "According to new estimates, the $870 million figure for 2013 can be divided into $365 million in sales from comics periodicals—traditional American comic books—sold almost entirely via the direct market or comic shop market, the network of about 2,000 comic shops around the country. Comichron also noted that about $25 million of the $365 million in periodical sales come from newsstands."

   Source: "Comics, Graphic Novels Market Hit $870 Million in 2013," by Calvin Reid, http://publishersweekly.com July 16, 2014

Computer Consulting

SIC 7379-05	NAICS 541512	Number of Businesses/Units 471,054

Rules of Thumb
➢ 50 to 65 percent of annual sales plus inventory

Pricing Tips
- Note: Many consulting businesses are one-man operations or are headed by someone who has the contacts and may basically be "the business." This person may be the goodwill, and without his or her presence the business may not be worth much. If this person stays while the business is slowly being transferred and an earnout is in place, the value may still be there.

Benchmark Data

Statistics (IT Consulting)

Number of Establishments	471,054
Average Profit Margin	8.1%
Revenue per Employee	$191,300
Average Number of Employees	4.3
Average Wages per Employee	$83,410

Products and Services Segmentation

Computer application design and development	34.8%
Computer systems design, development, and integration	28.2%
IT technical support services	13.7%
IT technical consulting services	9.1%
Other services	8.7%
IT computer and network management services	5.5%

Major Market Segmentation

Financial services	24.0%
Federal and state governments	23.0%
Manufacturing and retail	17.8%
Other sectors	12.0%
Communications an technical	11.7%
Healthcare	11.5%

26th Edition

C - Rules of Thumb

Industry Costs

Profit	8.1%
Wages	43.2%
Purchases	14.2%
Depreciation	0.8%
Marketing	1.5%
Rent & Utilities	4.5%
Other	27.7%

Market Share

International Business Machines Corporation	8.3%

Source: IBISWorld, May 2015

- "Of those that run multi-person businesses, most have fewer than three owners. Corporations have two to three non-owner employees. Almost 90% of firms earned $500,000 or less, while 4.4% earned a million or more. 75% of ICCA Consultants have over 15 years of experience in their field."

Source: Independent Computer Consultants Association, (ICCA), www.icca.org

Resources

Associations
- Independent Computer Consultant Association: www.icca.org
- TechServeAlliance: www.techservealliance.org/

Computer Programming Services—Custom
(See also Computer Consulting)

SIC 7371-02	NAICS 541511	Number of Businesses/Units 71,000

Pricing Tips
- "Traditional methods use some multiple of revenues for valuation; however, this is fraught with problems. Growth in revenues is a key aspect, prized in establishing higher value. Earnings are not unimportant, although high-growth companies may be more attractive even without earnings. Look for stability or managed growth in operations.
  "Because software companies must be nimble to respond to market actions, and are vulnerable to loss of key persons, control premiums (and lack of control discounts) and discounts for illiquidity are typically enhanced in this industry."

Industry Trend
- "Down—foreign competition at lower hourly rates is moving programming services jobs overseas."

Questions
- "1) Productivity of current workforce 2) Projects ongoing and anticipated 3) Strategic advantages of this business over the competition."

Rules of Thumb - C

Computer Services		
SIC 7378-01	NAICS 811212	Number of Businesses/Units 60,287

Rules of Thumb

➢ 55 percent of annual sales, plus fixtures, equipment and inventory

Benchmark Data

Statistics (Electronic & Computer Repair Services)

Number of Establishments 60,287
Average Profit Margin 5.3%
Revenue per Employee $137,200
Average Number of Employees 2.4
Average Wages per Employee $38,882

Products and Services Segmentation

Other electronic equipment (including medical equipment) repairs 41.6%
Computer and office machine repairs 36.9%
Communications equipment repairs 16.6%
Consumer electronics (including radio, TV and VCR) repairs 4.9%

Major Market Segmentation

Small and medium businesses 48.9%
Large companies 23.0%
Households 12.1%
Federal government 6.4%
Nonprofit organizations 4.8%
State and local governments 4.8%

Industry Costs

Profit 5.3%
Wages 28.5%
Purchases 35.1%
Depreciation 0.8%
Utilities 1.6%
Rent 4.9%
Other 23.8%

Source: IBISWorld, January 2015

Computer Stores		
SIC 5734-07	NAICS 443120	Number of Businesses/Units 18,599

Rules of Thumb

➢ 30 percent of annual sales plus inventory

Benchmark Data

Statistics (Computer Stores)

Number of Establishments 18,599
Average Profit Margin 4.1%
Revenue per Employee $306,000
Average Number of Employees 4.3
Average Wages per Employee $41,612

26th Edition

C - Rules of Thumb

Products and Services Segmentation

Laptop computers	35.0%
Desktop computers	32.0%
Printers, scanners and supplies	11.0%
Peripherals and other hardware	10.0%
Software	8.0%
Storage devices	4.0%

Major Market Segmentation

Households	59.2%
Businesses	22.3%
Educational institutes	12.5%
The government	6.0%

Industry Costs

Profit	4.1%
Wages	13.6%
Purchases	72.6%
Depreciation	0.7%
Utilities	3.2%
Rent	3.3%
Other	2.5%

Source: IBISWorld, November 2014

Computer Systems Design

SIC 7373-98	NAICS 541512	

Rules of Thumb

- ➢ 50 percent of annual sales plus inventory
- ➢ 2 to 4 times SDE plus inventory
- ➢ 3 to 6 times EBIT
- ➢ 3 to 7 times EBITDA

Pricing Tips

- "Very work-force intensive. Make sure the business can prosper without the owner. Contracts are important."
- "System design firms are often classified as 'programming' firms. More work is being done by temporary employment firms, renting IT professional staff."
- "Highly variable valuations. Biggest component of valuation is the management structure. Midmarket companies with excellent management structure can get very good multiples but a small operation which is highly owner driven may get very little. Having contracts with large customers can improve valuation significantly."

Expert Comments

"Talented people can easily leave and start their own gig. Contracts with a very wide customer base can be very important. Corporate clients are more valuable than consumer clients."

Rules of Thumb - C

"Design firms are being acquired by the large consulting houses. May be attractive for strategic reasons, such as industry niches and/or package familiarity."

"Highly knowledge driven industry. Risk can be very high depending on the importance of the role played by the current owner. If the owner's role is non-critical, then the business can be very lucrative."

Benchmark Data
- "$100,000 or more per employee"
- "$100,000 or more in revenues per technician and $200,000 or more per engineer"
- "Revenue and profit growth is more important than stability of earnings. Sales per employee is a key metric."

Expenses as a percentage of annual sales
Cost of goods	20%
Payroll/labor Costs	50% to 55%%
Occupancy	05%
Profit (estimated pretax)	20%

Industry Trend
- "Continuing growth as technology and tools become indispensable for businesses and individuals."

Questions
- "Reasons for the exit. Strategic growth plans. Customer retention plans. Employee specific compensation issues."
- "Who is (are) the key employee(s) who drives the sales? Are there any critical technical roles?"

Concrete Bulk Plants (Ready-Mix)

SIC 5032-30	NAICS 32732	Number of Businesses/Units 5,166

Rules of Thumb
➢ 30 to 35 percent of SDE plus fixtures, equipment and inventory

Benchmark Data

Statistics (Ready-Mix Concrete Manufacturing)
Number of Establishments	5,166
Average Profit Margin	4.0%
Revenue per Employee	$355,000
Average Number of Employees	14.0
Average Wages per Employee	$54,673

Products and Services Segmentation
Standard ready-mix concrete	65.0%
Specialty ready-mix concrete	35.0%

26th Edition

C - Rules of Thumb

Major Market Segmentation

Private nonresidential construction	35.0%
Residential construction	35.0%
Infrastructure, utilities and public works construction	25.0%
Other	5.0%

Industry Costs

Profit	4.0%
Wages	15.4%
Purchases	55.4%
Depreciation	3.5%
Marketing	0.1%
Rent & Utilities	1.7%
Other	19.9%

Market Share

Cemex SAB de CV	5.4%

Source: IBISWorld, August 2015

Consignment Shops

(See also Clothing Stores—Used, Resale Shops, Used Goods)

SIC 5932-04	NAICS 453310	Number of Businesses/Units 40,000

Rules of Thumb

➢ 15 to 20 percent of annual sales

➢ Note: Consignment shops are just that. They very seldom purchase inventory; rather, they place it on the sales floor and have agreements with the owner regarding price, and generally a schedule in which the price is reduced every month or so for a set period of time. After this period, the goods are usually returned to the owner. The shop works on essentially a commission or fee only if the goods sell.

Benchmark Data

- For additional Benchmark Data see Used Goods
- "What sells: clothing, bookcases, cookbooks. costume jewelry, kitchen gadgets, golf clubs. What doesn't sell: collectible dolls, fur coats, large paintings, vintage dinnerware, needlepoint art."

Source: National Association of Resale and Thrift Shops

Construction—Buildings

	NAICS 236	

Rules of Thumb

➢ 20 to 30 percent of annual sales plus inventory

➢ 1 to 2 times SDE plus inventory

➢ 1 to 3 times EBITDA

Rules of Thumb - **C**

Pricing Tips
- "With very small companies with 1 or 2 employees the norm lately has been to look at FMV of assets as bottom line for pricing purposes."
- "Value in construction trades business is dependent on many factors not normally associated with small business valuation."
- "In many instances in a challenging economy it is not unusual to sell one of these companies for the fair market value of their assets."

Expert Comments

"Small companies have been hit really hard in the economic downturn we have been in for the last few years."

"Make sure you understand the sales and marketing side of the business and how feasible it will be to remove the owner from the business without a serious decline in new and referral business."

Benchmark Data

Statistics (Home Builders)
Number of Establishments	191,664
Average Profit Margin	4.9%
Revenue per Employee	$206,900
Average Number of Employees	2.3
Average Wages per Employee	$67,149

Products and Services Segmentation
Vinyl siding exterior homes	27.8%
Brick exterior homes	26.4%
Stucco exterior homes	25.9%
Other exterior homes	11.6%
Wood exterior homes	7.8%
Aluminum siding exterior homes	0.5%

Major Market Segmentation
Private-sector clients (property developers)	65.2%
Private-sector clients (households)	29.8%
State or locally funded projects	2.7%
Federally funded projects	2.3%

Industry Costs
Profit	4.9%
Wages	38.8%
Purchases	35.9%
Depreciation	0.5%
Marketing	0.9%
Rent & Utilities	1.7%
Other	17.3%

Market Share
DR Horton Inc.	15.4%
Lennar Corporation	12.5%
PulteGroup Inc.	8.3%

Source: IBISWorld, July 2015

26th Edition

C - Rules of Thumb

- "In the final analysis, a construction business should always be worth the FMV of its hard assets."

Expenses as a percentage of annual sales

Cost of goods	20% to 30%
Payroll/labor Costs	25%
Occupancy	05% to 10%
Profit (estimated pretax)	25% to 45%

Industry Trend
- "The surviving companies will be slow to recover."
- "Stagnant"

Questions
- "What would happen to this company if we plucked you out of here today for 1–3 months? Would the business operate effectively?"

Construction—Electrical

NAICS 238210	Number of Businesses/Units 222,350

Rules of Thumb
> 2 times SDE plus inventory

Pricing Tips
- "Strong order book is essential. Wide range of customers."

Expert Comments
"Underpricing of bids is a serious risk but may be used to increase order book in preparation for sale. Good demand for sound business. Location is relatively unimportant."

Benchmark Data

Statistics (Electricians)

Number of Establishments	222,350
Average Profit Margin	4.5%
Revenue per Employee	$177,800
Average Number of Employees	4.2
Average Wages per Employee	$53,748

Products and Services Segmentation

Electric power and systems installation and servicing	65.0%
Telecommunications installation and servicing	18.0%
Other services	6.0%
Fire and security system installation and servicing	6.0%
Electronic control system installation and servicing	5.0%

Rules of Thumb - C

Major Market Segmentation

Commercial buildings	33.4%
Institutional, educational, and civic organization buildings	18.2%
Nonbuilding construction	14.3%
Industrial buildings	13.9%
Single-family homes	12.5%
Multifamily housing (e.g. apartment buildings)	7.7%

Industry Costs

Profit	4.5%
Wages	30.3%
Purchases	37.8%
Depreciation	0.8%
Rent & Utilities	2.1%
Marketing	2.6%
Other	21.9%

Source: IBISWorld, August 2015

Expenses as a percentage of annual sales

Cost of goods	50%
Payroll/labor Costs	30%
Occupancy	n/a
Profit (estimated pretax)	06%

Industry Trend
- "Directly dependent on construction industry but can work related areas if necessary to cover slack period."

Questions
- "1. Details of job costing, current and bids 2. List of staff, experience, and time with business 3. Usual financial and due diligence."

Construction—Excavation (site preparation)

NAICS 238910	Number of Businesses/Units 29,119

Rules of Thumb
- 25 percent of annual sales plus inventory
- 2.2 times SDE plus inventory
- 1.8 times EBIT
- 2 times EBITDA

Pricing Tips
- "Adjust for age/condition of equipment."

Expert Comments
"Due to the economy, construction and site prep companies are declining."

C - Rules of Thumb

Benchmark Data

Statistics (Excavators)

Number of Establishments	29,119
Average Profit Margin	4.1%
Revenue per Employee	134,500
Average Number of Employees	18.6
Average Wages per Employee	$32,401

Products and Services Segmentation

Earthmoving, excavation work, land clearing (Residential Bldg)	43.7%
Earthmoving, excavation work, land clearing (Non-Residential Bldg)	32.3%
Nonbuilding construction excavation	8.9%
Foundation Digging	8.2%
Trenching contractor	6.9%

Major Market Segmentation

Residential building market	43.0%
Non-residential building market	32.0%
Nonbuilding construction market	25.0%

Industry Costs

Profit	4.1%
Wages	24.5%
Purchases	33.4%
Depreciation	6.2%
Marketing	2.0%
Rent & Utilities	6.2%
Other	23.6%

Source: IBISWorld, May 2015

Expenses as a percentage of annual sales

Cost of goods	25%
Payroll/labor Costs	40%
Occupancy	10%
Profit (estimated pretax)	25%

Industry Trend

- "The construction industry is tied to the economic recovery."

Questions

- "Customer lists, future contracts, condition of equipment and any lawsuits?"

Construction—In General		
	NAICS 23	

Rules of Thumb

➢ 20 to 25 percent of annual sales plus inventory

➢ 1 to 2 times SDE plus inventory

Rules of Thumb - C

> ➢ 1.5 times EBIT
>
> ➢ 2 to 3 times EBITDA
>
> ➢ Note: "Some construction firms own significant equipment and some are run from storefronts, so Rules of Thumb are misleading. The business history is very important, as is the value of signed contracts to be completed, and understanding how a company bills its work in progress. Accounts receivable can average over 45 days, increasing the working capital required and decreasing the business value. Once again Rules of Thumb are not very useful."

Pricing Tips
- "Many times businesses in this sector will end up selling for the fair market value of their assets not including cash, receivables, or investments. When pricing these businesses you must consider the fair market value of the assets."
- "Good supply of buyers for firms doing over a million dollars in EBIT with 20 percent or better profit margins. Smaller ones are fairly difficult, and the best practice is to merge with larger company that doesn't have a presence in that area. Important for owner to stay after transaction. Individual to individual transactions are the most difficult."
- "Determining the sale price of a contracting or service-related business is difficult at best. One must consider how dependent the business is on the ongoing involvement of the owner, does the business have an established client base that produces repeat business that will continue post acquisition, does the business have a systematic sales and marketing function that will continue to produce new business without the owner present, and, does the fair market value of the equipment exceed the rule of thumb price?"
- "Stock vs. assets, employment agreements."
- "Construction companies are relatively hard to sell, with the exception of ones that have been established many years and enjoy an established name and reputation. These should be [priced at] depreciated value of fixtures and equipment and rolling stock, plus 10 percent of the sale price for goodwill, plus 25 percent of the part of the business period which has already been contracted for."

Expert Comments
"Construction and service-related businesses have a low cost of entry and require a minimum investment to start. Many of these businesses are centered around the owner's reputation and do not have a sales and marketing plan in place to develop new sales on a regular basis."

"Very competitive business, easy to enter, high profit margins, significant risk."

"Because of the many categories in construction, I generally applied the average value. Construction companies are difficult to sell and relatively difficult to replicate because of capital requirements."

"It takes a special buyer to take on a contracting or service-related business. Your most likely buyer on some occasions might be a competitor from

C - Rules of Thumb

another market that wants entrance into your market. In some fields the fact that a contractor is union is actually a plus because the contractor only needs to have the journeymen on payroll when they are on the job, and therefore ongoing payroll costs are reduced and profit is increased. Additionally, the union contractors get a significant amount of support from the union that translates into additional business and growth opportunities."

Benchmark Data

Statistics (Home Builders)

Number of Establishments	191,664
Average Profit Margin	4.9%
Revenue per Employee	$206,900
Average Number of Employees	2.3
Average Wages per Employee	$67,149

Products and Services Segmentation

Vinyl siding exterior homes	27.8%
Brick exterior homes	26.4%
Stucco exterior homes	25.9%
Other exterior homes	11.6%
Wood exterior homes	7.8%
Aluminum siding exterior homes	0.5%

Major Market Segmentation

Private-sector clients (property developers)	65.2%
Private-sector clients (households)	29.8%
State or locally funded projects	2.7%
Federally funded projects	2.3%

Industry Costs

Profit	4.9%
Wages	38.8%
Purchases	35.9%
Depreciation	0.5%
Marketing	0.9%
Rent & Utilities	1.7%
Other	17.3%

Market Share

DR Horton Inc.	15.4%
Lennar Corporation	12.5%
PulteGroup Inc.	8.3%

Source: IBISWorld, July 2015

Statistics (MunicipalBuilding Construction)

Number of Establishments	47,262
Average Profit Margin	2.5%
Revenue per Employee	$132,400
Average Number of Employees	19.2
Average Wages per Employee	$64,458

Rules of Thumb - C

Products and Services Segmentation
General contracting services	67.0%
Construction management services	11.5%
Remodeling contracting services	11.5%
Other construction activities	10.0%

Major Market Segmentation
Education sector	53.3%
Healthcare sector	26.5%
Recreation sector	11.4%
Public safety sector	6.3%
Religion sector	2.5%

Industry Costs
Profit	2.5%
Wages	49.8%
Purchases	18.2%
Depreciation	1.4%
Marketing	1.6%
Rent & Utilities	2.6%
Other	23.9%

Source: IBISWorld, April 2015

- "Many service-related contracting businesses will charge at least 2 times their direct costs as their hourly fee for service."

Expenses as a percentage of annual sales
Cost of goods	25%
Payroll/labor Costs	30% to 40%
Occupancy	05% to 10%
Profit (estimated pretax)	25%

Industry Trend

- "'This should be a good year for housing, buoyed by sustained job growth, rising consumer confidence that is back to pre-recession levels and a gradual uptick in household formations,' said NAHB Chief Economist David Crowe. 'We expect 2016 to be even better, due to a significant amount of pent-up demand and an economy that will be entering a period of reasonable strength and consistency.'

  "Single-family housing production is expected to post a 9 percent gain in 2015 to 704,000 units and jump an additional 39 percent to 977,000 units in 2016. On the multifamily side, production ran at 355,000 units last year, what could be considered a normal level of production, and is expected to continue in that range or modestly higher through 2015 and 2016. In another way of looking at the long road back to normal, by the end of 2016, the top 40 percent of states will be back to near normal production levels, compared to the bottom 20 percent, which will still be below 75 percent. 'What we are seeing, no matter what bucket you are in, the numbers are getting better,' said Denk. 'There's a broader recovery all around.'"

  Source: "Housing Recovery Slow and Steady in 2015, Will Pick Up Pace Next Year,"
  http://nahb.com/news_details.aspx?newsID=17232

- "This sector is closely tied to the ups and downs of the general economy."

C - Rules of Thumb

Seller Financing
- "5 to 7 years, however SBA loans up to 10 years can be obtained"

Questions
- "If for some reason you were unable to work for the next 6–12 months, what would happen to this business? Where do you get your business from? What systems do you have in place to generate new sales?"

Resources

Associations
- National Association of Home Builders: www.nahb.com

Construction—Specialty Trades
SIC 1799-99

Rules of Thumb
- ➢ 50% of Annual Gross Sales plus inventory
- ➢ 2 times SDE plus inventory
- ➢ 2 to 3 times EBIT
- ➢ 1 to 2 times EBITDA

Pricing Tips
- "Like most services businesses, the key is in the existing relationships. Two times SDE is fair as long as there is evidence that the relationships will transfer smoothly to the buyer."

Expert Comments

"Customers don't care about the provider's location and facilities, just that the job can be done at a reasonable cost. These businesses can be hard to market because specific experience—or a good amount of mentoring—is paramount to who runs the business next."

"This is a highly competitive business that is typically dependent on the owner's goodwill."

Benchmark Data
- "Service businesses will set hourly rates at 2 to 3 times their direct cost per employee per hour to cover overhead and markups."

Expenses as a percentage of annual sales

Cost of goods	25%
Payroll/labor Costs	40%
Occupancy	10%
Profit (estimated pretax)	25%

Industry Trend
- "This sector will improve as the economy improves."

Seller Financing
- 2 years

Questions
- "Reason for selling. What he/she does on a daily basis.Employee census. Worker's comp mode rate.Upside potential."
- "How do you get new jobs? Do you have a sales and marketing plan that generates new work on a consistent basis?"

Contract Manufacturing (See also Job Shops, Machine Shops)	
SIC 3999-06 NAICS 332710	Number of Businesses/Units 2,700

Rules of Thumb
- ➢ 3 to 4 times EBITDA plus reasonable owner's compensation
- ➢ 2 to 4 times SDE plus inventory

Pricing Tips
- "4 x EBITDA is just a rule of thumb. A range of 3 x to 8 x is realistic depending on a range of factors (history, custom concentration, future prospects, etc.)."

Expert Comments
"Competition is high and the key to gross profit margins is using technology to be low-cost manufacturer."

Expenses as a percentage of annual sales

Cost of goods	45%
Payroll/labor Costs	20%
Occupancy	15%
Profit (estimated pretax)	20%

Industry Trend
- "Outsourced manufacturing business on track for moderate growth in 2013 as OEMs seek to build on opportunities in consumer, industrial and automotive electronics markets. The contract manufacturing industry is expected to grow this year despite continued economic weakness worldwide, according to a new report from industry analyst IHS.

"In a report from its Outsourced Manufacturing Intelligence Service, IHS pegs the industry growth at 4.5% this year, to $404.5 billion. That's slower than the 5% growth the industry saw in 2012, but IHS predicts steady, though unremarkable, growth for contract manufacturers worldwide over the next three years. By 2016, the group says revenue will rise to nearly $452 billion as original equipment manufacturers seek to boost production to serve customers in consumer electronics, industrial and automotive markets."

Source: "Electronics Contract Manufacturing to grow 4.5% this year" Global Purchasing Staff, globalpurchasing.com, February, 2013

C - Rules of Thumb

Seller Financing
- "5 years max with a due on sale provision."

Questions
- "Customer concentration and who has technical skill to operate"
- "Discuss the outlook for the company. What opportunities exist for the buyer and why the seller isn't pursuing them."

Contractors—Masonry		
SIC 1741-01	NAICS 238140	Number of Businesses/Units 91,106

Rules of Thumb
- ➢ 27 percent of annual sales includes inventory
- ➢ 1 to 2 times SDE includes inventory

Pricing Tips
- "Commercial masonry is worth more than residential masonry."
- "Home masonry will go for 1X SDE, and B2B will go for 1.5X SDE."

Expert Comments

"Relationships with your builders help getting the contracts for work."

"The industry is changing to foreigners and they are bidding lower to get jobs."

"When home building is doing well, so is this industry; when the home building industry slows down, so does this industry."

Benchmark Data

Statistics (Masonry)
Number of Establishments	91,106
Average Profit Margin	5.0%
Revenue per Employee	$126,000
Average Number of Employees	2.7
Average Wages per Employee	$37,044

Products and Services Segmentation
Masonry contracting using brick or block	66.0%
Other (including work with concrete, marble and granite)	16.0%
Pointing, cleaning, and caulking	6.0%
Refractory contracting	6.0%
Stone contracting	6.0%

Major Market Segmentation
Residential construction market	45.0%
Commercial construction market	37.0%
Municipal construction market	13.0%
Other	5.0%

Rules of Thumb - **C**

Industry Costs

Profit	5.0%
Wages	28.6%
Purchases	41.0%
Depreciation	2.3%
Marketing	0.3%
Rent & Utilities	7.5%
Other	15.3%

Source: IBISWorld, November 2014

- "They estimate that they charge $2.00 per brick and built a very profitable company doing so."
- "Non-union is more salable than union."

Expenses as a percentage of annual sales

Cost of goods	20%
Payroll/labor Costs	50%
Occupancy	10%–15%
Profit (estimated pretax)	15%–20%

Industry Trend
- "Flat"

Questions
- "What % of bids do they get?"
- "Union or non-union labor?"
- "Relationships to the customers, are the contracts assignable, and when will you introduce the buyer to customers before closing?"
- "Make sure they have good foremen in place to run the crews going forward with a new buyer."
- "Understand the builders' contracts in place."

Convenience Stores

(See also Convenience Stores with Gas, Gas Stations/Mini-Marts)

SIC 5411-03	NAICS 445120	Number of Businesses/Units 44,987

Rules of Thumb

- 10 to 20 percent of annual sales plus inventory
- 2 to 2.5 times SDE plus inventory
- 2 to 3 times EBITDA plus inventory—C-store only
- 6 to 8 times EBITDA plus inventory—real estate + business
- 5 times EBITDA less cosmetic renovation to receive a national brand of fuel; inventory is separate and above
- Kiosk—1 to 2 times EBITDA plus real estate & fixtures & equipment
- Mini-Convenience—2 to 3 times EBITDA plus real estate & fixtures & equipment
- Limited-Selection Convenience Store—2 to 3 times EBITDA plus real estate & fixtures & equipment

C - Rules of Thumb

> Traditional Convenience Store—3 to 4 times EBITDA includes real estate & fixtures & equipment less inventory
>
> Expanded Convenience Store—4 to 5 times EBITDA includes real estate & fixtures & equipment less inventory
>
> Hyper-Convenience Store—same as Expanded Convenience Store

Pricing Tips

- "Additional revenue sources such as: ATM machines, game machines, fresh fruits and increased deli items, Lotto sales, money orders and even check cashing have become increasingly more important to convenience store retailers with the industry trending toward lower margins and increased competition over the past several years. Many stores are also offering petroleum product discounts to their customers if paying cash rather than using credit cards. This helps the retailer with cash flow as well as saving approx. 2% (or more in some cases) in credit card processing fees which is substantial especially in high-volume gasoline sales locations selling millions of gallons of petroleum products annually."
- "Stores doing less than $50,000 per month inside sales are not in high demand and bring next to nothing in today's market. Those doing $50k+ per month inside bring 2x's EBIT or more. Gas volume (outside sales in gallons) is less important due to low margins but can still draw customers who may spend money inside if gas is priced competitively."
- "Average price is between 2 and 3 times SDE, 3 to 5 times when real estate is involved. Business with nominal revenue, average under $1,000 per day in sales, is actually buying a job and sale price is 1 or 1.5 times, definitely under 2 times of SDE."
- "Always check the profit margins carefully other than overall sales."
- "Location of business. Competition in the immediate area. Types of products sold. Lottery commissions helpful."
- One industry expert reported: "Should strive for an overall 'weighted' inside gross profit margin of 30 percent. Included in this margin, you should attempt to get a margin between 50 percent and 60 percent for deli sales. Outside gasoline/fuel sales margins will vary all over the place depending on competition. You're in the ballpark, generally, if you get a bottom line profit of between 6.5 percent and 7.0 percent of total sales after taxes, depreciation and amortization."
- "Interstate location more desirable"
- "An up-to-date current property appraisal is helpful. Also, there is software available for measuring the potential value and potential revenue/gallonages of a new-build location, or for measuring the investment value of an existing location based on the gallonage, inside sales, quick food sales, and car wash sales."
- "The buyers/jobbers and lenders all accept the 5 times EBITDA."
- "Beer and wine license a plus; good deli counter a plus; 3,000+ sq. ft.; ample parking; easy in-out; extra storage; good corner location, ample inventory."
- "High sales volume with profit important; need loss leaders, especially milk and bread; good personnel; customer service important; open early morning; clean facility."

Rules of Thumb - **C**

Expert Comments

"Inside profit margins are not as sensitive as in other food operations. Folks shop for convenience, not price."

"Convenience stores in general have significantly dropped in price over the past few years. Demand for good stores is still very high but inside sales and rent are the most significant factors in deciding price and desirability."

"The fact that this is mostly a cash business, relatively less risky, easy to learn and replicate make this business appealing to many people. Some areas are obviously saturated and avoidable. In general, the industry is very marketable if and only if: seller has substantiating books and records for current 3 years and that daily inside sales are minimum $1,000–$1,500 (excluding extraneous revenues). Importance of location, traffic count and trading area demographic to this industry is no different than to any other retail business. Industry growth has been very stable."

"Easy to start up a convenience store location. Some areas are saturated with this type of business."

Benchmark Data

Statistics (Convenience Stores)

Number of Establishments	44,987
Average Profit Margin	1.4%
Revenue per Employee	$230,000
Average Number of Employees	3.4
Average Wages per Employee	$16,241

Products and Services Segmentation

Tobacco products	35.9%
Food service	19.4%
Packaged beverages	15.4%
Other	11.4%
Candy and snacks	10.6%
Beer	7.3%

Industry Costs

Profit	1.4%
Wages	7.1%
Purchases	78.5%
Depreciation	1.0%
Marketing	1.1%
Rent & Utilities	4.9%
Other	6.0%

Market Share

7-Eleven Inc.	24.0%

Source: IBISWorld, April 2015

- "According to NACS Constitution and Bylaws, the NACS Definition of a Convenience Store is:

C - Rules of Thumb

✓ '...a retail business with primary emphasis placed on providing the public a convenient location to quickly purchase from a wide array of consumable products (predominantly food or food and gasoline) and services.'

"While such operating features are not a required condition of membership, convenience stores have the following characteristics:

✓ While building size may vary significantly, typically the size will be less than 5,000 square feet;

✓ Off-street parking and/or convenient pedestrian access;

✓ Extended hours of operation with many open 24 hours, seven days a week;

✓ Convenience stores stock at least 500 SKUs; and

✓ Product mix includes grocery type items, and also includes items from the following groups" beverages, snacks, (including confectionery) and tobacco."

"While the top-performing chains on a whole continued to do well, the top 10%, or top decile, of stores had a few setbacks. Though its sales numbers were, as expected, higher than the other quartiles and higher than last year, the top-decile numbers were actually down in terms of return on capital employed, going from 19.16% in 2012 to 16.9% in 2013, according to NACS officials.

Top Decile vs. Top Quartile

2013	Top 10%	Top 25%
Store operating profit	$34,487	$26,593
Store operating profit per square foot	$16.15	$10.74
Break-even CPG	7.78c	7.66c
EBITDA	$31,923	$25,406
Net profit margin (pretax/sales)	2.61%	2.48%
Return on capital employed	16.90%	16.49%

In-Store Sales Contribution

Cigarettes	32.4%
Foodservice	18.0%
Packaged beverages	15.5%
Beer	7.9%
OTP	4.6%
Salty snacks	3.7%
Candy	3.1%
Packaged sweet snacks	2.0%
Milk	1.6%
Alternative	1.1%
All other	10.1%

In-Store Gross-Profit-Dollar Contribution

Category	Share of in-store gross-profit $
Foodservice	29.1%
Packaged beverages	19.6%
Cigarettes	14.4%
Beer	5.0%
Candy	4.5%
OTP	4.4%
Salty snacks	4.3%
Packaged sweet snacks	2.2%
Alternative	1.6%
Milk	1.3%
All other	13.6%

Direct store operating expenses

Item	2013 expense*	PCYA**
Wages and benefits	$17,147	3.4%
Credit-card charges	$5,728	1.3%
Utilities	$2,777	3.1%
Repairs and maintenance	$2,665	4.2%
Supplies	$980	-0.3%
Total DSOE	$40,956	4.4%
Facility expense	$9,175	8.3%
Rent/occupancy	$4,821	4.0%
Total DSOE & facility expense	$50,132	5.1%

* Per store per month
** Percent change from a year ago

Source: NACS® State of the Industry Summit Special Issue 2014

- "Beer Sales: Nearly 80 percent of convenience stores sell beer, accounting for nearly one-third of all beer purchased in the United States, about 93 percent of which is sold cold. In fact, the U.S. convenience store industry sells more than 2 billion gallons of beer a year—roughly one-third of all the beer purchased in the United States.

  "Candy Sales: Candy is a high-impulse item in convenience stores. In fact, many shoppers (49 percent) report that their candy purchases were unplanned, according to global research firm Envirosell.

  "Coffee Sales: More than three out of four adult Americans say that they drink coffee either daily or regularly, according to the National Coffee Association, and convenience stores are one of the preferred destinations for coffee drinkers. Consumers stop to buy coffee more than they fill up their cars, providing convenience stores with a great opportunity to build loyalty and repeat sales.

  "Technology: The integration of technology into convenience stores continues at a fast pace. Over the past decade, the convenience store industry has gone from being a technology laggard to a technology leader in using new technologies to deliver convenience.

  "While such operating features are not a required condition of membership, convenience stores have the following characteristics:
    - ✓ While building size may vary significantly, typically the size will be less than 5,000 square feet;
    - ✓ Off-street parking and/or convenient pedestrian access;
    - ✓ Extended hours of operation with many open 24 hours, seven days a week;
    - ✓ Convenience stores stock at least 500 SKUs; and
    - ✓ Product mix includes grocery type items, and also includes items from the following groups: beverages, snacks (including confectionery) and tobacco."

- "Average range of gross profit (GP) is 20% to 35% excluding gasoline revenue."
- "Two out of three (65 percent) of all convenience stores offer food prepared on site, and 91 percent offer commissary/packaged products."
- "Should strive for average 30 per cent 'weighted' inside margin on merchandise sales."
- "Rental less than $15 per square foot can make all the difference in a successful convenience store business."
- "C-stores annual sales $767,000; food service annual sales $115,000"

C - Rules of Thumb

Expenses as a percentage of annual sales

Cost of goods	60% or less— Good Store
Payroll/labor Costs	20% +/- (Owner operator will lower)
Occupancy	07% to 15% +/- (Rent or Mortgage Payment)
Profit (estimated pretax)	10% to 15% Gasoline Profit Should Cover Rent/Mortg

Industry Trend

- "While convenience stores have offered fresh, prepared foods for years, it is only over the last decade that the trend has accelerated. The reason is two-fold:
    - ✓ More and more time-starved consumers want on-the-go meal solutions, and
    - ✓ Retailers have found that foodservice can deliver new customers inside the store, and at a higher profit level than for items like gas."
- "The result is that convenience stores have continued to evolve from gas stations that happen to sell food to food retailers that happen to sell gas. The overall convenience store foodservice category includes: food prepared on-site, commissary/packaged sandwiches, hot dispensed beverages, cold dispensed beverages, and frozen dispensed beverages.

"Food Prepared On-Site—Many retailers have successfully turned their convenience stores into popular destinations for both hot and cold foods prepared onsite, such as deli sandwiches, flat breads, hoagies, breakfast sandwiches, hamburgers, pizza, grilled chicken sandwiches, salads, soups and wraps.

"A growing number of retailers use touch-screen ordering kiosks that allow customers to customize their selections, which streamlines speed of service and ensures the accuracy of orders. And to execute food prepared on-site effectively, foodservice management basics are a must: proper menu management, customer service and product consistency. Food prepared on-site leads the overall foodservice category, accounting for more than 62% of total foodservice sales in 2011.

"Commissary/Packaged Sandwiches—Convenience stores are stepping up their foodservice programs to keep up with competition from quick-service and fast-casual restaurants, as well as grocery store prepared meals. Many retailers offer a proprietary foodservice program where sandwiches, wraps and other fresh food items are prepared at a commissary.

"Hot Dispensed Beverages—Coffee is without a doubt the hot beverage of choice in convenience stores and the number one subcategory of the hot dispensed beverages category, generating 77% of the category's sales. This category typically delivers nearly three-quarts of its sales during morning service hours."

Source: "Convenience Stores Offer More Convenience," NACS Online—Research—Fact Sheets, www.nacsonline.com. This is a wonderful, informative Website.

Seller Financing

- "Seller financing for businesses is usually limited to 5 years. If real estate is involved, seller financing is usually limited to 10 years."
- "5 years all due and payable with 15-year amortization"
- 5 to 7 years

Rules of Thumb - C

Questions
- "Have your margins been shrinking over the past five years?"
- "Do you have accurate books so I can go to a bank for a loan?"
- "Any previous environmental issue, current leak test result, 3 years' tax return, lease agreement. Do you want to sell or test the market?"
- "Ask for 3 years of tax returns. Don't base buy decision on under-the-table numbers."
- "Amount of gross that's tobacco related. Lottery sales, any employee or customer thefts?"
- "Location, location, location; traffic count and number of rooftops dictate the best locations, along with traffic patterns, red lights, curb cut access, etc. Age and condition of petroleum and other equipment are important; environmental issues must be dealt with prior to closing. Phase I and II reports are almost always required for financing and property transfer. What is the mixture of sales? How do your sales break down concerning gas, merchandise/ cigarettes, beer, grill, deli? Have all of your EPA requirements been completed? How many robberies have you had since you bought the store? Do you have key people? Who supplies your gasoline? Who owns the gasoline equipment? Who is your wholesaler that supplies the majority of your groceries? Are there any convenience stores being built within two miles of the store?"

Resources

Websites
- CS News Online: www.csnews.com

Associations
- National Association of Convenience Stores—excellent site, lots of valuable information: www.nacsonline.com

---

Convenience Stores with Gas

(See also Convenience Stores, Gas Stations w/Convenience Stores/Mini-Marts)

SIC 5411-03	NAICS 447110	

Rules of Thumb

➢ Note: The information that follows is also in Gas Stations with C-Stores. It is a confusing issue, and perhaps there is no difference between a C-store with gas and a gas station with a C-store, but many experts still feel that there is. So here goes, again: Convenience stores with gas—these operations are more convenience stores than gas stations such as a 7-Eleven or Circle K. Gas stations with convenience stores (mini-marts)— these operations are more gas stations than convenience stores, such as Mobil, Shell and Exxon gas stations that have convenience stores. In many cases, the garages and stations themselves have been retrofitted to be convenience stores. These operations may include a car wash.

➢ 20 to 25 percent of annual sales plus inventory

➢ 2 to 2.5 times SDE plus inventory. 3.5 times SDE would be for SDE of $300,000+ on a consistent basis.

C - Rules of Thumb

- 1 to 2.5 SDE (with service bays) plus inventory.
- 2.25 to 3.75 times EBITDA (business only) higher multiples as EBITDA increases.
- 5 to 6 times SDE includes real estate
- 5 to 7 times EBITDA includes real estate
- "3.0 to 3.5 times EBITDA—including the real estate is a good rule of thumb for convenience stores with gas. 2.0 to 3.5 times EBITDA for leased sites. Current and future requirements from oil companies are reducing the overall number of stations across the country. Before you purchase any gas station make sure you ask the oil company what the future is of that particular site. Age and condition of the petroleum equipment and environmental issues are important considerations in selling these businesses. A Phase I & II are required for both purchased and leased sites if a loan is required through a bank or the SBA (very difficult in this environment).

Convenience Store with Gas, e.g., Circle K, Citgo

Index (multiple)		SDE	Gals/Mo
1.0x	to	$50K+	50K
2.25x	to	$90K+	75K+
2.75x	to	$150K+	100K+

The above value multiples do not include inventory (at cost).

- "7-Eleven convenience stores without gas are primarily controlled by the parent company (51%), thus your profit picture is relatively lower than the businesses shown above and therefore your multiples will be lower as well."

Pricing Tips

- "Based on EBIDTA, the multiplier could fluctuate from 0 to 2.5 depending on demographics, land and building size, additional room to expand other income centers, number of MPD's, quality of equipment, etc. If property is being purchased, we strongly recommend to hire the services of a reputable appraisal firm in order to obtain a valuation of it. This is normally ordered by the financial institution lending the funds."
- "Factors impacting value include: Location, Fuel Supply Contract and Length, Age of Tanks & Pumps, Environmental Issues, Liquor License"
- "The multiples used to be higher, however due to market conditions they have come down approximately 20% in the last two years. The eroding profit margin, measured as cents per gallon, has tightened up in the marketplace since then, resulting in the gas station owner being forced to look for volumes and margins elsewhere in the station. The snack shop/convenience store section has stepped up to the plate and accounts for about 80% of the profits, while the other 20% and all of the gasoline margin goes towards the costs of employees and such. Depending on the rent or the mortgage structure, the 80% figures adjust up or down. Do not let the huge sales volumes fool you; measure the gallons times the margin, and not the millions in actual sales/revenue figures."
- "Gross sales is not a good factor in pricing, since the profit margin varies between gas and grocery sales."
- "3 to 4 times EBITDA including the real estate is a common rule. Location, traffic count, brand, and population are important considerations."
- "It has nothing to do with total sales volume or revenue. It does have everything to do with average gallons sold, and margins per gallon; volatility in

Rules of Thumb - C

industry requires you map out gallons and margins per month for last 2 years. Majors tend to have flat fixed margins, minors and unbranded markets move between 2–4 cents to high of 25%–30% margins."
- "Dealer stations in our market sell for 2.2 to 2.5 post due diligence SDE for the business only. I value gas stations with the land by starting with SDE and deducting the buyer's required income for managing the station and any necessary reserves, and then I capitalize that amount by what I feel is the market cap rate. This is basically a real estate approach to the value."
- "Fewer and fewer stations surviving in today's competitive market."
- "Factors that most influence value are volume of gasoline sales, location, length, C-store versus service bays, traffic count and major brand identity."
- "Age of tanks; does station have canopy (is it cantilever or mech. attached); is it clean (environment); location, location, location."
- "The geographical site/location is key to a buyer in many offers and subsequent sells. Near freeways or interstates, high visibility corner locations or locations near major malls all come with a premium price tag."
- "The length of lease, the type of fuel supply contract (whether there is a contract with a major oil company or the buyer may purchase fuel on the open market) and the age and condition of the equipment will determine whether the site comes in at the low or high end of the range."
- "Sales and the gross profit on items like tobacco is indicative of the net"

Expert Comments

"The industry is experiencing a surge in mergers & acquisitions by national and regional chains. Mom and pop operations are slowly dwindling."

"Amount of Competition: More than the amount will be the brand of the competitors. Buyer should stay away from locations that have big brand names nearby known for price slashing. Amount of risk: Any business is subject to risk, but a professionally operated one will minimize this factor. Historical Profit Trend: Past history will not be relevant if positive factors are present such as demographics, land and building size, additional room to expand other income centers, number of MPD's, quality of equipment, etc., that will give the basis for success."

"Hard to replicate due to site work needed and tank cost"

"Expand the inside variety, sales, and profit, and depend less on the gas margins over which you have limited control."

"C-Stores are marketable if they are priced fairly. Up-to-date equipment, EPA compliance and motivation (reflected in the pricing) have a major influence on marketability. Good records to document sales both inside and outside are important factors too."

"A larger location is better. A full liquor license is harder to obtain. Tobacco products have a high cost and low profit. Higher rent costs."

"A convenience store is not too difficult to open by itself, especially if it's without gasoline. Convenience stores come in all kinds of formats: corner stores, main street, highway exits, inside malls, inside airports, inside college campuses, etc. Location is very important to get the walk-in traffic."

"High profit margin with varied merchandise and lots of smaller profit centers: cell phones, phone cards, money orders, lottery, Western Union, bill payment centers, deli, ATM, copy center, etc."

C - Rules of Thumb

Benchmark Data

- "What are the top three biggest business challenges you face today?
  Credit-card fees 56%
  Affordable Care Act 36.8%
  Continued economic weakness 36.8%
  Increased competition—c-stores 31.3%
  Increased competition—nontraditional retailers (food, drug, mass, dollar) 25.2%
  Minimum-wage increases 25.2%
  Employee turnover 24.5%
  Regulatory pressures 16.0%
  Declining fuel demand 14.7%
  Volatility/reduced margins on fuel .... 12.9%"
  Source: CSP Outlook Survey, CSP December 2014

- "Ownership of Convenience Stores Selling Fuel
  500+ Stores 16%
  201–500 Stores 6%
  51–200 Stores 6%
  11–50 Stores 9%
  2–10 Stores 5%
  1 Store .... 58%"
  Source: NACS/Nielsen 2014 Convenience Industry Store Count

- Miscellaneous Benchmark Data:
  - ✓ The U.S. convenience store industry has 151,000-plus stores that account for nearly $700 billion in sales.
  - ✓ As gas prices and the use of plastic at the pump have increased, consumers are increasingly concerned about the debit "holds" on their accounts.
  - ✓ While convenience stores have offered fresh, prepared foods for years, it is only over the last decade that the trend has accelerated. The result is that convenience stores have continued to evolve from gas stations that happen to sell food to food retailers that happen to sell gas.
  - ✓ Nearly 80% of convenience stores sell beer, accounting for more than 30% of all beer purchased in the United States.
  - ✓ With competition for consumers' hot dispensed beverage dollars is at an all-time high, convenience stores are one of the preferred destinations for coffee drinkers who want a quality cup of Joe quickly.
  - ✓ Candy Sales: Candy is a high-impulse item in convenience stores. In fact, many shoppers (49 percent) report that their candy purchases were unplanned, according to global research firm Envirosell.
  - ✓ Technology: The integration of technology into convenience stores continues at a fast pace. Over the past decade, the convenience store industry has gone from being a technology laggard to a technology leader in using new technologies to deliver convenience.
  Source: National Association of Convenience Stores

- Expenses Based on Sales
  Fuel sales: .... 1.3 million gallons, $3.08 million
  Gross profit margin: 6.9%
  In-store sales: .... $1.081 million
  Gross profit margin: 29.5%
  Pretax profit: .... $42,196, or 1.2 percent of revenue

Rules of Thumb - C

- "A good store should do a minimum of $750,000 to $1,000,000 in yearly sales plus lottery, and be at least 3,000 sq. ft. It should have a good deli counter and liquor, and a large parking lot with easy in and out. A free-standing building is better with extra storage."
- "Gross profit % of in store sales should be in the 30%–35% range; gasoline is almost a lost leader in many markets."
- "Determining benchmarks is very difficult because there are many factors that make a successful operation. Similarly, it is difficult to determine percentages of gross sales for various items, mainly because the gas prices fluctuate so much. An operation may have revenues of $3.5 million one year and $5 million the next year, without a material change in gas or store sales."
- "$480 per sq. ft. approx."
- "Factors that influence price and things to look for: Store sales should be greater than $30K per month to be considered a good business. When addressing the sales, do not add in the lottery sales. What percentage is the gross profit on average? The rent is a straight fee or a percentage of sales. Things to add into the value of this business: volume is greater than $40K per month, gross profit should be a minimum of 30 percent, appearance, part of a large gas station and/or car wash. Things to subtract in this business: volume is below $25K per month, gross profit is below 27 percent, competition in the neighborhood, part of a small gas station; e.g., Circle K or 7-Eleven, location, appearance."

Expenses as a percentage of annual sales

Cost of goods	70% or less—Good Store
Payroll/labor Costs	20% +/- (Owner-operator will lower)
Occupancy	05% to 07%
Profit (estimated pretax)	06% to 12%

Industry Trend

- "High competition amongst major convenience retailers. Bigger and better stores, more varieties and add-ons."
- "But, by far, the key message across most of the speaker programs was how the nation's changing demographics will impact business in the years ahead. The demographics of aging baby boomers, digitally-connected millennials and a larger multicultural population will have a profound effect on c-stores."

    Source: "Don't Put All Your Eggs in the Millennials' Basket" by Don Longo, Convenience Store News, 4/17/15

- "More than 75% of c-store retailers polled in the CSP Outlook Survey said business conditions in 2014 were 'good' or 'excellent,' the highest percentage in the history of the survey. More than 60% expect some or great improvement in 2015. Considering that more than 56% of survey participants this years were chains with one to 20 stores, it's an assessment that shows even small businesses—the c-store industry's core—are finally feeling an economic lift."

    Source: CSP, December 2014

- "Recent spiraling downward profits have weeded out significant numbers of weak businesses. Tight money, in turn, affects and lessens the overall asking price as well as the final price of stores. Fewer closings and they often take longer."
- "Very competitive industry with shrinking fuel margins forcing all profits to come from the inside sale of groceries, food, cigarettes and other items."

C - Rules of Thumb

Seller Financing
- "The most common financing is only for inventories for merchandise in the convenience store and fuel in the tanks. It normally will not exceed six months and will require some guarantee."
- "SBA and bank loans have become increasingly more difficult due to economic conditions and type of business"
- "7 years, on average 6 percent interest per annum."
- "As much as 50 percent of sales price could be financed—3 to 5 years typical."
- "Franchise—3 to 5 years (5 to 10 percent)"
- "4 to 7 years 6% interest"
- "Property—10 to 15 years (8 to 11 percent)"
- "7% to 8% interest"

Questions
- "Ask about sales trends, GP margins, gasoline margins and COGS."
- "• What is the present brand name and who supplies the gasoline? • What are the terms and length of the supply agreement? • What type of price is paid for the fuel? Rack, DTW, etc? • Report of gallons sold and purchased as well as pool margins for the last year. • What are the terms of the lease (if applicable)? Are there any subleases on the property? • What is the car count as per DOT? Is it a signalized corner intersection • Does the station have compliant tanks, piping and monitoring systems? • Are there any planned road changes? • Does the property have any existing right of way reservations? • Is there a recent appraisal? • Is the station environmentally clean? If not, is it under a federal cleanup program? • Is there a pending or executed foreclosure activity in the property? • Does the station have a generator capable of handling pumping of gas and coolers in C-Store in case of a disaster? • Is the station in an area of restricted zoning or a zoning moratorium on petroleum facilities? • Fuel service—size of canopy and if it connects to C-Store, quality of dispensers, point-of-sale readers, etc. • Quality and brand of MPD's (gas pumps) • Building size and type—kiosk, small, traditional, expanded, hyper • Hours of operation—24 hours x 7 days a week or less • Competition—How many stations are on the remaining three corners, within a two mile radius and what brands? • Store Size, layout and equipment. Is any of the equipment leased? • Number of SKU's (stock keeping units) in the C-Store—usually 2,870 average • Product mix of inventory—closely related to the demographics of the area • Overall pricing of items (high, average, low) • Is cashier enclosed with bulletproof glass? General area security • What income centers does the station have including food services? (see below) • What factors have influenced the volume for the gas, store, car wash, etc.? • How is the local trade area changing and why? Market Outlook • Property Taxes and Insurance cost • Residential density— important, otherwise it becomes a Monday to Friday gas station • Parking—how many spaces? • Visibility—must be free of obstructions • Ingress & egress • Car Wash—building size, length of tunnel, brand & quality of the equipment • Convenient pedestrian access & off-street parking • External appearance—cannot be an eye sore • Quality and cleanliness of public bathrooms • Are there any planned renovations?"
- "5 years' financial and gas sales history; phase I & II environmental reports"
- "Crime history, employee turnover and rent."
- "Be sure to ask the seller if he has signed a fuel purchase agreement with

Rules of Thumb - C

a jobber or oil company. Is the seller getting any rebates from the jobber or oil company? Is the seller getting any hold-back money from his cigarette suppliers? Are there any additional state or local or city taxes that are an add-on up and beyond what your competitors pay? And then the big one: What is the environmental status of the property? Are there any outstanding environmental issues? Does the state that the property is located in have a cleanup fund? Most states have an insurance fund that has a deductible from $10,000 to $50,000. However, some states do not have a fund and the owner of the property is required to buy separate insurance. This is a must to find out. You can sell the store and have everything done and won't be able to get the deal financed because of environmental issues. Be careful. Find all of this out first before you get into the deal too far."

- "Do you have tax returns for the past 3 years? Do your P&L's agree with the tax returns? Have you had any fuel contamination issues? If so, are they resolved? What is the pool margin (profit over the rack price)?"

Resources

Trade Publications
- Convenience Store Products: www.cspnet.com

Associations
- National Association of Convenience Stores—excellent site, lots of valuable information: www.nacsonline.com

	Franchise
Cost Cutters Family Hair Care (See also Barber Shops, Beauty Shops, Fantastic Sam's, Franchises, Great Clips, Hair Care)	
Approx. Total Investment	$116,095 to $317,465
SIC 7241-01 NAICS 812112	Number of Businesses/Units 850

Rules of Thumb
- ➢ 55 to 60 percent of annual sales plus inventory

Resources

Websites
- www.costcutters.com

Country/General Stores		
SIC 5399-02	NAICS 452990	

Rules of Thumb
- ➢ 20 percent of annual sales plus inventory

26th Edition

C - Rules of Thumb

Coupon Books (See also Direct Mail—Advertising, Franchises, Valpak)	
NAICS 541870	

Rules of Thumb
- ➢ 2 to 4 times EBITDA

Seller Financing
- "Not usually seller financed. If financed, 2 to 3 years."

Court Reporting Services		
SIC 7338-01	NAICS 561492	Number of Businesses/Units 170,905

Rules of Thumb
- ➢ 30 to 35 percent of annual revenues includes inventory

Benchmark Data

- Court Reporting Services in the U.S. (The report below is the latest available)

Statistics (Court Reporting Services)

Number of Enterprises	170,905
Average Wages per Employee	$23,647
Average Profit Margin	4.0%
Average Revenue of Enterprise	$106,258

Share of employer establishments by employment size, 2005

Employment Size	Share (%)
1 to 4 Employees	71.3

Industry Costs

Profit	4%
Depreciation	4%
Other	54.4%
Wages	37.6%

- "There are no major players in this industry."

   Source: IBISWorld, August 2009

- IBISWorld has discontinued updating this business. We have left the last report as it still contains information of interest.

- "According to the AOC study, which was done by the staff of the National Center for State Courts, the average state-employed court reporter earns $53,000 in salary and $1.25 for every page of a court record transcribed."

   Source: "N.C. weighs necessity of court reporters; 'it's all about the money' by Michael Gordon, *Charlotte Observer*, February 10, 2014

Industry Trend
- "Of the more than 50,000 court reporters in the United States, more than 70 percent work outside of the courtroom, according to the National Court Reporters Association."

Rules of Thumb - **C**

- "Statistics project that jobs in this field will grow more than 18 percent between 2008 and 2018—a good deal faster than the average for all occupations."
- "'Court reporting is forecasted by the U.S. Department of Labor to grow at the rate of 14 percent between now and 2020. With the present workforce so competitive, it is important that students learn about this unique and age-old profession that can take as little as two years to enter and one that offers a full-time average salary according to the U.S. Department of Labor Bureau of Statistics of $62,000 nationwide and upwards of $83,000 in the New York area' said Stuart M. Auslander, the school's director."

Source: http://www.ncra.org/News/newsdetail.cfm?ItemNumber=15025 April 2, 2014

Resources

Associations
- The U.S. Court Reporters Association: www.uscra.org
- American Association of Electronic Reporters and Transcribers: www.aaert.org
- National Court Reporters Association: www.ncraonline.org

	Franchise
Coverall Health-Based Cleaning Systems (Commercial Cleaning) (See also Franchises)	
Approx. Total Investment	$14,148–$47,656
NAICS 561720	Number of Businesses/Units 8,045

Rules of Thumb
- 2 to 3 times monthly volume
- Master/Area developer—sell for 3 to 5 times earnings plus some blue sky for size and potential of market (some cases).
- 4 times EBITDA

Pricing Tips
- "The four basic components of determining the value and price of a Master Franchise of Coverall include the collective principal amount of Franchisee Notes outstanding, the value of the exclusive rights to the population territory inclusive of the number of businesses with 5 or more employees, the value of the business structure (number of commercial accounts serviced and the number of franchisees) and the cash flow of the territory."

Expenses as a percentage of annual sales
Cost of goods	80%
Payroll/labor Costs	04%
Occupancy	01%
Profit (estimated pretax)	10%

Resources

Websites
- www.coverall.com

C - Rules of Thumb

Culligan International—Franchise/Dealership	Franchise
(See also Franchises)	
Approx. Total Investment	$35,000
NAICS 422490	Number of Businesses/Units 654

Rules of Thumb

> 80 to 120 percent of gross annual sales—dependent on several things: market size, current penetration rental base, water quality, etc.

Seller Financing
- "Frequently 7 to 10 years."

Resources

Websites
- www.culligan.com

Curves for Women (See also Fitness Centers, Franchises)	Franchise
Approx. Total Investment	$15,000 to $45,000
SIC 7299-06 NAICS 713940	Number of Businesses/Units 9,400

Rules of Thumb

> 1.5 to 2 times SDE includes inventory

> 30 percent of annual sales includes inventory

Pricing Tips
- "1.5 to 2 times SDE. The number of monthly check drafts and club size and location are important value factors along with membership trends."
- "Most clubs need 175–200 members to break even. 90% EFT is typical."

Expert Comments

"Acquisitions of existing franchises are generally excellent investments as a result of expected return on investment, market potential, and ongoing franchisor investment and research in the fitness industry."

"Other franchisors using the '30-minute-circuit' program have entered the marketplace with very mixed results. Current Curves locations have closed in market areas which were saturated."

Benchmark Data
- "1.5 employees per $100K sales"
- "It takes about 125 members to break even."
- "Usually owner-operated facilities are run at minimal expenses."

Rules of Thumb - D

Expenses as a percentage of annual sales

Cost of goods	05%
Payroll/labor Costs	20% to 25%
Occupancy	10% to 15%
Profit (estimated pretax)	25% to 30%

Seller Financing
- 3 years

Questions
- "What was your highest membership number? Review monthly membership history for last 3–5 years. Why do members join your club? Why do/don't they renew yearly membership? Explain club safety/parking lot issues if any. Review lease. Any complaints from adjoining tenants concerning music/noise issues? What are the nearest Curves Clubs to you? Other competing franchise clubs?"

Dairy Drive-Thru
NAICS 722515

Rules of Thumb
➢ 25 percent of annual sales plus inventory

Benchmark Data
- See Food Stores—Specialty

Dairy Queen (See also Franchises, Ice Cream/Yogurt Shops) — Franchise

Approx. Total Investment	$400,000 to $1,000,000
Estimated Annual Sales/Unit	$700,000
SIC 2024-98 NAICS 722513	Number of Businesses/Units 6,111

Rules of Thumb
➢ Price = 1.1 to 1.2 times annual sales for stores w/real estate
➢ Price = .45 times sales for leased facility. Rent = variable item
➢ "Walk-up"— two windows with real estate—1.24 (+/-) times annual sales
➢ Without real estate —.5 (+/-) times annual sales
➢ Full Brazier— with real estate—1.15 (+/-) times annual sales
➢ Without real estate—.5 (+/-) annual sales"

Pricing Tips
- "Dairy Queens: With Real Estate = 1.1X sales. IDQ leaning toward 'Corporate' type ownership, moving away from 'Ma & Pa' owners."

D - Rules of Thumb

Expert Comments
"Many players in this market"

Benchmark Data

Expenses as a percentage of annual sales

Cost of goods	31%
Payroll/labor Costs	25%
Occupancy	08%
Profit (estimated pretax)	15%

Seller Financing
- "Rarely seller financed"
- "5 years with balloon payment."
- "SBA financing—17 to 18 years with real estate; 7 to 10 years without real estate."

Questions
- Questions to ask seller: "Leased facility—rent important;owned facility—loan & taxes important"

Resources

Websites
- www.dairyqueen.com

Data Processing Services

SIC 7374-01	NAICS 541513	Number of Businesses/Units 67,328

Rules of Thumb
➢ 15 percent of annual sales plus inventory
➢ 2.2 times SDE plus inventory
➢ 2 times EBIT
➢ 2.2 times EBITDA

Pricing Tips
- "The Data Processing and Hosting Services industry has a medium level of capital intensity. For every $1.00 spent on wages, an estimated $0.19 is allocated toward capital expenditure in 2015. Although investment in capital has remained stable during the past five years, wages' share of revenue has risen. As a result, the industry's capital intensity level has declined during the five years to 2015.

  "The industry is labor-, skill- and knowledge-intensive but with significant need for computing and software-related equipment. Labor costs are the largest expense for industry operators, representing an estimated 43.0% of revenue in 2015."

Source: IBISWorld, January 2015

Rules of Thumb - **D**

- "A proprietary software component could raise the multiple to as much as 10 x."

Benchmark Data

Statistics (Data Processing & Hosting Services)
Number of Establishments 67,328
Average Profit Margin 13.3%
Revenue per Employee $196,900
Average Number of Employees 9.2
Average Wages per Employee $88,108

Products and Services Segmentation
Application service provisioning 23.8%
Other services and data processing 22.2%
Business process management and data processing provisioning 18.4%
Data storage and management services management services 11.1%
Website hosting services support services 10.1%
IT technical support services network management services 9.1%
IT computer network and network management services hosting services 5.3%

Major Market Segmentation
Non-financial enterprises 39.0%
Resellers 26.0%
Financial firms 16.0%
Government organizations 12.0%
Content providers 7.0%

Industry Costs
Profit 13.3%
Wages 44.7%
Purchases 14.5%
Depreciation 8.2%
Marketing 3.4%
Rent and Utilities 4.8%
Other 11.1%

Market Share
International Business Machines Corporation 12.5%
Hewlett-Packard Development Company LP 9.6%

Source: IBISWorld, June 2015

- "Location is not important. Skill sets and experience of employees is the key to larger contracts. Annual maintenance contracts based on number of 'seats' is more valuable than service contracts."

Expenses as a percentage of annual sales
Cost of goods .... n/a
Payroll/labor Costs 35%
Occupancy .... n/a
Profit (estimated pretax) 40%

26th Edition   219

D - Rules of Thumb

Industry Trend

- "The pullback in information technology (IT) spending immediately following the recession resulted in a slowdown of industry growth rather than a decline in revenue. The Data Processing and Hosting Services industry's performance will improve over the next five years due to renewed IT spending and increased outsourcing by nonindustry companies seeking to trim IT costs. "Consolidation within other industries will likely push more companies to a level of complexity in which the outsourcing of their IT needs is more convenient and affordable than maintaining those services in-house. Meanwhile, the increasing prevalence of internet-based media and services has continued driving this industry's revenue beyond prerecessionary highs."

   Source: IBISWorld, January 2015

- "More maintenance contracts vs. service contracts"

Questions

- "Ask for resumes of employees and meeting with a few top customers during due diligence."

Dating Services

SIC 7299-26	NAICS 812990	Number of Businesses/Units 4,884

Rules of Thumb

➢ 30 to 35 percent of annual sales

Pricing Tips

- "It's also heading to even bigger money. Last year, the mobile dating market reported revenue of almost $213 million, up 29% from the previous year, according to market research company IBISWorld. In the next five years, revenue is expected to nearly double to more than $415 million."

   Source: "Mobile apps tap the changing face of online dating," www.usatoday.com, February/2013

Expert Comments

"Regulators across the world have sought to regulate dating services, as they try to protect the growing number of individuals that use them. Mainstream sites such as eHarmony and Match.com, alone, have 20 million and 17 million worldwide users respectively."

Source: "Online dating: growth, regulation, and future challenges" by Elena Magrina, Policy Analyst at Inline Policy, 9/8/14

Benchmark Data

Statistics (Dating Services)

Number of Establishments	4,884
Average Profit Margin	13.2%
Revenue per Employee	$307,800
Average Number of Employees	1.7
Average Wages per Employee	$79,679

Rules of Thumb - D

Products and Services Segmentation

Online dating	48.7%
Mobile dating	26.2%
Matchmakers	14.2%
Singles events	6.7%
Other	4.2%

Major Market Segmentation

Consumers 25 to 34 years old	33.3%
Consumers 35 to 44 years old	25.8%
Consumers 18 to 24 years old	15.2%
Consumers 45 to 54 years old	12.1%
Consumers 55 to 64 years old	9.1%
Consumers 65 years and older	4.5%

Industry Costs

Profit	13.2%
Wages	26.2%
Purchases	8.7%
Depreciation	2.3%
Marketing	18.9%
Rent & Utilities	4.4%
Other	26.3%

Market Share

InterActive Corp	21.8%
eHarmony Inc.	13.5%
Zoosk Inc.	5.0%

Source: IBISWorld, April 2015

Online Dating Statistics

Total number of single people in the U.S.	54,250,000
Annual revenue from the online dating industry	$1,249,000,000
Average spent by dating site customer per year	$239
Percent of users who leave within the first 3 months	10%
Percent of male online users	52.4%
Percent of female online users	47.6%
Percent of marriages in the last year in which the couple met on a dating site	17%

Source: Reuters, *Herald News*, PC World, *Washington Post*, January 1, 2014

- "In less than two decades, online dating has soared and is 'in the growth phase of its economic life cycle,' says an IBISWorld report. Though 18- to 29-year-olds make up the biggest chunk of users, with 30- to 49-year-olds next in line, demand is expected to increase with the north-of-50 crowd, too. More than one-third of Baby Boomers are unmarried, and as more and more migrate to the digital world, the industry is beginning to target this unattached and largely underserved market."

    Source: "Mobile apps tap the changing face of online dating," www.usatoday.com, February 2013

Industry Trend

- "The Internet and dating will continue to be a match made in heaven. With consumers using the Internet more than ever before, demand for online dating

D - Rules of Thumb

services is on the rise. In particular, demand from niche dating networks and baby boomers is increasing, and a new wave of smartphone applications will bring the industry to more people."

Source: IBISWorld, April 2015

- "Millions of people first met their spouses through online dating. But how have those marriages fared compared with those of people who met in more traditional venues such as bars or parties? Pretty well, according to a new study. A survey of nearly 20,000 Americans reveals that marriages between people who met online are at least as stable and satisfying as those who first met in the real world—possibly more so.

    "In fact, people who met online were slightly less likely to divorce and scored slightly higher on marital satisfaction. After controlling for demographic differences between the online and real-world daters, those differences remained statistically significant, the team reports online today in the Proceedings of the National Academy of Science."

    Source: "Online Dating Really Can Lead to Love" by John Bohannon, http://news.sciencemag.org/2013/06/online-dating-really-can-lead-love, June 3, 2013

- "The challenge for the industry long term, experts suggest, is that its goals—making money and growing an audience—are somewhat at odds with those of its customers.

    "'It is kind of a weird category,' says Peter Farago, marketing vice president at Flurry Analytics, a firm that analyzes smartphone and app activity.'Success for the consumer is they pair off and meet someone and no longer use the service.'

    "Lesnick says the typical online dater stays with a service two to four months—paying an average of $20 a month (some as high as $60)—and then is gone."

    Source: "Mobile apps tap the changing face of online dating," www.usatoday.com, February/2013

Resources

Trade Publications
- Online Dating Magazine: www.onlinedatingmagazine.com

Day Care Centers/Adult (See also Assisted Living, Nursing Homes)		
SIC 8322-10	NAICS 624120	Number of Businesses/Units 5,984
Rules of Thumb		
➢ 70 to 75 percent of annual sales		

Pricing Tips
- "A higher price can be justified if the mix of clients is more private pay than Medicaid reimbursement or paid by other government programs. Additional revenue and profit and thus value/price can be obtained by adding services such as bathing, in home care service and transportation."

Expert Comments
"The time to reach breakeven is relatively long as this is still a relatively new segment of senior healthcare. The majority of adult day care centers are run by non-profit entities. The challenge for adult day care owners is to

Rules of Thumb - **D**

build a payer mix that is not dependent upon governmental programs (i.e., Medicaid) and to focus on the private pay client. Unlike the in-home non-medical care business, this is a 'bricks & mortar' investment with significant initial build-out cost but has a staffing model that is perfect for an absentee owner or an owner/operator."

Benchmark Data

Statistics (Adult Day Care)

Number of Establishments	5,984
Average Profit Margin	7.5%
Revenue per Employee	$48,800
Average Number of Employees	24.9
Average Wages per Employee	$21,864

Products and Services Segmentation

Social and medical model	44.0%
Social model	33.0%
Medical model	23.0%

Industry Costs

Profit	7.5%
Wages	44.5%
Purchases	17.6%
Depreciation	2.3%
Marketing	2.3%
Rent & Utilities	7.1%
Other	18.7%

Source: IBISWorld, June 2015

- "Center for Health Statistics Releases First Round of Reports on Adult Day Services" by Peter Notarstefano, December 13, 2013
"The Center for Disease Control National Center for Health Statistics (NCHS) released on December 12, 2013, the first in a series of reports from the National Study of Long-Term Care Providers (NSLTCP). The report, Long-Term Care Services in the United States: 2013 Overview, provides information on the supply, organizational characteristics, staffing, and services offered by providers of long-term care services including adult day services.
"The report also includes demographic, health, and functional characteristics of users of these services. This report includes information on findings adult day services centers, home health agencies, hospices, nursing homes, and residential care communities.
"Some Interesting findings:
  ✓ The largest share of adult day services centers (32.4%) were in the South.
  ✓ The largest number of adult day centers were located in Metropolitan areas (60.7%).
  ✓ 36.8% of the adult day centers were located in areas that had a census of less than 10,000 people.
  ✓ The majority of adult day providers were not for profits (54.9%).
  ✓ 47.3% of adult day programs served over 101 participants per day.

D - Rules of Thumb

- ✓ 69.4% of programs had full time personal care aides.
- ✓ 19.2% of programs had full time RNs, however; the study did not distinguish between medical model and adult day services models with each state.
- ✓ 63.5% of programs had social work services.
- ✓ 47.3% offered mental health or counseling services.
- ✓ 63.8% offered some type of therapeutic services.
- ✓ 70.1% provided skilled nursing services.
- ✓ 34.9% provided some type of pharmacy services.
- ✓ 24.4% of adult day programs have hospice services.
- ✓ New Jersey had the highest daily enrollment in adult day (12 participants per thousand).
- ✓ 36.5% of adult day participants were under 65.
- ✓ 27.2% were age 75 to 84.
- ✓ 16.9% were 85 years old and older.
- ✓ 59.6% of adult day participants were women.
- ✓ 31.9% of adult day participants had Alzheimer's disease or another dementia.
- ✓ 23.5% of adult day participants had a diagnosis of depression.
- ✓ 39.6% needed assistance with bathing (included both medical and social model programs).
- ✓ 36.2% needed assistance with toileting.
- ✓ "97% of the adult day programs that responded to the survey were either licensed or certified by their state or participated in the Medicaid program. The report shows that in 2012, about 58,000 paid, regulated long-term care services providers served about 8 million people in the U.S. Each day in 2012 there were 273,200 participants enrolled in adult day services centers, 1,383,700 residents in nursing homes, and 713,300 residents in residential care communities."

Source: "National Study of Long-Term Care Providers," http://nadsa.org/nsltcp/

Expenses as a percentage of annual sales

Cost of goods	0
Payroll/labor Costs	25%
Occupancy	20%
Profit (estimated pretax)	20%

Industry Trend

- "Not a wheelchair or walker was in sight at these so-called social adult day care centers [in New York]. Yet the cost of attendance was indirectly being paid by Medicaid, under Gov. Andrew M. Cuomo's sweeping redesign of $2 billion in spending on long-term care meant for the impaired elderly and those with disabilities.

"Managed care became mandatory last year for people receiving home services who are eligible for both Medicaid and Medicare. The idea is to try to control spending, but about a third of the 92,000 people so far enrolled in the system statewide [NY] are newcomers to such services, many responding to aggressive marketing by social day care centers.

"Centers collected over $25 million from managed care plans in the first nine

Rules of Thumb - **D**

months of 2012, at roughly $93 per person per session, according to state figures. The managed care companies are paid by Medicaid; in New York City, the rate is about $3,800 a month per member."

Source: "Day Centers Sprout Up, Luring Fit Elders and Costing Medicaid" by Nina Bernstein, www.nytimes.com, published April 22, 2013

Seller Financing
- "Yes, usually for three (3) years."

Questions
- "What is your capacity and current loading? What is your payer mix? Do you provide any benefits to your employees? Is your occupancy cost above or below market? Are you a franchise? Is the owner the operator or an absentee owner? Do you also provide in-home care services in addition to your base adult day care offering?"

Resources

Associations
- National Adult Day Services Association: www.nadsa.org

Day Care Centers/Children (See also Schools)

SIC 8351-01	NAICS 624410	Number of Businesses/Units 785,634

Rules of Thumb

➢ 50 to 55 percent of annual sales includes inventory

➢ 2.5 to 3 times EBIT

➢ 3 to 4 times EBITDA

➢ 2 times SDE includes inventory. Most childcare centers are acquired with the real estate. The 2 multiple of SDE is after the debt service required to buy the real estate.

➢ Depending on the size of the facility (licensed capacity), location, and demographics of the area, the rule of thumb is:
  Center Size
  <40 .... 1 to times SDE
  40 to 85 .... 2 to 3 times (depending on expansion possibilities) SDE
  100+ .... 3 to 4 times SDE

➢ Pricing ranges from 1.5 to 4 times EBITDA depending upon the size (licensed) of the facility. The larger the facility, generally the higher the multiple.

➢ Two times cash flow for smaller centers (licensed for under 75). Up to four times cash flow for larger centers (licensed for 100 +).

Pricing Tips
- "...industry experts say operating a child day care business can be an ongoing struggle to balance expenses with parents' ability to pay. Regulations

D - Rules of Thumb

can add to costs—sometimes before operators are able to recover the increase through higher fees."

- "Percentage of Annual Revenue—30% to 45% of annual revenue for the business value only
Percentage of Annual Revenue—140% to 300% of annual revenue for the value of the real estate and business together
Multiple of Sellers Discretionary Cash Flow (SDCF) for the business value only—For centers licensed for under 100 children: 1 to 2 times annual SDCF; for centers licensed for 100 to 250 children: 2 to 2.5 times annual SDCF; for very profitable centers licensed over 250 children: 2.5 to 3.5 times annual SDCF. SDCF is also referred to as Adjusted Profits. It is calculated as: EBITDA + the Owner's Compensation.
Multiple of Earnings before Interest, Taxes, Depreciation, & Amortization (EBITDA) for the business value only—3 to 4 times annual EBITDA
Based on licensed capacity—$1,000 to $2,500 per child for the business value only
Based on licensed capacity—$6,000 to $14,000 per child for the real estate and business together"
- "Need 120+ capacity to be marketable. Capacity utilization above 75%. Prefer operator owns real estate."
- "Businesses with EBITDA of less than $100,000 will generally sell at a much lower multiple say 2–3 times, where an EBITDA of $300,000 will be 3.5–4 times. Building type, location, occupancy levels play a more important role in sale price than just the profit; centers with daily fees of under $60 per day per child will struggle to sell at any price; centers with a license of 50–80 children are the most; sort out sizes."
- "Centers that are above 100 children capacity or those generating in excess of $200k can be as high as 4 times SDE. While smaller centers that have a capacity of 50 children or less or with an SDE of only $50k command only a 1–1.5 times SDE. If renting/leasing the real estate—in most areas the rent should not be more than $10 sq. ft. (i.e., 4,000 sq. ft. = $4,000 a month maximum). However larger cities and counties like Miami-Dade could go as high as $30 a sq. ft."
- "In successful centers the SDE is usually around 25–30% of gross sales"
- "State regulations play a major role in the valuation of a child care business. As a general rule, higher degree of regulation often leads to higher quality of child care and lower business value due to cost of regulatory compliance. Child care market rates are not keeping pace with the cost to meet state regulations."
- "Competition, and location, ease of access, and capacity of center important"
- "State quality/star ratings and licensed capacity are drivers influencing multiplier; rarely gets above 3.75 multiple unless licensed for over 160 children and has earnings to support debt service after director salary(s)"
- "For a quick check you can use license cap times area sales ($10,000 a kid times 100 kids= X)"
- "Site location is critical; curb cuts and ease of access in/out of center is very important; proper side of road for traffic flow during rush hour; tenure of center, tenure of teachers and their level of secondary education; strong director/mgr. very important; quality centers with consistent earnings achieve price points in the higher end of the price range than other centers."
- "Size matters. Licensed capacity less than 75 expect a 2 1/2 to 3 times EBITDA, over 100 expect a 4 +/- EBITDA multiple."

Rules of Thumb - D

Expert Comments

"Run it like a business—not as an educator or on passion."

"Cleaner centers tend to do better and keep a higher enrollment while smaller, dirtier centers are closing their doors. Bottom line—reinvest in the business. Keep the doors and walls free of used tape and staples."

"Replication more difficult in states with high regulatory compliance"

"It would take 6–12 months to start from ground up, dealing with DCF licensure, health department, fire department, etc."

"Be careful to make sure that the seller isn't being taxed twice on any reimbursements from any governmental agencies."

"There are numerous governmental agencies to deal with in transferring ownership of a center. It can take anywhere from a few weeks to a few months from the time of the offer until the deal actually closes."

"While it is relatively easy to replicate a child-care business, value can be created in a center that has a track record and has been in existence for decades."

"Lots of competition"

"Newer facilities will command a higher service cost. Make sure the educational program keeps pace with changes in the educational sector. Some businesses have dual licenses and are licensed by the Department of Education."

"Very expensive to start a medium to large center from the ground up"

"Many variables here; location is key factor; strong operators/directors can achieve 22%–28% EBITDA depending on location, state & federal programs, level of income in area, etc."

"Depending upon growth rate of young population base, the better the curriculum the more difficult the business is to replicate."

"Risk is increasing due to over-competition in some markets, high entry cost due to real estate cost and regulations."

"Other than 'occupancy costs' all other expenses are pretty proportional to enrollment or gross revenues and are easily managed as such. If rent can be tied to enrollment, then risk is greatly reduced (example: 10% of gross receipts for rent)."

"$1,000 to $2,500 per licensed child capacity depending on the success of current business"

"Real estate can be the largest value in a day-care transaction. Rent should be adjusted to reflect Fair Market Value (FMV) rent based on a) comparable information available or, b) a percentage of the real estate appraisal value and, c) cross-checked by making sure, if financed, that the rent will cover the debt services (and a return on the down payment)."

D - Rules of Thumb

Benchmark Data

Statistics (Day Care)

Number of Establishments	785,634
Average Profit Margin	13.3%
Revenue per Employee	$28,300
Average Number of employees	2.1
Average Wages per Employee	$14,255

Products and Services Segmentation

Child day care services	58.7%
Preschool programs	19.2%
Government contributions	13.1%
Other services and receipts	9.0%

Industry Costs

Profit	13.3%
Wages	50.4%
Purchases	13.3%
Depreciation	2.3%
Marketing	0.4%
Rent & Utilities	15.6%
Other	4.7%

Source: IBISWorld, May 2015

- "Benchmarks are only accurate if for the same state, licensed size or rating scale. It is not possible to accurately compare child care businesses located in different states operating under different laws and regulations."
- "The U.S. child care services industry includes about 53,000 commercial facilities with combined annual revenue of $20 billion, plus about 21,000 facilities run by nonprofit organizations with combined annual revenue of about $13 billion. Major companies include Bright Horizons Family Solutions, Knowledge Universe, and Learning Care Group. The industry is highly fragmented: the top 50 companies generate less than 20 percent of revenue... The industry is labor-intensive: annual revenue per worker is about $38,000."
- "Small centers (under 100) need to have an owner/operator to realize a profit. Over 100 and it can be run by an absentee owner. Any rent above $10–$12 a square foot is too much."
- "Approximately 2.3 million individuals earn a living caring for and educating children under age 5 in the United States, of which about 1.2 million are providing child care in formal settings, such as child-care centers or family child-care homes. The remaining 1.1 million caregivers are paid relatives, friends, or neighbors.

Provider Setting	Number of Workers	Percent of Workers
Center-Based Staff	550,000	24%
Family Child Care Home Providers	650,000	28%
Paid Relatives	804,000	34%
Paid Non-Relatives	298,000	13%
Total	2,301,000	100%

"Child-care providers earn an average wage of only $9.46 an hour. With average salaries of $19,670 a year for child-care workers, many individuals holding these jobs do not earn very much more than the 2007 federal poverty level of $17,170 annually for a family of three."

Source: "Child Care Workforce," www.naccrra.org

- "Rents $1,700–$5,000 per child per year; staff $8,500–$10,500 per child per year; $15,000–$30,000 per child for a good leasehold center"
- "Labor is 35% to 50% of revenue."
- "Minimum $1,000 net profit per full-time enrollment to $3,000."
- "State's license based upon square footage per child. Physical layout combined with rent is a large factor in determining profitability of a business."
- "Depends on area, but we've sold schools based on Lic Cap $10,000 to $16,000 per child."
- "Each state varies between $5,000—$10,000/student fees."
- "Labor expense of 35% to 45% is good."
- "20%–24% EBITDA; Strong, tenured director and teachers, high education level of staff, good visibility; payroll costs 43%–48% of sales."
- "Easier to sell small and large centers, harder to sell medium-size centers."
- "10% net operating profit"

Expenses as a percentage of annual sales	
Cost of goods	10%
Payroll/labor Costs	40% to 55%
Occupancy	10% to 20%
Profit (estimated pretax)	10% to 18%

Industry Trend
- "With low unemployment, the childcare industry will do well."
- "Will follow general economy"
- "Steady"
- "Federal health officials proposed to overhaul 500,000 child care centers across the country, beefing up safety standards including background and fingerprint checks for employees and requiring states to better monitor the facilities."
- "Roughly 1.6 million U.S. children attend child care centers on subsidies—paid in the form of vouchers to families—from the federal government."
- "Continued growth, especially in some ethnic groups. Pricing schedules will not increase due to economy. Parents will seek out alternative, less expensive child care options."
- "Depending upon the demographic area, some consolidation"
- "Number of centers will stay flat. Cost to open is high."
- "Solid growth; education requirements becoming more important and required"
- Growing industry, but it costs more to set up center because of real estate cost."
- "Regional and national chains will continue buyouts."

Seller Financing
- "5% to 10% seller financing; the rest of the financing is from SBA loans."
- "Three to five years w/o RE, 15 to 20 years with RE"
- "Most are 90 percent SBA financed."
- "Business only—7 to 10 years."

D - Rules of Thumb

Questions

- "Occupancy records, look at competitors' occupancy as well. The future is more important than the past!"
- "Capacity, enrollment, rates, revenue, estimated profitability, facility. Does business owner or closely related 3rd party entity own the real estate? Detailed info on staff (hire dates & their credentials). Center's distinguishing characteristics. Describe local competition (reputation/rates/size/enrollment as % of capacity/advantages/disadvantages). Reason for sale?"
- "Are you on the food program? Subsidized care? Gold Seal?"
- "Tell me about staff turnover, infractions reported to licensing agencies (and cures for infractions), inspection report violations and new or threatened competitors."
- "Does the provider have a contract with the children's parents? If yes, ask for the contract. Does the provider have a rate schedule? Is the same schedule used for all children or do some have a special rate? Determine which children have a different rate and the amount. If the provider does not have the rate schedule for the year in question, ask for the current rate schedule and then ask how it differed in the tax year under exam. Does the provider furnish year-end statements to the parents as to how much they paid in the tax year?"
- "Any state subsidies? Review price schedule. Listing of all licenses—NAEYC accredited? Any claims against center? Confirm enrollment counts. Discuss curriculum. Education/experience of staff."
- "What local, state & gov. programs are you getting funding from & how much per age group... then go & verify from the state & counties how much of this money you will NOT be getting during the 6–8-month probationary period post closing & what the risks are of losing this funding ST & LT. Be sure you properly calculate this loss into your working capital needs & be prepared for it post closing. Consult with state & verify playground has adequate square footage for licensed capacity stipulated on license (they do not always match)."
- "Licensing compliance, working ratios, teacher education qualifications, rates in terms of competition, private pay vs. government-supported care."

Resources

Websites
- Childcare Brokers: www.childcarebrokers.com

Associations
- National Association for Family Child Care: www.nafcc.org
- National Child Care Association: www.nccanet.org/
- National Association for the Education of Young Children: www.naeyc.org
- Association for Early Learning Leaders: www.earlylearningleaders.org

			Franchise
Deck the Walls (See also Franchises)			
Approx. Total Investment			$112,500 to $202,000
	NAICS 442299		Number of Businesses/Units 200+
Rules of Thumb			
➢ 35 percent of annual sales plus inventory			

Resources

Websites
- www.dtwfraninfo.com

Delicatessens (See also Restaurants)		
SIC 5812-09	NAICS 445110	Number of Businesses/Units 41,000

Rules of Thumb
- 40 percent of annual sales plus inventory
- 2 times SDE plus inventory
- "If the deli is open five days a week, it's 50 percent of annual sales; if it's open six days a week, it's 40 percent of annual sales; and, if it's open seven days a week it's 30 percent of annual sales."
- Retail: 40 percent of annual sales plus inventory
- Industrial: 50 percent of annual sales plus inventory
- Office Buildings: 50 percent of annual sales plus inventory

Pricing Tips
- "It's important to recognize the distinction between sandwich shops and a real delicatessen. A real deli sells cold cuts plus many other traditional deli items; it usually does make and sell sandwiches, but it represents only a portion of their business. A sandwich shop is like a Subway or Quiznos."

Resources

Associations
- International Dairy-Deli-Bakery Association: www.iddba.org

Delivery Services (Courier Services)		
SIC 4212-05	NAICS 492210	Number of Businesses/Units 175,112

Rules of Thumb
- 70 percent of annual sales plus inventory (if any)
- 2 times EBITDA for businesses under $1 million
- 3 times EBITDA for businesses from $1 to $5 million
- 4 times EBITDA for businesses over $5 million

Pricing Tips
- ". . . FedEx has more pricing flexibility because its deliveries are handled by independent contractors while UPS employs unionized drivers."

D - Rules of Thumb

Expert Comments

"It is worthy to note that the Frontier study (Frontier Economics, London) did research on 'why' businesses use and value express delivery for global shipments. Here are the value points for the global customer according to the study:
- ✓ Global Reach – ability to send items anywhere
- ✓ Reliability – Knowing the items arrive on time
- ✓ Transparency – Being able to track the items
- ✓ Speed – ability to reach destination quickly
- ✓ Security – Knowing the items move in a secure supply chain."

Benchmark Data

Statistics (Courier and Local Delivery Services)

Number of Establishments	175,112
Average Profit Margin	12.6%
Revenue per Employee	$142,900
Average Number of Employees	4.0
Average Wages per Employee	$33,436

Products and Services Segmentation

Ground deliveries	57.7%
Domestic air transit deliveries	30.2%
International air transit deliveries	8.8%
Messengers and local deliveries	3.3%

Major Market Segmentation

Retail trade	30.0%
Households	20.0%
Finance and insurance	15.0%
Other	15.0%
Government departments	10.0%
Healthcare	10.0%

Industry Costs

Profit	12.6%
Wages	24.3%
Purchases	12.1%
Depreciation	4.9%
Marketing	1.0%
Rent & Utilities	2.1%
Other	43.0%

Market Share

United Parcel Service Inc.	38.9%
FedEx Corporation	26.6%

Source: IBISWorld, June 2015

- "Of the online retailers profiled in the Top 500 Guide, 184 list UPS as their shipping carrier, 139 FedEx and 107 USPS, according to Top500Guide.com"

Rules of Thumb - **D**

Industry Trend
- "Overall ecommerce will continue to account for larger share of world trade. For example, the ecommerce share of trade volumes of developed countries could reach 40% in 2025 and up to 30% in emerging markets. In China alone according to a MasterCard study, cross-border online sales reached $2.92 billion in 2012 and their projection for 2015 is $8.11 billion. Finally, total ecommerce global is expected to grow by 20% the next two years and reach $2.3 trillion in 2017."

Source: "The Huge Growth for the Express Delivery Industry" 3/23/15 http://expressassociation.org/delivery_and_logistics_news/THE_HUGE_GROWTH_FOR_THE_EXPRESS_DELIVERY_INDUSTRY_194.asp

Resources
Associations
- Express Delivery & Logistics Association: www.expressassociation.org

		Franchise
Del Taco (See also Franchises)		
Approx. Total Investment		$672,700 to $1,620,500
Estimated Annual Sales/Unit		$1,200,000
	NAICS 722513	Number of Businesses/Units 525

Rules of Thumb
➢ 70 percent of annual sales plus inventory

Resources
Websites
- www.deltacofranchise.com

Dental Laboratories		
SIC 8072-01	NAICS 339116	Number of Businesses/Units 12,000

Rules of Thumb
➢ 45 percent of annual sales plus inventory
➢ 1 times SDE plus equipment and inventory
➢ 2 times SDE includes equipment & inventory

Benchmark Data
- "Let's start with the premise that for most laboratories labor is the largest single cost item, typically running between 45% and 60% of revenues. Keep this important concept in mind. Increasing the productivity of your technicians is not just the number of units you ship to clients. It requires increasing output without increasing the time the technicians spend working. If they build 40 units of porcelain in a 40-hour week, building 50 units in a 50-hour week is not increased productivity. It's actually worse because you are now paying overtime. Increasing productivity requires producing 45 units in that 40-hour

26th Edition

D - Rules of Thumb

week. If you are a crown and bridge lab, your goal should be to produce 3.75 complete finished units per technician per day. Removable labs should shoot for 3.25 units. A five-technician crown and bridge lab should average 18.75 per day."

Source: "Higher Productivity = Bigger Profits" by Chuck Yenker, www.dentalproductsreport.com. March 2010

- "Industry Asks FDA to Improve Regulation of Dental Restorations to Protect Patient Safety in $5.5 billion U.S. dental-restoration products industry. Most domestic dental laboratories are exempt from registering with the FDA, and most typically employ just 3.5 people."

    Source: National Association of Dental Laboratories and www.businesswire.com

Industry Trend

- "The Top 5 Dental Lab Trends of 2014:
    1. The gap between practice and lab grew even smaller
    2. Labs of every size realized they could handle more case types than they thought
    3. 3D printing continued to march forward
    4. All-digital started to be more than a marketing slogan
    5. Creativity still mattered"

    Source:"The Top 5 Dental Lab Trends of 2014" by Ryan Hamm 12/19/2014
    http://www.dentalproductsreport.com/lab/article/top-5-dental-lab-trends-2014

- "Nevertheless, as the number of people with private health insurance slightly increased at an annualized rate of 1.3% during the five years to 2014, demand for industry services propelled forward. Additionally, rapid technological changes, such as new filling, bonding and implant compounds, such as all-ceramic restorative systems; cutting edge computer-aided design and computer-aided manufacturing (CAD and CAM systems); and computer imaging, stimulated demand for industry services."

- "The Dental Laboratories industry is highly fragmented and has a low level of concentration. No company generates more than 5.0% of industry revenue, and the largest industry firm, National Dentex Corporation, accounts for about 3.6% of revenue. "In 2014, the largest four players generate less than 10.0% of industry revenue," says Turk. Over the five years to 2014, concentration has been stable; the number of industry firms has remained relatively flat, increasing at an estimated average annual rate of 0.2% to 6,850. Further, many industry players belong to regional and national dental laboratory associations, such as the National Association of Dental Laboratories, which prevents one operator from strengthening their market share."

    Source: www.PRWeb.com, February 28, 2014

Dental Practices		
SIC 8021-01	NAICS 621210	Number of Businesses/Units 185,179

Rules of Thumb

➤ 50 to 60 percent of annual sales includes inventory
➤ 1.3 to 1.8 times SDE includes inventory
➤ 4 times EBIT
➤ 4 to 5 times EBITDA
➤ 50 to 70 percent of annual collections subject to how weighted practice is towards managed care versus private fee for service (cash pay) and condition of equipment

Rules of Thumb - D

Pricing Tips

- "Profit margin should be between 35% and 45% for well-run practice. SDE should be 35% and pricing is dependent on SDE as well as demographics of the practice, per patient billing (over $500 is typical in a well-run practice). Practices with a routine and effective retention program, a healthy hygiene component (25%+ revenue) and gross revenues over $500,000 are more desirable and achieve higher enterprise values."

- "The perception that dentists take home a hefty profit is misleading, but changing the way dental practice expenses are publicized may change people's minds. . . . 'Since no other business would consider omitting compensation for the CEO or top wage earners from overhead figures, many outside the dental industry may perceive this as a 35–40 percent profit,' said Dr. David May, CDBP chair. 'This may explain why legislators and foundations feel that it is not an issue if dental insurance companies cut reimbursements 10–15 percent.'"

- "Upon a recommendation from CDBP, the HPRC agreed to stop publishing the 60 percent statistic that excludes owner dentists' salaries when calculating dental office overhead. With owner dentists' salaries included as a cost, practice expenses average around 90 percent of gross billings, dropping the profit margin down to 10 percent. The HPRC has published this statistic since 2006, but including it alongside the data that excludes owner dentists' salaries has led some to be confused by its interpretation.

    "'The commonly reported dental practice expense percentage of 60 percent, which excludes owner dentist salaries, if taken out of context, could lead to a mistaken perception about what it costs to operate a dental practice,' HPRC staff members Bradley Munson, Adriana Menezes and MaroVujicic, Ph.D., wrote in the research brief titled 'Dental Practice Expenses Much Higher When Owner Salaries Accounted For,' which can be found at ADA.org/1442.aspx. It does not take into account the value of the practice owner's time.

    "The previous calculation method ignored the difference between gross billings and actual receipts collected, also known as the collection rate, according to HPRC. When the collection rate is taken into account under the new measure, the average expense percentage increases to around 97 percent, HPRC reported in its research brief. 'Since more than 80 percent of active private practitioner dentists in the United States are practice owners, the traditional method underestimates the true cost of operating a dental practice.'"

    Source: "Dental Office Overhead: Practice expenses should include owner dentists' salaries," by Kelly Soderlund, ADA News staff, April 2013

- "Age of equipment, quality of three-party payer contracts, quality of location in terms of patients."

- "What should I scrutinize when looking at a practice? Look at the gross production of the office to determine if you can produce or have produced that amount of dentistry. Also look to see if collections are close to the level of production, what the overall overhead of the office is and what makes up that overhead. For the physical office, look to be sure the location is in an area that will support your vision of your practice and that the building is in good condition. Within the office, note the quality and age of the equipment and whether anything is in major disrepair. Eventually, you will review patient charts and reports to verify statistics like new patient flow and the amount of active patients. You will want to get some idea of what kind of treatment patients are accustomed to and what has been done for them. Despite the importance

D - Rules of Thumb

of working equipment, do not over-emphasize its value. You are primarily purchasing goodwill, or the ongoing patient flow and production of the office. Equipment is easily, and affordably, replaceable. A quality patient base, skilled staff and working office systems are not."

Source: Buying a Practice—FAQs, www.towniecentral.com/Dentaltown/Article

- "Solo practice should be grossing at least $500K–$700K. If less, probably an underperforming practice. Amount of hygiene (i.e., teeth cleaning) revenue can affect profitability. Value of equipment can vary, as some equipment is quite expensive (e.g., CEREC or digital radiography)."
- "Average general dentistry px sells for 60%–65% of gross, with +/- 25% standard deviation."
- "The average new dental start-up office (2,000 square feet with 5-6 treatment rooms, 2 fully equipped to start) costs between $450,000 and $550,000 to complete. The cost also includes some working capital and marketing allowances."
- "Would the cost of purchasing an existing dental office rival or exceed the cost of a start-up? Would you have to replace outdated equipment? What can you do to enhance your chances for selling your practice?"
- A 'must' purchase is the American Dental Association's *Valuing a Practice: A Guide for Dentists*. http://www.adacatalog.org/. Read it, learn it and memorize it!"
- "According to *Valuing a Practice*, a practice is likely to sell for between 40% and 65% of the average last 3 years of gross income. It varies by specialty, with prosthodontia being lowest, followed by perio and pedo. Endo is highest."

Expert Comments

"Expensive set up for new practice with high office renovation, plumbing and other construction costs.Easy financing available through many sources. Banks are very accommodating to dentists. There appear to be fewer dentists exiting dental schools who are interested in practice ownership."

"Dental practices are most marketable in desirable suburban areas and least in rural areas. Good profit for time practicing, typically 40% to 45% of gross, depending on practice."

"Fewer dentists from schools, trend to aggregate dental practices."

"More baby boomers, more demand. Easy to obtain start-up finance. But still buyers for good practices in desirable locations"

"Fee-for-service or insurance-based practice will cause multiples and marketability to increase/decrease."

"Much better market than for medicine"

"100% financing available.Start-up money available too.Plenty of buyers. Growth 14%."

Benchmark Data

Statistics (Dentists)

Number of Establishments	185,179
Average Profit Margin	17.5%
Revenue per Employee	$135,700
Average Number of Employees	5.2
Average Wages per Employee	$50,313

Products and Services Segmentation

Dental nonsurgical intervention services	50.1%
Dental visits and consultations	32.3%
Dental surgical intervention services	15.7%
Anesthesia services	1.0%
Other	0.6%
Medical and diagnostic testing	0.3%

Industry Costs

Profit	17.5%
Wages	38.1%
Purchases	10.7%
Depreciation	1.5%
Marketing	1.0%
Rent & Utilities	9.5%
Other	21.7%

Source: IBISWorld, May 2015

- Miscellaneous Facts
    - ✓ "Male dentists are practicing an average of 34 hours per week, while female dentists practice 27 hours per week.
    - ✓ There will be 15 new dental schools opening in the coming years.
    - ✓ Since 2005, dentists have experienced a 13% decline in their average annual income, even though spending on dental care by patients has increased each successive year.
    - ✓ By the year 2020 (just 6 years away), the majority of practicing dentists will be women, and over the next 10-20 years, this increased influx of women into the field of dentistry may be one of the most defining forces in the entire make-up, culture and practice organization in dentistry.
    - ✓ 60% of practicing dentists under the age of 44 are women.
    - ✓ The market for chairside milling is slowly, but steadily, increasing, with an expected compound annual growth rate (CAGR) of 10.5% between 2012 and 2019, which will increase the approximately 12,650 chairside milling units in use in the United States in 2012 to an estimated 22,087 by 2019.
    - ✓ Most graduating dentists are coming out of dental school with anywhere from 150-300K worth of student loan debt, and 41% of all graduating dentists say this debt load influences their practice choice (the reason many join a group practice as opposed to establishing a solo practice).
    - ✓ The average retirement age for dentists is now 68.3 years"
        Source: "Trends in Dentistry, Forces impacting the dental industry's course in 2014 and Beyond,"
        Inside Dental Technology

- "Approximately 1400 patients necessary to employ one full-time dentist. These must be active patients."
- "A highly profitable practice will have a 40 percent to 50 percent profit margin. A practice that hovers at a 30 percent profit margin is doing something wrong. Inefficient staffing, poor production, or too many unnecessary expenses can be the culprits."

Source: The Snyder Group, www.snydergroup.net

- "3 operatories, 1–2 hygienists"
- "$500 per patient billing and higher desirable"
- "Profitable enterprise with 35% to bottom line"
- "65% to 75% overhead"
- "Gross over $500,000 is a successful practice"

D - Rules of Thumb

Expenses as a percentage of annual sales
Cost of goods	07% to 10%
Payroll/labor Costs	30% to 40%
Occupancy	04% to 07%
Profit (estimated pretax)	30%

Industry Trend
- "New dentists entering the market are well trained but carry an average debt load of $200,000. With changing demographics and a shift from commercial dental insurance to public coverage, it's created a shift from solo dental practices to group or corporate practices.
  Here's a breakdown of current trends that will affect your dental practice:
  - ✓ Dental practices need to be more cost-effective and efficient to manage healthcare reform.
  - ✓ Hence – trend towards corporate-supported dental practices
  - ✓ Demographic changes require different patient care, insurance acceptance & training and technologies.
  - ✓ Shift in population from northern states to Sunbelt states.
  - ✓ Consumers are more sophisticated and well informed about their medical/dental care. They seek high-quality care without a premium.
  - ✓ Growing need to provide preventative and restorative dental services.
  - ✓ U.S. Govt. spending on dental care has increased—4 in 10 U.S. children have public dental coverage.

  "Are there enough dentists? Current workforce is aging—37% of dentists are over 55 years and an additional 27% are between 45–55 years. As the U.S. economy has improved, more and more dentists are retiring—leaving a void of new dentists. Dental schools are graduating more students, but the increase in new dentists might not meet the demand created by the growing publicly insured sectors. A recent survey conducted by the Association of State and Territorial Dental Directors found that less than ½ of dentists treated Medicaid patients in 25 of 39 states survey."

  Source: http://benevis.com/resources/dental-industry-trends-and-changes/ February 2, 2015

- "As the economy improves, patients will have more dentistry done."
- "Increasing due to the Health Care Reform allowing millions of disadvantaged persons in"
- "Dentistry remains a good profession. Excellent profit potential for those willing to work hard. Technology and new cosmetic procedures should keep productivity and demand high."
- "Growing demand.Trend to add more ancillary services (i.e., teeth whitening, cosmetics) to improve profitability."
- "Dependent on insurance coverage allocated to dental practices"
- "Improvements in technology, quality of materials, and education of consumers regarding services available and transparency in pricing will continue to accelerate."
- "Stable"
- "More female dentists"
- "Many dentists will be wanting to transition their practices."

Rules of Thumb - **D**

Seller Financing
- "Very good 3rd-party financing available—sometimes even 100 percent."
- "Bank financing is readily available. Terms are usually 100% of the price plus working capital over 7 to 10 years."

Questions
- "Patient demographics, Revenue per patient, hygienist revenue, employee turnover, recall system"
- "Why selling? What type of practice do you have (e.g., types of procedures)? What plans do you participate with? Number of treatment rooms?"
- "Ask about: What are the revenues comprised of? What 3rd party payer sources exist? Age and condition of equipment. How they market."
- "Besides all the typical questions, how many active patients do they have; do they want to stay on or leave; and if they own the real estate (50%–60% do), do they want to rent or sell it."
- "Are billing practices compliant? Any staffing issues, personal or professional?"
- "Age of practice and equipment, demographics of practice, call-back programs, average annual billing per patient."
- "Type of practice, hours worked, amount of hygiene revenue, number of operators, type of procedures commonly performed, payer mix, insurance contracts"
- "Many! Ask for operations data including number and types of procedures performed, demographics of patients, management systems and reports available in the practice, payer issues, regulatory requirements, technology issues, etc."
- "# FTE dentists? gross receipts? # lay staff? hygienist income as % of gross? # right-handed operators vs. # left-handed operators."

Resources

Trade Publications
- Dental Economics: www.dentaleconomics.com

Associations
- American Dental Association: www.ada.org

Diagnostic Imaging Centers		
	NAICS 621512	Number of Businesses/Units 17,486

Rules of Thumb
- ➢ 100 percent of annual sales includes inventory
- ➢ 3.25 times SDE includes inventory
- ➢ 4 times EBIT
- ➢ 5 times EBITDA

Pricing Tips
- "May be necessary to include A/R in the price for working capital needs. Age and type of equipment very important."

D - Rules of Thumb

Expert Comments
"Highly competitive and constant change taking place with reimbursement rates via Medicare."

Benchmark Data

Statistics (Diagnostic Imaging Centers)
Number of Establishments	17,486
Average Profit Margin	12.2%
Revenue per Employee	$172,800
Average Number of Employees	5.9
Average Wages per Employee	$56,385

Products and Services Segmentation
Computed tomography (CT) scanning	27.5%
Magnetic resonance imaging scans	27.1%
All other diagnostic imaging	21.4%
Ultrasound imaging	10.8%
Radiographic imaging (Including x-rays)	10.0%
Other services	3.2%

Major Market Segmentation
Private insurance payments	40.0%
Medicare and Medicaid payments	25.0%
Other	11.5%
Hospital payments	10.0%
Health practitioner payments	8.0%
Out-of-pocket payments	5.5%

Industry Costs
Profit	12.2%
Wages	32.8%
Purchases	41.9%
Depreciation	5.5%
Marketing	1.1%
Rent & Utilities	6.0%
Other	0.5%

Source: IBISWorld, December 2014

Expenses as a percentage of annual sales
Cost of good	10%
Payroll/labor Costs	25%
Occupancy	05% to 10%
Profit (estimated pretax)	40%

Industry Trend
- "IBISWorld expects the market for analytic and diagnostic services to return to growth in the five years to 2019. Scientific advances will yield new and improved service capabilities and the aging US population will increasingly require more and better diagnostic imaging services."

Source: IBISWorld, December 2014

- "Uncertainty. While the need for scans (CT, MRI, X-ray) will continue to go up, reimbursements will likely fall."

Rules of Thumb - D

Dialysis Centers

NAICS 621492	Number of Businesses/Units 37,893

Rules of Thumb
➢ 5 to 10 times EBITDA

Pricing Tips
- "Patient mix (types of payer sources) is key; geography is also important given differences in reimbursement in different areas and regulations."

Benchmark Data

Statistics (Emergency & Other Outpatient Care Centers)
Number of Establishments 37,893
Average Profit Margin 13.7%
Revenue per Employee $160,500
Average Number of Employees 16.0
Average Wages per Employee $56,237

Products and Services Segmentation
Other outpatient care centers 41.4%
Freestanding ambulatory surgical and emergency centers 27.9%
Kidney dialysis centers 22.1%
HMO medical centers 8.6%

Major Market Segmentation
Private insurance 39.8%
Government 35.4%
Other 14.6%
Contributions, gifts and grants 5.3%
Patients (out-of-pocket) 4.9%

Industry Costs
Profit 13.7%
Wages 33.5%
Purchases 21.8%
Depreciation 4.4%
Marketing 0.7%
Rent & Utilities 6.1%
Other 19.8%

Market Share
Fresenius Medical Care AG & Co. KGaA 10.3%
DaVita HealthCare Partners Inc. 8.9%

Source: IBISWorld, May 2015

- "Often owners will hear estimates based on amounts 'per patient' which can be inaccurate, as they may be based on very different types of programs in different areas with different payer groups."

26th Edition

D - Rules of Thumb

Expenses as a percentage of annual sales	
Cost of goods	0
Payroll/labor Costs	0
Occupancy	0
Profit (estimated pretax)	05% to 15%

Industry Trend

- "Experts say dialysis providers can realize savings and survive in two ways: they can pursue a consolidation strategy that allows them to spread their fixed costs over a greater number of centers. Or they can find ways to offer the same service more cheaply."

  Source:"Dialysis providers expect ACOs, payment cuts, consolidation" by Beth Kutscher, http://www.modernhealthcare.com/article/20141011/MAGAZINE/310119931 October 11, 2014

- "For 400,000 people across the country with failed kidneys, dialysis care is a matter of life and death. It is also a lucrative business, in part because Medicare pays for such treatment regardless of age. But as for-profit clinics and chains have grown to control about 85 percent of the dialysis market over the last decade, researchers have documented starkly higher mortality rates in centers owned by for-profits compared with nonprofits."

  Source: "Hospitals' Dialysis Plan Is Under New Scrutiny," by Nina Bernstein, www.nytimes.com February 12, 2014

- "The proposed sale of Eastern Maine Medical Center's dialysis clinics to a for-profit corporation roused concerns Tuesday about the safety of patients seriously ill with kidney disease. . . DaVita officials said the company's clinical outcomes are among the best in the industry, leading to fewer infections and lower mortality rates. The company serves about 142,000 patients nationwide. . . DaVita and competitor Fresenius Medical Care, which operates 10 clinics in Maine, run two-thirds of all dialysis clinics inthe country."

- "Strict regulations and the highly specialized nature of dialysis programs have led most hospitals across the country to sell their outpatient clinics. More than 80 percent of the nation's 5,000 dialysis clinics are now for-profit, according to an analysis of the industry by journalism nonprofit ProPublica. Financial incentives encourage for-profit operators to get into the dialysis game. The shift dates back to 1972, when Congress voted to extend Medicare coverage to nearly anyone diagnosed with kidney failure, including full payment for dialysis and kidney transplants."

- "Going through new update on conditions of participation and reimbursement changes over time, but still a very solid area given the long-term relationship with patients and relatively predictable cash flow."

Questions

- "Whether they are the medical director, and what relationships they have with patient referral sources, whether they would continue to work in the unit post transaction, etc."

Dick's Wings & Grill (See also Franchises)	Franchise
Approx. Total Investment	$100,000 per restaurant + a net worth of $500,000
NAICS 722513	Number of Businesses/Units 20

Rules of Thumb

➤ 35 percent of annual sales

Rules of Thumb - D

Resources

Websites
- www.dickswingsandgrill.com

Diners (See also Restaurants)		
	NAICS 722511	
Rules of Thumb		
➢ 30 to 35 percent of annual sales plus inventory		

Direct Mail—Advertising (See also Coupon Books, Valpak)		
SIC 7331-05	NAICS 541860	Number of Businesses/Units 2,867
Rules of Thumb		
➢ 40 to 50 percent of annual revenues plus inventory		
➢ 2 to 2.5 times SDE not including inventory		

Pricing Tips

- "Valpak used to be the gold standard for this industry at a multiple of 3. Considering new technology and the economy most have been selling at 2 X SDE or slightly less."

Expert Comments

"On-line coupon technology has hurt this industry."

"Marketability is high. Location and facilities are solid because this biz thrives in metropolitan areas and can be run out of your home."

Benchmark Data

Statistics (Direct Mail Advertising)

Number of Establishments	2,867
Average Profit Margin	5.2%
Revenue per Employee	$244,700
Average Number of Employees	17.4
Average Wages per Employee	$50,496

Products and Services Segmentation

Full direct mail services	49.7%
Other services	17.5%
Printing and fulfillment services	16.7%
Lettershop services	13.0%
Mailing list support services	3.1%

D - Rules of Thumb

Major Market Segmentation
Retail Stores	34.5%
Other	19.8%
Finance, banking and insurance institutions	18.0%
Restaurants and travel companies	15.7%
Business-to-business market	12.0%

Industry Costs
Profit	5.2%
Wages	20.8%
Purchases	35.1%
Depreciation	2.3%
Marketing	6.9%
Rent & Utilities	6.1%
Other	23.6%

Market Share
Valassis Communications Inc.	11.5%

Source: IBISWorld, July 2015

Expenses as a percentage of annual sales
Cost of goods	65%
Payroll/labor Costs	05% to 10%
Occupancy	05%
Profit (estimated pretax)	20% to 25%

Industry Trend
- "Continuing decline unless they can integrate current technology."

Questions
- "How many recurring agreements are in place? How large is your biggest client?"
- "How many active clients? What is your average net profit?"

Resources
Associations
- Direct Marketing Association: www.the-dma.org

Direct Selling Businesses		
SIC 5963-98	NAICS 4543	Number of Businesses/Units 681,436

Rules of Thumb
➢ 4.5 to 5 times EBITDA

Pricing Tips
- "It all depends on who is buying and who is selling. Buyer and seller motivation is key. If the seller is very successful and getting in the way of larger companies, that would tend to dramatically increase the price."

Rules of Thumb - D

Benchmark Data

Statistics (Direct Selling Companies)
Number of Establishments	681,436
Average Profit Margin	5.3%
Revenue per Employee	$57,900
Average Number of Employees	1.1
Average Wages per Employee	$8,260

Products and Services Segmentation
Home and family care products	46.4%
Wellness and personal care products	29.3%
Clothing and accessories	8.6%
Other products and services	8.6%
Leisure and educational products	7.1%

Industry Costs
Profit	5.3%
Wages	14.6%
Purchases	72.0%
Depreciation	1.0%
Marketing	1.7%
Rent and Utilities	4.5%
Other	0.9%

Source: IBISWorld, June 2015

- "$150,000 annual sales per employee"

Expenses as a percentage of annual sales
Cost of goods	60%
Payroll/labor Costs	01%
Occupancy	01% to 04%
Profit (estimated pretax)	07% to 10%

Industry Trend
- "Increasing consolidation"

Seller Financing
- "Both are common, many times it is a combination of the outside financing and seller financing."

Questions
- "You need to have detailed information on all the customers. See what the trends have been the last 3 years. Who are the suppliers? Many times the key supplier is the buyer. About the employees, how long they have been there and their roles in the company. Need to see all financial information including tax returns for the last 3 years. What equipment is being included, like trucks, forklifts and warehouse equipment? Are the bottles, racks, water coolers, and coffee brewers in good shape? What is the age of this equipment? What about accounts receivable? Need A/R aging reports, totals and for each customer."

D - Rules of Thumb

Distribution/Wholesale—Durable Goods
NAICS 423

Rules of Thumb
- 4 times EBITDA
- 2 to 2.5 times SDE plus inventory
- 4.5 times EBIT

Pricing Tips
- "Inventory (durable or non-durable) is critical to the sale and must be current, well managed with appropriate controls and real time valuation processes in place."
- "Worth approximately one-half of sales volume; watch out for large, stale inventory."
- "% of annual gross sales is a poor guide to follow. EBITDA drives ROI and ability to service debt."
- "Add cost of replacing current ownership with professional management to SDE, and then multiply this number by 4 to 6 to get price. Variance is for security of earnings, competition, assets, etc."

Expert Comments
"There are significant competitive cost barriers to entry into this industry, where size does matter along with quantity and quality of product lines, adequate logistical distribution channels, good supplier pricing and terms, adequate facilities sizing and location. Solid, well-diversified customer base mitigates risk and wards off competitive challenges."

Benchmark Data
- "Distribution costs are sensitive to energy prices. Direct competition from manufacturers is increasing which creates a challenge for many distributors and a need to find service and delivery differentiation for the clients."
- "Cost of goods should be less than 74%, with 70% as ideal; operating expenses of less than 20%; sales/assets ratio of 3.0; W/C ratio of 13% to 15% of revenues; current ratio of 3.0 or greater; A/R turnover ratio of 12.0; inventory turns of 6.0 or greater; sales per employee greater than $250,000; sales per sq. ft. in excess of $300,000."

Expenses as a percentage of annual sales
Cost of goods	70% to 80%
Payroll/labor Costs	10% to 20%
Occupancy	03% to 08%
Profit (estimated pretax)	08% to 15%

Seller Financing
- "Banks like the industry and will generally provide SBA 7(a) credit to qualified buyer and where consistent cash flow is evident."

Rules of Thumb - D

Questions
- "Does the business belong to any distributor buying groups/co-ops?"

Resources
Associations
- National Association of Wholesaler-Distributors: www.naw.org

Distribution/Wholesale—Electrical Products	
NAICS 423610	Number of Businesses/Units 15,025

Rules of Thumb
- ➢ 35 percent of annual revenues plus inventory

Pricing Tips
- "This category includes electrical components which tend to sell for less than the above figure which is the other category included in this entry—electrical equipment."

Benchmark Data

Statistics (Electrical Equipment Wholesaling)
Number of Establishments	15,025
Average Profit Margin	4.4%
Revenue per Employee	$902,300
Average Number of Employees	13.2
Average Wages per Employee	$78,185

Products and Services Segmentation
Other electrical equipment	32.5%
Wiring	23.7%
Lighting fixtures and light bulbs	16.1%
Relay and industrial controls	8.0%
Switchgear and switchboard apparatus	7.8%
Motors and generators	6.5%
Power and distribution transformers	5.4%

Major Market Segmentation
Industrial users	42.0%
Construction	31.0%
Utility	14.0%
Commercial, institutional and governmental	13.0%

Industry Costs
Profit	4.4%
Wages	8.5%
Purchases	70.0%
Depreciation	0.3%
Marketing	1.0%
Rent & Utilities	3.5%
Other	12.3%

D - Rules of Thumb

Market Share

WESCO International Inc. 2.9%

Source: IBISWorld, June 2015

Distribution/Wholesale—Grocery Products/Full Line		
SIC 5141-05	NAICS 424990	Number of Businesses/Units 5,318 |//
Rules of Thumb ➢ 3 to 4 times SDE ➢ 4 times EBIT ➢ 4 to 4.5 times EBITDA		

Pricing Tips

- "Use 25%–30% of GPM [gross profit margin] times 4 to arrive at goodwill price including all F F& E. To this number, add the dollar amount of net working capital, if any, to be included in the sale."

Benchmark Data

Statistics (Grocery Wholesaling)

Number of Establishments 5,318
Average Profit Margin 2.4%
Revenue per Employee $1,300,000
Average Number of Employees 26.7
Average Wages per Employee $56,956

Products and Services Segmentation

Other 23.5%
Fresh meat and meat products 20.0%
Canned food 17.7%
Frozen food 13.0%
Dairy products 10.0%
Specialty food 6.0%
Fresh fruits and vegetables 5.4%
Paper and plastic products 4.4%

Major Market Segmentation

Food service outlets 51.3%
Supermarkets and other grocery retailers 36.5%
Other wholesalers 9.0%
Other 3.2%

Industry Costs

Profit 2.4%
Wages 4.4%
Purchases 80.0%
Depreciation 0.4%
Marketing 1.1%
Rent & Utilities 1.6%
Other 10.1%

Rules of Thumb - D

Market Share

SYSCO Corporation	25.1%
C&S Wholesale Grocers Inc.	14.2%
US Foods	12.8%
Performance Food Group	8.1%
Wakefern Food Corporation	7.7%

Source: IBISWorld, September 2015

- "$285,000–$300,000 sales per employee would be a good benchmark for a successful wholesale distributor."

Expenses as a percentage of annual sales

Cost of goods	80% to 83%
Payroll/labor Costs	12%
Occupancy	05%
Profit (estimated pretax)	07% to 08%

Questions
- "Stability of gross profit margins?"

Distribution/Wholesale—Industrial Supplies

NAICS 423840	Number of Businesses/Units 10,290

Rules of Thumb
➢ 50 percent of annual revenues plus inventory
➢ 4 to 5 times EBITDA

Pricing Tips
- "Many distributorships for larger equipment do not order high dollar inventory until they receive a request from a customer to order that equipment. Therefore, inventory levels may not be extremely high as they try to not hold excess inventory. If the business you are evaluating is not operated this way and there is a large amount of inventory, you may need to consider that in your working capital calculations."

Expert Comments

"Companies that represent quality lines of products are desired. Contracts with customers to consistently provide their equipment or supplies or maintenance are a major plus."

Benchmark Data

Statistics (Industrial Supplies Wholesaling)

Number of Establishments	10,290
Average Profit Margin	5.0%
Revenue per Employee	$820,200
Average Number of Employees	8.1
Average Wages per Employee	$66,536

D - Rules of Thumb

Products and Services Segmentation

Abrasives, strapping and tape	31.0%
Industrial containers	19.0%
Mechanical power transmission supplies	16.0%
Other supplies	16.0%
Industrial valves and fittings	14.0%
Welding supplies	4.0%

Major Market Segmentation

Industrial users for production inputs	43.0%
Other wholesalers for resale	22.0%
Other	11.0%
Businesses for end use	10.0%
Retailers for resale	9.0%
Building contractors	5.0%

Industry Costs

Profit	5.0%
Wages	8.2%
Purchases	70.0%
Depreciation	0.7%
Marketing	1.0%
Rent & Utilities	3.2%
Other	11.9%

Source: IBISWorld, June 2015

Industry Trend

- "Consolidation of companies with revenues between $1,000,000 and $50,000,000 will be the trend as larger companies search for synergies and new customers through acquisition."

Questions

- "Who are your distributor agreements with? What restrictions do you have regarding geography and other products? How many additional products can your current sales force add to their sales book?"

Resources

Associations

- Industrial Supply Association: www.isapartners.org

Distribution/Wholesale—In General

Rules of Thumb

➢ 65 percent of annual sales plus inventory

➢ 2.75 times SDE plus inventory

➢ 3.2 times EBIT

➢ 3 times EBITDA

Pricing Tips
- "Distribution companies that are profitable with a strong history and diversified customer base can command high multiples."
- "Assumes SDE in excess of $500K. Where less than $500K, lower multiples; where over $1M, multiples exceed 3 and escalate as SDE increases."
- "Suppliers, how many, and will that continue for a new owner, under the same or better terms. Current contracts with customers and account concentration issues all of high importance in determining value."
- "Debt service will have great impact on ultimate rule of thumb multiple considering 'living wage' necessary by locality after debt is serviced."

Expert Comments
"Easy to replicate, lots of competition"

"Easy to market with use of the Web. For a savvy new owner with more technical abilities, an existing wholesale/distribution business can market to the world."

"Can be easy to replicate, the sales force is often key to success."

"Distributor with large, developed customer base is difficult to duplicate, thus enhancing the value. Seller-based financing is essential with the limitation on SBA financing where the major business asset is inventory."

Benchmark Data
- "High margins for the most part"
- "Low rent can be easy to achieve for these types of 'warehouse' businesses."
- "Cost of goods sold varies from 60%–70% depending on product."

Expenses as a percentage of annual sales	
Cost of goods	70%
Payroll/labor Costs	15%
Occupancy	05%
Profit (estimated pretax)	10% to 15%

Industry Trend
- "When marketing to the wholesale distribution industry, it is important to have a firm understanding of the current wholesale distribution market. With annual sales of about $5 trillion (down from $6 trillion in early 2011), the US wholesale distribution industry includes about 300,000 companies. For the period between 2010 and 2015, the output of the US wholesale distribution industry is forecast to grow at an annual compounded rate of 6 percent. A respected industry overview cited the industry's growth over the last decade as having been 'above average' as compared to other industries. If this sounds less than enthusiastic, here's the reality check they provide: during that 10-year period, while distributor revenue grew nearly 50% – with computers, electrical goods, and machinery leading the pack – retailers showed 40% growth, and the US economy saw 30% growth. Considering that the decade in question included the 'ugliest financial disaster since the Great Depression,' and that the US economy still managed to show 30% growth on average, we'd say 'above average' works well enough."

Source: http://www.thefrantzgroup.com/industry-marketing-experiences/wholesale-distribution-industry-overview/

D - Rules of Thumb

- "Wholesaler-distributors should plan on economic expansion in 2015, though generally at a milder pace than was evident in 2014. Wholesaler-distributors closer to the consumer side of the economy will likely see stronger growth than those in the business-to-business market. A faster rate of growth in the U.S. economy, and thus a great demand on wholesaler-distributors, should be anticipated for 2016."

   Source: "State of the Wholesale Distribution Industry" by Alan Beaulieu, http://www.naw.org/about/industry.php

- "Growing industry, particularly over the Internet"
- "Highly competitive . . . unless a unique product, specifically manufactured. Margins are declining as competition increases."
- "Always a demand for wholesale and distribution businesses."

Questions
- "What other products or lines can they distribute, are there any restrictions given by current suppliers?"
- "Get financials for past 3 years and year to date. What has changed in your industry? Do you sell to distributors? If so, what are the margins? What is the source of your product and is there an agreement to assure continued supply?"
- "What is the current method of finding and keeping customers? How do they expect the current sales to grow? Does China or overseas production cause any future issues for the current products sold?"
- "How many clients do you have and how many are 'regularly' serviced?"

Resources

Associations
- National Association of Wholesaler-Distributors: www.naw.org

Distribution/Wholesale—Janitorial

NAICS 423850	Number of Businesses/Units 2,247

Rules of Thumb
➢ 30 to 40 percent of annual sales plus inventory

Benchmark Data

Statistics (Cleaning & Maintenance Supplies Distributors)

Number of Establishments	2,247
Average Profit Margin	5.1%
Revenue per Employee	$579,600
Average Number of Employees	18.7
Average Wages per Employee	$49,014

Products and Services Segmentation

Paper and plastics products	54.4%
Chemical supplies	27.0%
Janitorial supplies and accessories	8.1%
Power equipment	7.1%
Other janitorial products	3.4%

Major Market Segmentation

Others	19.3%
Healthcare Centers	14.9%
Industrial buildings	14.6%
Janitorial service companies	14.5%
Schools, colleges and universities	13.7%
Government buildings	8.4%
Retail outlets, malls, department stores, grocery stores and other	7.9%
Commercial buildings	6.7%

Industry Costs

Profit	5.1%
Wages	8.5%
Purchases	61.1%
Depreciation	0.8%
Marketing	2.1%
Rent & Utilities	3.4%
Other	19.0%

Market Share

United Stationers Inc.	6.0%

Source: IBISWorld, February 2015

Distribution/Wholesale—Medical Equipment & Supplies

NAICS 42145	Number of Businesses/Units 13,506

Rules of Thumb

> 50 percent of annual revenues plus inventory

Pricing Tips

- "Pricing on medical equipment tends to be a higher percentage of sales than medical supplies. While the percentage of annual sales price might be a bit higher than the multiple in the Rule of Thumb above, the price based on percentage of annual sales for medical supplies could be lower."

Benchmark Data

Statistics (Medical Supplies Wholesaling)

Number of Establishments	13,506
Average Profit Margin	5.1%
Revenue per Employee	$689,400
Average Number of Employees	17.1
Average Wages per Employee	$104,560

Products and Services Segmentation

Surgical, medical and hospital instruments and equipment	53.4%
Surgical, medical and hospital supplies	24.1%
Orthopedic and prosthetic appliances and supplies	10.4%
Dental equipment, instruments and supplies	6.5%
Other	4.2%
Pharmaceuticals, cosmetics and toiletries	1.4%

26th Edition

D - Rules of Thumb

Major Market Segmentation

Hospitals	39.0%
Clinics	30.0%
Dentists	18.5%
Alternate care providers	12.5%

Industry Costs

Profit	5.1%
Wages	15.1%
Purchases	53.8%
Depreciation	0.7%
Marketing	2.0%
Rent &Utilities	3.6%
Other	19.7%

Market Share

Cardinal Health Inc.	7.1%
Owens & Minor Inc.	6.0%

Source: IBISWorld, April 2015

Distribution/Wholesale—Paper

NAICS 425120	Number of Businesses/Units 941

Rules of Thumb

➢ 3 to 4 times SDE plus inventory
➢ 4 to 5 times EBIT
➢ 5 times EBITDA

Pricing Tips

- "Use 25–30% of GPM [Gross Profit Margin] times 4 to arrive at goodwill price including all FF&E. To this number, add the dollar amount of net working capital to be included in the sale."

Benchmark Data

Statistics (Paper Wholesaling)

Number of Establishments	941
Average Profit Margin	1.2%
Revenue per Employee	$2,105,200
Average Number of Employees	14.6
Average Wages per Employee	$69,346

Products and Services Segmentation

Printing and writing paper	43.9%
Fine roll paper	28.8%
Other	15.1%
Newsprint	12.2%

Rules of Thumb - **D**

Major Market Segmentation

Book and magazine publishers	30.1%
Paper converters	21.5%
Commercial printing	19.0%
Newspaper publishers	16.0%
Other industries	11.5%
Exports	1.9%

Industry Costs

Profit	1.2%
Wages	3.3%
Purchases	81.0%
Depreciation	0.5%
Marketing	0.4%
Rent & Utilities	1.5%
Other	12.1%

Market Share

Xpedx	9.6%

Source: IBISWorld, February 2014

Expenses as a percentage of annual sales

Cost of goods	70% to 75%
Payroll/labor Costs	10%
Occupancy	04%
Profit (estimated pretax)	08% to 10%

Industry Trend
- "Stable"

Questions
- "Stability of gross profit margins, number of inventory turns per year. Percentage of slow moving inventory and the need for adjustments thereof."

Distribution/Wholesale—Tools	
NAICS 423171	Number of Businesses/Units 8,121

Rules of Thumb
- 55 percent of annual sales includes inventory
- 3.7 times SDE includes inventory

Pricing Tips
- "Higher multiples for the higher net profit industries"

Expert Comments
"Location is not typically important since there is not much drop-in traffic."

D - Rules of Thumb

Benchmark Data

Statistics (Tool and Hardware Wholesaling)

Number of Establishments	8,121
Average Profit Margin	4.5%
Revenue per Employee	$650,500
Average Number of Employees	11.0
Average Wages per Employee	$58,337

Products and Services Segmentation

Bolts, nuts, rivets and other fasteners (excludes nails)	42.1%
Hand tools and power tools	34.3%
Miscellaneous hardware	15.5%
Plumbing and hydronic heating equipment	5.0%
Cutlery	3.1%

Major Market Segmentation

Retailers	39.6%
Other wholesalers	23.8%
Building contractors and heavy construction	15.2%
Manufacturing and mining industries	11.3%
Businesses and others for end use	10.1%

Industry Costs

Profit	4.5%
Wages	9.1%
Purchases	65.2%
Depreciation	0.7%
Marketing	1.0%
Rent & Utilities	3.2%
Other	16.3%

Market Share

Stanley Black & Decker Inc.	8.2%
Ace Hardware Corporation	6.0%

Source: IBISWorld, February 2015

- "Very hands-on with the key customers. Must maintain knowledge of the products they need to service their clients."

Expenses as a percentage of annual sales

Cost of goods	74%
Payroll/labor Costs	08%
Occupancy	01%
Profit (estimated pretax)	15%

Industry Trend
- "Good"

Questions
- "Do you need a mechanical background or inclination to be successful?"

Rules of Thumb - **D**

Document Destruction

| | NAICS 561990 | |

Rules of Thumb
- ➢ 150 percent of annual sales includes inventory
- ➢ 4 times SDE includes inventory
- ➢ 6 times EBIT
- ➢ 6 times EBITDA

Pricing Tips
- "Prices range from 1.25 to 2.0 times gross revenues"
- "Mobile shredding operations include price adjustments to compensate for the age of the fleet."

Expert Comments
"In a world of daily data breaches, identity theft and privacy concerns, ensuring the protection of information is dire. Companies are looking for better protection in regard to the secure destruction of their private documents as confidentiality and security top businesses' list of importance."

"High revenue growth rates have attracted new market competition."

"This is a high growth industry, with low technology requirements and relatively few barriers to entry."

Benchmark Data
- "Well-run businesses can generate $250K–$300K revenue per vehicle in fleet."
- "EBITDA margins should exceed 30% for mobile operations and 35% for plant-based operations."

Expenses as a percentage of annual sales	
Cost of goods	40%
Payroll/labor Costs	25%
Occupancy	05%
Profit (estimated pretax)	30%

Industry Trend
- "Industry revenues should continue to grow. Consolidation has reduced the number of larger independently owned businesses."
- "Revenue trends exceed 20% growth due to heightened awareness of confidentiality and identity theft concerns. Many state regulations require shredding of confidential information."
- "Shredding Ahead: business booms as market demands document destruction"

Source: www.ezy-waysecurityshredding.com.au

D - Rules of Thumb

Questions
- "Age of fleet and the output of plant facilities are important. Industry standard equipment is a must."
- "What % of the business is recurring versus one-time purge service revenues? Is the service provided on-site at the customer location via a mobile shredding truck or destroyed in a plant environment off-site?"

Resources

Trade Publications
- Security Shredding and Storage News: www.securityshreddingnews.com
- Storage and Destruction Business:
  http://www.sdbmagazine.com/sdb0215-secure-information-destruction.aspx

Associations
- National Association for Information Destruction: www.naidonline.org/nitl/en

---

Dog Kennels (See also Pet Grooming)		
SIC 0752-05	NAICS 812910	Number of Businesses/Units 100,711

Rules of Thumb
- ➢ 1 times annual sales plus inventory
- ➢ 2 to 3 times SDE plus inventory
- ➢ 2.7 times EBIT

Pricing Tips
- "Multiplier can be anything from 1 to 3.5, most sold comps support a range of 2 to 3. Issues affecting multiplier selection are: longevity, occupancy rates for boarding kennels (similar to hotel/motel analysis), seller involvement, financing ability, state of facilities, location, etc. Grooming salons are in the 1 to 2 times multiplier; if seller is the groomer and no staff, there is no business goodwill."
- "Careful consideration of multiplier of 'add backs,' revenue trend, geographic location."
- "American Boarding Kennel Association (ABKA) uses 1 to 1.5 times gross sales plus real estate. These transactions can be very real estate intensive and often business does not support debt service. That needs to be taken into consideration when pricing. Location and zoning influence pricing considerably."
- "Multiplier depends largely on 1) type of facility (old/new), 2) geographic area (how difficult is licensing and zoning), 3) growth of business in the past 5 years, 4) how involved/important is the seller in the operation, 5) how large is real estate component (if high, price gets inflated, so business is priced for less)."
- "One way of calculating the market value of a boarding kennel would be to figure the present market value of just the real estate and add to that 1 or 1½ times the annual gross. Now, the difference between 1 and 1½ times would be determined by the area. For example, if the kennel is in a growing area, you would be more inclined to go 1½ times. If the kennel is in an area that is static, and there is reason to feel that the kennel will continue to do more business, then you could use one times the annual gross."

Expert Comments

"Competitors not only include other facility (i.e., real estate) based businesses, but an animal owner's friends, relatives, etc. that often 'watch the pet' cheaper. In home petsitters are gaining popularity, so they need to be considered in competition analysis. 'Barriers to entry' include zoning and land use laws, which are getting stricter raising the value of existing, properly zoned facilities. Industry itself continues to grow and has survived the recession fairly well. Very marketable business, but lots of unqualified buyers. Risk can be high, especially to a buyer with no prior industry experience. Lending can be challenge due to mixed-use properties. Seller's personal goodwill needs to be measured carefully against real business goodwill; high customer loyalty to seller causing a risk for buyer. If seller is the groomer, buyer can expect the grooming income to diminish drastically upon purchase. Often a real estate holding company (owned by the seller as well) owns the real estate and the business (operating company owned by the seller) pays rent to the holding company. When recasting, it's imperative to substitute that rent for Fair Market Rent in the area; sometimes this leads to an add-back, sometimes to a deduction. The business must be valued based on SDE that INCLUDES occupancy cost. One can't add back all the rent and then value based on that SDE; there is a cost for the real estate the business uses to generate income."

"Multiplier depends on the following factors: 1. Geographic location (determines marketability and desirability) 2. Seller's role and risk assessment of transfer 3. Historical revenue trends 4.Type and age of facility (older facilities are less desirable/not many buyers willing to buy 5. Real estate value (if high, business will most likely not generate enough to support debt service, hence fetches a lower valuation to still stay within a price range that it can actually be sold)."

"Dog daycares are experiencing heavy growth and thus competition, easy to replicate. Older boarding kennels with outdated facilities are difficult to market/sell, resort styles attract more buyers. Industry is growing, profit margins are historically high and continue as such. Zoning restrictions are growing limiting entry in some states. The smaller the business, the higher the risk for new owner. Customers tend to be very loyal to the owner, and do not deal with change in ownership well. Grooming salons are very high risk, as most customers will leave with the seller. The less the seller is involved in the business, the lower the risk. This is a personal service industry, and needs to be assessed as such."

"Barriers to entry depend largely on zoning and licensing. In some states it's very easy, some states very restrictive. Seller is the highest risk for buyer due to the personal nature of the business. Lots of interested buyers, financing the deal can be difficult. Industry growing as a whole; the trend is more toward the resort style/ communal play facilities. Older facilities are hard to market, small buyer pool."

Benchmark Data

- "Occupancy! A successful facility should have a year-round occupancy level of at least 50%. Per-run revenue can be measured; but, as many facilities also provide grooming and daycare services, not a reliable benchmark. Payroll below 40% of Gross Income. Overall, SDE should be close to, or above, 30% of Gross Income."
- "Boarding kennels: Year-round occupancy should be minimum of 50%, preferably over 55%. Average annual income per run/enclosure around $3500.

D - Rules of Thumb

Dog daycares: average number of dogs per day around 1 dog per 75 SF of (inside) area."
- "Analyze like a hotel, based on occupancy. Statistically, a decent operation should have at least a 50% occupancy (yearly). SDE should be 24% to 30% of gross sales, if business well managed."

Expenses as a percentage of annual sales
Cost of goods	03%
Payroll/labor Costs	40%
Occupancy	17%
Profit (estimated pretax)	30%

Industry Trend
- "Industry continues to grow, new services are being added. Customers spend more and more money on their pets, that have been elevated to a family member status."
- "Growth, more franchises, more 'resort' style facilities, more competition."

Questions
- "1. What are your day to day duties at the business? (how much does the customer base rely on the seller?) 2. Verify zoning and land use from the county department directly. 3. How much of the income do you produce personally (grooming, training, etc.)? 4. Staff and what level of authority do they have? 5. How do you think the clientele will react when they learn that you've sold? 6. Get confirmation on any septic, well, etc. issues. 7. Which licenses are required (besides regular business license) to operate?"
- "1. Determine if a successful kennel or not. 2. Pricing in comparison to competition and how often they are raised (industry notorious for not raising prices regularly) 3. Real estate issues: septic, water, inspections, set-backs, neighbors, noise ordinances, etc."
- "How involved is seller in day-to-day operations and with clients? License/zoning/inspections.Relationship with neighbors and veterinary clinics.Longevity of staff. If grooming is a part of the business, is it a groomer or the seller doing the work? How does the facility stand out from the competition in the area?"

Resources

Associations
- International Boarding and Pet Care Services Association: www.ibpsa.com
- National Association of Professional Pet Sitters: www.petsitters.org

Dollar Stores		
	NAICS 452990	Number of Businesses/Units 36,235

Rules of Thumb
- 15 to 20 percent of annual sales plus inventory
- 2 to 2.5 times SDE plus inventory
- 2 to 2.5 times EBITDA
- 1.5 to 2 times EBIT

Rules of Thumb - D

Pricing Tips
- "With the increase in competition, margins must be looked into carefully."
- "Sells easily, as mom-and-pops are moving in, and it's day hours only."
- "Very competitive market. More diversification and the astute marketers are moving to the $1–$5 spread."
- "There seems to be a downward pressure on profitability but the dollar stores are expanding into higher priced and higher margin items."

Expert Comments
"Stores do better in a down economy."

"Not too difficult to replicate; needs a large amount of inventory; the larger the store, the better the variety and the sales."

"Easy to replicate and possible margin squeeze"

Benchmark Data

Statistics (Dollar and Variety Stores)
Number of Establishments	36,235
Average Profit Margin	3.9%
Revenue per Employee	$223,900
Average Number of Employees	6.9
Average Wages per Employee	$20,396

Products and Services Segmentation
Others	25.0%
Groceries	22.4%
Drugs, health aids and beauty cosmetics such as lipsticks	13.2%
Soaps, detergents, cleaning supplies and paper related products	11.8%
Men's and womenswear, and other textile products	10.5%
Cosmetics such as moisturizers, and hygiene products	8.6%
Kitchenware and home furnishings	8.5%

Industry Costs
Profit	3.9%
Wages	9.2%
Purchases	71.5%
Depreciation	1.2%
Marketing	0.4%
Rent and Utilities	5.9%
Other	7.9%

Market Share
Dollar General Corporation	35.8%
Family Dollar Stores Inc.	18.9%
Dollar Tree Stores Inc.	16.4%
Big Lots Inc.	9.1%

Source: IBISWorld, March 2015

- www.buckstore.com/store-development is an excellent site and we suggest if more information about size, investment dollars, etc. is needed, this is the site to visit. In fact if you are even visiting dollar stores don't miss this site.

D - Rules of Thumb

"Prices at Dollar General for the same item tend to be 30 to 40 percent cheaper than a typical drugstore, and 15 to 20 percent cheaper than a standard grocery store, MacDonald said. Most of Dollar General's items are priced below $10, with about 25 percent of goods selling for $1 or less. Family Dollar's average transaction is about $10, with about 30 percent of merchandise priced at $1 or less, according to the companies."

Source: www.buckstore.com/dollar-stores by Chelsey Livingston, Staff Writer, May 2, 2014

- "Good ones do over $550 per sq.ft."
- "$400–$600 Sq. Ft."

Expenses as a percentage of annual sales

Cost of goods	70% to 75%
Payroll/labor Costs	15% to 17%
Occupancy	10%
Profit (estimated pretax)	20% to 25%

Industry Trend

- "In the wake of a second-quarter profit plunge of more than 30 percent, Matthews, N.C.-based Family Dollar Stores said it will shutter 370 underperforming stores later this year and cut prices on 1,000 products as it embarks on a strategic business review of its operations.

  "The 8,100 national dollar store chain also said it would curtail new store openings in the next fiscal years to 350 to 400 from its original projected estimate of 525 stores that it planned to open this year alongside 'reducing corporate overhead' that will result in job cuts in a bid to save in upwards of $45 million annually in operating costs to deliver stronger shareholder returns.

  "Highlights of the ongoing business review include:
    - ✓ A significant investment to lower prices on about 1,000 basic items.
    - ✓ Reducing its cost structure through the optimization of our workforce.
    - ✓ Closing approximately 370 underperforming stores.
    - ✓ Slow new store growth beginning in fiscal 2015 to improve ROI"

  Source: "Family Dollar Shutters 370 Stores," April 10, 2014, www.progressivegrocer.com

- "Showing that many Americans are still pinching pennies, the largest dollar store chains are planning to open more new stores nationwide in 2014 than they have since the economic recession started.

  "Dollar General Corp., which operates 11,061 stores in 40 states, wants to open 700 more of its yellow stores in the coming year. Plans are to also remodel or relocate another 525, said company spokesman Dan MacDonald. Competitor Family Dollar Stores Inc. runs 8,000 storefronts in 46 states, said spokesman Josh Braverman. Plans are to open 525 more stores and close 80 locations nationally in fiscal year 2014. The company's fiscal year started in September. Family Dollar says its average customer is a female head-of-household in her mid-40s earning $40,000 a year.

  "Seventy percent of Dollar General stores are in communities with populations of less than 20,000, according to the company. Family Dollar in the past has looked to open in strip shopping centers, in urban and suburban areas. Now Family Dollar prefers to build new stores to suit, company officials said."

  Source: Dollar Stores, Chelsey Levingston, www.buckstore.com/dollar-stores, May 2, 2014

- "Next to supercenters, dollar stores remain the fastest growing channel among food, drug, and mass retailing. No-frills stores, low prices, and a small, easy-

Rules of Thumb - **D**

to-shop and easy-to-access format gives shoppers a convenient option to big box discount retailers, like Wal-Mart. 'Dollar stores combine pricing power, efficient operations, and small stores to make the model work,' comments Skrovan."

Source: www.retailindustry.about.com/od/seg_dollar_stores/a/bl

Questions
- "Tax returns and all invoices"
- "Paperwork, and sit and observe"
- "Margins and vendor contacts"

Resources
Websites
- Dollar$tores: www.buckstore.com—a must see site

	Franchise
Domino's Pizza (See also Franchises, Pizza Shops)	
Approx. Total Investment	$119,950 to $461,700
Estimated Annual Sales/Unit	$800,000
SIC 5812-22 NAICS 722513	Number of Businesses/Units 10,040

Rules of Thumb
➢ 45 percent of the first $400K in annual sales, 50 percent of the next $100K ($400 to $500K) in annual sales, then 55 percent of the next $250K of annual sales (from $500 to $750K)

Resources
Websites
- www.dominosbiz.com

Donut Shops (See also Dunkin' Donuts, Restaurants—Limited Service)	
SIC 5461-05 NAICS 722515	Number of Businesses/Units 19,350

Rules of Thumb
➢ 45 to 50 percent of annual sales plus inventory (and can go much higher for a great store)
➢ 2 to 2.5 times SDE plus inventory

Pricing Tips
- "Higher coffee sales (60 percent of sales) produce higher value. Very low coffee sales produce lower values."
- "Length & cost of lease? Retail vs. wholesale business? Percentage of business that is coffee (the higher the percentage of coffee sales, the higher the price)"

26th Edition   263

D - Rules of Thumb

Benchmark Data

- For Additional Benchmark Information see Restaurants -- Limited Service

Statistics (Doughnut Stores)

Number of Establishments	19,350
Average Profit Margin	6.4%
Revenue per Employee	$85,900
Average Number of Employees	7.8
Average Wages per Employee	$22,480

Products and Services Segmentation

Donuts in bulk	25%
Coffee	20%
Other beverages	18%
Other items	18%
Yeast donuts	10%
Mini donuts and donut holes	5%
Other donuts	4%

Industry Costs

Profit	6.4%
Wages	26.1%
Purchases	39.0%
Depreciation	2.0%
Marketing	4.5%
Rent & Utilities	6.0%
Other	16.0%

Source: IBISWorld, June 2014

- "The store needs to be located on the morning side of traffic flow in order to do a high volume and to minimize … risk of failure. The donut business is not an absentee business."

Source: The Donut Factory

Expenses as a percentage of annual sales

Cost of goods	21% food (+ 4.2% paper goods)
Payroll/labor Costs	20% to 23%
Occupancy	10%
Profit (estimated pretax)	0

	Franchise
Dream Dinners (See also Franchises)	
Approx. Total Investment	$273,200 to $418,000
	Number of Businesses/Units 85

Rules of Thumb

- ➢ 40 percent of annual sales plus inventory

Resources

Websites

- www.dreamdinners.com

Rules of Thumb - D

Drive-in Restaurants (See also Restaurants)	
NAICS 722513	

Rules of Thumb
- ➢ 40 to 45 percent of annual sales plus inventory
- ➢ 5 to 6 times monthly sales plus inventory

Drive-In Theaters (See also Movie Theaters)	
NAICS 512132	Number of Businesses/Units 393

Rules of Thumb
- ➢ 2 percent of annual sales plus equipment and real estate

Benchmark Data
- "In 2013, there were 393 Drive-ins in the U.S., up from 366 in 2012."

Source: natoonline.org

Industry Trend
- "Drive-ins and small-town movie theaters have been challenged in the past few years since the movie industry has been phasing out film prints and implementing the use of digital protection. Adapting to digital, however, can cost theater owners $70,000–$80,000 per projector."
- "The most recent statistics from Drive-Ins.com say there are only 442 drive-in theaters left in the world—including 350 in the U.S. and 53 in Canada. The site says when drive-ins were at their peak in 1958, somewhere between 4,000 and 5,000 drive-ins were in operation in the U.S."

Source: Drive In Theaters by Tim Lammers, Drive-Ins.com

- "Drive-in theater closes after 66 years—A 66-year-old drive-in movie theater in St. Albans, Vt., has closed. Harold Ryan Jr. told the St. Albans Messenger that he was just 2 years old when his parents built the theater in 1948, and it was just the second theater of its kind in Vermont at the time. Admission was a quarter per person, and children under 12 were free. When the theater was first opened, the movies were on reels that had to be spliced together. Last year, distributors moved to a digital format, forcing theater owners to upgrade their projectors. That did not happen at the drive-in."

Source: "New England in brief," *Boston Globe*, July 8, 2014

Resources

Associations
- United Drive-in Theatre Owners Association: www.driveintheatre-ownersassociation.org

D - Rules of Thumb

Dr. Vinyl (See also Franchises)	Franchise
Approx. Total Investment	$44,000 t0 $69,500
NAICS 325211	Number of Businesses/Units 170+

Rules of Thumb
➢ 75 percent of annual sales plus inventory

Resources
Websites
- www.drvinyl.com

Dry Cleaners	
SIC 7212-01 | NAICS 812320	Number of Businesses/Units 37,366

Rules of Thumb

➢ 1 times to 1.2 times annual revenues. The larger dry cleaners, over $500,000 with a cash flow of 40% or more command higher prices. Typically, a dry cleaner doing $1 million or more in revenue annually will sell for 1.1 to 1.2 times revenue.

➢ SDE is usually 35%–40% of gross revenues.

➢ 70 to 80 percent of sales plus inventory. Plants with on-site laundry equipment will get a higher multiple. Plants with over-the-counter sales of $35,000 will receive higher multiples.

➢ 2.5 to 3 times SDE plus inventory

➢ 2 to 3 times EBIT

➢ 2.5 to 3 times EBITDA

➢ 2 times SDE for a poor unit, 2.5 times SDE for a "so-so" business, 3 times SDE for a good store, 3.5 times SDE for a "hot" unit with a good lease & equipment, 4 times SDE for a real "winner."

➢ "70% of annual gross sales if equipment is under five years old. If equipment is between six and 10 years old, it will be 60% of annual gross sales. If equipment is over 11 years old, it will be between 40% and 50% of the annual gross sales."

➢ "Purchase price ranges from 70% of annual sales to 100%. Single stores with full garment pricing (no discounts, no coupons) & having monthly retail sales over $35,000 will achieve the higher multiple. Retail pick-up stores (no equipment) 25% to 50% of annual sales."

➢ "One can get 3 times cash flow (SDE) if the owner is a manager and does not perform a specific job such as counter, dry cleaner or presser. If the owner does perform a specific job, such as dry cleaner, etc., the cash flow should include the owner's salary and the business would be valued at 2.5 times that cash flow."

> "Dollar for dollar (100 percent of sales) on a plant that has dry cleaning equipment and a single-buck or double-buck shirt unit, assuming all sales are over-the-counter, not from pick-up stores or hotels or other cleaners. 75 percent of sales for plant w/o shirt unit, & 50 percent of sales on pick-up stores, assuming sales are $125,000 or more."

Pricing Tips

- "Dry cleaning machine and shirt machine play a big key role in pricing. There will be a significant price different between a dry cleaner plant with an extra large size and good brand hydro carbon machine and very good condition shirt machine vs. dry cleaner with perc machine and no or older type shirt machine. Perc dry cleaner machine will be obsolete in 2020, therefore it has no value; it's the same with a shirt machine, if the owner does it with old press machine, creative old way vs. newer shirt machine. A good brand 60-lb. hydro- carbon dry cleaning machine and shirt machine will run approximately $80,000 to $100,000 after delivery and installation, and configuring, plumbing and electrical. Other important equipment overlooked are all pressers and the boiler—are they installed correctly and are they up to the current code?"
- "Dry cleaner plant with high volume over-the-counter (retail vs. wholesale) will get more SDE multiple. Ample parking is very important with 1 or 2 assigned parking spaces in the front."
- "Owner who is involved and works in the business will get lower SDE multiple vs. owner who only oversees the business and has all employees in place including front counter."
- "Location, age of equipment and is the equipment state of the art."
- "The price has a lot of qualifications. Larger revenues command higher multiples, age of equipment, location, type of dry cleaning done—discount or full price, delivery, fire restoration, etc."
- "The pricing should not be driven by multiples. Things to consider are: type of equipment, age of equipment, location, the premise lease, the gross sales, services provided and cash flow."
- "There are many factors that will determine value. In order of importance are verified retail sales, lease terms, equipment condition, breakdown of how sales occur (wholesale, discount, full retail, shirts vs. dry cleaning etc.). We also look at competition, tenant mix, parking, signage, customer lists and more."
- "Dry cleaners under $500,000 in sales sell dollar for dollar to sales. Higher volume dry cleaners can command a premium up to 20%–25%."
- "Break down gross sales between pickup stores, route sales, and wholesale accounts."
- "If the equipment is over 5 years old, the SDE multiplier should be 2 times."
- "The larger dry cleaners sell for a premium and earn a larger percent SDE. The smaller dry cleaners <$250k do not command a premium price and also earn a smaller percent of SDE."
- "The multiple used can be as much as 3 times if the owner just manages the business and does not perform any specific duties."
- "If the equipment is under five years old, use one (1) times SDE plus what equipment is valued as a going concern."
- "100%–110% of yearly gross, depending on equipment condition, age, etc., competition, and location."

D - Rules of Thumb

- "If the dry cleaner does its own shirts in-house with its own shirt equipment, the price can be 3 x SDE or 100% of gross sales. The value based on gross sales is assumed that all the sales come over the counter and not from an outside agency, such as hotels, tailor shops, or other dry cleaners and office convenience stores."
- "Sixty percent (60%) of annual gross sales if equipment is over 10 years old. Eighty-five percent (85%) of annual gross sales if equipment is under 5 years old."
- "The most common rule of thumb for determining the marketing price used by sellers and buyers (and brokers!) is still one times the annual gross sales for a full plant, and 50 percent of annual gross sales for a pickup store. The actual selling price is then a percentage up or down from that starting point (usually down), depending on specific features of the business. The more important features are the type and length of the lease; type, age and condition of equipment; ability to verify actual annual gross sales; and the location. Due to environmental issues, the most important feature is a lease that allows for dry cleaning with perc or petroleum on the premises and at least 10 years of term (five years with five-year option to renew). Most sellers today want to be 'cashed out' and outside financing is available. Many buyers feel that if they are paying cash with outside financing (usually with higher interest rates), then the seller should discount his selling price. Often when outside financing is available, the seller will still be required to provide a small promissory note to make up the difference between the agreed selling price, down payment, and funds provided by the lender."
- "'A business is worth what a buyer is willing to pay for it and what the seller is willing to sell it for.' We hear this a lot and cannot argue with this wisdom. The majority of dry cleaners are small cash businesses and family owned and operated. Many cannot provide substantial financial information with accurate cash flow/net profit figures. Consequently, buying decisions are based more on the buyer's approval of the location and equipment. If the contingencies for sales verification and satisfactory lease are met, then buyers can feel comfortable with the simple multiple of gross sales method. Depending on the variables present with each business, most desirable plants are selling for 75–99 percent of verifiable gross sales. Pickup stores are selling for 20–50 percent of sales, and routes can go for 15–40 percent."
- "Dry cleaning plants without laundry equipment have been selling for 75 to 85 percent of annual net total sales. Dry cleaning plants with laundry equipment have been selling for 85 to 100 percent of annual net sales. Also, selling price ranges from 2.65 to 3.5 x discretionary cash flow earnings before owner's compensation and debt service."

Expert Comments

"Dry cleaners with plants are very costly, with all the environmental and state and city requirements. Landlords who rent to dry cleaners are very careful about contamination, especially the dry cleaners with perc. machines that have the history of causing contamination. All the perc.machines will be replaced with hydrocarbon, wet dry cleaner machines, etc."

"Age of the equipment and the care of it is very important. The trend is for dry clean business owners to eliminate the use of perchlorethylene as the cleaning solvent. Buyers should take into consideration the cost of a new dry cleaning machine that will use the environmentally friendly solvents."

"The dry cleaning industry is consolidating with the Mom & Pops closing due to mega giant discount dry cleaners being built. Too many small dry cleaners have been built, however; good new locations are hard to find. The build out price of a dry cleaner is high due to the amount of equipment needed; older small dry cleaners cannot compete."

"Competition is driven by services. Amount of risk is low if services are high and a clean store is maintained"

"Dry cleaning is not difficult, just a lot of hard work!"

"Competition in the dry cleaning industry is very high and reputation and location are very important factors."

"Dry cleaners under $400,000 easy to replicate, dry cleaners over $750,000 very difficult to replicate, dry cleaners over $1 million, very very difficult to replicate"

"Good business, especially if the family of the owner is part of the mix."

"Competition from discount cleaners hurts the profit."

"Dry cleaning is a long-term business with not a lot of drastic ups and downs."

Benchmark Data

Statistics (Dry Cleaners)

Number of Establishments	37,366
Average Profit Margin	7.1%
Revenue per Employee	$63,300
Average Number of Employees	3.9
Average Wages per Employee	$19,393

Products and Services Segmentation

Retail dry cleaning and laundry services	64.2%
Commercial full-service laundry	15.7%
Commercial dry cleaning services	12.3%
Other	7.8%

Industry Costs

Profit	7.1%
Wages	30.8%
Purchases	19.8%
Depreciation	5.2%
Marketing	3.0%
Rent & Utilities	17.9%
Other	16.2%

Source: IBISWorld, April 2015

- "Dry cleaner agencies have higher COGS because the garment will be picked up and delivered by dry cleaner plants."
- "A well-designed dry clean plant can operate in smaller spaces then most businesses. $150 per square foot should be the gross sales to look for."

D - Rules of Thumb

- "The profitability of a dry cleaner depends on rent and payroll. The rent at a plant needs to be no more than 15% and payroll should be around 24%–26% to be profitable."
- "Typical breakeven for a dry cleaning store is approximately $150,000 annual sales. Average is $250,000."
- "Almost 36% of dry cleaners are utilizing coupons 'often' as part of their marketing strategy, according to results from this month's American Drycleaner Your Views survey. On the flip side, 30.1% of those surveyed say they do not use coupons at all as part of their marketing strategy, while 23.7% say they only use them 'on occasion.' Roughly 11% distribute coupons 'every few months.' Direct mail is the most popular way dry cleaners distribute coupons (61.2%), while some utilize the Internet through social media (41.8%); in-house e-mail (35.8%); or through e-mail services such as Groupon (13.4%). Some dry cleaners have taken the traditional approach by distributing coupons through the newspaper (19.4%), while some utilize other forms of distribution (25.4%), like door hangers, or featuring their coupons on grocery store receipts."
  Source: "Survey: 70% of Dry Cleaners Dish Up Discounts as Part of Marketing Strategy," by Carlo Calma, www.americandrycleaner.com, February 12, 2014
- "Rent and payroll are the most important expenses and need to be in line with sales."
- "Labor percentage should be at least 36% to 40% for an absentee owner."
- "Location with drive-thru"
- "Keep agency work to a minimum."
- "Large dry cleaners—$750,000 annual sales, avg. 3,000 sq. ft."
- "Each employee presser should generate between $1,300 and $1,800 of sales per week."
- "Supply costs (hangers, bags, cleaning solvent, etc.): approx. 6% to 8% of gross sales. Payroll costs for an owner-operated store: 30% to 35% of gross sales. SDE profit: approx. 25% to 32%."

Expenses as a percentage of annual sales
Cost of goods	30%
Payroll/labor Costs	25% (lower figure with owner working full time)
Occupancy	11% to 15% + RETaxes & CAM (top locations MA)
Profit (estimated pretax)	15% to 25%

Industry Trend

- "Dry cleaners with perc.machines will be closing down unless they are in great location and their volume is high. More and more bigger cleaners will be replacing the little cleaners, including discount cleaners. It is very difficult for discount cleaners to make a profit in a high cost area like California."
- "Sales will be up as more and more employees are trending to looking and feeling good about how they present themselves."
- "Tide is already known as a laundry detergent. Now, the brand is being expanded into a chain of franchised dry cleaners, with the first location in Minnesota now open in Apple Valley. The location touts its drive-thru and 24-hour service, including a dropbox where customers can leave laundry at any time along with 24-hour lockers where customers can pick up their dry cleaning anytime. Procter & Gamble owns the Tide brand. The franchise is being

developed in conjunction with Procter & Gamble's wholly owned subsidiary, Agile Pursuits Franchising Inc."

Source: http://www.twincities.com/business/ci_28020131/business-briefing-tide-dry-cleaners-opens-franchise April 30, 2015

- "Dry cleaning industry in general is consolidating. Larger dry cleaners are taking over market share from the smaller cleaners and offering discounting small dry cleaners cannot compete with."
- "I believe we are in the beginning of a growth phase. Consumer confidence, fabrics, clothing costs and economy are some of the reasons. It's easy to copy but hard to replicate a successful operation. Our industry is very detailed in nature. The removal of small stains, professional pressing, replacing missing or cracked buttons are all fairly easy tasks but you need someone on staff that will actually look for and complete. It is this consistency of quality and caring that will build your sales. Customer service is the primary reason people either stop coming or continue to become loyal customers."
- "In metropolitan areas, business will decline. In high-income areas, it will grow."

Seller Financing

- "Seller financing is a must, usually 50 to 60% down and the rest will be carried by the seller for 4 to 5 years with 5% to 7% interest depending on the monthly payment."
- "Combination of bank and seller carry financing."
- "Bank financing is difficult to get for dry cleaners although not impossible. Seller financing is preferred although a lot of sellers do not want to provide any financing."
- "5 to 10 years"
- "Sellers have not been keen to offer seller financing. Typical transaction is bank financed for all cash to the seller. Sometimes we can get sellers to carry back 10 to 15 percent of the purchase, subordinate to the bank."
- "Sellers on the east coast have to hold paper 99 percent of the time—usually 50 to 80 percent financed for 5 to 10 years."

Questions

- "Buyer should ask for all the brands and sizes of all the equipment including laundry machines and determine if the capacity will be enough in case of growth. Number of slots on conveyor line, discount or full service, prices for garment, delivery retail or wholesale. If they do delivery is the van included in the price? Tailoring—if so, who does it? How to handle work in process/accounts receivable."
- "Books and records, age of equipment and what solvent is being used."
- "How many hours are you working?"
- "Who are the biggest competitors?"
- "The age of the boiler and the dry cleaning machine. Anything newer than 10 years is good."
- "How has his business been trending in the last 3 years?"
- "Contamination from PERC"
- "Monthly sales important, any environmental issues, will landlord renew lease?"
- "Where do the gross sales come from: over-the-counter, pick-up stores, hotels, other dry cleaners, etc."

D - Rules of Thumb

Resources

Trade Publications
- National Clothesline: www.natclo.com
- American Dry Cleaner: www.americandrycleaner.com

Associations
- National Cleaners Association: www.nca-i.com
- Dry Cleaning and Laundry Institute: www.dlionline.org

Dry Cleaning Pickup Outlets/Stores (See also Dry Cleaning)

SIC 7212-01	NAICS 812320

Rules of Thumb
- 25 to 50 percent of annual sales
- 30 times weekly sales

Dry Cleaning Routes (See also Dry Cleaning)

SIC 7212-01	NAICS 812320

Rules of Thumb
- 15 to 40 percent of annual revenues

Dry Clean USA (See also Dry Cleaners, Franchises) — Franchise

Approx. Total Investment	$350,000 to $500,000
SIC 7212-01	NAICS 812320	Number of Businesses/Units 450

Rules of Thumb
- 55 percent of annual sales plus inventory

Resources

Websites
- Dry Clean USA: www.drycleanusa.com

Dunkin' Donuts (See also Donut Shops, Franchises) — Franchise

Approx. Total Investment	$240,100 to $1,667,750
Estimated Annual Sales/Unit	$900,000
SIC 5812-06	NAICS 722515	Number of Businesses/Units 10,800

Rules of Thumb - D

Rules of Thumb
- 60 to 100 percent of annual sales plus inventory
- 4 times SDE plus inventory
- 5 times EBITDA
- "Prices typically run 5 times EBITDA on groups of 3 or larger. Rule of thumb, which is still very strong in the marketplace, is about 1.25 times annual sales in very high coffee sale areas of New England. It is closer to 1 times sales in the Mid-Atlantic where coffee sales are still very good, but not as high as in New England. Where coffee sales are much less, values run about .75 times annual sales. These numbers can be affected (up and down) by unusually low or high rents, and/or the requirement to undergo a major remodel in the near future."

Pricing Tips
- "The higher values are ascribed to units with a greater percentage of coffee sales."
- "Dunkin' Donuts' minimum cash required is $750,000 with a net worth of at least $1,500,000. Minimum 5-store development required."

  Source: Dunkin' Donuts

- "The value is decreased if the unit or units require substantial remodeling in less than 4–5 years."
- "Sufficient length of leases and franchise agreements, percentage of businesses coming from coffee/beverages."

Expert Comments

"It is a well-known franchise, but there is stiff competition from Starbucks and McDonald's."

"The marketability is not as high as one would expect for such a profitable and growing business. The reason is that the franchisor has very strict requirements to approve a buyer."

Benchmark Data
- "Fourth quarter highlights include:
  - ✓ Dunkin' Donuts' U.S. comparable store sales growth of 1.4%
  - ✓ Added 260 net new restaurants worldwide including 141 net new Dunkin' Donuts in the U.S.
  - ✓ Revenue increased 5.5%
  - ✓ Adjusted operating income increased 8.4%; adjusted operating income margin of 50.1%
  - ✓ "Fiscal year 2014 highlights include:
  - ✓ Dunkin' Donuts U.S. comparable store sales growth of 1.6%
  - ✓ Added 704 net new restaurants worldwide including 405 net new Dunkin' Donuts in the U.S.
  - ✓ Positive Baskin-Robbins U.S. net store growth
  - ✓ Revenue increased 4.9%"

  Source: http://www.dunkinbrands.com/news/dunkin-brands-reports-fourth-quarter-fiscal-year-2014-results
  February 5, 2015

D - Rules of Thumb

- "How the Donut Divides" ... back-of-the-envelope financial estimates for running a shop that does about $87,000 in sales a month, which he says is about average in New England. Rent on retail space—10%; payroll—22.5%; miscellaneous costs (mortgage payments for the franchise, which can go for $1.5 million around here in New England) plus taxes, utilities, maintenance, etc.—19.1%; food and paper supplies—27.5%; fees to Dunkin Brands split between shared advertising fund and franchise fees)—10.9%; profit (if the shop runs efficiently)—10%.
  "Estimated sales breakdown is beverages—65%; sandwiches, bagels, and other products—27%; and donuts—8%."
  The above is from a very successful franchisee of Dunkin' Donuts with many stores. It is from an article in the *Boston Sunday Globe* written by Neil Swidey, "Time to Make the Empire," September 21, 2014.
  Note: Dunkin' Donuts is an icon of franchises in New England. There is one on almost every corner; and just say Dunkin' and everyone in New England knows what you are talking about. The donuts and coffee are also very good.
- "Food cost can be in the low 20's, as well as labor costs."
- "Food costs 20% to 24% or less, depending on business mix."

Expenses as a percentage of annual sales

Cost of goods	23% to 24% + 4% supplies (paper)
Payroll/labor Costs	22%
Occupancy	08% to 10%
Profit (estimated pretax)	15% to 20%

Industry Trend

- "Dunkin Donuts on Wednesday opened its first store in Reykjavik, Iceland, drawing crowds eager for a taste of the chain's baked goods and coffee. . . .Drangasker, the franchise holder, has the right to open as many as 16 restaurants in the country over five years, chief executive ArniPeturJonsson said. Dunkin's parent company, Canton, Mass.-based Dunkin' Brands Group, signed a deal in January to open more than 1,400 shops in China over the next two decades, plus 100 more in Mexico. Worldwide, the company has 11,000 locations in 36 countries."

  Source: *Bloomberg News* as reported in *Boston Globe*, August 6, 2015
- "Dunkin' Donuts plans to double its locations in the United States over the next 20 years, the company announced Wednesday.The coffee and doughnut chain currently operates nearly 7,000 stores nationwide. Each new store adds an average of 20 to 25 new employees, both full and part time a Dunkin' spokeswoman said."

  Source: "Dunkin' Donuts to double U.S. locations" by Annalyn Censky, CNNMoney

Seller Financing
- "7 years—usually are bank/SBA financed."

Questions
- "When are remodels due? Lease details are critical, and length of time remaining on the franchise agreements. Does the seller have expansion rights in adjacent areas?"
- "What percent of sales is beverages?"

Rules of Thumb - E

Resources

Websites
- www.dunkinfranchising.com

Eagle Transmission Shop	Franchise
(See also AAAMCO Transmissions, Auto Transmission Centers, Franchises)	
Approx. Total Investment	$194,000 to $292,500
SIC 7537-01 NAICS 811113	Number of Businesses/Units 27

Rules of Thumb
- 40 percent of annual sales
- 2.5 times SDE
- This franchise is primarily Texas based, but is expanding.

Benchmark Data
- "Cost to get to breakeven is the same as AAMCO—approx. $200,000 (this is my targeted bottom sale price)."
- "Franchises with an owner overseeing a manager in the expenses are still selling for 2.5 to 3 X SDE."
- "Franchised shops with SDE of at least $100,000 with high percentage retail are very marketable."
- "Franchised shops that historically are not breaking even with a manager in the expenses are very hard to sell."
- "If the location seems OK, the price seems to bottom out at about $125,000. Small independents are getting more and more difficult."

Resources

Websites
- www.eagletransmission.com

E-Commerce (Internet Sales)	
SIC 5731-24 NAICS 454111	Number of Businesses/Units 204,489

Rules of Thumb
- 30 percent of annual sales includes inventory
- 2 to 4 times SDE includes inventory
- 3 to 6 times EBITDA

Pricing Tips
- "Gross sales are not necessarily important to determine value because of tendency for very high gross margins. A business with little or no inventory is more valuable. Businesses with very high inventory are very difficult to value

26th Edition

E - Rules of Thumb

and sell; the business is the inventory."
- "High inventory businesses will be harder to sell. Higher multiples with SDE over $100K are more easily sold. The ease of the operation will determine marketability. Many are too complicated for the average buyer."
- "The more niche-related the product, the higher the multiple."
- "Typically, an e-commerce Website will sell for 2.75x SDE. However, there are variables that may increase the multiple or decrease the multiple. The more automated the Website and if capable of drop shipping, the multiple increases closer to 4x. Also, if there is inventory involved and additional staff is needed the multiple decreases."
- "Prices vary depending on age of business...at least three years is excellent...12 months is usually necessary."
- "Must understand and quantify Internet traffic, search engine rankings (organic vs. ppc), and which sites they sell product through (i.e., eBay, Amazon, internal Website, etc.)"
- "2.5–4x is the range, with the value changing based on barriers to entry such as vendor relationships, natural search positions, years in business, revenue size in general, etc."
- "The gross sales are usually not applicable to determine value because of low expenses."

Expert Comments

"Internet storefronts can easily be replicated. Finding a good source for product will always help reduce risk."

"The business will be more valuable if it is harder to replicate."

"Online shopping continues to grow, but so does the competition, so being able to differentiate oneself is a major coup."

"A unique product with aggressive marketing will usually succeed."

"Internet companies can be replicated structurally, but very difficult to replicate from an SEO stand point."

Benchmark Data

Statistics (E-Commerce & Online Auctions)

Number of Establishments	204,489
Average Profit Margin	3.9%
Revenue per Employee	$843,900
Average Number of Employees	1.8
Average Wages per Employee	$44,840

Products and Services Segmentation

Other merchandise	31.5%
Computer hardware	18.4%
Clothing, footwear and accessories	18.2%
Furniture and home appliances	9.1%
Medication and cosmetics	7.8%
Sporting goods, toys, hobby items and games	7.2%
Office equipment and supplies	5.5%
Food, beverages and alcohol	2.3%

Industry Costs

Profit	3.9%
Wages	5.4%
Purchases	61.1%
Depreciation	0.7%
Marketing	4.8%
Rent & Utilities	3.9%
Other	20.2%

Market Share

Amazon.com Inc.	16.1%

Source: IBISWorld, May 2015

- "Always look at current market comps when pricing as conditions may be subject to change."
- "On average, the gross margin is 20%. The expenses tend to be very low because many internet businesses are relocatable and do not require an office or warehouse."
- "Profits can be as high as 50–90%"
- "Because of the low overhead and ease of operations, many of these businesses have returns of 30%–40%."
- "Average conversion rate would be anything around 1% (that is 1% of all visits turn into orders). Anything over 2% is excellent."
- "Sales per square foot is the key. Sales divided by the square foot."

Expenses as a percentage of annual sales

Cost of goods	20% to 50%
Payroll/labor Costs	0% to 50%
Occupancy	0% to 10%
Profit (estimated pretax)	50% to 60%

Industry Trend

- "Upward trend"
- "Unlimited growth potential for the next 3–5 years"
- "Online shoppers in the United States will spend $327 billion in 2016, up 45% from $226 billion this year and 62% from $202 billion in 2011, according to a projection released today by Forrester Research Inc. In 2016, e-retail will account for 9% of total retail sales, up from 7% in both 2012 and 2011, according to the report, 'US Online Retail Forecast, 2011 to 2016,' by Forrester analyst SucharitaMulpuru. That represents a compound annual growth rate of 10.1% over the five-year forecast period.

  "The steady growth in the number of web shoppers also is helping to boost e-commerce sales. Forrester says that 192 million U.S. consumers will shop online in 2016, up 15% from 167 million in 2012. But the bigger factor in driving e-commerce growth is that each shopper will spend more on average, the report says. U.S. consumers in 2016 will each spend an average of $1,738 online, up 44% from $1,207 in 2012.

  "Many consumers will prefer the Web to bricks-and-mortar retailers in large part because of online deals, the report says—70% of holiday shoppers last year said they made purchases online rather than in stores because online retailers offered better deals."

Source: "E-retail spending to increase 62% by 2016" by Thad Rueter, Senior Editor, Internet Retailer

E - Rules of Thumb

Seller Financing
- "Recently it's buyer financing"
- 1–5 years

Questions
- "Ask the sellers before you analyze numbers if all the revenues generated are from products that either do not require a license to be sold, or, if they do require a license or some kind of special permission, that it transfers or can be transferred to a new owner. Look at 3 year trends in annual sales. Why are you selling? Ask to see payment gateway record for the past 3 years to help verify financials, i.e., company PayPal Account or other merchant gateway. Is all of the income shown on the company Payment Gateway Record only from income generated from that particular company?"
- "Do they have tracking information—Google Analytics, or other? What platform is the Website built on? Is the Website part of a brick and mortar business? If so, are funds co-mingled."
- "How does the business or system operate? Do you stock inventory? How easy and long does it take to learn the operation?"
- "Does the seller inventory the product? Who does the credit card processing and what are their fees? Who does the Web hosting and how much traffic can the Web site handle? How do they maintain their Internet rankings? What are they doing to increase their Web presence?"
- "How easy is it for a buyer to learn the business?"
- "Any repeat business? Percentage of revenue budgeted for advertising?"

Resources

Trade Publications
- Internet Retailer: www.internetretailer.com
- E-Commerce Times: www.ecommercetimes.com/

Electric Motor Repair		
SIC 7694	NAICS 811310	|//
Rules of Thumb		
➢ 33 percent of annual sales plus inventory		
➢ 3 times SDE plus inventory		
➢ 5 times EBIT		
➢ 4 times EBITDA		

Pricing Tips
- "Condition of equipment and customer concentration are significant factors."
- "Industry is always a mix of repair of customer motors and resale of new motors and related products. Rule of thumb for pricing is one-third of annual repair sales plus 15% of annual product sales, plus inventory. Most successful buyers for smaller businesses in the industry have electric motor background. Condition of equipment and extent of machine shop tools is important."

Rules of Thumb - E

Expert Comments

"This is a mature industry. The repair market (higher margins) is stable to declining slightly as increased costs force higher horsepower standard motors to be replaced (lower margins) rather than repaired. Other technological factors and the shift to more offshore manufacturing have resulted in no net growth and eroding profits. Successful shops have either good niche customer markets and/or services or a long- term approach to partnering with customers to reduce customer's motor operating costs. Sales growth for individual companies usually comes from taking sales away from competitors."

Benchmark Data

- $150,000 sales per employee is an average for companies with approximately 2/3 repair, 1/3 new sales.

Expenses as a percentage of annual sales

Cost of goods	25%
Payroll/labor Costs	25%
Occupancy	10%
Profit (estimated pretax)	05%

Industry Trend

- "Repair lags general industry trends. Emphasis on power generation and distribution including wind energy."

Questions

- "Technical strengths of shop employees? Concentration of customers? Where is future growth coming from?"
- "Buyer needs to establish the repeatability and retainability of current customers after change in ownership."

Embroidery Services/Shops

SIC 7389-42	NAICS 314999	

Rules of Thumb

➢ 55 to 60 percent of annual sales plus inventory

Engineering Services

	NAICS 54133	Number of Businesses/Units 162,133

Rules of Thumb

➢ 40 to 45 percent of annual revenues; add value of fixtures & equipment; may require earnout

E - Rules of Thumb

Benchmark Data

Statistics (Engineering Services)
Number of Establishments	162,133
Average Profit Margin	8.6%
Revenue per Employee	$187,400
Average Number of Employees	6.6
Average Wages per Employee	$87,330

Products and Services Segmentation
Industrial and manufacturing projects	21.5%
Transportation projects	18.5%
Commercial, public and institutional projects	13.5%
Miscellaneous federal government projects	12.5%
Other	10.5%
Residential building projects	9.5%
Project management services	8.0%
Municipal utility projects	6.0%

Major Market Segmentation
Private businesses	47.2%
Government bodies	31.1%
Engineering firms	6.1%
Construction firms	5.9%
Architectural firms	5.6%
Individuals	3.3%
Nonprofit organizations	0.8%

Industry Costs
Profit	8.6%
Wages	46.9%
Purchases	12.7%
Depreciation	1.4%
Marketing	1.2%
Rent and Utilities	3.9%
Other	25.3%

Market Share
AECOM	6.6%
Fluor Corp.	2.5%

Source: IBISWorld, June 2015

Environmental Testing
NAICS 541380

Rules of Thumb
- 60 percent of annual sales plus inventory
- 2 to 2.5 times SDE plus inventory

Rules of Thumb - **E**

Pricing Tips
- "SDE must at least be equal to new debt service using a 1.5 ratio, owner's salary and any capex requirements, or it's priced too high."
- "Be sure the accounting is on the accrual method so there is no confusion as to how values are arrived at."

Expert Comments
"Owner and his contacts are more the driving, networking force than the location or the facilities."

Benchmark Data
- "It can be a roll-up-your-sleeves kind of business."

Expenses as a percentage of annual sales	
Cost of goods	02%
Payroll/labor Costs	30%
Occupancy	03%
Profit (estimated pretax)	16%

Industry Trend
- "Steady, but real estate activities have a big influence."

Questions
- "Why did you get in the business and why are you getting out at this time?"

Resources
Websites
- Environmental Business International: www.ebionline.org

Environment Control (Commercial Cleaning Services) — Franchise

(See also Franchises)

Approx. Total Investment		$55,000
	NAICS 561720	Number of Businesses/Units 50

Rules of Thumb
➢ 42 percent of annual sales plus inventory

Pricing Tips
- The firm has 53 units in 19 states. Go to their Website for more information: www.environmentcontrol.com

Resources
Websites
- www.environmentcontrol.com

E - Rules of Thumb

Event Companies

| SIC 7389-44 | NAICS 812990 | Number of Businesses/Units 223,987 |

Rules of Thumb
- ➢ 3 times EBITDA plus asset value

Pricing Tips
- "Are there events on the books going forward? How many repeat clients?"

Benchmark Data

Statistics (Trade Show and Conference Planning)
Number of Establishments	4,934
Average Profit Margin	6.8%
Revenue per Employee	$177,300
Average Number of Employees	15.8
Average Wages per Employee	$42,662

Products and Services Segmentation
Convention and trade show planning	65.0%
Special events and other related services	35.0%

Major Market Segmentation
Other	35.3%
Consumer goods, sporting goods, travel and other consumer services	17.6%
Medical and healthcare	17.6%
Business services	10.4%
Producers of commodities, chemicals and engineered materials manufacturers	10.3%
Communications and information technology	8.8%

Industry Costs
Profit	6.8%
Wages	24.2%
Purchases	29.7%
Depreciation	1.4%
Marketing	19.1%
Rent & Utilities	6.2%
Other	12.6%

Market Share
The Freeman Companies	13.4%
Viad Corp.	5.5%

Source: IBISWorld, December 2014

Statistics (Party & Event Planners)
Number of Establishments	219,053
Average Profit Margin	9.8%
Revenue per Employee	$20,800
Average Number of Employees	1.0
Average Wages per Employee	$6,016

Products and Services Segmentation

Corporate social events	41.6%
Weddings	28.7%
Birthday parties	16.0%
Other	13.7%

Industry Costs

Profit	9.8%
Wages	28.2%
Purchases	21.0%
Depreciation	2.5%
Marketing	6.0%
Rent & Utilities	6.7%
Other	25.8%

Source: IBISWorld, September 2015

Industry Trend

- "Events are no longer a two or three-day project, but create a community that starts before the event begins and continues indefinitely after. Planners must think about a much longer lifecycle of their events than ever before. More are using technology to extend that lifecycle. The biggest barrier to the emergence of these connected communities is that planners may not have time to manage these communities as they are moving on to planning the next event. As this event trend develops, planners will have to incorporate strategies to manage these communities."

"As budgets have turned around and hotels are back to charging premium rates, more planners will be seeking out alternative venues for events.
Most communities have empty warehouses, hangars; blank canvasses with perhaps with fewer limitations than a traditional venue. There are zoos, parks, restaurants, rooftops, parking garage structures, all great locations for events, many with build in décor.

"I believe there will also be more local and regional events vs. national and international events. As travel cost and headaches related to travel have risen, and venue cost has been rising also, I predict that more planners will opt to look a bit closer to home for their events and meeting."

Source: "2015 Meeting and Event Trends for Event Planners" by Al Wynant January 7, 2015,
http://helloendless.com/2015-meeting-event-trends-event-planning/

Seller Financing

- 2 ½ years

Fabric Stores		
SIC 5949-02	NAICS 45113	Number of Businesses/Units 21,674
Rules of Thumb		
➢ 3 times monthly sales plus inventory		

F - Rules of Thumb

Benchmark Data

Statistics (Fabric, Craft & Sewing Supplies Stores)

Number of Establishments	21,674
Average Profit Margin	5.0%
Revenue per Employee	$77,900
Average Number of Employees	2.8
Average Wages per Employee	$11,344

Products and Services Segmentation

Fabrics	40.0%
Sewing and craft supplies	33.0%
Other	12.0%
Seasonal decorations	8.0%
Fabric home decor	7.0%

Industry Costs

Profit	5.0%
Wages	14.6%
Purchases	60.2%
Depreciation	0.9%
Marketing	2.1%
Rent & Utilities	5.5%
Other	11.7%

Market Share

Michaels Stores Inc.	47.7%
Jo-Ann Stores Inc.	26.5%
Hobby Lobby Stores Inc.	19.1%
Hancock Fabrics Inc.	6.0%

Source: IBISWorld, July 2015

Industry Trend

- "Question: What happened to fabric stores? Answer: Good women's clothes made from beautiful fabrics became cheaper as more people were making money on cheap labor, so there was less sewing going on. Also, a lot of stores that have gone were family-run businesses. The younger generation had no interest in continuing to run them."

Resources

Websites
- The Fabric Shop Network—an online resource: www.fabshopnet.com

---

Family Clothing Stores (See also Women's Clothing)

SIC 5651	NAICS 448140	Number of Businesses/Units 45,197

Rules of Thumb

➢ .75 to 1.5 times SDE plus inventory

➢ 2.4 to 2.8 times SDE includes inventory

➢ 40 to 45 percent of annual sales includes inventory

Rules of Thumb - **F**

Pricing Tips
- Women's Apparel— "try 23 percent of annual sales + inventory and/or 1.1 times SDE."

Benchmark Data

Statistics (Family Clothing Stores)
Number of Establishments	45,197
Average Profit Margin	4.9%
Revenue per Employee	$136,700
Average Number of Employees	16.8
Average Wages per Employee	$15,588

Products and Services Segmentation
Other womenswear	25.7%
Women's casual wear	25.5%
Men's casual wear	15.0%
Other menswear	13.1%
Women's formal wear	8.9%
Children's wear	7.8%
Men's formal wear	4.0%

Major Market Segmentation
Generation X	35.5%
Baby boomers	24.5%
Generation Y	22.5%
Seniors aged 65 and over	10.0%
Children aged 9 and under	7.0%
Commercial buyers	0.5%

Industry Costs
Profit	4.9%
Wages	11.3%
Purchases	65.2%
Depreciation	1.0%
Marketing	7.5%
Rent & Utilities	6.2%
Other	3.9%

Market Share
The TJX Companies Inc.	14.3%
Gap Inc.	11.3%
Ross Stores Inc.	10.9%

Source: IBISWorld, August 2015

Expenses as a percentage of annual sales
Cost of goods	46% to 52%
Payroll/labor Costs	14% to 18%
Occupancy	06% to 10%
Profit (estimated pretax)	12% to 15%

Seller Financing
- 5 to 10 years

26th Edition

F - Rules of Thumb

Family Entertainment Centers		
	NAICS 713120	
Rules of Thumb		
➢ 3 times EBITDA		

		Franchise
Fantastic Sam's (See also Barber Shops, Franchises, Great Clips)		
Approx. Total Investment		$136,100 to $247,100
	NAICS 812112	Number of Businesses/Units 1,145
Rules of Thumb		
➢ 35 to 40 percent of annual sales plus inventory		

Resources

Websites
- www.fantasticsams.com

		Franchise
Fast-Fix Jewelry and Watch Repairs (See also Franchises)		
Approx. Total Investment		$150,000 to $240,000
SIC 7631-01 & 7631-02	NAICS 811490	Number of Businesses/Units 160
Rules of Thumb		
➢ 80 to 85 percent of annual sales plus inventory		

Resources

Websites
- www.fastfix.com

		Franchise
FastFrame (See also Franchises)		
Approx. Total Investment		$150,000
SIC 7699-15	NAICS 442299	Number of Businesses/Units 227
Rules of Thumb		
➢ 32 percent of annual sales		

Rules of Thumb - F

	Franchise
FasTracKids	
(See also Schools—Educational/Non-Vocational, Children's Educational Franchises)	
Approx. Total Investment	$78,455 to $210,155
NAICS 624410	Number of Businesses/Units 270

Rules of Thumb
> 45 percent of annual sales plus inventory

Resources
Websites
- www.fastrackids.com/

		Franchise
Fast Signs (See also Franchises, Sign Companies)		
Approx. Total Investment		$178,207–$289,498
SIC 3993-02	NAICS 541890	Number of Businesses/Units 570

Rules of Thumb
> 42 to 46 percent of annual sales plus inventory

Resources
Websites
- www.fastsigns.com

Fire Suppression Systems Sales & Services		
	NAICS 238220	

Rules of Thumb
> 80 percent of annual sales plus inventory

> 2.2 times SDE plus inventory

Pricing Tips
- "Business does not have to be profitable to obtain price, but must have good accounts, preferably with contracts in place."
- "The value of the customers can depend on whether the owner is the primary contact or the employees."
- "Most of these businesses are small and run by a family. There are larger companies that are actively seeking to roll up smaller companies. Their primary interest is retaining the current customers and the pricing of the products and services. They are more focused on gross sales than SDE or EBITDA."

F - Rules of Thumb

Expert Comments

"Location of the business is not important as long as it is central to its customer base. In general these are not retail businesses and do not have walk-in traffic. They test/service/refill fire extinguishers and do installation and service of fire suppression systems. This has been a 'mom-and-pop' industry with businesses that have revenues of less than $1 million. There are several companies like Simplex Grinnell who are big players. It is an industry that is ripe for roll-up to increase revenues by adding customers, and consolidation is occurring in many markets."

Benchmark Data

- "Typical benchmarks are sales per customer. These range from $100 to a $1,000 per year. Customer concentrations can be of big concern. A large quantity of smaller companies and customers that represent less than 5% of revenue are preferred."

Expenses as a percentage of annual sales

Cost of goods	20%
Payroll/labor Costs	24%
Occupancy	05% to 06%%
Profit (estimated pretax)	15%

Industry Trend

- "Smaller businesses will be purchased by larger businesses."
- "Increasing NFPA requirements for portable extinguishers is driving the sale of new models with an opportunity to increase service. Businesses have to stay compliant with NFPA standards for insurance purposes."

Questions

- "Revenue per customer? Are there contracts in place for service? Employees interact with customers, so questions about their capabilities are important. Ask questions about relationships with local fire marshals and fire departments which can be very important. You want them on your side because they are often the enforcement arm for fire safety compliance."
- "Questions about customer concentration. There should be lots of small accounts as measured by revenue ($500–$1,000 per year). Large accounts suggest risk in transfer for the buyer."

Resources

Associations
- National Fire Sprinkler Association: www.nfsa.org
- National Fire Protection Association: www.nfpa.org
- Fire Suppression Systems Association: http://www.fssa.net/

Rules of Thumb - F

Fish & Seafood Markets

	NAICS 445220	Number of Businesses/Units 4,716

Rules of Thumb

> 20 to 25 percent of annual sales plus inventory

Benchmark Data

Statistics (Fish and Seafood Markets)

Number of Establishments	4,716
Average Profit Margin	3.3%
Revenue per Employee	$171,800
Average Number of Employees	2.8
Average Wages per Employee	$21,402

Products and Services Segmentation

Finfish	68.7%
Shellfish	27.3%
Other	4.0%

Major Market Segmentation

Consumers	65.5%
Single-location restaurants	27.2%
Chain restaurants	7.3%

Industry Costs

Profit	3.3%
Wages	12.4%
Purchases	69.8%
Depreciation	1.7%
Marketing	0.7%
Rent & Utilities	4.8%
Other	7.3%

Source: IBISWorld, January 2015

Industry Trend

- "The world seafood market, which encompasses fresh, canned and frozen seafood products, is expected to excess $370 billion by 2015, according to Global Industry Analysts. It is predicted the market will be fueled by a rising global population, increased discretionary incomes, and technological advances such as packaging and improved transportation. Demand will be particularly strong in developing regions including Latin America and Asia-Pacific. The overall market for aquaculture and fisheries is predicted to exceed 135 million tons by 2015, reports Global Industry Analysts.

    Source: "Fish and Seafood Markets," www.reportlinker.com/ci02030/fish-and-seafood.html

- "Going forward, the pace and robustness of the recovery will determine how overall sales improve for fish and seafood and which of the various categories will enjoy the highest growth. Packaged Facts projects that the retail market for fish and seafood will grow to $17.1 billion by 2017, with the overall compound annual growth rate for the retail fish and seafood market projected at 3.1% for the period."

    Source: www.packagedfacts.com/Fish-Seafood-Trends-7649917/

26th Edition

F - Rules of Thumb

Fitness Centers (See also Racquet Sports Clubs)

| SIC 7991-01 | NAICS 713940 | Number of Businesses/Units 89,708 |

Rules of Thumb

- 70 to 100 percent of annual sales plus inventory
- 2 to 3 times SDE plus inventory
- 4 to 5 times EBIT
- 3 to 4 times EBITDA
- "One year's annual revenues, usually reduced (or pro-rated) by memberships already contracted and paid for"
- "The clubs today have the electronic transfer money systems . . . One rule of thumb would be ten times the monthly amount . . . so if the club has $10,000 a month going through the electronic transfer, then the price would be $100,000 plus the value of the equipment . . . taking into consideration that the lease has sufficient time on it . . . most clubs today have $30,000 and up on the electronic transfer money. If there is 10 years on the lease, added value can be given for that."

Pricing Tips

- "This is a capital intensive business, so first break apart tangible and intangible assets. Sadly, the market value of used fitness equipment is generally low, so the primary value will be from cash flow; however, it will be easier to break this out first to better value large from smaller facilities. For intangible value average the cash flow quantity and quality. Use 2x SDE for intangible quantity and average that with 10x monthly contract revenues to reflect the quality (or dependability) of that cash flow. Finally, calculate the value of outstanding paid-in-full contracts and subtract that from the consideration."
- "Pricing varies by size. Smaller fitness studios with little infrastructure may sell for 3X EBIT. Larger businesses, with multiple locations, upscale clientele and solid management team, will be much higher."
- "If the business model is based on member's paying monthly through pre authorized payments this business can be very stable. Most facilities have a good value in assets if the owner takes care in maintaining the equipment. The greatest challenge is often from rising occupancy cost so if an owner can purchase the building they occupy or secure a long term favourable rental agreement, they can ensure their continued profitability. Many facilities have gone with great success to a model that includes multiple revenue streams (personal training, group fitness, nutritional consultation, juice bar, pro shop, etc.) to provide a better and more even cash flow."
- "Drivers are quality of equipment and facilities. 5% of annual revenues needs to go into CAPEX annually so best driver of value is EBITDA minus CAPEX (Capital Expenditures). Facilities get a lot of wear and tear and they need to be updated regularly. Retention also drives multiple and value. Facilities with excellent retention (better than 80%) will garner higher multiples and valuations than those at 60% or less. 60% is usually average retention rate for a quality facility 50% or less for poorer run facilities."
- "Be wary of value of smaller storefront facilities/franchises. Many are often upside down, meaning a multiple of EBITDA doesn't justify the original purchase price on the business."

Rules of Thumb - F

- "Multiples vary by size of the business. A small yoga or Pilates studio would likely generate a 3 times multiple of adjusted EBITDA, whereas a multi-location larger chain could generate a 5x multiple, or up to 1x revenue, assuming a 20% profit margin. Multiples will be lower if the owner teaches personally."
- "What condition is the equipment in? Is the lease within market rents?"
- "Fitness and/or health centers historically have been priced at 10 times the Electronic Transfer Money. Example: If the club has $15,000 a month on the electronic transfer money, times 10 equals $150,000 plus value of equipment. Equipment can be about $100,000 (depreciated), plus a ten-year lease is added value . . . so market price would be on or about $300,000.00 to $350,000.00 depending on condition of the facility . . . naturally all of this would be assuming the $15,000 cash flow covers the net, plus . . . "

Major franchise companies in the fitness business

Name	# of Units	Approximate Investment
Anytime Fitness	2,100	N/A
Curves	9,400	$39,170-$44,595
Gold's Gym	683	$895,000–$1 million
Snap Fitness	1,900	$77,000 to $242,000

Expert Comments

"Never get into fitness center ownership because of your knowledge of fitness alone. Be sure you have adequate sales and marketing resources to survive."

"Fitness is enjoying a lot of popularity right now, which has brought in a great deal of competition. It is about sales production, and often people get into it thinking it is about fitness, Because of their failures, the equipment, while expensive, isn't worth that much although recurring revenues from contracts in place are worth a great deal."

"The media spends a lot of time promoting fitness and diet. This is a business that isn't going away."

"In the CrossFit space specifically, competition is increasing to keep up with consumer demand, which has grown several fold over the past 5 years. Gyms can command a premium if they:
 ✓ have established themselves deeply in the local market and build strong brands
 ✓ have trainers that have built large and engaged followings
 ✓ have sent delegates to compete in the CrossFit games
 ✓ are in Tier 1 locations (but not crippled by rent)."

"This is a competitive industry with a lot of different segments; low-cost, low-service to high-touch, high-cost facilities. You need to understand where a facility fits in its competitive landscape."

"The biggest risk to fitness center business is capitalization. It takes 12–18 months to get to breakeven. They get hurt if they don't adequately capital their companies. Once you get to breakeven, 70–90% of the next dollar flows to the bottom line, so depending on its profitability trend, bringing a little bit of growth can be very accretive."

"These are excellent businesses to sell. It's a fun industry and fun business.

F - Rules of Thumb

There are lots of buyers."

"Health and fitness is on trend."

"Building from scratch or green fielding operations has much more risk associated with it."

"Location in affluent areas is key for successful Pilates or yoga studios. A long-term lease is also key. Private sessions are significantly more profitable than group classes, so a studio with a higher percentage of privates will be more profitable than one that focuses on group classes. Industry is highly fragmented, with few large industry players."

"There are a few big publicly held competitors in the marketplace which have a big effect on market areas that are densely populated. There are increasing numbers of franchise systems filling niche areas of the fitness industry. Though there is more competition, health club membership enrollment by the general population is still well below 20% nationwide. This, coupled with the increasing awareness of the need for regular exercise, bodes well for continued industry growth."

"The average rate of memberships per capita continues to grow in the U.S. Obesity is a major health concern, which employers and insurance companies are starting to battle by providing health club membership assistance. Full-service clubs are but one choice in a market that continues to grow with clubs that focus on niches of the industry (i.e., women only, children's performance, 24/7 convenience clubs, etc.)."

Benchmark Data

Statistics (Gym, Health & Fitness Clubs)

Number of Establishments	89,708
Average Profit Margin	8.9%
Revenue per Employee	$44,200
Average Number of Employees	8.0
Average Wages per Employee	$14,028

Products and Services Segmentation

Fitness and recreational sport center services	43.9%
Membership fees	41.9%
Personal training services	5.7%
Merchandise sales	2.8%
Roller and ice skating rink services	2.6%
Other	1.9%
Spa services	1.2%

Industry Costs

Profit	8.9%
Wages	32.1%
Purchases	20.0%
Depreciation	7.4%
Marketing	10.0%
Rent & Utilities	15.5%
Other	6.1%

Source: IBISWorld, April 2015

Rules of Thumb - **F**

- "Contract sales should be at least 75% of total revenues in a healthy sales environment."
- "The Scope of the Health Club Industry
    - ✓ Number of US Clubs: 32,150 (as of 01/14)
    - ✓ Number of US Health Club Members: 52.9 million (as of 01/14)
    - ✓ Number of US IHRSA Member Clubs: 5,900
    - ✓ 2013 Total US Industry Revenues: $22.4 billion
    - ✓ Approximate Number of Health Clubs Worldwide (in 66 markets): 165,300
    - ✓ Approximate Number of Health Club Members Worldwide: 138.7 million
    - ✓ 2012 Total Global Industry Revenues: $78.1 Billion (USD)"

    Source: http://www.ihrsa.org/industry-research/
- "Good benchmark numbers to look at are the total number of active members (paying monthly) and the average amount each of those member pay. Member growth and attrition over a three-year period can be a good indicator as to future performance."
- "Urban is $200 per square foot; suburban is $100 per square foot. Occupancy costs of 15% average; 20% OK but high; less than 10%, excellent. Location is key; need highly visible, easily accessible locations."
- "Profit of 10%–20%, membership attrition rate of 30% is average."

Expenses as a percentage of annual sales

Cost of goods	05%
Payroll/labor Costs	23% to 25%
Occupancy	20% to 25%
Profit (estimated pretax)	15% to 20%

Industry Trend

- "Remember Curves, very hot when it was introduced and now they are difficult to give away. Similar fitness centers models built on a program grow rapidly and will then collapse. They can be very profitable if you get in early and then get out after growing a number of units. Generic facilities will have greater staying power."
- "Physical inactivity is growing in the United States despite health club memberships growing, too, according to the Physical Activity Council's (PAC) 2015 Participation Report released Thursday.The report showed physical inactivity has reached a six-year high even though health club memberships across the country have grown during nearly the same period. According to a media release from the PAC, 82.7 million Americans (28.3 percent) were physically inactive in 2014, an increase of 0.7 percent from 2013."

    Source: "PAC Report: American Physical Inactivity Reaches Six-Year High, Club Memberships Increase" by Eric Stromgren, www.clubindustry.com 4/23/15
- "Ten Fitness Trends to Look Out for in 2015
    - ✓ More people will utilize wearable technology to monitor and record biometric data.
    - ✓ Online video-on-demand workout programs will become increasingly common.
    - ✓ Online personal training goes mainstream.
    - ✓ 'Functional training' will recede from our lexicon and the concept of loaded movement training will become more popular.
    - ✓ Group-based training programs will be personalized to each individual

F - Rules of Thumb

- participating in the workout.
- ✓ Participation in one-on-one personal training will decline at large health clubs in favor of small group or semi-private training programs.
- ✓ Workout programs will move away from pure High-intensity Interval Training (HIIT) and start featuring more intelligent program design that allows for proper recovery from the stresses of exercise.
- ✓ Trainers and clients will begin to use biomarkers to track progress from an exercise program.
- ✓ Competitive formats like American Ninja Warrior, parkour, Spartan Race and obstacle course races will continue to grow in popularity.
- ✓ Old-school group-exercise programs and full-service health clubs will make a comeback."

Source: "10 Fitness Trends to Look Out For in 2015" by Pete McCall, MS, https://www.acefitness.org/blog/5145/10-fitness-trends-to-look-out-for-in-2015 12/15/14

- "Growth! As the population becomes older, there is an increased need to maintain fitness levels to maintain overall health."
- "The trend in the industry is towards smaller facilities that are providing a much higher level of service (Personal Training Studios). These facilities are able to change significantly more that the old barn style facility due to the extra service and don't suffer as much by the rise in the value of real estate."
- "Industry now maturing as a natural bi-product of its exponential growth (13 gyms in US in 2005 to over 10,000 worldwide in 2014). Phasing out of poorer performing gyms as gyms that have the most loyal and engaged communities best positioned to thrive over the long term. Continued integration of diet (paleo) in business models."
- "Growing—more segmentation."
- "Yoga is becoming segmented by type within larger markets. When considering competitors, focus on competitors that offer a similar type of yoga. Pilates is much smaller industry, but growing rapidly."

Seller Financing

- "Conventional lenders see fitness centers like restaurants, assets that are not worth much if they have to be liquidated. It will require a solid history of cash flows to attract one to finance a deal. Because of this, seller financing is often used in creative ways."
- "These businesses usually sell with some form of vendor financing up to 35% of the purchase price."
- "Outside financing more common"
- "If you have a large chain, there is little seller financing needed. If you have one facility, you may need to provide significant financing."
- "Some banks will provide financing."

Questions

- "Do you use Mind Body Online for scheduling? How are instructors paid? Are the instructors on payroll (which they should be) vs. 1099s?"
- "What is your retention rate of members and employees. Employee retention drives member retention."
- "Match bank statements with monthly remits and request supervised access to the membership software."
- "What is the attrition level? How many members are on long-term contracts?

Request the monthly remit amounts for trailing 12-month period."
- "Do you know of or have you heard of any rumors about any potential competition coming within 15 miles of this club? Why selling?"
- "Does the company buy or lease its exercise and weight equipment? Leasing is very common. How many members are there on average? It should be about 3,000. What is the referral rate for new members? It should be about 75%–80%. What is the member attrition rate? It is usually about 30%–37%."

Resources

Websites
- Club Industry: www.clubindustry.com
- HealthClubs.com: www.healthclubs.com

Associations
- IDEA Fitness: www.ideafit.com
- International Health, Racquet &Sportsclub Association: www.ihrsa.org

---

Flower Shops (Florists)		
SIC 5992-01	NAICS 453110	Number of Businesses/Units 35,662

Rules of Thumb
- ➢ 30 to 35 percent of annual sales includes inventory
- ➢ 2 times EBITDA

Pricing Tips
- "Review the Profit and Loss Statement to determine if wire service revenues and expenses (FTD, Teleflora, etc.) are tracked on separate line items to ensure that the sales are not overstated and cost of goods is not understated."
- "A premium should be given for stores with a significant number of commercial accounts (especially if there is a credit card on file for ease of billing) which helps protect revenues from big box stores that also sell flowers and plants."
- "Florists with a significant number of weekly or house accounts are very attractive in the marketplace and can command slightly higher multiples. Below market rent can also justify higher multiples. Conversely, shops located near grocery stores with large floral departments or near big box discounters should expect lower multiples."

Expert Comments

"Owning a flower shop continues to be a desirable lifestyle business for creative entrepreneurs who wish to provide an artistic and meaningful contribution to their community."

"The floral industry has been deeply affected by the economy and online 'orders.' Grocery stores and discount warehouses have also taken market share from retail florists."

F - Rules of Thumb

Benchmark Data

Statistics (Florists)

Number of Establishments	35,662
Average Profit Margin	4.2%
Revenue per Employee	$72,200
Average Number of Employees	2.2
Average Wages per Employee	$15,782

Products and Services Segmentation

Arranged cut flowers	57.6%
Giftware and other	18.9%
Potted plants	11.8%
Unarranged cut flowers	11.7%

Industry Costs

Profit	4.2%
Wages	21.9%
Purchases	45.4%
Depreciation	1.8%
Marketing	3.4%
Rent & Utilities	9.9%
Other	13.4%

Source: IBISWorld, January 2015

Establishments by Employment Size

Number of Employees	Share of Establishments
0 to 4	89.7%
5 to 9	7.4%
10 to 19	2.2%
20 to 99	0.6%
100 or more	0.1%

Source: IBISWorld, January 2014

Statistics (Online Flower Shops)

Number of Establishments	5,861
Average Profit Margin	1.3%
Revenue per Employee	$122,400
Average Number of Employees	5.2
Average Wages per Employee	$28,150

Products and Services Segmentation

Floral arrangements	57.6%
Gift basket and other	23.9%
Plants	11.8%
Floral network services	6.7%

Industry Costs

Profit	1.3%
Wages	23.8%
Purchases	45.4%
Depreciation	3.7%
Marketing	16.2%
Rent & Utilities	3.9%
Other	5.7%

Market Share

Florists' Transworld Delivery Inc.	29.9%
1-800-Flowers.com Inc.	24.5%

Source: IBISWorld, August 2015

- "Robin and David Heller, owners of Flowers by David in Langorne, Pa., and Florists For Change members, know they can't compete with $5 bouquets at supermarkets, whose cut-flower market share is 32 percent, or the order-gatherers, who have 12 percent. (Independent florists like the Hellers still claim 40 percent.)"

    Source: "Small florists struggle for differentiation from Internet middleman" by Virginia A. Smith, *Philadelphia Inquirer*, May 3, 2014

- "Weddings: account for approximately 10% of retail florists' business. Sympathy: accounts for approximately 22% of retail florists' business. Corporate sales: make up approximately 17–22% of retail florists' sales."

    Source: Floriculture Industry Overview/Society of American Florists

- "For a florist to be profitable, the rent should not exceed 15% of gross sales."
- "Local business is generally more profitable than wire-service-generated income."

Expenses as a percentage of annual sales

Cost of goods	33%
Payroll/labor Costs	20%
Occupancy	10%
Profit (estimated pretax)	20%

Industry Trend

- "Still struggling in the post-recession, local flower shops aren't just competing with supermarkets, discounters and do-it-yourselfers. They're fighting to survive as a growing number of online middlemen known as 'order gatherers' sweep into the marketplace and take orders local florists used to receive. Sounds like an old story: Brick-and-mortar battle booming Internet competitors. But florists say these third-party retailers are using deceptive advertising and failing to give consumers a fair deal.

    "They aren't shops. They take orders online and from toll-free numbers, add the standard 20 percent commission and other fees (an amount florists claim is too high), and then relay the order to a florist in the recipient's hometown—Penny's, say—to be filled and delivered. By the time Penny's gets it, the commission and fees have been deducted from the $80 order, which now worth $50. After Pannepacker deducts his $10 delivery fee, he's left with $40 - half the original order—to make the beautiful flower arrangement the customer chose from the order-gatherer's Website.

    "The ranks of U.S. florists have dwindled from 27,341 in 1992 to 15,307 in 2011, the latest figures available, according to the Society of American Florists, whose 15,000 members represent all sectors of the flower industry, including order gatherers. John Zhang, marketing professor at the University of Pennsylvania's Wharton School, likens the plight of florists to the airline ticket, hotel reservation, and travel industries, which all have been transformed by third-party Websites."

    Source: "Small florists struggle for differentiation from Internet middleman" by Virginia A. Smith, *Philadelphia Inquirer*, May 3, 2014

- "Floral Departments ranked 6th in growth among all supermarket departments."

F - Rules of Thumb

Seller Financing
- 2 to 5 years

Questions
- "Percentage of local business versus wire service?"

Resources

Websites
- Some free information, but lots of data available for a fee: www.aboutflowers.com

Trade Publications
- Florists' Review: www.floristsreview.com

Associations
- Society of American Florists—for members only: www.safnow.org
- Wholesale Florist & Florist Supplier Association: www.wffsa.org

Food Processing & Distribution

NAICS 233310	

Rules of Thumb
- Processing:Branded—5 to 7 times EBITNon-Branded—4.5 to 6 times EBIT
- Distribution:Branded and Non-Branded—4 to 5 times EBIT

Pricing Tips
- "Rate of growth; gross margins—higher is better; customer concentration—high is a threat; management continuity, high synergies."

Food Service—Contractor

NAICS 722310	Number of Businesses/Units 28,955

Rules of Thumb
- 40 to 45 percent of annual sales plus inventory
- 2.5 to 3 times SDE plus inventory
- 3.5 times EBIT
- 3.5 times EBITDA

Pricing Tips
"Location.Location.Location. A rule of thumb: 1 person will occupy a building for every 200 sf of total building space. This number is very important to calculate a frequency rate depending on the building usage/mix (customer count and average ticket is key); also if there are multiple buildings in the center, assume 1 person for every 450 sf of buildings more than 25 yards away from primary building will frequent the shop."

"A better operator can create 25% to 40% more sales quickly. You can still sell potential in this industry."

Expert Comments

"More and more operators are getting as close to office and workforce personnel as possible with smaller units. This will create pressure on price and profit."

"There is a low amount of competition for drinks, snacks, light & quick meals, but over the years there have been many franchise, lunch delivery & catering operations fighting for this market. The building owners see the shops in their buildings as an amenity in small buildings and are very accommodating. Large buildings, however, see this as a revenue source. As markets change so do the value and view of these type of shops change for the building owners & managers. When you find an accommodating landlord, take advantage of it because the odds are the tides will turn and the lease could be working against you."

Benchmark Data

Statistics (Food Service Contractors)

Number of Establishments	28,955
Average Profit Margin	5.5%
Revenue per Employee	$79,700
Average Number of Employees	19.8
Average Wages per Employee	$21,850

Products and Services Segmentation

Cafeteria dining services	30.0%
Retail outlets and concessions	26.0%
Food and nutrition services	13.0%
Other	12.0%
Catering and banquet	11.0%
On-site restaurants	8.0%

Major Market Segmentation

Educational institutions	29.0%
Business and industry	28.0%
Healthcare	22.0%
Sports and entertainment	12.0%
Other	5.0%
Airlines and airports	4.0%

Industry Costs

Profit	5.5%
Wages	27.6%
Purchases	44.3%
Depreciation	1.8%
Marketing	2.0%
Rent & Utilities	5.5%
Other	13.3%

F - Rules of Thumb

Market Share
Compass Group PLC	29.0%
Aramark Corporation	22.0%
Sodexo	18.6%
Delaware North Companies Inc.	6.1%

Source: IBISWorld, March 2015

- "Keep occupancy cost under 10% • get all food service in the building and if possible the inter center • operation should be set up to run with a very low amount of employees • food cost will be higher because customers are expecting a discount for their loyalty; not willing to pay for the convenience as you would expect. • get the vending in the center for all the building."

Expenses as a percentage of annual sales
Cost of goods	35% to 39%
Payroll/labor Costs	16% to 19%
Occupancy	04% to 10%
Profit (estimated pretax)	15% to 20%

Industry Trend
- "This industry has nice potential over the next few years as landlords struggle to fill empty office & industrial space, but the secret is out so there will be more operators interested in these smaller spaces."

Seller Financing
- "There is very little outside financing the sales, and lack of increased sales volume prohibits banks from participating in the financing. Will most likely be owner financing."
- "3 to 5 years is common with about 30% down."
- "Finance no longer than the current lease term. 3 to 5 years is average."

Questions
- "#1) The lease is very important (get a copy and read it slowly). #2) Agreement with company is very important (get a copy and read it slowly). #3) What are the sales trends for the last 2 years? #4) What improvements or repairs are needed? #5) Count the people in the building. #6) Get information on employees. #7) Make a spreadsheet of the compatible operations. #8) Outside setting is a big value. If they don't have it, can you add outside set? #9) Do you like the food they sell? #10) What equipment will you need and is there room for it? #12) Make sure the common areas are kept up nicely. #13) How many hours does the owner work? #14) Call health department for inspection ASAP. #15) Can you increase the hours? #16) Equipment age is important. #17) When is the last time seller had a price increase?"

Food Service Equipment and Supplies
NAICS 423440

Rules of Thumb
- 45 percent of annual sales plus inventory
- 2.5 times SDE plus inventory
- 4.5 to 5 times EBIT
- 5 to 6 times EBITDA

Rules of Thumb - **F**

Pricing Tips
- "10 times EBITDA for dealerships"
- "All assets saleable? Obsolete equipment?"

Benchmark Data
- "It comes as no surprise that anticipated labor pressures will have an effect on a foodservice operator's bottom line, rippling out to other aspects of the business. In fact, 80 percent of the operators surveyed report they have changed their purchasing behaviors in the past year due to the business concerns outlined above. Along those lines, 41 percent of operators altered their approach to food purchases, 38 percent changed their approach to purchasing foodservice equipment and 34 percent say they altered their approach to procuring supplies."
  Source: "Food Service Equipment & Supplies," fesmag.com/research/industry-forecast/11581-2014
- "40% + gross margins"
- "$200,000/employee"

Expenses as a percentage of annual sales	
Cost of goods	30%
Payroll/labor Costs	30%
Occupancy	05% to 07%
Profit (estimated pretax)	10%

Industry Trend
- "Cautious consumers and mixed economic indicators combined with the impact of a harsh winter will result in the foodservice industry experiencing a moderate 2014 but point to a somewhat promising 2015."
  Source: "2015 Equipment and Supplies Industry Forecast: Balancing the Salty with the Sweet" by Joseph M. Carbonara, www.fesmag.com 9/2/14
- "Today's foodservice operator faces no shortage of business pressures. Rising food costs remain a key pressure point for all operators. And the fact that foodservice sales are forecasted to grow anywhere from 3 percent to 3.6 percent in 2014, depending on which study you read, means the industry will likely remain in a take-share mode for the foreseeable future. That means foodservice operators will continue to carefully monitor their foodservice purchasing habits.
  "Breaking down changes to supplies purchasing by segment, 35 percent of commercial operators report using more private label products and buying more specially priced items. In contrast, 35 percent of non-commercial operators report steering more of their purchases through a buying group or group purchasing organization. And 32 percent of non-commercial operators report placing smaller supply orders.
  "Foodservice operators continue to invest in their businesses. In fact, 85 percent either made an equipment purchase in 2013 or plan to do so in 2014. Further, 90 percent of operators said they plan to buy new equipment rather than used items. Beyond the item's quality, condition and age, key factors when deciding to purchase a used item include the equipment type, cost/value ratio, availability, how the equipment was previously used and whether a warranty is necessary."
  Source: "Food Service Equipment & Supplies," fesmag.com/research/industry-forecast/11581-2014

F - Rules of Thumb

Resources

Trade Publications
- Food Service Equipment & Supplies Magazine: www.fesmag.com
- Foodservice Equipment Reports: www.fermag.com

Food Stores—Specialty

NAICS 44529	Number of Businesses/Units 51,737

Rules of Thumb

- Food Stores—Specialty consists of several types of retail food stores including:
- Candy Stores—30 to 35 percent of annual sales plus inventory
- Bakeries—40 to 45 percent of annual sales plus inventory
- Dairy Stores—25 percent of annual sales plus inventory
- Other—35 to 40 percent of annual sales plus inventory

Pricing Tips
- "This category also includes the following retail businesses: confectionery products, gourmet foods, organic and health foods, packaged nuts, spices and soft drinks."
- "In general, these businesses will sell for 30 to 35 percent plus inventory."

Benchmark Data

Statistics (Specialty Food Stores)

Number of Establishments	51,737
Average Profit Margin	5.7%
Revenue Per Employee	$78,300
Average Number of Employees	2.3
Average Wages per Employee	$13,814

Products and Services Segmentation

Candy, chocolate and snacks	27.4%
Bakery products	23.2%
Other	15.3%
Refrigerated/frozen meats and eggs	9.8%
Dairy products	9.6%
Coffee and tea	9.5%
Gourmet prepared foods	5.2%

Industry Costs

Profit	5.7%
Wages	18.8%
Purchases	53.2%
Depreciation	2.0%
Marketing	2.0%
Rent & Utilities	10.3%
Other	8.0%

Source: IBISWorld, May 2015

Rules of Thumb - **F**

Statistics (Ethnic Supermarkets)

Number of Establishments	24,466
Average Profit Margin	1.4%
Revenue per Employee	$207,400
Average Number of Employees	5.9
Average Wages per Employee	$19,842

Products and Services Segmentation

Other food items	38.9%
Meats	16.5%
Produce	14.0%
Non-food items	9.7%
Beverages (including alcohol)	9.3%
Dairy items	7.4%
Frozen foods	4.2%

Industry Costs

Profit	1.3%
Wages	9.6%
Purchases	70.2%
Depreciation	1.8%
Marketing	0.6%
Rent & Utilities	4.4%
Other	12.0%

Source: IBISWorld, December 2014

- "All in all, specialty food products represent nearly 15 percent of the total market share of all foods sold domestically at retail. When the Specialty Food Association began its annual research about 12 years ago, Tanner said that market share was only 4 percent. The association anticipates reaching 20 percent market share within the next five years.
  "For manufacturers, average annual sales in 2014 were $2.9 billion, with 48 percent showing growth of 20 percent or more for that year. Nearly two-thirds of those manufacturers are co-packing private-label items for retailers. Among importers, a majority of sales gains were in the 1 percent to 19 percent range. For distributors, mean annual sales were $7.2 million, and 46 percent said they grew sales 20 percent or more last year. Brokers reported higher average sales and SKU counts in 2014 than in previous years.
  "Specialty food retailers also had a good year in 2014, with the average square footage of specialty stores growing to 6,072 square feet. 'I think that's because they're getting more business and they're putting in more departments than they have been in the past,' Tanner said."
  Source: https://www.specialtyfood.com/news/article/flourishing-specialty-food-industry-hits-109b-sales/

Industry Trend

- "The popularity of organic food in recent years has led many large food companies to acquire small organic businesses. The past year alone saw a surge in specialty food business acquisitions, with sales including Annie's Homegrown to General Mills, Mom Brands to Post, and Rudi's Organic Bakery to Hain Celestial.
  "Some in the industry believe consumers are being fooled into thinking their favorite organic brands are not connected to food giants and that these larger

F - Rules of Thumb

businesses are hurting a movement that is based on avoiding conventional foods. While these mergers have led to wider access to organic foods and lower prices, some analysts predict organic standards will weaken as a result."
Source: https://www.specialtyfood.com/news/article/should-large-companies-run-organic-food-businesses/

- "Total retail and foodservice sales of specialty foods swelled to nearly $109 billion in 2014, a growth of 22 percent since 2012, marking a banner year for the industry. The Specialty Food Association and Mintel International presented the findings of the 2015 State of the Specialty Food Industry in a live webinar Wednesday, painting a promising picture of the growth and sustainability of specialty foods.

"Additionally, 15 segments within the industry saw sales exceeding $1 billion. Presenters noted the report does not include sales information from notoriously private Whole Foods Market and Trader Joe's; were those companies' data included in the study, it is estimated that sales numbers would be markedly higher."
Source: https://www.specialtyfood.com/news/article/flourishing-specialty-food-industry-hits-109b-sales/

Resources

Websites
- Specialty Food: www.specialtyfood.com

Food Trucks (See also Catering Trucks)

NAICS 722330	Number of Businesses/Units 4,318

Rules of Thumb
➢ 25 to 30 percent of annual sales plus inventory

Pricing Tips
- "In terms of cost, there is a wide range for starting up an outside dining establishment. Street kiosks can be started for only a few thousand dollars. Street kiosks generally cost $3,000 to purchase a food car, $500 for the food ingredients, and around $1,000 to get the necessary permits and rent a space on the street.

"An actual food truck will likely run into the tens of thousands of dollars. As with any business venture, the costs can be quite low to get a bare bones operation off the ground or extremely high if all the bells and whistles are added immediately. In terms of dollars, the range could be anywhere from $50,000 to $200,000. The higher end of that range would be considered pretty outrageous for anything but a high-end establishment that might also want a food truck presence to cater to its customers. On the lower end, anything below the $50,000 range could start to cause concerns about the reliability of the transportation or quality of the food and preparation equipment.

"A very reasonable range for getting a food truck off the ground is likely between $70,000 and $80,000. A reasonably priced food truck, such as one that is only a few years old and can reasonably be 'remodeled' to fit a new food focus, will make up the bulk of the cost at around roughly $60,000. Going new would add considerable expense that might not be worth the risk of a new venture. The additional costs include fuel and maintenance, business permits, kitchen equipment purchases or rental expenses, food supplies, insurance, advertising dollars and any employee expenses.

"Opening a physical space in one location will run anywhere from $100,000 to $300,000 at the low end. The key benefit is that diners know where to find the establishment each day."

Source: "The Cost of Starting a Food Truck," *Forbes*, September 27, 2012

- "A big difference between food trucks and catering trucks is that the food truck is many times named after a restaurant or recognizable chef. This is often difficult to transfer and most likely neither the restaurant nor chef will be willing to allow a stranger to operate under their name. In other words a good portion of the value (and goodwill) is the name. If franchises such as Chili's or one of the steakhouse franchises get into the food truck business—that would be transferable with franchisor approval. Some food trucks do not use a well-known name, but rather specialize, such as the grilled cheese sandwich truck that did so well on a TV show. A food truck specializing in a particular food category would be transferable, again with permission."
- "Food trucks might be a fad, but they may also be a very successful business model."
- FOOD TRUCKS

  Pros
  1. The growth of the mobile restaurant unit is a long-term trend (Source: NRA) 2. Excellent marketing tool for an existing restaurant 3. A throwback to the Good Humor Man and the 'Roach Coach.' 4. A positive option in a commercial neighborhood with no restaurants nearby. 5. Similar to the open air markets in Europe. 6. Ease of entry and lower start-up cost at $70,000–$120,000 for a new truck. 7. Can be a positive contribution to the less affluent community 8. An affordable dining alternative for college students.

  Cons
  1. Not fair to existing restaurant owners who have to pay rent, taxes, etc. and have had to adhere to strict building codes, especially sanitation (5 sinks, etc.) with the Board of Health. 2. Sanitation codes need to be strictly enforced—temperatures, hygiene, etc. 3. The business is very weather dependent—New England vs. Florida.

Benchmark Data

Statistics (Food Trucks)

Number of Establishments	4,318
Average Profit Margin	9.0%
Revenue per Employee	$58,900
Average Number of Employees	3.5
Average Wages per Employee	$22,107

Products and Services Segmentation

American	38.3%
Latin American	24.6%
Asia and Middle Eastern	18.1%
Other	9.6%
Dessert	9.4%

F - Rules of Thumb

Industry Costs

Profit	9.0%
Wages	37.3%
Purchases	36.0%
Depreciation	1.4%
Marketing	1.8%
Rent & Utilities	8.9%
Other	5.6%

Source: IBISWorld, September 2015

Outfitting a Truck/Major Expenses

Medium used truck price	$43,000
Truck decals	$5,000
Electronics	$500
Permits	$500

- Most Common Truck Specialties
    1. Cheeseburgers
    2. Mexican/Tacos
    3. Desserts
    4. American Classics
    5. Sandwiches

Source: Matthew Twombly, NGM Staff Sources; Todd Schifeling, University of Michigan; Daphne Demetry, Northwestern University, Roaming Hunger; National Restaurant Association

- "Patrons shared this enthusiasm while feeling that food trucks provide good—but not great—value. In fact, food truck cuisine isn't cheap. Customers spend an average of $9.80 at lunch and $14.99 at dinner per person. Only 8 percent of lunch patrons spend less than $8, while 45 percent of dinner patrons spend less than $10. Still, some 50 percent of lunch and dinner diners feel that the value is excellent or good.

    "Food trucks operate in a similar manner. The average food truck business generally requires $55,000 to $75,000 in startup costs. This is substantially less than the $250,000 to $500,000 (or more) required to launch a brick-and-mortar eatery. Food trucks can also get to market more quickly and have much lower operating costs than Main Street restaurants...This included: 272 customers in person at food truck sites in San Francisco, including 168 customers and 104 dinner customers."

Source: www.network.intuit.com

Industry Trend

- "The food truck business has grown 80% since 2009, and it's on the way to becoming a billion-dollar industry by 2020."

Source: Matthew Twombly, NGM Staff Sources; Todd Schifeling, University of Michigan; Daphne Demetry, Northwestern University, Roaming Hunger; National Restaurant Association

- "The food truck industry has only grown in strength over the past five years and is one of the best performing segments in the broader food-service sector. The industry's remarkable rise began in 2008, just as the recession hit, as hundreds of new vendors recognized changing consumer preferences favoring unique, gourmet cuisine."

Source: http://foodtruckjobs.mobile-cuisine.com/food-truck-industry-growth-trends/

- "According to research firm IBISWorld, in the past five years, food-truck sales nationwide grew at an annual rate of 9.3%, to $857 million, as the trend spread to cities from Los Angeles to Boston."

Source: "Meal Impact" by Alice Park, Time, June 1, 2015

Rules of Thumb - F

- "With gourmet-style dishes at fast-food prices, they attract customers ranging from train drivers to Nobel Prize laureates, said Daphne Demetry, a doctoral student at Northwestern and one of the study's authors. 'We're changing the way in which we eat and how we eat,' Demetry said. 'Food trucks used to be called "roach coaches," and now they're serving elite food.'"
    Source: "Food trucks fuse high, low cuisine as they evolve" by Yasmeen Abutaleb, *Boston Sunday Globe*, August 17, 2014

- "Emergent Research expects food trucks to generate between 3 and 4 percent of total restaurant revenue—about $2.7 billion—by 2017, a fourfold increase from 2012. In other words, food trucks are not a fad but a viable market segment with significant competitive advantages over quick-serve, fast-food and take-out food vendors. To delve deeper into the trend, Emergent Research recently interviewed a cross section of food truck operators and their customers."
    Source: www.network.intuit.com

- "David Weber, president of the New York City Food Truck Association, explained that the ratio is more like 25 to 1 the other way. That's because despite the inherent attractiveness of cute trucks and clever food options, the business stinks. There are numerous (and sometimes conflicting) regulations required by the departments of Health, Sanitation, Transportation and Consumer Affairs. These rules are enforced, with varying consistency, by the New York Police Department. As a result, according to City Councilman Dan Garodnick, it's nearly impossible (even if you fill out the right paperwork) to operate a truck without breaking some law."
    Source: "The Truck Stops Here" by Adam Davidson, *Bloomberg's Businessweek*, May 12, 2013

- "So it's not really surprising that new research conducted by The NPD Group finds that money spent on food-truck meals is money that could have gone to a traditional quick-service restaurant. In fact, half the adults surveyed said they would have gone to a QSR had they not eaten food from a truck or cart. Another 20% say they would have skipped the meal altogether, so in that sense food trucks are expanding the IEO universe while also taking sales from other options.
"NPD finds that the most-often-cited reasons for patronizing a food truck or cart is the availability of 'interesting' foods. That makes sense to anyone who has enjoyed a Pork Burger at Los Angeles' Flatiron Truck: a 5-oz. pork patty with bacon-tomato jam, pickled red onions, arugula and Manchego cheese in a brioche bun. Brick-and-mortar restaurants can compete with menu items like that, but not with 'convenience,' which is the second-most-mentioned reason for food-truck dining."
    Source: Source: "Food trucks and the changing face of quickservice," *Asian Restaurant News*, August 21, 2013

Football Teams (Professional)		
SIC 7941-05	NAICS 711211	Number of Businesses/Units 31

Pricing Tips

- "The average National Football League team is worth $2 billion, the highest value in all of the 18 years *Forbes* has tracked professional football team values. The $2 billion average is 38% more than a year ago, the biggest year-over-year increase since *Forbes* began tracking NFL values. The gain was

F - Rules of Thumb

fueled primarily by a $39 million increase in national revenue for each of the league's 32 teams. The vast majority of this national revenue increase came from the start of the league's new broadcasting deals. The NFL has the highest TV ratings and national broadcasting revenue of any U.S. professional sports league.

"For the ninth consecutive year, the Dallas Cowboys are in the top spot as the NFL's most valuable team, thanks to record NFL revenue last season of $620 million. With a current value of $4 billion, the Dallas Cowboys are now also the most valuable sports franchise in the world, for the first time since 2007.

"Rounding out the top five in the NFL are the New England Patriots (No. 2), worth $3.2 billion, and Washington Redskins (No. 3), worth $2.85 billion, New York Giants (No. 4), valued at $2.8 billion and the San Francisco 49ers (No. 5), valued at $2.7 billion. What the NFL's most valuable teams have in common are their presence in large markets and their stadiums, which provide them with more premium seating and sponsorship revenue than most teams generate. The 49ers had the largest one-year increase in value (69%) of any NFL team because in 2014 the team relocated into revenue-rich Levi's Stadium."

Source: www.forbes.com September 14, 2015

		Franchise
Foot Solutions (See also Franchises, Shoe Stores)		
Approx. Total Investment		$200,000 to $225,000
	NAICS 448210	Number of Businesses/Units 201
Rules of Thumb		
➤ 60 to 65 percent of annual sales plus inventory		

Resources

Websites
- www.footsolutions.com

		Franchise
Framing & Art Centre (See also Franchises, Picture Framing)		
Approx. Total Investment		$118,200 to $179,400
SIC 5999-27	NAICS 442299	Number of Businesses/Units 50
Rules of Thumb		
➤ 60 percent of annual sales plus inventory		
➤ Note: This is a Canadian franchise company		

Benchmark Data
- For Benchmark Data see Picture Framing

Resources

Websites
- www.framingartcentre.com

Franchise Food Businesses (See also Franchises)

| | NAICS 722 | |

Rules of Thumb

- (This category is dominated by McDonald's, Burger King, Wendy's, KFC, Domino's, Pizza Hut, Arby's, Dairy Queen, Taco Bell & Denny's—others are Subway, Blimpie's, Baskin Robbins & Schlotzsky's)
- 52 to 60 percent of annual sales plus inventory
- 2.5 SDE plus inventory
- 4 times EBIT
- 3.5 times EBITDA
- Asset value plus 1 year's SDE plus inventory

Pricing Tips

- "Franchise resales can skew these metrics higher depending on the quality of the franchise or the current 'hotness' of the franchise concept."
- "Rule of thumb: will list for 60% of gross and sell for 60% of list. Add cost of franchise fee on top of selling price. Non-traditional sites ... very lease dependent!"
- "Establish seller-adjusted cash flow and multiply times 2.5 to 3.5"
- "The multiples are a bit above the level for the industry in which the franchisee participates."
- "Stability of income, down payment & quality of franchisor"
- "Labor costs typically represent 15 to 20 percent of gross food sales. Food costs generally run from 28 percent to a high 40 percent for red meat on the menu. Pizza shops run about 28 to 30 percent. Rent should not exceed 10 percent."
- "Check the franchise agreement. Who pays transfer and training fees? Does the franchisor have the first right to purchase the business? Will the transition require the facilities to be upgraded to franchisor's current standards? If yes, the upgrade cost can be substantial."

Benchmark Data

- "Food Costs 25%–30% of sales. Labor Costs 25%–28% of sales. Rent (total occupancy including CAMS, taxes and insurance) 8%–10% of sales"
- "QSR 25–30 % food cost"
- "$600 to $800 per sq. ft. is respectable."

Expenses as a percentage of annual sales	
Cost of goods	30%
Payroll/labor Costs	19%
Occupancy	07%
Profit (estimated pretax)	22%

Seller Financing

- "5 to 7 years; however, SBA loans up to 10 years can be obtained."

Questions

- "What would you do to improve sales? Would you do it again?"

F - Rules of Thumb

Resources

Websites
- We Sell Restaurants Blog: http://blog.wesellrestaurants.com/

Franchises	
	Number of Businesses/Units 784,000 +

Rules of Thumb

We have listed franchises with a "quick" rule of thumb, or range, usually expressed as a percentage of sales. For many of them we have based it on quite a few actual sales; others may have been based on just a few; and in some cases just one where we felt it was appropriate. They can be a good starting point for pricing the business.

➢ Many of the franchises are well known while others are very new with just several units. By the time this goes to press, some of the franchises may have folded, sold or merged. We try to keep this as up-to-date as possible. We could use your help. To contribute to our ever-growing list, just go to our Web site and click on Franchise Update. Complete the form that will show up and email to us at tom@bbpinc.com. Also if you find that a franchise has disappeared or merged, etc., please let us know. Obviously the big changes such as Mail Boxes to UPS Stores will be caught by us or by our researchers (hopefully).

➢ Keep in mind that Rules of Thumb are just that. Every business is different and Rules of Thumb will never take the place of a business valuation or even an opinion of value. But, they will give you a quick ballpark idea of what the business might sell for everything else being equal. A rule of thumb will tell you whether a seller is in the ballpark when he or she tells you what they think their business is worth or what they want to sell it for.

➢ For up-to-date information and for those companies where the number of units is not shown, track down their Web site. Read the footnotes where indicated. Also, additional information is usually available under its own listing in this Guide. We have listed many of the franchises listed below, and others where information was available, by itself alphabetically by name within the Rules of Thumb section. In some cases, there is the Estimated Annual Sales per Unit and the Approximate Total Investment.

➢ Remember that Rules of Thumb are not intended to create a specific value or to be used for an appraisal. They supply a quick "ballpark" price range. They can provide a starting point for pricing a business or a sanity check after performing an informal valuation. Read the How to Use Section of the Guide, in the front, to gain some insight on how to make some adjustments to make the rule of thumb a bit more accurate.

➢ Several other factors can greatly influence the selling price of a franchise. One is the question of the transfer fee levied by the franchisor and who pays it. This amount can be substantial, so find out the information on this prior to going to market. The second is the franchisor requiring a major change in outside appearance and a change in the interior of the unit -- or both. This should also be investigated before attempting to sell it. The costs involved in either requirement can be substantial.

Rules of Thumb - F

Name of Franchise	Selling Price as a % of Sales
AAMCO Transmission	40%–42%
A & W Restaurants	45%
Ace Cash Express	1.25%
Ace Hardware stores(1)	45%
Adam and Eve Stores	35%
Aero Colours	70%
All Tune & Lube	20%–25%
Allegra Printing	70%
AlphaGraphics	60%–65%
American Poolplayers Association (2)	1.4 SDE
Andy onCall	25%
Anytime Fitness	2.5 SDE
Atlanta Bread Company	25%–30%
Baskin-Robbins Ice Cream	46%–56%
Batteries Plus	30%–35%
Beef O'Brady's	25%
Beltone Hearing Aids	50%
Ben & Jerry's	35%–40%
Between Rounds Bagel Deli & Bakery (3)	
Big Apple Bagels	35%–40%
Big City Burrito	55%–60%
Big O Tires	35%
Blackjack Pizza	40%
Blimpie's	45%–50%
Boba Loca	30%
Bruster's Ice Cream	45%–50%
Budget Blinds(4)	50%–55%
Burger King	35%
Car X Auto Service	35%–40%
Carl's Jr.	40%
Cartridge World	30%–35%
Carvel Ice Cream/Restaurants	55%
CertaPro Painters	45%
CheeburgerCheeburger	35%–40%
Chick-Fil-A	60%–70%
Closets by Design	45%
Closet Factory	45%–50%
Cold Stone Creamery	30%
Cost Cutter's Family Hair Care	55%–60%
Coverall North America (5)	2–3 times mo. sales
Culligan Dealerships	80%–120%
Curves for Women (6)	30%
Dairy Queen	45%
Deck the Walls	35%
Del Taco	70%
Dick's Wings and Grill	35%
Domino's Pizza	45%–50%
Dream Dinners	40%
Dr. Vinyl	75%
Dry Cleaners USA	55%
Dunkin' Donuts (7)	60%–100%
Eagle Transmission Shops (8)	40%
Environment Control	42%
Fantastic Sam's (9)	35%–40%
Fast Fix (Jewelry)	80%–85%
Fast Frame	32%
Fast Signs	42%–46%
FasTrac Kids	45%

26th Edition 311

F - Rules of Thumb

Foot Solutions	60%–65%
Framing & Art Centre	60%
Friendly Computers	30%
Friendly's Restaurant	40%
Gatti's Pizza	30%–35%
Geeks on Call	60%
General Nutrition Centers	40%
Godfather's Pizza	25%–30%
Goin' Postal	30%–35%
Goodyear Store (Business Opportunity)	35%
Grease Monkey International	58%
Great Clips	1–1.5 SDE
Great Harvest Bread Co. (10)	
Great Steak	55%–60%
Grout Doctor	85%–90%
Harley-Davidson Motorcycles(11)	85%–90%
Home Helpers	40%–45%
Home Team Inspection	35%
Honest-1 Auto Care	70%–75%
House Doctor	24%
Hungry Howie's Pizza & Subs	35%
Huntington Learning Center	60%
i9	65%–70%
Jani-King	25%–30%
Jersey Mike's Subs	50%
Jiffy Lube	45%–50%
Jimmy John's	65%–70%
Johnny Rockets	70%–75%
Jon Smith Subs	20%
Juice It Up	20%–25%
Kentucky Fried Chicken (KFC)	30%–35%
Kumon Math & Reading Centers	80%–90%
Kwik Kopy (printing)	50%–60%
Lady of America	45%–50%
Laptop Xchange	80%–85%
Lenny's Subs	15%–20%
Liberty Tax Service	45%–50%%
Li'l Dino Subs (12)	64%
Little Caesar's Pizza	55%
Logan Farms (honey-glazed hams)	30%
MAACO Auto Painting and Bodyworks	40%
MaggieMoo's Ice Cream (13)	25%
Maid Brigade	45%
Mail Boxes, Etc. (See UPS Stores)	40%–45%
Mama Fu's	30%
Marble Slab Creamery	45%
Martinizing	55%–60%
McGruff's Safe Kids ID System	52%
Meineke Car Care Center	30%–35%
Merry Maids	45%
Midas Muffler	30%–35%
Minuteman Press	65%
Miracle Ear Hearing Aids	60%
Molly Maid	40%
Money Mailer	40%–45%
Mountain Mike's Pizza	27%
Moto Photo	72%
Mr. Gatti's Pizza	25%–30%
Mr. Jim's Pizza	35%–40 %

Rules of Thumb - F

Mr. Payroll	130%
Mr. Rooter Plumbing (14)	
Mrs. Fields Cookies	68%
Murphy's Deli	50%
Music Go Round	40%
My Favorite Muffin	30%–35%
Nathan's Famous	100%
Nature's Way Café	45%
Natural Chicken Grill	25%–30%
New York Pizzeria	35%–40%
Obee's Soup/Salad/Subs	55%–60%
Oil X Change	30%
Once Upon A Child	25%
Orange Julius	32%
Original Italian Pie	35%–40%
OXXO Dry Cleaners	65%
Pak Mail	50%
Panera Bread	35%–40%
Papa John's Pizza (15)	35%–40%
Papa Murphy's Pizza	38%–40%
Parcel Plus	25%
Petland	50%
Pillar to Post—Home Inspection	25%–30%
Pizza Factory (16)	30%–35%
Pizza Inn	45%
Planet Beach	35%–40%
Play It Again Sports	40%–45%
Precision Tune Auto Care	35%–40%
Pump It Up	30%
Purrfect Auto	45%
Quaker Steak & Lube	45%
Quizno's Classic Subs (17)	25%
Red Robin Gourmet Burgers	30%–35%
Renaissance Executive Forums	70%
Rocky Mountain Chocolate Factory	50%–55%
Rita's–Ices, Cones, Shakes	80%–130%
Roly Poly Sandwiches	34%
Safe Ship	40%
Samurai Sam's Teriyaki Grill	45%
Sarpino's Pizza	50%
Sears Carpet & Upholstery Care	35%
Senior Helpers	40%–45%
ServiceMaster Clean	55%–60%
Servpro	90%–95%
Shell Rapid Lube (Business Opportunity)	50%
Signarama	55%–60%
Sir Speedy (printing) (18)	55%–60%
Smartbox Portable Self Storage	45%–50%
Smoothie King	40%–45%
Snap Fitness	40%
Soup Man (Original)	30%
Subway (19)	50%–60%
SuperCoups	40%–45%
Superior Inspection	1.3%
Swisher (restroom hygiene service)	75%
Sylvan Learning Center	1.7 X SDE
Synergy Home Care	30%–35%
Taco John's	30%
Tan USA	60%–65%

F - Rules of Thumb

TCBY	40%–45%
The Maids	40%–45%
Togo's Eatery	60%
Topz Healthy Burgers	40%
Tropical Smoothie Café	50%–55%
Two Men and a Truck	40%–45%
U Save (auto rental) (20)	10%
UPS Stores	35%–40%
Valpak Mailers	40%–45%
Valvoline Instant Oil Change	50%
Wild Birds Unlimited	30%–35%
Wine Kitz (Canada)	55%
Wingstop Restaurants	33%
Wireless Toyz	45%–50%
Worldwide Express	50%–55%
Your Office USA	60%
You've Got Maids	60%
Ziebart International (auto services)	42%
Zoo Health Club	20%

(1) Sales seem to indicate that smaller sales bring a higher multiple (50% +) than stores with sales over $1 million, which seem to bring lower multiples. Price is plus inventory which may be the cause of lower multiples for larger stores. (2) $1,000 to $1,800 per team in sales; selling price - $2,000 to $2,500 per team (3) 3–4 times earnings (4) 2 times annual EBIT, plus inventory & equipment (5) Master/Area developer—Sell for 3 to 5 times earnings plus some blue sky for size and potential of market (some cases).(6) Prices for Curves for Women seem to be all over the place. Some sales have been reported at 75+% of sales. One sale reported was 1.31 times sales for four units. (7) Dunkin' Donuts shops now sell for 75–125% of annual sales, depending mainly on geography. It's about 125% in New England, 100% of sales in the Mid-Atlantic States, and lower in the South and Midwest.There really is not a Dunkin' Donuts market in the West, however they are now moving into the West Coast market. A sale in Colorado was reported that sold for 22% of sales. (8) Eagle is a Texas-based franchise www.eagletransmission.com. They are the strongest transmission franchise in the Dallas area with 21 locations and are a minor player in Houston and Austin. The attraction is the royalties at 4% in Dallas and 6% in Houston and Austin, and the training is "hands on" locally. (9) These stores sell for maximum 2 times SDE versus $120,000 to $150,000 + for new. 10 to 12 sales have been reported at 2 times SDE for absentee owner stores (most are) and 2 times SDE + manager's salary of owner operated.(10) 3.3–3.4 times SDE (11) Netted $2,100,000 and seller retained 20% of ownership (12) One sold for 80% of sales, but it was located in an office building with vending rights. (13) One MaggieMoo's Ice Cream &Treatery sale was reported at 92%, three years old, great location, growth at 15% approx a year; but only 15% down payment (14) 1–4 times SDE plus hard assets. The number between 1–4 depends on several factors such as the owner operating a truck, etc. (15) The only sale reported of Papa John's was a 3-store chain which sold for $475,000 with $150,000 down and grossed $1,191,700. (16) Pizza factory has approximately140 units in the 10 western states. (17) Quiznos, which has struggled as a higher-priced alternative to Subway, has closed an estimated 1,000 of its U.S. shops (the company won't confirm the number) and has begun putting mini-stores in gas stations in a bid to boost sales—from www.msn.com April 2011 (18) One sale was reported at 70% of sales. (19) "As a former multi-unit Subway franchisee and a Development Agent, now a business broker for Subway stores, there are many different formulas I have seen. 30 to 40 weeks' sales, or 60 to 70% of sales is a popular one. Actual sales price depends on supply and demand and is closer to 70% of sales in So. CA." "On stores with gross sales of $300,000 to $500,000, multiple of 40% of annual sales.On stores with sales of $500,000+, multiple of 50% of annual sales. Franchisor would like 30% as a down payment on resales." (20) Price does not include cost of vehicles, and revenues do not include auto sales.

Rules of Thumb - F

Pricing Tips

- "Rule of thumb for the Franchise Industry varies with the sub-industry. Typically you will find that franchise concepts trade for 1x to 2x above the rule of thumb for the specific sub industry. i.e., if an independent Auto Repair shop trades for 3x, a franchise concept can trade for 4x to 5x. The determining factor for whether a franchise concept trades for 1x over the sub industry or 2x depends on the strength of the franchise system."
- "Middle Market can vary wildly depending on size of the system and industry."
- "'When I started and you talked about the value of a franchisee, people talked about 4.5 to 5.5 times EBITDA,' said Bill Kraus, senior managing director of GE Capital, Franchise Finance. 'That might still be true. But for consolidators that have a lot of scale, prices are in the 7s now.'"
- "Presumes profitability on top of market-rate wages to the owner(s) for the time spent working in and on the business. I have observed about 90 business categories of franchised enterprises. It is hard to generalize about 'franchised enterprises' in general. Other considerations can be time left on the license and franchiser transfer fees. Still another consideration can be the history and SIZE (number of units regionally—nationally) reflecting the strength of the brand."
- "Varies depending on the type of franchise, the revenues, net income or SDE, age of business, and several other possible factors."
- "Branded businesses tend to sell at higher prices than non-franchised businesses. Example—Maid Services, 10% to 20% higher. Has everything to do with the track record of the franchiser. Some franchisers fail, at least 25% to 40%. This can vary based on the category. Some new franchisers will take anyone's money anywhere in the U.S. Some potential franchisees get impressed with an idea at a trade show and walk away from their background. Ethics vary."
- "Pricing the franchise resale obviously depends on the franchise. Is the franchise value added or—as in some cases—value subtracted? Does franchising add value to the business or would the same business—independent of a franchise label—bring as high a price in the marketplace? When calculating a multiple of annual sales, is it before subtracting the royalty fees, or are they included in the annual sales? After all, 6 percent of just $500,000 in annual revenues is $30,000, but just $12,000 at 40 percent of annual sales. The $12,000 probably doesn't have much of an impact on pricing unless the sales are really astronomical.

"McDonald's has always been the franchise that everyone compares others to, but that has changed recently. However, it probably hasn't hurt the price of a McDonald's—it is still a very strong brand. One disadvantage of franchising is that, like Burger King, the company gets sold several times, and the direction of the new owners can play havoc with operational support, advertising and growth of the company. In most cases, franchisees have no control over this. The strength of a franchise is the success of the brand name and the reputation created in the marketplace. Many franchises have been able to create that brand-identity and awareness to add a lot of value to the price of one of the units. And, if you want to buy a very popular franchise in a particular geographical marketplace, you have to pay the going rate.

"Some prospective business buyers like the security and the support of a franchise. Still others want the independence of owning and controlling their own business. Buying an independent business provides just that. No

F - Rules of Thumb

answering to the franchisor, no royalties and no heavy advertising fees, no forced purchasing from certain suppliers—and no politics. Owning your own independent business also allows you to expand, change, add or delete products and/or services. Independent businesses can be very quick to adjust to changes. Franchises, especially large ones, are very cumbersome and slow to adapt to new trends and ideas.

"The choice is a personal one. Some very strong independent operators have chosen, after years of independence, to buy a franchise, while some franchisees felt stifled and changed to an independent business.

"As for pricing a franchise, we don't see much of a difference between an independent business and the franchised one, except for the very big players, where the franchise label probably adds a lot of value, maybe 10 to 20 percent, based on the same gross. On the other hand, the fledging franchise with just a few units has some real problems on the resale side. If it's fairly new, there are plenty of new units available, the name doesn't really mean anything yet, and the age old question is asked—why is the business for sale? In cases like this, the percentage multiples might be reduced by the same figure as is added for the well-known brand name—most likely lower.

"Despite what the franchise industry would like us to believe, not all franchises are successful. What has always struck us as strange is the buyer who is very number-oriented and turns down a very good business due to some slight anomaly in the financial statement from two years ago, but will be the same buyer who purchases a franchise (a new one) where he has seen no books and records and has no idea whether the location will work out or not."

Source: *The Business Broker* (Business Brokerage Press)

- Key Considerations When Pricing a Franchise

"Lease Terms—If the lease doesn't contain a provision for at least 10 years remaining, the price can be affected accordingly.

"Franchise Rights—If there aren't at least 10 years left in the franchise agreement, a price adjustment downward should be made. This may not be applicable in those states where the franchisor may not terminate the agreement unless there is a default.

"Territorial Rights—If the franchise agreement does not provide for territorial rights, this could be a minus. In other words, if the franchisor can open additional units in the immediate area, the value of the existing franchise could be diminished. However, if the franchisee has additional territorial rights then the value may be increased.

"Business Mix—If the bulk of the sales is in low-profit items, value may be diminished; whereas if high profit items make up a substantial part of the business, value may be increased. Is there wholesale business? Do one or two customers make up a majority of the business? Business mix should be considered.

"Remodel Requirements—Does the franchise agreement state that the business has to be remodeled periodically? How often and how much remodeling? The value of the business may be reduced by the cost of the remodeling, depending on when it has to be done.

"Hours of Operation—Does the franchisor require specific hours and days open? Some franchisors, especially food related, donuts/convenience stores, may state that the business has to be open 24 hours a day, seven days a week. The shorter the hours, the better the price.

"Location—Obviously, the better and more desirable the location, the better the price.

Rules of Thumb - F

"Cash Flow—The price of a small business may be based on its sales history rather than on reported profitability. Some businesses are just not operated efficiently from a cash management point of view. Certainly, strong cash flow benefits the price asked, but a poor cash flow coupled with strong historical sales does not necessarily detract from the price."

Excerpted from a presentation to the American Institute of Certified Public Accountants by Bernard Siegel, Siegel Business Services, Philadelphia, PA.

Expert Comments

"People in general, regardless of industry, are choosing to use/consume from a brand name more each year, moving away from independent companies more. That trend is not expected to change anytime soon."

"Call other franchisees in the system to validate. Speak with both those who are successful and those who might be struggling to get a realistic expectation."

"Regarding the ease of replication—typically it's difficult because one must develop a concept, develop the business structure, develop the systems, and prove the model in multiple locations before expanding thru franchising. It takes a lot in the beginning but it offers great value down the road to investors looking for such proven models!"

"A franchisee must be committed to following the franchise system. Franchisees that sway from the franchise standards seem to struggle. The learning curve for a franchise is much, much quicker than a typical business with systems, controls and procedures normally in place. This makes is much simpler for the franchisee to expand the business in size and/or locations"

"Investigate the franchiser."

"Besides brand strength, the business system of the franchiser has a lot to do with success. Franchisees (new & re-sales) have to follow the business system."

"Owner needs to be able to follow systems and be a team player."

Benchmark Data
- "This varies greatly depending on the business and the specific industry it's in within the franchise industry. I can't really generalize since so many various industries are included in franchising."
- "I value most business based on multiple of SDE plus assets."

Industry Trend
- "'Our forecast for the franchise sector continues to be presented with a note of caution because recent employment actions by the National Labor Relations Board create a cloud of uncertainty over the franchise sector, which could impede the growth of the number of franchise businesses, and thus franchise employment and output,' said James Gillula, managing director, IHS Economics.

  "Highlights from the forecast include:
  ✓ Projected growth of the number of franchise establishments in 2015 is

F - Rules of Thumb

- projected to reach 781,931 an increase of 1.6 percent, matching the pace of growth in 2014.
  - ✓ As employment growth economy-wide continues to strengthen, employment in the franchise sector will continue to outpace growth in businesses economy-wide, as it has in each of the last four years. Franchise employment is expected to reach 8,820,000 jobs, a 2.9 percent increase, while total private nonfarm employment will increase 2.7 percent.
  - ✓ The 2015 forecast for economic output of franchise businesses in nominal dollars continues to show an increase of $890 billion or a 5.4 percent increase— ahead of the $845 billion (5.0 percent) gain in 2014. The gross domestic product (GDP) of the franchise sector will increase by $521 billion or 5.2 percent in 2015, an increase over the $496 billion generated in 2014.
  - ✓ This will exceed the growth of U.S. GDP in nominal dollars, which is projected at 4.2 percent. The franchise sector will contribute approximately 3 percent of U.S. GDP in nominal dollars."
- "Franchise businesses will continue to increase and create jobs at a faster pace than the overall economy in 2015, as it has in each of the last four years, the International Franchise Association said today. According to the quarterly update of the Franchise Business Economic Outlook prepared by IHS Economics, employment and output growth for the franchise sector will increase over the previous year, echoing the yearly forecast released in January."

  Source: "Franchise Employment Growth Continues to Outpace Economy-Wide Hiring" by Jenna Weisbord, http://www.franchise.org/franchise-employment-growth-continues-to-outpace-economy-wide-hiring 4/10/15

- "More than half of franchisees struggle to make a decent living, and nearly two-thirds wouldn't recommend investing in their franchise system, according to a new survey sponsored by a coalition of unions pushing to reform the franchise business model. In addition, 42 percent of franchisees surveyed were dissatisfied with their franchise system. The survey was conducted for the coalition Change to Win by FranchiseGrade.com, which surveyed more than 1,100 operators over a one-month period in February and March."

  Source: "Survey: Franchisees struggle to make a living" by Jonathan Maze, *Nation's RestaurantNews*, 5/4/2015

- "Continue to grow, certain franchise sectors will do much better than others: home care, children's services, fitness, personal services and quick-serve restaurants."
- "The franchise industry solicits studies regularly and the most recent (2015) shows the franchise industry growth to continue this year in the 4–5% range. It also shows that the franchise industry produces more jobs in the U.S. than any other industry."
- "According to the recently released Monitor 200 report from Restaurant Finance Monitor big franchisees are getting bigger, often diversifying into new brands to achieve their growth. In 2013, the average franchisee among the report's 200 largest operators reported $143.5 million in total revenue from 109 locations, both of which were up approximately 30 percent from their averages of $109 million and 84 locations in the 2009 report.
- "'This period of consolidation among restaurant franchisees is almost unprecedented,' said Jonathan Maze, editor of Restaurant Finance Monitor, in a statement. 'A number of these companies operate more units or have more revenue than most restaurant brands.'"

  Source: "Landing the big franchisees" by Mark Brandau, nrn.com, August 11, 2014

- "Over the course of 25 years, while the establishment of new franchise locations has been relatively flat, the share of new locations has increased through the efforts of franchise brokers."
- "It is getting harder to start an 'unbranded' business. It is easier to open multiple locations with a branded business. Franchising is being driven on a commercial & consumer level. Despite the economy, new franchisers are entering all markets—everywhere nationwide."
- "Continued growth and interest as confidence in corporate jobs decreases."

Seller Financing
- "Outside financing for the majority, but sellers seem to be carrying part of the deal lately."
- "In the sale of an existing franchise, it is usually a combination of personal funds, outside financing and seller financing. In the sale of a new unit or location, there is no seller financing."
- "Most franchises, especially existing profitable franchises, can be financed."
- "Combination of both as in an SBA loan and a seller carryback."
- "Outside financing for new locations, both for resales."

Questions
- "Would you invest in this opportunity if you had it to do again?"
- "The same questions that apply to any business for sale, plus: Have you reached your financial expectations that you had when you purchased the franchise? How long have you owned the franchise? Have you had problems or issues with the franchisor? Has the franchisor provided the support and services they agreed to? How many new franchises have been sold in the past 2 years?"

Resources

Websites
- Entrepreneur 2014 Franchise 500: www.entrepreneur.com/franchise500
- Franchise Gator: www.franchisegator.com
- Franchise Grade: www.franchisegrade.com
- FranNet: www.frannet.com
- FranchiseKnowHow: www.franchiseknowhow.com
- Franchise Grade: Franchisegrade.com

Trade Publications
- Franchise Times: www.franchisetimes.com
- Blue MauMau: www.bluemaumau.org

Associations
- International Franchise Association: www.franchise.org
- American Association of Franchisees & Dealers: www.aafd.org
- American Bar Association—Forum on Franchising: www.americanbar.org/groups/franchising.html

F - Rules of Thumb

Freight Forwarding

SIC 4731-04	NAICS 488510	Number of Businesses/Units 80,896

Rules of Thumb
- 50 percent of annual sales
- 2.6 times SDE

Expert Comments
"Just sold a niche market, owner plus one employee freight forwarder, for $1.1 million at these figures."

Benchmark Data

Statistics (Freight Forwarding Brokerages & Agencies)
Number of Establishments	80,896
Average Profit Margin	4.8%
Revenue per Employee	$347,200
Average Number of Employees	4.2
Average Wages per Employee	$48,178

Products and Services Segmentation
Domestic freight transportation arrangement services	51.9%
International freight forwarding and customs brokerage services	35.1%
Non-vessel operating common carrier services	9.2%
Other	3.8%

Major Market Segmentation
Manufacturers	62.0%
Importers and wholesalers	23.0%
Others	15.0%

Industry Costs
Profit	4.8%
Wages	13.9%
Purchases	48.9%
Depreciation	0.8%
Marketing	0.8%
Rent & Utilities	3.7%
Other	27.1%

Source: IBISWorld, April 2015

Questions
- "Do you need a customs license?"

Friendly Computers (See also Franchises) — Franchise

Approx. Total Investment		$56,980
	NAICS 811212	Number of Businesses/Units 260

Rules of Thumb
- 30 percent of annual sales plus inventory

Rules of Thumb - F

Resources

Websites
- www.friendlycomputers.com

Friendly's Restaurant (See also Franchises)	Franchise
Approx. Total Investment	$475,000 to $1,977,100
Estimated Annual Sales/Unit	$1,150,000
NAICS 722511	Number of Businesses/Units 325

Rules of Thumb
- 40 percent of annual sales plus inventory

Resources

Websites
- Friendly's Restaurant: www.friendlys.com

Fruits and Vegetables (Wholesale)	
SIC 5148-01 NAICS 424480	Number of Businesses/Units 4,615

Rules of Thumb
- 25 percent of annual sales plus inventory
- .50 to 1 times SDE plus inventory
- .75 times EBIT
- .75 times EBITDA

Pricing Tips
- "What is the average 'per basket or package' profit the company normally charges/expects?"
- "How much commission/profit does wholesaler charge its customers per basket/box? It usually is about $2.50 to $3 per . . . anything less makes the wholesaler merely a shipping company."
- "Actual gross sales achieved is not an important analysis tool . . . since there is usually an inverse relationship between sales volume & amount of profit that may be achieved (for instance, the more a box of tomatoes costs, the less profit may be added on). Better to determine how many packages/boxes of product are handled weekly & what 'profit per unit' is achieved."

Expert Comments
"It is perhaps one of the least expensive businesses to start & operate, but just as easy to destroy without a strong paying customer base. One can grow this business through adding of multiple delivery trucks & yet not even have to rent warehouse space."

26th Edition

F - Rules of Thumb

Benchmark Data

Statistics (Fruit & Vegetable Wholesaling)
Number of Establishments	4,615
Average Profit Margin	4.3%
Revenue per Employee	$759,800
Average Number of Employees	22.3
Average Wages per Employee	$39,525

Products and Services Segmentation
Vegetables	42.8%
Bananas	16.0%
Apples	14.7%
Watermelons	6.9%
Grapes	6.6%
Strawberries	5.4%
Oranges	4.6%
Peaches	3.0%

Major Market Segmentation
Retailers	43.2%
Other wholesalers	25.0%
Foodservice providers	23.1%
Others	8.7%

Industry Costs
Profit	4.3%
Wages	5.2%
Purchases	78.5%
Depreciation	1.1%
Marketing	0.2%
Rent & Utilities	5.1%
Other	5.6%

Source: IBISWorld, March 2015

- "How much is profit per package/box? Is a buyer used?"
- "Is there adequate storage area for holding buy-in/specials?"

Expenses as a percentage of annual sales
Cost of goods	40% to 50%
Payroll/labor Costs	30%
Occupancy	10%
Profit (estimated pretax)	10% to 20%

Industry Trend
- "If the 'hothouse effect' is a reality to our environment & fuel prices continue an upward trend, the produce business will be adversely affected."
- "Smaller wholesalers either going out . . . or taking on additional food lines."

Seller Financing
- "Both Outside Financing and Seller Financing depending on what the corporate tax returns look like and the amount/age of equipment owned by the company. "

Rules of Thumb - **F**

Fruit & Vegetable Markets (Produce)

	NAICS 445230	Number of Businesses/Units 12,627

Rules of Thumb
- 35 to 40 percent of annual sales

Benchmark Data

Statistics (Fruit and Vegetable Markets)
Number of Establishments.. 12,627
Average Profit Margin 2.9%
Revenue per Employee $141,800
Average Number of Employees... 2.5
Average Wages per Employee $17,476

Products and Services Segmentation
Vegetable (excluding potatoes, dry beans and lentils) 34.7%
Fruit... 23.5%
Other... 16.2%
Potatoes... 14.5%
Meat, fish, seafood and poultry (including prepackaged meats) 3.8%
Dairy products and related foods (including milk and cheese) 3.6%
Delicatessen items (including deli meats)... 2.5%
Frozen foods (including frozen packaged foods)... 1.2%

Industry Costs
Profit 2.9%
Wages... 12.3%
Purchases... 75.0%
Depreciation... 1.0%
Marketing 1.1%
Rent & Utilities 3.0%
Other.. 4.7%

Source: IBISWorld, July 2015

Resources

Trade Publications
- The Packer: www.thepacker.com

Fuel Dealers (Wholesale)

	NAICS 424720	

Rules of Thumb
- 1.5 times SDE plus inventory
- 1.5 EBITDA

Pricing Tips
- "Wholesalers/distributors are large-volume, low-margin operators; therefore the price is 1–2 times EBITDA."

F - Rules of Thumb

Benchmark Data
- "Typical wholesaler does $30 million in annual sales."

Resources

Trade Publications
- Butane Propane News: www.bpnews.com

Associations
- National Propane Gas Association: www.npga.org

Funeral Homes/Services

SIC 7261-02	NAICS 812210	Number of Businesses/Units 30,614

Rules of Thumb
- 200 percent of annual sales includes inventory and real estate
- 5 to 6 times SDE includes inventory and real estate; 4 times SDE without real estate
- Under 75 funerals per year, 3 to 4.5 times EBITDA; 75 to 150 funerals, 4 to 5 times EBITDA; and 150 + funerals, 4.5 to 6 times EBITDA
- 6 to 6.5 times EBITDA if real estate is included. If real estate is not included, long-term triple net lease is a must (8 to 10 percent of sales); purchase price would be 4 times EBITDA or approx. 1 times trailing 12 months sales
- 6 times EBIT includes real estate

Pricing Tips
- "The standard in the industry for those that deal with funeral homes regularly is to use a multiple of 4.5 to 6 times historical EBITDA. However, since most business brokers use SDE to arrive at a value please update the business reference guide with the correct SDE multiple, it should be 1.5 to 3 times SDE."
- "The standard within the industry is to use a multiple of EBITDA, typically 4.5 to 6 to determine a purchase price for everything including real estate. When determining EBITDA make sure to adjust the earnings by subtracting out the Cash Advance Items as they are a pass through and can inflate the earnings figure. These are things that are provided to families at cost—such as obituaries, flowers, cemetery expense,etc. As to what multiple to use, that is where the 'art' comes in, but some things to consider: condition of building, age of vehicles, is it the only one in town or is there a lot of competition, how much is in the prepaid funeral accounts, has revenue been increasing, decreasing or flat, what about market share. A funeral home that has been updated, has newer vehicles, is the only one in town that has 3–5 years annual revenue in prepaid accounts with flat to increasing revenue and market share would be closer to a 6. One that has not been updated since the 70s, with 10-year-old vehicles, and declining revenue in an area with a lot of competition would obviously get a much lower multiple."
- "Valuations formulas are very difficult to use to obtain highest possible value. Knowing the highest value requires understanding how the business will fit into

Rules of Thumb - F

- a buyer's operational strategy and what the buyer's costs will be to operate."
- "Funeral homes that are larger in size and have more traditional funeral services are slightly more valuable than the standard Rules of Thumb."
- "Valuations can be negatively affected by high cremations or eroding market share. Valuations can be positively affected by strong real estate values, high growth areas, or increasing market share."
- "There are a handful of general methods used to value funeral home businesses. For example, one rough rule of thumb is valuing the funeral home business at $10,000 per call. Of course, this method fails to account for average revenue per call. Obviously, a funeral home with 200 calls doing 90% traditional funerals is worth more than a 200 call firm with a 60% cremation rate.

  "Another valuation method that is employed is to multiply earnings before interest, taxes, depreciation and amortization (EBITDA). Usually, a multiplier factor of from 1.8 to 3 is used. For example, if a firm had average earnings of $500,000 before interest, taxes, depreciation and amortization, under this method the firm would be worth anything from $900,000 to $1,500,000 depending on the multiplier that is used. The choice of which multiplier to employ may depend on the particular facts of the funeral home business such as whether its market share is increasing, how effective its pre-need program is, etc."
- "You need to understand the value or non-value of pre-needs."

Expert Comments

"1. **200 percent of annual sales includes inventory and real estate.**

"The rule of thumb has been around for a long time, but it always used to be a range of '1.5 to 2 times annual sales including inventory and real estate,' plus the math of 2X is easier than 1.5X to do in your head.

"There are two big issues with this method. First, it does not take into account cash advance items. These are items that the funeral home purchases for the family and puts on the contract, but there is no markup. These items are easily identified in a contract analysis, or if the funeral home has accurate P&L's, as they should be line items.

"Things like obituaries, flowers, death certificates, opening/closing the grave, crematory fee, required permits, etc. can add up to between $1,000 to $2,000 per service. Since there is no profit to the funeral home, there should be no markup/multiple assigned to these items when trying to value a funeral home. If anything, a slight discount should be applied, because many funeral homes give families 30 days to pay, so they are giving an interest-free loan to the families served.

"As an example, most industry participants use a multiple of EBITDA to value a funeral home. If we compare the two, here is what we get (assuming we already subtracted out cash advance items).Revenue is $1,000,000 so two times sales would be a value of $2,000,000. However, using EBITDA it would be $1,800,000 (a funeral home can be run at a 30% EBITDA, so in this case $300,000 and the average multiples used are 4 to 6, so 6 times $300,000= $1,800,000). While it is only 10% overpriced using this method, if cash advance items are not subtracted first, it can be 20–30% overpriced.

F - Rules of Thumb

"If we used the 1.5 times sales, we would be at $1,5000,000 and since EBITDA multiples are 4-6 most of the time we use a multiple of 5, since it is in the middle of the range. A $300,000 EBITDA x 5= $1,500,000. We have a match!! This is the area that 90%+ of the deals actually get done.

"2. 5 to 6 times SDE includes inventory and real estate, 4 times SDE without real estate

"The issue with this rule of thumb as it is written is that it is also the same as (or even higher than) the EBITDA method listed in the guide and since the SDE method adds back all the owner's earnings and the EBITDA method allows for a reasonable owners salary, obviously one of the methods in the guide is wrong.

"The one that is wrong here is the SDE as it over-inflates the value of the funeral home, and since most general business brokers use the SDE method, it is causing a lot of funeral homes to be listed, but not sold. If we stick with the fictional funeral home doing $1 million in revenue, it would not be out of the question for an owner or manager to have a salary of $90,000/year and use of a company car. So, if using SDE, that $90,000 is added back in and say $10,000 for use of a car, we would be adding back in $100,000 which could increase the sale price by up to $600,000 or more above the EBITDA method.

"If we stick to the fictional funeral home we have been using in the previous example, the EBITDA was $300,000 and at a multiple of 6 would value the funeral home at $1,800,000; a multiple of 4 would be $1,200,000. The SDE method would add back the $100,000 owner's compensation/benefits and give us a figure of $400,000. Based on that, to arrive at a similar valuation as the EBITDA method, you are looking at an SDE multiple between 3 and 4.5 times (3 x $400,000=$1,2000,000 and 4.5 x $400,000 = $1,800,000). This range would bring it in line with the EBITDA method, allow general business brokers to arrive at a realistic value and get deals done.

"3. Under 75 funerals per year 3 to 4.5 times EBITDA; 75 to 150 funerals, 4 to 5 times EBITDA; and 150+ funerals, 4 to 6 times EBITDA

"These numbers are pretty close. The lower multiples for the smaller businesses are because nobody really wants a firm under 100 services per year, as there is typically not enough money to hire another licensed funeral director; so the buyer is really buying a job and may be better off to just stay working somewhere else and making about the same amount of money, getting some time off, and having no financial risk.

"4. 6 to 6.5 times EBITDA if real estate is included. If real estate is not included, a long-term triple net lease is a must (8 to 10 percent of sales); purchase price would be 4 times EBITDA or approx. 1 times trailing 12 months' sales.

"Obviously, this one is on the high end of the EBITDA range. Because this is the top of the range, the real estate, furniture, fixtures, equipment, and vehicles better be in pristine condition. If not, the cost to update, repair or replace these items should be subtracted from the valuation arrived at.

"Also, while a long-term lease is a must, the difference between a gross lease and a triple net lease depends on if you are the buyer or seller, although the 8-10 of net sales is about the right percentage.

"5. 6 times EBIT includes real estate

"Again, top of the range."

"Competition is average, as most families continue to use the same funeral home as they have in the past. However, there is a bit more competition from low-cost Internet based cremation companies starting to affect the industry. I rank the risk as average since this is a fairly stable industry. The profit trends have been declining sharply with the rapid rise in cremation versus traditional burial. This has resulted in a drop in revenue and profits which in turn has lowered values of the businesses themselves. Location and facilities I ranked as good, most funeral home real estate is well cared for and most people know where the funeral home in there town is. Marketability I ranked as good; there are buyers for fairly priced funeral homes and the SBA is typically willing to finance them. I ranked the industry trend as poor, only because it is rapidly changing from traditional funeral/burial to cremation. Owners will have to adapt to the changing preferences of the baby boomers, or they will find other options such as having a memorial service and or luncheon at a banquet facility and not involve the funeral home. I ranked ease of replication as very hard, as it is very expensive to start a funeral home and often zoning issues can be a challenge. In addition most funeral homes allow families to pre-plan their funeral; once this is done people rarely use a different funeral home."

"Competition varies greatly from region to region with more in urban areas and little to none in rural areas so I put it at average. Amount of Risk: Since death is certain but we do not know when it will occur, I put the risk at average. Historical Profit Trend: The profit trend is down; as more people choose cremation or limited burial options, revenues have been declining at most firms. Location and Facilities: Most of the time the funeral home is one of the nicest buildings in a town. Marketability: For all but the smallest of funeral homes, if it is priced fairly, it is pretty easy to find a buyer. Industry Trend: While cremation has lowered revenues, the coming increase in the number of deaths gives the industry trend a lift, since the increase is still a few years out, I give the trend a fair rating. Ease of Replication: This is hard because most families will return to the same funeral home year after year unless they are given a reason to change. Because of this, it does not make a lot of sense to spend a million dollars+ to see if you can change their minds. Plus if a funeral home has a good prepaid funeral program in place, they can lock up a market, as most people who prepay, use the funeral home they prepaid at."

"Very high barriers to entry. Funeral home buyers are typically easy to find. Outside financing is a challenge."

Benchmark Data

Statistics (Funeral Homes)

Number of Establishments	30,614
Average profit Margin	10.6%
Revenue per Employee	$132,300
Average Number of Employees	3.8
Average Wages per Employee	$35,020

F - Rules of Thumb

Products and Services Segmentation

Traditional pre-burial services	31.3%
Merchandise sold	28.7%
Other	22.1%
Body preparation services	7.5%
Direct cremation services	5.5%
Transportation	4.8%

Industry Costs

Profit	10.6%
Wages	26.6%
Purchases	30.0%
Depreciation	4.7%
Marketing	3.2%
Rent & Utilities	5.6%
Other	19.3%

Market Share

Service Corporation International	12.9%

Source: IBISWorld, April 2015

- "A typical single location funeral home can be run at an EBITDA in a range of 28-32%. Any more than that, and they are likely not putting money back into the facility and equipment."
- Employment of funeral service workers is projected to grow 12 percent from 2012 to 2022.

U.S. Bureau of Labor 2013 Occupational Employment Statistics (May 2013)

	Employment	Annual Mean Wage
Funeral Service Managers	8,810	$68,420
Morticians, Undertakers, and Funeral Directors	24,280	$47,100
Funeral Attendants	33,400	$22,530
Embalmers	4,390	$41,590

Expenses as a percentage of annual sales

Cost of goods	20%
Payroll/labor Costs	28% to 30%
Occupancy	10% to 20%
Profit (estimated pretax)	30% to 35%

Industry Trend

- "Funeral Homes are going to have to adapt to these changes with additional offerings such as receptions and luncheons either at the funeral home, or at an off-site location coordinated by the funeral home. Funeral Directors need to start thinking like event planners and come up with ways to engage the families they serve, perhaps letting their buildings be used for weddings, community meetings, etc. For many funeral homes this will require a significant investment in remodeling their facilities to accommodate these alternative uses."
- "The rise in nontraditional funeral services and cremation has resulted in lower revenue per call and less cash flow to the business. This will result in lower

valuations and some firms will need to close or merge with competitors as they will not need to have as large of a building in the future. Firms will need to adapt to these changes and focus on educating the public on the importance of honoring and celebrating a life lived by having a service. These services will be nontraditional and more of a celebration; they may be held at the funeral home or offsite. Successful funeral directors in the future will become more like event planners."

- "In the death-care industry, as practitioners call it, SCI (Service Corporation International) casts a long shadow. Based in Houston and publicly traded on the New York Stock Exchange (NYX), it operates more than 1,800 funeral homes and cemeteries in the U.S. and Canada. It has 20,000 employees and a market capitalization of $4 billion. For 40 years, SCI has gobbled competitors as the pioneer consolidator of a fragmented industry. Although it has overreached at times, suffering a corporate near-death experience after a late-1990s debt binge, SCI is hungry once again."

    Source: "Is Funeral Home Chain SCI's Growth Coming at the Expense of Mourners?" by Paul M. Barrett, October 24, 2013, www.businessweek.com/articles/2013-10-24

Seller Financing

- "The standard is outside financing for 75-80% of the purchase price, with the seller carrying back the balance in the form of a non-compete agreement over several years. Since this is a relationship based business, the non-compete helps to protect the buyer and helps to insure the seller will assist in transitioning the relationships in the community to the new buyer."
- 10–15 years
- "15–20 percent of purchase price for 10 years"
- 7–10 years

Questions

- "Ask if the firm has ever been cited by the state regulators for anything, ask if they have ever been cited by the FTC. Ask to see copies of the facility license from the state and make sure it is current."
- "Make sure to ask about the prepaid funeral accounts and the last time they were audited. Make sure your attorney has a clause in the purchase agreement that states you are only assuming the prepaid funeral liabilities specifically disclosed and that can be verified. Get advice from someone experienced in the business."
- "Why is seller selling? How long has seller owned the business? How many competitors are there in the market? What are the demographics in the market? Are there any key employees in the business?"
- "Check volume trends and average sales trends for at least 5 years."
- "Will he stay and help with the transition? Continuing former owner's goodwill is extremely important typically."

Resources

Associations
- International Cemetery, Cremation & Funeral Association: www.iccfa.com
- National Funeral Directors Association: www.nfda.org

F - Rules of Thumb

Furniture and Appliance Stores

SIC Furniture Stores 5712-16 / Appliance Stores 5722-02

NAICS Furniture Stores 442110 / Appliance Stores 443111

Rules of Thumb
➢ 2 times monthly sales plus inventory

Pricing Tips
- Large privately held profitable furniture stores may bring as much as one times annual sales.

Benchmark Data
- "Industry average is about $325 in sales per sq. ft."

Furniture Refinishing

| SIC 7641-05 | NAICS 811420 | Number of Businesses/Units 23,064 |

Rules of Thumb
➢ 50 percent of annual sales plus inventory

Benchmark Data

Statistics (Furniture Repair & Reupholstery)
Number of Establishments 23,064
Average Profit Margin 6.8%
Revenue per Employee $53,700
Average Number of Employees 1.4
Average Wages per Employee $18,570

Products and Services Segmentation
Office and institutional furniture repair 36.7%
Upholstery repair of household furniture 31.4%
Other furniture repair services 17.8%
Wooden household furniture repair 14.1%

Major Market Segmentation
Households 55.0%
Businesses 43.0%
Government 2.0%

Industry Costs
Profit 6.8%
Wages 34.8%
Purchases 30.2%
Depreciation 1.7%
Marketing 1.5%
Rent & Utilities 7.6%
Other 17.4%

Source: IBISWorld, August 2015

Rules of Thumb - **F**

Furniture Stores

| SIC 5712-16 | NAICS 442110 | Number of Businesses/Units 42,355 |

Rules of Thumb
> ➢ 60 percent of annual sales includes inventory

Pricing Tips
- "Analyze gross profit margin & ratio of repeat clientele to new customers."

Benchmark Data

Statistics (Furniture Store)

Number of Establishments	42,355
Average Profit Margin	2.5%
Revenue per Employee	$274,100
Average Number of Employees	5.2
Average Wages per Employee	$32,905

Products and Services Segmentation

Living room furniture	51.5%
Dining room furniture	19.1%
Other furniture	15.9%
Bedroom furniture	13.5%

Industry Costs

Profit	2.5%
Wages	12.2%
Purchases	58.2%
Depreciation	0.9%
Marketing	3.4%
Rent & Utilities	9.0%
Other	13.8%

Market Share

Ashley Furniture Industries Inc.	6.3%
Inter IKEA Systems BV	5.3%

Source: IBISWorld, June 2015

- "U.S. furniture stores posted a 7.8% increase in furniture, bedding and accessories sales in 2013, growing revenue to a combined $34.1 billion, up from $31.7 billion the year before. That growth wasn't as impressive as the 9.9% gain in 2012 for the previous Top 100, but it blew away the meager increase for all U.S. furniture stores and led to a major capture of additional market share."

Source: The Research Store, http://site.reedbusinessstore.com/ft.html

Expenses as a percentage of annual sales

Cost of goods	30%
Payroll/labor Costs	15%
Occupancy	20%
Profit (estimated pretax)	35%

26th Edition

G - Rules of Thumb

Industry Trend

- "Two furniture retailers placed in the top five 2014 Hot 100 Retailers list for the first time ever. In the annual list compiled by Kantar Retail and published by the National Retail Federation, Wayfair came in second and Conn's HomePlus fourth. Additional furniture retailers on this year's list include Overstock.com, Jordan's Furniture, Nebraska Furniture Mart, and Crate and Barrel."
  Source: "Six Trends about the Furniture Industry We're Loving Right Now" by Caroline Platkiewicz, http://www.blueport.com/blog/six-trends-about-the-furniture-industry-were-loving-right-now 10/7/14
- "Top 100 stores post 8.3% sales increase in 2014."
  Source: http://www.furnituretoday.com/article/519893-top-100-furniture-stores

Questions

- "What is the reason for selling? Will the purchaser assume ownership of the client base? Is there already a fully functional Website?"

Resources

Trade Publications
- Bedding Today: www.furnituretoday.com/

Garage Door Sales & Service

SIC 5211-02	NAICS 444190	Number of Businesses/Units 31,639

Rules of Thumb

➢ 25 percent of annual sales plus inventory

Benchmark Data

Statistics (Garage Door Installation)

Number of Establishments	31,639
Average Profit Margin	18.1%
Revenue per Employee	$75,000
Average Number of Employees	2.1
Average Wages per Employee	$28,806

Products and Services Segmentation

Retrofits and upgrades	68%
Installation in new commercial construction	2%
Installation in new residential construction	10%
Repair and maintenance work	20%

Major Market Segmentation

Homeowners	62%
Garage door merchants	26%
Construction firms	12%

Rules of Thumb - **G**

Industry Costs

Profit	18.1%
Wages	35.3%
Purchases	25.9%
Depreciation	2.3%
Marketing	1.0%
Rent & Utilities	5.0%
Other	12.4%

Source: IBISWorld, January 2014

Garbage/Trash Collection (See also Waste Collection)

SIC 4953-02	NAICS 562111	Number of Businesses/Units 11,707

Rules of Thumb
➢ 1.5 to 2.5 times annual sales

Pricing Tips
- "In the larger cities, garbage routes are selling from $30 to $34 for each dollar taken in per month. Perimeter routes around the larger cities sell for $18 to $22 for each dollar taken in per month, with the smaller communities selling from $14 to $18 for each dollar taken in during the month. If the dump is owned by the garbage collector, you should also add the amount of the land and permit value."

Benchmark Data

Statistics (Waste Collection Services)

Number of Establishments	11,707
Average Profit Margin	8.8%
Revenue per Employee	$230,700
Average Number of Employees	17.8
Average Wages per Employee	$46,420

Products and Services Segmentation

Residential waste collection services	35.3%
Nonresidential waste collection services	25.2%
Other	18.3%
Transfer and storage facility services	8.2%
Hazardous waste collection services	5.2%
Recyclable material collection services	4.3%
Construction and demolition site waste collection services	3.5%

Major Market Segmentation

Individuals and households	38.7%
Retail and office businesses	29.6%
Industrial companies	15.4%
Government and not-for-profit organizations	10.1%
Construction and demolition companies	6.2%

26th Edition

G - Rules of Thumb

Industry Costs

Profit	8.8%
Wages	20.4%
Purchases	21.9%
Depreciation	7.4%
Marketing	1.0%
Rent & Utilities	7.2%
Other	33.3%

Market Share

Waste Management Inc.	27.9%
Republic Services Inc.	19.3%

Source: IBISWorld, June 2015

Industry Trend

- "The US waste management industry includes about 24,000 establishments (single-location companies and units of multi-location companies) with combined annual revenue of about $86 billion."

  Source: www.firstresearch.com

- "The top two companies, Waste Management and Republic Services accounted for 39 percent of total industry revenue. All of the publicly traded companies together comprised 61 percent of total revenues. All told, the private sector represents 78 percent of the industry while the municipal sector controls the remaining 22 percent. This is a sharp contrast to 1992 when municipalities controlled 35 percent of industry revenue."

  Source: "Waste Market Overview & Outlook 2012," *Waste Business Journal*

Garden Centers/Nurseries

(See also Landscape Services, Lawn Maintenance and Service)

SIC 5261-04	NAICS 444220	Number of Businesses/Units 13,281

Rules of Thumb

- ➢ 3–5 times Seller's Discretionary Earnings plus inventory
- ➢ 25 percent of sales plus inventory

Pricing Tips

- "Customer database indicating the amount of recurring revenue per customer"

Expert Comments

"This is a maturing industry but the right business location and a good marketing and management of finances makes all the difference. Affluent customer base is necessary to compete effectively with mass merchants. A service component of the business is helpful but increases risk."

Rules of Thumb - **G**

Benchmark Data

Statistics (Nursery and Garden Stores)
Number of Establishments	13,281
Average Profit Margin	2.7%
Revenue per Employee	$242,500
Average Number of Employees	8.7
Average Wages per Employee	$29,569

Products and Services Segmentation
Equipment	51.4%
Grain and animal feed	19.1%
Chemicals	17.2%
Plants	8.3%
Tools and other supplies	4.0%

Major Market Segmentation
Consumers aged 45 to 64	45.0%
Consumers aged 66 and older	26.0%
Consumers aged 44 and younger	11.0%
Farmers	10.0%
Corporate entities	8.0%

Industry Costs
Profit	2.7%
Wages	12.1%
Purchases	53.3%
Depreciation	1.6%
Marketing	1.6%
Rent & Utilities	4.6%
Other	24.1%

Source: IBISWorld, June 2015

How many year-round employees does your organization have?
5 or fewer	55%
6 to 10	20%
11 to 15	10%
20 to 25	3%
More than 25	12%

Source: www.todaysgardencenter.com/magazine

- "In very good news for the garden industry, the vital second quarter {of 2013} saw strong increases in all categories (sales volume, average sales per customer and customer traffic) for a strong majority of garden centers. A full 70.6 percent saw increases in sales per customer. That's even more solid in light of the 64 percent who report increases in traffic and 66.7 percent that had increased sales volume. Since more than half of garden center revenue comes from this quarter (53.2 percent on average, according to the survey), strong increases in sales, average sales and traffic have an outsized impact on the overall industry's health."

Source: Today's Garden Center 2013 State of the Industry Survey, http://www.todaysgardencenter.com/business-management/state-of-the-industry/2013-state-of-the-industry-survey-its-a-good-year/

G - Rules of Thumb

- "A new survey question added last year and continued in 2013 asking households how much they spent at each type of retailer selling lawn and garden products confirmed that big-box stores and mass retailers account for the largest share of lawn and garden retail sales. The 2013 National Gardening Survey found that U.S. households spent more at Home Improvement Centers (27% of the total gardening retail market) and at Mass Merchants (20%) than they did at local Garden Centers and Nurseries (17%) or local Hardware Stores (15%). Many industry insiders have speculated about this shift in market "channel" share for years, and the 2013 National Gardening Survey has confirmed their suspicions. With a collective 47% share, large national chains now drive the L&G market."
    Source: Garden Market Research, http://www.gardenresearch.com/home?q=show&id=3737
- "30-40,000 per parking space.$120,000 per FTE. Inventory turn of 4 or more is good, but needs to improve to 5 to 8. GMROII of $5 or better must be attainable."

Expenses as a percentage of annual sales

Cost of goods	48%
Payroll/labor Costs	28%
Occupancy	05%
Profit (estimated pretax)	04%

Industry Trend

- "The highly anticipated trends report, published annually since 2001, finds that gardening goes hand-in-hand with a healthy lifestyle. People see both outdoor and indoor spaces as extensions of themselves and are making conscious decisions to use plants and garden products as 'tools' to increase their overall well-being and lead a sustainable lifestyle. In 2015, the report says brands are being held to ever higher standards, as customers demand that products are not only reliable but have a positive impact on the planet. Brands that help consumers make positive environmental, personal and community impacts will pull ahead.

"According to the report, the idea of 'going green' takes on a dual meaning in 2015. As more states decriminalize marijuana, consumers will also invest time in 'growing their own.' 'First it was "eat your garden." Then it was "drink your garden." Now, it's "smoke your garden,"' says McCoy. 'Marijuana is going to become a great ornamental plant as people continue to customize their garden and outdoor space to meet their needs.'

"What are some of the components that are fueling this sustainable lifestyle and contributing to eco-friendly gardens and outdoor spaces? Garden Media identified nine new trends driving major industry shifts:

1. The new consumers
2. Wellbeing
3. Garden-tainment
4. Bite-sized decadence
5. Rebel-hoods
6. Color pops
7. Portable gardening
8. Bed head style
9. Smoke your garden"

    Source: http://www.gardenmediagroup.com/clients/client-news/435-gmg-releases-2015-trends

Rules of Thumb - **G**

- "Landscape Firms Scale Up To Remain Competitive—Landscape service trends appear to be improving. In fact, according to First Research, the output of the U.S. landscaping industry is forecast to grow at a compounded annual rate of 4 percent through 2016, indicating steady growth in the longer term. I made an informal tally of the mergers and acquisitions over the last three years and they filled up three pages single-spaced! About 80 percent of those were in the landscape sector, reflective of the fact that regional landscape firms are rapidly scaling up to achieve the economies of scale necessary to compete with the behemoth created by the Brickman's and Valley Crest merger."
    Source: "2015 State Of The Industry: Current Green Industry Trends" by Charlie Hall, http://www.greenhousegrower.com/business-management/2015-state-of-the-industry-current-green-industry-trends/ 1/19/15

Seller Financing
- 5 to 15 years

Questions
- "Here are some key questions to get answered in analyzing garden centers:
    - ✓ How many months are you open for business (determine season)? If not open all year, which months are you open?
    - ✓ What method do you use to value your ending inventory (e.g., cost)?
    - ✓ What makes up your inventory in the winter months?
    - ✓ How are obsolete/damaged goods accounted for?
    - ✓ What is your policy regarding returns and allowances for plants?
    - ✓ Do you have a slow season? Which months? What other sources of income do you have during the slow season?
    - ✓ Who are your major suppliers (any related parties)?
    - ✓ What services do you provide? (landscaping, lawn service, delivery, plant rental, etc.?)"
    Source: The above is excerpted from an IRS Audit Technique Guide (Market Segment Specialization Program—MSSAP).
- "What am I not seeing in your numbers? Is unaccounted cash being removed from the business? How current and complete is your customer database?"

Resources

Websites
- Today's Garden Center: http://www.todaysgardencenter.com/

Trade Publications
- Garden Center Magazine: http://www.gardencentermag.com/

Gas Stations—Full-and/or Self-Serve		
(See also Gas Stations with Convenience Stores/Mini Marts)		
SIC 5541-01	NAICS 447190	Number of Businesses/Units 13,753
Rules of Thumb		
➢ 10 to 15 percent of annual sales plus inventory		

26th Edition

G - Rules of Thumb

- 2.5 to 3 times SDE plus inventory
- 2.5 to 3.0 times EBIT
- 2.5 to 3.5 times EBITDA (business only)
- 1.5 to 2.5 SDE (with service bays, business only) plus inventory
- 5 to 6 times SDE includes real estate
- 5 to 7 times EBITDA—business and real estate
- "4 to 6 times EBITDA including the real estate is a good rule of thumb for convenience stores with gas. 2 to 3.5 times EBITDA for leased sites. Age and condition of the petroleum equipment and environmental issues are important considerations in selling these businesses. A phase I & II report are required for both purchased and leased sites."

Pricing Tips

- "Buyers are looking for high volume gas stations; the norm is the higher the gasoline volume per month the more attractive the business becomes. That being said you also need to be aware of the margin on each gallon of gas sold. Find out if the tanks underground have been inspected in the last year and meet or exceed EPA and local standards. Ask if any leaks or hazardous waste has been found/detected on the premises in the last ten years. If the gas station has a convenience store associated the value is higher, if there is a car wash the value increases again."
- "Service Stations are more than dispensers of gasoline. The typical station has one or more of the following sources of revenue:
  - ✓ Gasoline
  - ✓ Diesel fuel
  - ✓ Sale of Vehicles
  - ✓ Car Wash
  - ✓ Mini-Markets
  - ✓ Lottery
  - ✓ Check Cashing
  - ✓ Propane
  - ✓ Scales
  - ✓ Repair Shops with or without Tow
  - ✓ Towing
  - ✓ Kerosene"

  Source: www.irs.gov/business/small/article

- "The multiples used to be as high as 4.5 to 5 times the SDE in 2003. The eroding profit margin, measured as cents per gallon, has tightened up in the marketplace since then, resulting in forcing the gas station owner to look for volumes and margins elsewhere in the station. The snack shop/convenience store section has stepped up to the plate and accounts for about 80% of the profits, while the other 20% and all of the gasoline margin goes towards the costs of employees and such. Depending on the rent or the mortgage structure, the 80% figures adjust up or down. Do not let the huge sales volumes fool you; measure the gallons times the margin, and not the millions in actual sales/revenue figures."
- "3 x SDE or 2–3 times EBIT are the best; the percentage of annual gross sales doesn't reflect a fair price."

Rules of Thumb - G

- "3 to 4 times EBITDA including the real estate."
- "Margins are getting squeezed in some areas, therefore must be taken into consideration."
- "Gross sales is not a good factor in pricing, since the profit margin varies between gas and grocery sales."
- "3 to 4 times EBITDA including the real estate is a common rule. Location, traffic count, brand, and population are important considerations."
- "It has nothing to do with total sales volume or revenue. It does have everything to do with average gallons sold, and margins per gallon; volatility in industry requires you map out gallons and margins per month for last 2 years. Majors tend to have flat fixed margins, minors and unbranded markets move between 2–4 cents to high of 25%–30% margins."
- "Multiple of 2 x SDE is mid-point of the range 1.75-2.25 x SDE, and does not include the real estate. This range is applicable to Arizona statewide, and it narrows when considering 3 identifiable markets within AZ: Phoenix metro, Tucson metro, and rural. Real estate, when included, may be priced separately and added to SDE multiple, or 'digested' in the business valuation by a higher range of multiples. Real estate valuations may be considered by the same 3 Arizona markets, but should also consider the class of property, i.e., A, B & C. The full range when including real estate is approx. 5 x SDE for a C-class property in rural AZ, to 14x for a Class-A property in Phoenix metro."
- "Dealer stations in our market sell for 2.2 to 2.5 post due diligence SDE for the business only. I value gas stations with the land by starting with SDE and deducting the buyer's required income for managing the station and any necessary reserves, and then I capitalize that amount by what I feel is the market cap rate. This is basically a real estate approach to the value."
- "2 or 3 times net SDE—most stores have horrible records . . . proof of numbers is through gas receipts and store invoices. Gallons per month, pool margin, inside sales, other income and do the tanks meet 2009 standards."
- "Factors that most influence value are: volume of gasoline sales, location, length, C-store versus service bays, traffic count and major brand identity."
- "Age of tanks; does station have canopy (is it cantilever or mech. attached); is it clean (environment); location, location, location."
- "The geographical site/location is key to a buyer in many offers and subsequent sells. Near freeways or interstates, high visibility corner locations or locations near major malls all come with a premium price tag to the buyer."
- "Stand-alone gas stations are dwindling in number as it is difficult to survive on just gasoline alone. Most stations are also service garages and/or have some other profit center to generate income."
- "Gas only: 2 to 2.5 times SDE plus inventory
  Gas with food market: 2.5 to 3 times SDE plus inventory
  Gas with car wash/food mart: 2.5 to 4 times SDE plus inventory
  Gas with garage/repair: 1.5 to 2 times SDE plus inventory"

Expert Comments

"Major oil companies are getting out of owning properties and managing labor. More and more newer immigrants are getting into locations as owners across the country. Oil companies primarily want to be in the fuel supply business as their core profit driver."

G - Rules of Thumb

"A gas station is not easy to replicate by any means, with all the environmental regulations and what have you. The profit trend is definitely downwards, with non-branded or independent owners who primarily buy product on the open spot market being hammered the most. The branded market seems to want to try to chase non-branded independents out of the market with their pricing on racks."

"With the way the economy is now, it's very tough to generate a decent profit out of a gas station, Customers looking for cheaper gas, cheaper groceries, increased use of credit cards—all this affects the business; and with the big oil companies like Racetrac and QT opening stores every day, they are affecting independent gas stations big time."

"It is getting very expensive to build a new ground-up facility. Average does cost close to $2 million, therefore it is not that easy to replicate. Not to mention the uphill battle with most urban zoning requirements which causes lengthy delays and adds to the soft costs."

"Gas stations are easy to market, especially with the real estate. Competition is declining, since some stations choose to close rather than face environmental upgrades. Profit trends downward on gasoline, with gas profit paying some to most of costs only. Marts/snack shops/stores are major moneymaking factors."

Benchmark Data

Statistics (Gas Stations)

Number of Establishments	13,753
Average Profit Margin	1.0%
Revenue per Employee	$931,500
Average Number of Employees	8.6
Average Wages per Employee	$23,725

Products and Services Segmentation

Diesel	49.2%
Gas	41.8%
Other	5.6%
Automotive services (e.g. repairs, car washes and general parts)	2.5%
Nonautomotive fuel	1.8%

Major Market Segmentation

Consumers	68.8%
Businesses	26.1%
All other	5.1%

Industry Costs

Profit	1.0%
Wages	2.7%
Purchases	79.1%
Depreciation	0.6%
Marketing	0.3%
Rent & Utilities	2.9%
Other	13.4%

Market Share

Royal Dutch Shell PLC 9.9%

Source: IBISWorld, September 2015

- "Retailers know consumers will go somewhere else to save a few pennies a gallon, so they keep the difference between the selling price and their fuel costs as low as possible, according to the 2013 Retail Fuels Report by NACS, the Association for Convenience and Fuel Retailing. Indeed, while 71% of a store's total sales are motor fuels, only 36% of profit dollars are generated by fuels, the trade group said in its report. Many gas station owners try to make up for the thin gasoline margins through sales of other products, such as snacks and drinks."
- "If the gas station does 150k+ gallons per month with a gas margin of .20 cents or higher per gallon and the convenience store is doing at least $45k per month, this would be recognized as a good opportunity."

Source: National Association of Convenience Stores

- "Good locations should do upwards of $400 per sq. ft."
- "Adding prepared meals in the store tends to increase the bottom line since these items have a high profit margin."
- "$450–$500 per sq. ft."
- "Traditional benchmarks still are looked for when considering the early stage feasibility of buying an operating station: fuel volume (gals/mo.) and store sales without lottery. Given the complexity of the variables and trends, these have become less valid in assessing the future success of a gas station business. A better starting point I believe is the overall historical SDE. Capitalizing this to a price must consider the value of the real estate and the quality of the property, including location. Estimated pretax profit (below) is historically understated with private companies in AZ, hence the need to determine SDE. The number provided is representative of the pretax profit, but seldom a valid representation of the financial benefit accruing to the owner."
- "Auto repair facilities, not found too easily any more, are more profitable per square foot than markets. However, auto repairs must be run right, and carry a lot of headaches with them."
- "A good gas station should pump at least 1.2 million gas gallons yearly."
- "Gross profit per gallon is what generates the income."

Expenses as a percentage of annual sales

Cost of goods.. 75%
Payroll/labor Costs... 08% to 10%
Occupancy.. 05% to 10%
Profit (estimated pretax) .... 03% to 05%

Industry Trend

- "Privately owned gas stations historically have some of the thinnest profit margins in retailing, but in 2013 they experienced their strongest margins in years, according to preliminary data from Sageworks, a financial information company. Net profit margins, on average, increased to nearly 3%, compared with 1.6% in 2012. At the same time, sales among private gas stations were relatively flat, increasing only about 1% from 2012.

"A financial statement analysis by Sageworks shows that gas stations in 2013 experienced less pressure on their margins from key costs (costs of goods sold, or COGS), which were about 87% of sales, on average. Fuel expense

G - Rules of Thumb

is the biggest component of COGS. Third-party data indicate that wholesale prices for resale ('rack' prices) fluctuated through the year, ranging from $2.587 a gallon to $2.989 a gallon for regular but ending 2013 slightly lower than they were at the start of the year."

Source: "Why Gas Station Owners May Be Smiling," Forbes 1/21/2014

- "In south Florida trend is to larger stores, 2000 sq. feet or more. More food service inside the larger C-store; repair bays are history."

Seller Financing
- "3 years, on average 8 percent interest per annum."
- "As much as 50 percent of sales price could be financed—3 to 5 years typical."
- "Franchise—2 to 3 years (5 to 10 percent)"
- "Property—10 to 15 years (8 to 11 percent)"

Questions
- "5 years' financial and gallonage history; phase I & II environmental reports"
- "Any new competition?Security & safety?Road construction?Introduction to vendors."
- "Gallons history, margins history, both for last four years; plot against spot prices to see how tight street pricing gets on that street."
- "The quality of their historical financial statements, including both income statements and balance sheets. This is both for prospective buyer due diligence and lender requirements."
- "As much paperwork as possible to get to the truth"
- "Status of the underground tanks."
- "Some Key Questions:
A buyer would want to ask the current owner if the oil company owns the property or if the land is leased to the oil company. The value of the business will be less if the land is leased from another entity. The reason is that when the lease expires, even if there are options, the oil company may decide not to renew. Make sure the oil company owns the property; worst case make sure the lease for the station runs at least for another 10 years (when the oil company does not own the land). Buyers should also be concerned about the types of tanks that are underground—are they steel or fiberglass? If the owner has steel tanks, find out why the tanks have not been replaced with fiberglass. Ask the current owner if there have been any leaks or contamination. If the answer is yes, find out when and to what extent. Has the problem been corrected?"
- "One should also find out who is responsible for any and all contamination that lies above or below the surface of the site. Always require, in an offer to purchase agreement, a clause that states that the buyer will perform as part of the due diligence a Phase I report by an accredited environmental or chemical engineer who has a license to do so, with the results approved to the buyer's satisfaction. If a Phase II or III report is required, it is strongly suggested that it be done as well."

Resources

Trade Publications
- National Petroleum News: www.npnweb.com

Gas Stations w/Convenience Stores/MiniMarts
(See also Gas Stations, Convenience Stores w/gas)

SIC 5541-01	NAICS 447110	Number of Businesses/Units 103,237

Rules of Thumb

- Note: The information that follows is also in C-Stores with Gas. It is a confusing issue, and perhaps there is no difference between a C-store with gas and a gas station with a C-store, but many experts still feel that there is. So here goes, again: Convenience stores with gas—these operations are more convenience stores than gas stations such as a 7-Eleven or Circle K. Gas stations with convenience stores (mini-marts)— these operations are more gas stations than convenience stores, such as Mobil, Shell and Exxon gas stations that have convenience stores. In many cases, the garages and stations themselves have been retrofitted to be convenience stores. These operations may include a car wash.
- 20 to 25 percent of annual sales plus inventory
- 80 percent of annual sales with real estate plus inventory
- 4 to 5 SDE with mini-mart (minimum 800 sq. ft.), 200K gals/mo., with the mini-mart $35K+/mo.
- 3 to 5 times EBIT
- 2.5 to 3.75 times EBITDA (business only)
- 3 to 4 times EBITDA
- 4 to 7 times EBITDA—business and real estate, with car wash or large convenience store included
- 7 times EBITDA with real estate

Pricing Tips

- "1) What type of gas supply agreement is in place; rack deal gets a high price, dtw(dealer tank wagon) average price, commission agent low price. Buy a commission agent gas station only if there is a 10 or more year lease.
2) Gas volume and pool margin on gas
3) Convenience store gross profit preferred 30% or higher
4) Independent or brand name. Independent are valued at a higher price.
5) If it has a car wash it has a higher value.
6) Low rent high value.
7) If diesel is also sold, higher value as pool margin on diesel is high
8) The more the revenue stream, the higher the price."
"Location, years history of proven growth, modern facility and, attention to competition."
- "The number and breadth of variables makes ROT pricing invalid, and largely misleading—we don't use it."
- "1) Valuation is 2–3 times Net income for owner-operated gas stations and for absentee owned 3–4 times.
2) Potential buyers must consider rent, pool margin on gas, mechanics on salary or commission.

G - Rules of Thumb

   3) Age of the car wash equipment. Most car washes last 10 years.
   4) Land owned by the oil company is a plus; if third party owns the land, check the underlying lease between the oil company and the landlord.
   5) Check transfer fee and security deposit charged by the oil company"

- "Gas Stations with C Stores or Car Washes bring a higher multiple on the West Coast. You may pay more for a business as you purchase, but when it comes time to sell you'll receive a higher multiple as well. The norm right now is 3.5 to 4x SDC and 4 to 5x EBITDA, most require at least 80% cash down."
- "Evaluate competition, neighborhood demographic changes anticipated, and revenue trends. Adjust multiple for inferior facility as well as superior facility to comparable sales."
- "The value of gas stations, at least in the Northeast, is impacted strongly by the age and viability of the underground storage tanks. These can cost $200,000 or more to replace and many single-walled tanks are required by the state governments to be removed from the ground. Another significant determinant of value is the fuel supply agreement. If the location is controlled by a fuel distributor or oil company, the business is usually worth less because a new owner will not have the ability to buy fuel on the open market."
- "The multiples used to be higher, however due to market conditions they have come down approx. 20% in the last two years. The eroding profit margin, measured as cents per gallon, has tightened up in the marketplace since then, resulting in forcing the gas station owner to look for volumes and margins elsewhere in the station. The snack shop/convenience store section has stepped up to the plate and accounts for about 80% of the profits, while the other 20% and all of the gasoline margin goes towards the costs of employees and such. Depending on the rent or the mortgage structure, the 80% figures adjust up or down. Do not let the huge sales volumes fool you; measure the gallons times the margin, and not the millions in actual sales/revenue figures."
- "2 to 3 x SDE are the best multiples; the percentage of annual gross sales doesn't reflect a fair price."
- "It has nothing to do with total sales volume or revenue. It does have everything to do with average gallons sold, and margins per gallon; volatility in industry requires you map out gallons and margins per month for last 2 years. Majors tend to have flat fixed margins, minors and unbranded markets move between 2–4 cents to high of 25%–30% margins."
- "Multiple of 2x SDE is mid-point of the range 1.75-2.75x SDE, and does not include the real estate. may be priced separately and added to SDE multiple, or 'digested' in the business valuation by a higher range of multiples. Real estate valuations may be considered by the same 3 Arizona markets, but should also consider the class of property, i.e., A, B & C. The full range when including real estate is approx. 5X SDE for a C-class property in rural AZ, to 14x for a Class-A property in Phoenix metro."
- "Dealer stations in our market sell for 2.2 to 2.5 post due diligence SDE excluding property(California). I value gas stations with the land by starting with SDE and deducting the buyer's required income for managing the station and any necessary reserves, and then I capitalize that amount by what I feel is the market cap rate. This is basically a real estate approach to the value."
- "Age and condition of the petroleum equipment and environmental issues are important considerations in selling and buying these businesses. A phase I & II report are required for both purchased and leased sites. Standard SBA loans

Rules of Thumb - **G**

are becoming more challenging as we all are aware, find the bank or lending institution in your area who provides the best opportunity for a bank/SBA loan for gas stations and convenience stores."
- "Some factors that detract are small lot size and access issues."
- "The most valid pricing comes from capitalizing adjusted cash flow, or SDE. If the gas station acquisition includes the real estate, this either needs to be broken out and priced in addition to the business, or digested in the capitalization calculation. Severely reduced transaction volume, little or no new construction, and poorly defined interest rate scale to define risk (& CAP rates) due to government intermediation make the standard approaches to pricing uncertain."
- "Profit margin on gasoline should be more than 6 cents per gallon. Store gross margins will average 20% to 25%. Pricing is based on DE, not gross, since margins are small and reflective of competition."
- "Normally 7 times EBITDA with real estate and 4–5 times without real estate in Midwest"
- "5–7 times with real estate for stores doing $70k+ inside and 70k+ gallons per month"
- "SDE should be at or about $100,000 before businesses will generate strong buyers' interest."
- "2 to 3 times EBITDA for business alone or 3 to 5 times business with property"
- "Gasoline volume and gasoline margin are key indicators of value; beer/wine license receives a higher price; store size greater than 1000 sq. ft. gets a higher price; length of time and type of fuel contract; franchised vs independent impacts price but depends on area."
- "Factors that increase the value include a long-term lease, no contract with a major oil company (so the buyer can negotiate his own contract), strong convenience store and/or strong co-brand. Factors that decrease the value include strong competition, lack of space for development, small lot size, full-service gasoline requirements."
- "The rule of thumb when valuing a convenience store with real estate is 5–6 x EBITDA; without real estate, it is 2–3 x EBITDA plus inventory. Questions to ask from the seller are: Is the store branded (Mobil, BP, Shell etc.) and if so how long is the contract to the brand? You need to know this, because the buyer may want to change the brand, and there will be a financial obligation to the brand to get out of the commitment."
- "6–7 times EBITDA with the real estate included for a branded decent store doing over $50,000 inside sales and 50,000 gallons per month."
- "Individual operator buyers are looking for stores that are management run/absentee owned where they can get in and run the stores themselves. This enables them to know what is walking in and out of the store, alleviate high payrolls, plus another 12% payroll tax, maybe some workers compensation, better be able to know about markups, etc. There are lots of buyers for these stores, which is driving price up versus the traditional EBITDA method of valuation."

Expert Comments

"To buyers: work in a station for a minimum 6 months before buying one. Make sure you have 2–3 months working capital after the purchase.

G - Rules of Thumb

"To sellers: start preparing two years prior to selling so you have clean financials. Not having proper financials will lead to lower valuation. Prepare a good management/employee team so the station is on auto pilot."

"Gas stations are a retail business with a very high barrier to entry. Same inventory keeps changing hands as opening a new location is tough due to zoning laws and regulations and it costs over $2 million to get a new one started. It's a recession free business. You don't need a lot of employees, mostly one, unless you have a great hot food program."

"Municipalities dictate barriers to entry. Licensing (privileged licenses) are provided to qualified applicants only."

"This industry is dominated by large national and regional players with deep pockets."

"Use a broker, and find a specialist for the market you're going into. Business standards of practice, jobber relationships, environmental regulations, etc., vary greatly among regions of the country and the various states."

"Gas stations have a high barrier to entry therefore the same inventory changes hands with very few new sites opening."

"The overall appetite for profitable businesses in this class is trending upward."

"Amount of risk in purchasing this business is relatively low. The multiple for that reason is higher than most businesses. Do your homework; make sure you understand all facets of this business. Most gas station owners I know work about 15 hours per week. Their average return is approx. $145,000 to $190,000 SDC annually."

"Major oil companies are selling off their company-owned stations. More foreign buyers are coming into the marketplace. Oil companies primarily want to be in the fuel supply business as their core profit driver."

"A gas station is not easy to replicate by any means, with all the environmental regulations and what have you. The profit trend is definitely downwards, with non-branded or independent owners who primarily buy product on the open spot market being hammered the most. The branded market seems to want to try to chase non-branded independents out of the market with their pricing on racks."

"It is getting very expensive to build a new ground-up facility. Average cost $2+ million, therefore it is costly to replicate. Not to mention the uphill battle with most urban zoning requirements which causes lengthy delays and adds to the soft costs."

"Gas stations and car washes are becoming more available in the listing base and not selling near as quickly as in the past. Financing is difficult to acquire as the main reason, also the drop in profitability along with rising rent factors are making gas stations less appealing. Some independent stations choose to close rather than face environmental upgrades. Profit trends downward on gasoline, with gas profit paying some to most of costs only. Marts/snack shops/stores are major moneymaking factors."

"Hard to replicate due to site work needed and tank cost"

"Good high-volume single stores are hard to find and they are usually older stores"

"Gas stations are perhaps the closest thing we have to perfect competition in the world. Prices are readily visible and there are almost always plenty of competitors to give the customer a choice. The risk level is relatively low because there are few fluctuations in volume from year to year. There is some risk in the fuel margin, as the margin is highly dependent on what the commodity market for fuel is doing. Profits remain steady in the fuel and in the stores, with the possibility for a little rise in profitability in the Northeast with the exit of two major oil companies (Shell and Mobil) from the retail business and the removal of some of their fuel price subsidies. Regulations continue to be a burden that erodes the profitability of the typical location, but the consolidation of the industry has somewhat offset that. Good gas stations are highly marketable— there is a seemingly endless supply of buyers, usually foreign-born (Indian, Pakistani, Lebanese, etc.). The industry is mature and consolidating, and gas will someday go away as a fuel source, so it is in a long and slow decline. The gas station/c-store model is fairly easy to replicate. Gas stations with service bays are not so easy to replicate."

"High competition, but owner operators can compete on service and quality of products."

"The gas station industry is consolidating and going through the same types of changes that are occurring with hardware stores, pharmacies and local general stores. These other types of stores are being challenged by stores like Home Depot, Walgreens and Wal-Mart. The small, local, full-service gas station is being supplanted by large Hess, Mobil, Exxon or Shell stations that have large convenience stores, car washes and co-brands. These large stores are able to pump a lot more volume than the older sites and therefore need less margin to survive. This is compounded by the fact that the larger stores have stronger ancillary revenues from their convenience stores and other revenue sources. A modern store is more easily marketable. The older sites are being transformed into other retail uses, like banks and coffee shops."

"The gas station industry continues to consolidate rapidly. With the exit of big oil companies like Chevron, Mobil and Shell from gasoline retail, we will likely see consolidation continue for three to five years and then possibly see the industry fragment slightly. Large multi-site operators will buy many of the major oil companies' locations, with some being left over for the smaller operators. Consolidation will continue to hurt the small mom & pop operation and help the large-volume highway and busy main thoroughfare locations."

"Gas stations and C-stores have been in high demand and as a result prices paid have been exaggerated compared to many businesses. Some buyers try to buy low and then re-sell in 2–3 years and make their profit when they sell. Make sure to verify financials."

"This is a $570 billion annual gross sales yielding net over $5 billion profit industry. The trend indicates historically stable growth, easy to replicate

G - Rules of Thumb

and also relatively easy to market as long as seller has books and records to substantiate the operational profit. In general, success of store clearly depends on location, condition of gasoline equipment and fixtures, traffic count & patterns, demographic of immediate trading area. However one has to be cautious in selection of a business site. There are often victims of small stores facing dreadful competition with a big box gas store like Wawa or Sheetz. A retailer has to have crucial research, not limited to a county economic development agency, to find out any possible agenda for an incoming competitor in the area, prior to deciding to purchase a store."

"High barrier to entry due to amount of capital needed to build stations; large entry of foreign investors; often find sellers with inadequate financial statements."

"Huge superstores make it hard to compete in large populations. Good stores are hiding in smaller communities with less competition. If you find a store in a good location, you can bet one of the big boys will also think it is a good location and soon join you. Make sure you are landlocked or closest to the Interstate."

Benchmark Data

Statistics (Gas Stations with Convenience Stores)

Number of Establishments	103,237
Average Profit Margin	1.1%
Revenue per Employee	$566,800
Average Number of Employees	7.2
Average Wages per Employee	17,823

Products and Services Segmentation

Regular gasoline	58.9%
Groceries	12.8%
Mid-grade and premium gasoline	12.1%
Other	10.7%
Diesel	5.5%

Industry Costs

Profit	1.1%
Wages	3.2%
Purchases	89.0%
Depreciation	0.9%
Marketing	0.2%
Rent & Utilities	3.3%
Other	2.3%

Source: IBISWorld, May 2015

- "Looking at demographics, drivers aged 18 to 34 are most likely to visit c-stores this summer, according to the NACS survey. Seventy-eight percent of consumers surveyed in this age group expect to purchase a snack while traveling this summer; 74 percent plan to buy a drink; 73 percent will use the bathroom; and 40 percent will buy a sandwich or meal."
  Source: http://www.csnews.com/product-categories/fuels/more-summer-vacationers-will-take-road?cc=1
- "Average profit pretax is about 10%. Gas volume should be minimum 1.2 million gallons per year. $600,000 in convenience store sales with 30–40% gross profit. Car wash must do minimum $100–$150k per year"

Rules of Thumb - G

- "Case by case, customer count to average sale +$12.00 per transaction."
- "Gross profit % of in-store sales is an important metric, and many of the major players will use gasoline as a lost leader to get you in the store."
- "Benchmarks for success depend upon revenue centers on the property and the sales mix among the centers, most easily illustrated by considering fuel and c-store. Fuel sales for a metro station might be 60-80% of sales with a profit margin of 2–4%, and the balance under-the-roof at 30% gross margin. (Fuel margins are expressed in pennies/gallon, called blended or pooled margin—easily converted into percent.) Rural stations tend to function more as a grocery store where fuel is the convenient item. These might do 80–90% under the roof and 10–20% or so in fuel. Store margins in rural settings can approach 40%, and fuel pooled margins $.30/gal. (vs., currently, $.12-.18/gal. in metro settings) Additional products and services also are a factor in this evaluation, e.g., carwash, alcohol sales, QSR (franchised or not), quick lube, etc."
- "Gross Profit margins in C-Stores should not be less than 30%, for delis not less than 50%, car wash GP margins 90%. Gasoline pool margins should be a min. of $.15/gallon."
- "There are 123,289 convenience stores selling fuel in the United States, and these retailers sell an estimated 80% of all the fuel purchased in the country. Overall, more than 58% of the convenience stores selling fuel are single-store operators—more than 70,000 stores across the country."

  Source: www.nacsonline.com/Research/FactSheets
- "Most gas stations with C Stores are open seven days a week, some 24 hours, most 6 am to 11 pm. Food costs on average show a 34% gross profit. Number of employees normally shows 2 FT employees throughout the day per shift."
- "100,000 gallons of gas sold per month is a minimum for a profitable station. $50,000+ per month is minimum for the convenience store sales."
- "Fuel margins in the Northeast average somewhere around 15 cents per gallon. Convenience store margins are around 25%–30%. A successful business can be measured by sales and margin. Any store with 1 million+ gallons and $750,000+ in store sales (provided the rent is reasonable) is an attractive location."
- "$400 per sq. ft. if they are good."
- "Some sellers value stores close to 8–10x the inside sales per month."
- "Monthly stores sales greater than $60K/month; gasoline volume greater than 150,000 gallons a month with a weighted margin of 10 cents or more."
- "Gross profit % of instore sales should be in the 30–35% range; gasoline is almost a loss leader in many markets. Fuel margins vary widely and can be from 5 cents to 15 cents/gallon depending on the market and cost pricing."
- "$250 to 280 per sq. ft."
- "The economics of the transformation make sense. A good price on fuel might get people in the door once or twice a week. Great coffee, brick-oven pizza, and gelato could pull them in daily."

Expenses as a percentage of annual sales

Cost of goods	65% to 80%
Payroll/labor Costs	08% to 15%
Occupancy	06% to 16%
Profit (estimated pretax)	04% to 10%

G - Rules of Thumb

Industry Trend

- "Freedom to choose where to stop was cited by 59 percent of those stating they will travel by car this summer, also a 7-percent jump. Once consumers do stop, c-stores are certain to benefit. Three-quarters (76 percent) of vacationers on the road this summer plan to stop to use the bathroom; 69 percent expect to get gas; and 67 percent expect to get food or drinks, reported NACS. Those in the 18-to-34 age group are expected to visit c-stores the most."
  Source: http://www.csnews.com/product-categories/fuels/more-summer-vacationers-will-take-road?cc=1
- "Positive trend. More discount retailers like Sheetz, Wawa, Royal Farm will try to get into inner cities from where they were kept out earlier due to high population density. Convenience stores will be expanded with hot food items added replicating the 7-Eleven model along with a car wash if there is room."
- "The trend is towards the larger, modern stores with more inside sales offerings including fast food, and multiple fueling locations outside."
- "Continuing consolidation with the industry (M&As). More stores going to food service sales. In AZ, not a lot of alternative fuels added to the sites."
- "Continued improvement and profitability with reasonable reduction in risk."
- "Speedway LLC will soon extend its convenience store footprint from nine states to 23, securing a foothold in most regions of the Northeast and Southeast. Following months of speculation, the division of Marathon Petroleum Corp. (MPC) announced Thursday an agreement to purchase Hess Corp.'s 1,256-store retail division for a total cash consideration of $2.87 billion. "The transaction is expected to close late in this year's third quarter, assuming regulatory approvals are obtained. Once the deal is complete, Speedway will have 2,733 company-owned stores, enough to become the second-largest c-store operator in the United States, according to Gary Heminger, president and CEO of MPC."
  Source: "Speedway to Acquire Hess Retail Network," by Brian Berk, Convenience Store News, 5/22/14
- "Lots of stores which sold in the last 3–5 years will be re-selling again as owners find it hard to profit, but they will find it hard to re-sell as well."
- "This will continue to be a very stable and attractive business for the next few years."
- "Positive"

Seller Financing

- "A combination of seller financing and outside financing recently. Less amount today for Request of Seller."
- "If real estate is part of the seller's assets, outside financing. If it's the business only with a lease, you can still get SBA financing, but often times the seller will need to provide 'filler' or 'gap' financing."
- "70% of the purchase price plus inventory paid by the buyer at closing and 30% seller financing for 2–4 years at 6–7% interest rate."
- "Usually outside financing. A percentage of inventory may be asked to carry for a short term."
- "Usually finance, 20–25% for three years at 6% interest."
- "SBA and bank loans have become increasingly more difficult due to economic conditions and type of business."
- "7 to 10 years on average 6 percent interest VIR, per annum. As much as 50 percent of sales price could be financed by the seller"
- "Loans on Property—10 to 15 years (7 to 11% interest)"

Rules of Thumb - G

Questions
- "How much financing can the seller do? What is your gas pool margin? Do you have a supply agreement with an oil company or are you independent? What is the gross profit on your convenience store sales? How old is the car wash equipment? If repair, how old is the equipment in the bays? Do you have emission/inspection? Do you have any fleet contracts for gas? Do you own the ATM or is it leased? What is your lotto commission? If buying real estate also: how old are the tanks, any road widening plans, how much insurance premiums does he pay. What is the workers comp insurance premium especially if there is a repair shop with the gas station? Who is the nearest competitor?"
- "Ask for 5 years' financial statements and tax returns; petroleum equipment detail; environmental assessments."
- "1) Potential buyers must consider rent, pool margin on gas, if mechanics are on salary or commission.
- 2) Age of the car wash equipment. Most car washes last 10 years.
- 3) Land owned by the oil company is a plus; if third party owns the land, check the underlying lease between the oil company and the landlord.
- 4) Check transfer fee and security deposit charged by the oil company."
- "Monitor stores in their neighborhood, read Convenience Store Decisions, Convenience Store & Petroleum, watch competition in the market and new land opportunities."
- "Any hazardous waste issues, or leak detection signals. How old are the dispensers and POS system in place? Does the oil company require any upgrades, if so what are they and the dollar amount to do so. How stable is the current station for longevity."
- "What would you do different to enhance sales?"
- "What is the age and material of tanks? Is there contamination? Who is responsible for that? Is the site part of a state clean-up fund? What are the gallon sales? Fuel margin? Store sales and margin? Lottery sales and net lottery income?Any ancillary sales (air, vending, ATM, etc.)"
- "Will they participate in financing?"
- "How much is rent? What is the monthly gross profit? What is the pool margin on gas after credit card fees?"
- "Gas volume, profit margin, store sales, lottery sales, rent. Length of lease is important, any zoning issues, any plans for the road to change, any new competition expected."
- "5 years' financials by profit center; petroleum equipment information; real estate appraisals; phase I & II environmental reports."
- "Everything about sales, income and the underground equipment"
- "Gasoline volume, cents per gallon margin (very important), store sales, store margin, lottery net income, ancillary income, environmental status, size, age and material of tanks, zoning, traffic count, competition."
- "Audited financial statements? Environmental issues?New development in area—competitors?"

Resources

Websites
- American Petroleum Institute: www.api.org

G - Rules of Thumb

Trade Publications
- Retail Business Review: www.conveniencestoresgasstations.retail-business-review.com
- Convenience Store News: www.csnews.com
- Convenience Store/Petroleum News: www.cspnet.com
- National Petroleum News: www.npnweb.com

Associations
- New York Association of Convenience Stores: www.nyacs.org
- PA Petroleum Association: www.ppmcsa.org
- National Association of Convenience Stores: www.nacsonline.com
- Arizona Petroleum Marketers Association: www.apma4u.org
- Gasoline & Automotive Service Dealers Of America: www.gasda.org

		Franchise
Gatti's Pizza (See also Franchises, Pizza Shops)		
Approx. Total Investment		$450,000 to $1,000,000
Estimated Annual Sales/Unit		$1,000,000
SIC 5812-22	NAICS 722513	Number of Businesses/Units 110

Rules of Thumb
➢ 30 to 35 percent of annual sales plus inventory

➢ Company also offers a larger restaurant: GattiTown—$2,900,000 to $3,200,000

Benchmark Data
- Size—3,000 to 8,000 sq. ft.
- Gatti town—18,000 to 25,000 sq. ft.

Resources
Websites
- www.gattispizza.com

		Franchise
Geeks on Call (See also Franchises)		
Approx. Total Investment		$53,350 to $82,150
	NAICS 811212	Number of Businesses/Units 123

Rules of Thumb
➢ 60 percent of annual sales plus inventory

Resources
Websites
- www.geeksoncall.com

Rules of Thumb - **G**

Franchise
General Nutrition Centers (See also Franchises)

Approx. Total Investment	$165,000 to $200,000
SIC 5499-04	NAICS 446191	Number of Businesses/Units 3,100

Rules of Thumb
➢ 40 percent of annual sales plus inventory

Resources

Websites
- www.gnc.com

Gift Shops (See also Card Shops)		
SIC 5947-12	NAICS 453220	Number of Businesses/Units 71,500

Rules of Thumb
➢ 25% to 35% of annual sales plus inventory
➢ 2.2 to 3 times SDE includes inventory
➢ 3 to 4 times EBITDA
➢ Inventory @ cost + FF&E + 1 to 2 times SDE

Pricing Tips
- "If the store has a good location, has a customer tracking system and a good Website that is providing at least 10% of annual sales, the values above will hold. Fortunately..., most buyers believe that they could run & manage a retail gift business. It is a 'fun' business; most folks don't go into a gift shop 'unhappy.' It is a 'feel good' business."
- "Inventory should be valued separately and include any costs associated with shipping inventory to the point of sale and preparing it for sale. Example: beads are bought in bulk. They are heavy and require extra costs to ship and require time and cost to re-package and weigh into smaller sellable units."
- "1. Location weighs heavily. 2. Products are very important in relation to value. Is the store a card + gift shop? Does it carry high-end American crafts and upscale gifts, gifts + toys? The mix is important along with profit margins."

Expert Comments

"Gifts make people smile. An owner needs to be able to have joyous empathy with their customers—especially those looking for that 'special gift' for someone special to them. And, you need to have good taste for what your customers may want. Providing services such as gift baskets and shipping can add to the business, especially with developing corporate sales."

"For smaller stores, unreported cash sales may exist. For larger stores, management, location and experienced buyers are key. Volume/type of

G - Rules of Thumb

products sold is very important. Merchandise buyers can make or break profitability, image, etc."

"Relatively easy to get into a craft business but difficult to obtain and maintain profitability. Smaller independently owned stores tend to be operated by owners with a passion for the craft rather than a passion for business."

Benchmark Data
- For additional Benchmark Data see Card Shops
- "The open hours make for a long work day. Most successful stores are owner run to keep wages in balance. Also, most stores use part-time help to keep the hours at lower wages."
- "Gross sales benchmark of $125K per employee"
- "Rent at 10% of GAS (Gross Annual Sales); Sales per Square Foot at $150–$175; Sales per Employee at $75,000–$125,000; Advertising at 3%–4% of GAS."
- "Small store sales are usually $200–$300 per sq. ft. Larger stores $300–$500 per sq. ft. Small stores should average $125,000 per employee."

Expenses as a percentage of annual sales

Cost of goods	48% to 55%
Payroll/labor Costs	08% to 18% (larger stores)
Occupancy	06% to 08%/mall stores 08% to 12%
Profit (estimated pretax)	20% to 25% sole proprietor; 05% to 10% larger

Industry Trend
- "More use of good Websites to sell more to repeat customers that do not have to actually come back into the store. Also, building up customer list with reminders and specials."
- "While spending on gifts, greeting cards and souvenirs will pick up over the next five years due to revived income levels, industry revenue will continue to decline. Competition from free virtual outlets like social networking sites and online greeting cards Websites will constrain the industry's growth over the next five years. Furthermore, more consumers will shop at discount retailers instead of specialty stores, further cutting into revenue growth."

Source: IBISWorld, March 2014

- "I don't have the statistics, but I believe there are fewer gift shops in business every year. The successfully operated gift stores appear to be in tourist locations and affluent communities. It is extremely difficult to secure unique gift products to sell, and many gift products are available at major retailers and discounters nationally at often discounted prices, making it virtually impossible for small stores to compete."
- "Survival is extremely difficult."
- "Large stores have survived recession, etc. Small stores are becoming extinct due to rising costs, difficulty in obtaining knowledgeable/motivated employees, the inability to buy with volume discount, difficulty moving old inventory, poor buying decisions."

Seller Financing
- "Seller financing is used"
- 3 to 7 years

Rules of Thumb - G

Questions
- "Look for a business that you would like to own and be proud to say that you owned it. The decision should be a blend of #1) what the seller has been doing for the last 3 years and #2) what ways do you see to improve and grow the business."
- "Any unusual trends, seasonal or one-time hot selling items included in gross sales revenue? Explain the competition in detail. Discuss thoroughly the theft and/or shrinkage issues. Any convictions recently? Who is really responsible for purchasing duties?"
- "For small stores—What are your cash sales and are any expenses paid with cash? What do you 'love' and 'hate' about owning this store? Both answers may surprise you!"

Resources

Associations
- The Retail Gift Card Association: www.thergca.org
- Craft and Hobby Association—a good site: www.craftandhobby.org

	Franchise
Godfather's Pizza (See also Franchises, Pizza Shops)	
Approx. Total Investment $100,000 to $300,000 depending on business model	
Estimated Annual Sales/Unit	$384,000
SIC 5812-22 | NAICS 722513	Number of Businesses/Units 600

Rules of Thumb
➢ 25 to 30 percent of annual sales

Resources

Websites
- www.godfatherspizza.com

	Franchise
Goin' Postal (See also Franchises, Mail & Parcel Centers)	
Approx. Total Investment	$48,865 to $139,500
SIC 7331-01 | NAICS 561431	Number of Businesses/Units 350

Rules of Thumb
➢ 30 to 35 percent of annual sales plus inventory

Resources

Websites
- www.goinpostal.com

G - Rules of Thumb

Golf Carts—Sales & Service (See also Golf Courses, Golf Shops)

| SIC 5571-02 | NAICS 441228 | Number of Businesses/Units 1,500 |

Rules of Thumb
> 25 to 30 percent of annual sales plus inventory

Golf Courses

SIC Private: 7997-06—Public: 7992-01

| | NAICS 713910 | Number of Businesses/Units 12,014 |

Rules of Thumb
> Rule of Thumb (Private): 2.5 to 5 times SDE plus inventory

> Rule of Thumb (Public): Net income multipliers—8 to 11, typically 9 to 10

> 4 times golf-related income (green fees, golf carts, driving range—does not include pro shop or food & beverage)

Pricing Tips

- "Prices for U.S. golf courses climbed 57 percent in 2013, according to Steven Ekovich, vice president for investments at Marcus & Millchap's National Golf and Resort Properties Group. Among operational, regulation-length golf courses with at least 18 holes valued at $250,000 to $75 million, the average sale price was $4.25 million last year. While that's still below the 2006 average of $7.33 million, it's up from the market low of $2.7 million reached in 2012.
"The average golf course sales price has risen to $4.25 million from a low of $2.7 million in 2012. 57% rise in prices for U.S. golf courses in 2013; $4.25 million average price of a U.S. golf course in 2013; 144 net course closings last year (2013)"
Source: "Golf Courses See Green Again,"Nadja Brandt and Michael Buteau, *BloombergBusinessweek*, April 17, 2014

- "Fourth, I finally realized that golf is part of the hospitality industry and that I'm a terrible host. I'm not a people person. I don't schmooze well. Our green fees were $17 weekdays, $22 weekends; and when an elderly man demanded his 'senior discount,' I snapped that I was practically giving away the golf as it was, and I'd be damned if I'd let the AARP crowd bankrupt me."

- "Real estate value big determinant in price of a golf course"

- "Personal property + equipment (FF&E) usually accounts for 3 to 10 percent of the purchase price depending on the amount of equipment leased and type of operation (daily fee vs. private). From 4 to 7 percent of price is typical."

- "Profit estimated—40 percent."

- "Due to weather-related conditions, a 5-year average for cash flow should be used— capital reserves of 5 percent should always be accounted for."

- "Add to price for additional assets such as development land. Also check rounds of golf, P&L and type of facilities."

- "Be careful to look at non-golf income for 'normal' distribution."

Benchmark Data

Statistics (Golf Courses & Country Clubs)
Number of Establishments	12,014
Average Profit Margin	2.1%
Revenue per Employee	$75,600
Average Number of Employees	27.4
Average Wages per Employee	$28,967

Products and Services Segmentation
Memberships	42.0%
Golf course green use	22.0%
Food and beverages	21.0%
Other sales and services	9.0%
Equipment rentals and sales	6.0%

Industry Costs
Profit	2.1%
Wages	38.4%
Purchases	19.3%
Depreciation	9.8%
Marketing	1.5%
Rent & Utilities	6.6%
Other	22.3%

Source: IBISWorld, August 2015

Expenses as a percentage of annual sales
Cost of goods	20%
Payroll/labor Costs	45%
Occupancy	15%
Profit (estimated pretax)	20%

Industry Trend

- "A separate Sports and Fitness Industry Association report, citing a Physical Activity Council study, said golf participate rate dropped 2.5% last year to 24.7 million players on a golf course, and has seen an average annual decline of 2.8% the past five years."

  Source: "If you want a bargain on golf equipment, now's the time to buy" by Andria Cheng, http://blogs.marketwatch.com/behindthestorefront/2014/05/20/dicks-sporting-goods-troubles-mirror-golf-industrys-challenges/ 5/20/14

- "Once the go-to activity for corporate bonding, the sport is suffering from an exodus of players, a lack of interest among millennials and the mass closure of courses. The tangled personal life of Tiger Woods, who for years was golf's biggest ambassador, also hasn't helped. All that has taken a toll on the companies that make and sell golf equipment, including Dick's Sporting Goods Inc. and Callaway Golf Co.
  "About 400,000 players left the sport last year, according to the National Golf Foundation. While almost 260,000 women took up golf, some 650,000 men quit. A severe winter on the East Coast worsened the situation this year by delaying the start of golfing season for many. Slow sales of clubs and other gear dragged down results for Dick's this week, sending its stock on the worst tumble since the retail chain went public in 2002.

G - Rules of Thumb

"There also are fewer places to play golf these days. Only 14 new courses were built in the U.S. last year, while almost 160 shut down, the National Golf Foundation said. Last year marked the eighth straight year that more courses closed than opened."

Source: "Golf Market Stuck in Bunker as Thousands Leave the Sport" http://www.bloomberg.com/news/articles/2014-05-23/golf-market-stuck-in-bunker-as-thousands-leave-the-sport

- "Average net profit margins for privately owned golf courses and country clubs (NAICS 713910) have been negative for several years. Over the last 12 months, for example, golf courses and country clubs lost about 2 cents for every dollar of revenue generated by memberships, club shop sales and restaurant meals. That's about the same as in 2013 and only slightly better than the -4% margin, on average, for 2012. Sales, meanwhile, increased in 2012 for the first time in five years and grew about 4%, but then reversed course in 2013 and were basically flat over the last 12 months, according to Sageworks' data."

Source: "Think Playing Golf Is Tough? Try Operating A Course" by Mary Ellen Biery, http://www.forbes.com/sites/sageworks/2014/06/29/golf-courses-operating-with-weak-sales-negative-profit-margins/

- "More than a third of facilities (37 percent) report working with increased budgets in 2013, according to the data, while a third (34 percent) reported working with fewer financial resources than in 2012. Nearly another third (29 percent) reported their budgets remained stable. For those courses with flush budgets, 33 percent reported the increase ranged from 1 percent to 10 percent, and only 1 percent experienced a jump of more than 20 percent. On the opposite end, the majority (24 percent) of those who had to make do with fewer resources saw those cuts range from between 1 percent and 10 percent. Only 2 percent reported a drastic slide of 20 percent of more."

Source: "State of the Industry," www.golfcourseindustry.com, January 16, 2014

- "For the most part, superintendents were in line with their three-year outlooks. According to the data, the percent of golf course facilities that remained in the black rose consistently during the last three years, from 62 percent in 2011 to 68 percent in 2012 and 70 percent in 2013. Likewise, courses that turned a profit increased during that time period, from 32 percent in 2011 to 38 percent in 2012 and nearly half (42 percent) in 2013.

"So what are the biggest roadblocks to economic bliss? According to superintendents, the top three factors impacting the future health of their facilities include lack of marketing, slow play, and round discounting by competitors.

"It's been a long tough road out of the mire that was The Great Recession. Five years later the majority of golf courses indicate they're still are up to normal staffing levels, and nearly half say their overall and capital budget, as well as revenues, have yet to return to pre-recession levels.

"While the overall 2013 State of the Industry data would point that the industry is on the road to recovery, only a slim number of courses indicated they'd recovered fully (11 percent) and were actually ahead of pre-recession business levels (10 percent)."

Source: "State of the Industry" www.golfcourseindustry.com 1/16/14

- "Course operators in the transition zone from the Carolinas to Arizona are learning that spray painting acre after acre of their dormant Bermuda grass, instead of overseeding, keeps golfers happy and, perhaps more critically, money in the bank. In the Southeast, where water is relatively abundant and cheap, facilities are saving tens of thousands of dollars. But out west where the opposite is true, some courses are hanging on to hundreds of thousands they used to spend.

"'Agronomically and financially, it's a no-brainer,' says Shaun Emerson, director of agronomy at Desert Mountain Golf Club in Scottsdale, Arizona. 'Of course, there's a cost to paint but nothing like there is with overseeding, which we figure in the Southwest runs somewhere between $300,000 and $400,000. When you paint, you save on water, labor, seed costs, fertilizer, wear and tear on equipment, and then your transition [back to active Bermuda grass] is so much better.'"

Source: "A Bit Easier Being Green" by Trent Bouts, www.golfbusiness.com May 2013

Seller Financing
- 5 to 7 years

Questions
- Questions to ask seller: "Is there adjoining acreage that could be used for golf community homes? This can greatly increase value of the golf course."

Resources

Websites
- Golf Course Industry: www.golfcourseindustry.com

Trade Publications
- Golf Courses and Country Clubs: A Guide to Appraisal, Market Analysis, Development, and Financing by Arthur E. Gimmy, MAI, and Martin E. Benson, MAI, published by The Appraisal Institute: www.appraisalinstitute.org

Associations
- National Golf Course Owners Association: www.ngcoa.org

Golf Driving Ranges & Family Fun Centers		
SIC 7999-31	NAICS 713990	Number of Businesses/Units 54,151

Rules of Thumb
➢ Golf Driving Ranges—70% to 75% of annual sales including inventory

Benchmark Data

Statistics (Golf Driving Ranges & Family Fun Centers)

Number of Establishments	54,151
Average Profit Margin	4.1%
Revenue per Employee	$74,200
Average Number of Employees	2.6
Average Wages per Employee	$19,422

Products and Services Segmentation

Other	31.6%
Amusement and recreation services	30.5%
Coin operated games and rides	14.0%
Amateur sports teams and club services	6.7%
Meals and beverages	5.5%
Fitness and recreational sport center services	5.1%
Registration for sports tournaments and matches	3.8%
Golf course and country club services and memberships	2.8%

G - Rules of Thumb

Industry Costs

Profit	4.1%
Wages	26.2%
Purchases	27.5%
Depreciation	1.3%
Marketing	1.0%
Rent & Utilities	16.0%
Other	23.9%

Source: IBISWorld, May 2015

Golf Shops (See also Golf Courses)		
	NAICS 451110	

Rules of Thumb
- 30 percent of annual sales plus inventory

Benchmark Data
- "The specialty golf channel is now dominated by the national chains. 76% of all square footage and 34% of the door counts are owned by multi-door retailers with store footprints over 10,000 square feet.
- "Key findings from research done by the Longitudes Group in 2014:
    - ✓ 47% of the gear sold last year in the U.S. golf market flowed through the off-course channel, including $2.28 in apparel/soft goods and $2.98 in hard goods.
    - ✓ Total square footage of off-course retail increased by 1.9% to 8.6M square feet, while the number of total off-course stores decreased by 8.6% to 869 stores."

Source: "2015 Off-course retail report shows a mixed bag of growth & contraction" by Longitudes group, 2/19/15

Industry Trend
- "What's done is done. What's in the past should stay in the past, and what's most important now is to take the recent gains and focus on the future. That's the prevailing attitude circulating through much of the golf industry, one that's persevered through thick and thin these past few years. Five years post the Great Recession, it appears many turf maintenance programs have begun to shed their budgetary shackles and focus again on growing turf and the game of golf."

Source: Golf Course Industry's "State of the Industry, 1/16/14

Questions
- "Is the seller willing to allow the buyer a 10% rejection on the inventory (or some other fixed amount)?"

Resources

Websites
- National Golf Foundation: www.ngf.org
- Professional Golfers Career College: www.progolfed.com

Rules of Thumb - G

Goodyear Tire Stores (See also Tire Stores)

NAICS 441320

Rules of Thumb
- ➢ 35 percent of annual sales plus inventory

Gourmet Shops (See also Food Stores—Specialty)

| SIC 5499-20 | NAICS 445299 | Number of Businesses/Units 3,000 |

Rules of Thumb
- ➢ 20 percent of annual sales plus inventory

Benchmark Data
- For Benchmark Data see Food Stores—Specialty

Grease Monkey (See also Auto Lube/Tune-up, Other Lube Franchises) — Franchise

| Approx. Total Investment | $190,000 to $300,000 |
| NAICS 811191 | Number of Businesses/Units 250 |

Rules of Thumb
- ➢ 50 percent of annual sales plus inventory

Resources

Websites
- www.greasemonkeyshine.com

Great Clips (See also Barber Shops, Fantastic Sam's, Franchises) — Franchise

| Approx. Total Investment | $109,150 to $208,300 |
| NAICS 812112 | Number of Businesses/Units 3,600 |

Rules of Thumb
- ➢ 1 to 1.5 times SDE plus inventory

Benchmark Data
- "According to Goggins, (Vice-President of Development for Great Clips) the company's earnings claim shows franchisees spend $150,000 on average to open a salon, ringing up $306,000 annually. That nets them a tidy $54,000."

Resources

Websites
- www.greatclipsfranchise.com

G - Rules of Thumb

Great Harvest Bread Company (See also Franchises)	Franchise
Approx. Total Investment	$328,986 to $482,766
NAICS 311811	Number of Businesses/Units 200

Rules of Thumb
> 3.2 to 3.4 times SDE plus inventory

Resources

Websites
- www.greatharvest.com

Great Steak (See also Franchises)		Franchise
Approx. Total Investment		$153,050 to $456,000
Estimated Annual Sales/Unit		$425,000
SIC 5812-19	NAICS 722513	Number of Businesses/Units 100

Rules of Thumb
> 50 to 55 percent of annual sales plus inventory

Resources

Websites
- www.kahalamgmt.com

Green Businesses (See also Sustainable Businesses)	
NAICS 541620	

Pricing Tips
- "My expertise is in what I call an 'industry horizontal.' Environmentally sustainable businesses can exist in virtually any industry. I've sold a furniture company, a toy manufacturer, a retail store, a recycled product manufacturer, a body care product company, etc. The multiples and Rules of Thumb for those are the same as the industries they are a part of, the difference being that their environmental sustainability makes them value at the higher end of the range than average."

Industry Trend
- "Continued growth especially in sectors such as renewable energy and organic food products. Organic body care products and natural and organic clothing are up and coming in this space as well."

Rules of Thumb - **G**

Ground Transportation Companies (Motorcoach/Limousine)
(See also Bus Companies, Limousine Services)

	NAICS 484110	

Rules of Thumb
- 50% of Annual Gross Sales plus inventory
- 2 to 3 times SDE plus inventory
- 3 times EBITDA plus vehicle value for small to midsize operations; 4 times EBITDA plus—for over 15 vehicles

Pricing Tips
- "You must look at ODCF before you use a multiple. It is important to know if the vehicles are owned, leased or financed. Depreciation will not be a total add-back because you must factor in the life of the vehicle so that only a portion of depreciation is added back. You must reduce Fair Market Value by outstanding debt."
- "Maintenance records?Facility?"
- "Who controls the groups? The quality of the drivers and how long have they been with the company? Are the groups preformed or do they sell into them? Condition of equipment counts."

Expert Comments
"It is a business with low barriers to entry. Now that the economy is improving, this is a discretionary expenditure that has started to increase."

Benchmark Data

Statistics (Airport Shuttle Operators)
Number of Establishments	4,022
Average Profit Margin	7.7%
Revenue per Employee	$61,900
Average Number of Employees	2.6%
Average Wages per Employee	24,944

Products and services segmentation
Local shuttle services for business	53.5%
Local shuttle services for leisure	41.6%
Long-distance shuttle services	3.2%
Other	1.7%

Industry Costs
Profit	7.7%
Wages	40.1%
Purchases	29.1%
Depreciation	4.5%
Marketing	1.1%
Rent & Utilities	4.6%
Other	12.9%

Source: IBISWorld, March 2015

G - Rules of Thumb

- "Driver earnings vary by city. For example, in New York City, median UberX drivers make between $26 and $30 per hour. In Chicago, that average is closer to $16 per hour. UberBlack drivers earn more per hour—except in New York, where UberX is slightly ahead.

  "Overall, median hourly earnings for Uber drivers tend to be higher than hourly wages for other taxi and chauffeur jobs, and are sometimes 50–100% higher. However, Uber contractors are not reimbursed for driving expenses like gasoline, depreciation, or insurance, while employed drivers often are."

  Source: Source: "The Numbers Behind Uber's Exploding Driver Force" by Brian Solomon, http://www.forbes.com/sites/briansolomon/2015/05/01/the-numbers-behind-ubers-exploding-driver-force/ 5/01/15

- "A net profit of 20% would be considered good even though there is a great deal of wear and tear on the vehicle. In addition to having rides to and from airports, executive trips, wedding trips, prom trips, engagement trips, sporting engagement trips, etc. This business is very attractive for barter and is used extensively in barter organizations."

Expenses as a percentage of annual sales

Cost of goods	30% to 40%
Payroll/labor Costs	30%
Occupancy	10%
Profit (estimated pretax)	20%

Industry Trend

- "Uber's active driver base has grown from basically zero in mid-2012 to over 160,000 at the end of 2014. The number of new drivers has more than doubled every six months for the last two years. Most of that exponential growth has come from the cheaper UberX service, which in most areas lets drivers use their own cars to pick up riders. UberBlack, the commercial-licensed black car service, has seen steady but not exponential growth.

  "On average, Uber drivers are younger, more educated, more white, and (slightly) more female than the rest of U.S. taxi workers. 49.2% of Uber drivers are under 40 years old, vs. 28.4% of taxi drivers. Yet nearly 37% have college degrees, and 10.8% have postgraduate degrees too (vs. 14.9% and 3.9% of taxi drivers, respectively).

  "More than 40% of Uber drivers self-identify as White non-Hispanic, vs. 26.2% for taxi drivers. Women make up nearly 14% of Uber drivers, more than the 8% of female taxi drivers, but much less than their 47.4% portion of the rest of the U.S. workforce. Women also work fewer hours, on average, than male drivers."

  Source: "The Numbers Behind Uber's Exploding Driver Force" by Brian Solomon, http://www.forbes.com/sites/briansolomon/2015/05/01/the-numbers-behind-ubers-exploding-driver-force/ 5/01/15

Seller Financing

- "Based on the price of the vehicle and the down payment, the term should be 5 to 7 years."

Questions

- "What has been your biggest frustration?"

Resources

Trade Publications

- Limousine, Charter, and Tour: www.lctmag.com

Rules of Thumb - **G**

Grout Doctor (See also Franchises)	Franchise
Approx. Total Investment	14,405 to $37,415
NAICS 811411	Number of Businesses/Units 73

Rules of Thumb
➢ 85 to 90 percent of annual sales plus inventory

Resources

Websites
- www.groutdoctor.com

Guard Services (See also Security Services/Systems)	
SIC 7381-02 NAICS 561612	Number of Businesses/Units 35,000

Rules of Thumb
➢ 30 percent of annual sales plus inventory
➢ 3 times SDE includes inventory
➢ 3 times EBITDA

Pricing Tips
- "Non-union are worth more"
- "If guards are 1099's, business is worth less."

Expert Comments
"As crime increases, so does security."

"It is easy to lose a client if you have to go to bid every year."

Benchmark Data
- For additional Benchmark Data see Security Services/Systems
- "Cost is different for an armed guard, for an event security, or 24-hour security service."

Expenses as a percentage of annual sales
Cost of goods	05%
Payroll/labor Costs	70%
Occupancy	05% to 10%
Profit (estimated pretax)	15% to 20%

Industry Trend
- "'Formal training of the nation's one million-plus private security officers is widely neglected, a surprising finding when contrasted with other private occupations such as paramedics, childcare workers, and even cosmetologists,' said Mahesh Nalla, lead investigator and MSU professor of criminal justice.

G - Rules of Thumb

"The research also states that security guards say they're unprepared to handle problematic people and physical altercations and to protect themselves. It strongly endorses the need for systematic and standardized training in the $7 billion-a-year industry.

"'It's reasonable to conclude that private security continues to be an under-regulated industry despite the increase in the roles private security guards play in people's lives and the fact that they greatly outnumber sworn police officers in America,' Nalla said."

Source: "Security guard industry lacks standards and training," www.gsnmagazine.com, 6/9/14

Questions

"Most guard companies have major clients; explain anything over 20%, could become an earnout event."

"Relationship to customers?"

Gun Shops and Supplies

SIC 5941-29	NAICS 451110	Number of Businesses/Units 6,490

Rules of Thumb

➤ 30 to 35 percent of annual sales plus inventory

Benchmark Data

Statistics (Gun & Ammunition Stores)
- Number of Establishments 6,490
- Average Profit Margin 15.4%
- Revenue per Employee $123,800
- Average Number of Employees 4.0
- Average Wages per Employee $25,819

Products and Services Segmentation
- Ammunition 25.0%
- Pistols 24.0%
- Rifles 22.0%
- Equipment and accessories 15.0%
- Shotguns 8.0%
- Revolvers 6.0%

Industry Costs
- Profit 15.4%
- Wages 21.2%
- Purchases 38.9%
- Depreciation 3.7%
- Marketing 1.2%
- Rent & Utilities 5.1%
- Other 14.5%

Source: IBISWorld, January 2015

- "While NSSF (National Shooting Sports Foundation) sells copies of the entire report, here are the highlights:

- ✓ 84 percent of retailers surveyed reported that overall sales in 2012 exceeded sales from the previous year.
- ✓ 76.9 percent of retailers surveyed said sales of AR-style modern sporting rifles in 2012 exceeded sales from the previous year (60.1 percent), the largest increase in the firearms category.
- ✓ Retailers surveyed said that 25.8 percent of their customers were first-time firearm buyers in 2012 compared to 25 percent in 2011 and 20.8 percent in 2010.
- ✓ For the third year in a row, the number of female customers increased. For the year 2012, 78.6 of retailers surveyed said more women came to their stores, compared to 72.8 in in 2011 and 61.1 in 2010.
- ✓ Firearms most often purchased by women were a semiautomatic handgun followed by revolvers, modern sporting rifles, shotguns, traditional rifles and muzzleloaders."

Source: "National gun dealer survey shows unique buying trends for ARs, women," by Lee Williams, *Herald-Tribune*, May 17, 2013

Average Annual Firearm Production (U.S.)

Weapon	Production
Rifle	1,425,500
Shotgun	777,125
Revolver	352,625
Pistol	889,125
Total Average Yearly Production	3,444,375

Firearm Sales Statistics

Guns and ammunition manufacturing annual revenue	$11,000,000,000
Number of weapons and ammunition manufacturers in the U.S.	465
Number of retail gun dealers	50,812
Number of background checks for gun purchases in 2013	17,000,000
Percent of U.S. households that own a gun	32%
Annual number of Americans who used a firearm for protection	645,000
Percent who felt laws limiting gun ownership infringe on the public's right to bear arms	49%

Source: www.statisticbrain.com, research date 1/1/2014

Industry Trend

- "In spite of the fact that gun ownership is becoming increasingly restrictive due to government legislation in both the United States and Canada, opening and operating a retail business that buys, sells, and trades guns still has the potential to be profitable. In addition to gun sales you can also sell ammunition and hunting-related products as well as offer a gun repair service. Promote the business by establishing alliances with gun clubs and shooting ranges as well as firearm instructors, as these clubs and individuals can refer your business to others. Starting this type of business will require a substantial investment and you will also have to clear a few legal hurdles before you can open. A well-promoted and operated gun shop could return the owner a six-figure yearly income."

Source: "Gun Shop—Business At A Glance" www.entrepreneur.com

- "Months after the shooting that killed 26 at a Connecticut elementary school, General Electric (GE, Fortune 500) has halted its lending programs for purchases from gun shops, the company said Wednesday. GE Capital,

H - Rules of Thumb

which provides consumer financing services, had previously provided lending services to gun shops to help consumers finance firearm purchases. Earlier this year, the company sent letters to shops notifying them that the program would be terminated for future purchases. It will not affect financing for guns bought at major retailers like Wal-Mart (WMT, Fortune 500) and Dick's Sporting Goods (DKS, Fortune 500), which sell guns along with a range of other items."

Source: "GE Capital halts lending for gun shop purchases" by Melanie Hicken, www.money.cnn.com April 24, 2013

Resources

Associations
- National Shooting Sports Foundation: www.nssf.org

Hardware Stores

SIC 5251-04	NAICS 444130	Number of Businesses/Units 20,492

Rules of Thumb
➢ 45 to 50 percent of annual sales plus inventory
➢ 3 to 3.5 times SDE plus inventory
➢ 3.5 times SDE includes inventory

Pricing Tips
- "As with all companies, there is not just one set of multipliers that can be used to estimate their values. The hardware store multipliers found in the marketplace are affected by the size of the company and its level of profitability. The above multipliers represent an average of all sizes of hardware stores at all levels of profitability. However, the multipliers at different levels of revenues assuming that the company has an average level of profitability are: 1) The average store with revenues between $500,000 and $1,000,000 and an SDE of approximately 15% of revenues, will have revenue multipliers of .51, cash flow multipliers of 3.8 including inventory, or 1.5 times cash flow + inventory. 2) The average hardware stores with revenues between $1 million and $2 million and an SDE of approximately 14% of revenues will have revenue multipliers of .43, cash flow multipliers of 3.2 including inventory, or 1.6 times cash flow + inventory. 3) The average store with revenues between $2 million and $4 million and an SDE of approximately 9% of revenues will have revenue multipliers of .34, cash flow multipliers of 3.6 including inventory, or 1.6 times cash flow + inventory. Stores that have higher levels of profitability than the average SDE margins noted above will have higher revenue multipliers and stores with lower levels of profitability will have lower revenue multipliers."
- "The above multipliers apply to average hardware stores with less than $600k in revenues that have an SDE profit margin (SDE/Sales) of 12%–20%. If the SDE margin is less than 12% the Revenue Multiple will be .46 and the Cash Flow Multiple will be 4.6. If the SDE profit margin is greater than 20% the Revenue Multiple will be .55 and the Cash Flow Multiple will be 3.0. The average store with revenues between $600k and $1,200k generally earns a Revenue Multiplier of .51 and a Cash Flow Multiplier of 4.3. However, the SDE profit margin must be between 11% and 16%. If it is below 11% the

revenue multipliers are .48 and the Cash Flow multipliers are 4.7. If the SDE profit margin is more than 16%, the Revenue multipliers are .54 and the Cash Flow Multipliers are 3.7. Stores with revenues from $1,200k to $2,000k earn Revenue Multipliers of .35 and Cash Flow Multipliers of 3.0 for SDE profit margins in the 9%–15% range. For stores with SDE profit margins less than 9%, the Revenue Multipliers will be .28 and the Cash Flow Multiplier will be 3.6. If the SDE Profit margins are greater than 15% the Revenue Multiplier will be .40 and the Cash Flow Multiplier will be 2.9. All the above multipliers include inventory."

- "1.9 times SDE plus inventory. Inventory, however, should be between 25% and 30% of Total Revenues. If inventory is more than 30%, the seller will not get full price on the surplus inventory."
- "Smaller stores with revenues less than $600,000 and SDE less than $100,000 are generally not worth much more than the value of their inventory."

Expert Comments

"Lowe's, Home Depot, and the recession continue to chip away at the market for the independent. The number of independent hardware stores has declined 10% since before the start of the recession. However, the attrition has leveled out in 2011 and 2012 and there has even been slight growth in the total number of stores. Even still, hardware stores are still in demand. Profitable stores with positive growth in the last few years will sell fairly quickly. Replication is difficult due to the high capital intensity of the business. Markets are very saturated."

"Stores with revenues below $600k are very difficult to sell. Profits provide low incomes to the owner. Stores should be franchised to gain any advantage in this market."

"Even though most stores have seen revenue declines, the demand for profitable stores is still strong."

"Stores in good locations will still bring premium prices. Rural locations are often insulated from the effects of big boxes."

"Franchised hardware stores continue to be in demand even though sales have declined. Buyers seem willing to forgive a slight downturn in sales this year, just because most stores are experiencing declines."

"Reasonably profitable hardware stores sell very quickly."

"Heavy industry consolidation by the big boxes means that small operators must be aligned with a major franchisor. Local dealer advertising groups are also a must. Plenty of help on the store floor, convenient parking, knowledgeable staff, and quick service are far more important to today's hardware shoppers than price. Therefore, small neighborhood stores that possess those characteristics will survive the big boxes quite well."

Benchmark Data

Statistics (Hardware Stores)

Number of Establishments	20,492
Average Profit Margin	2.8%
Revenue per Employee	$178,700
Average Number of Employees	6.9
Average Wages per Employee	$23,275

H - Rules of Thumb

Products and Services Segmentation

Hardware, tools, plumbing and electrical supplies	57.7%
Lumber and other building materials	16.3%
Lawn, garden and farm supplies	9.2%
Other	9.1%
Paint and sundries	7.7%

Major Market Segmentation

Do-it-yourself consumers	69.5%
Contractors	19.0%
Do-it-for-me consumers	11.5%

Industry Costs

Profit	2.8%
Wages	13.6%
Purchases	60.6%
Depreciation	1.1%
Marketing	1.7%
Rent & Utilities	4.0%
Other	16.2%

Market Share

True Value Company	22.0%
Ace Hardware Corp.	20.9%
Do It Best Corp.	18.1%

Source: IBISWorld, July 2015

- "Stores with less than $100 in revenues per square foot of retail space are typically underperforming. A quality store will generate $150 per square foot and super stores over $200 per square foot."
- "For stores in the $1 million to $1.5 million range, payroll on the average should be about 12% of Gross Revenues. However, payroll for stores in the rural areas can be in the 10%–11% range, and in the big cities payroll may be in the 13%–18% range."
- "Inventory around 2.0–2.5; Sales are $100–$150/ Sq. Ft. Best run stores with revenues in the $1 million to $1.5 million range can turn inventory at 3.0 times and sales at $200/ Sq Ft. Stores in rural areas have labor costs ranging 12–13% of sales and rent 4–5%; big cities pay 16–20% and rent is 7–10% of sales. The difference is in the gross profit margins. Rural stores are doing 38–41% and big city stores are doing 42–48%."
- "Should turn their inventory 2.5 to 3 times per year. Fixtures and equipment should not exceed 16 percent of the average stock carried per year. These stores are sold for fixtures and equipment at depreciated value plus the inventory at wholesale cost. Markup runs from 35 to 40 percent."

Expenses as a percentage of annual sales

Cost of goods	50% to 60%
Payroll/labor Costs	12% to 15%
Occupancy	05% to 08%
Profit (estimated pretax)	01% to 03%

Industry Trend
- "The Hardware Stores industry is picking up steam and heading toward prerecessionary highs. Over the five years to 2014, industry revenue has increased at an average annual rate of 3.2% to $22.6 billion. Low disposable income, homeownership rates and low home-improvement spending have hampered revenue growth. These drivers have picked up significantly, especially in 2012, when signs of recovery began to show. Continued recovery and increases in these drivers are expected to help industry revenue slowly grow by 0.3% in 2014."

Source: IBISWorld, May 2014

- "Very stable industry growth. The next few years should see growth at about 3% per year."
- "Computerization, renovation, innovation. Do or die."

Seller Financing
- "A good, qualified buyer should bring at least 25% down to the table. In such cases a ten year amortized note is fairly common."

Questions
- "Have you increased the markup on your merchandise in the last two years? Sellers often begin increasing prices just before they sell a business to pump up the bottom line. The increased prices makes it look like revenues are increasing from one year to the next, when in fact, it is just because merchandise is being sold at a higher price. It often takes a year or two before the customers finds out that prices were increased and decide to shop elsewhere. If you bought such a store based on the pumped up bottom line in the current year, you might find that your customer base disappears the next year."
- "How do you value your ending inventory on the books? Is there concealed inventory or understated inventory? How often do you do a physical inventory? Is your cash register point-of-sale system read barcodes? Is your inventory counts computerized? "
- "If an Ace Hardware store—are you Vision 21 compliant? Hardware wholesales (Ace, True Value, Do It Best) have operating benchmarks that they require their dealers to adhere to. These include store signage, decor, color schemes, updated computers, attendance at hardware shows, participation in advertising groups etc. These requirements are expensive. It is not uncommon that a buyer will have to pay to upgrade the store to those standards immediately after purchasing the store."
- "Is your computer database current? Are inventory counts accurate?"

Resources

Websites
- Home Channel News: www.homechannelnews.com/section/hardware-stores

Associations
- National Retail Hardware Association: www.nrha.org

H - Rules of Thumb

Harley-Davidson Motorcycle Dealerships		
(See also Motorcycle Dealerships)		
SIC 5571-06	NAICS 441228	

Rules of Thumb

- "85 to 90% of annual sales. In this case the agency netted $2,100,000 and seller retained 20 percent of ownership."
- 3.5 SDE plus net assets plus inventory
- 1 to 6 times EBITDA

Benchmark Data

- For Benchmark Data see Motorcycle Dealerships

Industry Trend

- "Harley-Davidson is America's largest heavyweight motorcycle manufacturer, holding 55% share of the market, which is expected to grow by 2%-2.5% this year. Harley already holds a massive share in the U.S. heavyweight motorcycle market (601+ cc), and despite the entry of new players in the country such as the resurgent Indian motorcycles, Harley has managed to grow its share each year since 2009.
  "The U.S. heavyweight motorcycle market is expected to cross 310,000 unit sales this year, up 2.1% year-over-year. However, industry volumes are still much lower than the 543,000 unit sales in 2006, which could mean that there is room for growth, especially as the unemployment rate slides and disposable incomes grow. Following a negative 2.1% contraction in the U.S. GDP in Q1, the country's GDP returned to positive growth in the second and third quarters, increasing by 4.6% and 3.5% respectively. Also, the unemployment rate has dropped to a six-year low of 5.8% in the U.S. Given Harley's iconic brand image and loyal customer following, the company's volume sales are expected to rise with an increase in the heavyweight motorcycle market size."
  Source: http://www.forbes.com/sites/greatspeculations/2014/12/19/harley-davidsons-success-story-in-the-u-s/

- "Dealers worldwide sold 57,415 new Harley-Davidson motorcycles in the first quarter of 2014 compared to 54,254 motorcycles in the year-ago quarter. In the U.S., dealers sold 35,730 new Harley-Davidson motorcycles in the quarter, up 3.0% compared to sales of 34,706 motorcycles in the year-ago period. In international markets, dealers sold 21,685 new Harley-Davidson motorcycles during the first quarter, up 10.9% compared to 19,548 motorcycles in the year-ago period, with sales up 20.5% in the Asia Pacific region, 8.2% in the EMEA region and 8.9% in the Latin America region, and down 2.4% in Canada."
  Source: www.webbikeworld.com April 22, 2104

Questions

- "Why are you selling? What are the strengths and weaknesses of your business? Are there any add-backs? What is your reputation in the marketplace? What is the upside potential?"

Resources

Websites

- www.harley-davidson.com

Rules of Thumb - **H**

Health Food Stores (See also General Nutrition Centers)

| SIC 5499-01 | NAICS 446191 | Number of Businesses/Units 83,021 |

Rules of Thumb
➢ 1 to 1.5 times SDE plus inventory
➢ 40 percent of annual sales plus inventory

Benchmark Data

Statistics (Health Stores)
Number of Establishments	83,021
Average Profit Margin	5.7%
Revenue per Employee	$111,600
Average Number of Employees	2.4
Average Wages per Employee	$26,077

Products and Services Segmentation
Vitamin and mineral supplements	26.6%
Orthopedic equipment	20.0%
First-aid products	18.9%
Sports nutrition products	12.0%
Convalescent care products	11.9%
Other	10.6%

Industry Costs
Profit	5.7%
Wages	23.3%
Purchases	58.1%
Depreciation	1.5%
Marketing	2.4%
Rent & Utilities	4.5%
Other	4.5%

Market Share
General Nutrition Centers Inc.	8.2%
Vitamin Shoppe Inc.	6.2%

Source: IBISWorld, July 2015

Industry Trend

- "'On-the-go convenience has replaced all-in-one convenience for grocery-buying consumers,' Webster (Justin Webster, Hillphoenix Design specialist) explained.'Increasingly, consumers would rather make more frequent trips to smaller stores where they can pop in and out with ease.' That's one of the drivers behind drug stores netting 54 percent of quick-trip shopping experiences, according to Chicago-based market researcher IRI. Small-format dollar stores claim 46 percent of those short shopping trips, IRI reported — compared with 25 percent of traditional grocers. The bottom line: Conventional grocery stores have lost 15 percent of their market share in the last five years to competing warehouses, dollar stores and drugstores, Phil Lempert, a Santa Monica, Calif.-based grocery and retail analyst told *USA Today*."

H - Rules of Thumb

"Aided by store-based nutritionists, shoppers will look for fresher and healthier options, even on the go, so sales of fresh juices and pre-cut produce will keep climbing. 'Ready, fresh, now is on the minds of millennials looking for instant gratification in healthy, fresh alternatives that are also convenient,' Webster explained."

Source: http://supermarketnews.com/store-design-construction/consumer-driven-trends-center-convenience-health-and-smaller-stores-2015

- "'Natural and organic food sales are the fastest-growing percentage of the grocery industry,' Springer said. 'More people are paying attention to what they eat, and special diets have found their way into supermarket aisles. It's happening everywhere. There are opportunities in towns big and small.'"

Source: "New, existing health food stores aim to meet area's fast-growing demand" Janice Podsada, www.omaha.com April 30, 2013

- "Locations in 2013: 58,377. Locations added in the five years to 2018: 5,769. Rising demand for dietary supplements, the emergence of healthcare legislation, and the aging of the American population will boost demand for the Health Stores industry during the next five years. Rapid growth in the supplement and sports nutrition segments and the recent uptick in available real estate have encouraged operators to open additional locations despite mounting competition from mass merchandisers and online retailers."

Source: IBISWorld.Com

Resources

Associations
- Specialty Food Association: www.specialtyfood.com

Hearing Aid Sales

SIC 5999-79	NAICS 446199	Number of Businesses/Units 7,217

Rules of Thumb
- ➢ 40 to 45 percent of annual revenues plus inventory
- ➢ 4 times EBITDA

Pricing Tips
- "Larger practices with multiple offices and support infrastructure sell at higher multiples. The more trained audiologists and dispensers that a practice maintains, the more stability the practice will offer to purchasers."
- "Transition agreements for long periods are common."

Expert Comments
"Market for audiology and hearing aids is expanding as baby boomers enter the market. Franchises such as Miracle Ear (1,300 franchised units) and Beltone reduce obstacles to entry and increase ease of replication."

Rules of Thumb - **H**

Benchmark Data

Statistics (Hearing Aid Clinics)
Number of Establishments	7,217
Average Profit Margin	7.1%
Revenue per Employee	$215,400
Average Number of Employees	1.8
Average Wages per Employee	$59,074

Products and Services Segmentation
Digital hearing aids	65.0%
Analog hearing aids	15.0%
Other	13.0%
Batteries and accessories	7.0%

Major Market Segmentation
Consumers older than 65	41.9%
Consumers aged 55 to 65	25.6%
Consumers aged 45 to 54	14.0%
Consumers aged 18 to 34	7.0%
Consumers aged 35 to 44	7.0%
Consumers younger than 18	4.5%

Industry Costs
Profit	7.1%
Wages	27.5%
Purchases	45.1%
Depreciation	1.2%
Marketing	2.5%
Rent & Utilities	7.5%
Other	9.1%

Market Share
Amplifon USA	6.8%

Source: IBISWorld, July 2014

- "Cost of Goods sold should not exceed 35%"
- "$300,000 per dispenser"

Expenses as a percentage of annual sales
Cost of goods	35%
Payroll/labor Costs	20%
Occupancy	05%
Profit (estimated pretax)	18%

Industry Trend
- "Following are five trends to follow in the New Year:
    1. Awesome New Products: More powerful digital processing technologies, improved integration of wireless features, constant improvements in sound processing software, and integration with mobile phones will continue to result in fantastic new products.

26th Edition

H - Rules of Thumb

2. **Consumers in the Driver's Seat:** As the new products get new markets of customers excited, the "consumerization" of the hearing business will accelerate.
3. **Hot Competition/Lower Prices/Lower Margins:** More choices mean more competition for manufacturers. As digital technologies continue to deliver higher performance at constantly lower costs, hearing product providers will have to deliver more and better products at even lower prices.
4. **Bigfoot and Big Brother:** Big Brother in the form of federal governments providing various subsidies to consumers will play an even larger role in driving demand for hearing aids.
5. **The Audiologist Squeeze–Adapt or Die:** Audiologists, hearing-aid dispensers and other hearing health professionals have been the heart and soul of the hearing products business since its inception."

Source: "2015 Hearing Industry Outlook: Only the Strong Survive" by David Copithorne 12/31/14
http://hearingmojo.com/2015-hearing-industry-outlook/

- "However, these stronger sales come with some caveats for private practice dispensing professionals for three major reasons. First, the 2014 sales increase of 3.4% in the private sector is slightly lower than the 4.2% increase in 2013. Second, Costco's hearing aid sales have grown by approximately 20% per year for the past 5 years, and are included in HIA's private sector unit sales. When taking Costco's sales out of the equation (Figures 2 and 3), HR estimates that private practice sales probably increased by around 1.5% in 2014, 2.7% in 2013, and 1.5% again in both 2011 and 2012. Third, as noted in The Hearing Review's recent dispenser survey (April 2014), average sales prices (ASP) have been flat or slightly declining for the past several years, meaning that gross revenue increases for many private practices have been relatively difficult to come by."

Source:" Hearing Aid Sales Increase by 4.8% in 2014; RICs Continue Market Domination"
http://www.hearingreview.com/2015/01/hearing-aid-sales-increase-4-8-2014-rics-continue-market-domination/

- "Looking at the entire US market, three-quarters (74.0%) of all hearing aids were BTEs, and 52.2% were of the RIC or RITE styles. Traditional BTEs constituted 21.8% of the market. ITEs made up just over one-quarter (26.0%) of all hearing aids dispensed, led by full- and half-shell ITEs (11.6% of total market), ITCs (7.8%), and CICs (6.3%)."
"The Department of Veterans Affairs (VA) accounted for 20.6% of all units—or 617,371 out of 2.99 million hearing aids—dispensed in the United States during 2013, for a growth unit rate of 7.3% over 2012. When ignoring dispensing activity at the VA, private-sector dispensing unit growth increased by 4.2% in 2013. On average, private-sector professionals dispensed a higher percentage of RIC/RITEs than VA professionals (54.3% private sector vs 44.1% VA) and lower percentages of traditional BTEs (20.6% vs 26.2%) and ITEs (25.1% vs 29.6%)."

Source:"Hearing Aid Sales Rise by 4.8% in 2013; Industry Closing in on 3-Million Unit Mark,"
www.hearingreview.com, 1/21/14

- "The market, driven by technological advancements in cochlear implants, bone-anchored hearing-aids and the introduction of wireless Bluetooth capability from Starkey, GN Resound and Cochlear America, is expected to touch almost $8 billion in annual sales by 2018."

Source: headsets.tmcnet.com

- "More than 28 million Americans have some degree of hearing loss, a number that could reach 78 million by 2030."

Source: Hearing Industries Association (HIA)

Seller Financing
- 3 years

Questions
- "Is this business free from liens/encumbrances with vendors that would prohibit the sale of the practice?"
- "Are any loyalty agreements or right of first refusals in place?"

Resources

Websites
- audiologypracticeforsale.com

Trade Publications
- Audiology Online: www.audiologyonline.com

Associations
- Hearing Industries Association (HIA): www.hearing.org

Heating Oil Dealers
NAICS 454310

Rules of Thumb
- 25 percent of annual sales plus inventory
- 2.5 times SDE plus inventory
- 3 to 3.5 times EBIT
- 3 to 4 times EBITDA.

Pricing Tips
- "Gross profit per gallon is the main value driver....the higher the better."
- "Most of these businesses are bought on a retained gallonage basis, typically around 1 X gross profits plus assets. Location, customer mix, automatic vs. will call delivery are important issues. Impacted by weather."
- "There is slow turnover in this industry, as most dealers are 2nd or 3rd generation in the business."
- "Industry buyers used to price on the basis of gallons delivered, especially automatic gallons. They now price at 4 to 5.5 times EBITDA, based upon number of automatic vs. 'will call' customers, margins per gallon, location, competition from discounters, condition of equipment, etc."
- "Low margin, high risk business since there is credit risk involved."
- "Most industry buyers want to acquire on the basis of 'retained gallons,' where the buyer offers a limited amount of cash up front and pays only for customer gallons that actually get delivered over a period of time. This puts the risk on the Seller and often requires the Seller to remain in the business for some period. It also, however, allows the Seller to get top dollar for his business due to the 'no risk' nature of the deal to the Buyer. Industry buyer will also pay cash up front, but only for customers who are on some type of automatic delivery

H - Rules of Thumb

(automatic, service, and budget customers). These customers are less price sensitive and will typically stay through any transition in ownership."

- "It depends on the amount of hard assets. Gross profits generally drive the value of these businesses. The higher the gross profit, the higher the value. Gross profit per gallon is a key ratio. Some things that detract from value are high real estate values (land & bldgs.), and other outdated petroleum bulk plants, & petroleum equipment. Any environmental problems are a concern."

Expert Comments

"Customers switching to other fuels due to high price of product; environmental concerns; industry image old."

"Customer satisfaction/loyalty is inversely proportional to price of fuel oil."

"Mature industry with significant environmental regulations. Price spikes similar to summer of 2008 hurt the industry. Growth generally comes through acquisitions. More consolidation for the future."

"Competition is relatively high due to: 1. Discounters, 2. Overcapacity of oil to be delivered, trucks, personnel in a mild winter and every summer; 3. The consolidation in the industry."

"Replication is easy at an entry level if the entrant is near a distribution point and sells on a 'cash on delivery' basis. Otherwise, it takes years to develop a strong customer base on automatic delivery."

Benchmark Data

- "Gross profit per gallon"
- "As heating oil prices rise, savings from switching to gas heat grow—PSE&G's average customer would pay $1,122 for the year beginning last October, the company announced when it set its yearly rate last May. It would take 757 gallons of oil to produce the same amount of heat as gas."
- "Gross profit per gallon is a key benchmark. The higher the better."
- "Less desirable companies (discounters) are very difficult to sell."
- "Should exceed $.60/gallon in most markets and higher in metro areas."
- "EBITDA is the most common benchmark. Another would be number of automatic gallons x margin per gallon x a multiple of 1 to 1.5 but in the end, industry buyers will look at EBITDA."
- "Gross profit per gallon is a good benchmark. Should be in the $.50 to $.70 gallon range in rural markets, and higher in the metro areas."
- "Most successful full-service companies in Connecticut and Massachusetts target margins of 45 to 55 cents per gallon but 'discounters' will work on margins as low as 25 to 30 cents by keeping their overhead low, not delivering too far from a terminal, and not offering oil burner service, credit, automatic delivery, budget plans, etc."

Expenses as a percentage of annual sales

Cost of goods	60% to 70%
Payroll/labor Costs	10% to 15%
Occupancy	02% to 05%
Profit (estimated pretax)	05% to 10%

Industry Trend
- "Slow decline as customers switch to other fuels."
- "Heating oil usage will decline based on increasing price, conversion to natural gas, and growth of alternative energy sources. The industry is consolidating, and many small businesses (<1,000 customers) are having a difficult time competing."
- "The industry is in the midst of consolidation, as larger companies employ economies of scale and best practices, placing great pressure on the 'mom and pop' companies started in the 50s and 60s."

Seller Financing
- "Typically Outside financing; most of these companies are sold on a retained gallonage basis."
- We typically get cash at closing for fixed assets, and finance the intangibles over 2 to 5 years."
- "2 or 3 years"
- "5 to 7 years"

Questions
- "Are there any environmental concerns; compliance with government regulations."
- "5 years' financials and gallonage history; customer base breakdown by class of customer and type of delivery (automatic or will call); asset listing; phase I & II environmental reports."
- "How many gallons do you deliver? What are your average margins per gallon? How many gallons delivered are to automatic customers, service customers, budget plan customers, and 'will call' customers."

Resources

Websites
- American Petroleum Institute (API): www.api.org

Trade Publications
- Oil & Energy Magazine: www.nefi.com/oilandenergy.php

Associations
- PetroleumMarketers Association of America (PMAA): www.pmaa.org
- PA Petroleum Association: www.ppmcsa.org
- Empire State Energy Association: http://www.eseany.org/index.php

Heavy Equipment Sales & Service		
	NAICS 811310	

Rules of Thumb
➢ 50 percent of SDE plus fixtures, equipment and inventory

H - Rules of Thumb

Hobby Shops (See also Toy Stores)

SIC 5945-08	NAICS 451120	Number of Businesses/Units 24,092

Rules of Thumb
- The Hobby and Toy category in IBISWorld also includes: Craft Supplies, Hobby Goods, Traditional & Electric Games, and Magic Supplies (See Benchmarks for percentages of each). The percentage of annual sales and the multiple of SDE would be about the same as listed below plus inventory.
- 20 percent of annual sales plus inventory
- 1.5 times SDE plus inventory

Pricing Tips
- "Don't buy too much inventory. In the hobby business, October through January are the busiest sales months while many find February, March, August and September are slower. When approaching a heavy selling season, you need to increase inventory. When it ends, you need to move whatever seasonal or outdated inventory that did not sell out the door as quickly as you can."

Source: www.nrhsa.org

Benchmark Data

Statistics (Hobby & Toy Stores)
Number of Establishments	24,092
Average Profit Margin	5.9%
Revenue per Employee	$134,900
Average Number of Employees	5.1
Average Wages per Employee	$15,033

Products and Services Segmentation
Traditional toys and games	33.0%
Electronic and video games	31.8%
Hobby and craft supplies	30.7%
Other products and services	4.5%

Industry Costs
Profit	5.9%
Wages	11.3%
Purchases	69.8%
Depreciation	3.1%
Marketing	2.1%
Rent & Utilities	3.7%
Other	4.1%

Market Share
Toys "R" Us Inc.	35.3%
GameStop Corporation	23.8%
Michaels Stores Inc.	21.3%
Jo-Ann Stores Inc.	6.9%

Source: IBISWorld, April 2014

- "The gross profit margin for the average hobby shop is around 35 percent, before expenses and taxes. Net profit margins are usually less than 10 percent."

Source: National Retail Hobby Stores Association

Rules of Thumb - **H**

Industry Trend

- "Continuing a trend from the past five years, independent hobby and toy stores will find it increasingly challenging to compete with mass merchandisers and department stores, which offer lower prices and convenience. Over the next five years, changing consumer preferences will create tough market conditions for industry operators, as children begin to demand more adult-focused products, like electronics and media players. Still, greater demand from baby boomers and increasing disposable incomes will benefit the industry."

   Source: IBISWorld, April 2014

- "It's been tough going for independent hobby shops, which, much like independent bookstores, have been squeezed out by national chains. Toys R Us, Michaels Arts & Crafts and Jo-Ann crafts store together occupy about 83 percent of the $17 billion industry, according to research firm IBISWorld. The recession triggered a dramatic slowdown in toys and hobby spending, and more than 2,600 stores closed between 2007 and 2012.

   "'They're vanishing,' said Fred Hill, president of the Hobby Manufacturing Association. 'The market itself is shrinking.' Big-box stores like Walmart and Target pose a threat to the small shops because they sell hobby items cheaper and have a wider customer base, according to experts at IBISWorld.

   "'Hobby shops are not like a convenience store or liquor store or drugstore,' said Hill, who manufactures model trains and owns two hobby stores in Southern California. 'We have very limited appeal.'

   "But independent hobby stores say they offer what no Walmart or Target can—a place for hobbyists to go not just to buy a model rocket or plane, but also learn the best way to fix it when it breaks and upgrade it with a new paint job. Hobby stores also organize radio-controlled car races, hobby classes and competitive robotics teams. 'You get that nurturing support,' Pozzi said. 'That's what a hobby store is about.'"

   Source: "San Jose hobby shop makes a comeback" by Heather Somerville, www.mercurynews.com/business March 8, 2013

Resources

Trade Publications

- Model Retailer magazine : www.modelretailer.com

Associations

- Craft & Hobby Association: www.craftandhobby.org/eweb/
- National Retail Hobby Stores Association: www.nrhsa.org

Home-Based Businesses

Rules of Thumb

> The best way to price a home-based business is to first find out if the business is dependent on the owner. If so, it may be impossible to price as it may have little or no value. However, if the business is transferable it may have value. Prepare an SDE figure and then create a multiple (see Introduction for more information on SDE and a corresponding multiple) to arrive at an approximate price. If the business corresponds to a business listed in this Guide, see if the information there helps.

26th Edition

H - Rules of Thumb

Industry Trend
- "After 37 years of following small and home business launches, the National Mail Order Association (NMOA) predicts a new explosion in people starting a business because of layoffs and fears of salary reductions. 53 percent of small (businesses with one or more owners but no paid employees) businesses in the U.S. are 'home- based' businesses."

Home Centers (See also Hardware Stores, Lumberyards)

NAICS 444110	Number of Businesses/Units 12,241

Rules of Thumb
- 40 to 45% percent of annual sales includes inventory
- 2 times SDE plus inventory

Pricing Tips
- "Sales indicate that smaller sales bring higher multiple than stores with sales over $1 million. Price is plus inventory."
- "Home centers are a hybrid hardware/lumberyard. Typically they will do 50% lumber and 50% hardware. They focus primarily on the do-it-yourself customers, although they will also deal with the pro contractors. Home centers will usually have little higher prices in lumber than a pro lumberyard. However, they are usually in nicer locations and well-defined commercial areas. Lumberyards need much more yard space and therefore are often located in areas where acreage is cheap, i.e., in the more undeveloped areas. Home centers will usually have retail store space in the 10,000 to 20,000 sq. ft. range with a modest sized outdoor lumber area."

Expert Comments
"The high capital costs for inventory and fixtures and the lack of good locations are significant barriers to entry."

Benchmark Data

Statistics (Home Improvement Stores)
Number of Establishments	12,241
Average Profit Margin	9.8%
Revenue per Employee	$222,200
Average Number of Employees	62.0
Average Wages per Employee	$26,040

Products and Services Segmentation
Lumber and other building and structural materials	29%
Tools, equipment, paint and flooring	20%
Lawn, garden and farm equipment supplies	14%
Household appliances, kitchen goods and housewares	12%
Plumbing fixtures and supplies	10%
Electrical supplies	9%
Hardware	3%
Other	3%

Rules of Thumb - H

Major Market Segmentation

Professionals	38.5%
Do-it-yourself	37.5%
Do-it-for-me	24.0%

Industry Costs

Profit	9.8%
Wages	11.7%
Purchases	69.5%
Depreciation	1.2%
Marketing	3.0%
Rent & Utilities	2.4%
Other	2.4%

Market Share

Home Depot Inc.	46.7%
Lowe's Companies Inc.	33.8%
Menard Inc.	5.0%

Source: IBISWorld, November 2014

- "Sales per square foot of retail space should be greater than $250. Margins should be greater than 33%; payroll should be less than 17%–18% to be profitable. Must have well-defined marketing programs in place. Should have advertising greater than 2% of sales, preferably 3% or more."
- "A good home center may do $300–$400/sq. ft. per year in sales."

Expenses as a percentage of annual sales

Cost of goods	65% to 70%
Payroll/labor Costs	12% to 15%
Occupancy	05% to 06%
Profit (estimated pretax)	10% to 15%

Industry Trend

- "Home centers have been less impacted than lumberyards during the last two years. The primary reason is that profits come mostly from the hardware side of the business, which has been 'hit' less hard than lumber sales."

Questions

- "Why are you selling? Are there any potential franchise or refurbishment costs that may be included in the sale?"
- "Does any one contractor represent more than 10% of your lumber business? This is a personality business. If the old owner goes, the customer might leave too."

H - Rules of Thumb

Home Health Care—Care-Giving

(See also Home Health Care—Equipment & Supplies)

NAICS 621610	Number of Businesses/Units 331,203

Rules of Thumb

- ➢ 50 percent of annual sales plus inventory
- ➢ 2 to 4 times SDE plus inventory
- ➢ 4 to 6 times EBIT
- ➢ 3 to 5 times EBITDA

Pricing Tips

- "Health Care and related service businesses such as home health care, doctor's offices, PT clinics, personal transportation, etc. can vary slightly. Each is considered on a case by case basis due to the complexities and variables of each owner and their business. I do not use hard and fast numbers on health related businesses without meeting with an owner first."
- "Must be aware of reimbursement"
- "A good business should have at least a 20-point margin. If not, the business may be a lot more valuable to a seasoned acquirer than the numbers show."
- "Multiples can be higher for high-cash-flow companies due to high interest from acquirers."
- "Price the same as service industry in general."
- "Need to watch for employee and customer related litigation."

Expert Comments

"Nature of this industry breeds competition, but lack of necessary operational and marketing skills means that only a few gain the critical mass necessary. Successful companies need to be good at personal marketing and dealing with employees."

"It is easy to start a home health company but difficult to get past the critical point of $1 million–$2 million in sales. Businesses past that point see a lot less competition than the smaller ones."

"Service business with low asset base, competition is increasing due to ease of entry."

"The above ratings are for mid-market companies. For smaller companies, barriers to entry are minimal, and profit and growth trends are not as favorable."

Benchmark Data

Statistics (Home Care Providers)

Number of Establishments	320,480
Average Profit Margin	7.3%
Revenue per Employee	$52,800
Average Number of Employees	4.3
Average Wages per Employee	$26,927

Rules of Thumb - H

Products and Services Segmentation

Traditional home healthcare and home nursing care	57.3%
Home hospice	22.6%
Homemaker and personal services	6.1%
Other	4.9%
Home therapy services	9.1%

Major Market Segmentation

Medicare	50%
Medicaid	30%
Out-of-pocket	10%
Private insurance	8%
Other	2%

Industry Costs

Profit	7.3%
Wages	51.0%
Purchases	7.5%
Depreciation	1.1%
Marketing	1.3%
Rent & Utilities	3.9%
Other	27.9%

Source: IBISWorld, February 2014

Statistics (In-Home Senior Care Franchises)

Number of Establishments	10,723
Average Profit Margin	13.5%
Revenue per Employee	$61.200
Average Number of Employees	19.5
Average Wages per Employee	$26,318

Products and Services Segmentation

Homemaker and personal services	6.1%
Home hospice	22.6%
Other services	4.9%
Home nursing care	66.4%

Major Market Segmentation

Medicare	21.9%
Private Insurance	13.0%
Out-of-pocket	40.2%
Medicaid	17.8%
Other sources	4.7%
Other government (e.g. Veterans Affairs, Indian Affairs, etc.)	2.4%

Industry Costs

Profit	13.5%
Wages	43.0%
Purchases	8.5%
Depreciation	3.1%
Marketing	4.5%
Rent & Utilities	3.2%
Other	24.2%

H - Rules of Thumb

Market Share
Home Instead Inc.	7.0%
Interim HealthCare Inc.	5.7%

Source: IBISWorld, September 2014

- "In 2013 the average revenue for Home Care Assistance locations open at least 36 months was $2,022,405! Every day, 4,000 people turn 85. Of those, 70% will need daily care of an average of 3 years. In 2013, the median Home Care Assistance location grew by $290,000. Top performing sites grew by over $750,000. The market for home care will double in the next 5 years."

Source: From an ad for Home Care Assistance, June 2014

- "And since its enactment, Medicare has been far and away the largest single source of revenue in home health care services, accounting for 37 percent of the total. The rest is accounted for by way of private insurance and out-of-pocket costs, which made up 22 percent, 19 percent from Medicaid and 20 percent paid for by money from local governments."

Source: Senior Care Industry Analysis 2014—Cost & Trends, www.franchisehelp.com

- "The average hourly rate for a certified home health aid is $32.37."
- "Profit margin should be 20% or more."
- "People intensive. Payroll can be about 60% of revenues, which also means that acquirer should be a good people manager."

Expenses as a percentage of annual sales
Cost of goods	05%
Payroll/labor Costs	50% to 55%
Occupancy	05%
Profit (estimated pretax)	20% to 27%

Industry Trend

- "Senior care, home care, senior delivery services, anything that makes seniors' lives easier and their families' lives more manageable, will be in great demand going forward. The less government control, the better the profit margin."
- "Thanks to the aging of the baby boomer generation born in the late 1940s and 1950s, the American population is getting older. Between 2010 and 2050, the senior population will swell dramatically. As the boomer population reaches age 65, the senior population is projected to reach 88.5 million—well over twice the number of seniors in 2000 and twenty percent of the total population of the United States. 8,000 people will turn 65 every day in 2011. This increasing elderly population has and will necessitate more senior healthcare. In fact, in the late 2000s, there were more than 17,000 providers of home healthcare to 7.6 million people, servicing anything from temporarily illness, to disabilities, to terminal illness.

"Although it is currently far more common for a family member to take care of a senior, rather than a nursing home or home health care, as the population ages dramatically it will be far more difficult and the burden will be more onerous on younger family members. This will lead to an increased need for both nursing homes and home health care. In 1990, there were 11 possible caregivers for every family member needing care. But by 2050 it is projected this ratio will reach four to one. In 2006, 23 percent of Americans provided care for someone over fifty, and it is predicted that nine million seniors will require long-term care in the foreseeable future. This along with the relatively high cost of nursing homes and hospitals has led to a boon in the home health care industry. "Home health care can be less stressful and more convenient for seniors, as well as more affordable. In addition, in a survey, 89 percent of seniors expressed a desire to remain in their homes as long as physically possible, which would provide more future home health care business."

Source: "Senior Care Industry Analysis 2014—Cost and Trends," www.franchisehelp.com

- "Home health care advocates point to what they see as an irony in efforts to contain medical costs. The highest cost care is hospital care: the more days a patient stays, the higher the tab. With home health, the idea is to release the patient to the home where regular care can help prevent readmissions.
"Outside the industry, though, there is less concern. The Medicare Payment Advisory Commission, in its latest report to Congress, contended that there is sufficient access to home health care with more than 12,000 agencies, that the quality of services is generally good, and that average provider profit margin are high enough.
"Margins vary widely, according to the commission, with some negative and others above 20 percent. The average in 2011 was 14.8 percent. Smaller agencies didn't fare as well as larger agencies, possibly because of economies of scale, and nonprofits didn't fare as well overall as for-profit agencies.
"That calculation doesn't factor in all provider costs, however, and net margins are actually far smaller and declining, said William Dombi, vice president for law for the National Association for Home Care and Hospice. Decreasing reimbursements will lead to some providers going out of business, he said, and less access to care for some people."

Source: "Home health care firms foresee boom, challenges," www.timesleader.com June 1, 2013

- "Home Health Care Industry Focus—In 1994, approximately one in eight Americans was age 65 and older. But by 2030, one in five Americans will be a senior citizen. From 2010 to 2030, the number of baby boomers age 65 to 84 will grow by an estimated 80 percent while the population age 85 and older will grow by 48 percent. In addition, between 1994 and 2020, the nation's population of 85 years and older is projected to double to 7 million, and then increase to between 19 and 27 million by 2050. So it's easy to see why those in the home health care industry see another boom on the horizon—one of ever-increasing demand for services."

Source: www.missouribusiness.net/iag/focus

Seller Financing
- "SBA financing is the first choice for both parties. This is more affordable for the Buyer and the least risk for the Seller."

Questions
- "Be prepared to be fully invested and do whatever it takes for your clients. What do you worry about the most and how can I grow this?"
- "Is the business a franchise, is there restricted territory, is there a fair amount of outstanding AR, are the employees 1099 or W-2, etc. All items can be addressed and resolved."
- "Who runs the operations (i.e., people) and will they be staying post acquisition?"

H - Rules of Thumb

Home Health Care—Equipment and Supplies		
(See also Home Health Care Rental)		
SIC 8082-01	NAICS 532291	Number of Businesses/Units 21,000
Rules of Thumb		
➢ 85 percent of annual sales plus inventory		
➢ 4 times EBITDA excluding rental equipment depreciation		
➢ 4 times EBIT		
➢ 4 times SDE plus inventory		

Pricing Tips
- "Know the payer source—% of Medicare. Know the product mix—# of respiratory patients. Know the referral concentration—# of referring physicians. Know the monthly new-patient setups."
- "Payer mix rental vs. sales"
- "Depends on type of contracts (Medicare-Medicaid, private pay, nursing home, etc.) and length of contracts."
- "The age of the equipment may make it subject to obsolescence. A careful inventory of equipment located in patient homes must be made and evaluated by an expert."
- "Multiples of EBITDA range from 3 to 5. Much of the pricing depends on product mix, e.g., respiratory, DME, infusion, sleep apnea, etc."
- "Competition is high because the market is huge and growing. Risk is low because established businesses have patient referral sources. Profits are slightly down due to more third-party 'paperwork' requirements. Marketability is high, since many large companies are growing by acquisition. Industry is growing due to an aging population."

Expert Comments
"Substantial pressure on margins due to Medicare implementing cost controls and national competitive bidding."

Benchmark Data
- See additional Benchmark Data under Home Health Care (care-giving and nursing)
- "20% + EBITDA margins. Need to show annual growth in sales and profits. Stable referral sources."

Expenses as a percentage of annual sales
Cost of goods	35%
Payroll/labor Costs	20%
Occupancy	05%
Profit (estimated pretax)	35%

Industry Trend
- "Medicare sees significant cost savings when it preserves spending on home medical equipment, according to a new study unveiled at The VGM Group's

Rules of Thumb - **H**

Heartland Conference this week.The study, conducted by Brian Leitten of Leitten Consulting, found, for example, that for every $1 that Medicare pays for mobility equipment, it saves $16.78 in treatment for avoided falls. 'The message is clear: HME does save Medicare money and helps beneficiaries live where they want to be—at home,' said John Gallagher, vice president of government relations for VGM, in a press release.

"Other examples from the study: For every $1 Medicare spends on supplemental oxygen therapy, it saves $9.62 in treatment for COPD-caused medical complications; and for every $1 Medicare spends on CPAP therapy, it saves $6.73 for the treatment of OSA-related complications."

Source: "Medicare saves with HME, study says," www.hmenews.com, 6/12/14

- "Continued consolidation due to competitive bidding."
- "Declining profits because of Medicare pricing pressures"

Questions
- "Any outstanding Medicare audits? Are they accredited?"

Resources

Websites
- www.hmenews.com

Home Health Care Rental

(See also Home Health Care—Equipment and Supplies)

SIC 5999-20	NAICS 532291	Number of Businesses/Units 7,739

Rules of Thumb
➢ 4 times EBITDA

Pricing Tips
- "Payor mix (Medicare, Medicaid, commercial, etc.). How many 'capped' patients?"

Expert Comments

"Industry demand is growing but margins continue to decline as CMS (Center for Medicare & Medicaid Services) reduces reimbursement to providers."

Benchmark Data

Statistics (Home Medical Equipment Rentals)

Number of Establishments	7,739
Average Profit Margin	9.0%
Revenue per Employee	$134,700
Average Number of Employees	4.8
Average Wages per Employee	$39,270

26th Edition

H - Rules of Thumb

Products and Services Segmentation
Oxygen and respiratory therapy equipment	70.0%
Mobility aid equipment	20.0%
Diabetic therapy equipment	5.0%
Other medical equipment	5.0%

Major Market Segmentation
Medicare insured individuals	50.0%
Other insured individuals	26.2%
State and local governments	16.8%
Out-of-pocket individuals	7.0%

Industry Costs
Profit	9.0%
Wages	28.8%
Purchases	9.3%
Depreciation	42.0%
Marketing	1.2%
Rent & Utilities	5.0%
Other	4.7%

Market Share
Lincare Holdings Inc.	22.2%

Source: IBISWorld, February 2015

- "Historically, high O2 (oxygen concentrators), high Medicare businesses were preferred, but this has changed with reimbursement reductions and added legislation from CMS."

Expenses as a percentage of annual sales
Cost of goods	10%
Payroll/labor Costs	20%
Occupancy	04%
Profit (estimated pretax)	18%

Industry Trend
- "Continued pricing pressures and uncertainty of Medicare reimbursement rates. Implementation of competitive bidding will further erode profit margins."

	Franchise
Home Helpers (See also Franchises, Home Health Care—Care-Giving)	
Approx. Total Investment	$47,150 to $86,400
NAICS 621610	Number of Businesses/Units 658

Rules of Thumb
➢ 40 to 45 percent of annual sales plus inventory

Resources

Websites
- www.homehelpers.cc

ADVERTISEMENTS

26th Edition

ADVERTISEMENTS

Selling Middle Market Businesses

"This is a must for anyone who wants to learn about the larger business transaction."

Selling Middle Market Businesses: Guidebook for Intermediaries, by Russ Robb, **captures the entire process of selling middle market businesses from the intermediary's point of view.**

What does this book include?
- Over 400 pages of forms, tips, techniques and wisdom
- Examples of the proposal letter, confidentiality agreement, fee agreement, term sheet, letter of intent, and much more.
- Chapters on:
    - ✓ Targeting The Buyer
    - ✓ Preparing The Selling Memorandum
    - ✓ Sellers Dilemmas & Mistakes
    - ✓ Valuation Techniques
    - ✓ Value Drivers
    - ✓ Negotiating
    - ✓ Putting the Deal Together
    - ✓ Case Studies
    - ✓ Glossary, Sample Forms & Agreements

Learn more or order online at
businessbrokeragepress.com/shop/books/

Selling Middle Market Businesses: Guidebook for Intermediaries $160

businessbrokeragepress.com . 800.239.5085

Business Reference Guide **2016**

ADVERTISEMENTS

Pratt's Stats
is your source for private company comparables.

Pratt's Stats is the profession's leading source for private company merger and acquisition transaction data. Rely on Pratt's Stats' industry-standard market comparables to price your next assignment or benchmark performance.

Become a member of the Contributor Network

- **Complimentary access** – For each deal you contribute you'll get 3 free months of access to Pratt's Stats. Search 24,200+ transactions and utlize the Pratt's Stats Analyzer to complete your analysis

- **Complimentary subscription to Pratt's Stats Private Deal Update** – A quarterly publication that analyzes private company acquisitions by private buyers from the Pratt's Stats database

- **Listing in BVR's referral database** – As a contributor your name will be added to our referral database, easily searchable by broker location, industry specialty, or name

Join the Contributor Network at:
bvresources.com/contribute
or contact Zac Cartwright at
(971) 200-4840 or zacc@bvresources.com

26th Edition

ADVERTISEMENTS

accurate pricing.
thorough reports.
supplemental income.

ValuTrax™ utilizes a variety of traditional business brokerage valuation methods, including market methods, buyer's test method and multiple of discretionary earnings method, to offer business transaction professionals an accurate and easy to use small business valuation model.

Simply follow a 13-step process to quickly determine an indication of value of a business in a "typical" asset sale.

How does it earn you money?

ValuTrax™ generates professional pricing reports that could be sold for more than twice the cost of an annual subscription.

ValuTrax™ Annual Subscription.. $299*

Potential Income from the sale of
just one professional pricing report
generated by ValuTrax™... $500 to $1000

*15-day Money Back Guarantee: If you are not completely satisfied with ValuTraxTM, just cancel your subscription within the first 15 days and you will receive a full refund of your annual subscription fee.

Learn more
To find out more about ValuTrax, visit us online at
valutrax.net

WWW.VALUTRAX.NET

businessbrokeragepress.com   .   800.239.5085

Business Reference Guide **2016**

ADVERTISEMENTS

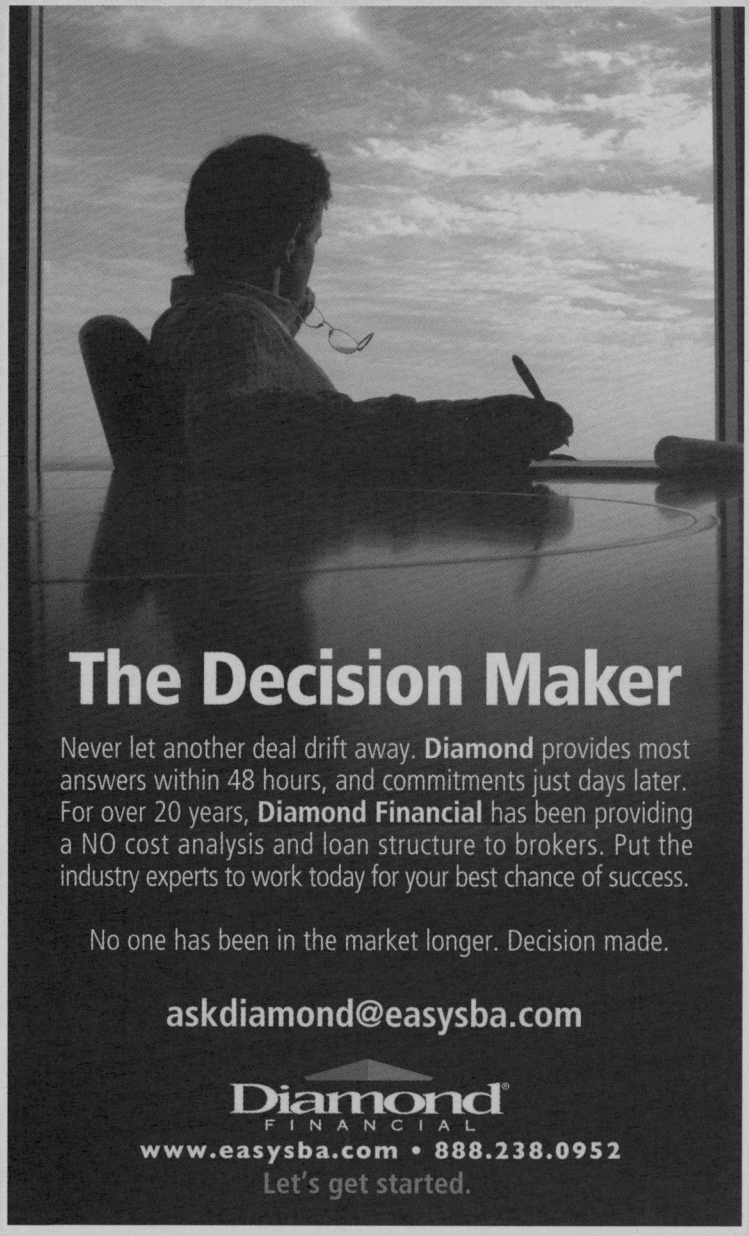

26th Edition

ADVERTISEMENTS

PeerComps was created to provide business intermediaries with a cost effective tool which allows them to provide an accurate business valuation for each and every listing, using the most reliable information available on comparable transactions for small businesses.

OUR BUSINESS VALUATION TOOL uses transaction data for our comps database to help our subscribers obtain an accurate and reliable business valuation in 15 minutes or less. Our database and valuation tool focus on "main street businesses with annual revenues between $250,000 and $5 million."

RELIABLE DATA must come from reliable and unbiased sources. Our transaction data has been gathered from national, regional and local SBA lenders across the United States. The data encompasses all major industry classifications and even includes specialized industries such as professional practices, franchises, online businesses, etc.

To learn more please contact Lori Mize at 813.391.5039 or lori@peercomps.com.

701 S. Howard Avenue, Suite 203 | Tampa, FL 33606
813.391.5039 | PeerComps.com

ADVERTISEMENTS

GCFValuation

GCFValuation has earned a reputation of reliability, sound judgment, and expertise in appraising businesses. Our firm has a full staff of in-house appraisers with the credentials that meet the IRS and SBA defined Qualified Appraiser requirements.

Business Valuation... More Than Just Numbers!

Business valuation services for:

- Business Intermediaries
- SBA Lenders
- CPA's
- Attorneys

If you are searching for an appraiser, please consider **GCFValuation** for your next engagement.

701 S. Howard Avenue, Suite 203 | Tampa, FL 33606
888.893.1803 *toll free* | **gvalue.com**

Mergers | Acquisitions | Litigation Support

26th Edition

ADVERTISEMENTS

CAPITAL BUSINESS SOLUTIONS™
Connecting Buyers and Sellers Around the World

IS IT TIME TO SELL OR EXPAND YOUR BUSINESS?

WE CAN HELP!

Business Valuations, Financing

Complete Franchise Development

Sales and Marketing

Lender Pre-Qualification

CAPITAL BUSINESS SOLUTIONS

An International Business Brokerage Alliance
www.capitalbbw.com
800-690-8993

THE RESULTS DRIVEN INDUSTRY LEADER

ADVERTISEMENTS

less of this   more of this

Meet with clients more. Join Murphy Business.

We Do It For You...

Have you ever wondered how much more successful you could be if you had the support where others handled the posting of your listings, provided you with the industry research and pricing guidelines and did your marketing and lead generation follow up for you?

We do that for you...we provide all the back office support you'll need to allow you to do what you do best - meet with clients and broker deals.

As a business broker, you already know how costly and time consuming it is for you to do all of that work, and how it takes time away from meeting with sellers and buyers. That's why we're offering a special program for existing business brokers to join our company and benefit from all our support, ongoing training and services.

Expand your business and join North America's premier business brokerage firm, Murphy Business & Financial Corporation LLC.

If you'd like to learn more, we'd welcome the opportunity to discuss Murphy Business with you in greater detail.

**Call Sandee Devine today at 888-561-3243 or
email at s.devine@murphybusiness.com**

Murphy Business & Financial Corporation LLC
513 N. Belcher Road • Clearwater, FL 33765
(888) 561-3243 • www.murphyfranchise.com
www.murphybusiness.com

26th Edition

ADVERTISEMENTS

Ready for an online makeover?

Deal Studio offers customized, ready-made websites EXCLUSIVELY for business brokers and intermediaries. These sites not only look great, but they are also:
- dynamic,
- full of content,
- built to be indexed by search engines, and
- automatically updated with current seller and buyer content every week.

**We don't just create websites–
we create online marketing hubs for business brokers.**

Deal Studio was created to give business brokers and intermediaries a full studio of marketing tools and integrated systems. These tools can be custom selected in order to meet your unique requirements when it comes to marketing, systems, and budget. Deal Studio has the skills, the track record and experience you need.

Don't just take our word for it, read what our clients are saying at
deal-studio.com/client-testimonials

Learn more at deal-studio.com

ADVERTISEMENTS

How Many Buyers Does it Take to Sell a Business?

Just one, of course. But finding the right match means having a sufficient pool of candidates on hand to begin your search. At Transworld Business Advisors, we have a large bank of business buyers ready to transact when presented with the right opportunity.

We're experts at pairing buyers and sellers of businesses of all kinds. We'll streamline the process to complete the sale quickly and smoothly. And with thousands of sales to our credit, Transworld Business Advisors has the experience to maximize the sales price every time, giving sellers the most bang for their buck.

So contact Transworld Business Advisors today and select the perfect buyer from our database of candidates tomorrow.

TRANSWORLD
Business Advisors
Business Sales • Franchises • Mergers & Acquisitions

800.205.7605 | tworld.com

26th Edition

ADVERTISEMENTS

What's A Business Really Worth?

BIZCOMPS® 2014 (PDF Version)
24th Annual Study of Recent Small Business Sales in the US & Canada, and provides you the valuable data needed to help determine the worth of a business. The study is in electronic book format with over 140 individual business ratio profiles. It can be viewed on an iPad or your computer, and any portion may be printed. The study will be sent as a PDF file on a flash drive.

For further information see our website at: www.bizcomps.com

BIZCOMPS ® is an independent, authoritative study of the multiples and terms of small business sales.

BIZCOMPS® 2014 is an annual study of over 12,553 actual businesses sold in the last ten years totaling over $4.7 billion dollars. All business sales data for the entire U.S.A. and Canada is contained in one data base accessible on-line. The study is provided as an electronic book in PDF format.

They are compared by:
- Sales price to gross sales
- Sales price to seller's discretionary earnings
- Actual down payment versus all cash
- Rent as a percent of gross sales
- The value of furniture, fixtures and equipment
- The value of inventory at time of sale
- Percent down payment
- Number of employees
- Profit as a percent of gross sales
- Number of days to sell business
- Franchise information
- General location of business

Several interesting businesses are included in this year's study, such as: heating and air conditioning contractors, manufacturers, distributors, silk screen printing, sign manufacturers, printers, taxicab fleets, accounting services, convenience stores, travel agencies, day care centers, check cashing, donut shops, coin laundries, dry cleaners, one-hour photo labs, trucking companies, janitorial services, video rental services, etc.

This study is useful to business brokers, business appraisers, attorneys, accountants, lenders, business sellers and buyers. It has increased 12% from the previous year and is an invaluable source of comparison data.

The PDF can be viewed on an iPad or your computer, and any portion may be printed.

TO ORDER: Send your check to BIZCOMPS , P.O. Box 97757, Las Vegas, NV 89193 (702) 454-0072

BIZCOMPS® 2014 please send me your Transaction Sale Study (PDF Version) @ $365.00 plus $5.00 postage.
E-MAIL address: _____

NAME: _____
BUSINESS: _____
ADDRESS: _____
CITY: _____ STATE _____ ZIP _____
PHONE: _____ COUNTRY _____

Name on card (print): _____
Card Number: _____
Exp. Date: _____ ☐ MC ☐ Visa ☐ AMEX
Signature: _____

ADVERTISEMENTS

Looking for Quality Leads?
Let BusinessBroker.net Help!

Free 30 Day Trial Offer! Sign-up today to become a MEMBER of BusinessBroker.net, a leading business-for-sale Website.

- Top "Business for Sale" Search Positions in Yahoo, Google, and Bing.
- We've been successfully serving the broker community since 1999 and pride ourselves on excellent customer service.
- Be included in over 32,000+ Business-for-Sale Listings and over 1,400 Broker Members.
- Market Yourself to Buyers and Sellers in our Broker Directory.
- Free 30-Day Trial offer. After Trial, just $39.95 per month - flat fee.

Sign Up Today

Just visit us at www.BusinessBroker.net or CALL US at
1-877-342-9786
We look forward to hearing from you!

www.BusinessBroker.net | 1-877-342-9786

26th Edition

ADVERTISEMENTS

BIZCOMPS®
Business Sale Statistics

Online Version

What's A Business Really Worth?

BIZCOMPS® 2015 (Online Version)
25th Annual Study of Recent Small Business Sales in the US & Canada, and provides you the valuable data needed to help determine the worth of a business.

BIZCOMPS® is an independent, authoritative study of the multiples and terms of small business sales.

For further information see our website at: www.bizcomps.com

BIZCOMPS® 2015 is an annual study of over 13,000 actual businesses sold totaling over $3.8 billion dollars. All transactions have occurred over the last ten years. All business sales data for the entire U.S.A. and Canada is contained in one data base. A free transaction analyzer is also available. Data is available 24/7. One year's subscription is $539.

They are compared by:
- Sales price to gross sales
- Sales price to seller's discretionary earnings
- Actual down payment versus all cash
- Rent as a percent of gross sales
- The value of furniture, fixtures and equipment
- The value of inventory at time of sale
- Percent down payment
- number of employees
- Automatic updates from the internet
- Profit as a percent of gross sales
- Number of days to sell business
- Franchise information
- General location of business

Several interesting businesses are included in this year's study, such as: heating and air conditioning contractors, manufacturers, distributors, silk screen printing, sign manufacturers, printers, taxicab fleets, accounting services, convenience stores, travel agencies, day care centers, check cashing, donut shops, coin laundries, dry cleaners, one-hour photo labs, trucking companies, janitorial services, video rental services, etc.

This study is useful to business brokers, business appraisers, attorneys, accountants, lenders, business sellers and buyers. It has increased 12% from the previous year and is an invaluable source of comparison data.

TO ORDER: Send your check to BIZCOMPS, P.O. Box 97757, Las Vegas, NV 89193 (702) 454-0072

BIZCOMPS® 2015 please send me: One year's subscription to the Bizcomps Online Data Base: $539.00. A password
(702) 974-4550 (fax) will be sent to your E-MAIL: _____

NAME: _____
BUSINESS: _____ Name on card (print): _____
ADDRESS: _____ Card Number: _____
CITY: _____ STATE _____ ZIP _____ Exp. Date: _____ ❏ MC ❏ Visa ❏ AMEX
PHONE: _____ COUNTRY _____ Signature: _____

ADVERTISEMENTS

Nationwide Valuations offers both business valuations and machinery and equipment appraisals.

Make Nationwide your one stop valuation source.

Services include but not limited to:
- Small Business Administration (SBA) Financing
- Machinery and Equipment Appraisals
- Merger & Acquisition
- Management Planning
- Buy/Sell Agreements
- Exit Planning
- Estate Tax and Gift Tax
- Personal financial/Estate Planning
- ESOP Valuations
- S Corp Election
- 5500 Valuations for Y/E ROBs reporting
- Succession Planning
- Stock Option Granting
- Charitable Contributions

888.750.5259 • info@nationwidevaluations.com
5445 DTC Parkway, Penthouse 4 • Greenwood Village, CO 80111

26th Edition

ADVERTISEMENTS

EARN COMMISSIONS SELLING FRANCHISES

Contact us to learn more today!
Call: (888) 977-IFPG ext 106
Visit: www.IFPG.org

ADVERTISEMENTS

A.F.B.B.B.E.
Alliance for a Better Business Brokering Experience

Valued representation is the meaning behind our Organization and Ethics Policy, with the focus on client needs. Our goal is not to meet client expectations but to exceed them by means of REPLETE- Responsiveness, Education, Partnership, Loyalty, Trust and Exection.

The strength of our Organization is its talented and caring members. These professionals are part of your community and committed to making a difference in the quality of lives of families- the very foundation of our counties economy and strength. It is through that entrepreneur spirit that this Country went from a vast wilderness to the most powerful economic structure in the world.

Honesty, Knowledge, Dedication and Respect are qualities you can expect from any member of the A.F.B.B.B.E. You will receive a "White Glove" service regardless of the size of the transaction. Rather you are a Mom & Pop business or a Multi-Million producer; first time buyer or large Investor, expect to have all your questions answered to your satisfaction and in a timely manner. Expect to have your communications responded to promptly.

When you work with a Broker-Member you unleash the power of Synergistic outreach to find the best possible representation through to a successful conclusion of your transaction. We are your advocates.

"Success through Partnership"
Join the movement today

844-232-2220
businessbrokeralliance.com

26th Edition

ADVERTISEMENTS

Business Reference Guide **2016**

ADVERTISEMENTS

INDUSTRYEXPERT

Some of the most useful information about buying and selling businesses comes from business brokers and from people who have extensive knowledge about specific industries.

We are constantly seeking out these Industry Experts and rely on their information to keep us up to date on the latest developments in their areas of expertise.

Our **Industry Expert** program allows you to share your expertise in such a way that benefits brokers across the nation and around the world, while also offering you valuable benefits that increase your visibility to potential clients and referral sources.

Seach for an Industry Expert or Apply to be an Industry Expert at
IndustryExpert.net

26th Edition

ADVERTISEMENTS

Want to create a consistent pipeline of prepared saleable businesses?

Want to eliminate most deal killers before they occur?

Let BTA assist you in building a pipeline of saleable businesses!

Through our proprietary owner education and consulting services we assist owners in being prepared for the eventual sale of their largest illiquid asset, their business. We provide our BTA partners a unique opportunity to attract and prepare owners by providing unique tools and resources including our BTA Transition Readiness Survey and our co-branded webinars and workshops that differentiate their practice and create a saleable pipeline.

www.BusinessTransitionAcademy.com • (844)-4MY-EXIT

Business Reference Guide **2016**

Rules of Thumb - **H**

Home Inspection

	NAICS 541350	Number of Businesses/Units 25,738

Rules of Thumb

➢ 45 percent of annual sales includes inventory

Benchmark Data

Statistics (Building Inspectors)

Number of Establishments	25,738
Average Profit Margin	17.6%
Revenue per Employee	$76,300
Average Number of Employees	1.5
Average Wages per Employee	$27,672

Products and Services Segmentation

Home inspection services	46.1%
Specific element inspection services	18.6%
Commercial building inspection services	16.6%
Other	11.3%
New home construction inspection services	7.4%

Major Market Segmentation

Home buyers and sellers	35.8%
Parties seeking repairs or maintenance	23.7%
Commercial building construction market	16.8%
The government	13.7%
New home builders	10%

Industry Costs

Profit	17.6%
Wages	36.2%
Purchases	14.8%
Depreciation	2.7%
Marketing	6.8%
Rent & Utilities	4.1%
Other	17.8%

Source: IBISWorld, October 2014

- "While it is difficult to scientifically predict your market potential, there are some general guidelines which you might find useful. As a rule of thumb, roughly 15,000 existing homes are sold annually per 1,000,000 population size, or 1.5%. Calculating the percentage of these homes, the percentage that are inspected can be as high as 95% in major cities and along the East and West coasts, and as low as 10%–25% in more rural areas. Try to obtain from local officials and real estate salespeople the figures for the population in your region and the percentage of homes there that are inspected. Then apply the following formula to estimate your current home inspection business opportunity: (Population x .015) x % of homes inspected = # of home inspections conducted per year

"For example, if (1) one million people live in your area and you determine that roughly (50%) fifty percent of the homes sold are inspected, then you

H - Rules of Thumb

can estimate that about (7,500) seven thousand five hundred inspections are conducted annually. This is a minimum figure, because it does not include inspections of newly built homes and, as the market and consumer awareness grow, the number of home inspections overall will grow as well.

"Now check your local Yellow Pages to determine the number of home inspectors working in your area, and divide the number of annual home inspections by that figure. Twenty (20) inspectors in our example above would mean that each inspector would average about three hundred seventy five (375) inspections per year. This is only a general picture, however, since multi-inspector firms account for a larger market share, while part-time inspectors will do fewer. The average home inspection fee nationally is $240, and so a home inspector in this scenario could project to earn an annual gross income of $90,200. It is quite feasible, however, for well-trained inspectors to earn well over $100,000."

Source: International Society of Home Inspectors, http://www.ishionline.org/

Resources

Associations
- National Association of Home Inspectors—a good site: www.nahi.org
- International Society of Home Inspectors—an excellent site with lots of good information: www.ishionline.org

Homeland Security

Rules of Thumb
- 100 percent of annual sales includes inventory
- 3.5 times SDE includes inventory
- "Defining a company as Homeland Security is tricky. Government contractors are typically more Homeland Security companies than traditional security companies. Since this industry is already in the hundreds of billions, and is expected to grow exponentially over the next decade, I would recommend a new category."

Pricing Tips
- "Funded contracts are worth a minimum of 1x revenue."
- "There is a tremendous difference between backlog and funded backlog. Funded backlog should receive a very high premium on that number. If customer is Federal Government, and you are supplying them with a unique technology, there is a tremendous amount of value, even after the life of the product, in parts. This will add longevity to any product pipeline."

Expert Comments

"As the government grows, the industry will grow exponentially."

"The Homeland Security industry is experiencing consolidation. Therefore competition is increasing in certain areas where companies have historically not seen any. Companies with proprietary technology, particularly

Rules of Thumb - H

technology currently being used by the government, are greatly increasing in value."

"The recent government funding for Homeland Security products has made this a growing industry for many years to come. Large Homeland Security contractors, many who are also defense contractors, are seeking small companies with patented products to be able to capture more government products."

"Location is irrelevant. It is important to have a plan for foreign sales."

Benchmark Data
- "A patented product with a history of orders can realize as much as 30x earnings."
- "Multiple of earnings for funded contracts is typically 7–8x's."
- "1 to 3 times revenue"

Expenses as a percentage of annual sales
Cost of goods	30%
Payroll/labor Costs	20%
Occupancy	10%
Profit (estimated pretax)	25%

Industry Trend
- "There is a steady demand for security products and technology for well into the future. The trend is clearly toward exponential growth."
- "Growing, but a lot going to the larger industry players."

Questions
- "Can you export this service or technology? Are you an 8a company? How do you market this product? (Most do not, and have a few key contacts)."
- "How much of his orders are funded? How much is coming from GSA schedule? Can you see an invoice? Does the government pay him promptly?"
- "What is the amount of your funded backlog? How much of your equipment is rejected each year? Do you know how many pieces of your equipment are deployed and actively used? What patent or market protection do you have?"

Resources

Trade Publications
- Government Security News: www.gsnmagazine.com

Home Nursing Agencies (See also Home Health Care—Care-Giving)

NAICS 621610

Rules of Thumb
➢ 4 times EBITDA

➢ 2–4 times Seller's Discretionary Earnings plus inventory

H - Rules of Thumb

Pricing Tips
- "Very stable pricing. Depends on contracts and customer types"
- "Multiples of EBITDA commonly used for home nursing agencies run from as low as 1 to 5 times 12 month trailing EBITDA."

Expert Comments
"This is part of the growing healthcare segment. As the population gets older, the need for in-home services grows."

Benchmark Data
- "With the aging of America, and the growing need for health care services, this is a growth industry. Low cost of entry equals a competitive environment."

Expenses as a percentage of annual sales	
Cost of goods	0
Payroll/labor Costs	50% to 60%
Occupancy	10%
Profit (estimated pretax)	15% to 20%

Seller Financing
- "10%–20% seller financed; 2 to 5 years"

Questions
- "Percentage of business under contract; percentage of business under long-term care"

Resources

Associations
- National Association for Home Care and Hospice: www.nahc.org

---

Home Team Inspection Service (See also Franchises, Home Inspection) — Franchise

Approx. Total Investment		$37,400 to $70,600
SIC 7389-96	NAICS 541350	Number of Businesses/Units 160

Rules of Thumb
➢ 35 percent of annual sales plus inventory

Benchmark Data
- For Benchmark Data see Home Inspection

Resources

Websites
- www.hometeaminspection.com

Rules of Thumb - H

Honest-1 Auto Care (See also Franchises)	Franchise
Approx. Total Investment	$153,500 to $372,500
NAICS 811111	Number of Businesses/Units 26

Rules of Thumb
> ➢ 60 to 65 percent of annual sales plus inventory

Resources

Websites
- www.honest-1.com

Hospital Laundry—Supply (See also Uniform Rental)	
NAICS 812331	

Rules of Thumb
> ➢ 50 percent of annual sales plus inventory

Pricing Tips
- An industry expert states that for laundry with hospital contracts a rule of thumb is 50 percent of gross annual sales. This is because that market is a very competitive one.

Benchmark Data
- For additional Benchmark Data see Uniform Rental
- "The size in value of the laundry market, including: healthcare, hospitality, and federal government is $10.5 billion annually, as follows:

Total Laundry Market Size and Value by Segment

Segment	Percent
Healthcare	45.9%
Hospitality	52.8%
Federal Government	1.3%
Total	100.0%

- "As indicated, the size of the federal government market is small compared to the total laundry market. The statistics related to this market are as follows: healthcare—hospitals: 4,915, 823,560 beds; healthcare—nursing homes:17,000, 1.6 million beds; hospitality—hotels: 53,500 rooms; and federal government—1,231 locations."

  Source: "Competition in the Laundry Industry," www.sourceamericalaundry.mindtouch.us/

- The Textile Rental Services Association (TRSA) estimates the following costs that hospitals spend for on-premise laundry services:
  - ✓ fringe benefits, taxes, insurance—12%
  - ✓ fuel oil, natural gas—7%
  - ✓ depreciation—2%

H - Rules of Thumb
  ✓ maintenance—2%
  ✓ water and sewer—1%
  ✓ electricity—1%
  ✓ interest on investment, administration, and support—5%

Source: www.trsa.org

Resources

Associations
- Textile Rental Services Association (TRSA): www.trsa.org

Hotels & Motels		
SIC 7011-01	NAICS 721110	Number of Businesses/Units 55,807
Rules of Thumb		
➢ 250 to 300 percent of annual sales plus inventory		
➢ 8 times SDE		
➢ 8 to 10 times EBITDA		
➢ 2.0 to 3.5 times annual room revenues—average 2.5		
➢ Outside corridors—2.0 to 2.5 times annual room revenues		
➢ Inside corridors—2.5 to 3.0 times annual room revenues		
➢ Seldom seen—3.5 times annual room revenues		
➢ $20,000 per room		
➢ 10 to 12 percent cap rate		

Pricing Tips
- "Lease arrangements, age of equipment, management in place, length of existence."
- "Most hotel buyers look at a multiple of room revenue. One of the few industries that is not based on EBITDA. On very large properties a cap rate is sometime used."
- "Smaller, limited-service property (100 rooms and less) buyers tend to value hotels based on annual room revenue (2.5–3 times) whereas larger, full-service property buyers tend to value hotels on cap rates (9-12%)."
- "Independent older properties: 1.5–2 times annual room revenue. Moderate franchise, 30–70 rooms: 2–3 times room revenue. Larger franchise properties, 70+ rooms: 4–5 times room revenue, but more often around a 10 cap rate."
- "Most independent, exterior-corridor properties will sell for 1.5–2.0 times gross sales, while franchise or flagged properties will sell for 3 times gross sales. In major metro markets with higher real estate values, these numbers will be pushed up."
- "Hotels should be priced only after taking into consideration an ample FF&E Reserve of 4 to 5 percent of revenues (in addition to Repairs and Maintenance expense). Anticipate third-party financing of 60 to 70 percent of the purchase price and debt service coverage (1.25-1.5) can be proven. Some like to

Rules of Thumb - H

analyze based on ADR and Occupancy Rates and some base on times gross revenue only. Land lease or exterior corridor properties are going at 2x gross revenue and some interior franchise units may go as high as 3.5x."
- "Usually use a rule of thumb from 2.0 to 3.0 of gross sales. In extreme cases, up to 3.5 for excellent franchised property. Age and condition of property as well as FF&E makes a difference. We use several approaches to actual valuation of a property. Adequate (approx. 5%) for reserves. RevPAR (Revenue per Available Room) seems to be the thing today, not gross sales."
- "Hotels are based on many things, since you just don't buy a hotel business. You have real estate attached 100% of the time. Revenue per available room, occupancies, average daily rates play important parts. In general, a hotel would sell according to the amount of rooms built. In general, you could take revenue per available room per year and multiply that by number of rooms then multiply that number by anywhere from 3 to 10 to get a price; of course this would depend upon what type of flag the hotel was flying. Food and beverage operations both in hotels and free standing are similar. Basically a good rule of thumb is to take the replacement cost of the FF&E plus leasehold improvements, then add this amount to 50% of revenue or 3x seller's discretionary cash or bottom line after seller add-backs."
- "Most appraisers use only the land plus building, plus FF&E for total valuation. We prefer to consider all of these, but add a value for the going business based on the gross and net income."
- "Beach properties: 3 ½ to 5 times sales. Oceanfront: 4 to 5 times gross sales."
- "Large capital investment on front end makes the property susceptible to new, better-located competition. Need ongoing reserve for replacement of FF&E."
- "Location and franchise make a great difference. Also, we must consider extended-stay motels."
- "Check contracted room business and QA score if franchised."
- "We use several approaches to establish value. One is the Performance Index Method—developing a valuation table showing (a) cap rate (b) economic value (c) value per room (d) multiple of room revenue and (e) multiple of total revenue. One can then determine economic value by using either desired cap rate (best method), per room rates, X gross or Y total revenue. We also use discounted future earnings, discretionary cash flow, book value, market value and rule of thumb. We usually provide a range of values based on profitability, income risk, desirability, business type, business trend in location, competition, industry, terms of sale, along with a few other factors."
- "Our general analysis using a high and low range utilizes several approaches to value (1) the income approach (2) excess earnings (3) discounted future earnings (4) discretionary cash (5) book value (6) market value (7) rule of thumb—then we have value comparisons and then a correlation and final opinion of value range and finally an opinion of value. We base the above on: profitability, income risk, desirability, business type, leasehold, and product exclusivity. A factor is assigned to each of the above for both high and low range."
- "Room revenue multiplier (2x to 6x), net operating income multiplier (6x to 12x). The multiplier you choose determines the capitalization rate."
- "Location—highway changes—age—obsolescence—market conditions—affiliation."

26th Edition

H - Rules of Thumb

Expert Comments

"High cost of entry."

"One must be aware of trends but be careful it is not a fad. Location is a key ingredient, items like parking, traffic lights, visibility. Highly competitive for some, so locating near target audience is crucial."

"Buy low, sell high. Market is good. Money is still cheap, multiples are still down. Try to find a property 5 years old or less selling at the right price and you will score yourself a win in the buyer markets."

"Mid-market and nice economy franchises are in demand as well as independent properties. Less need for pools and restaurants on site. Most people are busy and just need a nice clean place to lay their heads and be on their way."

"Expensive to build new. Pie isn't getting any bigger with more properties taking a piece of the pie. Property value has decreased which makes property not worth as much as say 3–5 years ago."

"Constant upgrades and increased same class competition can strangle cash flow."

"The trend is toward limited service, manageable properties under 80 rooms, as they are able to be owner operated with limited staff, and the economy does not affect the properties as readily."

"There is a large pool of buyers for hotel properties but these buyers are discretionary and will not overpay. Good locations are nice but susceptible to newer, nicer developments which can hurt business. Mid-markets with median competition are favorable."

"There is a lot of competition in the hospitality industry. Many properties turn a mediocre profit, but the appreciation in property value is usually the benefit. Buy a property, maintain it for 3–5 years, sell it for a profit."

Benchmark Data

Statistics (Hotels and Motels)

Number of Establishments	53,336
Average Profit Margin	17.7%
Revenue per Employee	$103,900
Average Number of Employees	30.2
Average Wages per Employee	$26,960

Products and Services Segmentation

Guest room rentals from hotels with 25 or more rooms	62.7%
Motels	12.6%
Food and alcohol sales from hotels with 25 or more rooms	12.5%
Conference room rentals from hotels with 25 or more rooms	4.2%
Other revenue from hotels with 25 or more rooms	4.2%
Hotels with fewer than 25 rooms and other accommodations	3.8%

Major Market Segmentation

Domestic leisure travelers	48.5%
Business travelers	24.0%
International leisure travelers	14.0%
Meeting, events and incentive travelers	13.5%

Rules of Thumb - H

Industry Costs

Profit	17.7%
Wages	26.0%
Purchases	29.9%
Depreciation	6.9%
Marketing	2.0%
Rent & Utilities	7.6%
Other	9.9%

Source: IBISWorld, August 2015

Statistics (Boutique Hotels)

Number of Establishments	2,471
Average Profit Margin	17.1%
Revenue per Employee	$91,200
Average Number of Employees	29.8
Average Wages per Employee	$32,013

Products and Services Segmentation

Lodging	69.0%
Food and beverages	17.0%
Lounges	7.5%
Spa and wellness services	6.5%

Major Market Segmentation

Business travelers	68.0%
Leisure travelers	29.3%
Other travelers	2.7%

Industry Costs

Profit	17.1%
Wages	35.1%
Purchases	31.9%
Depreciation	6.0%
Marketing	2.6%
Rent & Utilities	5.6%
Other	1.7%

Market Share

Starwood Hotels & Resorts Worldwide Inc.	18.9%
Kimpton Hotel & Restaurant Group, LLC	14.1%

Source: IBISWorld, January 2015

Penn State Index of U.S. Hotel Values (2016)

	Value Per room	Annual % Change
Overall	$132,277	8.0%
Luxury	$430,401	7.2%
Upper Upscale	$218,585	7.2%
Upscale	$158,347	7.9%
Upper Midscale	$116,974	7.1%
Midscale	$75,645	9.3%
Economy	$42,473	14.6%

Source: "Penn State Index of U.S. Hotel Values, The Pennsylvania State University

H - Rules of Thumb

- "Hotels are based on many things, since you just don't buy a hotel business. You have real estate attached 100% of the time. Revenue per available room, occupancies, average daily rates play important parts. In general, a hotel would sell according to the amount of rooms built. Usually use a rule of thumb from 2.0 to 3.0 of gross sales. In extreme cases, up to 3.5 - 4.0 for excellent franchised property. Age and condition of property as well as FF&E makes a difference. We use several approaches to actual valuation of a property. Adequate (approx 5%) for reserves. RevPAR (Revenue per Available Room) seems to be the thing today, not always room revenues."
- "Hotels are valued differently as to who the buyer is. For owner-operator they may look at 2–3 times annual gross revenues, while investors will look at cap rates, and existing hospitality groups will look at market share and price per room costs for an acquisition versus the cost of building new."

Expenses as a percentage of annual sales

Cost of goods	01% to 10%
Payroll/labor Costs	20% to 30%
Occupancy	50% to 60%
Profit (estimated pretax)	10% to 22%

Industry Trend

- "High number of rooms under construction that raises the bar for older properties to compete."
- "Lots of short sales and foreclosures brought the market values down but the properties are making a resurgence. Very few rundown franchises any more. Punch list requirements keeping properties above board. If not they convert to an independent."
- "There's an interesting disconnect going on in the hotel industry at the current time. While industry fundamentals are creeping steadily back to their heady days subsequent to the 'Great Recession,' new hotel construction is not along for the ride.
- "Meanwhile, hotel profits are skyrocketing. 'There is a lot of optimism in the industry,' Woodworth said. 'Next year should be one of the greatest years we have seen in quite some time.' Already, average revenue per available room growth is growing. 'Rate growth and occupancy levels are going to be well above their long-term averages,' he said. 'We have well above average profit increases pretty much out as far as we can see.'"

  Source: Mark Woodworth, PKF Hospitality Research, and as reported by the *Dallas Morning News*
- "Trend is toward moderate priced property and extended stay with free perks like breakfast and wi-fi."
- "Slowly getting to be a buyer's market"

Seller Financing

- "Mostly outside financing...but many times deals are made with extremely creative and sophisticated financing models."
- "Outside financing since there is a large asset in the real property included. Any owner financing is 10–20% at tops. If a seller is willing to finance more than that, be very leary."
- "Not usually seller financed currently"

Rules of Thumb - **H**

- 20 years
- 5 to 10 years
- "20 to 30 year amortization, 5-year balloon."
- "10 to 20 years—depends on age and size of property. One assumption—seller financing seldom exceeds time of original note. Last five sales have all been different with different interest rates."

Questions
- "PIP requirements? STAR reports?"
- "ADR, occupancy, RevPar, punch list, recent inspection reports"
- "Are there capital expense items that need attention? How much contracted room business do they have? How much room business do they have on the books and for how long a period of time? What was their last QA score if it is a franchise hotel? Do they know of any new highways being constructed in the future that may divert traffic to or away from the hotel? Any new competition coming up in the area?"
- "Contract on the brand franchise? Age of equipment? Age of property? And all paperwork?

Resources

Websites
- Hotel Management: www.hotelmanagement.net
- Hotel Business: www.hotelbusiness.com
- National Real Estate Investor: http://nreionline.com/property-types/hotel

Trade Publications
- Hotels and Motels: Valuations and Market Study, published by the Appraisal Institute: www.appraisalinstitute.org
- Lodging Magazine: www.lodgingmagazine.com

Associations
- American Hotel & Lodging Association : www.ahla.com

			Franchise
House Doctors (See also Franchises)			
Approx. Total Investment			$169,975 - $457,975
	NAICS 236118	Number of Businesses/Units	43

Rules of Thumb
➢ House Doctors is a handyman service specializing in minor home repairs
➢ 24 percent of annual sales plus inventory

Resources

Websites
- www.housedoctors.com

H - Rules of Thumb

Hungry Howie's Pizza & Subs — Franchise

(See also Franchises, Pizza Shops, Sandwich Shops)

Approx. Total Investment		$219,700 to $371,500
Estimated Annual Sales/Unit		$550,000
	NAICS 722513	Number of Businesses/Units 550

Rules of Thumb
- 35 percent of annual sales plus inventory

Benchmark Data
- For Benchmark Data see Pizza Shops & Sandwich Shops

Resources

Websites
- www.hungryhowies.com

Huntington Learning Center (See also Franchises) — Franchise

Approx. Total Investment		$98,300–$198,200
	NAICS 611691	Number of Businesses/Units 279

Rules of Thumb
- 60 percent of annual sales

Resources

Websites
- www.huntingtonfranchise.com

HVAC—Heating, Ventilating & Air Conditioning

	NAICS 238220	Number of Businesses/Units 107,376

Rules of Thumb
- 25 to 40 percent of annual sales plus inventory
- 2 to 3 times SDE plus inventory
- 3 to 4 times EBIT
- 2.75 to 3 times EBITDA

Pricing Tips
- "Residential service companies with good amount of annual preventative maintenance agreements command higher sell price. Heavy new construction

Rules of Thumb - H

is risky, with commercial new construction riskier than residential new construction. Mix between service and new construction should be no more than 80/20 to maintain higher sell multiples. Home Performance (Energy Audits) are on the rise in Midwest region, and help differentiate residential HVAC Companies. (Requires 2–3 year total investment of $400,000–$600,000). Home Automation is a good complimentary product/service offering for residential HVAC Companies. (Requires 2–3 year total investment of $200,000–$300,000)."

- "Higher percentage of business associated with residential 'service work' drives value. Number of active residential service (maintenance) agreements holds value. Heavy dependence on new construction depletes value. Commercial service work helps value, if ongoing activity by commercial accounts can be proven. Certain HVAC contractors are involved in energy conservation services, which are not proven popular (or sustainable) in all states at this time."
- "Mix drives value. There is an enormous range of pricing based on the mix of business. Prices for these businesses range from under 10% of revenue to over 100% of revenue. This is an enormously fragmented industry and therefore every company mix, set of controls, recurring nature, and margins will drive value."

Expert Comments

"The value of qualified HVAC companies (and trade companies in general) are on the rise, due to the lower number of people interested in becoming HVAC technicians/tradesman. The average cost of this service will rise significantly over the next 10 years, making this industry prime for consolidations, mergers and buyouts."

"Competition: highly fragmented, over 50,000 contractors. Risk: a required recurring market. Historic profit trend: as varied as there are contractors. Location: proximity to market important, but not a driving factor as services provided off-site. Marketability: tough to carry sustainability based on typical owner influence. Growth: somewhat mature, slow-growth industry. Ease of replication: these businesses are easily replicated."

Benchmark Data

Statistics (Heating and Air-Conditioning Contractors)

Number of Establishments	107,376
Average Profit Margin	3.8%
Revenue per Employee	$151,800
Average Number of Employees	5.3
Average Wages per Employee	$46,383

Products and Services Segmentation

New construction HVAC installation	59.0%
HVAC maintenance and repairs	28.0%
Existing structure HVAC installations (i.e. replacements)	7.3%
Refrigeration system installations, maintenance and repairs	5.7%

H - Rules of Thumb

Major Market Segmentation

Single-family homes	28.9%
Healthcare and institutional buildings	13.3%
Educational buildings	12.6%
Other	12.5%
Manufacturing and industrial buildings	10.5%
Office buildings	10.1%
Apartment buildings	6.1%
Retail	6.0%

Industry Costs

Profit	3.8%
Wages	31.4%
Purchases	39.9%
Depreciation	2.1%
Marketing	0.8%
Rent & Utilities	5.5%
Other	16.5%

Source: IBISWorld, July 2015

- "Sales per employee, including administrative:
    - ✓ High = $250,000
    - ✓ Medium = $225,000
    - ✓ Low = $175,000
    - ✓ Sales per Service Truck:
    - ✓ High = $350,000*
    - ✓ Medium = $300,000
    - ✓ Low = $250,000

*Accessory sales are a must for higher service sales per truck. (i.e., Surge Protectors, Compressor Savers, UV Lights, Filtration, etc.)"

"Sales per Field Technician Employee:
- ✓ Optimal = $350,000
- ✓ Average = $250,000
- ✓ Poor < $175,000
- ✓ "Field Techs to Inside Support Ratio:
- ✓ Optimal = 5/1
- ✓ Average = 3/1
- ✓ Poor = 2/1"

Expenses as a percentage of annual sales

Cost of goods	35% to 65%
Payroll/labor Costs	10% to 22%
Occupancy	02% to 03%
Profit (estimated pretax)	05% to 15%

Industry Trend

- "Consolidation will occur over next ten years, due to added cost of retaining qualified employees."
- "Wider spread between 'haves' and 'have nots.' Larger and stronger are consuming the mid-size and weaker. Home energy services are on the rise,

Rules of Thumb - H

but spotty acceptance per state. Home energy services have high barriers to entry, due to high certification and equipment costs."
- "Here's what's happening:
  - ✓ Plumbing companies moving into the HVAC business
  - ✓ HVAC companies adding plumbing to their service offerings
  - ✓ Contractors adding specialty services to their businesses. Some examples include irrigation, lawn fertilization, water softeners, bottled water, geothermal market, water-well drilling
  - ✓ Business scope changes—large, residential new-construction contractors change to primarily commercial
  - ✓ Single-family home contractors beginning to do multi-family condos
  - ✓ Service and repair contractors entering the single-family market
  - ✓ Single-family specialists moving into multi-family construction
  - ✓ Radiant work is becoming more marketable in upscale homes, particularly in the Northeast. It's used in just under 25% of homes in Canada, and the trend is moving south."

Source: "An Industry Forever Changing" by Eddie Hollub, *Contracting Business*, www.contractingbusiness.com

Seller Financing
- "Combination of both. Outside financing is accepted, as this can be recession proof business. Sellers willing to finance, if they know the customer base is solid. (good amount of preventative maintenance agreements and recurring business)"
- "Seller financing is more common, because most sellers have not properly prepared to sell, leaving themselves in a vulnerable position."

Questions
- "Ask for no less than five years of Tax Returns or Financials. Ask for proof of PMA's. Ask for employee descriptions and longevity. Ask for list of recurring customers."
- "Number of service agreements. Number of active accounts over 5–10 years. Are equipment (HVAC system) warranties held 'in house,' or are they held by manufacturer(s)? What is/are the manufacturer's policies regarding transfer of business ownership as it relates to warranties? List of key employees and why they are key? (easy for one key man to buy a truck and start installing/servicing to feed himself). Are there any employee agreements in place?"

Resources

Trade Publications
- Air Conditioning Refrigeration News: www.achrnews.com
- HVACNews.com: www.hvacnews.com

Associations
- Kentucky Association of Master Contractors: www.kyamc.com
- The Indoor Environment and Energy Efficiency Association: www.acca.org

I - Rules of Thumb

i9 Sports (See also Franchises)	Franchise
Approx. Total Investment	$44,900 to $69,900
NAICS 713990	Number of Businesses/Units 130

Rules of Thumb
➤ 65 to 70 percent of annual sales plus inventory

Resources

Websites
- www.i9sportsfranchise.com

Iceberg Drive Inn (See also Franchises)	Franchise
Approx. Total Investment	$132,500 to $556,000
NAICS 722513	Number of Businesses/Units 16

Rules of Thumb
➤ 40% to 45% of annual sales plus inventory

Resources

Websites
- www.icebergdriveinn.com

Ice Cream Trucks (See also Catering Trucks)	
NAICS 722330	

Rules of Thumb
➤ 1 times SDE plus fair market value of the truck(s) plus inventory

Pricing Tips
- "How much do you make selling ice cream? 'If it's raining outside, you can make as little as $3, but on a good day, you can earn $500. These days, though, the high gas prices are eating into my profit...'"
  Source: "Selling ice cream, bringing back memories" by Cindy Atoji Keene, *Boston Globe*, July 27, 2008
- "Today, ice cream trucks are owned by small regional companies that rent to independent drivers, or individuals who go it alone. Some, including Tanner, buy a fleet and rent to drivers such as Phillips, who take home 35 percent of their daily sales—minus the $12 daily truck rental fee and gas costs. Tanner gets the other 65 percent to cover operational and stocking costs: he supplies 64 varieties of ice cream from various suppliers to every truck. Phillips said that, so far, her best day netted more than $400 in sales. She's been working six days a week, now aiming for $500."
  Source: *Boston Globe*, August 18, 2005. Dated, but still informative.

Rules of Thumb -

Benchmark Data

- For Benchmark Data see Catering Trucks
- "... While the profits don't quite cover tuitions, Toll (Taylor) says it's a huge help in paying for books and other expenses. She says the truck (ice cream) can rake in up to $1,000 on a good day."
   Source: "Paying for College With an Ice Cream Truck" by Gabrielle Karol, June 5, 2013, www.smallbusiness.foxbusiness.com/entrepreneurs

Industry Trend

- "Good Humor's trucks will soon be hitting the road again after a decades-long hiatus, but the iconic ice cream brand's fleet will be announcing its presence with tweets instead of clanging bells. Customers looking for an ice cream fix will be able to summon the classic Good Humor trucks by tweeting @GoodHumor. And, in another modern twist, the throwback trucks will be blasting pop music and rock songs instead of ringing their iconic chime bells."
   Source: "Good Humor's iconic ice cream trucks are making a big comeback" by Tom Huddleston, Jr., http://fortune.com/2015/06/23/good-humors-ice-cream-trucks/

Resources

Associations

- International Association of Ice Cream Distributors and Vendors (IAICDV): www.iaicdv.org
- International Dairy Foods Association: www.idfa.org

Ice Cream/Yogurt Shops (See also Baskin-Robbins, Carvel, etc.)

SIC 5812-03	NAICS 722515	Number of Businesses/Units 20,000

Rules of Thumb

- ➢ 60 percent of annual sales plus inventory
- ➢ 2.2. times SDE plus inventory (franchised only)
- ➢ 3 times EBIT
- ➢ 3 times EBITDA
- ➢ 15 to 20 times weekly sales (independent only)

Pricing Tips

- "Length of lease a major factor and property ownership desirable"
- "Condition of premises, age of equipment, and location of shopping center critical to resale value."
- "2.5 x SDE applies to franchised ice cream stores with minimum 8+ year lease remaining with transfer fee included in the price. If less than 8 year lease or if seller requires buyer pay transfer fee, appropriate modifications need to be made. Non franchised ice cream businesses sell at 15-20x weekly sales assuming condition and lease (8+) years are acceptable."
- "Franchised ice cream operations have consumed the marketplace, and independent stores are virtually unsellable. Well-run franchised operations have good resale value, although seasonal in many marketplaces."
- "These stores are usually sold for a little less than one half year's gross sales.

Rules of Thumb

If it is a franchise store, such as Dairy Queen, Arctic Circle, or A&W, 15 percent can be added to the asking price. Net profit usually runs from 18 percent to 22 percent. Lease on the property should not exceed 6 percent (upper limit) of gross profit."

Expert Comments

"Location-driven business with increasing competition in the marketplace. Co-branding is an ideal situation for this concept to offset the seasonality and utilize the facility to a greater degree."

"Franchised operations protect many of the negatives, but increasing availability of premium desserts and ice cream limit expansion possibilities."

Benchmark Data

- For more Benchmark Information see Restaurants—Limited Service

Statistics (Frozen Yogurt Stores)

Number of Establishments	3,459
Average Profit Margin	6.3%
Revenue per Employee	$110,000
Average Number of Employees	5.9
Average Wages per Employee	$15,845

Products and Services Segmentation

Self-serve yogurt	69.0%
Full-service yogurt	21.0%
Other products	10.0%

Industry Costs

Profits	6.3%
Wages	14.8%
Purchases	50.7%
Depreciation	4.2%
Marketing	3.0%
Rent & Utilities	13.0%
Other	8.0%

Market Share

Menchie's	12.2%
Sweet Frog	11.5%
Yogurtland	10.9%
TCBY	9.1%
Orange Leaf Frozen Yogurt	7.7%
Red Mango	6.8%
Pinkberry	5.8%

Source: IBISWorld, April 2015

- "Product cost is lower in many franchises that manufacture product on site. However, those franchises typically have higher labor costs."
- "Limit retail operations to 1200 s/f or less."
- Estimated Annual Sales (2012-2013): Cold Stone Creamery: $330,000; Baskin Robbins: $200,000; Ben & Jerry's: $300,000

Rules of Thumb - I

Expenses as a percentage of annual sales

Cost of goods	28%
Payroll/labor Costs	22%
Occupancy	10%
Profit (estimated pretax)	05%

Industry Trend

- "It's not just frozen yogurt that's pulling away ice cream lovers—consumers are also enjoying gelato, Italian ice, custard, smoothies and other frosty concoctions."
- "Traditional ice cream sales have been slowly declining and seem poised to hit their lowest levels this year since the mid-1990s. Production of regular ice cream peaked in 2002 at about 14 quarts per person each year, according to government figures. That has fallen to 11.6 quarts per person, a 13% drop. Seven of the 10 biggest ice cream chains had fewer stores in 2012 than they had in 2011, according to research firm Technomic. Cold Stone Creamery has shuttered more than 100 stores since 2009. At Baskin-Robbins, revenue and store count have fallen every year since 2008."

    Source: "The Decline of an All-American American Treat," finance.yahoo.com, 6/21/13

- "Dramatically increasing product costs will strain profitability, increase in number of franchised concepts will cause competition unseen in the marketplace in its history."

Questions

- "Equipment servicing questions, employee history, historical sales"
- "Owner operated or absentee?Any wholesale accounts."
- "Sales by month to determine fluctuations; manager, if any, and salary, with benefits.Changes in product cost and related change in selling price of products.Sales trends, on a month-to-month basis.Must speak to company district manager, if a franchise, about his/her requirements of a new buyer."

Resources

Associations

- International Dairy Foods Association: www.idfa.org

Ice Hockey Teams (Professional)

SIC 7997-05	NAICS 711211	

Pricing Tips

- "The average NHL team is worth about $282 million, 18% more than a year ago. But over one-third if the league is operating in the red."

    Source: *Forbes* magazine (This publication has a lot of valuable information) www.forbes.com/nhl

Benchmark Data

- For Benchmark Data for professional sports teams see Baseball Teams

I - Rules of Thumb

Incentive Companies
| | NAICS 561520 | |

Rules of Thumb
- ➤ 3 to 5 times EBITDA—multiple expands as free cash flow number rises.

Pricing Tips
- "Is the future business under contract with cancellation clauses?"
- "How many programs are on the books for the next 12 months? Are they serving various industries or concentrating on one sector? Diversity is better. Three types—travel, merchandise, debit card. Points tracking & redemption, etc. = big interest in online registration and digital offerings."

Industrial Safety and Health
Rules of Thumb
- ➤ Manufacturing—5 to 7 times recasted EBIT less debt
- ➤ Distribution—4 to 6 times recasted EBIT less debt

Information and Document Management Service Industries
| | NAICS 541513 | |

Rules of Thumb
- ➤ 4 to 6 times normalized EBITDA

Information Technology Companies
| | NAICS 541512 | |

Rules of Thumb
- ➤ 100 to 150 percent of annual sales
- ➤ 2.5 to 4 times SDE
- ➤ 3 to 4 times EBIT
- ➤ 3 to 6 times EBITDA

Pricing Tips
- "Must understand vendor contracts, customer contracts, assignability, and how important employees are to the company having certain certifications."
- "The range of value varies widely by size of company and deal structure. Smaller companies (under $1 million in revenue) tend to see SDE multiples around 2.5 times SDE. Larger companies with more than $1 million EBITDA tend to see multiples of 4 times EBITDA, and are more likely to use EBITDA as the earnings metric. Companies in the middle of the foregoing range tend to be valued around 3 to 3.5 times SDE or EBITDA. Revenue is not

Rules of Thumb -

a significant factor, except that most buyers will place a ceiling at 1 times revenue. Companies with recurring revenue and predictable earnings will be valued higher, such as IT Managed Service Providers, SaaS, DaaS, and hosted services with annual contracts and recurring income. Staff, technical capabilities, and sales team strength tend to be value drivers as well."

- "IT companies with recurring revenues will sell at higher multiples and are very attractive to buyers. EBITDA ranges between $1MM and $4MM tend to receive a multiple of EBITDA of 4-7 approximately 80% of the time. These companies typically operate on very high margins. Therefore, a company with revenues of $3MM may very well have profits between $1MM and $1.5MM."
- "Depending upon software subscriptions renewals, EBIT can be as high as 10."
- "Might increase multiple if selling company has secured gov't contracts especially if in secured agency."
- "Consider any off-balance sheet value, i.e., IP, Gov't contracts, valued customer relationships, unique vendor relationships."
- "Is there an SLA (Software License Agreement) for each type/copy of software being used? Are the SLA's assignable? Has the vendor given written permission to assign them and under what conditions? Has the company been reported to the Software Consortium as a company using unlicensed software? Is the technology based on open standards and/or proprietary? Is there a complete inventory list of all software and hardware being used in the business? What 3rd parties are hosting applications and providing IT Services?"
- "Off-balance sheet items such as: customer/client lists, developed technology, R&D yet to be commercialized, patents, proprietary products, future potential to grow the business."
- "Ask questions about client relationships that will remain, about product & market development, about other competitive advantages."

Expert Comments

"The world is becoming more computer and software dependent. Companies that address hardware, software, managed services, and data center storage are all poised to be in an industry that will experience vast growth into the future. Technology can get old very quickly, so companies must stay relevant."

"Overall the industry enjoys above average characteristics, but not necessarily the home-run characteristics of previous time periods. Overall the industry is trending up, but is more favorable to companies with modern methods of business. Older companies that continue to do business the way they did 5 years ago tend to suffer and see reduce valuation."

"Location makes very little difference. Novelty and future utility are the key growth factors."

"Historical profit trends are key. Also regarding the marketability is a factor if it has intellectual property value to sell."

"If an IT services company has aligned with a leading technology provider, they frequently experience tremendous growth in business equity. I have seen the ownership of professional services companies sell their equity within just a few years and realize a return on investment multiple of 10 or higher."

I - Rules of Thumb

Benchmark Data

- "Most important in the IT area would be sales growth trends."
- "Gross margin, utilization of consultants, percent recurring revenues"

Expenses as a percentage of annual sales
Cost of goods	05%
Payroll/labor Costs	75%
Occupancy	05% to 10%
Profit (estimated pretax)	15% to 20%

Industry Trend

- "Significant growth overall for hardware, software, services, and storage."
- "Managed Service Providers, SaaS, DaaS, and other fully hosted services and cloud-based services will continue to gain momentum. Old-line technology companies (break-fix, staffing, hardware support, etc.) will decline in popularity and valuation."
- "Budgets are still growing for IT. Sales revenue should grow."
- "Steady but moderate growth. Demand for Information Technology is ever increasing. Growing demand for additional storage and retrieval of data."

Seller Financing

- "While seller financing and earnout can be common, the industry tends to be a good fit for SBA 7(a) financing. This allows buyers to pay lower valuations in exchange for sellers receiving all cash at closing. When there is upside to be achieved or downside to mitigate, then revenue-based earnouts can be more effective here than other industries because fixed and variable expenses can often be more predictable."
- 3 years

Questions

- "Describe your streams of revenue and your contract lengths. Are your key salespeople operating with a non-compete agreement? Who has the primary contacts with your top 10 customers?"
- "Do you have contracts with your client companies? How many users are under contract? Is this hardware, software, etc...? How do your technical representatives work in your company? Where are they located? Do they have individual specialties? How are they paid? Who sells to the customers? Who takes care of client concerns? What do you use to back-up data? Where do you co-locate storage and back-up? Do you own all or part of a data center?"
- "Stability of staff, will owner(s) stay on for a reasonable period"
- "Why are they selling, revenue and earnings track record, size of customer's geographic footprint, who are their technology partners, etc...?"
- "Must have references and be able to demo product(s)"

Injection Molding
NAICS 333249

Rules of Thumb

➤ 4.5 to 6 times EBITDA

Rules of Thumb - I

Inns (See also Bed & Breakfasts)

| SIC 7011-02 | NAICS 721110 | Number of Businesses/Units 14,000 |

Rules of Thumb
➢ 8 times SDE including inventory

Pricing Tips
- "The smaller the inn and lower the business income, the more the real value factor weighs heavy in the formula. The larger the inn and the higher the business income, the less weight this factor affects total value. Many of the larger inns have been selling in the 8 to 10 capitalization rate of net income, less any needed repairs, and up to a 20% discount if seller financing is not involved."
- "Inns & B&Bs (businesses as opposed to real-estate driven small properties—small is 3 rooms or less): 4.2 times gross room sales, a little higher for dinner service; 4.51 times room sales. Factors affecting price are area, size, style & owner's quarters. Dinner food service makes a property more difficult to sell. Everyone wants a B&B."
- "For motels & lodging, a commonly used rule of thumb is the GIM (Price/Gross Annual Income) which varies from 3.5 to 5.0. For these kinds of properties, a CAP rate of 10 percent is typical. More important is the cash flow for an inn to be economically feasible; the inn must have enough income to pay the expenses, debt service, and enough left over for the owners to live on."
- "On larger inns, use 8 (bank-financed) to 10 (seller-financed) cap rate on Net Operating Income (NOI) before debt & depreciation. For smaller inns, take the asset value of the underlying real estate & furnishings, add it to 3 times the net operating income and add $20K to $40K for the aesthetics & tax benefits. Work backward to see if NOI can support debt service and reduce accordingly."
- "Must have private baths now. Operating expense can range from $3K to $10K per room depending on occupancy and size of building. Income is usually $5K to $20K per guest room depending on location (occupancy & room rate) and amenities."
- "Leased [inn] properties priced at 30–60 percent of gross sales. Owned properties priced at 50 percent plus of gross sales."
- "Buyer should have a sense of good taste, common sense & hospitality ... cash flow is not great, it will mostly cover living expenses (mostly tax deductible) and there is real estate appreciation potential which you can retain tax free to the degree it is your primary residence. Future of business is excellent—has a great appeal to over-50, early-out, college-educated baby boomers; a lot of teachers. Buyer profile doesn't generalize to other typical businesses."
- "...In business w/leased property, monthly rent & terms of lease are a major factor. Food cost should be plus or minus 30 percent. Labor cost should be plus or minus 25 percent. Also, how much debt does the business have? How much do the owners pay themselves? How many hours do they work?"

Benchmark Data
- For additional Benchmark Data see Bed and Breakfasts
- "In the middle part of U.S., B&Bs are selling for $80K–$100K/guestroom on average. The popular East & West Coast locations could be up to twice that

I - Rules of Thumb

amount. The larger the inn, the less value/guestroom. Values and expenses vary greatly due to the non-standardized structure of the buildings and locale."
- "Operating expenses 40 to 50 percent"

Expenses as a percentage of annual sales

Cost of goods	15% (food, cleaning supplies & linens)
Payroll/labor Costs	10% not including owner
Occupancy	07% to 10%
Profit (estimated pretax)	10%

Industry Trend
- "B&Bs primarily cater to affluent, baby boomer and millennial travelers. That market appears to be growing. This is also the market that the next generation of innkeepers is coming from."

Seller Financing
- "On inns that are < $700K, conventional commercial financing is available. Over $700K, the seller and the SBA is usually involved. Typically it's buyer 10%, seller 25% and lender 65%."
- "Most large inns are seller financed, typically with 20 percent down and terms @ 9 percent, 30-year amortization with a 7-year balloon."
- 5 to 10 years
- Some owner financing, full owner financing—20-year amortization, 5–10-year balloons, 7 years normal

Questions
- "Ask the broker/seller how their B&B will work for you w/the buyer's down payment."

Resources

Websites
- This is a Web site offering inns for sale.: www.bb-4-sale.com

Associations
- Michigan Lake to Lake Bed and Breakfast Association: www.laketolake.com
- Professional Association of Innkeepers International: www.innkeeping.org

Insurance Agencies/Brokerages

SIC 6411-12	NAICS 524210	Number of Businesses/Units 424,246

Rules of Thumb
- ➢ 125 to 150 percent of annual sales includes inventory
- ➢ 150 to 200 percent of Commission Revenue
- ➢ 3 to 5 times SDE plus inventory
- ➢ 4 to 6 times EBIT
- ➢ 4 to 6 times EBITDA

Rules of Thumb -

> "A. Standard Multi-Lines Independent Insurance Agency
>   a) under $1 million commission, Multiple of Gross Commission Income—1.25 to .85, depending on carriers represented.
>   b) over $1 million commission and fee income, EBITDA, 3 to 9 times.
>   B. Non-Standard Auto Insurance Agency. Insurance Commission Income, excluding add-on coverage's, times last year's retention, .2 to 1.0 times commission income.
>   C. Surplus Lines Agency; .80 to 1.0 times commission."
> 100% of annual commissions; applies to multi-line agencies doing $100,000– $200,000 in gross commissions
> 1.0 to 1.5 times annual renewal commissions
> 1.5 times annual commissions (property & casualty)
> 2 times annual revenues (standard agency)
> "Agencies with more revenue ($1.5M + in commissions) are typically valued at 5–8 times EBITDA. This roughly translates into 1.5–2.0 + times commission revenues. Hard markets yield more contingent income and increased pricing on carrier premiums. EBITDA margins after recasting should come in between 15%–40% depending on size; any brokers above $2 million in commissions due to economies of scale issues."

Pricing Tips

- "There are really no Rules of Thumb. Each agency is so different; they each have their own valuations depending on many variables involved. Perhaps the average agency sells for 2x total revenues (without subtracting expenses), but 95% of agencies probably fall in the range of 1x to 3x revenues, depending on the quality of business, location and a number of other factors."
- "Although competition is high, there are significant barriers to entry. Personal expertise is essential, as is good sales ability. Gaining contracts from insurance companies (carriers) is essential, and difficult for someone starting an agency from scratch to do."
- "As of the start of 2015 the industry had experienced several years of increasing premiums, thus boosting agency revenues even if the number of accounts had not increased. However, the expectation was that the increase in commercial lines premiums was likely to reverse, and personal lines premiums were likely to be flat. If this expectation comes to pass, then industry growth in 2015 will slow substantially.

"Pricing as of the start of 2015 is above the historical norm. Typical small agencies are selling for 1.5 to 2.0 times annualized commission revenue, with particularly desirable agencies selling for even more. Pricing for smaller agencies is usually based on a multiple of commissions, partially because the profitability of the book of business in the hands of the seller is much more relevant than its current profitability in the hands of the current owner. Pricing for larger agencies is usually based on a multiple of free cash flow, approximated by EBIT, plus an adjustment for reasonable compensation for the owner. Typical multiples are 6.0 to 7.0, with some sales at 8.0 or higher. Pricing is rarely in terms of seller's discretionary earnings. It is a seller's market as of the beginning of 2015, with more interested buyers than potential sellers. Although Rules of Thumb are commonly used in the industry, the actual transaction price will depend on the specific book of business, loss ratios, and

I - Rules of Thumb

the buyer's expected account retention after the sale."
- "Pricing is 1.0 to 1.25 times annual commission for agencies under $250K in revenue. 1.5 times when revenue is $250K– $1MM. Then 2 times annual commission when revenue is over $1MM."
- "The size of an agency plays a very important part in calculating the market value of an insurance agency. Agencies with revenue of over $3M usually go for 2 to 2.5X revenue. Revenue from $1M to $3M go for 1.75 to 2X. Agencies with revenue from roughly $250K to $1M go for 1.5X. Anything less than $250K goes for closer to 1 or 1.25X revenue. Of course retention, seller's transition plans, carrier appointments, and type of business also play a part in the value of an agency."
- "Expected account retention by the buyer is critical. Loss ratios of less than 50% are a significant plus."
- "Allstate will buy back the book at 1.5x commissions. Typical selling is between 2.3 and 2.55 x commissions (excluding bonuses). New buyer must qualify with personality profile."
- "Most agencies sell for between 1 and 2 times gross commissions earned by the agency. Factors affecting price: Insurance companies represented, types of insurance sold, persistency of the block of business, and loss ratios on the blocks of different types of insurance issued."
- "Don't confuse SDE with EBITDA with adjusted EBITDA. This is one of the biggest mistakes that I see made by other brokers. Many brokers also simply market an agency at 2 x revenue regardless of the quality of the book of business and available financing. There are many factors that can influence the market value such as the carriers, lines of business, client demographics and non-commission based income. Financing and deal terms are also critical to getting an agency sold and getting the highest price. Personal lines P&C agencies can be sold at fixed prices based on the low risk of a broad customer base. Commercial lines P&C and employee benefits agencies have larger accounts and are often structured with an earnout or retention-based payment on large accounts."
- "Expected account retention by the buyer is critical. Loss ratios of less than 50% are a significant plus. Smaller agencies are often sold as a book of business that will be combined with an existing agency, after which the seller's location may be shut down. These books of business are usually sold as a multiple of commissions, with the multiple perhaps as high as 2.0. Larger agencies are usually sold as a multiple of SDE, often including an earnout component that can bring the total price to 7.0 or higher in the event of stellar future performance (hard to achieve)."
- "Key factors to consider when adjusting the value of an agency are length of time the current owner is willing to stay on board, renewal retention, size of book, and carriers represented. Buyers are willing to pay a premium for agencies where the current owner is willing to stay on for 2 or more years. Agencies with commission income over $2M will usually sell for multiples such as 2 to 3 times gross commission due to larger brokerage firms being potential buyers."
- "Non-standard auto: 1.10 times commission large agencies: 1.65 times commission"
- "Agencies with SDE of 25% or higher, after inclusion of the buyer's likely cost to hire a replacement for the departing seller, are likely to sell for higher multiples of commissions, and sometimes higher multiples of SDE as well."
- "The insurance brokerage industry is highly diverse and the valuation process can be complicated. Valuation multiples can range from <1 to 3 times commission revenue and 3.5 to 8 times EBITDA. Deal structures will also vary

Rules of Thumb - I

depending on the risk of the agency or book of business."
- "Multiples vary greatly based on type of ins. agent: Standard, Non-Standard, Surplus Lines. Agencies with commission income over $1.5 million will be higher multiple based on many operational factors and composition of client. Brokered business, non-standard auto, and agency finance are assigned lower multiples. Retention rates and industry concentration should be reviewed carefully. Insurance company relationships are critical requiring review of loss ratios with each company represented, special commission arrangements, possibility of contract cancellation. Degree of differentiation in level of service and breadth of services offered is key separator from the competition."
- "1 to 3 times annual commission for property & casualty books of business. Varies based on ratio of standard vs. non-standard business."
- "Expected retention by the buyer is critical. Loss ratios are very important. Benefits business is very hard to value because of uncertainty regarding health care reform."
- "Start with the recasting. Determine the DE and adjusted EBITDA. Identify fixed expenses and opportunities for a strategic buyer to consolidate overhead. The average agency should have a DE/revenue of > 40%. If the prospect is not at that level, need to figure out why. Look at the risk factors: revenue history, carriers represented and commission rates, lines of insurance (personal, commercial, life/health; each also has subdivisions that are relevant), average renewals, average policy size and size existence of any large policies (greater than $10k premium), carrier loss ratios (should be under 50%), employment agreements with producers (potential for employee to walk with customers), etc. Contact third-party financing options and determine the amount and rate they will finance so you can look at debt service coverage (most deals happen with an ROIC > 40% so the terms may shift against the seller if you don't pre-arrange a reasonable deal structure). Low risk agencies (e.g. stable, standard personal lines) can be sold at fixed terms for higher multiples (typically > 4.5 x adjusted EBITDA). Higher risk (e.g. commercial lines with large accounts) may be structured with an earnout and lower price. Just like any business, the value is driven by the proforma earnings, risk and terms of the sale."
- "Larger P&C agencies will sell for 6–7.5X pro-forma EBITDA to nationals. Smaller agencies will sell as books of business for 2–3X gross commissions."
- "Niche agencies often receive higher value compared to main street agency."
- "It is no longer a strong seller's market. Prices have come down, but there is no consensus by how much."
- "Insurance agencies typically sell for a multiple of the premium income (gross sales) which can vary between 2 and 4 times this number but usually is 2 times since this multiple depends on many factors, such as the type of insurance markets the agency is appointed with, the retention rate of their policies, the commission earned on renewals for the existing book and how long this agency has been operating."
- "Working capital adjustment 30 to 60 days."
- "Pricing for smaller agencies is often between 1.5 and 2.0 times annual commissions. Pricing is often between 6.0 and 7.0 times adjusted EBITDA."
- "P&C insurance agencies: 2X standard PL book, 1.75X smcomm book; 1.5X large account book; multiples may be higher or lower depending on financial benchmarks to peer groups."
- "Brokered Business—1.0 times commission. Non-Standard Auto (direct bill)—1.0 to 1.25, (agency bill/premium finance)—.5 to .8 times commission."
- "Length of time in business, reputation, possible cross-selling opportunities in the future, etc."

Rules of Thumb

- "Brand-name carriers, licensed personnel, revenue per client, revenue per employee, target accounts."
- "Pricing today is higher than it was 10 years ago. Typical pricing is 150% to 200% of annual commissions for smaller agencies, and 6 to7 times EBITDA for medium and larger agencies. Balance adjustments range between net zero to one-month's net working capital. Tax complications can be severe for a 'C' corporation, or an agency that has been a 'C' corporation any time during the prior ten years."
- "Agencies with volume above $1.5 million will sell closer to 8 times EBITDA and/or 1.5 to 2.0 times commission revenues. Direct-bill premiums have a value of 30% higher than agency-bill policies, better retention."
- "The insurance products and companies represented by the agency are an important component of value. Commissions generated from the sale of securities sell at much lower multiples. An analysis of the client mix is necessary to determine the nuances of valuation."
- "Direct-bill policies have a value of 30% greater than agency-bill policies, due to retention. Personal lines have greater value than commercial lines due to the relationship with clients and commission to the producer. Agencies with state-of-the-art Internet-based management systems and transactional filing seem to generate greater revenue per employee."
- "Contract persistency is critical to the continuation of fees. The demographics of the clientele base should be carefully analyzed. The range of valuation multiples is very wide and varies by the type of revenue stream and how it's paid. Regulation violations by the owner can severely reduce the price."
- "Renegotiations of agency contracts by companies as a condition of approving the new agent destroy value and kill deals. The time is perhaps right, though, because the industry is at the point in its cycle when they want all the business they can get on almost any terms. Companies often have a 'pocket' buyer, who is the only buyer they will agree to. Approval often means acceptance of a reduced commission rate. Traditional agencies aren't worth the time and effort."
- "One interesting exception has come to my attention, and that is brokerage-based agencies that deal extensively in employee benefits, particularly employee group health insurance. The business tends to be high volume, stable, and consistently profitable. The contractual relationships that have been set up by many of the major HMOs etc. with brokers have volume and quality factors such that two agencies, each receiving $3 in revenue, if combined, may receive $12–$15. Beyond that, various sources have identified this as a fertile field for cross-selling opportunities and other incremental revenue."

Expert Comments

"Account retention by the buyer, post-sale, is critical. Sellers should be willing with account retention. Buyers should make sure the seller's employees are not likely to leave and compete with the new owner of the agency. If they do, account retention can suffer significantly."

"FL has no national carriers writing new property coverage. FL agents have no carriers willing to insure both auto and homeowner coverage. Few standard carriers willing to insure property over $100,000 value. Most larger property coverage placed in Surplus Lines Brokerage Market."

"Smaller agencies are often sold as a book of business that will be combined with an existing agency, after which the seller's location may be shut down. The books of business are usually sold as a multiple of commissions, with the multiple perhaps as high as 2.0 x commissions. Small agencies with few potential local buyers that must be kept open after the sale are less profitable to a buyer and may sell for as low as 1.0 x commissions. Larger agencies are usually sold as a multiple of EBIT, often including an earn out component that can bring the price to 7.0 or higher if difficult to achieve goals are reached post sale."

"The insurance brokerage industry is very competitive, however there can be significant barriers of entry for new competition and the revenues are recurring."

"There is high buyer demand. Banks have been aggressive acquirers. The industry is going through consolidation. It is a good time to be a seller."

"Existing brokers choose to grow their business by purchasing mature books of business from retiring brokers."

"Insurance agencies are generally very marketable. One reason is the ease with which one agency can often be consolidated with another."

"P&C personal lines independent agency competition is high due to direct writers Geico and Progressive, and profit margins continue to shrink due to carrier expense ratio pressures. Barriers to entry are relatively low if you buy into the industry, but high to start up a company from scratch due to appointment requirements by national carriers. Profitable and portable books of business are highly marketable at realistic multiples of EBITDA."

"Personal lines property/casualty premiums are increasing annually. Commercial lines property/casualty premiums are static or declining. Medical benefits premiums are increasing annually."

"Since buyers are counting on the existing client base staying with the agency post sale, property & casualty agencies are generally quite salable regardless of the amount of competition in their market area. Independent agencies competing with them are quite often the buyer, and are able to achieve operating economies of scale that can make the acquisition quite a bit more profitable than proforma financial statements from the seller would indicate. For this reason, even a marginally profitable agency can often command a healthy multiple of revenue when sold. The most common concern of buyers is account retention post sale. Agencies with difficult accounts to retain will almost always sell for less. Account retention is so important that sales are often structured with a significant part of the price based on account retention post sale. It should be noted that starting an independent insurance agency today can be quite difficult, but combining an existing agency with another is often quite beneficial. The resulting profits can be greater than the sum of the parts."

"Lot of competition in personal lines. Location is more important if the agency business is more personal lines. Commercial lines, location not much of a factor. What markets/contracts the agency has will limit them to the type of business the agency can focus on. Agencies are easy to sell to other agencies that want to expand. Larger insurance brokerages can absorb a book of business without much increase in overhead."

I - Rules of Thumb

Benchmark Data

Statistics (Insurance Brokers and Agencies)

Number of Establishments	424,246
Average Profit Margin	12.0%
Revenue per Employee	$155,400
Average Number of Employees	2.3
Average Wages per Employee	$50,632

Products and Services Segmentation

Commercial P&C insurance	32.4%
Personal P&C insurance	25.0%
Health and medical insurance	13.2%
Life and accident insurance	11.3%
Other annuity and insurance	8.8%
Insurance administration and risk consulting	6.0%
Annuities	3.3%

Major Market Segmentation

Businesses	45.7%
Individuals aged 45 to 54	11.8%
Individuals aged 35 to 44	11.1%
Individuals aged 65 and older	10.1%
Individuals aged 34 and younger	8.7%
Individuals aged 55 to 64	46.1%
Government	4.3%

Industry Costs

Profit	12.0%
Wages	32.7%
Purchases	1.9%
Depreciation	1.3%
Marketing	1.3%
Rent & Utilities	1.5%
Other	49.3%

Market Share

Aon Corporation	2.6%
Marsh & McLennan Companies Inc.	2.2%
Arthur J. Gallagher & Co.	1.8%
Willis Group Holdings	0.9%

Source: IBISWorld, September 2015

- "Above average agencies (top quartile) often put 25% of revenues on the bottom line, after adjusting for discretionary use of funds and reasonable owner's compensation. The best agencies often put around 40% of revenues on the bottom line. These agencies are highly sought after as acquisition targets. They usually have at least $5 million in annual revenues."
- "Revenue per employee should be $125,000 or higher. Spread (which is the difference between revenue per employee and compensation per employee) needs to be $30,000 or higher."
- "Agencies with SDE of 25% or higher, after inclusion of the buyer's likely cost to hire a replacement for the departing seller, are likely to sell for higher multiples of commissions, and sometimes higher multiples of SDE as well."

Rules of Thumb - I

- "Better Standard agencies with focus on commercial risks can generate $150k revenue per employee. Better Standard agencies with focus on personal lines risks can generate $100k per employee. Non-Standard Auto agencies can generate $50–$60k per employee."
- "Well-run agency averages $140k per employee."
- "Pertaining to personal lines P&C agencies, the agency should typically have one CSR per $125–$150k in revenue. Pertaining to commercial lines P&C agencies, the agency should typically have one CSR per $200k+ in revenue."
- "$125,000 commission revenue per employee in larger commercial agency. Trends downward as agency size decreases."
- "An agency in the top quartile should be able to put a 25% EBITDA on the bottom line."
- "Low loss ratio.High level of standard vs. non standard business 75%+."
- "The most relevant benchmark is agency profit of 25% or more, adjusted to correct for excess owner compensation plus all the myriad ways an owner typically benefits financially from ownership."

Expenses as a percentage of annual sales

Cost of goods	15%
Payroll/labor Costs	30% to 50%
Occupancy	05% to 12%
Profit (estimated pretax)	15% to 30%

Industry Trend

- "As long as the stock market stays up, and the economy stays strong, these agencies will remain highly sought after acquisition targets. If the economy turns down, the seller's market may end, but they are likely to weather the storm better than the average small closely held business."
- "Agencies will become more productive as the market continues to harden. This will be done through the staff handling the same accounts, while adding new revenue because of increased rates. Also, there should be improved automation and streamlining of the work that is done. Paperless systems are becoming the norm in many firms today. Insurance companies will be pressured to follow the lead from agencies and become more automated, as well. Because insurance carriers are not as automated as agencies, often a lot of the burden falls on the agents."
  Source: "Insurance Industry Trends for Agencies to Exploit in 2014," by Catherine Oak, January 27, 2014
  www.insurancejournal.com/magazines
- "The industry will continue to consolidate due to the demand for purchasing agencies."
- "The current trend is the market continues to harden. This really began sometime in the second half of 2013. The past hard market was firmly in place from about 2000 through 2003. Prior to this almost a whole generation had lived under soft market conditions! The current soft market has been in various lines in various regions for a number of years, since about 2007.
  "Managing the agency in a way that exploits these trends will lead the firm to success. With hard markets, there is a lot of work quoting for not a lot of reward in increased premiums and thus, commissions. In order to keep revenues up, agencies will still need to sell more – either cross sell or sell additional coverages to new customers. Value added services should be offered and a fee charged, to increase revenue."
- "The value of agencies is finally increasing because of today's improving economy and the ability to get credit lines from banks."
- "Many small to medium-sized firms cannot individually maintain the number of

I - Rules of Thumb

quality markets they need to compete today with larger firms. Consolidators, networks and clusters provide that service, so the agency can compete.

"Clusters vary in size, style, capability and appearance. Generally speaking, the individual agency can maintain some, if not all their autonomy. These entities can also be a way for new people opening their own agencies to own their own firms. Some cluster organizations even provide perpetuation for their members within the group or umbrella entity. This option is becoming much more popular for agency owners than selling out. Then the cluster members can become the perpetuation plan for retiring principals of agency owners in the cluster."

> Source: "Insurance Industry Trends for Agencies to Exploit in 2014," by Catherine Oak, www.insurancejournal.com/magazines, 1/27/14

- "P&C—minimal growth; health—shrinking competition and revenues due to reduced compensation rates under PPAC (Obama's healthcare law)."
- "Standard agencies' revenue will improve as business revenue increases. Small standard agencies will be relegated to small business. Consolidation will continue with regional brokers acquiring strong local standard agencies."
- "Continued industry consolidation. Carriers want agents to write more business with them or risk the chance of being dropped."
- "The insurance business will continue to be highly competitive and rest on the ability of the agency to service their clients at a high level. Rates are important, but service and keeping the clients satisfied is the way to grow an agency."

Seller Financing

- "There are about 6 or so specialty lenders who target this industry and it's desirable to lenders."
- "Seller financing is very common when one independent agency buys another. If a national buyer is involved the up-front cash is often a large portion of the sale, with the balance in an earn-out. The earn-outs can be very hard to achieve in full."
- "Mostly a mix of the two with outside financing carrying the majority of the note."
- "Usually financed through Seller financing, however there are numerous cash buyers"
- "Varies. Usually some type of earnout provision is structured."
- "Midsize to larger deals there is no seller financing requirements."
- "Most sales have some component of an earnout based on retained business (future commissions). May make it necessary for seller to stay on for a period of time after sale to increase likelihood business will stay with new ownership."
- "Down payment—25 to 50 percent; balance—24 to 60 months, plus interest at 2 percent over prime"
- "50% of gross commissions for three years"
- "3 to 5 years"
- "Sometimes owner financing on renewals. For instance, 1.50 times renewals. This can be tricky because buyer may take the cream of the crop and seller is left holding the bag."

Questions

- "What is your retention? How are your loss ratios? In your opinion, how likely is it that a new owner will be appointed by the carriers?"
- "Reason for selling. How long in business? Annual retention. Are key personnel willing to stay?"
- "Will you help with account retention post sale?"

Rules of Thumb - I

- "Why are you selling? What carriers do you represent? Do employees have non compete agreements? Type of business written?Age of clientele?"
- "Can I see your CSRP report? This is the agency report card."
- "Are you willing to remain with the business for 2 to 4 years?"
- "What insurance companies do you represent and what premium and loss ratio have you had with each for last 3 yrs.? Employees and date of hire?Persistency? Top 10 clients and commission revenue from each? Copies of all producer agreements?Cash or accrual basis tax payer? Itemized list of commission receivables and premium payables?"
- "What is the product mix? (personal lines, commercial lines, benefits, and general description of any specialization). 'S' vs. 'C' corp status. Have tax issues been assessed? Will an asset sale generate tax issues for the seller? Are the employees subject to enforceable non-piracy agreements?"
- "Are you willing to do an earnout?"
- "Do your producers have vesting rights to their books of business?"
- "Size of book? Mix of book by product line? Expense ratio for agency?Loss ratio for P&C book?New business growth? Licenses held? Carrier appointments held? Written premium by carrier?"
- "Companies represented, percentage of cancellations with each carrier, the appointment with the carriers must be transferable, how long at same location, key employees: do they have a non-compete agreement in force now, or will they sign one before the sale?"
- "Will buyer inherit the client base, will seller give up the renewal and trail commissions of existing clients? What is the likelihood of existing clients canceling their contract after knowing that the ownership changed hands?"
- "Are your carriers A-rated?"
- "Copies of company's statements including production, loss ratios, possibility of transfer of appointments with insurance carriers, income taxes for last 3 years, how you get customers,"

Resources

Websites
- Independent Insurance Agents and Brokers of America: www.independentagent.com
- Insurance Information Institute—lots of information and data: www.iii.org
- AgencyEquity: www.AgencyEquity.com

Trade Publications
- American Agent and Broker: www.propertycasualty360.com/American-Agent-Broker
- Insurance Journal: www.insurancejournal.com/magazines

Associations
- American Association of Insurance Services: www.aaisonline.com
- Florida Association of Insurance Agents: www.faia.com
- Professional Insurance Agents: www.pia.org
- The Council of Insurance Agents and Brokers: www.ciab.com
- American Association of Insurance Management Consultants: www.aaimco.com

I - Rules of Thumb

Insurance Companies (in general)
(See also Insurance Companies—Life, Property & Casualty)
NAICS 524210

Rules of Thumb
➢ 1 to 2 times capital and surplus

Pricing Tips
- "A ton of information is required, beyond the company's financial statements and tax returns, such as reports submitted to the insurance department of the states the company does business in; actuarial reports on the adequacy of amounts in reserve to pay claims; rating of company by one or more insurers-rating organizations; status of any significant lawsuits pending against the company; its reputation in the industry; and its relationship with its sales force. Just getting an opinion as to value involves hundreds of hours of document review and analysis."

Benchmark Data
- For Benchmark Data see Insurance Companies—Life, Property & Casualty

Resources
Trade Publications
- Insurance Networking News: www.insurancenetworking.com

Insurance Companies—Life (See also Insurance Agencies)	
NAICS 524210	Number of Businesses/Units 9,414

Rules of Thumb
➢ 1 to 2.5 times capital and surplus

Benchmark Data

Statistics (Life Insurance & Annuities)
Number of Establishments	9,414
Average Profit Margin	7.1%
Revenue per Employee	$2,288,900
Average Number of Employees	38.8
Average Wages per Employee	$103,791

Products and Services Segmentation
Other	28.8%
Variable deferred annuities	21.7%
Fixed rate deferred annuities	12.9%
Individual whole life premiums	12.5%
Group life premiums	8.2%
Individual universal life premiums	7.0%
Immediate annuities	5.7%
Individual term life premiums	3.2%

Rules of Thumb - I

Major Market Segmentation

Individuals aged 45 to 54	23.5%
Individuals aged 35 to 44	22.2%
Individuals aged 65 and older	20.2%
Individuals aged 34 and younger	17.4%
Individuals aged 55 to 64	16.7%

Industry Costs

Profit	7.1%
Wages	4.6%
Purchases	64.1%
Depreciation	0.8%
Marketing	0.3%
Rent & Utilities	0.3%
Other	22.8%

Market Share

MetLife Inc.	4.8%

Source: IBISWorld, May 2015

Insurance Companies—Property & Casualty
(See also Insurance Agencies)

NAICS 524126	Number of Businesses/Units 18,100

Rules of Thumb

➢ ½ to 3 times capital and surplus

Pricing Tips

- "I have a Property & Casualty company for sale with stockholders' equity of $145 million; the asking price is 1.6 to 1.7 times stockholders' equity. Price dropped due to an adjustment in some bad risks that were eliminated."

Benchmark Data

Statistics (Property, Casualty and Direct Insurance)

Number of Establishments	18,100
Average Profit Margin	12.9%
Revenue per Employee	$989,100
Average Number of Employees	34.2
Average Wages per Employee	$85,359

Products and Services Segmentation

Private passenger auto	36.3%
Other	17.2%
Homeowners multiple peril	15.1%
Other liability	8.7%
Workers compensation	8.5%
Commercial multiple peril	6.9%
Commercial auto	5.0%
Fire	2.3%

26th Edition

I - Rules of Thumb

Major Market Segmentation

Other commercial market	42.3%
Private vehicle market	36.3%
Other private market	13.9%
Commercial vehicle market	5.0%
Other insurance carriers	2.5%

Industry Costs

Profit	12.9%
Wages	8.7%
Purchases	1.8%
Depreciation	1.1%
Marketing	1.3%
Rent & Utilities	1.4%
Other	72.8%

Market Share

State Farm Mutual Automobile Insurance Company	11.9%
Allstate Insurance Company	5.2%
Liberty Mutual Group Inc.	5.2%
The Travelers Companies Inc.	4.3%

Source: IBISWorld, September 2015

Questions
"What is their stockholders' equity? What management do they have? What is their marketing ability?"

Internet Hosting—Colocation

Rules of Thumb
➢ 3 to 4 times EBITDA

Pricing Tips
- "Prices are down from 2 years ago."

Expert Comments
"Industry was growing by 50% per year prior to the economic downturn. Still growth in the industry."

Benchmark Data
- "Most are netting between 33% and 44% of gross income."

Expenses as a percentage of annual sales

Cost of goods	n/a
Payroll/labor Costs	n/a
Occupancy	n/a
Profit (estimated pretax)	33%

Industry Trend
- "Massive growth"

Internet Related Businesses
Rules of Thumb
➢ 80% of Annual Gross Sales

Pricing Tips
- "Market values on Internet-based business vary based on so many different points; every deal is different."
- "Internet-based companies are currently trading at: 2.3–3.8 X the true net income of that company. Example: Business ABC has a net income of $100k/year. That company would trade for somewhere in the ballpark of $230k–$380k, assuming there is no inventory included. Now remember each deal is different!"

Industry Trend
- "The Internet is growing ever-so-fast! The trend over the few years is clearly on an upswing! Every single company/business out there needs an Internet presence, and if you don't have one, you're missing out on a major market share of your industry."

Seller Financing
- "Currently the Internet Merger & Acquisitions space is an either all cash business or with a little seller financing thrown into the mix! Traditional banks are not at the point yet where they can evaluate how to protect their asset (the domain and its content). Unless you have free and clear real estate to put up as collateral, you're not getting a bank loan on an Internet company."

Investigative Services (See also Guard Services, Security Services/Systems)

	NAICS 561611	Number of Businesses/Units 8,000

Rules of Thumb
➢ 70 to 75 percent of annual sales

Benchmark Data
- For Benchmark Data see Security Services/Systems

Investment Advice

	NAICS 523930	

Rules of Thumb
➢ 1.5 times SDE
➢ 1 times annual sales

Pricing Tips
- "Contract persistency is critical to the continuation of fees. The demographics of the clientele base should be carefully analyzed. The range of valuation

J - Rules of Thumb

multiples is very wide and varies by the type of revenue stream and how it's paid. The numbers above are considered to be averages. Regulation violations by the owner can severely reduce the sales price."

Expert Comments

"Industry consolidation and company marketing efficiencies are promoting the move away from commissioned sales force."

Benchmark Data

Statistics (Financial Planning and Advice)

Number of Establishments	75,602
Average Profit Margin	26.7%
Revenue per Employee	$226,600
Average Number of Employees	2.3
Average Wages per Employee	$75,119

Products and Services Segmentation

Business and government financial planning and management	41.3%
Personal financial planning and advice	33.0%
Other Services	15.8%
Personal investment management	21.0%

Industry Costs

Profit	26.7%
Wages	34.1%
Purchases	4.3%
Depreciation	1.1%
Marketing	1.2%
Rent & Utilities	2.9%
Other	29.7%

Market Share

Morgan Stanley Wealth Management	19.8%
Wells Fargo & Company	18.4%
Bank of America Corporation	13.5%
Ameriprise Financial Inc.	13.2%

Source: IBISWorld, April 2015

	Franchise
Jani-King (See also Coverall, Franchises, Janitorial Services)	
Approx. Total Investment	$8,170 to $74,000
NAICS 561720	Number of Businesses/Units 11,022

Rules of Thumb

> 25 to 30 percent of annual sales plus inventory

Resources

Websites
- www.janiking.com

Rules of Thumb - J

Janitorial Services (See also Coverall, Jani-King, Maid Services)

| SIC 7439-02 | NAICS 561720 | Number of Businesses/Units 901,261 |

Rules of Thumb
- 45 to 50 percent of annual sales plus inventory
- 1.5 times SDE plus inventory
- 1 times one month's billings; plus fixtures, equipment and inventory
- 4 times monthly billings; includes fixtures, equipment and inventory

Pricing Tips
- "1.5 to 1.75 times SDE including a working inventory for commercial janitorial service companies. 1.25 to 1.60 times SDE including a working inventory for maid service/residential businesses. Commercial companies with Gross Sales in excess of $3 million–$20 million could fetch a 3-6 time multiple of SDE. Companies with long terms (3-5+ years) client contracts have more weight. Fully staffed with supervision in place has more weight. Government contracts offer nice security for buyers but are difficult to transfer. Minority owned businesses carry less weight if client contracts are based on such ownership. W-2 Employees carry more weight than 1099's. Quality of books and records are important."
- "Janitorial (Contract Cleaners)—1.5 times net, depending upon the amount of hired help. An industry evaluation is 3 to 5 times the monthly gross depending upon the equipment and the type of accounts; e.g., government vs. private . . . a very conservative approach which could vary widely on a monthly basis. Government contracts could offer more start-up security for a prospective purchaser."

Benchmark Data

Statistics (Janitorial Services)
Number of Establishments	901,261
Average Profit Margin	5.9%
Revenue per Employee	$28,100
Average Number of Employees	2.1
Average Wages per Employee	$15,150

Products and Services Segmentation
Standard commercial cleaning	61.2%
Other	20.3%
Residential cleaning	8.3%
Damage restoration cleaning	4.9%
Floor care services	3.0%
Exterior window cleaning	2.3%

Major Market Segmentation
Offices	32.0%
Educational facilities	30.4%
Retail complexes	12.3%
Residences	8.3%
Government	6.2%
Industrial plants	6.1%
Healthcare facilities	4.7%

26th Edition

J - Rules of Thumb

Industry Costs

Profit	5.9%
Wages	53.5%
Purchases	19.8%
Depreciation	1.1%
Marketing	1.2%
Rent & Utilities	3.3%
Other	15.2%

Market Share

ABM Industries Inc. 5.3%

Source: IBISWorld, August 2015

- Benchmarking Survey Report
  This survey was conducted and produced by the research department at the CM B2B Trade Group, the parent of CM/Cleaning & Maintenance magazine. It is being sponsored as a service by P&G ProLine™, Proctor & Gamble's complete line of floor care, carpet care, daily cleaner, and specialty cleaner products.

  "The survey found the following averages of interior building area cleaned in square feet per FTE (full-time equivalent employee) per hour, with no obstructions:

2–4 year college/university	12,466
Schools/districts (K–12)	11,388
Private office building	10,853
Government facility	7,835
Medical facilities	5,931

"Median square footage per FTE per hour was as follows:

2–4 year college/university	5,000
Schools/districts (K–12)	4,000
Private office building	4,500
Government facility	4,000
Medical facilities	2,050"

Source: "Benchmarking Survey: Which Facility Has Best Cleaning Production?"
by Nicole Lemperle, Associate Editor, CM Cleaning & Maintenance Management.

Expenses as a percentage of annual sales

Cost of goods	03%
Payroll/labor Costs	45%
Occupancy	07%
Profit (estimated pretax)	40%

Industry Trend

- "The cleaning industry is one of the fastest growing service industries in the United States. It is predicted that cleaning services will experience a five percent growth rate between 2008 and 2018, and this growth will be largely due to the health care industry, where elderly care needs will only increase over that period. In addition, personal consumption for cleaning, laundering and repair of clothing is predicted to increase at a compound annual rate of 3 percent from 2010 to 2015."
- Source: "Cleaning Industry Analysis 2014—Cost & Trends," by Andrew Weber, www.franchisehelp.com

Rules of Thumb - J

- "Janitorial and Maid Service businesses seem to be on the rise. Purchasers coming out of the corporate world are finding it easy to transition into these industries. As the long as the economy keeps trending positive, these industries should thrive."

Seller Financing
- "SBA and Private Equity Group financing is certainly an option. Most small units are sold with at least 80-90% cash down."

Resources

Trade Publications
- C M Cleaning & Maintenance Management—informative site based on the magazine: www.cmmonline.com

Associations
- Building Service Contractors Association International: www.bscai.org
- International Janitorial Cleaning Services Association: www.ijcsa.org
- International Sanitary Supply Association: www.issa.com

Jersey Mike's Subs (See also Franchises, Sandwich Shops)	Franchise
Approx. Total Investment	$243,337 to $492,732
Estimated Annual Sales/Unit	$650,000
SIC 5812-19 NAICS 722513	Number of Businesses/Units 800

Rules of Thumb
> 50 percent of annual sales plus inventory

Benchmark Data
- For Benchmark Data see Sandwich Shops

Resources

Websites
- www.jerseymikes.com

Jewelry Stores	
SIC 5944-09 NAICS 448310	Number of Businesses/Units 68,845

Rules of Thumb
> 4 to 6 times EBIT if inventory included
> None—too inventory intensive

Pricing Tips
- "What return on assets would be expected if current owner left city?"

26th Edition

J - Rules of Thumb

- "A destination upscale jeweler has a much better 'chance' of being sold as a going business."
- "Highly capital intensive—inventory on hand most critical in pricing"
- "Price is based on amount of inventory, current value, years in business, and profit of operations now and after sale is completed."
- "No magic formula—jewelry is a high-capital requirement for inventory and hiring personnel; trust & confidence of owners not readily transferable. Will seller sell without inventory—or one year's supply based on sales volume that is high enough to be attractive—example: annual sales of $500,000 with inventory at cost of $200,000 is attractive if business has growth and is currently profitable."

Benchmark Data

Statistics (Jewelry Stores)

Number of Establishments	68,845
Average Profit Margin	6.8%
Revenue per Employee	$193,000
Average Number of Employees	2.6
Average Wages per Employee	$26,615

Products and Services Segmentation

Diamond Jewelry	42.0%
Other merchandise	20.7%
Watches	15.1%
Gold jewelry	9.6%
Pearl and other gemstone jewelry	8.1%
Loose gemstones, including diamonds and colored gemstones	4.5%

Industry Costs

Profit	6.8%
Wages	13.8%
Purchases	53.8%
Depreciation	0.9%
Marketing	2.7%
Rent & Utilities	9.1%
Other	12.9%

Market Share

Signet Jewelers Ltd.	16.6%
Tiffany & Co.	5.2%

Source: IBISWorld, July 2015

Expenses as a percentage of annual sales

Cost of goods	55% to 58%
Payroll/labor Costs	22%
Occupancy	n/a
Profit (estimated pretax)	06%

Industry Trend

- "After struggling during the recession, the industry has somewhat recovered during the five years to 2014. Industry revenue is expected to rebound from recessionary lows at an average annual rate of 3.7% to about $36.0 billion during the five years to 2014. Additionally, the number of jewelry stores

Rules of Thumb - **J**

is expected to grow 0.9% annually during the five-year period to 70,527 locations."

Source: IBISWorld, June 2014

- "A store's website remains the No. 1 marketing tool for retailers, cited by 75 percent of respondents, down slightly from 80 percent last year."

Source: "Exclusive Report: Sale rebound continues" Michelle Graff, www.nationaljeweler.com April 9, 2013

Seller Financing
- "Not seller financed—inventory too portable—high risk"
- 3 years

Resources

Websites
- National Jeweler: www.nationaljeweler.com

Trade Publications
- Instoremagazine: www.instoremag.com

Associations
- Jewelers of America (JA): www.jewelers.org

	Franchise
Jiffy Lube International	
(See also Auto Lube/Tune-up, Other Lube Franchises)	
Approx. Total Investment	$220,000 to $400,000
NAICS 811191	Number of Businesses/Units 2,032

Rules of Thumb
➢ 45 to 50 percent of annual sales plus inventory

Benchmark Data

Resources

Websites
- www.jiffylube.com

	Franchise
Jimmy John's Gourmet Sandwiches	
(See also Franchises, Sandwich Shops)	
Approx. Total Investment	$330,000 to $519,400
Estimated Annual Sales/Unit	$850,000
SIC 5812-19 NAICS 722513	Number of Businesses/Units 1,950

Rules of Thumb
➢ 65 to 70 percent of annual sales plus inventory

J - Rules of Thumb

Benchmark Data
- For Benchmark Data see Sandwich Shops

Job Shops/Contract Manufacturing (See also Machine Shops)		
	NAICS 332710	

Rules of Thumb
- ➢ 1.5 to 2 times SDE plus inventory
- ➢ 3 to 5 times EBIT
- ➢ 4 to 5 times EBITDA

Pricing Tips
- "Customer concentration is an issue for most job shops and contract manufacturers. A customer over 30% or two customers over 50% is a major problem."
- "4 x EBITDA is just a rule of thumb. A range of 3 x to 8 x is realistic depending a range of factors (history, custom concentration, future prospects, etc.)"
- "Best rule of thumb in this industry to use as a barometer is FMV of FFE&M plus 1X EBITDA."
- "Job shops with full range of capabilities (turning, milling, grinding, stamping, etc.) are more desirable."

Expert Comments

"While some people consider ease of replication is easy they are wrong, wrong, wrong. The business might be easy to start but very difficult to get big-name customers until the company has established a track record."

"Competition is high and the key to gross profit margins is using technology to be low-cost manufacturer."

"Recent influx of orders from OEM's has contributed to better backlog. Receivable aging improving and more shops able to get 33%–50% deposits. Not as much used equipment in the field as prior years. Competitive edge goes to automated shops with palletized tool changing machining centers, wire EDM, etc."

"In some cases, the machinery & equipment has a higher value than the business."

Benchmark Data
- For additional Benchmark Data see Machine Shops
- "Revenues per man-hour can be all over the place because newer, numerical controlled machines are much more productive. The higher the revenues per man-hour the 'better' the business."
- "Most modern shops set up to have one employee service two machines."
- "Determine unused capacity. Buyers will want to determine potential without major capital investment."

Rules of Thumb - J

Expenses as a percentage of annual sales

Cost of goods	40% to 50%
Payroll/labor Costs	25% to 28%
Occupancy	03% to 05%
Profit (estimated pretax)	12%

Industry Trend

- "Custom fabricators need to juggle highly variable demand cycles from myriad customers, and to do that they need capacity. Judging by the 2015 Capital Spending Forecast, they're building that capacity with more equipment. Projected capital spending growth has slowed from the dramatic rebound seen post-recession—2015 projections are up only 3.5 percent over 2014—but the spending has shifted."

Projected Operating Level by Plant Size

Employees	Higher	Lower	Same as 2014
1–19	59.8%	7.0%	33.2%
20–49	61.2%	3.1%	35.7%
50–99	68.0%	0.8%	31.2%
100–249	71.4%	6.7%	21.9%
250–499	65.3%	6.1%	28.6%
500–999	71.4%	3.6%	25.0%
1,000+	64.3%	14.3%	21.4%
Average	64.5%	5.2%	30.4%
2014 Average	57.1%	5.9%	37.0%
2013 Average	60.5%	7.0%	32.5%"

Source: "2015 metal fabrication forecast: Steady as she grows" by Tim Heston 12/8/2014
http://www.thefabricator.com/article/shopmanagement/2015-metal-fabrication-forecast-steady-as-she-grows-article

Seller Financing

- "Most deals to have some seller financing, usually 3 to 5 years at an interest rate between CD rates and bank loan rates. Our current experiences are interest rates in the 3% to 4% range."

Questions

- "Find out the seller's motivation. Could be issues related to hiring skilled machinists or constant battles with customers paying on time."
- "Discuss the outlook for the company. What opportunities exist for the buyer and why the seller isn't pursuing them."
- "Backlog, WIP, age, qualifications & tenure of staff, condition of equipment (look at line items for R&M closely to avoid machinery held together with band aids), need for CAPEX near and mid-term, etc.?"
- "Will the business be sustainable when owner leaves? Any known environmental issues?"

Resources

Trade Publications

- Design2Part Buyers Guide: www.D2PBuyersGuide.com

J - Rules of Thumb

John Deere Dealerships

Pricing Tips

- "Rules of Thumb are totally inappropriate. If DOT then dealership has future but if not DOT, the days are numbered and must be acquired by an adjoining dealership. Market share is huge to JD and rebates reducing to those not DOT or not achieving market share objectives. Need 40% equity so forget about high leverage deals. Be careful and look at aging of inventory and losses hidden in leases and conditional sales contracts—dealers are exposed.

  "DOT is the term used for their Dealer of Tomorrow standards. The goal is to deal with $50 million plus dealers only. They no longer want 'Joe' who is a good salesman to be a dealer. They want organizations with sufficient size that they can afford to employ a full management team—general manager, controller/VP-Finance, sales manager, parts manager, and aftermarket manager. At $50 million, you can afford most of these people and at $100 million, you can afford better people and real economies of scale set in."

Johnny Rockets (See also Franchises)		Franchise
Approx. Total Investment		$539,525 to $975,575
Estimated Annual Sales/Unit		$1 million plus
	NAICS 722513	Number of Businesses/Units 335

Rules of Thumb

➢ 70 to 75 percent of annual sales plus inventory

Pricing Tips

- "Some have sold for 100 percent of sales."

Resources

Websites
- www.johnnyrockets.com

Jon Smith Subs (See also Franchises, Sandwich Shops)		Franchise
	NAICS 722513	Number of Businesses/Units 8

Rules of Thumb

➢ 20 percent of annual sales plus inventory

Rules of Thumb - K

	Franchise
Juice It Up (See also Franchises)	
Approx. Total Investment	$159,979 to $391,448
NAICS 722515	Number of Businesses/Units 80

Rules of Thumb
➢ 20 to 25 percent of annual sales plus inventory

Resources

Websites
- www.juiceitup.com

	Franchise
KFC (Kentucky Fried Chicken) (See also Franchises)	
Approx. Total Investment	$1,300,000 to $2,500,000
Estimated Annual Sales/Unit	$945,000
NAICS 722513	Number of Businesses/Units 4,200

Rules of Thumb
➢ 30 to 35 percent of annual sales plus inventory

	Franchise
Kumon Math & Reading Centers (See also Children's Educational Franchises, Schools—Educational/Non-Vocational)	
Approx. Total Investment	$77,187–$149,319
NAICS 611691	Number of Businesses/Units 1,450

Rules of Thumb
➢ 80 to 90 percent of annual sales plus inventory

Pricing Tips
- " ... franchisees say you have to have at least 200 [students] to make a center go."

Source: "Branding Brawl" by Beth Ewen, *Franchise Times*, March 2013

Benchmark Data
- By the Numbers:
  Change at Kumon North America centers since 2008
  Average selling price of existing center, to $106,000 from $86,000 .... up 24%
  Average enrollment, to 174 students from 145 .... up 20%
  Number of centers, to 1,514 from 1,305 .... up 16%
- "They're requiring centers to locate in retail locations, not the church basements or community centers where they might have operated before. They are requiring operators to spend $600 per quarter on local marketing, and

K - Rules of Thumb

opening five days a week and eight hours a day, not the few part-time hours that centers used to do."

Source: "Branding Brawl" by Beth Ewen, *Franchise Times*, March 2013

Industry Trend

- "Kumon, the world's largest after-school math and reading franchisor, is ranked as the number one tutoring franchise in *Entrepreneur* magazine's annual Franchise 500 issue for the 13th year in a row. The company assisted more than 370,000 students this year in math and reading, an increase in student enrollment from 355,000 last year. Kumon plans to continue helping more children with the opening of new centers across the United States, Canada and Mexico in 2014."

Source: "Entrepreneur Magazine Ranks Kumon No. 1 Education Franchise for 13th Consecutive Year," www.franchising.com/news/20140108

Kwik Kopy Business Center (See also Franchises, Quick Printing)		Franchise
Approx. Total Investment		$219,578 to $248,626
	NAICS 323111	Number of Businesses/Units 18

Rules of Thumb

➢ 50 to 60 percent of annual sales plus inventory

Lady of America (See also Fitness Centers, Franchises)		Franchise
Approx. Total Investment		$9,250
	NAICS 713940	Number of Businesses/Units 500

Rules of Thumb

➢ 45 to 50 percent of annual sales plus inventory

Resources

Websites
- www.loafitnessforwomen.com

Landscaping Services (See also Lawn Maintenance & Service)		
SIC 0782-04	NAICS 561730	Number of Businesses/Units 497,912

Rules of Thumb

➢ 45 to 50 percent of annual revenues plus inventory

➢ 1.5 times SDE; plus fixtures and equipment (except vehicles) & inventory

➢ 2 to 4 times EBITDA (may be higher for larger firms)

Pricing Tips

- "Multiples of EBITDA range from 2 to 6 depending on size, profitability and industry segment."

Rules of Thumb - L

- "Landscape contractors need substantial capital investments for equipment. Startup costs of $100,000 are needed to compete in this industry. 'It's a difficult field unless you're a really large company' said Crabtree, who has been in the industry for over 15 years. Profit margins are typically 5%."

   Source: www.urbanforest.org

Expert Comments

"Competition is fierce and ease of replication is as easy as owning a lawnmower and weed whacker. Much better once the company reaches several million in sales."

"Set yourself apart from the competition. Get long-term contracts. Focus on maintenance."

Benchmark Data

Statistics (Landscaping Services)

Number of Establishments	497,912
Average Profit Margin	6.5%
Revenue per Employee	$80,300
Average Number of Employees	2.0
Average Wages per Employee	$32,509

Products and Services Segmentation

Maintenance and general services-commercial	51.0%
Maintenance and general services-residential	31.0%
Design-build-installation services	13.8%
Other	8.4%
Arborist services and other services	4.2%

Major Market Segmentation

Single-family residential markets	67.1%
Commercial markets	22.1%
Multifamily residential markets	6.5%
Government and institutional markets	4.3%

Industry Costs

Profit	6.5%
Wages	40.6%
Purchases	29.2%
Depreciation	3.5%
Marketing	1.3%
Rent & Utilities	4.8%
Other	14.1%

Source: IBISWorld, July 2015

- "In the Lawn and Landscape State of the Industry 2013 survey, respondents reported business in the following sectors: 67% single family residential, 25% commercial/industrial, 7% multi-family, and 3% governmental/institutional.
"The survey showed that companies had the following business lines in 2013: maintenance (45%), design build (18%), lawn care (12%), irrigation (6%), tree care & ornamental (6%), and snow and ice removal (5%). The industry average net company profit for those surveyed in 2013 was 10%.

L - Rules of Thumb

"The contractors surveyed reported profit margins in 2012 as follows: 26% made a profit margin between 5-9.9%; 21% made a profit margin between 1-4.9%; 20% made a profit margin between 10-14.9%; and 14% made a profit margin between 15-19.9%."

Source: www.landcarenetwork.org/PLANET/Media/Statistics

Expenses as a percentage of annual sales	
Cost of goods	50%
Payroll/labor Costs	30%
Occupancy	05%
Profit (estimated pretax)	10% to 15%

Industry Trend

- "Although tempered by the recent economic recession, and subsequent decline in consumer spending, residential housing and construction activity, the landscaping services market in the US is expected to recover and reach $80.06 billion by 2015.

  "The need to beautify commercial/residential property as a place for relaxation, entertainment or work, has long nourished the interest in landscaping. The worth added to the value of property by decorative structures, ponds, patios, and green-winding pathways too cannot be undermined. Keeping in view the growing popularity and importance of landscaping as an art, science, and commercial value proposition, it is of little surprise that landscaping services has now become one of the most important domains in the overall services industry."

  Source: "2015: Landscaping Market to Hit $80 Billion"
http://www.landscapeonline.com/research/article/13920

- "The Global Industry Analysts Report says 'the landscaping services market in the U.S. is expected to recover and is poised to reach U.S. $80.06 billion by 2015.'

  "It's not just the big boys that are more optimistic about business conditions, According to a fall survey of Green Industry PRO readers, 58% expect maintenance sales to grow this year while 49% expect lawn care sales to grow. On the other hand, less than 10% expect maintenance and/or lawn care sales to dip.

  "Since 90% of landscape companies employ fewer than 20 people, we're talking about a lot of average-size companies that are feeling pretty good about their chances of remaining competitive."

  Source: "Slow but Steady" by Gregg Wartgow, Green Industry Pro, www.greenindustrypros.com

Seller Financing

- "Generally difficult to finance because of lack of assets."

Questions

- "Does the company have contracts with its clients? Are all employees legal? How many customers are built on relationships with the seller, and what will happen to them if he sells?"

Resources

Trade Publications

- Lawn and Landscape: www.lawnandlandscape.com
- Turf Magazine: www.turfmagazine.com
- Landscape Management: www.landscapemanagement.net

Rules of Thumb - L

Associations
- National Association of Landscape Professionals: www.landscapeprofessionals.org
- Association of Professional Landscape Designers: www.apld.org

Land Surveying Services		
SIC 8713-01	NAICS 541370	Number of Businesses/Units 19,077

Rules of Thumb
> 40 to 80 percent of annual fee revenues; plus fixtures, equipment and inventory; may require earnout

Benchmark Data

Statistics (Surveying and Mapping Services)
Number of Establishments	18,735
Average Profit Margin	8.4%
Revenue per Employee	$120,300
Average Number of Employees	3.2
Average Wages per Employee	$45,803

Products and Services Segmentation
Property line, boundary and cadastral surveying	27.7%
Construction surveying	21.6%
Engineering services	6%
Topographical and planimetric surveying and mapping	15.9%
Geospatial photo processing from aircraft and satellites	9.9%
Other services	11%
Subdivision layout and design services	7.9%

Major Market Segmentation
Construction firms	25.0%
Federal government departments and agencies	20.0%
Land subdivision and development firms	20.0%
Professional technical firms	15.0%
City, county and state surveying offices	10.0%
Energy, utility and mining companies	10.0%

Industry Costs
Profit	8.4%
Wages	38.1%
Purchases	17.8%
Depreciation	2.7%
Marketing	1.1%
Rent & Utilities	9.8%
Other	22.1%

Source: IBISWorld, December 2014

Industry Trend
- "Overall employment of surveyors, cartographers, photogrammetrists, and surveying technicians is expected to grow much faster than the average for all occupations through the year 2016. The extensive availability and use of

L - Rules of Thumb

sophisticated technologies, such as remote sensing and GPS, will continue to increase the precision and productivity of these workers. Opportunities for surveyors, cartographers, and photogrammetrists should remain concentrated in engineering, surveying, mapping, building inspection, and drafting services firms."

Source: "Latest trends in the Economic Outlook for Land Surveyors," www.landsurveyor4hire.com

- "The executive director of the National Society of Professional Surveyors (NSPS) told members of a Congressional subcommittee that the U.S. Department of Labor's recent decision to categorize survey crew members as 'laborers and mechanics' was 'detrimental to the surveying profession,' and requested Congress' help in reversing DOL's decision."

Source: "Press Release from the National Society of Professional Surveyors concerning the Davis-Bacon Act," www.amerisurv.com, June 19, 2013

Resources

Trade Publications
- Professional Surveyor magazine: www.profsurv.com

Associations
- The National Society of Professional Surveyors: http://www.nsps.us.com/

Laptop Xchange (See also Computer Stores)		Franchise
Approx. Total Investment		$183,750 to $267,800
	NAICS 443142	Number of Businesses/Units 20

Rules of Thumb
> ➢ 80 to 85 percent of annual sales plus inventory

Resources

Websites
- www.laptopxchange.com

Law Firms		
SIC 8111-03	NAICS 541110	Number of Businesses/Units 468,202

Rules of Thumb
> ➢ 90 to 100 percent of annual fee revenue; firms specializing in estate work would approach 100 percent; may require earnout.
> ➢ 4 times SDE includes inventory
> ➢ 3.5 times EBIT
> ➢ 3.5 times EBITDA

Pricing Tips
- "A lot will depend upon the consultants, and how loyal they are to the firm."

Rules of Thumb - L

- "Whether the multiplier is in the lower or the higher level of the range depends primarily on how much repeat business is expected, the nature of the law practice, the number of clients and the transferability of client relationships. If there is a great deal of repeat business and client loyalty that can be transferred, the multiplier will be higher. In the sale of a law practice, a portion of the clients will not stay with the practice by reason of the close personal relationship usually developed between client and attorney. This must be considered when determining the multiplier. The multiplier may then be raised or lowered depending on the stability of the flow of future revenue expected."

Source: "Valuing Professional Practices and Licenses"

Expert Comments

"It is difficult to replicate, as the good businesses have reputations built over many years."

Benchmark Data

Statistics (Law Firms)

Number of Establishments	468,202
Average Profit Margin	18.1%
Revenue per Employee	$205,600
Average Number of employees	2.9
Average Wages per Employee	$77,114

Products and Services Segmentation

Commercial law services	43.6%
Other services	26.0%
Criminal law, civil negligence and personal injury	16.9%
Real estate law	8.1%
Labor and employment	5.4%

Major Market Segmentation

Business and corporate clients	66.1%
Households	29.1%
Government and not-for-profit clients	4.8%

Industry Costs

Profit	18.1%
Wages	37.7%
Purchases	1.8%
Depreciation	0.9%
Marketing	1.6%
Rent & Utilities	6.0%
Other	33.9%

Source: IBISWorld, April 2015

Enterprises by Employment Size

No. of Employees	Share %
1 to 4	88.3
5 to 9	5.6
10 to 19	2.8
20 to 99	2.1
100 to 499	0.8
500+	0.4

Source: IBISWorld, May 2014

26th Edition

L - Rules of Thumb

Expenses as a percentage of annual sales

Cost of goods	0
Payroll/labor Costs	0
Occupancy	0
Profit (estimated pretax)	30%

Industry Trend

- "Consistent with past practices, firms continued to raise their rates in 2014, albeit at a fairly modest level of 3.1 percent. And, also consistent with past experience, clients continued to push back, keeping strong pressure on firm realization rates. Over this ten-year period (2005 through November 2014), firms increased their standard rates by 35.9 percent from an average of $348 per hour to $473 (or an average increase of about 3.6 percent per year). At the same time, reflecting mounting client push back to these rate hikes, the collected rates achieved by law firms increased by a somewhat more modest 28.2 percent over the ten-year period, from an average of $304 per hour to $390 (or an average increase of about 2.8 percent per year). While the market for law for law firm services has clearly been impacted by external factors, there has also been an important shift in the internal dynamics of the market that has become increasingly apparent in recent years. Specifically, there is now strong evidence that the U.S. legal market has segmented into discernible categories of highly successful and less successful firms, and that the performance gaps between those categories has been steadily widening."

    Source: http://www.law.georgetown.edu/academics/centers-institutes/legal-profession/upload/FINAL-Report-1-7-15.pdf

- "For practically everyone else in Big Law, the future looks chaotic. Client fee pressures will be matched by the cost overhang of the pre-recession go-go era. Young lawyers will increasingly struggle to establish a foothold. To protect their personal pocketbooks, firms are lengthening the path to partnership amid an oversupply of fresh labor. The Bureau of Labor Statistics estimates that during the decade ending in 2020, the U.S. economy will create 73,600 lawyer positions. Law schools are pumping out 25,000 graduates a year, suggesting an excess of 176,400 JDs no one really needs."

    Source: "Law firms are merging and growing like conglomerates. Sharp young minds keep flooding into law schools. But as D.C.-based Howrey discovered, Big Law is about to get small," by Paul M. Barrett, *Businessweek*

- "Fast growing. Litigation is becoming larger and larger, especially in the medical, accounting and technical fields."

Questions

- "What is their backlog? Customer concentration?"

Lawn Maintenance & Service (See also Landscaping Services)

SIC 0782-06	NAICS 561730	Number of Businesses/Units 39,000

Rules of Thumb

- ➢ 50 to 60 percent of annual sales plus inventory
- ➢ 2 to 2.75 times SDE plus inventory
- ➢ 1.7 to 3 times EBIT
- ➢ 2 to 4 times EBITDA

Rules of Thumb - L

Pricing Tips
- "Multiples vary based on several factors, with the most important being the percentage of recurring revenues. Lawn care (fertilization & weed control companies) and landscape maintenance companies receive higher multiples than construction-oriented businesses. Larger companies (lawn care companies with revenues in excess of $1 million and maintenance companies with revenues in excess of $2.5 million tend to get higher multiples. Companies with EBITDA margins in line with industry benchmarks will usually get a higher multiple."
- "The age and condition of the fleet of vehicles and equipment used in the business may negatively impact the valuation if a buyer would expect to need a high level of capital expenditures."
- "Companies with a larger working capital requirement (more money tied up in accounts receivable) may receive a lower valuation."
- "Install/enhancement revenue does count...it is repetitive in nature."
- "Pre billing or post billing of clients....pre bill is more valuable."
- "Depending on size, 2–4 times EBITDA for large company, could be higher"
- "The baseline multiple of SDE for commercial landscape maintenance businesses is typically between 2.5 and 3 plus inventory. The range of the multiple depends on the customer concentration, type of customer, quality of equipment and management in place. Landscape construction and residential landscape maintenance businesses have much lower value compared to commercial landscape businesses. I have found that financial buyers typically pay more than strategic buyers since they are buying their way into the industry. The real value in landscape service companies relates to the recurring nature of the revenue including both the monthly maintenance fees and extras that are derived from the monthly maintenance customers."
- "Larger companies = higher value. Equipment Fair Market Value should be added to gross sales and SDE multiplier formulas."

Expert Comments

"Recognize the importance of both residential and commercial to cash flows due to terms."

"Landscape maintenance companies are marketable since the industry has been impacted less compared to other businesses in the current economy. Their margins have been reduced, but businesses still need to maintain their properties."

"Generally difficult to finance because of lack of assets"

"Maintenance is fairly easy to learn."

"Easy entry, many small companies and large companies. Those that are professionally operated are successful."

Benchmark Data
- For additional Benchmark Data see Landscape Services
- "Many companies in this industry classify labor costs as a part of direct costs in calculating gross profit. Benchmark profit percentages are: maintenance companies 10-15%, lawn care (fertilization and weed control companies) 15-30%, construction (design-build companies) 10-20%."

L - Rules of Thumb

- "Enhancements can/should be around 20% of the gross service revenue annually. 2-man residential crew should max generate $150k annually."
- "Residential route can do up from $180,000 to $225,000 in revenue."
- "Labor 28% to 30% off season & 40% in season. Hourly labor rate commercial $30.00 per hour, specialty labor $45 to $55 for specialty (irrigation, fertilization, install)"
- "50% gross profit or more"
- "$75K per employee"

Expenses as a percentage of annual sales

Cost of goods	20% to 45%
Payroll/labor Costs	35% to 45%
Occupancy	02% to 05%
Profit (estimated pretax)	10% to 15%

Industry Trend

- "The industry weathered the Great Recession better than many observers expected. Business is recovering nicely and is expected to continue to expand as the construction sector strengthens. A robust merger & acquisition market has developed and is expected to continue in the near future led by high profile private equity transactions involving the industry's largest participants."
- "Continued growth, low barrier of entry going to allow for small companies to enter the market...limited financing will keep the industry fragmented"
- "Continued pressure on gross profits due to customer budget issues, increasing fuel costs and workers comp rates."
- "More smaller companies, easy entry."

Seller Financing

- "Smaller companies are usually sold with substantial seller financing, but transactions involving $2–$3 million purchase prices are often financed with SBA loans."
- "Seller financing...guarantees arenot the norm despite the rumors otherwise"
- "Financing usually at the street value of the assets for 2 or 3 years"
- "25% to 50% seller financing over 5 years"

Questions

- "The most important question is why are you selling. Multiples are relatively low and so the pay off from a sale is often limited compared to the cash flow experienced owners can generate. As a result, it is very important to understand why an owner is selling and is it a good reason."
- "What is your monthly service revenue? What types of properties do you do? (Residential or Commercial) What type of grass (blue, zosia, augustine, bahaia)? How many people in your crews? How many stops a day are they doing? Does your price per property include trimming, trees and shrubs (which drive labor)?"
- "Do they pre-bill or post bill service? Is service billed monthly with cuts of 42 per year? What is the mix of service by commercial and residential? Density of the routes drives fuel and therefore labor and fuel consumption."
- "What % of revenue is maintenance versus new construction? Maintenance has much more value. What is the % of revenue from commercial maintenance versus residential maintenance? Commercial maintenance has more value. What is the customer concentration? Who maintains the relationships with the

customers? What is the quality and maintenance history on the vehicles and equipment?"
- "What is the turnover of customers? How much business is the owner responsible for?"
- "What is your customer concentration? Who manages the customer accounts? Who holds the contractor's license? Will key employees agree to stay?"

Resources

Websites
- Lawn & Landscape: www.lawnandlandscape.com

Trade Publications
- Lawn and Landscape magazine: www.lawnandlandscape.com
- Landscape Management magazine: www.landscapemanagement.net
- Turf Magazine: www.turfmagazine.com

Associations
- National Association of Landscape Professionals: www.landscapeprofessionals.org
- AmericanHort: www.americanhort.org

	Franchise
Lenny's Subs (See also Franchises, Sandwich Shops)	
Approx. Total Investment	$216,500 to $369,000
SIC 5812-06 NAICS 722513	Number of Businesses/Units 152

Rules of Thumb
➤ 15 to 20 percent of annual sales plus inventory

Resources

Websites
- www.lennys.com

	Franchise
Liberty Tax Service (See also Accounting/Firms/Tax Practices, Franchises)	
Approx. Total Investment	$57,800 to $71,900
NAICS 541213	Number of Businesses/Units 4,500

Rules of Thumb
➤ 45 to 50 percent of annual sales plus inventory

Resources

Websites
- www.libertytaxfranchise.com

L - Rules of Thumb

Franchise
Li'l Dino Subs (See also Franchises, Sandwich Shops)

Approx. Total Investment	$47,400 to $240,800
NAICS 722513	Number of Businesses/Units 15

Rules of Thumb
➢ 64 percent of annual sales plus inventory

Pricing Tips
- "One sold for 80 percent of sales, but it was located in an office building with vending rights."

Benchmark Data
- For Benchmark Data see Sandwich Shops

Limousine Services (See also Ground Transportation, Taxicab Businesses)		
SIC 4119-03	NAICS 485320	Number of Businesses/Units 137,306

Rules of Thumb
➢ 50 to 55 percent of annual revenues plus vehicles

➢ 2 to 2.5 times SDE plus vehicles

➢ 4 times EBITDA—companies with corporate accounts under contract plus vehicles.

➢ 3 times EBITDA plus vehicles

Pricing Tips
- "You need to look at Owner's Discretionary Cash Flow (also known as Seller's Discretionary Earnings). You also need to know whether the limousines are owned outright, financed or leased. Depreciation expense becomes an important consideration because the owned vehicles wear down rapidly and must be replaced to keep the business looking 'up to date.'"
- "A profitable business should net 15% to 20% because the margins are high."
- "The figure needs to be adjusted for the fair market value of the vehicles less the outstanding debt."
- Note: Depreciation is usually considered an "add-back" and is therefore part of the Seller's Discretionary Earnings/EBIT/EBITDA. However, in this type of business it should not be added back as it is a necessary business expense. Vehicles are the mainstay of the business and replacement is ongoing business.

Expert Comments
"No real barriers to entry. It is easy to finance vehicles and create a website."

"Any person can get started by buying one vehicle and building from there."

Rules of Thumb - L

Benchmark Data

- "Most respondents, 55%, were small fleet operators (1–10 vehicles); followed by medium-sized fleets 32% (11–50 vehicles); and large fleets, 13% (51-plus vehicles).
- "The average operator/limousine company gross profit margin in 2014 was 20.7%, up from an average of 18.7% in 2013, an average of 16.7% in 2012 and 10% in 2011."

Source: 2015-2016 LCT Fact Book

- Note: See Taxicab Businesses for additional Benchmark Data

Expenses as a percentage of annual sales

Cost of goods	30% to 35% (Auto Purchases)
Payroll/labor Costs	25% to 35%
Occupancy	05% to 10%
Profit (estimated pretax)	10% to 20%

Industry Trend

- "The bill would require that all drivers for (Transportation Network Companies) TNC's, such as Uber and Lyft, undergo a background check and maintain levels of insurance on an equitable basis to what is required of the taxi and livery industry. These provisions are at the heart of the debate. A lower standard on background checks creates a public safety issue for passengers. Maintaining lower levels of insurance and regulation for Uber and Lyft creates an inequity in the cost of doing business, and thus a competitive disadvantage for the taxi and livery industry."

Source: "Boston Legislation Seeks to Regulate TNCs" by Tom Halligan 7/22/15 http://www.lctmag.com/regulations/news/294876/boston-legislation-seeks-to-regulate-tncs

- "The number of new limousine companies entering the industry has been growing, but the number of mergers and acquisitions among established companies has risen as well. The estimated gross limousine industry revenue in 2014 is $3.3 billion, up 11.5% from 2013."

Source: 2015-2016 LCT Fact Book

- ". . . estimates that iPads save the company up to 8% on annual fuel costs and up to 25% savings in paper costs. It also reduces chauffeur phone calls to operations by 20%. Moreover, there are many benefits that can't be tied to hard dollars, but operators know from feedback and observation that iPads are spurring better customer service, customer relations, and most importantly, customer satisfaction."

Source: "Touch & Go: Tablet Access Speeds Up Operations," www.lctmag.com/technology/article/107388

Seller Financing

- "Seller should expect 50% down and offer 10-year amortization with a 3-year balloon at 6% interest."

Questions

- "You will want to see the repair and maintenance records for all the vehicles. You will want to know if there have been any accidents. You will want to know if there is outstanding litigation or workmen's compensation issues. What background checks and drug tests are performed on new hires?"
- "Look at the maintenance logs; have a mechanic check all vehicles."

26th Edition

L - Rules of Thumb

Resources

Trade Publications
- Limousine, Charter, and Tour: www.lctmag.com

Associations
- National Limousine Association—a lot of excellent information, with a study for members only: www.limo.org

Liquefied Petroleum Gas (Propane)

SIC 5984-01	NAICS 454312	Number of Businesses/Units 1,700

Rules of Thumb
- 130 percent of annual sales plus inventory
- 3 to 4 times SDE plus inventory
- 4 times EBIT
- 6 times EBITDA (Good double-check is 2.5 to 3.5 gross profit)

Pricing Tips
- "EBITDA multiples can range from 3.5 to over 7.0 X, depending on the specific characteristics of the company being sold; there are many variables to consider; multiple does not include inventory or A/Recs."
- "High % of company-owned tanks in the field, automatic delivery, high gross margin per gallon are all important factors in determining value."
- "Multiple of gallons 1–2X; multiple of gross margin 1–2.5X; add value .for high number of company- owned lease tanks, relatively new trucks (less than 5 years), high percentage of residential accounts, backup management and infrastructure, current safety programs, current equipment/storage controls."

Expert Comments

"Large amount of capital needed for infrastructure & equipment, as well as for trucks and tanks; seasonal sales volume affects working capital requirements, depending on time of year."

"Hire a professional intermediary who has extensive experience in the propane industry as offers for these types of businesses vary widely."

"Supply displacements during peak winter season; high level of technical expertise required to safely install tanks and equipment; CDL requirements"

"Capital-intensive business; desirable alternative clean-burning fuel; larger national companies are aggressively looking for acquisition opportunities."

"Even though the barriers to entry are increasing, smaller companies' marketability is decreasing."

"The propane industry is very capital intensive in that most companies want to own and control the tanks at customer locations. For this reason, the business is difficult to enter. Price spikes and supply displacements are also issues during the peak winter months. There is a high level of technical expertise needed to install and service propane equipment. Drivers and technicians must pass rigorous training programs and DOT requirements."

"Extremely mature industry with little innovation"

Benchmark Data
- "COGs and GP margins vary greatly from company to company, area by area; as such there is no real average. GP can vary from $ 0.35 cents per gallon sold to well over $2.00 per gallon, depending on many factors. Net Income and EBITDA amounts and percentages can also vary greatly."
- "Gross profit per gallon is a key factor. Average gp/gallon should now be exceeding $1.00/gallon in most areas."
- "The business is a delivery business, so the more efficient the delivery, aka gallons per bobtail, the higher the profit."
- "EBITDA per gallon greater than $0.15"
- "Can vary considerably by company, depending on customer mix between residential, commercial, farm & industrial type customer."

Expenses as a percentage of annual sales	
Cost of goods	40% to 50%
Payroll/labor Costs	15% to 25%
Occupancy	02% to 05%
Profit (estimated pretax)	15%

Industry Trend
- "Tougher competition from natural gas, especially since natural gas pricing has gotten so much cheaper and more natural gas lines are being built."
- "Slow growth as customers shift away from heating oil in rural areas. Some upside potential in Autogas applications, particularly for fleets."
- "EIA's estimate for winter energy expenditures for homes heating with propane in the Midwest is $2212, which is $759 higher than projected in October 2013. The estimate for average U.S. expenditures for homes using fuel oil is $2243, $197 higher than forecast."
  > Source: Household Heating Expenditures Expected to Rise 54% Over Winter." www.bpnews.com
- "Slow but steady growth in most areas as people shift away from heating oil. Propane is a viable clean-burning alternative fuel choice with many advantages over other fuels."

Seller Financing
- "100% all cash transactions typically (except for Invent & A/Recs which are paid within 90–180 days typically); non-compete allocations vary somewhat and these payments are sometimes tied to a payout period of 3–5 years"
- "Typically uses outside financing"
- "Typically cash at closing for fixed assets; intangibles are sometimes financed over five years."
- "Five years"

Questions
- "5 years' financials and gallonage history; gross profit per gallon by segment of business; complete list of assets including tank inventory, bulk plants, trucks, etc.; real estate appraisal."

L - Rules of Thumb

- "Customer concentration, competition, age of fleet, tenure/age of employees, reason for exit"
- "Company ownership of customer tanks & cylinders is an important consideration. Where the company owns most of the customer field equipment, and there are good gross profits, a much better value can be obtained."
- "Lease tank coverage, age of equipment, age and volume of bulk storage, type of customer base."

Resources

Websites
- Propane Education & Research Council: www.propanecouncil.org

Trade Publications
- LP Gas Magazine: www.lpgasmagazine.com
- Butane/Propane News (BPN): www.bpnews.com
- Propane Canada: www.northernstar.ab.ca

Associations
- PERC—Propane Education & Research Council: www.propanecouncil.org
- National Propane Gas Association: www.npga.org

Liquor Stores/Package Stores (Beer, Wine & Liquor Stores)

SIC 5921-02	NAICS 445310	Number of Businesses/Units 45,984

Rules of Thumb
- ➢ 35 to 45 percent of annual sales plus inventory
- ➢ 2 to 3 times SDE plus inventory
- ➢ 2.5 to 3.5 times EBITDA
- ➢ 3 times EBIT

Pricing Tips
- "Old inventory or lack of long, reasonable lease creates an un-marketable store."
- "The % to gross is between 40–50% depending on factors such as rent, payroll, gross profit. SDE will fluctuate as well between 2.5–3.25%."
- "Retail sales are more profitable and will drive a better selling price than wholesale sales."
- "Competition in area, employee benefits, hours of operation."
- "Location, rent, and payroll expense will be the first questions asked. Gross profit is right behind them. Be prepared."
- "Number of active licenses in town. Size and appearance of stores compared to competition. Lease terms, renewal clauses, options to buy. Lottery income."
- "This type of business sells for higher multiples in states where they restrict the number of licenses per town, such as in Massachusetts. In these areas large stores with over $1 million in sales may sell for as much as 45% of sales or 4X SDE."
- "Liquor stores will often sell for a price equivalent to 6 months' worth of sales."
- "As always, watch for high lease rates as a percentage of sales. Overall lease

rates in excess of 8% depress multiples and pricing, all other factors being equal."

- "Depending on fixed overhead expenses, to include the percentage of rent to gross sales, a formula of 3–5 times monthly sales will also be considered. Generally we take 3–5 of the formulas used and average them based on gross sales, cost of rent, current margins, and break even point for an owner operator, or investor."
- "I generally use 2–3 times SDC plus inventory plus any add-backs."
- "I use 2 times SDE plus inventory at cost. Often times the price is 1 times SDE if there has been a decline in sales."
- "Pay close attention to inventory amount, turns, owner operated or use of employees, rent cost as a percentage of gross sales, margins on gross sales. 25%–28% will be closer to a true value. These areas listed will create various ranges when they are higher or lower than good working averages. Inventory should allow for 9–10 turns per year. Occupancy cost/sales should be no more than 7%–8% using the above ratios and multipliers."
- "Is store high volume because of lower margins? What percentage of store is fine wine? Is this percentage growing? Are there any other package goods licenses available in town? What is the town's position on awarding malt beverage and beer licenses? Is store on right-hand side of road heading home?"
- "7 to 9 months of sales plus inventory is a general rule of thumb for a liquor store."
- "Total Gross sales, minus all expenses, add back owner's salary and any personal expenses paid for by the business=Seller's Discretionary Cash flow. Take that figure and start with a 2 multiple for a small store and increase in .25 increments for strong lease, increasing sales, high wine sales."

Expert Comments

"Must purchase existing store in New Jersey. Location key factors and historical trends of store."

"Work with the seller to verify sales. Pay attention to details; do not try to reinvent the wheel."

"Inexperienced operators quickly realize the tight margins and long hours. Those without retail experience and or industry knowledge should keep an industry consultant close by. Stores with $2M–$3M revenue are highly in demand. Maryland is a three-tier system allowing for individual ownership of licenses, allowing for stiff competition. It appears in Maryland everyone wants to own a liquor store."

"Location is very important, for the businesses success. In addition, multiple locations, allowing for larger case quantity purchases, will provide a better pricing and profit model for an owner. Thus, a buyer should provide for ongoing working capital to operate the store in order to take advantage of quantity case pricing. This is important to the success and ongoing survival of the store, particularly if there is a large-volume store close by, which is viewed as a competitor. Margins are shrinking in the industry at both the retail and wholesale levels. Hence, many small stores are struggling to survive, due to their occupancy cost being high, in relation to both their sales and margins. The lower margins drive the cost of occupancy up, which cannot be adjusted, when the owner is locked into a specific lease period. Hence, we are seeing many small operators, at best, buying a job. When they get into the business, they overlook the need for additional working

L - Rules of Thumb

capital and potential negative cash flow for an extended period of time, when starting a store, from 'scratch'".

"Liquor stores with annual revenue of $1.5M and above are very much in demand."

"Liquor stores are controlled in that locations are limited. Any store must have $200,000 in inventory to be very successful and to take advantage of distributor discounts on large purchases."

"Liquor laws vary state to state and have a great bearing on competition, barrier to entry, marketability and profit trend. Colorado retailers, as an example, are facing legislative battles to stop grocery chains and convenience stores from selling full-strength beer and wine. Distributors are pressuring for changes to how sales tax is collected. Government in general is looking for ways to increase revenue through taxation changes. Conversely, liquor stores are perceived as recession resistant and therefore popular targets of acquisition. The public is more focused on a good shopping experience in stores. Customer service, presentation and cleanliness matter more now than ever before. SBA lending is difficult to find even for profitable stores."

"Ease of Replication—In most cases, creating a new liquor store is very hard. Unless someone has a license or can obtain an existing one, it is impossible to open a liquor store. Competition, for this reason, is not a major factor. Since the competitive set is already in place, potential buyers already know who they are up against."

"Wine stores have a higher percentage of gross profit margin. Growing stores with great leases tend to sell for more money."

Benchmark Data

Statistics (Beer, Wine & Liquor Stores)

Number of Establishments	45,984
Average Profit Margin	2.4%
Revenue per Employee	$287,600
Average Number of Employees	3.7
Average Wages per Employee	$20,861

Products and Services Segmentation

Distilled spirits, brandies and liqueurs	39.0%
Wine	27.9%
Beer	22.8%
Tobacco and smoking accessories	7.6%
Other	2.7%

Industry Costs

Profit	2.4%
Wages	7.2%
Purchases	75.1%
Depreciation	0.7%
Marketing	0.8%
Rent & Utilities	4.5%
Other	9.3%

Source: IBISWorld, July 2015

Rules of Thumb - L

- "Rental amount biggest factor in success. Can not exceed 7 percent of gross sales. Store will not be profitable at or above that level."

Percent of Total Sales Tendered by Liquor Stores

Spirits and Liquors	40%
Beer	30%
Groceries, Cigarettes, Cigars	25%
*The answers to the above are represented as a % of gross.	
Payroll Staff	7%
Occupancy Expense	3–7%
Cost of goods	75%

- Profit includes many variables so not easy to determine"
- "Gross margins on retail sales should be at least 25%"
- "Rental is a key component of the business. If the rent is too high a percentage of Gross Sales, business will not thrive."
- "Typical employee expense is still 7% of revenue. This does not include owner compensation. Occupancy expense has been historically 3–6%, but I am seeing rents above that in shopping centers (7–8.2%). In order to show profitability with higher rent expense you must have gross profit upwards of 25% and revenue of upwards of $2M."
- "Typical net from a liquor store is 10–15% for a working owner. Rent and margins can greatly affect this figure though."
- "Product costs should not exceed 80%, based on purchase, or sales volume. Smaller locations should keep product costs no more than 72–75%. Occupancy costs are very critical to the operation, as well as the location."
- "Gross Profit 25%–30%, occupancy expense 7%–8%, payroll not to exceed 7%, wine sales making up of at least 40% of revenue and stores between 5,000–10,000 square feet."
- "$250 per square foot annually"
- "$300,000–$500,000 per year gross sales, for an 1800–2400 square foot space."
- "Successful stores are showing a GPM of 25% or better. Those stores are typically focusing on wine sales where margins are higher."
- "Occupancy costs must remain within 7% for a successful operation."
- "Benchmarks: Location to populated neighborhoods, gross margins of 25% or better. 1–2 part time employees, owner operator, unless 3 units are owned by same owner."
- "Blended margins can be confusing without understanding product mix and demographics. POS systems [Point of Sale] a real pain with constant price changes but discourages employee theft."
- "Normal product mix in sales is 60% liquor and 40% wine."
- "Turn inventory 9 to 10 times a year."
- "3,500 sq. ft., ample parking, easy in and out, free-standing building, prefer basement and/or extra storage, some food items, buying co-op with regular ads, pricing"
- "The typical store grosses about $350,000/year. Overall gross profit margins in liquor stores generally are between 21 to 24 percent, the exceptions being very large (over $1,000,000/year) discount stores that operate on lower margins—and wine specialty stores."

Expenses as a percentage of annual sales

Cost of goods	65 to 80%
Payroll/labor Costs	05% to 12%
Occupancy	05% to 15%
Profit (estimated pretax)	08% to 15%

26th Edition

L - Rules of Thumb

Industry Trend
- "Bad financial times equal more liquor store sales."
- "I expect the marketability to remain consistent, although multiple licensing bills in Maryland has made proprietors uneasy."
- "Some consolidation expected as larger stores are built to combat nationals like TotalWine."
- "Growing, more wine sales and specialty stores."
- "More liquor store owners owning multiple stores versus one store/one owner. Families and chain stores are aggressively purchasing liquor stores."
- "The market will remain to have high demand, primarily for stores with revenue of $1 million+."

Seller Financing
- "Inventory cash at closing $ for $ at cost. Business 1/3 to 1/2 down short term feller financing only way to sell."
- "After 2008 seller financing was the only source, but within the last two years SBA has become more flexible."
- "Seller financing is the best option."
- "7 to 10 years at 2 over prime"
- "Many stores can be bank financed but sometimes the seller will finance the inventory for 1 year."
- "5 years on business, 30 to 120 days on inventory"
- "I would suggest that the buyer pay 100% of the inventory cost plus put 50% down for the business. The seller can offer 6%, ten-year amortization with a three-year balloon."

Questions
- "Review the sales and expenses over a two or three year period. See what trends are, up or down. Is theft a problem? Most sellers are either burnt out or not making money."
- "Rent expense, payroll, gross profit, category mix of gross and length of lease term?"
- "Seller—true margins, sales trends and mix; buyer—any experience in industry, reason for purchasing "
- "What are your margins, what is are product percentages (beer/wine/liquor), what are your lottery commissions, what is your rent, how many hours do you work, what is the competition in your area"
- "How long in business. Any deliveries? Lottery yearly commission. Hours worked by seller or his or her family."
- "1. Lease terms and amount 2. Sales by year, for last 3 years 3. Margins and net profit. 4. Provide copies of all invoices and bank statements for a minimum of 2 years. 5. Will they be willing to owner finance a portion of the sale price. 6. Will they allow you to view the closing of the store each day, with regards to their bookkeeping, for 1–2 weeks. 7. Why are they selling the business. 8. What would they do to grow the business. 9. What 2 things do they not like about the business and how would they fix them, if they had the time and money. 10. How much time of a training period will the seller provide and would they be available, by phone, for additional support, up to one year, at an agreed upon day and time."

Rules of Thumb - L

- "Blend of merchandise sales by wine, liquor and beer and by size of units sold. Special deals they receive from distributors. Under the table labor and vendors. Is there a co-op to buy at best price?"
- "Closest competition, term of lease, payroll cost, how computer system controls inventory and ordering. Do they work on margins or markup? How do store margins compare to any stores within 2–3 miles? How did they arrive at selling price? How would they grow the business, and how long will they provide training and distance for a covenant not to compete?"
- "Is there an option on the property or is it owned by the seller? What competition is nearby? Are there any other licenses available in the town? Do you owe any back taxes or fees that would hold up the transfer of the liquor license?"
- "What are your sales tax numbers and are you current?"
- "Lease rate, term, options, NNN cost, assignability, product mix percentages, margin overall and for each category, operating entity type, length of time in business, why selling, knowledge of competition, inventory control systems in place."
- "Security/surveillance system in place?Theft/shrinkage."
- "How often do you order from your distributors? What is your markup on beer, wine and liquor? What percentage of your sales are beer, wine, liquor and other?"
- "How much income was derived from buying smart? Additional sources of revenue, if any and amount? Request copies of sales tax reports from state, to verify the numbers represented. How many suppliers are used and terms available if any? Has there been or is there any liquor store in the process of being opened in the area? What type of terms will the landlord provide, for a long-term lease with options? Does it justify being opened each day at 9:00 a.m. vs. 10:00 a.m. and what have the sales trends, by day, been during that extra hour? Obtain a certificate of good standing, from the state, relative to all taxes being paid and current, particularly the sales taxes. How does the buyer figure margins, markup, gross profit and/or product cost? Much confusion among individuals relative to this topic."
- "Ask to review bank statements, sales tax reports and purchase invoices to confirm unreported cash sales."
- "Rent, cost of goods sold, payroll, lottery commissions, inventory ordering, are they on POS?"
- "Why are they selling? Days and hours they work? Margins? Payroll paid off books? Case vs. broken-case pricing and what percentage of business is broken-case purchases? Cost of broken-case purchasing? Is this cost calculated before or after establishing margin on product sold? Also, any taxes paid on product purchases and are they, too, calculated before calculating margins or added on after this formula?"
- "Does the store cash checks? Does the store have lottery? Does the store sell fine wines? If so, it has higher margins. Is it a discount store? Does it sell lots of half-pints?"

Resources

Associations
- National Alcoholic Beverage Control Association: www.nabca.org

L - Rules of Thumb

Franchise
Little Caesars Pizza (See also Franchises, Pizza Shops)

Approx. Total Investment	$265,000 to $681,500
Estimated Annual Sales/Unit	$830,000
NAICS 722513	Number of Businesses/Units 3,900

Rules of Thumb
> 55 percent of annual sales plus inventory

Resources
Websites
- www.littlecaesars.com

Lock & Key Shops		
SIC 7699-62	NAICS 561622	Number of Businesses/Units 21,165

Rules of Thumb
> 40 to 45 percent of annual sales plus inventory

Benchmark Data

Statistics (Locksmiths)

Number of Establishments	21,165
Average Profit Margin	4.3%
Revenue per Employee	$56,700
Average Number of Employees	1.5
Average Wages per Employee	$19,268

Products and Services Segmentation

Nonresidential security system installation and repair	51.4%
Residential security system installation and repair	23.4%
Key cutting and duplication services	8.6%
Resale of locks and security merchandise	8.3%
Other services	4.4%
Residential and nonresidential system services with monitoring	3.9%

Major Market Segmentation

Businesses	52.7%
Households	30.6%
Government entities	10.9%
Not-for-profit organizations	5.8%

Industry Costs

Profit	4.3%
Wages	33.9%
Purchases	35.2%
Depreciation	1.6%
Marketing	2.9%
Rent & Utilities	5.0%
Other	17.1%

Source: IBISWorld, August 2015

Rules of Thumb - **L**

Resources

Associations
- Institutional Locksmiths' Association: www.ilanational.org
- Associated Locksmiths of America: www.aloa.org

Logan Farms Honey Glazed Hams (See also Franchises)	Franchise
Approx. Total Investment	$338,475 to $418,125
NAICS 445210	Number of Businesses/Units 11

Rules of Thumb
- ➢ 30 percent of annual sales plus inventory

Resources

Websites
- www.loganfarms.com

Lumberyards (See also Building Materials/Home Centers)	
SIC 5211-42 NAICS 444190	Number of Businesses/Units 52,025

Rules of Thumb
- ➢ 40 percent of annual sales includes inventory
- ➢ 4 to 6 times SDE includes inventory
- ➢ 4 times EBIT
- ➢ 4 to 6 times EBITDA

Pricing Tips
- "These comments would apply to lumberyards dealing with contractors, sometimes called 'ProYards,' not home centers (DIY business) . . . if profits (EBT) are 5%–10% of sales, the business would likely sell for 1.5 times book value; less profitable lumberyards sell for book value, or in an asset sale. In an asset sale, if profits are above 5% EBT, use lesser of cost or market on the inventory and FMV on equipment and real estate used in the business, plus one year's EBT for goodwill/non-compete."
- "The major buyers were offering to pay for the best yards 5.5 x EBITDA"
- "There are several types of lumberyards: the publicly traded 'big box' Home Depot, Lowe's types, whose value is daily shown on the NYSE; and the more prevalent independently owned 'Pro' type lumberyard, usually in or close to a metro area with sales in excess of $5 million, that has as its customers primarily professional contractors (most new-home builders), remodel/repair contractors, and commercial/industrial customers. These Pro yards have a minimum of 80% of their business with professionals and a maximum of 20% with DIYers. The smaller town lumberyards generally serve DIYers (60%) and Pro accounts (40%). The demand for lumberyards since 2006 has diminished

L - Rules of Thumb

to now be almost nonexistent. With the housing 'meltdown' and poor economy, there is little interest in a capital-intensive business with a large, expensive, slow-turning inventory, expensive equipment and large accounts receivable. The value of a lumberyard has also changed drastically. It used to be, prior to 2006, that a good, profitable Pro type lumberyard would bring 1.5 times its book value, or from 5–6 times EBIT. Now a good lumberyard, if still profitable, would likely sell for its book value and, maybe even less, its liquidation value. Even a strategic acquisition may bring only these prices. I do not see anything on the horizon that would restore higher prices for these businesses. Home Depot and Lowe's are selling for about 50% to 60% of their highs of 2005–2006 so they too are showing signs of the tough economy."

Expert Comments

"Lumberyards are very difficult to duplicate. High dollar investment keeps most competition out of a market. It also requires a minimum of 2 acres to runs a $5 million lumberyard. Cost of land these days makes it impossible to start a new store. Most stores have been in existence for decades and have a very low cost basis on the facilities."

Benchmark Data

Statistics (Lumber & Building Material Stores)

Number of Establishments	52,025
Average Profit Margin	3.2%
Revenue per Employee	$460,100
Average Number of Employees	5.0
Average Wages per Employee	$41,596

Products and Services Segmentation

Lumber and other structural building materials	55.4%
Hardware, tools, plumbing and electrical supplies	22.1%
Doors and windows	9.9%
Flooring and roofing materials	8.4%
Other	4.2%

Major Market Segmentation

Professional Contractors	60.0%
Do-it-for-me customers	20.0%
Do-it-yourself customers	10.0%
Other	10.0%

Industry Costs

Profit	3.2%
Wages	9.4%
Purchases	60.5%
Depreciation	1.0%
Marketing	1.6%
Rent & Utilities	4.0%
Other	20.3%

Source: IBISWorld, April 2015

Rules of Thumb - M

- "Stores with 60% hardware and 40% lumber are considered home centers. If sales are 60% lumber or more and 40% hardware, it is a lumberyard. Lumberyards earn 20–23% margin on lumber compared to 23–26% for homecenters. Lumberyards have very high levels of accounts receivable (60–80% of monthly sales). When housing starts are in decline, contractors are slow to pay their bills. Lumberyards will see their receivables jump from 30–45 day turnover to 50–60 day. That can add $200,000 to receivables very quickly and kill any cash flow the lumberyard has. Bad debt write-offs can quickly run into the tens of thousands of dollars. Lumberyard owner should have an unused line of credit equal to 50% of monthly sales. This will allow him to weather receivable increases, winter sales declines and so on."
- "Sales per employee vary from $200,000 to $400,000."
- "Sales typically are over $500 per square foot and $300,000 per employee for lumberyards with retail space of more than 8,000 sq. ft."

Expenses as a percentage of annual sales	
Cost of goods	75%
Payroll/labor Costs	20%
Occupancy	03% to 05%
Profit (estimated pretax)	02% to 05%

Seller Financing
- "Very few sell on owner financing; the sales are generally to existing lumber dealers."

Questions
- "Why selling? Have audited 5 years' financials?"
- "Look carefully at profit, and if future earnings are possible."

Resources

Associations
- National Lumber & Building Material Dealers Association: www.dealer.org

	Franchise
MAACO Auto Painting and Bodyworks (See also Franchises)	
Approx. Total Investment	$150,000 to $300,000
NAICS 811121	Number of Businesses/Units 457

Rules of Thumb
> 40 percent of annual sales plus inventory

Resources

Websites
- www.maacofranchise.com

M - Rules of Thumb

Machine Shops (See also Contract Manufacturing, Job Shops)

| SIC 3599-03 | NAICS 332710 | Number of Businesses/Units 20,096 |

Rules of Thumb
- 50 to 65 percent of annual revenues includes inventory
- 2 to 3 times SDE plus inventory
- 4.5 to 7 times EBIT
- 3 to 5 times EBITDA

Pricing Tips
- "Client concentration remains an issue. Deduct 1X for any concentration over 50%. Proprietary processes and expertise in working exotic metals/materials, add 1–2 X. ISO and other certifications along with lean processes, add 1X. Five axis CAPEX adds 1–2X. Important to examine the excess earnings approach when valuing a machine shop. Retrofit Bridgeports and other more labor intensive equipment, deduct 1–2X. In general, the larger the shop the higher the valuation multiples."
- "Some buyers want excess capacity, some buyers won't pay for it. Frequently you see a high percentage of sales with one or two customers look for contracts. Many short run or prototype shops do not have repeat business. Productions shops have contracts with a consistent flow of business. Quality certifications like ISO 9000 help the multiple. It means they have processes and controls in place. Look at tenure of machinist. Skilled machinists are hard to find."
- "Unique industry relative to valuation. Capital asset base, CAPEX, client concentration, value add services and industries served all contribute to fluctuations in value. Medical and aerospace concentration bringing highest multiples. EBITDA under $1M values 3–5X. Over $2M, 4–7X. Inventory typically included in working capital."
- "EBITDA under $1M will generate lower multiples while anything over $2M will generate 4–6X. CAPEX requirements and working capital may adjust price commensurately."
- "4–5 times SDE on a machine shop with sales trending in a positive direction"
- "Multiple of SDE seems to be a good starting point, backlog, AR, WIP; diversification boosts asking price."
- "WIP is extremely important as are raw materials. Certifications are becoming very important for strategic buyers."
- "Machine condition and level of technology are significant influences."
- "Wide range of customers a plus. Certifications extremely important most times."
- "Many are good solid businesses; important to remember work in progress when negotiating the transaction."
- "Backlog, client concentration, WIP, CAPEX, line-item expense for repairs & maintenance, availability of qualified labor, client industry trends, etc. are all issues a potential buyer should investigate in valuing a shop."
- "Short-run shops having design capabilities and doing prototyping may demand a premium. Different geographical areas will have varying availability of qualified machinists. Look for stable work force that is not near retirement.

Rules of Thumb - **M**

Be sensitive to difference between a machinist and a 'CNC machine operator.' Backlog, client concentration and industry(s) served can also have large effects on valuation."
- "Strategic buyers tend to look for excess capacity."
- "Short-run prototyping shops concentrating in the medical industry tend to sell for higher multiples."
- "Look for customer concentration. Determine sales mix between commercial and military/defense contractors. Age and type of equipment will affect valuation. Production capacity is important."

Expert Comments

"Barrier to entry becoming higher as cost of high tech equipment increases and good programmers less abundant. OEM's are experiencing slightly better growth and accordingly machine shop's backlogs are increasing. Gross income per employee should be in the $200K per range. Does the shop do a lot of prototyping/short runs or is it more of a mid to long run shop? Cost savings realized from longer runs."

"Get involved with an industry association. Meet other owners. Stay abreast of new technology. Have equipment checked out as part of due diligence. Find out about quality issues with major customers. Focus on the retention of employees after the transaction is completed."

"Competition is dependent on capabilities. Niche marketing is common. Risk is high because of CAPEX. The industry is seeing a resurgence with the improving economy and 'some' products being re-shored. This has been a tough industry but on the mend. Profitability is up. Ease of replication is hard because of cost of equipment and the quality standards that many customers now require."

"Backlogs are on the rise but net sales still relatively flat—off approximately 2% in 2012. Private equity investing more heavily in this space with roll-ups. Cost of new 4 and 5 axis machining centers increases barrier to entry. While the northeastern U.S. has its share, more machine shops in South and Midwest."

"Close attention should be paid to run rates per hour on machinery. Rent & labor will be split above and below COGS line. Percentages listed assume direct labor in COGS and admin; labor below the line."

"Industry requires significant capital expenditures. Sales tied closely to demand from OEMs."

"It's not an easy business these days. On-time work that is high in quality is very important."

"Many small (<$1,000,000) machine shops grow dependent on 1–3 customers or industry single."

"A tough economy makes it a tough climate for many. Those with aerospace contracts do pretty well and seem to hold their own."

"CAPEX represents a large barrier to entry in today's robotic world. OEMs fuel the industry to a large extent. Proprietary processes can add value."

M - Rules of Thumb

"Revenues and profitability are trending upwards in northeast U.S. Barrier to entry high with well-equipped shops, low with antiquated equipment like retrofit CNC Bridgeports, etc. Abundance of bankers searching for businesses has grown demand as their background of lending to mfg. makes this industry 'seem' a fit. Risk of high client concentration always a concern with contract manufacturing."

"Need to be $10 million shop to get good buyers"

Benchmark Data

Statistics (Machine Shops)
Number of Establishments	20,096
Average Profit Margin	7.9%
Revenue per Employee	$187,400
Average Number of Employees	13.2
Average Wages per Employee	$51,389

Products and Services Segmentation
Milling	41.3%
Turning	24.4%
Other	20.0%
Grinding	9.3%
EDM and ECM	5.0%

Major Market Segmentation
Other markets	30.0%
Heavy machinery, automotive and off-highway vehicle markets	27.6%
Defense markets	16.0%
Commercial airline markets	14.9%
Medical markets	11.5%

Industry Costs
Profit	7.9%
Wages	27.7%
Purchases	33.9%
Depreciation	3.9%
Marketing	0.8%
Rent & Utilities	3.8%
Other	22.0%

Source: IBISWorld, June 2015

- "Watch for inconsistencies in reporting of COGS, i.e., is all occupancy under the line? Is only production labor in COGS? Is inventory accurately represented? Total inventory value of raw material, WIP and finished goods should be 10–15%. Average growth last 5 yrs. has been 5–6%; watch for inconsistencies."
- "$100,000 sales/employee/year"
- "Geographic location is important to buyers since machinery is expensive to move."
- "Many shops like to get X dollars per hour per machine and then work towards 70%–80% capacity per machine or better."
- "There are no major players in this industry."

Expenses as a percentage of annual sales

Cost of goods	50% to 60%
Payroll/labor Costs	30% to 35%
Occupancy	03% to 07%
Profit (estimated pretax)	05% to 15%

Industry Trend
- "Industry indications are growth through 2020."
- "'In large part, the decline in manufacturing technology orders is due to smaller manufacturers feeling a sense of economic uncertainty and therefore hesitant to make any kind of capital investment,' said AMT President Douglas K. Woods. 'In addition, the energy industry has curbed its spending, accounting for about half of the year-to-date decline in orders, and aerospace did not perform as well as expected in the first quarter. We expect the downturn to ease thanks to strong performance in the automotive and medical industries, with industrial production and a stronger PMI also indicating resilience in manufacturing.'"

  Source: 7/13/15 by Bonnie Gurney http://www.amtonline.org/newsroom/AMTPressRoom/july132015usmtonewsreleaseformaymanusmtonewsreleaseformaymanu.htm

- "I see pockets of this industry doing very well and improving. There is some re-shoring going on where companies that moved their products to China (for example) are finding out the lead times and rising costs are not as lucrative as it once was."
- "As small shops leave the market, there will be opportunities for the medium to large shops."

Seller Financing
- "Typically bank financed with reserves for earnout if there exists significant client concentration"
- "Generally it is a blend of seller financing and outside financing unless the business is asset heavy."
- "Only small shops typically seller financed. Averages vary. Most deals SBA 7(a) 10 yrs. at P + 1–2.5 pts."

Questions
- "Backlog, client concentration, CAPEX, aging of receivables, organized labor, profit margins per category of equipment."
- "Any equipment need to be replaced, account concentration issues are very important to be informed of."
- "Personal salary & benefits, any unutilized or underutilized assets"
- "Will the owner stay on and will they finance, most important. Backlog and contracts also critical."
- "Historical trends and future client relationships.Machinery obsolescence, etc."

Resources

Associations
- Fabricators and Manufacturers Association, International: www.fmanet.org
- The Association for Manufacturing Technology: www.amtonline.org
- Precision Machine Products Association: www.PMPA.org

M - Rules of Thumb

MaggieMoo's Ice Cream and Treatery		Franchise
(See also Franchises, Ice Cream/Yogurt Shops)		
Approx. Total Investment		$225,000 to $375,000
Estimated Annual Sales/Unit		$200,000
SIC 2024-98	NAICS 722515	Number of Businesses/Units 159
Rules of Thumb		
➢ 25 percent of annual sales plus inventory		

Resources

Websites
- www.maggiemoos.com

Maid Brigade (See also Franchises, Janitorial Services, Molly Maid)		Franchise
Approx. Total Investment		$52,500
	NAICS 561720	Number of Businesses/Units 420
Rules of Thumb		
➢ 45 percent of annual sales		

Resources

Websites
- www.maidbrigadefranchise.com

Maid Services (See also Janitorial Services, Maid Brigade, Molly Maid, etc.)	
NAICS 561720	
Rules of Thumb	
➢ 35 to 40 percent of annual sales plus inventory	
➢ 1.5 times SDE plus inventory	

Benchmark Data

For Benchmark Data see Janitorial Services
- "The Growing Residential and Commercial Cleaning Industry—The residential and commercial cleaning industry is a $94 billion market comprised of 500,000 companies, employing hundreds of thousands in labor force. The industry has enjoyed a 5.5% annual growth rate over the past five years and is projected to grow at a similar or greater rate over the next ten years.

  "Despite its extraordinary size and growth, the cleaning industry is largely dominated by family-owned, mom and pop operators. Over 80% of the cleaning services sector is comprised of small, family-owned business units that operate without a comprehensive set of standards and regulations.

"According to Marketdata Enterprises, a research and analysis firm focused on the services sector, an average cleaning company employs five or less employees and grosses under $150,000 in annual revenue. The cleaning business is a 'low tech' business characterized by ease of entry. An individual cleaning company can be started with as little as $1000 in capital and be in operation a few days later. As such, most of the operators lack the necessary knowledge, experience and training to deliver a professional standard of service.

"According to Marketdata Enterprises, the cleaning services sector has one of the highest customer loss rates, running as high as 45 percent per year. This translates into one of every two customers changing their cleaning provider at least once per year. Some studies indicate that more than 60 percent of building managers are not satisfied with their service provider. A recent survey conducted by the BSCAI Services Magazine identifies the 'low standard of quality' as the number one industry problem.

"One of the major reasons for the high customer dissatisfaction rate is the general lack of professionalism in the industry. The large majority of cleaning companies are small mom and pop" business units that lack the knowledge, training and experience demanded today. Frustrated with the low standard of quality, homeowners, renters, property management companies and commercial businesses are searching for a company that can offer them a service of uncompromising quality and professionalism."

Source: AW Cleaning Services, awcleaning.com.
Although this site is a bit self-serving for AW, it is very informative.

Mail and Parcel Centers (Business Centers)

SIC 7389

NAICS 561431	Number of Businesses/Units 28,206

Rules of Thumb

- 40 to 45 percent of annual sales includes inventory, less direct cost of goods sold (pass-throughs, e.g., stamps, money orders, UPS charges)
- 2 to 3 times SDE for national franchises includes inventory
- 2.75 times EBIT
- 2.5 to 3 times EBITDA

Pricing Tips

- "Those netting up to $40,000 sell at a 1 multiple. Those netting $50,000 to $60,000 sell for a 1.5 multiple of provable net income. From $70,000 to $85,000 of provable net, the multiple is usually 2. Those netting $90,000 and up, the multiple is usually 2.25 to 2.5."
- "Pre-paid mailbox rentals will need to be prorated and credited back to the buyer unless negotiated out. Either way—it will affect value. Pass-throughs don't count toward annual sales."

M - Rules of Thumb

- "Ratio of individual customers (only see them at Xmas) to business customers (regular, daily or weekly)."
- "The rental rate is very important to the valuation of mail and parcel centers. Some mail and parcel centers can be located off major streets because they are destination locations. Franchise businesses are usually worth more than independent stores because of name recognition, brand value. These businesses are appealing to people who want flexible hours and no night hours. Also, most stores are open only a few hours on Saturdays. Sales are usually fairly predictable for mature stores."
- "Since it is a generally low barrier to entry, an established store that has well passed the breakeven is the best situation. An owner operator in this industry can see near 30% SDE so long as fixed costs are not too damaging."
- "Desirable cities demand higher prices because box rental customers will pay more."
- "Franchises will sell for higher % of annual gross sales. High-volume UPS stores sell for over 1x STR (Subject to Royalty)."
- "Rent is a very important factor, as it is a fixed cost. Stores below a certain minimum of sales diminish in value exponentially as they find it more and more difficult to cover the fixed costs."
- "Length of time in business, sales are growing or declining, competition coming or going."

Expert Comments

"Easy to own and easy to operate."

"Risk can be high if owner does not audit the weekly Electronic Funds Transfers (EFT's) statements from the bank. The carriers make 'mistakes' in their favor that you must then call & argue with them to change."

"Perception of mail centers is they are easy to learn and easy to run."

"This is a good service business that is somewhat recession resistant."

"The main suppliers to the industry are the biggest competitors. They give out accounts like candy. You can only make it if you provide a real service along with the shipping."

"These businesses are proven concepts today; and generally, mail and parcel centers are lower risk than many other businesses."

"Competition is high—even from the suppliers (UPS, FEDEX) providing individual accounts to your customers."

"Barriers to entry are not strong. A new store does not cost much to open. Establishing the business is the tough part. Competition is everywhere. Your suppliers (e.g., FedEx, UPS) are also your competition. All office supply houses are your competition."

Benchmark Data

Statistics (Business Service Centers)

Number of Establishments	28,206
Average Profit Margin	5.7%
Revenue per Employee	$108,000
Average Number of Employees	3.2
Average Wages per Employee	$29,733

Rules of Thumb - M

Products and Services Segmentation

Copying and reproduction services	48.6%
Postal and shipping services and mailbox rentals	27.2%
Packaging and labeling services and other	12.9%
Printing Services	11.3%

Major Market Segmentation

Small Businesses	60.0%
Households	20.0%
Corporate clients	20.0%

Industry Costs

Profit	5.7%
Wages	27.7%
Purchases	37.0%
Depreciation	3.1%
Marketing	1.5%
Rent & Utilities	10.5%
Other	14.5%

Market Share

United Parcel Service Inc.	18.4%
FedEx Corporation	10.7%

Source: IBISWorld, December 2014

- "Must have an average 50% mark up on shipping (USPS, Fed Ex, UPS, etc.)"
- "There are a lot of startup stores or lower performing stores whose annual sales are under $200K. Be careful if it goes below $150K in annual sales, as fixed costs will eat up your profit."
- "Location is important, do not need a lot of SF. Keep the rent low."
- "Mailbox rentals should cover all operating expenses."
- "Must be earning at least 50% gross profit or better. The sales must exceed a certain level (usually 10 times rent) before a profit can really be seen. A good store has a decent budget for advertising."
- "Most stores must be doing at least $150,000 in annual sales before they start showing any real profit. Advertising is very important; stores should not skimp on advertising. The client base is primarily within a radius of a few miles."

Expenses as a percentage of annual sales

Cost of goods	45% to 50%
Payroll/labor Costs	15% to 20%
Occupancy	10% or less
Profit (estimated pretax)	20%

Industry Trend
- "Trend toward more services—like opening, scanning and emailing mail to customers."

Seller Financing
- 3 years

M - Rules of Thumb

Questions
- "What competition is nearby. Get a standard disclosure form completed."
  "Is the notary income being reported? If not, look at notary's journal to get idea of volume. Any accounts receivable (business accounts)? Any 'trade' for mail box rental? Do you want to slap customers who complain about you selling stamps for a penny or two more than the post office?"   "Do they charge for packing labor? How much? If not, this is a pure profit area to explore! It does depend on their markup otherwise."   "What services are offered? How many mailboxes do they have, how many are rented, how much are they rented for, and when was the last time they raised the rates?"
- "Do you know of any new competition coming soon?"

Resources
Associations
- Association of Mail and Business Centers: www.ampc.org

Mail Order		
SIC 5961-02	NAICS 454110	Number of Businesses/Units 9,537

Rules of Thumb
- ➢ 6 times EBIT
- ➢ 5 times EBITDA
- ➢ 80 percent of annual sales includes inventory

Pricing Tips
- "6 to 7 times EBITDA in 2005, $8 million transaction B-2-B mail-order house, $10 million in sales, national accounts, 100% interest transferred."
- "Valuation of firm typically based on house account quality (house database of customers) and EBITDA sustainability and growth"

Expert Comments
"Straightforward estimate of risk-reward. Margins declining, but from high past levels. Ease of replication reduces going concern values. Consolidation occurring."

Benchmark Data

Statistics (Mail Order)
Number of Establishments	9,537
Average Profit Margin	3.1%
Revenue per Employee	$598,400
Average Number of Employees	21.3
Average Wages per Employee	$42,647

Products and Services
Health and beauty products	31.8%
Other	22.7%
Clothing, jewelry and accessories	14.9%
Computer hardware, software and office supplies	14.1%
Sporting goods, hobby goods, toys and games	9.8%
Furniture and household goods	6.7%

Rules of Thumb - **M**

Industry Costs

Profit	3.1%
Wages	7.1%
Purchases	64.1%
Depreciation	0.8%
Marketing	5.5%
Rent & Utilities	4.2%
Other	15.2%

Source: IBISWorld, September 2015

- "$300,000 revenue per sales employee."
- "Sales personnel should generate revenue of about $1.3 million per employee."

Expenses as a percentage of annual sales

Cost of goods	60% to 67%
Payroll/labor Costs	01%
Occupancy	01%
Profit (estimated pretax)	09% to 10%

Industry Trend

- "The Mail Order industry has experienced slight contraction over the past five years, largely due to rising competition from online retailers and minimal improvements in disposable income among frequent mail order customers. While consumer sentiment and disposable income are expected to take a positive turn, individuals will turn to brick-and-mortar retail stores and internet stores for the majority of their purchases. More struggles are projected for the industry in the five years to 2019, as industry catalog mailers will likely struggle to tap into the growing percentage of consumers who favor e-commerce over traditional mail orders. Therefore, IBISWorld forecasts industry revenue to decline steeply in the next five years."

    Source: IBISWorld, October 2014

- "Over the past five years, the bulk of the industry's revenue has shifted from catalog to Internet sales."

    Source: www.firstresearch.com

- "When 75 U.S. Senators agree on anything, a political earthquake is underway, and by that measure Congress seems poised to require retailers to pay in-state sales taxes, regardless of whether they have a physical presence in the state. Conventional wisdom holds that the new requirement would equalize the ground between online stores like Amazon.com and brick-and-mortar competitors like Best Buy. But according to Wired, Amazon seems rather OK with it all.

  "The U.S. Senate passed a non-binding resolution last week by a 75–22 vote that cleared the way for consideration of a final bill. A vote is expected soon, and the action now seems to be setting the exemption threshold, according to Inc.com.

  "'It could turn out that forcing Amazon to collect sales tax nationwide could be the worst thing to happen to brick-and-mortar retail,' Wohlsen argued. 'Competing with Amazon was tough enough when it was just a company in Seattle with a big warehouse in Kentucky. What happens when one of the world's biggest stores, online or off, suddenly moves right into your backyard?'"

    Source: "Sales tax threat stalks online mail-order empires, but will it really hurt them?"
    by Eric Schulzke, *Deseret News*, www.deseretnews.com April 24, 2013

26th Edition

M - Rules of Thumb

Questions
- "What experience do you have in the catalog or direct marketing industry?"

Resources

Associations
- National Mail Order Association—an excellent site, loaded with information: www.nmoa.org

	Franchise
Mama Fu's Asian House (See also Franchises, Restaurants—Asian)	
Approx. Total Investment	$407,000 to $663,000
SIC 5812-08 NAICS 722513	Number of Businesses/Units 17

Rules of Thumb
> ➢ 30 percent of annual sales plus inventory

Resources

Websites
- Mama Fu's Asian House: wwwmamafus.com

Management Consulting	
NAICS 54161	Number of Businesses/Units 808,105

Rules of Thumb
> ➢ 2.5 times SDE

Benchmark Data

Statistics (Management Consulting)
Number of Establishments	808,105
Average Profit Margin	9.7%
Revenue per Employee	$117,400
Average Number of Employees	2.2
Average Wages per Employee	$59,903

Products and Services Segmentation
Process and operations management	36.9%
Corporate strategy	20.3%
IT strategy	20.2%
Organizational design	13.1%
Financial advisory	7.1%
Marketing and sales	2.4%

Major Market Segmentation

Other	24.5%
Financial services companies	21.3%
Consumer products companies	14.8%
Government organizations	14.6%
Manufacturing companies	9.7%
Energy and utilities companies	6.7%
Individuals	4.3%
Nonprofit organizations	4.1%

Industry Costs

Profit	9.7%
Wages	50.7%
Purchases	9.2%
Depreciation	0.9%
Marketing	1.8%
Rent & Utilities	3.7%
Other	24.0%

Market Share

Accenture PLC	3.3%
Deloitte Touche Tohmatsu	2.6%
McKinsey & Company	2.6%

Source: IBISWorld, May 2015

Manufacturing—Aluminum Extruded Products
NAICS 331318

Rules of Thumb
- 50 percent of annual sales plus inventory
- 6 times SDE plus inventory
- 5 times EBIT
- 4 times EBITDA

Pricing Tips
- "Nature of contract with metal supplier; this is a low added value business."

Benchmark Data
- "At least a ratio of added value/salaries cost (total) of 2.0."

Expenses as a percentage of annual sales

Cost of goods	70%
Payroll/labor Costs	35%
Occupancy	05%
Profit (estimated pretax)	08%

Industry Trend
- "Growing"

Questions
- "Customer base, nature of metal contracts"

M - Rules of Thumb

Manufacturing—Chemical

| SIC 2899-05 | NAICS 32599 | Number of Businesses/Units 1,794 |

Rules of Thumb
- .5 to 2 times annual sales includes inventory
- 4 to 9 times EBITDA

Pricing Tips
- "Industry is very diverse (some businesses are state-of-the-art/cutting edge, some are very mature, and everything in between), therefore pricing depends on a variety of factors."

Expert Comments
"Chemical industry in U.S. on upward trend because of natural gas availability in the U.S., making for lower raw material costs in many cases"

Benchmark Data

Statistics (Chemical Product Manufacturing)
Number of Establishments	1,794
Average Profit Margin	7.0%
Revenue per Employee	$675,700
Average Number of Employees	34.5
Average Wages per Employee	$62,917

Products and Services Segmentation
Other chemical products and preparations	34.5%
Custom compounding of resins	29.2%
Photographic films, papers and plates	11.2%
Water treating compounds	9.2%
Photographic chemicals	5.7%
Automotive chemicals	5.1%
Evaporated salt, excluding table salt	2.7%
Gelatin, excluding ready-to-eat desserts	2.4%

Major Market Segmentation
Manufacturing sector	31.2%
Automobile industry	23.6%
Households	21.8%
Construction sector	18.7%
Other	4.7%

Industry Costs
Profit	7.0%
Wages	9.5%
Purchases	52.2%
Depreciation	1.8%
Marketing	0.1%
Rent & Utilities	1.9%
Other	27.5%

Source: IBISWorld, July 2015

Rules of Thumb - M

- "EBITDA multiples are the most common benchmark, but exhibit wide variation."
- "Benchmarks are not common, given the diverse nature of the industry."

Expenses as a percentage of annual sales	
Cost of goods	25%
Payroll/labor Costs	n/a
Occupancy	n/a
Profit (estimated pretax)	10%

Industry Trend

- "Compared to June 2014, U.S. chemical production was ahead by 4.0 percent on a year-over-year basis, an improving comparison. Chemical production remained ahead of year ago levels in all regions."

    Source: "U.S. Chemical Production Activity Rebounded in June" by Patrick Hurston, 7/21/15
    http://www.americanchemistry.com/Media/PressReleasesTranscripts/ACC-news-releases/US-Chemical-Production-Activity-Rebounded-in-June.html

- "Chemical industry is always churning. M&A activity is always happening."
- "American chemistry is the global leader in production, providing over fifteen percent of the world's chemicals and representing twelve percent of all U.S. exports. It is also one of America's largest manufacturing industries, an $812 billion enterprise providing 793,000 high-paying jobs. For every one chemistry industry job, nearly 7.5 others are generated in other sectors of the economy, including construction, transportation, and agriculture, totaling nearly seven million chemistry-dependent jobs.
- "'2014 has proven to be another year of robust and sustained expansion for the American chemical industry, now larger than either the motor vehicle or aerospace industries,' said ACC President and CEO Cal Dooley. 'With continued access to abundant supplies of natural gas from shale deposits, the economics of shale gas continue to create a new competitive edge that is revitalizing the industry, and the U.S. is now the most attractive place in the world to invest in chemical manufacturing.'"

    Source: ad for American Chemistry Council's 2014 edition of the *Guide to the Business of Chemistry*, www.americanchemistry.com

Seller Financing

- 5 years

Questions

- "Normal due diligence type issues plus environmental/regulatory issues which are somewhat unique to the industry, and impact of overseas competition."

Resources

Trade Publications

- IHS Chemical Week: www.chemweek.com
- Plastics News: www.plasticsnews.com
- Chemical & Engineering News: cen.acs.org
- ICIS: www.icis.com

Associations

- The Society of Chemical Manufacturers and Affiliates (SOCMA): www.socma.com
- American Chemistry Council: www.americanchemistry.com

26th Edition

M - Rules of Thumb

Manufacturing—Custom Architectural Woodwork and Millwork
NAICS 337212

Rules of Thumb
> ➢ 3 times SDE includes inventory

Pricing Tips
- "Growth and customer list affects multiple dramatically."

Expert Comments
"China is becoming a big factor."

Benchmak Data

Expenses as a percentage of annual sales

Cost of goods	50%
Payroll/labor Costs	30%
Occupancy	10%
Profit (estimated pretax)	10%

Industry Trend
- "China will affect every aspect of this industry. Must have niche to prosper."
- "Most owners are getting older, and the industry will consolidate."

Manufacturing—Electrical
NAICS 33531 — Number of Businesses/Units 2,112

Rules of Thumb
> ➢ 5 times EBITDA

Pricing Tips
- "Client relationships and strength of long-term contracts is a major factor. Patents and proprietary processes must be evaluated. Work force productivity factor, min. of $250K per man-year is essential."

Benchmark Data

Statistics (Electrical Equipment Manufacturing)

Number of Establishments	2,112
Average Profit Margin	5.3%
Revenue per Employee	$362,300
Average Number of Employees	52.8
Average Wages per Employee	$59,653

Products and Services Segmentation

Motors and generators	30.5%
Switches	28.4%
Relays and industrial controls	26.5%
Transformers	14.6%

Major Market Segmentation

Exports	40.3%
Wholesalers	20.0%
Utilities	16.0%
Downstream manufacturers	15.0%
Retailers	8.7%

Industry Costs

Profit	5.3%
Wages	16.7%
Purchases	50.1%
Depreciation	1.5%
Marketing	0.2%
Rent & Utilities	1.4%
Other	24.8%

Market Share

ABB Ltd.	10.1%
Eaton Corp.	9.2%
General Electric Company	8.9%

Source: IBISWorld, September 2015

- "Use of third-party contract manufacturers continues to grow as more and more traditional manufacturers outsource."

Expenses as a percentage of annual sales

Cost of goods	64%
Payroll/labor Costs	07% to 08%
Occupancy	04%
Profit (estimated pretax)	12%

Seller Financing
- 5 years

Manufacturing—Electrical Connectors
NAICS 334510

Rules of Thumb
➢ 3 times EBITDA

Pricing Tips
- "Transferring the customers and good accounting of inventory are very important."
- "Contract mfg. companies sell for 3X SDE or under. Companies with proprietary products are 4–7 X SDE depending on growth."
- "The customer list and management talent are key."

Expert Comments
"The industry is very cyclical."

M - Rules of Thumb

Benchmark Data
- "No customer bigger than 30%"

Expenses as a percentage of annual sales
Cost of goods	40% to 45%
Payroll/labor Costs	30%
Occupancy	10 to 15%
Profit (estimated pretax)	10%

Industry Trend
- "Major consolidation"

Questions
- "How much engineering work do you do?"

Manufacturing—Food
NAICS 311

Rules of Thumb
➢ 4 to 7 times EBITDA

Pricing Tips
- "Pricing Tips include brand, years in business, strong customer base and length of relationship with customers, vendor certifications (i.e., certified organic, 100% natural, etc.)"
- "Earnings multiples depend heavily on: brand, customer concentration, size, recurring revenue, clientele, vendor certifications, working capital requirements, earnings stability, owner involvement, product category and differentiation, equipment age/condition (future CAPEX), and barriers to entry."

Expert Comments
"Food manufacturing businesses have high marketability"

"Generally there is little or no proprietary content."

Benchmark Data
- "Branded vs. private label, any notable long-term customers?"
- "Wide range, depending on product category, sales channel, branded vs. private label, etc."
- "Food manufacturing gross margins (after material costs and direct labor) should be at least 40%, and preferably at least 50%."

Expenses as a percentage of annual sales
Cost of goods	30% to 40%
Payroll/labor Costs	10% to 15%
Occupancy	05%
Profit (estimated pretax)	05% to 10%

Rules of Thumb - **M**

Industry Trend
- "Stable"
- "Food manufacturing businesses are somewhat recession-proof, making the industry appealing to buyers in the current economic environment."

Seller Financing
- "Depends on the size of the deal. Average seller financing is 2–10 years"

Questions
- "Revenue, COGS, liabilities, owner involvement? Sales channel? Who are your customers? How long have you been supplying to these customers? Do you have contracts with clients? Any client that accounts for more than 10% of your sales? What is the production capacity? Type of equipment?"

Resources

Websites
- Food Manufacturing: www.foodmanufacturing.com

Trade Publications
- Food Engineering: www.foodengineeringmag.com/

Manufacturing—Furniture/Household

(See also Manufacturing—Wood Office Furniture)

SIC 2599-01	NAICS 33712	Number of Businesses/Units 4,210

Rules of Thumb
➢ 4 to 7 times EBITDA

Pricing Tips
- "Size, growth, condition of plant, how profitable it is, place in the market, and management can play a part."

Benchmark Data

Statistics (Household Furniture Manufacturing)

Number of Establishments	4,210
Average Profit Margin	4.2%
Revenue per Employee	$198,500
Average Number of Employees	27.1
Average Wages per Employee	$37,086

Products and Services Segmentation

Upholstered household furniture	44.4%
Institutional furniture	21.9%
Non-upholstered wood household furniture	20.0%
Metal household furniture	9.0%
Household furniture (except wood and metal)	2.5%
Wood television, radio and sewing machine cabinets	2.2%

26th Edition

M - Rules of Thumb

Major Market Segmentation

Retailers	41.9%
Wholesalers	30.9%
Contract outfitters	13.1%
Exports	11.8%
End users	2.3%

Industry Costs

Profit	4.2%
Wages	18.9%
Purchases	63.1%
Depreciation	0.9%
Marketing	0.7%
Rent & Utilities	2.4%
Other	9.8%

Market Share

Ashley Furniture Industries Inc.	10.3%

Source: IBISWorld, August 2015

Resources

Associations
- The Business and Institutional Furniture Manufacturers' Association—a worthwhile site: www.bifma.com

---

Manufacturing—General	
SIC 3999-03	Number of Businesses/Units 11,500

Rules of Thumb
- 40 to 60 percent of annual sales includes inventory
- 3 times SDE (depending on size & quality) includes inventory
- 3 to 4 times SDE; must manufacture product; not be a job shop
- 3 to 5 times EBITDA
- 4 to 5 times EBIT
- Hard Assets + 1.5 to 2 times EBIT

Pricing Tips
- "Work in progress is very important to consider as is determination of how it will be (or will not be) transferred to buyer. Freight and shipping charges important to consider as well. Contracts and the stability and transferability of those contracts is critical to the multiple. Inventory and pricing of inventory to the buyer should be carefully analyzed."
- "Factors to look for: sales/profitability trends; years in operation; fixed asset value. Risk factors: technology, competition, and industry trends. Exclusive products and patents can raise the multiple."

Rules of Thumb - M

- "Pricing a manufacturing business can be complex. There are many, many factors that need to be addressed including inventory, work in progress, condition of equipment, contracts in place, just to name a few. These and so many other factors can create large variances in the value."
- "Niche or proprietary products, processes, etc. require a premium. Repetitive long-term contracts generate a premium. ISO 2000 procedures in place deserve a premium. Discount for client concentration, labor unions and 'me too' products or services. Watch out for warranty exposure, product liability exposure, excessive WIP and old or obsolete inventory."
- "If the business is in a niche industry with a high barrier to entry it would likely see a higher multiple. Customer concentration can have a significant influence on the multiple, or may require a significant earnout. Exclusive products and patents can raise the multiple. How many competitors manufacture the same product? Companies facing little or no offshore competition will command a higher price. Values for job shops are lower than for companies with a product line."
- "On-hand inventory is critical as is work in progress. PO's not yet started and upcoming can add value. Contracts are very important, much more so than long-term/loyal customer. Raw materials important to consider. Ask about employees; keyman and are they IC's or employees."
- "Multiples are a starting point. Other variables are age and turnover of inventory, customer contracts or relationships in place for future revenues, age and quality of FF&E, ease of operations and learning curve, proprietary or niche products, market competition."
- "There has been increased demand for manufacturing businesses which is helping to push multiples higher."
- "Factors of importance: Is being an engineer critical to ongoing success? What impact if any does Chinese manufacturing have on this business? Is the customer base spread out?"
- "Does it have solid and/or proprietary product lines? Can it be operated without the current owner? Are outside vendors/contractors used in the manufacturing process? Do they sell to large well-known companies or distributors? And are these relationships ongoing and transferable? Can it be relocated or folded into an existing company?"
- "4–5 x SDE for product manufacturer. 3 x SDE & inventory & machinery & equipment."
- "Multiple would vary depending upon EBITDA range. For EBITDA's in excess of $4 million you might see a multiple of 4.5 or 5. EBITDA above $5 million would normally be a multiple of 6 or more."
- "Most accurate method is to deduct cost of professional employees to replace current ownership, and then use a multiple of 4 to 6 times net earnings (EBIT) depending on industry, security of earnings, assets, growth potential, etc."
- "We look at the calculation for owner benefit/cash flow and apply a 2 to 3 times multiple plus the current market value of furniture, fixtures and equipment and inventory at cost. Since manufacturing is very equipment intensive, using a pure EBITDA or cash flow multiplier does not adequately give a fair evaluation, in our opinion."
- "Transferability of the customer base and maintenance capital expenditures are the two biggest issues to close a deal."

M - Rules of Thumb

Expert Comments

"Location, rent and lease term must be clearly understood from the start. It can be dificult to replicate a running operation, therefore a business that may not currently be profitable may have substantial value to certain buyers."

"The burden of structural costs (corporate tax liability, employee benefits, tort litigation, regulatory compliance, etc.) is a competitive disadvantage relative to foreign competitors. The manufacturing sector's profitability is affected by cyclical movements in the economy. Profits, as a percentage of stockholders' equity, typically fall during a recession, but are coming back up. According to *FortuneMagazine*, private equity firms now have more than $1 trillion of available capital, which should mean more deals at higher prices."

"Barriers to entry can be the equipment, good employees, and customer base; it's critical to have a good understanding of these issues."

"As usual the seller will need to provide documentation on sales, distributors, vendors, operations and financials. The buyer will need to verify everything."

"Many of us believe that outsourcing to China and other places around the world will continue to slow down. We are seeing more manufacturing being brought back to the USA. These factors will have a positive impact on the value and sale of manufacturing businesses."

"Ease of replication is critical. Buyers tend to desire patents, sellers tend to have been too frugal to have incurred costs associated with patents."

"Highly competitive in some industries, so are the products proprietary or is it a niche this business has found?"

"Profitability & sales trends important—FMV of equipment/machinery, inventory, real estate = financing."

"Unlike some industries, an unprofitable manufacturer may drive value due to its bolt-on capabilities. Overhead can be eliminated and capacity and customers can potentially be transferred to another company."

Benchmark Data

"3-4 x adjusted-verifiable net"

"$100/sq. ft. is about average for sales/sq. ft. "

"$1k sales per square foot, but it depends on what you are selling, power transmission products vs. electronics."

"Revenues per employee over $175,000.Gross Profit after direct labor, COGS, etc. of 35% or more."

"According to a recent *Inc. Magazine* report, the average sales/employee was $203,985. However, this number varies between $150,000 and $250,000."

"40% or higher Gross Margins. 10% or higher EBITDA"

"Proprietary products are most important."

Rules of Thumb - **M**

"No customer bigger than 20%"

"Gross margin >45%; Inventory turns >4"

Expenses as a percentage of annual sales

Cost of goods	45% to 60%
Payroll/labor Costs	15% to 20%
Occupancy	03% to 08%
Profit (estimated pretax)	05% to 10%

Industry Trend

- "Manufacturing seems to be a sought after industry from buyers in all price ranges."
- "According to IndustryWeek, the 'SMAC Stack' adoption will gain speed: A manufacturing comeback is being driven by SMAC—social, mobile, analytics and cloud. The SMAC Stack is becoming an essential technology tool kit for enterprises and represents the next wave for driving higher customer engagement and growth opportunities. The need to innovate is forcing cultural change within a historically conservative 'if it's not broke don't fix it' industry, and SMAC is helping early adopters in the manufacturing market increase efficiencies and change."
- "Growth including onshoring and manufacturing moving from China to U.S. and Mexico."
- "The trends should be upward based on: 1) natural gas costs have come down, 2) labor costs are going up in developing countries, and 3) new automation technology continues to increase productivity and require fewer skilled workers."
- "Small manufacturing seems to be holding its own."
- "For the company with the special products and customers the trend for success is positive."
- "Some key findings from the Manufacturing Institute:
    - ✓ Manufacturing is driving productivity growth in the U.S. economy, increasing at two and a half times the rate of the service sector.
    - ✓ Companies with under 100 employees make up over 94% of all U.S. manufacturers.
    - ✓ U.S. manufacturers invest a far greater percentage of revenue in research and development than other industries.
    - ✓ Manufacturing employees earn a higher average salary and receive greater benefits than workers in other industries.
    - ✓ U.S. manufacturers have reduced energy usage and emissions to below the level from 1990.
    - ✓ U.S. manufacturers are responsible for 47% of the total U.S. exports.
    - ✓ The U.S. is the number one destination for foreign direct investment by a wide margin.
    - ✓ The U.S. manufacturing sector is so huge that if it were its own country, it would rank as the tenth-largest world economy."

    Source: www.themanufacturinginstitute.org
- "The strong have survived. Companies have made cuts so they are now more productive and efficient without some of the 'fat'."

M - Rules of Thumb

Seller Financing
- "Some seller financing is typical for a business in this industry selling for less than a few million dollars."
- "Finance can include SBA bank finance with typically 25% down where the buyer may put down 15% and the seller carry the balance of 10%. The alternative is seller finance where a large percentage of transactions have been structured under. This typically involves 50% down with a personal guarantee and a lien on the assets of the business."
- "Primarily outside with some small seller participation."
- "Manufacturing companies with lots of (paid off) equipment and a good lease along with good financials may get a loan as long as the buyer is financially strong and has direct industry experience. Seller financing is usually required to some degree, with or without a bank loan."
- "It's about 50/50 outside financing to seller financing."
- 3 to 6 years

Questions
- "Buyers should ask how much working capital is required and if any equipment upgrades will be needed in the near future."
- "What is the quality of your management team, are your books and records audited by a national or large regional firm, are you a planner and can you show me your strategic plan vs. execution, etc."
- "Customer concentration. By whom are technical and sales relationships owned? Environmental?Quality control standards?ISO compliance?Risk of obsolescence?Competitive products/threats?"
  - ✓ "Do you have a business plan?
  - ✓ Who are your key employees? Will they stay?
  - ✓ What skills/knowledge do I need to run this business successfully?
  - ✓ How much working capital is required?
  - ✓ Are any equipment upgrades needed in the near future?
  - ✓ Is there any pending legislation you are aware of that may affect this industry?
  - ✓ What is your customer concentration?
  - ✓ What are the biggest challenges facing your business today?"
- "Raw materials-how much, will the current pricing continue? Long term lease can be important; find out the status and if it is assignable or if a new one at the same or better rate is possible. Check the details carefully of all customer contracts."
- "Reason for selling. What he/she does on a daily basis.Employee census. Worker's comp mode rate Upside potential."
- "Do they have patents on their products?"
- "Is your product certified and if so what kind of certification"
- "How is your business protected from off-shore competition?"
- "Insurance considerations—is the business properly insured?"
- "Value and margin of backlog; asset value and basis for value; product line breakdown & mix; 3 to 5 years P&L and balance sheets."

Rules of Thumb - M

Resources

Associations
- The Manufacturing Institute: www.themanufacturinginstitute.org
- The National Association of Manufacturers: www.nam.org
- The Manufacturers Alliance for Productivity and Innovation: www.mapi.net
- The Association of Equipment Manufacturers: www.aem.org
- First Coast Manufacturers Association: www.fcmaweb.com
- Florida Manufacturing Extension Partnership: www.floridamep.org

Manufacturing—General Purpose Machinery		
	NAICS 3339	

Rules of Thumb
- 4.5 times EBITDA

Manufacturing—Guided Missile and Space Vehicle		
	NAICS 336414	Number of Businesses/Units 124

Rules of Thumb
- 100 + percent of annual sales
- 3 to 4 times SDE plus inventory
- 6 to 10 times EBIT
- 5 to 8 times EBITDA

Pricing Tips
- "Pricing is heavily impacted by third-party lending criteria and formal appraisals/evaluations. Buyers and sellers are sensitive to industry standards and trends as well as a certain segment being sensitive to environmental issues and political correctness."
- "Usually need to sell as a stock sale due to the qualifications and licenses held by the seller."
- "Value increases with the company's ability to meet high quality controls and production deadlines as specified by military and military contractors. Extremely high barriers to entry in this industry keep values high."

Expert Comments
"Visual appeal of facility as well as the level of technology in equipment is very important."

Benchmark Data

Statistics (Space Vehicle & Missile Manufacturing)
Number of Establishments	124
Average Profit Margin	9.8%
Revenue per Employee	$365,600
Average Number of Employees	552.6
Average Wages per Employee	$116,027

26th Edition

M - Rules of Thumb

Products and Services Segmentation
Missile systems	43.7%
Space systems	32.9%
Propulsion systems	13.2%
Other missile and space vehicle parts	12.1%

Major Market Segmentation
US military	61.0%
Domestic civilian market	29.1%
Exports	9.9%

Industry Costs
Profit	9.8%
Wages	31.5%
Purchases	41.3%
Depreciation	1.8%
Marketing	0.1%
Rent & Utilities	1.9%
Other	13.6%

Market Share
Lockheed Martin Corporation	31.7%
Raytheon Company	23.2%
The Boeing Company	11.4%
Orbital ATK Inc.	7.5%
GenCorp Inc.	6.4%

Source: IBISWorld, March 2015

- "Quality of production is paramount in this industry along with on-time delivery."
- "There are no common benchmarks or Rules of Thumb. Most businesses in this industry are unique, requiring special detailed analysis."

Expenses as a percentage of annual sales
Cost of goods	31% to 35%
Payroll/labor Costs	50%
Occupancy	15%
Profit (estimated pretax)	20% to 21%

Industry Trend
- "Uncertainty prevails due to government activity and controls. Economic uncertainty is still a lingering issue."
- "Trend is up due to war on terrorism."

Seller Financing
- "A mixture of 10% to 20% seller financing, a typical 20% and up buyer cash down payment, and 3rd party financing."
- "Five years at a premium over bank rates."

Questions
- "How are you going to pay for this business? If I carry back a note, what security are you going to provide and how many months of cash will you have at closing?"

Rules of Thumb - M

- "Are the key employees willing to stay on post sale? Are qualifications and certifications up to current standards and valid?"

Manufacturing—Machinery		
	NAICS 333	

Rules of Thumb
- ➢ 100 percent of annual sales includes inventory
- ➢ 4 times EBIT
- ➢ 3 times EBITDA

Pricing Tips
- "Average of last 3 years' EBITDA plus stockholders comp, multiplied by 2 to 4 depending on profit history and market share."
- "Valuation method for work in process.Inventory turnover.Nature and situation of officer's account with business.Indebtedness.How easy for the firm to get bonded on basis of financial credibility."
- "A manufacturer of industry-specific machinery generally employs 50 to 500 people. A high price is 1 x sales figure (valid if market dominant worldwide). A good price is equal to total assets. A frequently observed price is twice net assets (Stockholder's Equity) or 5 times EBITDA for a firm in good standing. Multiple of net earning is meaningless since most owners minimize net earnings through various perks."

Expert Comments

"The machinery business is highly dependent on global market share (high), skills, reputation with customers based on customer service and availability of spare parts. Management predicament is: How to control a high global market share when you are a business with between 50 and 500 employees?"

"Any sales require customized engineering, manufacturing and assembly, plus installation and start-up which are always cursed with delays."

Benchmark Data
- "Take sales figure minus costs of raw materials and components, which is added value. Divide added value by total salaries cost including management. If result is consistently above 2.0, it is a well-managed business. Watch out: In figures in expenses below, we consider total salaries costs, not labor costs (meaningless)."
- "Added value/salaries cost >2. Added value/sales figure >50%.Sales per employee >$250,000. Identified competitors are few, and far away."
- "Sales per employee: $120,000 to $250,000; varies a lot as function of manufacturing integration. Our experience (300 clients during last 10 years) is that 80% of the world machinery industry is mismanaged because of lack of market focus and deficient customer service. The remaining can be highly profitable, and utilize market downturns to acquire competitors (most of our own business)."

M - Rules of Thumb

Expenses as a percentage of annual sales

Cost of goods	60%
Payroll/labor Costs	25%
Occupancy	05%
Profit (estimated pretax)	10%

Industry Trend
- "It is moving to fast-growing economies where the biggest market is China, India, other NICs."
- "Favorable"

Questions
- "How many customers? Since when? How many customers amount to 50% of sales? How far away do they sell?"
- "Loans and advances to/from officers in balance sheet. Do they own their real estate (facility)? If so, is it undervalued in assets (historic value)?"

Manufacturing—Marine Products
NAICS 336612

Rules of Thumb
- 85 percent of Annual Gross Sales plus inventory
- 2.1 times SDE
- 3.2 times EBIT
- 3.9 times EBITDA

Pricing Tips
- "EBITDA must be adjusted to show owner's discretionary cash flow. The multiple that is used varies by industry segments, geographical location, and specific business and must be determined in a subjective manner by one knowledgeable of current market conditions."

Expert Comments

"Niche products are key to success and to reducing competition."

"Only the strong survived during the recession, which was particularly difficult for the marine industry from 2008 thru 2012. The weaker competitors fell away so the last couple of years have experienced a sharp increase in business for the survivors."

"Location is also key. In order to control shipping costs it is important to be located in active boating areas. Marine related manufacturing is typically a complex business with extensive processes creating attractive barriers to entry."

"Manufacturing has been enhanced by technological systems which have greatly improved over the last 25 years. CADCAM systems and computerized equipment have greatly improved productivity in the industry."

Rules of Thumb - **M**

Benchmark Data
- "Sales per employee with a strong management team in place: $120,000 to $180,000 depending on WIP production. A mix of customers is key with no one customer >20%."

Expenses as a percentage of annual sales
Cost of goods	32%
Payroll/labor Costs	25%
Occupancy	06%
Profit (estimated pretax)	21%

Industry Trend
- "With Memorial Day marking the kickoff to the summer boating season, the National Marine Manufacturers Association (NMMA) reported today healthy growth for the $35.4 billion U.S. recreational boating industry, with an estimated 171,500 new powerboats sold in 2014, an increase of 6.4 percent over 2013.

  "The popular outboard boat segment, which includes pontoons, aluminum and fiberglass fishing boats, and small fiberglass cruising boats, comprised approximately 84.4 percent of the overall powerboat market. Outboard boats were the most popular type of new powerboat sold in 2014. In addition to new powerboats, new sailboats sold at retail increased 33.9 percent to 7,500 units and new personal watercraft sales increased 21.6 percent to 47,900 units.

  "95% of boats on the water (powerboats, personal watercraft, and sailboats) in the U.S. are small in size at less than 26 feet—boats that can be trailered by a vehicle to local waterways. It's not just new boats Americans are buying, there were an estimated 940,500 pre-owned boats (powerboats, personal watercraft, and sailboats) sold in 2014."

  Source: "Boat Sales Strong with Summer on the Horizon" 5/19/15 http://nmma.org/news.aspx?id=19879

Seller Financing
- "Depending on the records, banks are doing SBA deals recently. If not, 60 to 70% down with 30 to 40% seller financing is common."

Questions
- "Customer concentration and % of rev from the top 10 customers"
- "Equipment needs to be up to date—updating equipment in this industry can be a large expense."
- "Are the contracts with manufacturers transferable to the new owner?"
- "Who is the competition?"
- "How is the business protected from offshore competition?"
- "Consider the WIP situation as these types of products can have significant amounts invested in work in progress."
- "Insurance considerations—is the business properly insured? Consider the value and margin of the backlog and make sure it is accounted for regarding insurance needs."
- "What are the capital expenditures required to maintain and grow the business?"

M - Rules of Thumb

Resources

Associations
- Marine Industries Association of South Florida: www.miasf.org
- National Marine Manufacturers Association: www.nmma.org

Manufacturing—Metal Fabrication	
SIC 1791-04	NAICS 238390

Rules of Thumb
- ➢ 70% to 80% of Annual Gross Sales plus inventory
- ➢ 4 to 4.5 times SDE plus inventory
- ➢ 5 to 6 times EBIT
- ➢ 4 to 6 times EBITDA

Pricing Tips
- "Products, type of metal fab and recurring revenue have material impact on value."
- "Equipment is a real expense so valuation will be dinged or improved based on how frequently seller updates equipment. Useful life of CNC equipment is typically 5–7 years depending on how hard it's used. CAPEX is a real expense of the business which keeps EBITDA multiples down. If they have any proprietary products, it improves value. Most contract manufacturers don't have proprietary products though.

  "Having spoken to over a hundred owners, I can attest that each is very unique. Confirm they don't have customer concentration and identify gross margins for their work. 40–50% gross margins are healthy.

  "Aerospace and defense fabrication typically garners better margins and multiples. It is common to have customer concentration in this space where one customer makes up 20–50% of sales. This dings value about a turn of EBITDA. Size matters too…$2M in EBITDA and below is limited to 5X and below. $2M–$5M is 5.5–6 and more than $10M of EBITDA 5.5–7X. 7X is very rich and that business will need a lot of other things going for it like heavy services (subassembly, kitting, supplier management, painting and e-coating, etc.)."
- "Adjustments to the multiple are: 1. Trend of revenues, gross margin and net 2. Customer concentration. Anything over 10% is a deduct 3. Industry & geographic concentration. The more diversified the better 4. Number of products and services offered 5. Is the owner the business?"
- "Typical 3–7 times EBITDA depending on the business, industry and the buyer. 1.5 times gross profit plus net book value combined with the normal three valuation approaches."
- "EBITDA must be adjusted to show owner's discretionary cash flow. The multiple that is used varies by industry, geographic location, and specific business, and must be determined in a subjective manner by one knowledgeable of current market conditions."

Rules of Thumb - M

Expert Comments

"There is significant variety in this industry. It's best not to rely on a rule of thumb, but focus on the specific attributes of the unique metal fabricator."

"The customers of these businesses regularly get competitive pricing from the market. It's not uncommon that you'll have a customer and lose a customer and get them back. The point is there is not a lot of pricing power for the owner."

"Pure welding and fabrication businesses that need less equipment are easier to sell than those that require more annual CAPEX spend."

"Proprietary products and processes can protect a company from competition, both domestic and overseas."

Benchmark Data
- For additional Benchmark Data see Manufacturing—Metal Stamping
- "5% of gross revenue goes into CAPEX each year. It is a real expense of the business. Gross margins from 30% to 55% are found depending on market and type of metal fabrication. Less than 30% GM is too commodity based and will trade for lower multiple (4 or less) 40–50% gross margin will trade 5X or above."
- "50 employees should generate $10M in revenues. You want to make sure you can pass commodity price increases along to customers."

Expenses as a percentage of annual sales	
Cost of goods	30% to 40%
Payroll/labor Costs	24% to 30%
Occupancy	20%
Profit (estimated pretax)	15% to 20%

Industry Trend
- "More reshoring is going on in U.S. The trend for more metal parts fabrication domestically is growing."

Seller Financing
- "Outside financing unless there is customer concentration."
- "90% outside financing, usually 5%-10% seller financing. They're usually asset heavy so financing is readily available."
- 3 to 5 years
- 5 years

Questions
- "What are gross margins? What are quality systems? How many new clients do you get a year? What percent of revenues have gone into CAPEX the last three years? Is your scrap revenue on your income statement?"
- "Check on your ability to sell metal fabricated parts. Getting new sales is important. Often owners are very good at building and challenged at selling. This is competitive and it's hard to get someone to change suppliers if they are doing a good job. Therefore, you're looking for new part numbers from OEMs. Buyers should ask about their quality programs, operating team, safety record and sales/customer retention history."

M - Rules of Thumb

- "Do you have any payment or performance bonds in place? Retainage? What is your backlog? Growing?"

Resources

Associations
Precision Metalforming Association: www.pma.org
Fabricators & Manufacturers Association Intl. (FMA): www.fmanet.org
American Welding Society: www.aws.org
The Society for Mining, Metallurgy and Exploration: www.smenet.org

Manufacturing–Metal Stamping	
NAICS 332119	Number of Businesses/Units 2,401

Rules of Thumb
➢ 5 times SDE plus inventory
➢ 3 times EBIT
➢ 4 times EBITDA

Pricing Tips
- "Length of time in business. Customer base and spread of customer base by percentage."

Expert Comments
"Depending upon products being developed"

Benchmark Data

Statistics (Metal Stamping & Forging)
Number of Establishments	2,401
Average Profit Margin	6.2%
Revenue per Employee	$369,800
Average Number of Employees	45.9
Average Wages per Employee	$55,776

Products and Services Segmentation
Forged metal products	36.2%
Stamped metal products	33.8%
Custom rollformed metal products	24.2%
Powder metallurgy products	5.8%

Major Market Segmentation
Aircraft and aerospace markets	35.0%
Other Markets	33.1%
Off-highway and agriculture markets	21.6%
Ordnance market	10.3%

Industry Costs

Profit	6.2%
Wages	15.7%
Purchases	53.5%
Depreciation	2.7%
Marketing	0.1%
Rent & Utilities	2.8%
Other	19.0%

Market Share

Alcoa Inc.	11.3%
Precision Castparts Corp.	9.9%

Source: IBISWorld, April 2015

Expenses as a percentage of annual sales

Cost of goods	50%
Payroll/labor Costs	15%
Occupancy	15%
Profit (estimated pretax)	20%

Industry Trend

- "Lots of this work is going to China."

Questions

- "How long in business? Cost of goods sold? Lease and rent? How long have employees been there? Diversification of customer base?"

Manufacturing—Metal Valve and Pipe Fitting

(See also Manufacturing—Valves)

	NAICS 332919	

Rules of Thumb

> 7 times EBIT

> 100 percent of annual sales

> Assets plus 1 to 2 times EBITDA

Expert Comments

"High capital investment"

Benchmark Data

- "Four inventory turns, 50 percent gross margin"

Expenses as a percentage of annual sales

Cost of goods	50%
Payroll/labor Costs	20%
Occupancy	30%
Profit (estimated pretax)	15%

M - Rules of Thumb

Manufacturing—Miscellaneous Electrical and Components

NAICS 335999	Number of Businesses/Units 870

Rules of Thumb
➢ 8 times SDE

Pricing Tips
- "Customer concentration and special skills required by owner drive the price model."

Benchmark Data

Expenses as a percentage of annual sales
Cost of goods	50%
Payroll/labor Costs	25%
Occupancy	15%
Profit (estimated pretax)	10%

Manufacturing—Office Products

NAICS 339940	Number of Businesses/Units 493

Rules of Thumb
➢ 5 to 8 times EBIT
➢ 1 times sales plus inventory

Pricing Tips
- "Key to higher valuation is the company's customer base. Does it include either:
  (a) One or more office superstores? (Staples, OfficeMax or Office Depot)
  (b) One or more national wholesalers? (United Stationers, etc.)
  (c) One or more contract stationers?"
- "Customer concentration—many office-product manufacturers have one major customers—a Staples, for example. This may impact valuation if too dependent. Manufactured vs. imported product—companies whose manufacturing base is not vulnerable to imports (from China or Taiwan) are more valuable than those who are."
- "There is no rule of thumb for the office products industry, but in general, pricing is affected by the size of the company. The larger the EBIT, i.e., over $5 million, then the higher the multiple. If a manufacturer of office products sells half to Staples et al and half to Wal-Mart et al, it is not a pure play in the office products business, so the price would be discounted accordingly. A better, more valuable, company would sell 100 percent to office product dealers, not 50 percent to mass merchants, 50 percent to office products. Other factors: breadth of product line, channels of distribution—how broad and complete is that industry, customer and supplier mix (80/20)? Dependency on family members means lower value; union is negative. Is M&E up to date? Growth rate correlation. Is company financeable, or only soft assets?"

Rules of Thumb - **M**

- "1. Customer profile—are the products well-entrenched in the office superstore channel? 2. Uniqueness of product—are items basic commodities or are they unique or distinctive? If the latter, valuation may go up."

Benchmark Data

Statistics (Art & Office Supply Manufacturing in the U.S.)
Number of Establishments	493
Average Profit Margin	3.7%
Revenue per employee	$274,600
Average Number of Employees	19.5
Average Wages per Employee	$44,238

Products and Services Segmentation
Pencils and art goods	38.3%
Pens and mechanical pencils	27.1%
Marking devices	18.2%
Carbon paper and linked ribbon	16.4%

Major Market Segmentation
Wholesalers	55.0%
Exports	20.7%
Retailers	17.9%
Other industries	6.4%

Industry Costs
Profit	3.7%
Wages	16.3%
Purchases	43.3%
Depreciation	3.4%
Marketing	1.3%
Rent & Utilities	5.2%
Other	26.8%

Market Share
ACCO Brands Corporation	18.2%
Crayola LLC	16.8%
Newell Rubbermaid Inc.	14.4%

Source: IBISWorld, August 2015

Seller Financing
- "Not very often. If it is a good company, it is a cash deal."
- 3 years

Manufacturing—Ornamental & Architectural Metal		
SIC 3446-04	NAICS 332321	|//
Rules of Thumb		

> 3 to 7 times EBITDA depending on the company, industry and buyer.

26th Edition 495

M - Rules of Thumb

Questions
- "Do you have to pay union or David-Bacon linked wages for government work?"

Manufacturing—Personal Health Products	
NAICS 325412	

Rules of Thumb
- 5 times SDE plus inventory
- 6 times EBIT
- 5.5 times EBITDA

Pricing Tips
- "30% of GPM [gross profit margin] x 5 should roughly equal a fair valuation."

Benchmark Data
- "$200,000 sales per employee"

Expenses as a percentage of annual sales
Cost of goods	40%
Payroll/labor Costs	12%
Occupancy	05%
Profit (estimated pretax)	10% to 12%

Questions
- "Market share and stability of GPM [gross profit margin]"

Manufacturing—Pharmaceutical Preparation & Medicine	
NAICS 325412	Number of Businesses/Units 4,039

Rules of Thumb
- 75 percent of annual sales
- 5 times SDE
- 4 to 5 times EBIT
- 6 times EBITDA

Pricing Tips
- "Biotech, smaller pharma and R&D based companies are valued using a discounted cash flow of expected earnings less R&D expense and capital expenditures."
- "Depends on the market size and developmental maturity of products in the pipeline"
- "Because of products manufactured, it is important that the products are not on the FDA hit list."

Rules of Thumb - M

- "Much of what the company is valued at will depend on how many products they manufacture, the concentration of clients to the gross revenues, the cost margin for each product, the number of short runs versus the number of long runs, and the opportunity for expansion through existing clients."

Expert Comments

"Seek outside advice for estimates of value. A thorough investigation of competing products is worth the effort. Consider taking an upfront retainer to cover some hard costs. Often when a company wants to sell it's because they are running out of cash. Therefore, it's critical to consider the company's burn rate alongside the length of the listing agreement."

"Value in this industry predicated on intellectual property, which means replication is or should be difficult. The industry has been riding a three-year upswing where values and multiples have gone up substantially dovetailing several significant successes. Profit trends are historically lower as many companies are purchased by larger companies prior to the launch of their products. Marketability can be good but is hampered but a limited pool of buyers. This is a very high risk industry but also high reward which can bring in competitors vying for the same treatment space."

Benchmark Data

Statistics (Brand Name Pharmaceutical Manufacturing)

Number of Establishments	2,759
Average Profit Margin	19.5%
Revenue per Employee	$908,800
Average Number of Employees	53.9
Average Wages per Employee	$88,152

Products and Services Segmentation

Other	45.7%
Oncological products	10.8%
Antidiabetes products	9.4%
Mental health products	9.2%
Respiratory agents	7.9%
Autoimmune products	6.9%
Lipid regulators	5.3%
Antihypertensives	4.8%

Major Market Segmentation

Chain pharmacies	37.3%
Exports	31.5%
Independent pharmacies	12.8%
Food and grocery stores	8.4%
Long-term care providers	5.5%
Mail service providers	4.5%

Industry Costs

Profit	19.5%
Wages	10.4%
Purchases	33.8%
Depreciation	2.2%
Marketing	3.0%
Rent & Utilities	4.0%
Other	27.1%

26th Edition

M - Rules of Thumb

Market Share
Johnson & Johnson	15.5%
Pfizer Inc.	15.1%
Amgen	13.1%
Merck and Co., Inc.	10.9%
AbbVie Inc.	9.8%
Eli Lilly & Company	6.9%

Source: IBISWorld, September 2015

Statistics (Generic Pharmaceutical Manufacturing)
Number of Establishments	1,280
Average Profit Margin	12.6%
Revenue per Employee	$837,000
Average Number of Employees	58.0
Average Wages per Employee	$91,231

Products and Services Segmentation
Pharmaceutical preparations for other drugs	33.6%
Pharmaceutical preparations for metabolic drugs	13.5%
Pharmaceutical preparations for cardiovascular drugs	11.6%
Pharmaceutical preparations for central nervous system drugs	10.1%
Medicinal and botanical products	9.6%
Biological products (except diagnostic)	9.5%
Pharmaceutical preparations for psychotherapeutic drugs	6.3%
In-vitro diagnostic substance products	5.8%

Major Market Segmentation
Wholesalers to chain stores	27.8%
Hospitals and clinics	17.3%
Third-party logistics providers	15.0%
Wholesalers to mail-order retailers	14.0%
Consumers	9.0%
Wholesalers to independent stores	8.9%
Other wholesalers	8.0%

Industry Costs
Profit	12.6%
Wages	10.7%
Purchases	47.8%
Depreciation	2.2%
Marketing	4.2%
Rent & Utilities	2.9%
Other	19.6%

Market Share
Actavis PLC	7.4%
Teva Pharmaceutical Industries Ltd.	7.1%
Mylan Inc.	6.7%
Sandoz Ltd.	5.2%

Source: IBISWorld, September 2015

- "Biotech and R&D companies do not follow the same matrix as many other companies because they are typically pre-revenue companies. Nonetheless, they carry intellectual and enterprise value which can be significant, even the smaller companies, to the right buyer. Finding the right buyers/bidders is the key to realizing the full value of the selling company."

Rules of Thumb - M

- "Development stage: number of drugs in pipeline, and the stage of development"
- "Pharmaceutical businesses are premium now that many trademarked items are available and companies are getting top dollar. FDA requirements are hard, and it can take months to get a company approved for manufacturing."

Expenses as a percentage of annual sales	
Cost of goods	30% to 35%
Payroll/labor Costs	30% to 32%
Occupancy	15% to 20%
Profit (estimated pretax)	20% to 30%

Industry Trend
- "More and more U.S. companies are being sold outside the U.S. and this is expected to continue with the standardization of product approval requirements. This is driving values up, especially for many of the smaller companies. Yet it also is becoming more important to research competitors before selling a business in this industry because they are not just found in the U.S. Management should be able to tell you what the competitive landscape looks like and any knowledgeable buyer will want to know in pre-due diligence."
- "Consolidation of existing companies and emergence of many new entrants"

Seller Financing
- "Senior debt can be very hard to get as there is often very little in the way of hard assets and profitability"
- 5 years

Resources
Websites
- FiercePharma: www.fiercepharma.com

Manufacturing—Plastic and Rubber Machinery
NAICS 333249

Rules of Thumb
➢ 9 times EBITDA

Pricing Tips
- "Look at customer concentration; determine age and condition of equipment; look at industry diversification."

Expenses as a percentage of annual sales	
Cost of goods	50%
Payroll/labor Costs	12%
Occupancy	08%
Profit (estimated pretax)	15%

M - Rules of Thumb

Manufacturing—Plastic Products

| SIC 3089-10 | NAICS 3261 | Number of Businesses/Units 6,428 |

Rules of Thumb
- 3.5 times SDE
- EBITDA is 4X to 7X depending upon size, product mix (less for automotive or appliance, more for medical, and size of products produced (more for companies with larger products, less for smaller products).
- EBIT is 5X to 8X, depending upon same considerations as EBITDA
- Both totals assume customer amounts of Working Capital (inventory+A/R+other current minus A/P+Accruals) transfers with the business.

Pricing Tips
- "The larger the operation, the higher the multiple. Customer concentration is also a huge factor; dependence on large customers significantly lowers valuation expectations. Companies deriving more than 50% of their revenues from medical products/customers will command a significantly higher multiple. Companies that derive more than 50% of their sales from automotive or appliance customers have lower multiples. Also, for injection molders, general metric is EBITDA minus CapEx since these companies have to invest annually in equipment."
- "Good company should have net profits in the 15%–20% range. Multiples in the range of 5 to 7 times EBITDA are possible for good companies. Niche businesses can be very attractive. A model with some manufacturing in the U.S. and some in China also works well."
- "Pricing depends on whether molding company has proprietary products or is a custom molder. Any proprietary products enhance the value. Concentration of customers is critical. High concentration = high risk. Machines vary significantly in capacity and are very expensive. They should be well-maintained and no more than 15 years old, depending on hours of usage. Capacity utilization is a critical questions. With aging baby boomers, technical staffing is becoming an issue due to lack of apprenticeships. Mold makers are 'dying' out. Few millennials are interested in becoming mold makers or molders. If a company relies on an aging in-house mold maker, be cautious. ISO certification is becoming more important, not only as a process control, but also as a marketing tool. ISO certified companies command a premium. Labor and insurance costs are rising, as is off-shore competition, and therefore robotic systems for removing and packaging parts add efficiency and command a premium. Molding is price competitive. Secondary operations, such as sonic welding, stamping, painting and assembly, are often the most, or only, profitable operations. It's important to look the markets being served by the molder and whether the customers face production cycles or seasonal variations. Buyers should be knowledgeable in plastics operations. Otherwise, it's a very big learning curve."
- "Contract manufacturers are worth less than manufacturers of proprietary products. Value is also dependent upon the type of processes used by the manufacturer. In order of value, from lowest to highest, based on processes used, thermoformers are the lowest value range, then blow-molders, then extruders, then rotational molders, then injection molders. The size of the equipment also is a factor in value; manufacturers who only produce small

Rules of Thumb - **M**

parts are much less valuable than those who can produce large parts/products. Any company focused on the automotive industry will command less interest from acquirers."
- "Manufacturers who can produce their products from recycled materials also have an advantage."

Expert Comments

"A lot of consolidation in the U.S. With competition from China, it is becoming easy to lose business."

"Location matters. When shipping plastic products, most shipments 'dimension out' before they weigh out, which means most manufacturers are located within 500 miles of their customers. Many larger manufacturers build/buy factories near their larger customers. Also, 10 to 15 years ago, this industry suffered heavily from off-shoring manufacturing to Asia. However, most of the new work is staying in the USA, leading to a resurgence in the industry. Plus, the Great Recession wiped out many, many companies leaving those in operation today in a much better position than pre-2008."

"It is a competitive industry but there is high demand for a well-run company. Proprietary niches are attractive. General commodity products get very little attention or value."

"The plastics manufacturing industry in the U.S. has been heavily influenced by the automotive industry. With the decline of the U.S. 'Big 3' manufacturers, plastic products manufacturers have had a tough haul since 2005. There have been many failures, thus reducing the value of equipment since the market has been flooded by used equipment. We have seen a steady decline in values of the past few years. With many huge companies in bankruptcy (Collins & Aikman, et al), equipment values are depressed as are company values. Size matters as well. Furthermore, the resins used by plastics manufacturers are all petroleum based; the price of raw materials has doubled in the past 12 months. If a processor has fixed prices (as many suppliers to the Big 3 do), this is a death sentence."

Benchmark Data

Statistics (Plastic Products Miscellaneous Manufacturing)

Number of Establishments	6,428
Average Profit Margin	2.4%
Revenue per Employee	$270,900
Average Number of Employees	55.0
Average Wages per Employee	$44,700

Products and Services Segmentation

Fabricated plastic products for transportation applications	20.7%
Consumer, institutional and commercial fabricated plastic products	19.3%
Plastic packaging (except film, sheet, foam and bottles)	15.8%
Fabricated plastic products for building applications	15.0%
Other plastic products	13.8%
Reinforced and fiberglass plastic products	6.7%
Fabricated plastic products for electrical/electronic applications	4.6%
Plastic plumbing fixtures	4.1%

M - Rules of Thumb

Major Market Segmentation

Automotive manufacturers	30.1%
Hardware and home improvement wholesalers	23.7%
Electrical and electronic manufacturing	18.4%
Plumbing fixture wholesalers	13.4%
Furniture and furnishing wholesalers	10.1%
Other	4.3%

Industry Costs

Profit	2.4%
Wages	16.5%
Purchases	46.6%
Depreciation	5.2%
Marketing	0.3%
Rent & Utilities	3.1%
Other	25.9%

Source: IBISWorld, July 2015

- "Has to be a niche product with good profit margins—at least 50%; medium volume businesses tend to be successful; high volume is difficult to sustain in the U.S. Revenue per employee should be at least $200,000."

Expenses as a percentage of annual sales

Cost of goods	60% to 74%
Payroll/labor Costs	08% to 20%
Occupancy	05% to 10%
Profit (estimated pretax)	07% to 12%

Industry Trend

- "Slow growth"
- "As customers settle into the new era of customized and repeatable manufacturing, the demand for precision parts likely will go up. In 2015, expect to see more of a focus on intricate plastic components, as well as manufacturing methods that are incredibly accurate. It's a new age for innovation, and everything from customized plastic gears and sprockets to bearings and clamps will be in high demand."

Source: "Top 5 Trends for Plastic Manufacturers in 2015" by David Nelson, December 12, 2014

- "2015 to 2018 are expected to be very good years for plastics manufacturers."
- "Lots of niches and continued growth. Companies in fast-growing niches like drones, medical manufacturing do well."
- "Most molders serve a given niche. The industry will rise and fall with the general economy."

Seller Financing

- "Typically these businesses are financed with outside financing, especially senior debt. They are asset-laden businesses and customarily easy to finance."

Questions

- "Most plastics companies are terrible at marketing. Ask the owner how they sell/market their products. Also ask what makes them different from their competitors."
- "Customer concentration.Size, in tons, of equipment. How do they sell their products?"

Rules of Thumb - **M**

Resources

Websites
- American Chemistry: www.americanchemistry.com
  - Injection Molding ReSource: www.injection-molding-resource.org

Trade Publications
- Plastics News: www.plasticsnews.com
- Plastics Technology Magazine: www.ptonline.com
- Plastics & Rubber Weekly: www.prw.com
- Plastics Engineering Magazine: www.plasticsengineering.org

Associations
- Society of the Plastics Industry: www.plasticsindustry.org
- Society of Plastics Engineers: www.4spe.org
- Manufacturers Association of Plastics Processors: www.mappinc.com

Manufacturing—Powder Metallurgy Processing

NAICS 332117

Rules of Thumb
- 50 to 60 percent of annual gross sales includes inventory
- 5 times EBIT
- 4.5 times EBITDA

Pricing Tips
- "Price could vary widely depending on growth prospects."
- "If EBIT is 12% of sales, the multiple at 60% is 5X. Most of these businesses now are not bringing double digits down to the EBIT line, but they still have a lot of assets, most of which would be hard to sell."
- "Industry is under significant stress due to the concentration in the auto industry. Companies with less exposure are performing better and will be more marketable than businesses with auto exposure over 50%."
- "Prices vary widely by product type, primary customer markets, and gross margins achieved."
- "Industry and customer concentration is a major influence in transactions."
- "None have any merit due to profitability variations; sanity check at 80 percent of revenue."
- "Gross margins consistency and diversification of the customer base add value to PM business."
- "Value is, and should be, a function of projected future cash flow."
- "Investment value drives this and other manufacturing markets. 5 to 6 times EBITDA (adjusted for synergy) is typical, but never a firm rule."
- "Transactions are driven by technology fit, growth prospects, profitability and other attributes of the selling company. Other key factors are: management, technology & systems, markets, and equipment age & mix. Markets served may have an influence and older smelting furnaces may detract slightly."

M - Rules of Thumb

Expert Comments

"Basic changes in the industry and individual company concentration will control the rate of

recovery."

"The industry is 70% automotive based which has had a significant effect on companies with a high percent of sales in this market segment. Non-automotive PM manufacturers are experiencing much better results."

"Profit margins have been squeezed in recent years due to movement offshore and increased volatility in raw material costs. In addition, the cost of capital equipment has increased faster than industry sales growth"

"The current trend to move manufacturing to China and India is affecting the key customer groups of many PM companies."

Benchmark Data
- "Sales per employee = $125,000 (varies with primary materials in products delivered)."

Expenses as a percentage of annual sales	
Cost of goods	30%
Payroll/labor Costs	40%
Occupancy	20%
Profit (estimated pretax)	10%

Questions
- "Percent breakdown of customer types by market segment. How large are the top 10 customers? What percent of sales do the top 10 account for? How large is the engineering and tooling staff? What experience does the technical staff have? How long have they been with the company?"
- "Customer trends; industry concentration; changes in key technical, management personnel and direct production supervisors."

Manufacturing—Prefabricated Wood Buildings

NAICS 321992	Number of Businesses/Units 843

Rules of Thumb
➢ 100 percent of annual sales includes inventory

Pricing Tips
- "Modular plants sell at a premium. Log home companies sell at a discount."
- "Dealer network is important, or if selling direct, quality of sales staff."

Expert Comments

"Difficult to develop designs and engineering and establish a reputation, so it is not easy to start business from scratch."

"The log and timberframe industry has suffered more than the building

Rules of Thumb - **M**

industry in general because it is such a custom building market that has a higher unit cost than more traditional construction and has been adversely affected (log structures in particular) by tightening energy and building code requirements."

Benchmark Data

Statistics (Prefabricated Home Manufacturing)

Number of Establishments	843
Average Profit Margin	2.2%
Revenue per Employee	$188,900
Average Number of Employees	47.2
Average Wages per Employee	33,952

Products and Services Segmentation

Manufactured mobile homes	55.3%
Prefabricated wood buildings	33.6%
Nonresidential mobile buildings	11.1%

Major Market Segmentation

Retail trade	60.3%
Wholesale trade	36.6%
Exports	3.1%

Industry Costs

Profit	2.2%
Wages	18.2%
Purchases	62.2%
Depreciation	0.9%
Marketing	1.1%
Rent & Utilities	5.2%
Other	10.2%

Market Share

Berkshire Hathaway Inc.	28.0%
Champion Enterprises Inc.	10.0%
Cavco Industries Inc.	7.8%

Source: IBISWorld, August 2015

- "Gross profit over 35%"
- "$1 million to $1.5 million sales per salesperson"

Expenses as a percentage of annual sales

Cost of goods	50%
Payroll/labor Costs	15%
Occupancy	03% to 05%
Profit (estimated pretax)	05%

Industry Trend

- "The U.S. wood product manufacturing industry includes about 14,000 companies with combined annual revenue of about $67 billion. Demand is closely tied to the level of home construction. The profitability of individual

M - Rules of Thumb

companies depends on efficient operations, because many products are commodities. Large companies enjoy economies of scale in purchasing. Small companies can often compete successfully by focusing on a local market."

Source: http://www.firstresearch.com/Industry-Research/Wood-Product-Manufacturing.html

- "Housing business is cyclical. Expect flat sales due to being in down cycle."

Questions
- "Warranty policy and expense. How much warranty exposure is there? Does company have a favorable reputation for taking care of warranties?"
- "What is your backlog? How many leads have you received over each of the last 5 years? How do you sell your product —through a dealer network or direct or both? What patented processed do you have? Do you have challenges meeting energy or structural/building codes? What info do you have for your sales performance by region for the last 5 years? How many competitors do you have and where are they located? Do you sell internationally? Brand name, length of time in business and type of building system are extremely important."

Resources

Associations
- Building Systems Council of National Association of Home Builders: www.nahb.org/page.aspx/category/sectionID=454

Manufacturing—Products from Purchased Steel

NAICS 3312

Rules of Thumb
➢ 3 to 5 times SDE includes inventory

Expert Comments
"Product line is the main importance along with the ability to deliver."

Benchmark Data
- "Payroll costs, equipment maintenance and age of equipment"

Expenses as a percentage of annual sales
Cost of goods	15%
Payroll/labor Costs	35%
Occupancy	20%
Profit (estimated pretax)	20%

Industry Trend
- "If you have a niche business, you will do well. If you are a job shop, chances are you will struggle."

Questions
- "How many customers does he have and what is the percentage of his business?

Manufacturing—Scientific Instruments

Rules of Thumb

➢ "Company value is 3 to 6 times EBITDA."

Pricing Tips

- "Where are the products in the life cycle? What new products are about to be introduced? Do they have strong patents? What is the competitive situation?"

Expenses as a percentage of annual sales

Cost of goods	50%
Payroll/labor Costs	25% to 30%
Occupancy	15%
Profit (estimated pretax)	10%

Manufacturing—Showcase, Partition, Shelving, and Lockers

	NAICS 337215	

Rules of Thumb

➢ 2 to 3 times SDE plus inventory

Pricing Tips

- "Customer concentration and any special skills required to operate can make for a big difference in pricing."

Expert Comments

"Economy changes the profitability very quickly here."

Benchmark Data

Expenses as a percentage of annual sales

Cost of goods	35%
Payroll/labor Costs	40%
Occupancy	15%
Profit (estimated pretax)	10%

Manufacturing—Signs (See also Sign Companies)

SIC 7389-38	NAICS 339950	Number of Businesses/Units 5,851

Rules of Thumb

➢ 45 to 50 percent of annual sales plus inventory

➢ 2 to 2.5 times SDE plus inventory

M - Rules of Thumb

Benchmark Data

Statistics (Billboard and Sign Manufacturing)

Number of Establishments	5,851
Average Profit Margin	3.6%
Revenue per Employee	$175,700
Average Number of Employees	12.5
Average Wages per Employee	$46,653

Products and Services Segmentation

Billboards	43.4%
Digital signs	38.6%
Alternative displays	9.5%
Transit displays	8.5%

Major Market Segmentation

Other	25.8%
Amusements and miscellaneous services	18.8%
Financial services, insurance and real estate	13.8%
Media and advertising agencies	10.5%
Miscellaneous retailers	8.8%
Public transportation, hotels and resorts	8.2%
Restaurants	7.6%
Communications	6.5%

Industry Costs

Profit	3.6%
Wages	26.9%
Purchases	39.6%
Depreciation	3.3%
Marketing	0.7%
Rent & Utilities	3.0%
Other	22.9%

Source: IBISWorld, August 2015

Industry Trend

- "The International Sign Association's initial ISA Sign Industry Market Monitor shows anticipated growth in large-format printers, dynamic digital signage, electric signage, and wayfinding signage throughout 2014 and into 2015. The ISA Sign Industry Market Monitor, sponsored by the National Association of Sign Supply Distributors (NASSD), assesses key drivers to compile data that shows changes in the market.
    - ✓ Large-format printers will enjoy stronger than average growth in both 2014 (.47) and 2015 (.59). Its growth will come largely as the manufacturing sector bounces back, posting anticipated growth of 4% in 2014 and 5% in 2015.
    - ✓ Dynamic digital signage also will grow in 2014 (.21) and 2015 (.48), thanks largely to hardware and software revenue. Display mounts are forecast to increase gradually each year, averaging 2.9% growth annually through 2017. All other cable and miscellaneous hardware revenue is expected to increase an average of 2.4% each year during the same time period. Installation (2.4%) and project management revenue (2.0%) also show growth.

Rules of Thumb - **M**

✓ Electric signage will experience a stronger year in 2014 (.74) but 2015 reflects a less aggressive growth rate (.48). Growth in this sector will largely will come from increases in out-of-home advertising, which is expected to grow 18% in 2014 and 15% in 2015. Other key factors include retail output, which is expected to increase 3% in 2014 and 4% in 2015; manufacturing output (3%, 2014 and 5% 2015); and professional services output (2% each year).

✓ Wayfinding signage (.71 in 2014 and .45 in 2015) will find its growth driven by new construction of highways and streets, which increases by 3% in 2014 before flattening in 2015, as well as growth in manufacturing, retail and professional services sectors."

Source: ISA Sign Industry Market Monitor

Resources

Associations
- International Sign Association (ISA): www.signs.org

Manufacturing—Small (See also Manufacturing—General)

Rules of Thumb
➢ 4 to 5 times SDE plus inventory

Pricing Tips
- "For manufacturing companies with sales of $1 million to $5 million, a crude rule of thumb is 3 to 4 times SDE, assuming the company is reasonably well established and viable. As company size goes up, the multiple will go up."
- "Factors to look for: sales/profitability trends; SDE (and trends); industry trends; years in operation; fixed asset value, seller financing. Risk factors: technology, competition, industry trends."

Manufacturing—Specialty Vehicle

Rules of Thumb
➢ 4 times SDE includes inventory

Pricing Tips
- "Evaluate inventory closely as there is a tendency to accumulate difficult-to-use inventory."
- "Look for amount of booked business. Lead times from getting the order to shipping the finished vehicle can run 12 months or more."
- "Evaluate financials closely. Many in this industry do not know what their true costs are."

Expert Comments
"It is difficult to acquire the expertise to build these vehicles. Many can build them—few can build them well."

M - Rules of Thumb

"Homeland Security issues make this a growth industry. It is fairly easy to replicate the 'physical facility,' but the real market advantage comes from experience in designing, building and using these vehicles."

Benchmark Data
- "Difficult to estimate sales per employee, but should probably be $175,000–$200,000 per hourly production employee."

Expenses as a percentage of annual sales	
Cost of goods	55%
Payroll/labor Costs	25%
Occupancy	05%
Profit (estimated pretax)	10%

Industry Trend
- "Much of the business is tied to Homeland Security. If there are attacks on our soil, demand will increase. Otherwise budget cutbacks will dampen demand."
- "The market for mobile command centers, bomb trucks, SWAT trucks, etc. will continue to be strong as long as the U.S. has to fight terrorists. Many corporations are developing mobile marketing vehicles which will also help drive demand."

Questions
- "Who has design experience in the company? Who has the mfg. experience in the company? How do you accurately cost jobs?"
- "What portion of the business is municipal, corporate, & private? Who are the key employees with industry experience? What is your marketing/sales plan? What is your backlog of business?"

Resources
Websites
- www.vehiclesuccess.com/links

Manufacturing—Sporting Goods & Outdoor Products	
NAICS 339920	
Rules of Thumb	
➢ 4 to 7 times EBITDA	

Pricing Tips
- "Brand and customer concentration are extremely important factors in valuing a manufacturer of outdoor and/or sporting products. These consumer products include hunting equipment, ammunition, fishing equipment, camping gear, sporting goods, outdoor apparel, etc. Patents are also an important value driver by increasing barriers to entry and making these consumer products harder to imitate. Customer diversity and relationships with key distributors are important. Brand awareness and time in the market place also add value.

Rules of Thumb - **M**

Many manufacturers outsource to contract manufacturers overseas to control costs and create a variable cost model. It's important to understand the sustainability of these supplier relationships."

Expert Comments
"Trade association reports show that consumers continue to spend money on sporting goods, even in tough economic times."

Benchmark Data
- "Gross margins tend to be very high for these manufacturers, well north of 50%, especially when they outsource manufacturing. Therefore, do not use revenue Rules of Thumb."
- "Cost of Goods—30% to 50%"

Manufacturing—Stainless Steel Food Service Fabrication	
NAICS 333319	

Rules of Thumb
> 3 to 6 times EBITDA depending on the company, industry and buyer.

Questions
- "Are you a custom fabricator also? Do you install? Do you sell other food-service equipment? Do you sell to the cruise lines?"

Manufacturing—Turbine and Turbine Generator Set Units	
NAICS 333611	

Rules of Thumb
> 8 to 10 times EBITDA

Pricing Tips
- "Use cap rate, similar to pricing commercial real estate."

Expert Comments
"This industry is, for a number of reasons, going to grow dramatically over the next decade. The economic model is very similar to that of commercial real estate—high upfront capital costs followed by extremely consistent cash flows, with upside appreciation potential. Smart money will get in early and ride the wave."

Benchmark Data
- "Revenue per kilowatt hour, capacity factor, PPA rate"

Industry Trend
- "Significant growth as the industry consolidates and becomes institutionalized."

M - Rules of Thumb

Manufacturing—Valves

| NAICS 332911 | Number of Businesses/Units 1,215 |

Rules of Thumb
- ➢ 5 times EBITDA

Pricing Tips
- "Special consideration given for special products, market share, industry recognition."

Expert Comments
"A lot of competition with 'commodity' type valves; the more specialized, the less competition"

Benchmark Data

Statistics (Valve Manufacturing)
Number of Establishments	1,215
Average Profit Margin	7.5%
Revenue per Employee	$384,100
Average Number of Employees	76.7
Average Wages per Employee	$62,571

Products and Services Segmentation
Industrial valves	43.8%
Fluid power valves and accessories	29.3%
Other	15.2%
Plumbing fixture valves, fittings and trim	11.7%

Major Market Segmentation
Exports	39.9%
Oil and gas	15.2%
Chemical manufacturing	10.7%
General manufacturing and processing industries (other)	9.8%
Waterworks	9.7%
Power generation	8.7%
Construction	6.0%

Industry Costs
Profit	7.5%
Wages	16.5%
Purchases	44.8%
Depreciation	2.3%
Marketing	1.3%
Rent & Utilities	0.2%
Other	27.4%

Source: IBISWorld, August 2015

Expenses as a percentage of annual sales

Cost of goods	60%
Payroll/labor Costs	20%
Occupancy	20%
Profit (estimated pretax)	15%

Industry Trend
- "Trends toward specialization"

Seller Financing
- 5 years

Manufacturing—Wood Kitchen Cabinets and Countertops

	NAICS 337110	

Rules of Thumb
➢ 2 to 2.5 times SDE plus inventory

Pricing Tips
- "Some wood cabinet manufacturers have state-of-the-art equipment that increases the efficiency of the business. Analyzing and adding the value of the equipment is a component of the above."

Expert Comments
"The sales trends are determined by the general economy of the geographic area. When housing starts are booming, demand is high."

Manufacturing—Wood Office Furniture

SIC 2499-02	NAICS 337211	

Rules of Thumb
➢ 2.5 to 3 times SDE includes inventory

➢ 2.5 to 3 times EBITDA

Pricing Tips
- "Very cyclical business"
- "Rules of Thumb do not work well for an industry this diverse."
- "Customer list drives the value."

Expert Comments
"Really depends where you are on the food chain; these vary from high- to low-margin businesses."

"Very dependent on economic cycles and affected by China"

M - Rules of Thumb

Benchmark Data

Expenses as a percentage of annual sales
- Cost of goods 40%
- Payroll/labor Costs 30%
- Occupancy 20%
- Profit (estimated pretax) 10%

Industry Trend
- "More consolidation and offshore competition"

Questions
- "How much design work and fashion trends?"

Resources

Associations
- Business and Institutional Furniture Manufacturers Association : www.bifma.org

---

	Franchise
Marble Slab Creamery (See also Franchises, Ice Cream/Yogurt Shops)	
Approx. Total Investment	$250,000 to $403,000
Estimated Annual Sales/Unit	$225,000
SIC 2024-98 NAICS 722515	Number of Businesses/Units 366

Rules of Thumb
> 45 percent of annual sales plus inventory

Resources

Websites
- www.marbleslab.com

Marinas (See also Boat Dealers)	
SIC 4493-06 NAICS 713930	Number of Businesses/Units 3,898

Rules of Thumb
> 10 to 12 times SDE plus inventory

> 10 times EBIT

> 11 to 12 times EBITDA

> 10 + times SDE plus inventory ("The real estate is included in the 10 + SDE figure. It is almost always owned. Very seldom is it leased, and then usually as part of a concession which has been bid out, say by the National Park Service or the TVA or something like that.")

Rules of Thumb - M

Pricing Tips
- "This is a very complicated business. Estimating the selling price has many factors such as: dock leases, leases with resorts, years of operation, strength of mid-level management, survey of the vessels, competition, market, etc. Bottom line, it would be foolish to use a multiplier without a great deal of study."
- "Be very careful using multipliers as the price of waterfront land greatly distorts the valuation of a marina. The best rule of thumb is to ensure that slip rental and boat storage income will suffice to cover debt service, allowing the buyer to make a living off the other services offered by the marina."
- "Waterfront property makes the earnings multiple much higher than most businesses. That and the fact that marinas are very difficult to start from scratch anymore"
- "There are so many businesses within a marina that a % of gross is misleading at best. The pricing is driven by the real estate (waterfront property) and is usually at least 10 x EBITDA. The ROI is terrible. One is buying a lifestyle."

Expert Comments

"It is a tourist related industry. If the location requires costly travel and the economy is soft, the sales will be down."

"Location and facilities are critical but vary greatly."

"These businesses are notoriously hard to make a living at. They are hard work for very little return. I always tell purchasers they are buying a lifestyle and that they will probably work harder than they ever have. This is not a 'retirement' business."

"Profits are being squeezed as discretionary income is not quite as high. Marinas are hard to sell as one is looking for a buyer that is basically not dependent on the income stream from the marina. As you get more boats, there are fewer places to put them, and permitting issues make starting a marina from scratch ever more difficult."

Benchmark Data

Statistics (Marinas)

Number of Establishments	3,898
Average Profit Margin	13.4%
Revenue per Employee	$154,300
Average Number of Employees	7.1
Average Wages per Employee	$38,474

Products and Services Segmentation

Pleasure craft dockage, launching, storage and utilities services	40.9%
Fuel and merchandise sales	20.8%
Other	17.6%
Repairs and maintenance services	12.8%
Food and beverage sales	7.9%

26th Edition

M - Rules of Thumb

Industry Costs

Profit	13.4%
Wages	25.1%
Purchases	5.0%
Depreciation	7.3%
Marketing	2.7%
Rent & Utilities	19.4%
Other	27.1%

Source: IBISWorld, September 2015

- "A marina is usually a combination of many businesses, each with its own benchmarks. You have a storage business, a service business, a gas station, boat sales, brokerage sales and sometimes a restaurant, all with different Rules of Thumb."
- "Each business in a marina has its own benchmark. The restaurant operation should be leased out to an operator as it is virtually impossible to run a marina and a restaurant at the same time."
- "Slip rental income and storage fees should cover 100% of debt service. Owner compensation and other benefits would come from sales and service charges and appreciation of real estate value(s)."

Expenses as a percentage of annual sales

Cost of goods	60% to 65%
Payroll/labor Costs	20%
Occupancy	05% to 12%
Profit (estimated pretax)	05% to 10%

Industry Trend

- "With innovative design and consumer preferences for outboard power, many manufacturers are seeing the fishing boat replace the fiberglass I/O as the de facto family runabout.

  "'Reality is there are a lot of people that fish, [and] there are a lot of people that don't, but they want those dual consoles, they want those center consoles for the ease of boating' said Rob Parmentier, president and CEO of Larson Boat Group. 'You can put a lot of people on board, they have less canvas, they are easier to clean, a lot of them are easier to get in and out of. You can use them as kind of an SUV, and they have the technology of the outboard power, which has completely surpassed that of I/O.'"

  Source: "Market Trends: Family, outboard trends favor fishing boats" by Jonathan Sweet, 6/9/15
  http://www.boatingindustry.com/top-stories/2015/06/09/freshwater-phenomenon/

- "As the economy rebounds, so will the lot of the marina improve. We are looking at discretionary income here, and that disappears in a poor economy."

Seller Financing

- "It is extremely difficult to obtain bank financing, since the assets can literally float away. Large down-payments and seller's financing is the rule."
- "Seller financing used as banks are loath to take any risks at all. They don't want foreclosure auctions which will only bring in a fraction of their loan."
- 15 years

Rules of Thumb - M

Questions
- "Be ready for a lot of hard work. Ask about environmental history. Be careful of new boat sales as the floor plans/interest thereon will eat you up. Competition results in razor thin margins. Stick to brokerage if possible."
- "Why are you selling? Are you environmentally 'clean'? What would you do differently if you were starting again?"
- "The number 1 question would be to cover all environmental issues. A Phase 1 would probably be called for."
- "Do you have any environmental issues, are your storm water plans up to date?"

Resources
Associations
- Boat Owners Association of the U.S.: www.boatus.com
- National Marine Manufacturers Association: www.nmma.org
- American Boat Builders and Repairers Association: www.abbra.org
- Association of Marina Industries: www.marinaassociation.org

Marine/Yacht Services (Boat/Repair) (See also Marinas)	
NAICS 811490	Number of Businesses/Units 99,311

Rules of Thumb
- ➢ 100 percent of annual sales includes inventory
- ➢ 2.3 times SDE includes inventory

Pricing Tips
- "Determine value of furniture, fixtures & equipment; any warranty work involved?"

Expert Comments
"The mega-yacht (80-foot to 180-foot boats) is a major growth industry, especially in south Florida."

Benchmark Data

Statistics (Boat Dealership and Repair)
Number of Establishments	99,311
Average Profit Margin	3.5%
Revenue per Employee	$122,200
Average Number of Employees	1.3
Average Wages per Employee	$11,726

Products and Services Segmentation
New boats	56.3%
Parts and repair services	19.0%
Other	14.0%
Used boats	10.7%

26th Edition

M - Rules of Thumb

Industry Costs

Profit	3.5%
Wages	9.6%
Purchases	73.0%
Depreciation	0.6%
Marketing	1.3%
Rent & Utilities	4.7%
Other	7.3%

Market Share

MarineMax Inc.	4.4%

Source: IBISWorld, December 2014

Expenses as a percentage of annual sales

Cost of goods	30%
Payroll/labor Costs	15%
Occupancy	07%
Profit (estimated pretax)	40%

Industry Trend
- "Growth"

Questions
- "Customer base, length of time in industry, employee turnover, specific services performed"

	Franchise
Martinizing Dry Cleaning (See also Dry Cleaning, Franchises)	
Approx. Total Investment	$305,000 to $593,700
NAICS 812320	Number of Businesses/Units 422

Rules of Thumb
➢ Note: Also known as One Hour Martinizing
➢ 55 to 60 percent of annual sales plus inventory

Benchmark Data
- "He said a franchisee could open a store for anywhere from $293,500 to $476,000, including the franchise fee and purchase of in-house dry cleaning equipment. A typical investment for a franchisee to open a store would be $390,000."
- "Four percent of the sales from a franchised store's gross sales go back to the company."

Source: "Martinizing Cleans Up" by Jeff McKinney, www.greenearthcleaning.com

Resources

Websites
- www.martinizingfranchise.com

Rules of Thumb - **M**

McGruff's Safe Kids ID System
			Franchise
Approx. Total Investment			$7,995 to $9,995
		Number of Businesses/Units	26

Rules of Thumb
> 52 percent of annual sales plus inventory

Resources

Websites
- McGruff'sSafe Kids ID Systems: www.mcgruff-tid.com/

Meat Markets
SIC 5421-07	NAICS 44521	Number of Businesses/Units 9,600

Rules of Thumb
> 40 percent of annual sales plus inventory

> 2.5 times SDE includes inventory

> 5 times monthly sales plus inventory

Benchmark Data

Statistics (Meat Markets)
Number of Establishments	9,600
Average Profit Margin	3.4%
Revenue per Employee	$181,400
Average Number of Employees	4.4
Average Wages per Employee	$21,117

Products and Services Segmentation
Broilers	42.1%
Beef	25.8%
Pork	23.6%
Turkey	7.4%
Other red meat and fish	0.5%
Other chicken	0.6%

Industry Costs
Profit	3.4%
Wages	11.6%
Purchases	68.0%
Depreciation	1.7%
Marketing	1.7%
Rent & Utilities	5.0%
Other	8.6%

26th Edition

M - Rules of Thumb

Market Share
Omaha Steaks International Inc.	6.8%

Source: IBISWorld, October 2015

Expenses as a percentage of annual sales
Cost of goods	50%
Payroll/labor Costs	15%
Occupancy	10%
Profit (estimated pretax)	15%

Industry Trend

- "Newspapers and news Websites have spent considerable ink (or kilobytes) this year talking about the rising prices of meat and poultry products, and some pundits questioned if there would come a price point where consumers had to stop buying meat altogether. If there is such a cliff, the market hasn't found it yet.
"In reality, consumers bought meat at supermarkets or restaurants as much as they ever have. They may have reallocated their shopping dollars or switched proteins, but they kept meat on the plate more often than not. 'Everything that we see says that demand is holding up, so the consumer wants to buy beef,' says John Lundeen, executive director of market research for the National Cattleman's Beef Association."

   Source: http://www.preparedfoods.com/articles/115134-top-meat-and-poultry-trends-in-2015

- "As a result, Packaged Facts estimates that retail sales of meat and poultry products topped $85 billion in 2012, up from nearly $73 billion in 2008. Looking ahead, sales are projected to grow to $98.3 billion by 2017. Supporting that growth will be an economic recovery that, while it has been very slow, is underway and likely to pick up steam with each passing year."

   Source: www.packagedfacts.com

- "Boutique butchers are now opening in cities across the country, from Brooklyn to Los Angeles, selling high-end, grass-fed meats to health-conscious consumers and foodies chasing trends, such as the charcuterie craze."

   Source: "Family-run Denver butcher shop celebrates 90 years in business," www.denverpost.com/news
   May 25, 2013

Resources

Websites
- North American Meat Institute: www.meatami.org

Associations
- National Cattlemen's Beef Association: www.beef.org

Medical and Diagnostic Laboratories	
NAICS 621511	Number of Businesses/Units 32,676

Rules of Thumb
- ➢ 1 times Annual Gross Sales
- ➢ 3 to 4 times SDE plus inventory
- ➢ 4 to 5 times EBIT
- ➢ 4 to 5 times EBITDA

Rules of Thumb - M

Pricing Tips
- "Good diversity of accounts, good 3rd party payer contracts a must"
- "Multiple of SDE increases with profit levels."
- "Client concentration, market penetration and ability to expand"

Expert Comments

"It would take over four years to replicate a new diagnostic clinic and that long to obtain a good strong client base."

"Difficult to acquire accounts since physician groups don't like to make changes. 3rd party payer contracts are difficult to obtain"

"This is a marketing business. Location, ease of service, and networking with doctors and attorneys is a must."

Benchmark Data

Statistics (Diagnostic & Medical Laboratories)
Number of Establishments	32,676
Average Profit Margin	17.9%
Revenue per Employee	$186,200
Average Number of Employees	8.9
Average Wages per Employee	$61,069

Products and Services Segmentation
Diagnostic imaging services	45.0%
Routine medical testing	31.5%
Anatomical pathology testing	12.0%
Other services	6.5%
Esoteric medical testing	5.0%

Major Market Segmentation
Private insurance payments	43.5%
Medicare and Medicaid payments	19.5%
Hospital payments	10.5%
Health practitioners payments	8.0%
Other	7.0%
Out-of-pocket payments	5.5%
Other healthcare providers payments	4.5%
Workers' compensation payments	1.5%

Industry Costs
Profit	17.9%
Wages	32.7%
Purchases	30.0%
Depreciation	1.8%
Marketing	1.5%
Rent & Utilities	6.5%
Other	9.6%

Market Share
Quest Diagnostics Inc.	14.4%
Laboratory Corporation of America Holdings	11.7%

Source: IBISWorld, June 2015

M - Rules of Thumb

- "The purchase of your reagents and the building of your client list are the most important factors. This is a marketing business to some degree."
- "Sales are measured on a per-technician basis. Each MRI tech should produce a certain level of revenue."
- "Broad, even client base a big plus. Ability to expand beyond immediate geographical region without significant working capital requirements."

Expenses as a percentage of annual sales
Cost of goods	15% to 20%
Payroll/labor Costs	44% to 45%
Occupancy	03%
Profit (estimated pretax)	30% to 35%

Industry Trend

- "Handheld ultra-sound scanners that are as 'cheap as a stethoscope' is the goal of a $100 million development project. Just as the clinical laboratory industry is seeing entrepreneurs pour hundreds of millions of dollars into projects intended to create miniature medical laboratory testing devices, so also is radiology and imaging a target for ambitious entrepreneurs. The vision of biotechnology entrepreneur Jonathan Rothberg, Ph.D. is to have patients take a trip to their neighborhood drugstore rather than an imaging center the next time they need an ultrasound or MRI."

    Source: "Biotech Entrepreneur Ready to Spend $100 Million to Design Cheap and Easy-to-Use Handheld Ultrasound Scanners that Can Be Used in Drugstores" by Andrea Downing Peck 8/3/15

- "Healthcare has been shifting from curative care to detection, prevention and personalized care over the past five years, which has benefited the diagnostic and medical laboratories industry. Moreover, the trend of preventive care stimulates demand for industry services, as more physicians monitor patients' blood and tissue, and test for health ailments with technology like MRI scans. However, the recession caused fewer individuals to have employer mandated health insurance and greatly limited industry revenue growth over the period. Nevertheless, during the next five years, the industry is expected to benefit from healthcare reform and the growing aging population, which will boost revenue. Geographic access to physicians has improved during the past five years, whereas laboratories have not diffused to rural areas as quickly."

    Source: IBISWorld, April 2014

- "Flat to slightly growing"
- "More personal injury MRIs"

Seller Financing

- "Yes, about 25% of the selling price can be seller financed over three to four years."

Questions

- "Payer contracts, employee retention, distributor contracts for goods sold"

Resources

Trade Publications
- Clinical Laboratory and Pathology News and Trends: www.darkdaily.com

Associations
- American Society for Clinical Laboratory Science: www.ascls.org

Rules of Thumb - M

Medical Billing

	NAICS 541219	Number of Businesses/Units 3,940

Rules of Thumb
➢ 75 to 80 percent of annual sales plus inventory
➢ 3 times SDE
➢ 4 times EBIT
➢ 4 times EBITDA

Pricing Tips
- "Specialties of clients are a very important factor."
- "The value of medical billing companies is heavily dependent upon the billing rates they charge their clients and the length of the contract. Billing rates are typically in the 5% to 8% range for larger accounts, but can be as high as 15% and as low as 2%."

Expert Comments
"Buyers should educate themselves on upcoming changes within the industry and find out the specific area of medicine that each client practices, example: surgeons, clinics, dialysis centers, etc."

"This is a highly competitive industry that has a strong financial outlook with the changes in the health care field and complicated coding and billing procedures."

Benchmark Data

Statistics (Medical Claims Processing Services)

Number of Establishments	3,940
Average Profit Margin	26.7%
Revenue per Employee	$131,900
Average Number of Employees	2.5
Average Wages per Employee	$48,013

Products and Services Segmentation

Claims processing	60.0%
Claims investigations	15.0%
Policy and claims examinations	15.0%
Back-office, administrative support and consulting	10.0%

Major Market Segmentation

Healthcare providers	60.0%
Private insurers	25.0%
Government insurers	15.0%

M - Rules of Thumb

Industry Costs

Profit	26.7%
Wages	36.6%
Purchases	1.4%
Depreciation	1.7%
Marketing	1.0%
Rent & Utilities	2.4%
Other	30.2%

Market Share

HMS Holdings	33.9%

Source: IBISWorld, October 2015

- "Sales per FT employee are typically around $100,000."

Expenses as a percentage of annual sales

Cost of goods	0
Payroll/labor Costs	50%
Occupancy	05%
Profit (estimated pretax)	25%

Industry Trend
- "Very positive trend for the industry as a whole with larger companies looking to do roll-ups of smaller companies as the industry is consolidating."

Seller Financing
- "Seller financing is more typical although outside financing may be possible."

Resources

Associations
- Healthcare Billing and Management Association: www.hbma.org

---

Medical Practices		
SIC 8011-01	NAICS 621111	Number of Businesses/Units 410,798

Rules of Thumb

➢ 35 to 40 percent of annual gross sales includes inventory

➢ 1 to 3 times SDE includes inventory

➢ 1.5 to 2 times EBITDA

➢ 3 to 3.5 times EBIT

➢ "35 to 50 percent of annual fee revenue; applies to small practices; may require earnout"

➢ "20 to 60 percent of annual fee revenue; applies to practices with fee revenues of $125,000 plus; may require earnout"

➢ "45 to 55 percent of one year's gross collections, based on location, age and contracts"

Rules of Thumb - M

Pricing Tips

- "The rule of thumb in any of the medical fields (i.e., accepting Medicare) is 1.5 x dividends as defined by IRS RR59-60. (You can call it 1.5 x EBITDA, but that is slightly incorrect for non-capital, asset-heavy businesses). Includes normal inventory but not excess inventory. %-of-gross hasn't applied to medicine in decades since the doctorshortage began.
"From SDE, I will subtract the estimate of the cost of employing one person at the same level of licensure, with the same work schedule, and with the same experience and sophistication as the current owner, at a market rate of compensation. This provides a perspective as if the owner was instead employed, and the balance was a return on investment to ownership. Another way to look at this is the result is the income available to the owner if the owner couldn't work and had to hire an equivalent replacement licensed professional to see the patients. This remainder income is equivalent to what the IRS defines as 'Dividends' in RR59-60. Dividends will be the income stream analyzed in the Income Approach."
- "If the practice is located near a hospital it will increase the value. Since there are so many specialties, a family practice might be easier to sell."
- "Income and expense and compensation expectations vary widely among practice types. A family practice is significantly different than say a cardiology practice or oncology practice. Compensation expectations differ significantly. $220K may be a good salary for a general practitioner, but less than half the expected compensation for a specialist like an interventional pain management specialist. Also, average number of hours worked vary between specialties."
- "The payer mix (private insurance, Medicare/Medicaid and cash (fee for service) influences value. Practices heavy in Medicare or Medicaid reimbursements tend to have a lower valuation than those with a more balanced mix or are more heavily weighted in fee for service and/or private insurance. Revenue trends, condition of facility and site and the level of technology used in the practice also play a role in valuation."
- "The value of medical practices is generally at an all-time low. Decisions regarding what, where, when and how to practice are influenced by numerous factors, including: personal preferences, market forces, state and federal policies and programs, and institutions that constitute the health care system and medical education infrastructure. Increasing retirement, plus the trend toward shorter working hours, increases the supply of practices for sale, and decreases the available FTE workforce available as buyers. The increasing rate of boomer retirement and decreasing count of new physicians contributes to a reduction of value of practices for sale. A significant shortfall of physicians could develop over the next 15 or more years in the absence of increased output from U.S. medical schools, increased recruitment of foreign-trained physicians, or both. The American College of Physicians is concerned that the practice environment for those in medical practice has become so encumbered with regulation and practice hassles, at a time when reimbursement for care provided by physicians is declining, that physicians are finding it increasingly difficult to provide for their patients.
"Of particular concern when determining value of a medical practice is ensuring not only that the purchase price is Fair Market Value, but also that the valuation method does not take into account the volume or value of referrals that the selling physician has made or may make to the purchaser, such that the purchase price could be challenged as a kickback or inducement. The OIG has provided guidance on the question of how to value a physician practice or other healthcare provider. The ailing economy is leading many Americans to skip doctor visits, skimp on their medicine, and put off tests. Employment by

M - Rules of Thumb

hospitals is paying more, and insurance-reimbursement and gross income is often dropping, so the results of the Income Approach of valuation identifying 'dividends' [(SDE minus market rate compensation of one working owner) x 1.5 (i.e., 66% Cap rate)] is becoming more important for more specialties. 'Percentage of annual gross sales' or 'SDE multiplier' as valuation Rules of Thumb are obsolete, if ever valid. Growth rates are available through the Congressional Budget Office reports; rarely above 2% historically. Medical practice is riskier—and demands higher Cap rates—than other professional practices like accounting, law, architecture and engineering which are not subject to clinical malpractice risks, or subject to Medicare or insurance company changing reimbursement limitations or denials.

"Many practices can't even sell at the value of the liquidated assets, since jobs pay more without asset purchase. The impact of specialty and location is profound, as is the FTE work-schedule and leverage of employed licensed providers. Medicare is continually reducing reimbursement, which impacts other insurances which often base their payment on a percent of Medicare (i.e., 80–120% of Medicare), so dependence on insurance reimbursement is an important consideration in value. In addition; specific diagnosis and procedure ('ICD/CPT') billing-code reimbursement changes—like what has happened in dermatology, ophthalmology, allergy, cardiology, and other specialties—have further reduced reimbursement and profits during the past decade. Cash and cosmetic practices are usually worth more since there is a higher profit for less work, and often provide a better lifestyle, but even those can be difficult to sell. Many specialties are having trouble attracting new doctors no matter the income, so guaranteed wages are increasing, sales are becoming more difficult, and values are dropping. Make sure to read the white papers on supply and demand available on many specialty professional association websites. The best overhead statistics are usually available at http://www.NSCHBC.org. The best market rate compensation stats are usually available at http://www.MGMA.com. The Goodwill Registry on sale-data is helpful in some cases, but the often-quoted running—average 10-year median goodwill—value as a percentage of gross is irrelevant; as the average of many specialties reflects the midpoint of 10 years' steady decline. You need to acquire the full database and evaluate the underlying data to be useful; and look in particular at the Price:SDE data. The effect of the Medicare cuts which began in 2005 can distort the Registry summary statistics and needs to be adjusted; and you need to remove results from court-valuations, divorces and other non-transactional data.

"Medical record charts are not a true 'asset' of the medical practice since they can't be put on the balance sheet as an asset using the Asset Approach valuation methodology. Medical record valuation is only used to specifically allocate intangibles, assuming they exist at the time of the valuation. The physician has the physical chart but usually cannot legally sell or dispose of it without the patient's consent (per state statutes), only transfer 'custodianship.' So the physician is basically a 'custodian' of the medical record rather than an owner of an asset with independent value. When paper charts are involved, I have come to the opinion that the value of the chart is zero because of the attendant custodianship liability costs. With EMR, a digital record may need to be converted from one digital platform to another either by custodianship transfer or technology succession, in which case a printout and re-entry may be required, probably exceeding in labor costs any physical value to the original digital chart.

"The billing process in a medical practice is very complex, both in generating the charges using appropriate diagnosis and treatment codes, and in recording the payment and adjustments for uncollectable amounts. 'Accounts

Rules of Thumb - M

Receivable' represent past gross charges for services rendered and as yet uncollected or adjusted-off. These receivables must be discounted to reflect both insurance company reimbursement disallowances, plus the decreasing value over time due to difficulty in collections of past due accounts. In other words, the historic collection ratio of the practice does not yet include the 'standing wave' of uncollectable accounts at practice end, or at a particular point in time, as in a valuation at a particular date."
- "PPACA (i.e., Obamacare) has made it worse, with escalating salaries, reducing dividends, and therefore value."
- "Don't try to use boilerplate broker contracts to sell medical practices, as it is easy to violate state or federal regulations; have all the paperwork and terms done by a medical practice transaction specialist attorney."
- "EBITDA doesn't apply well to medical practices without significant invested capital or capital assets. 'Dividends' per IRS RR59-60 is most applicable for these small service businesses. I usually see cap rates on pretax dividends of 65% or more."
- "Adjusted expenses and adjusted SDE are critical to determining profit potential."
- "Wide variety of sales price depending on type of practice. Primary care 30%–40%, specialty 20%–30%, non-physician owned (e.g., phys. therapy, NP/PA owned family practice) might sell for more 40%–50%. The more specialized the practice the harder to sell, x for goodwill, lower price ratios. Critical to compare after-debt service cash flow to doctor compensation range for that particular specialty. Different doctors have widely different compensation expectations. Focus on gross collections not gross billing."
- "1 to 1.35 times SDE plus inventory and accounts receivable are not included."
- "AGS, SDE, EBIT and EBITDA multiples really no longer apply. The best current formula is [2.5–4 times (SDE minus compensation for owner labor)]. The 2.5 multiplier is for insurance-based practices, and the 4 multiplier is for the best of cash practices. Insurance reimbursement trends are downwards, hurting values significantly. The reason AGS, SDE and EBITDA don't apply is the owner might be active or passive. It is illogical to think that a practice with $1,000,000 AGS has the same value to ownership if the owner works there 50 hours per week or is an absentee owner; which is why you have to subtract the market-rate comp for owner labor prior to applying the multiplier. Many specialties have merely liquidation value or close to it because of shortages, the ease of opening a competing practice, and hospital income & overhead guarantees via forgivable loans in lieu of practice purchase. Value issues are very, very localized. Rule of thumb: the sale should pay for itself to the buyer within 5 years with profits above comp for labor."

Expert Comments

"It's pretty easy to set up a medical practice from scratch in any underserved market, if you know how."

"Number of specialists per 100K population varies. Obamacare and healthcare reform is causing turmoil in industry. Industry is constantly evolving in response to government laws/regulations. Above-average practices can usually sell okay. Underperforming practices may have virtually no value and be unable to sell."

"Sell at Fair Market Value (FMV) to avoid the Anti-Kickback Statute or Stark Law. Ensure physician compensation is at FMV. Inquire as to the payor mix of the physician or physician practice to be bought and inquire as to any regulatory issues regarding the physician or physician practice to be bought."

M - Rules of Thumb

"Managed care, political pressure on lowing reimbursements, regulatory pressures, uncertainties all are playing a part in valuation declines in the healthcare industry."

"Physicians are very smart but often choose their advisors poorly. Selecting a team of trustworthy advisors (legal, accounting, transactional) is key to success."

"Affordable Care Act is creating a great deal of uncertainty, causing the incumbents to analyze their options. This uncertainty is creating opportunities to restructure, monetize or roll-up existing businesses."

"Medicare reimbursements dropping. Many practices picking up cosmetic and other ancillary profit centers."

"Competition is high and hospitals are offering better guarantees for startups."

Benchmark Data

Statistics (Primary Care Doctors)

Number of Establishments	184,629
Average Profit Margin	11.3%
Revenue per Employee	$207,100
Average Number of Employees	6.7
Average Wages per Employee	$80,007

Products and Services Segmentation

Diagnosis of general symptoms	32.0%
Diagnosis, screenings, preventative care	26.0%
Other	17.0%
Diagnosis of symptoms related to the musculoskeletal systems	12.0%
Disease treatment	7.0%
Diagnosis of symptoms related to the respiratory system	6.0%

Industry Costs

Profit	11.3%
Wages	38.7%
Purchases	14.6%
Depreciation	1.5%
Marketing	0.5%
Rent & Utilities	3.9%
Other	29.5%

Source: IBISWorld, June 2015

Statistics (Specialist Doctors)

Number of Establishments	226,169
Average Profit Margin	12.6%
Revenue per Employee	$171,200
Average Number of Employees	6.6
Average Wages per Employee	$88,069

Rules of Thumb - M

Products and Services Segmentation

Other	48.7%
Internal medicine	19.6%
Pediatrics	9.4%
Obstetrics and gynecology	6.0%
Anesthesiology	5.6%
General surgery	4.3%
Emergency medicine	3.7%
Dermatology and cosmetic surgery	2.7%

Industry Costs

Profit	10.1%
Wages	51.6%
Purchases	19.5%
Depreciation	1.5%
Marketing	0.5%
Rent & Utilities	3.9%
Other	12.9%

Source: IBISWorld, June 2015

- "Per bed, per full-time employee (FTE); per physician; per square foot; per machine; per member per month (PMPM)."

Physician salaries—Annual earnings from patient care

Highest paid specialties

Orthopedics	$421,000
Cardiology	$376,000
Gastroenterology	$370,000
Anesthesiology	$358,000
Plastic Surgery	$354,000

Lowest paid

Rheumatology	$205,000
Internal medicine	$196,000
Diabetes & endocrinology	$196,000
Family medicine	$195,000
Pediatrics	$189,000

Source:"Precarious future for primary care,"by R. Michael Rosenblum, *Boston Globe*, June 23, 2015

- "Practice benchmarks vary with specialty. Look up statistics/benchmarks for the practice type in question. A psychiatry practice may be a solo operation in 200SF with no support staff and almost no assets. A cosmetic plastic surgeon may have $500K in equipment and an in-house accredited surgical suite with a lot of staff. An oncology or allergy practice may have a great deal of value in drug inventory, whereas a pediatric practice may have no drug inventory. So for some practice types (e.g., psychiatry) the cost of goods sold is very small. Others have significant COGS. For most practice types expect a support staff ratio of 3-5 per full time doctor."
- "Profit for physician practices should be above 50%"
- "Revenue per procedure, cost per procedure, revenue per FTE physician, cost per FTE physician, revenue per work relative value unit (wRVU), cost per work relative value unit (wRVU) and compensation per work relative value unit (wRVU)"
- "Keep overhead less than 65%, labor less than 20%."

M - Rules of Thumb
- "The average profit margin is 14% with revenue per employee at $160,000 to $170,000."
- "Collections to compensation by specialty; work RVUs (Relative Value Units) per physician by specialty; accounts receivable collection rate; hours worked per week by specialty; professional component revenue percentage by specialty; technical component revenue by specialty; new patient visits by physician by specialty; number of patients by diagnosis per physician; length of stay by physician by specialty; readmission rate per physician by specialty; etc."
- "Depreciation is at 1.2% to 1.6%, Average revenue should be from $1,000,000 to $1,300,000."
- "75% reimbursement rate"
- "Benchmarks vary widely for 20+ specialties from pediatricians to neurosurgeons. Two good data sources by specialty are the National Association of Healthcare Consultants Statistics Reports (for practices with 10 or fewer doctors) at www.HealthCon.org, and the Medical Group Management Association at www.MGMA.com for larger groups."
- Note: www.healthcon.org is an excellent site and has a lot of data; however, one must purchase it, and non-members pay a lot more than members.

Expenses as a percentage of annual sales
Cost of goods	n/a
Payroll/labor Costs	25% to 40%
Occupancy	05% to 10%
Profit (estimated pretax)	20% to 30%

Industry Trend
- "Increased merger & acquisition (M&A) activity, and steady growth in revenue."
- "Other important changes in physician practice arrangements that occurred between 2012 and 2014 include:
  - ✓ The share of physicians who were practice owners decreased from 53.2 percent to 50.8 percent.
  - ✓ The share of physicians who were in solo practice decreased 18.4 percent to 17.1 percent.
  - ✓ The share of physicians who were directly employed by a hospital increased from 5.6 percent to 7.2 percent
  - ✓ The share of physicians who were in practices that had at least some hospital ownership increased from 23.4 percent to 25.6 percent."
  Source: http://www.ama-assn.org/ama/pub/news/news/2015/2015-07-08-majority-americas-physicians-work-small-practices.page
- "Other types of practices hospitals have acquired include (in order of quantity):
  - ✓ Cardiology
  - ✓ Orthopedics
  - ✓ General Surgery
  - ✓ Endocrinology
  - ✓ Gastrointestinal
  - ✓ Urology
  - ✓ Oncology
- "Hospitals report both offensive and defensive reasons for acquiring medical practices. These included:

Rules of Thumb - **M**

- ✓ Expanding service capabilities
- ✓ Meeting community need
- ✓ Insurance-related purposes
- ✓ Increased efficiency and alignment
- ✓ Increased Market Share
- "Other characteristics hospitals look for in an acquisition target include:
  - ✓ Reputation of the practice
  - ✓ Strategic value of the practice
  - ✓ Location of the practice
  - ✓ Quality of physician(s) in practice
  - ✓ Referral patterns
  - ✓ Existing relationships between hospital and practice

  Source: http://www.jacksonhealthcare.com/media-room/articles/physician-trends/physician-practice-acquisition-trends-2015/
- "The market trend is lower profits for the next few years."
- "A lot of turmoil due to regulatory changes. More practices trending to self-pay practices. Many doctors moving away from Medicaid and Medicare due to regulatory burden and low reimbursement. Still a very large part of the economy. Healthcare will still be strong in years to come. Likely to see more boutique practices and more capitation practices."
- "Demand for services and costs to provide services increasing while reimbursements decreasing."
- "Increasing competition; industry will tend to consolidate."
- "PPACA is driving physicians into employment, reducing available buyers."
- "Not all succession planning involves total retirement from the practice of medicine."
- "As hospitals began acquiring physician's practices, many believed that integrating physicians under one roof would reduce costs by increasing efficiency and streamlining patient care. But a new online poll conducted by the American College of Physician Executives (ACPE) shows the move toward physician integration may be actually driving up costs. The findings echo results of a recent report by the Medicare Payment Advisory Commission that shows the same clinical services cost more when performed as an outpatient procedure at a hospital instead of a doctor's office."
- "Lower supply of physicians/buyers, many practices going unsold, less people entering the field"

Seller Financing
- "100% financing is readily available through specialty bank departments."
- "Outside financing is more typical."
- "Lenders look very favorably towards funding these deals. Many have special terms available for financing professional practices."
- 5 to 10 years
- "If Medicare patients are seen, limit payout terms to one year to comply with laws."

Questions
- "Historical productivity, payor mix. Unaudited financial statements are common in the industry."

M - Rules of Thumb

- "An important fact is the type of medical practice, general or specialty! Number of Medicare and Medicaid patients? Billing process and whether in house or farmed out."
- "For buyers: try to buy so practice cash flows with no longer than a 10-year loan. For sellers: keep gross and profits up."
- "Ask Seller: practice type, hours worked, number of patient encounters/week per provider, support staff ratio per doctor, outpatient revenue vs. inpatient revenue, payer mix, services provided."
- "Accounts receivable in collections amount should be under 25%. Insurance accepted and type of billing to insurance companies. Employee retention and turnover."
- "What are the ACO plans in this community? Is your ICD/CPT coding federally compliant? Are your provider employment and compensation plans and PECOS registrations state and federally compliant?"
- "History of staff, provider contracts, billing procedures type of patients"
- "Hours worked. Use of mid-level providers/physician extenders payer mix reimbursement trends up/down ancillary profit centers."
- "Sustainability of projected revenue stream, based on probability of patients remaining with practice, level of reimbursement yield, regulatory restrictions on ASTC, etc."
- "Many!! Really understand the specialty, procedures, technology, provider team, management systems and team, payment systems and concerns, regulatory requirements, etc."
- "Atypical services, local hospital trends, specialty trends, insurance plans of note, %Medicaid, % Medicare, hidden income, technology & surgical obsolescence, if hospital will help recruit or is a potential buyer."
- "Why are you selling? Are you willing to recommend me to your patients, colleagues, and the community? Are you willing to provide full disclosure and transparency and assist to the fullest extent in transferring the value in the practice?"
- "Where do you get patients?"
- "One should look at whether the business is primary care or surgery/specialty, and what portion of the business is professional (fees) vs. technical (diagnostic or pharmaceutical/medical goods). Specific reimbursement trends are based upon specialty, provider supply (i.e., the supply of physicians to the population) and other indicators of demand for services, such as utilization demand for services in the market service area of the practice. Things that make business sense are often illegal in medical practice, so services, leases, referral sources, etc. need to be scrutinized for Stark II and Medicare compliance. CPT coding errors can greatly affect value."

Resources

Trade Publications

- Medical Economics: www.memag.com
- Physicians Practice: www.physicianspractice.com
- The BVR/AHLA Guide to Healthcare Valuation: www.amazon.com
- Medscape: www.medscape.com

Rules of Thumb - M

Associations
- American Medical Association: www.ama-assn.org/ama
- Medical Group Management Association: www.mgma.com
- National Society of Certified Healthcare Business Consultants: www.nschbc.org
- American Academy of Family Physicians: www.aafp.org

Medical Spas

NAICS 812199	Number of Businesses/Units 21,956

Rules of Thumb
- 50% of Annual Gross Sales plus inventory
- 2.5 times SDE includes inventory
- 3.5 times EBIT
- 5 times EBITDA

Pricing Tips
- "1) It is critical to understand if the business had prepaid services as a liability. Many med spas have balance sheet complications due to large prepaid services that are paid in advance and delivered over a year or more. Any assumed liability by the buyer should be counted as consideration. 2) Because of equipment obsolescence, equipment leasing is common. 3.0 multiple assumes the seller pays off the leases or if the buyer assumes the leases, the assumed amount counts as consideration/purchase price. 3) Med spas with niche services such as hair replacement may bring a higher multiple, especially if they have a relationship with a well-known hair restoration/hair replacement surgeon."

Expert Comments
"Med spas provide a niche between spa/beauty treatments and invasive plastic surgery. With the aging population of baby boomers, more women and men are investing in non-invasive 'image enhancement.' Spending money on microdermabrasion, laser hair removal, Botox and other services is considered more acceptable than ever. Medical doctors see the category as attractive, as the services are almost always elective and do not involve insurance money and its associated regulations."

Benchmark Data

Statistics (Health and Wellness Spas)

Number of Establishments	21,956
Average Profit Margin	8.5%
Revenue per Employee	$45,300
Average Number of Employees	16.9
Average Wages per Employee	$20,594

26th Edition

M - Rules of Thumb

Products and Services Segmentation

Massage and bodywork treatments	32.0%
Skin-care treatments	25.0%
Hair and nail treatments	21.0%
Retail	12.0%
Other	10.0%

Major Market Segmentation

Adult women	55.4%
Seniors	18.0%
Adult men	16.6%
Teenagers and children	10.0%

Industry Costs

Profit	8.5%
Wages	45.1%
Purchases	15.7%
Depreciation	4.0%
Marketing	3.1%
Rent & Utilities	14.2%
Other	9.4%

Market Share

Massage Envy	9.6%

Source: IBISWorld, October 2015

- "Market data estimates that revenues of the 2,100 U.S. medical spas reached $1.94 billion in 2012, and will hit $3.6 billion by 2016. Average revenues per facility are $924,000—with about 80% coming from procedures and 20% from retail product sales. The market is forecast to grow 18% per year. Fully 58% of med spas expected sales to grow more than 5% last year.

 "Females account for 83% of med spa clients, but the share of men is growing. The most requested esthetician services include: facials, waxing, microdermabrasion, chemical peels and other anti-aging treatments. There are 183,000 estheticians licensed to practice in the U.S. (they are not MDs).

 "The average profit margin of a med spa is 14% of net sales. Start-up costs range from $700,000 to $1 million, with up to half of that devoted to buying or leasing the latest laser machines. These machines wind up being obsolete in 2–3 years as technology changes so rapidly. Labor costs take up another big chunk of expenses."

    Source: "$1.9 Billion Medical Spas Market Poised For Growth," www.prweb.com January 2013

- "Advertising expenses are generally 25% of revenue and drive the business. 2–3 sales consultants per million in sales. Owner is often helping sell for a single location. 1 clinician per $150,000–$200,000 in sales. Laser hair removal tends to be the largest revenue category (50%+)."

Expenses as a percentage of annual sales

Cost of goods	05%
Payroll/labor Costs	30%
Occupancy	08% to 10%
Profit (estimated pretax)	25% to 30%

Rules of Thumb - **M**

Industry Trend
- "Eight biggest spa trends for 2015:
    - ✓ Wellness and preventive treatments
    - ✓ Specialty spas
    - ✓ Personalization
    - ✓ Treatments for men
    - ✓ Express, express, express
    - ✓ Social fitness
    - ✓ Expanded spa boutiques
    - ✓ Continued care

  "'In the past, spas were trying to please everyone,' says Debra Koerner, co-founder of Well World Group, a spa consultancy firm. 'They were expanding their menus and offering an overwhelming number of services.' Fast forward to 2015. 'In the bigger cities, in particular, we're seeing more niche properties and new franchises open up that offer convenience and affordability, specializing in one thing—whether massages (Massage Envy now has 1,000 locations across 49 states.), brows, lashes, hair or feet.'"

  Source: http://www.marketwatch.com/story/8-biggest-spa-trends-for-2015-2015-01-14

- "One of the biggest factors influencing spa industry trends for 2015 is the Baby Boomers. The Baby Boomer generation in the U.S. will account for about 40% of all spending. That demographic of individuals, ranging from age 45 to 65, has a large focus on combating aging and slowing the process. In 2015, it is likely that there will be an increase of spa treatments to help with aging. Acupuncture is being more widely introduced into the Western world spas and while it is known to have positive mental health benefits, it can also rejuvenate skin! If you're able to get past nerves of needles, you should consider adding acupuncture as an offered service at your spa or wellness center."

  Source: http://www.floridaspaassociation.com/blog/spa-industry-trends-2015/

- "Approximately 2,100 'medical spas' or 'med spas' are now operating in the United States. Medical spas only emerged ten years ago and exploded in number between 2007 and 2009. However, a major shakeout took place as franchises failed and the recession hit—exposing overoptimistic revenue assumptions and poor management. As primary care MDs seek to replace lost income, and as baby boomers age, demand should grow for minimally or non-invasive cosmetic procedures made possible by new laser equipment."

  Source: "$1.9 Billion Medical Spas Market Poised For Growth," www.prweb.com January 2013

Seller Financing
- 3 to 5 years

Questions
- "Revenue/service mix. Liability for prepaids. Equipment leases. Reason for selling."
- "1) Are there prepaids? 2) What unique services do you offer? 3) equipment leases 4) revenue/service mix 5) licensing/regulatory requirements 6) Do you need doctor/nurse to oversee operations? 7) Insurance"

Resources

Associations
- Day Spa Association (DSA): www.dayspaassociation.com

M - Rules of Thumb

Medical Transcription	
NAICS 561410	Number of Businesses/Units 86,596

Rules of Thumb
- 75 to 80 percent of annual sales
- 3 to 3.5 times SDE
- 4.5 to 5 times EBITDA

Pricing Tips

- "MTSO's are almost always sold as a percentage of revenue with not too much attention paid to net profit but a great deal to gross profit. Most of the buyers are rolling up revenue and are therefore most concerned about the quality of the revenue and the cost of production (COGS.) MTSOs with revenue under $1.5M can generally expect to get about 75–80% of revenue as a purchase price, while those doing revenue of $1.5M plus can expect to see 80–100% of revenue.

  "The lower the risk profile of the customer base the greater the percentage of revenue one can expect. Customer concentration and risk of losing the customer to EHR are central to evaluating this risk profile. If the work is post EHR, that is the MTSO is working within the healthcare provider's EHR, then the buyer is going to perceive the revenue to be less at risk of loss to EHR.

  "Earnouts are virtually always a part of any MTSO transaction. Typically the buyer will come in with 50–60% cash and the seller will carry the balance on an 18–36 month earnout tied to ongoing revenue. A greater risk profile will equate to a larger earnout, a lower profile to less earnout.

  "Offshore, onshore or hybrid production models: The easiest MTSO to sell is where all the customers are U.S. based but most are OK with some or much of the production work being done offshore. If offshore production is allowed, many more buyers, especially from India, will come to the table with offers. Ideally the business has customers paying onshore rates but the buyers believe they can move much of the production off shore while keeping the customer pricing closer to onshore rates."

- "Medical Transcription Service Organizations (MTSO) doing under $1M in revenue will average about 75% of revenue. As they near the $2M revenue mark, they sell closer to 100% of revenue. Revenue, rather than EBITDA or SDE, is generally the multiple used. Where a given MTSO ends up on the 75–100% of revenue range is determined by size, quality of the book of business, customer concentration, technology used and how open the seller and customers are to offshoring labor. MTSOs achieve optimum valuations when they have a low customer attrition profile and where the buyer has maximum flexibility in moving the business to another technology platform and to the production vendor (i.e., offshore or onshore) of their choice."

- "The market for Medical Transcription companies will vary according to several factors: the higher the 'price per line' the more a buyer is willing to pay; technology can influence price if the work is highly automated; the size of the service with regard to annual revenue and diversity of its customer base. These factors in combination can create a range of value from 75% of gross sales to 120% of gross."

Rules of Thumb - **M**

Expert Comments

"The Medical Transcription industry has witnessed declines in revenue and profitability due to low-cost offshore labor, improvements in speech recognition technology and the government mandated adoption of Electronic Health Records."

"Three trends have significantly eroded medical transcription profitability and growth: offshore labor has brought line rates charged customers down from the heights of 16–18 CPL to 7–10 CPL; EMR vendors like EPIC and GE have taken much market share from traditional transcription; speech recognition technologies have resulted in turning many traditional transcriptionists into editors."

Benchmark Data

Statistics (Document Preparation Services)

Number of Establishments	86,596
Average Profit Margin	16.5%
Revenue per Employee	$32,700
Average Number of Employees	1.4
Average Wages per Employee	$16,290

Products and Services Segmentation

Medical Transcription	51.2%
Desktop publishing	24.1%
Other transcription & secretarial	14.2%
Document editing and proofreading	10.5%

Major Market Segmentation

Healthcare providers	53.9%
Small service-related business	19.8%
Other	11.0%
Individuals and households	10.1%
Federal, State and Local Government	5.2%

Industry Costs

Profit	16.5%
Wages	49.1%
Purchases	17.5%
Depreciation	2.1%
Marketing	1.8%
Rent & Utilities	7.0%
Other	6.0%

Market Share

Nuance Communications Inc.	10.1%

Source: IBISWorld, September 2015

- "Gross profit and EBITDA are very much tied to how much of the production is done offshore and or how much of the production is being processed via a speech engine. Use of technology and offshore labor will have a huge impact on how profitable the business is."

M - Rules of Thumb

- "For work being produced through onshore labor, line rates should be 12–15 CPL with labor costs at 7–9 CPL and platform cost at about 1.5 CPL. Offshore production line rates are about 6 CPL, mostly in India followed by the Philippines. When production is done offshore, frequently the customer can get a line rate of 10–12 CPL. In hospitals speech recognition technologies are used to produce 70–80% of the work. In this case the customer may pay 10–12 CPL while cost of production (i.e., the editor plus the technology) might be more like 4 CPL for the editor/labor and 2–3 CPL for the speech engine."
- "Well-run MTSOs with only onshore operations can see gross profit margins in the 30–40% range; those with offshore operations can increase these margins by 10 points to the 40–50% range."
- "Medical transcriptionists continue to be an aging population. Part of this is impacted by the aging nature of the U.S. workforce overall. However, when compared to estimates of the 2006 age distribution of the U.S., the MT profession reflected in this survey trends older. This creates an immediate concern regarding the creation of not only a replacement workforce, but a workforce that can match the demands of the expanding healthcare industry."
- "The industry generally prices the transcription work on the basis of a 65 key strokes per line rate. Averages are running close to $.125 per line in the USA. The higher quality firms have been able to achieve as high as $.22 per line. This, of course, makes them more desirable and worth more to the buyer. Most of the firms use transcriptionists who are independent contractors and pick up the work from home-based computers from the servers of the MT firm. Work is turned around on a 24–48 hour basis in most cases."

Expenses as a percentage of annual sales

Cost of goods	50% to 70%
Payroll/labor Costs	0
Occupancy	0
Profit (estimated pretax)	15% to 20%

Industry Trend

- "Consolidation of smaller MTSOs by the large players, such as Nuance and lots of mid-sized regional/national players. More revenues will be lost to EHR and speech recognition technologies but the declines in revenue are tapering off from the big declines of the past few years of government incentivized EHR adoption."

Seller Financing

- "Occasionally for the smaller MTSO, the buyer will purchase with an SBA loan and the seller will hold a note for 15% of the transaction rather than the typical earn-out structure."
- "Transactions typically involve 50–60% cash down with the seller doing a 24–36 month earnout for the balance."

Questions

- "Please describe each customer that accounts for more than 15% of your revenue. Have you or do you anticipate losing any business to EMR or to other competitors? Is your production being done onshore or offshore? Are you open to selling to someone with an offshore workforce? What platform, if any, are you using? Are your customer contracts assignable?"

Rules of Thumb - M

Resources

Associations
- The Association for Healthcare Documentation Integrity: www.ahdionline.org
- American Health Information Management Association: www.ahima.org

	Franchise
Meineke Car Care Centers (See also Auto Mufflers, Franchises, Midas)	
Approx. Total Investment	$200,000 to $250,000
Estimated Annual Sales/Unit	$700,000
NAICS 811112	Number of Businesses/Units 975

Rules of Thumb
➢ 30 to 35 percent of annual sales plus inventory

Benchmark Data

Average Meineke Center—Sales: $700,035*

Cost of Goods Sold	26.5%	$185,509
Direct Labor (Inc. P/R Tax)	18.90%	$132,307
Variable Expenses	4.75%	$33,252
Fixed Expenses	14.40%	$100,805
Royalty	5.2%	$36,402
Advertising	7.6%	$53,203
Average earnings after Royalty and Advertising fees	22.65%	$158,558*

	Franchise
Merry Maids (See also Franchises, Janitorial Services, Maid Services, etc.)	
Approx. Total Investment	$60,150 to $87,750
NAICS 561720	Number of Businesses/Units 1,650

Rules of Thumb
➢ 45 percent of annual sales plus inventory

Resources

Websites
- www.merrymaids.com

M - Rules of Thumb

Franchise
Midas International (See also Auto Mufflers, Franchises, Meineke)

Approx. Total Investment	$220,000 to $425,000
Estimated Annual Sales/Unit	$1 million +
NAICS 811112	Number of Businesses/Units 3,000+

Rules of Thumb
➢ 30 to 35 percent of annual sales plus inventory

Resources

Websites
- www.midasfranchise.com

Middle Market Businesses (In General)

Rules of Thumb
➢ 2 to 5 times SDE plus inventory
➢ 3 to 5 times EBIT
➢ 3 to 5 times EBITDA

Pricing Tips
- "Only accept audited financials. Always retain qualified legal and accounting professionals early on in the process to uncover any 'hidden' issues that you may not discover on your own. Determine whether the industry sector of the business you are considering is trending up or down and what the long-term direction of the specific business's product line(s), within that industry, is projected to be. Determine what your exit strategy would be if you were to obtain control of the business."

Expert Comments
"Middle market businesses have very sophisticated competitors and are quite risky. Therefore, they are historically more profitable than smaller, main street operations. Because of the high cost of entry, there is a limited market for many of these businesses. Additionally, these companies tend to often be quite specific in their product line and hold a large market share in their respective geographic location."

Benchmark Data
- "Look for 'visionary' leadership and highly structured accounting and marketing departments. Look closely at employee costs and how 'deep' the middle management is, i.e., is middle management highly motivational or just high cost? Are all processes and procedures of the company in place or is everyone 'flying by the seat of their pants'? And which of these will be better for your given situation?"

Rules of Thumb - M

Expenses as a percentage of annual sales

Cost of goods	20% to 30%
Payroll/labor Costs	25% to 30%
Occupancy	10%
Profit (estimated pretax)	30% to 40%

Questions
- "What are their companies' goals for the future and how have they prepared to make that a reality? Have they prepared a contingency plan in the event of unforeseen developments and what are their contingencies?"

		Franchise
Minuteman Press (See also Franchises, Print Shops)		
Approx. Total Investment		$100,000 to $150,000
	NAICS 323111	Number of Businesses/Units 975

Rules of Thumb
➢ 60 to 65 percent of annual sales plus inventory

Resources

Websites
- Minuteman Press: www.minutemanpress.com

Mobile Home Parks		
SIC 6515-01	NAICS 531190	Number of Businesses/Units 96,500

Rules of Thumb
➢ 3 to 8 times monthly income

Pricing Tips
- "Eight times gross or $8,000 per space (pad), depending upon the amenities, e.g., carports, recreation center, landscaping, paving, size of pad (space), closeness to city, etc."
- Note: Mobile-home parks are generally real-estate-intensive—a real estate license is probably necessary to handle the sale.

Industry Trend
- "Such properties are not only good investments now but are set to become more so in the future, (Mark) Weiner said. Developers rarely build new ones anymore, and in particularly desirable communities, they're being closed to make the way for more lucrative housing instead. But Weiner said in California, demographic trends suggest both retirees and working-class residents will demand such communities as affordable options. 'We feel we meet the needs of low-income housing in every community we serve,' he said."

Source: http://www.bizjournals.com/sacramento/news/2015/01/14/emerging-investment-trend-mobile-home-parks.html

M - Rules of Thumb

Modeling Agencies		
SIC 7363-01	NAICS 711410	Number of Businesses/Units 6,748

Rules of Thumb
> ➢ 20 percent of annual sales

Pricing Tips
- "Smaller agencies may be one-person businesses and the goodwill may be difficult to transfer. Earnouts may be necessary."

Benchmark Data

Statistics (Model Agencies)
Number of Establishments	6,748
Average Profit Margin	2.8%
Revenue per Employee	$103,100
Average Number of Employees	1.4
Average Wages per Employee	$38,753

Products and Services Segmentation
Commissions from model representation	60.5%
Performance or project related contract	20.5%
Other	14.1%
Product Licenses	4.9%

Major Market Segmentation
Consumer goods	64.0%
Publishers	17.0%
Other	12.5%
Fashion designers	6.5%

Industry Costs
Profit	2.8%
Wages	37.6%
Purchases	23.3%
Depreciation	2.0%
Marketing	3.0%
Rent & Utilities	6.0%
Other	25.3%

Market Share
Wilhelmina International Inc.	6.0%

Source: IBISWorld, November 2014

Rules of Thumb - M

	Franchise
Molly Maid (See also Franchises, Janitorial Services, Maid Services, etc.)	
Approx. Total Investment	$85,600 to $131,000
NAICS 561720	Number of Businesses/Units 620

Rules of Thumb

> 35 to 40 percent of annual sales plus inventory

Resources

Websites
- www.mollymaid.com

	Franchise
Money Mailer (See also Advertising Material Distribution Services, Franchises)	
Approx. Total Investment	$50,000 to $75,000
NAICS 541870	Number of Businesses/Units 210

Rules of Thumb

> 45 to 50 percent of sales plus inventory

> "If a cooperative direct mail business, such as Money Mailer or Supercoups is making $100,000, it could be sold for $150,000 to $225,000, and $250,000 if it was a perfect situation. Now, on the other hand, if it is a Valpak, I believe you could get up to 3 times what it is making because Valpak is the undisputed leader."

Resources

Websites
- www.moneymailer.com

Montessori Schools (See also Children's Educational Franchises)	
NAICS 611110	

Rules of Thumb

> 35% of Annual Gross Sales plus inventory
> 1.5 to 2 times SDE
> 3 to 4 times EBITDA

Pricing Tips

- "The demographics profile—is it changing? Are the tuition rates within market—too low such that when increased will significantly affect enrollment and profits? Verify financials through due diligence by a knowledgeable CPA. Is the owner the director or simply the administrator overseeing operations? Are maintenance expenses being performed by the owner that would have to be assumed by the buyer? Is the enrollment going to change because of the personal goodwill of the owner and/or a director or key teacher who might leave? Why is the owner selling? Have there been any incidents or outstanding events that have not been disclosed. Verify continuation of enrollment due to possible aging of children in the area served. Is there a new school moving in or under construction nearby? Certifications of the teachers and their salaries. Teacher to student ratio. Are there foreseeable expenses in bringing the facility into code? What is the ethnic background of the owner/director and parents/students as compared to the buyer? Historic enrollment, actual enrollment, and maximum enrollment."

- "The larger schools with enrollment of 100 tend to sell for 3 times EBITDA, perhaps 4 times if the facility is in a location not easily replicated; the owners typically run them semi-absentee. Smaller schools are typically run by an 'owner/director' and are sold as a typical service business 1.5 to 2 times SDE."

Expert Comments

"Focus on why the facility is for sale and what the owner plans to do after sale."

"Most successful if enrollment is over 200 students, has a solid curricula with stable teachers in a high-income demographics"

Expenses as a percentage of annual sales	
Cost of goods	n/a
Payroll/labor Costs	25% to 35%
Occupancy	30% to 45%
Profit (estimated pretax)	20% to 35%

Industry Trend

- "For an educational movement trying to use a century-old pedagogical method developed by an Italian Catholic, Maria Montessori, to teach Jewish tenets, mixing metaphors is the point. Arguing that the traditional Jewish day-school model they grew up with is outmoded and too clannish for 21st-century Judaism, a new generation of parents and educators are flocking to Montessori preschools and elementary schools that combine secular studies with Torah and Hebrew lessons.

"Jewish Montessori schools, which began to catch on about 15 years ago, have also surged in popularity across the country. In Boca Raton, Fla., there are centrist Orthodox, Chabad Orthodox, Reform and Conservative Montessori preschools; Orthodox day schools have started Montessori programs in Houston and Cincinnati; and several New Jersey towns with large Jewish populations now have Montessori schools. The American Montessori Society says there are more than 4,000 Montessori schools in the United States; most are private (and secular, although some are associated with other religions) but a few are public. Ms. Petter-Lipstein said her group was tracking more than 40 Jewish Montessoris in North America and about 30 in Israel."
Source: "Montessori Schools Surge in Popularity Among New Generation of Jewish Parents," by Vivian Yee, February 21, 2014, www.nytimes.com

- "Growing in areas where there are children in the pre-K through third grade. Trends down if they are above this level and there are good public schools. There is a very strong demand for special education for handicapped children"

Seller Financing
- "We have sold large facilities with enrollment of more than 200 students for 3X EBITDA. Smaller are more difficult and sell for about 2X"
- 5 years

Questions
- "Ethnic ratio of students and the owner/director. Qualification and tenure of teachers. Are any of the teachers interns that will have to be replaced or higher paid later on?"

Resources
Websites
- www.montessori.edu
- www.montessori.org

MotoPhoto (See also Franchises) — Franchise

NAICS 81292	Number of Businesses/Units 16

Rules of Thumb
- ➢ 60 percent of annual sales plus inventory

Resources
Websites
- www.motophoto.com

Motorcycle Dealerships (See also Harley-Davidson Dealerships)

SIC 5571-06	NAICS 441228	Number of Businesses/Units 8,047

Rules of Thumb
- ➢ 12 to 14 percent of annual sales plus inventory
- ➢ 2 to 3 times SDE plus inventory
- ➢ 3 to 4 times EBITDA

Pricing Tips
- "2x to 5x SDE; includes parts, garments, & accessories inventory (PG&A); can include used vehicles, but not new vehicles. High multiples for Harley dealerships, and lower multiples for Japanese or other brands."
- "The EBIT multiple above assumes that all new vehicle inventory is subject to floor plan financing that will be assumed by the buyer. Normal working capital acquired."
- "The actual value of the franchise type of cycle business is fixtures and equipment plus the price of used cycles that have been taken in (prior to shop work being done) at the used motorcycle book price, plus the new cycles,

M - Rules of Thumb

plus 5 years' to ¾ year's net profit. One note of caution: contact franchisor to determine what is exactly required to satisfy their requirements for opening or buying a dealership; e.g., flooring requirements and financial strength."

Expert Comments

"Several years ago motorcycle dealerships were easy to sell. Some regions of the country have experienced a downward trend in sales. The southeastern U.S. is still very strong. Currently, smaller dealerships can be very difficult to sell."

"The original equipment manufacturers (Honda, Harley-Davidson, Yamaha, Suzuki, Kawasaki, etc.) control the number of dealers permitted in a marketplace. An existing dealership can block the establishment of a competing dealership of the same brand within a geographical proximity to the existing dealership."

Benchmark Data

Statistics (Motorcycle Dealership and Repair)

Number of Establishments	8,047
Average Profit Margin	1.4%
Revenue per Employee	$418,400
Average Number of Employees	7.3
Average Wages per Employee	$37,742

Products and Services Segmentation

New motorcycles, motor scooters and motor bikes	53.5%
Motorized sports vehicles including all-terrain vehicles	24.5%
Used motorcycles, motor scooters and motor bikes	13.5%
Other	5.2%
Independent repairers (excluding dealerships)	3.3%

Major Market Segmentation

Male consumers	68.5%
Business	15.5%
Female consumers	15.0%
Government	1.0%

Industry Costs

Profit	1.4%
Wages	9.1%
Purchases	74.6%
Deprecation	0.5%
Marketing	2.0%
Rent & Utilities	2.4%
Other	10.0%

Source: IBISWorld, August 2015

- "Vehicle sales 70% of gross; PG&A 15% of gross; service 12% of gross; finance & insurance sales 3% of gross."
- "GP% on new unit sales 18%; GP% on used unit sales 20%; F&I Income per major unit sold $500; GP% on parts & accessories 36%–40%"

Rules of Thumb - **M**

Expenses as a percentage of annual sales

Cost of goods	85%%
Payroll/labor Costs	05%
Occupancy	01%
Profit (estimated pretax)	02% to 03%

Industry Trend

- "Sales are up again (slightly) and 2014 marks the fourth consecutive year of slight increases in U.S. motorcycle sales. The 2014 sales total for street bikes, dual-sport and off-road motorcycles is 483,526. That is up about 3.7% from the 465,783 total reported in 2013.

  "The largest increase in sales was for off-road motorcycles, which is rather surprising. Dual-sport bikes remain popular but scooter sales were down yet again. U.S. scooter sales in 2013 were reported down by 6,363 units, which would mean a decrease of -18.6% from 2012 and 2014 indicates another 3.5% drop. Harley-Davidson reported 47,149 motorcycles sold in Q4 2014. That includes 26,957 sold in the U.S., a 1.6% decrease from the previous year. 20,192 were sold outside the U.S., a 9.2% increase. 2014 has been a momentous year for the Husqvarna brand. Enjoying record figures in sales and turnover, a total number of 16,337 motorcycles were sold."

  Source: http://www.webbikeworld.com/motorcycle-news/statistics/motorcycle-sales-statistics.htm

- "Reports indicate that 2013 U.S. motorcycle sales were up slightly by 1.4% in 2013 at 458,972 compared to the 2012 total of 452,386 (includes street, off-road, dual-sport and scooter sales). This is a very mild increase and the overall sales totals are still flat, especially compared to the peak years of 2004 through 2006, when more than twice as many motorcycles were sold in the U.S."

  Source: www.webbikeworld.com February 4, 2014

Questions

- "PG&A inventory and new vehicle value requirements for a new buyer can be the most difficult and complex aspect to understand. A good deal of time should be spent understanding what inventory is there and how much is really needed. Inventory should turn on an average of 4x to 6X per year in a healthy dealership. Slower turns suggest the business is carrying too much inventory or is very seasonal."

	Franchise
Mountain Mike's Pizza (See also Franchises, Pizza Shops)	
Approx. Total Investment	$197,000 to $598,000
Estimated Annual Sales/Unit	$525,000
SIC 5812-22 NAICS 722513	Number of Businesses/Units 160

Rules of Thumb

➢ 30% of annual sales plus inventory

Resources

Websites
- www.mountainmikes.com

M - Rules of Thumb

Movie Theaters

SIC 7832-01	NAICS 512131	Number of Businesses/Units 4,446

Rules of Thumb

➢ 4 times SDE

➢ 6 times annual adjusted earnings, 1000 plus seating

➢ 4 to 6 percent of annual sales; add fixtures & equipment

➢ 35 percent plus inventory for theaters with only one or several screens

Pricing Tips

- Concession sales usually make up 24 percent of movie-theater sales. It has been said that, without concession sales, the movie theater business would not be viable.

Benchmark Data

Statistics (Movie Theaters)

Number of Establishments	4,446
Average Profit Margin	12.5%
Revenue per Employee	$132,400
Average Number of Employees	28.4
Average Wages per Employee	$12,845

Products and Services Segmentation

Admissions	67.0%
Food and beverage sales	28.7%
Other	4.3%

Industry Costs

Profit	12.5%
Wages	9.7%
Purchases	37.0%
Depreciation	6.7%
Marketing	4.3%
Rent & Utilities	12.7%
Other	17.1%

Market Share

Regal Entertainment Group	17.6%
AMC Entertainment Inc.	16.8%
Cinemark Holdings Inc.	12.2%

Source: IBISWorld, June 2015

Industry Trend

- "As films earn less revenue, the studios that produce them earn less. Because of this, studios start taking a larger cut of the profit made from ticket sales, leaving the exhibiting theater with less. This is why the price for tickets and even concessions (where a movie theater earns the vast majority of its profit) have risen, while the earnings at the box office continue to fall."

Rules of Thumb - M

"While the advancements in home theaters have been great and are likely only to improve, nothing in your living room will compare to a move theater's 70 ft screen and hundreds of speakers. Most movies are made to be screened on a larger-than-life scale, and that's a trick television will likely never be able to copy."

Source: "Could Netflix Kill the Movie Theater Industry?" by Sarah Moran, screenrant.com, October 5, 2014

- "The strong growth in global box office would increase the proportion of the box office revenue to 42% of the total filmed entertainment revenue by 2017, from 40% in 2008. The shift is more evident in the emerging markets, while in the developed markets, the revenue share of box office to the total filmed entertainment sector is expected to rise only marginally.

"The recent slate of films and lack of major blockbusters has hindered the growth of box office revenues over the past few years. However, there are numerous major titles scheduled for release in 2015 and 2016 which can potentially boost box office revenues in both developed markets and emerging markets as demand for blockbuster US content continues to increase with further globalization and access to content."

Source: Cinema Operator Industry Report, www.redcapgroup.com

- "Wall Street usually shows little love for the movie business with its typically low, and unpredictable, profit margins. But in a combined look at the studio and exhibition businesses this morning, MoffettNathanson Research's Michael Nathanson and Robert Fishman tell investors that it's time to take a fresh look—as long as they proceed with caution. They lowered profit estimates for major exhibition chains Regal and Cinemark, citing expectations for weaker domestic summer box office results vs 2013. They project a full-year decline of 1.6% to $10.7B followed by a 5% jump in 2015 to $11.3B and then a drop of 2.6% in 2016 to $11.0B."

Source: "Film Business is Recovering, But It Won't Be Steady: Analysts," by David Lieberman, April 7, 2014, www.deadline.com

Resources

Websites
- Motion Picture Association of America: mpaa.org

Trade Publications
- "Business of Show Business: The Valuation of Movie Theaters," published by the Appraisal Institute: www.appraisalinstitute.org

Associations
- National Association of Theatre Owners: www.natoonline.org

Moving and Storage		
SIC 4214-01	NAICS 484210	Number of Businesses/Units 14,864
Rules of Thumb		
➢ 50 percent of annual sales		

26th Edition

M - Rules of Thumb

Benchmark Data

Statistics (Moving Services)

Number of Establishments	14,864
Average Profit Margin	6.3%
Revenue per Employee	$160,100
Average Number of employees	6.2
Average Wages per Employee	$35,143

Products and Services Segmentation

Residential moving	50.0%
Commercial moving	30.5%
Moving with storage	10.5%
Specialty goods moving	9.0%

Major Market Segmentation

Consumers	67.0%
Corporate customers	23.0%
Government	10.0%

Industry Costs

Profit	6.3%
Wages	22.2%
Purchases	37.0%
Depreciation	5.1%
Marketing	2.5%
Rent & Utilities	6.0%
Other	20.9%

Market Share

UniGroup Inc.	10.7%
Sirva Inc.	5.7%
Atlas World Group Inc.	5.3%

Source: IBISWorld, June 2015

- "The combined storage space in all those 48,500 facilities we have equals 2.3 billion square feet. That's 78 square miles, or more than three times the size of Manhattan. To put it another way, there are 7.3 square feet of storage space for every single person—man, woman, and child—in the U.S. This means it is possible for everyone in the entire country to be standing inside a storage unit at the same time.

"As of mid-2013, 87.4% of self storage units were occupied (percentage based on units rented per facility). Almost 9% of American households currently rent a self storage unit, even though 65% of them have a garage, 47% have an attic and 33% have a basement."

Source: "Important Self Storage Industry Trends Moving Companies Shouldn't Miss," http://blog.hireahelper.com/self-storage-industry-trends-for-movers/

Industry Trend

- "They are popping up all over, these garages-for-rent. The Self Storage Association will proudly tell you that self storage has been the fastest growing segment of the commercial real estate industry over the last four decades, while Wall Street analysts consider the industry to be recession-proof. There

Rules of Thumb - M

are 59,500 self storage facilities worldwide. Of these, 48,500 are in the U.S."
Source: "Important Self Storage Industry Trends Moving Companies Shouldn't Miss,"
http://blog.hirehelper.com/self-storage-industry-trends-for-movers/

Resources

Associations
- American Moving and Storage Association—an informative site: www.promover.org

	Franchise
Mr. Jim's Pizza (See also Franchises, Pizza Shops)	
Approx. Total Investment	$75,000 to $150,000
Estimated Annual Sales/Unit	$440,000
SIC 5812-22 NAICS 722513	Number of Businesses/Units 75
Rules of Thumb	
➢ 35% of annual sales plus inventory	

Resources

Websites
- www.mrjimspizza.net

	Franchise
Mr. Payroll (See also Franchises)	
Approx. Total Investment	$68,800 to $328,000
NAICS 522390	Number of Businesses/Units 92
Rules of Thumb	
➢ 130 percent of annual sales	

Resources

Websites
- www.mrpayroll.com

	Franchise
Mr. Rooter Plumbing (See also Franchises)	
Approx. Total Investment	$80,000 to $188,800
SIC 1711-05 NAICS 238220	Number of Businesses/Units 241
Rules of Thumb	
➢ 1 to 4 times SDE plus hard assets; the number between 1 and 4 depends on several factors, such as the owner operating a truck, etc.	

26th Edition

M - Rules of Thumb

	Franchise
Mrs. Fields Original Cookies (See also TCBY)	
SIC 5461-02	NAICS 311812	

Rules of Thumb

➢ 40 percent of annual sales plus inventory

Resources

Websites
- www.mrsfieldsfranchise.com

	Franchise
Murphy's Deli (See also Delicatessens, Franchises)	
Approx. Total Investment	Net worth of $200,000
NAICS 722513	Number of Businesses/Units 80

Rules of Thumb

➢ 50 percent of annual sales plus inventory
➢ Multiples have ranged from 40 percent to 60 percent

Resources

Websites
- www.murphysdeli.com

	Franchise
Music Go Round (See also Franchises)	
Approx. Total Investment	$253,550 to $325,300
SIC 5736-08	NAICS 451140	Number of Businesses/Units 34

Rules of Thumb

➢ 40 percent of annual sales plus inventory

Resources

Websites
- www.musicgoround.com

Music Stores (Record Stores, Musical Instruments)		
SIC 5736	NAICS 451140	
		Number of Businesses/Units Musical Instruments 10,275
		Number of Businesses/Units Record Stores 4,877

Rules of Thumb

> 25 percent of annual sales. Retail is generally higher, but the trend of this business is decidedly down, especially for the small independent store.1 to 2 times SDE plus inventory. If just a record/CD store it may be difficult to sell period. Music is now being downloaded over the Internet and records/CDs are becoming almost obsolete. If the music store sells sheet music, musical instruments, etc. SDE multiple might be higher.

Pricing Tips

- "Inventory of tapes, CD's, DVD's at FMV (used) is in addition to the above."
- "Usually in a store of this kind inventory turns about twice a year. The store should be located in an area where rent will not exceed 4 percent of the gross sales. National average shows a gross profit of approximately 54 percent before expenses of wages, repairs, maintenance, advertising, bad debts, utilities, insurance, taxes, etc. National average net profit is approximately 10 to 18 percent."
- "The leading music retailers are now box stores (Walmart and Best Buy), and music-only stores are no longer a player in the industry."

Source: www.en.wikipedia.org

Expert Comments

"Independent brick and mortar locations are a dying breed."

Benchmark Data

Statistics (Musical Instrument and Supplies Store)

Number of Establishments	10,275
Average Profit Margin	1.8%
Revenue per Employee	$169,300
Average Number of Employees	3.3
Average Wages per Employee	$22,252

Products and Services Segmentation

Violins, drums, guitars, and other instruments	49.7%
Pianos and organs	16.2%
Instrument rentals	14.1%
Audio equipment, components, parts and accessories	12.3%
Sheet music	5.4%
Other goods (includes tapes, CDs and audiobooks)	2.3%

Major Market Segmentation

Students	43.0%
Hobbyists	35.0%
Professional	21.0%
Churches	1.0%

M - Rules of Thumb

Industry Costs

Profit	1.8%
Wages	13.2%
Purchases	70.0%
Depreciation	1.0%
Marketing	2.2%
Rent & Utilities	7.3%
Other	4.5%

Market Share

Guitar Center Inc.	29.7%

Source: IBISWorld, January 2015

Statistics (Record Stores)

Number of Establishments	4,877
Average Profit Margin	1.2%
Revenue per Employee	$102,200
Average Number of Employees	3.8
Average Wages per Employee	$14,987

Products and Services Segmentation

Compact Discs (CDs) and Audiotapes	46.4%
Digital Video Discs (DVDs)	45.8%
Vinyl	7.8%

Industry Costs

Profit	1.2%
Wages	14.7%
Purchases	63.1%
Depreciation	1.2%
Utilities	2.0%
Rent	7.7%
Other	10.1%

Market Share

Trans World Entertainment Corporation	8.2%

Source: IBISWorld, December 2014

Expenses as a percentage of annual sales

Cost of goods	35%
Payroll/labor Costs	25% to 30%
Occupancy	15%
Profit (estimated pretax)	20% to 25%

Industry Trend

- "CDs are dead. That doesn't seem like such a controversial statement. Maybe it should be. The music business sold 141 million CDs in the U.S. last year. That's more than the combined number of tickets sold to the most popular movies in 2014 (Guardians) and 2013 (Iron Man 3). So 'dead,' in this familiar construction, isn't the same as zero. It's more like a commonly accepted short-

Rules of Thumb - M

cut for a formerly popular thing is now withering at a commercially meaningful rate. And if CDs are truly dead, then digital music sales are lying in the adjacent grave. Both categories are down double-digits in the last year, with iTunes sales diving at least 13 percent."

Source: "The Death of Music Sales," by Derek Thompson January 25, 2015 http://www.theatlantic.com/business/archive/2015/01/buying-music-is-so-over/384790/

- "Bettendorf, Iowa—When Jim Foster opened his piano store 30 years ago, he had 10 competitors selling just pianos. When he closed Foster Family Music in late December, not one was still selling pianos in the Quad-Cities area of Iowa and Illinois. . . . Stores dedicated to selling pianos like Foster's are dwindling across the country as fewer people take up the instrument and those who do often opt for a less expensive electronic keyboard or a used piano. . . But after gently falling over the years, sales have plunged more recently to between 30,000 and 40,000 annually."

Source: Associated Press as reported in the *Boston Globe*, January 3, 2015

Resources

Associations

- International Music Products Association: www.namm.com

		Franchise
My Favorite Muffin (See also Big Apple Bagels, Franchises)		
Approx. Total Investment		$254,300 to $379,628
	NAICS 722513	Number of Businesses/Units 70

Rules of Thumb

➢ 30 to 35 percent plus inventory

Resources

Websites

- www.myfavoritemuffin.net

Mystery Shopping Companies		
	NAICS 561990	Number of Businesses/Units 700

Rules of Thumb

➢ 50 percent of annual sales—the larger the company, the higher the percentage of annual sales over 50 percent.

Pricing Tips

- Large mystery service companies can sell for considerably more than 50 percent of sales.

Benchmark Data

- "How much can someone realistically expect to earn as a mystery shopper?

N - Rules of Thumb

Compensation for mystery shopping significantly varies depending on a number of factors, including the type of industry, the level of difficulty required to complete the assignment and the detail required by the mystery shoppers. Compensation for the typical shop ranges from $5 to $20. Some complex assignments, such as video mystery shop, can pay $75 or more.

"It is hard to find out more specifics on which companies get mystery shopped and how much shoppers are paid because shoppers are not allowed to divulge specific information, such as the name of the company they've shopped or how much they make per assignment. The shoppers are required to sign confidentiality agreements at the request of the mystery shopping providers and their customers."

Source: www.mysteryshop.org

Resources

Associations
- Mystery Shopping Providers Association (MSPA): http://www.mspa-na.org/

Nail Salons (See also Beauty Salons)

SIC 7231-02	NAICS 812113	Number of Businesses/Units 54,250

Rules of Thumb
➢ 25 percent of annual sales plus inventory

Benchmark Data
- For additional Benchmark Data see Beauty Salons

Nail Tech Demographics

Ethnicity	Percentage
Vietnamese	51%
Caucasian	40%
Black or African-American	05%
Hispanic or Latina	03%
Other	01%

Gender	Percentage
Male	6%
Female	94%

How many nail technicians work at this location (including yourself)?

Number of Technicians	Percentage
I am the only technician	56%
2 nail techs	17%
3 nail techs	08%
4 nail techs	06%
5 nail techs	02%
6 nail techs	04%
7+ nail techs	07%

Who are your clients?	Percentage
Girls under 20	06%
Women 21–25	11%
Women 26–35	19%
Women 36–45	27%
Women 46+	34%
Men	03%

Rules of Thumb - N

What percentage of your business is appointments vs. walk-ins?	Percentage
Regular appointments	49%
Standing appointments	36%
Walk-in appointments	13%
Other (filling in for another tech, for example)	02%

On Average what is your total weekly income?	Average
Service Income	$645
Tip Income	$129 (21%)
Incentives or earnings from retail sales	$85
Other bonuses or income earned in the salon	$106

Which best describes your current employment situation?	Percentage
Salon owner doing nails (not a booth renter)	40%
Nail technician (booth renter)	24%
Nail technician (employee)	11%
Salon manager or nail dept. manager (doing nails)	3%
Cosmetologist	3%
Student or apprentice	3%
Salon owner not doing nails	4%
Other	12%

What license(s) do you have?	Percentage
Nail technician/manicurist	78%
Cosmetologist	18%
Esthetician	8%
I am not licensed	5%
Barber	1%
Other	7%

How many nail technicians work in your salon?	Percentage
Just me	54%
2 nail techs	17%
3 techs	10%
4 techs	07%
5 techs	04%
6 techs	02%
7+ techs	06%

- "30% of booth renters pay their rent weekly, and the average weekly rent is $145/week. 70% of booth renters pay their rent monthly, and the average monthly rent is $343/month.
- "No surprise—the biggest growth for nail techs was in social platforms that emphasize the visual: Pinterest, Instagram, and YouTube. 67% of Americans use social media, but 92% of nail techs do. In two years, Pinterest has gone from 0% to 88%. Personal use of social accounts exceeds business use, but both are growing. Business use of LinkedIn has grown 440% in 2014."

Source: "Nails Magazine," 2014–2015 The Big Book, nailsmag.com

- "More experienced workers usually earn $50 to $70 per day, sometimes even $80. Their pay, though, still typically amounts to significantly less than minimum wage, given their long hours."

Source: "High Price of Pretty Nails: Workers are Underpaid and Unprotected," *New York Times*, May 10, 2015

Industry Trend

- "As far as small businesses go, it is relatively easy to open a nail salon. Just a few thousand dollars is needed for things like pedicure chairs with whirlpool

26th Edition 557

N - Rules of Thumb

baths. Little English is required, and there are few licensing hoops to jump through. Many skip them altogether. Overhead is minimal: rent and some new bottles of polish each month—and the rock-bottom wages of workers. Beyond the law barriers for entry, manicurists, owners and others who have closely followed the nail industry are hard pressed to say definitively why salons have proliferated."

Source: "High Price of Pretty Nails: Workers are Underpaid and Unprotected—A Boom In Nail Salons" the *New York Times* Sunday, May 10, 2015

Resources

Trade Publications
- Nails Magazine—interesting and useful site, has an interesting survey of the nail salon business: www.nailsmag.com

Nathan's Famous (See also Franchises) — Franchise

Approx. Total Investment		$50,000 to $1,000,000
	NAICS 722513	Number of Businesses/Units 300

Rules of Thumb
> 85 to 90 percent of annual sales plus inventory

Benchmark Data
- Units range from 120 sq. ft. to 3,000 sq. ft.

Resources

Websites
- www.nathansfamous.com

Natural Chicken Grill

	NAICS 722513	Number of Businesses/Units 14

Rules of Thumb
> 25 to 30 percent of annual sales plus inventory

> Note: This more of a business opportunity than a franchise. The initial fee is $20,000 in two payments of $10,000 There is also a $1,000-a-month charge after a unit has been open for three months. There is no royalty. The cost shown above is plus the build-out of the store. The cost includes training, set-up, consultation, etc. Units range from 1,500 sq. ft. to 3,500 sq. ft.

Rules of Thumb - **N**

Nature's Way Café (See also Franchises)

	Franchise
Approx. Total Investment	$129,500 to $253,900
NAICS 722513	Number of Businesses/Units 8

Rules of Thumb
- ➢ 45 percent of annual sales plus inventory

Resources

Websites
- www.natureswaycafe.com

Newspaper Routes

	NAICS 454390	

Rules of Thumb
- ➢ 90 to 100 percent of annual sales plus inventory
- ➢ $50 to $100 per daily/Sunday subscriber

Newsstands

SIC 5994-01	NAICS 451212	

Rules of Thumb
- ➢ 25 percent of annual sales plus inventory

Nursing Homes (See also Assisted Living Facilities, Retirement Homes)

SIC 8051-01	NAICS 623110	Number of Businesses/Units 17,913

Rules of Thumb
- ➢ 45 percent of annual sales plus inventory
- ➢ 2.5 times SDE plus inventory
- ➢ 3 times EBIT
- ➢ 4 times EBITDA

Pricing Tips

- "Return on investment—cash on hand is the guiding rule. Cost per bed varies from $20,000 to $60,000. Cost of upgrading facility a strong factor."
- "Pricing is based on a CAP Rate percentage based on NOI. NOI as defined in the HUD 232 analysis is much different than EBITDA. NOI calculates for management in place but also accounts for CAP EX or a 'reserve' plus a proprietary income of 15% before you arrive at NOI. Then you need to look

26th Edition

N - Rules of Thumb

at national and regional comps to see what CAP Rate nursing homes are currently selling for and then you can do the math. This method is almost always spot on for value."
- "In Florida (and other states) the licensing requirements have changed drastically, making entry into this industry very difficult, which in turn may raise the pricing multiple somewhat."

Expert Comments

"Licensing issues"

"Many states have moratoriums on new licenses, so this means that if buyers want in they must buy an existing home or at least a license that is in limbo. We have found marketability to be very high having sold every one we've ever listed. Profits overall are probably slightly down but good homes will have some private pay and their profits are holding up just fine."

Benchmark Data

Statistics (Nursing Care Facilities)
Number of Establishments	17,913
Average Profit Margin	8.0%
Revenue per Employee	$73,900
Average Number of Employees	104.1
Average Wages per Employee	$30,743

Products and Services Segmentation
For-profit skilled nursing facilities	43.6%
For-profit nursing homes	33.0%
Nonprofit skilled nursing facilities	10.3%
Nonprofit nursing homes	7.8%
Government nursing homes and skilled nursing facilities	4.7%
Hospice centers	0.6%

Industry Costs
Profit	8.0%
Wages	41.9%
Purchases	17.0%
Depreciation	2.6%
Marketing	0.4%
Rent & Utilities	7.0%
Other	23.1%

Source: IBISWorld, October 2015

- "With nursing homes the big thing is payor mix. Average to below average homes will run 90%+ Medicaid. An all-Medicaid home will not be extremely profitable. A good home must have some private pay, at least 10%, and a good mix of Medicare, say around 20%. If this is the case you'll have a home doing 15%+ bottom line EBITDA. Another good benchmark is to look at average Medicaid rate. If the average Medicaid rate for a year is $140/day that home is struggling to make ends meet (unless there is a ton of private pay/Medicare). If the average Medicaid rate is $185/day then that's a home getting higher acuity residents and they will be very profitable."

Rules of Thumb - O

Expenses as a percentage of annual sales

Cost of goods	15%
Payroll/labor Costs	40% to 50%
Occupancy	10%
Profit (estimated pretax)	15% to 20%

Industry Trend

- "Skilled nursing facilities' occupancy rate continued to tick up in the first three months of 2014, while absorption flipped into positive territory for the first time in almost a decade, according to the latest quarterly figures from the National Investment Center for the Seniors Housing & Care Industry.
  "Nursing care occupancy reached 88.4% in the first quarter of this year, based on numbers gathered by NIC's MAP® Data and Analysis Service. This was an increase of 0.4 percentage points from the last quarter of 2013. The increase is in line NIC's forecast models, which predicted occupancy in seniors housing to exceed 90% this year, NIC President Robert Kramer told McKnight's recently.
  "The occupancy rate for independent living (90.2%) already has passed this benchmark, according to the data released Friday. Assisted living occupancy was at 89.1% in the first quarter."
  Source: "Skilled nursing edges toward 90% occupancy, absorption rate makes first gain in nearly a decade, NIC data show," by Tim Mullaney www.mcknights.com April 14, 2014

- "The health care legislation includes a list of changes to nursing services for seniors and the disabled, including an infusion of federal funding to help state programs provide more care through home- and community-based settings, which, presumably, will result in a reduction in nursing home care. The industry is expected to experience lower demand, which will be moderately offset by an increase in the number of insured. Overall, sales are expected to grow by 1.5 percent on average per year through 2015, reaching $109.5 billion. This is slightly lower than the previous five-year average growth rate of 1.7 percent annually."

Seller Financing

- 10 years
- "SBA will allow a seller to be ballooned at 7 years (amortization can be 7 years or longer). HUD will allow seller financing (up to 50% of the amount buyer puts down - example: 20% down buyer and seller can contribute 10% each) but it MUST be a non-recourse loan, which makes it very difficult for the seller to collect if the buyer doesn't pay. If you're using SBA lending the seller note will have to be 7 years or longer."

Resources

Associations
- American Health Care Association: www.ahca.org

Office Staffing and Temporary Agencies (See also Staffing Services)

SIC 7363-03	NAICS 561320	Number of Businesses/Units 61,678

Rules of Thumb
- ➢ 6 to12 times EBITDA

O - Rules of Thumb

Benchmark Data

Statistics (Office Staffing & Temp Agencies)

Number of Establishments	61,678
Average Profit Margin	5.1%
Revenue per Employee	$45,700
Average Number of Employees	54.1
Average Wages per Employee	$31,399

Products and Services Segmentation

Industrial and factory staffing	34.7%
Office, clerical and administrative staffing	24.7%
Professional and managerial staffing	12.0%
Healthcare staffing	9.2%
Information technology staffing	8.4%
Other	7.5%
Engineering and scientific staffing	3.5%

Major Market Segmentation

Industrial	38.5%
Retail and other service-oriented sectors	21.0%
Other professional markets	13.0%
Technical sectors	12.0%
Healthcare sector	9.2%
Other	6.3%

Industry Costs

Profit	5.1%
Wages	68.2%
Purchases	10.8%
Depreciation	0.2%
Marketing	1.0%
Rent & Utilities	2.5%
Other	12.2%

Source: IBISWorld, September 2015

Office Supplies and Stationery Stores

SIC 5943-01	NAICS 453210	Number of Businesses/Units 11,869

Rules of Thumb

➢ 25 percent of annual sales plus inventory
➢ 1.5 times SDE plus inventory
➢ 12 percent times EBIT

Pricing Tips

- "Check inventory levels and FF&E carefully. Owners of these types of businesses tend to hide cash flow in excessive inventory and FF&E."

Rules of Thumb - O

Benchmark Data

Statistics (Office Supply Stores)
Number of Establishments	11,869
Average Profit Margin	1.9%
Revenue per Employee	$189,000
Average Number of Employees	7.4
Average Wages per Employee	$20,684

Products and Services Segmentation
Office supplies and equipment	44.6%
Office machines	28.5%
Technology	13.0%
Services	8.2%
Office furniture	5.7%

Major Market Segmentation
Small businesses	27.8%
Households for education purposes	22.5%
Large businesses	16.8%
Households for general purposes	15.3%
Other	8.5%
Households for satellite work	7.2%
Federal, state and local government	1.9%

Industry Costs
Profit	1.9%
Wages	11.0%
Purchases	58.2%
Depreciation	0.8%
Marketing	2.1%
Rent & Utilities	5.3%
Other	20.7%

Market Share
Staples Inc.	39.3%
Office Depot Inc.	37.6%

Source: IBISWorld, April 2015

- "Historical sales against same store performance would be a good measurement. Adequate advertising budget (5% of gross is desirable). Gross sales per square foot of $200/year would be good, $250/year would be very good, $300/year or more would be excellent."

Industry Trend

- "Office-supply retailers are grappling with controlling costs as they battle increased competition and technological shifts that are reducing demand for traditional supplies such as pens, paper clips and paper. Profitability among privately held office-supply, stationery and gift retailers (NAICS 4532) declined between 2012 and 2013, according to recent data from Sageworks, a financial information company. In fact, preliminary estimates from Sageworks' financial statement analysis of 2013 data show net profit margins swung from positive to

O - Rules of Thumb

negative in 2013. Office-supply retailers are typically one of the least profitable retail industries anyway, according to Sageworks, but last year they saw overhead expenses and costs of goods sold increase relative to sales.

"'There's a big shift in the landscape within this industry, particularly because there's less need for these office products now that everyone's going digital,' said Sageworks analyst James Noe. Privately held office-supply, stationery and gift retailers operated with a net loss, on average, of 1.2% of sales in 2013, compared with a net profit margin of 3.7% in 2012, according to Sageworks' industry data."

Source: "Office-Supply Stores Seeing Profit Margins Erased," by Mary Ellen Biery, www.forbes.com April 13, 2014

Oil and Gas Related Businesses

Rules of Thumb
➢ 4 times EBITDA

Pricing Tips
- "Industry rule of thumb for:
  Roustabout (SIC 1389)
    - ✓ 2x SDE plus FFE & inventory
    - ✓ 3–4x SDE
    - ✓ 75–90% of sales (100%+ when talking over $10+mil in sales)"

  "Drilling (water well) (SIC 1781) [O&G companies need water wells and core samples]
    - ✓ 2xSDE plus FFE & inventory
    - ✓ 3x SDE
    - ✓ 3.5x EBITDA
    - ✓ 150% of sales

  "Excavation/Construction (NAICS 213112) [specifically for O&G industry with MSAs (other excavations site preps {SIC 1794} are vulnerable to the housing/real estate market and deem lower pricing)]
    - ✓ 1.5x SDE plus FFE & inventory
    - ✓ 3–4x SDE
    - ✓ 80–90% of sales"
- "Adjust for age/condition of equipment."
- "The typical discount for all cash versus terms applies."
- "The oil and gas industry is a very broad cross section of industry segments and varies widely in size. Value parameters will vary widely and are probably most associated with individual market segments such as manufacturing or services."
- "The typical measure of earnings used is EBITDA. The multiple will range between 3.2X and 4X for transactions up to $20 million. The variance is based upon qualitative factors such as customer concentrations, equipment age and condition, middle management depth and experience, safety records, and nature of services being performed. Equipment rental companies will be higher in the range while companies providing products or services with

material intensive cost of sales will be somewhat lower, again depending upon qualitative factors.

"A key factor is the number of Master Service Agreements (MSA's) a company has in place. These are master agreements with an oil company. They do not guarantee any certain volume of work, but rather indicate the manner in which work will be performed, liabilities and hold harmless, rate sheets, insurance coverage required, etc."

Expert Comments

"Industry trends are heavily influenced by commodity based pricing of the underlying oil and gas products. The industry may be subject to boom-bust cycles."

"Characterized by boom-bust cycles. Can be very profitable in good times, but trends may follow commodities and politically managed petroleum prices."

"High risk if a few top accounts take the majority of the sales. Lose one and lose 70–90% of the business."

"The oil and gas sector is very cyclical over 7- to 8-year cycles, normally. Natural gas and oil prices dictate the demand for services; hence, the profitability and revenues within the industry. Replication of products and/or services is difficult without sufficient industry knowledge."

Benchmark Data
- "Roustabout—(SIC 1389)
    - ✓ Payroll 40–45%
    - ✓ Profit 25%

    Drilling (water well)—(SIC 1781) [O&G companies need water wells and core samples]
    - ✓ Payroll 15%
    - ✓ Profit 50%
    - ✓ Excavation/Construction—(NAICS 213112)
    - ✓ Payroll 15%
    - ✓ Profit 20–25%"
- "The cost of goods sold percentages vary widely. Companies providing materials in addition to their service or value added features tend to have much lower gross profit per dollar of revenues."

Industry Trend
- "Difficult profitability issues will likely remain over the short term. The long-term trend has been positive, but there are substantial periods of high volatility."
- "Currently in a strong downturn, but upturn is expected to follow price recovery over next 6 months to 3 years."
- "Steady to upward. The industry has historically seen boom-bust cycles. Today it is clearly booming."
- "Steadily increasing in revenues and earnings, depending upon the demand and pricing of oil and natural gas fluctuations."

O - Rules of Thumb

Seller Financing
- "Normally a combination of owner and institutional financing"
- "Most have significant third-party financing, with some seller financing, frequently in the form of an earnout or clawback. The factors affecting that are usually the customer diversity or customer concentration."

Questions
- "Equipment should be the number one question—age/condition. Ask for service maintenance logs. Find out the turnover rate. How often is the equipment replaced with better and newer equipment? Get a third-party equipment appraisal."

Resources

Websites
- American Petroleum Institute: www.api.org

Trade Publications
- The Oil & Gas Journal: www.ogj.com
- Hart Energy: www.hartenergy.com
- Shale Play Water Management: www.shaleplaywatermanagement.com

Associations
- American Association of Professional Landmen: www.landman.org
- PMAA—Petroleum Marketers Association of America: www.pmaa.org
- Pipe Line Contractors Association: www.plca.org
- Society of Petroleum Engineers: www.spe.org

Once Upon A Child		Franchise
(See also Clothing Stores—Used, Consignment Shops, Franchises)		
Approx. Total Investment		$204,200 to $309,500
SIC 5932-05	NAICS 453310	Number of Businesses/Units 245

Rules of Thumb
➢ 25 percent of annual sales plus inventory
➢ 30 percent of annual sales includes inventory

Optical Stores (See also Optometry Practices)		
	NAICS 446130	Number of Businesses/Units 16,156

Rules of Thumb
➢ 50 to 60 percent of annual sales includes inventory (Sales do not include regular exam fees)
➢ 2 times SDE includes inventory (Sales do not include regular exam fees)

Pricing Tips
- "Another benchmark is 1 x SDE, plus tangible assets."
- "Adjust price up or down depending on how updated the equipment is."
- "How many days do they perform exams? For whom?"

Expert Comments

"Very limited buyer pool; must have OD degree and state license."

"The aging population will increase the demand for eyecare."

"National chains seem to be weaker. Mom and pops seem to be hanging in there, so they may be keeping optometrists busy."

"Surgery has made the industry shrink. However many chains have contracted, giving independents some breathing room. Walmart still looms."

Benchmark Data

Statistics (Eye Glasses & Contact Lens Stores)

Number of Establishments	16,156
Average Profit Margin	5.0%
Revenue per Employee	$140,800
Average Number of Employees	5.3
Average Wages per Employee	$26,890

Products and Services Segmentation

Prescription eyeglasses	64.9%
Nonprescription eyewear	14.4%
Contact lenses	10.8%
Other	6.5%
Eye examinations	3.4%

Industry Costs

Profit	5.0%
Wages	18.9%
Purchases	39.5%
Depreciation	1.5%
Marketing	5.0%
Rent & Utilities	10.0%
Other	20.1%

Market Share

Luxottica Group S.p.A.	27.4%
National Vision Inc.	7.8%
Highmark Inc.	7.5%

Source: IBISWorld, June 2015

- "$300 average revenue per exam"
- "$250 revenue/patient is low. $500 is very good."
- "Should give exams at least one full day a week. The more days they offer exams, the better."
- "The retail industry is highly fragmented but concentrated at the top: 90 percent of companies operate a single store, but about a dozen chains operate more than 100 and account for half of industry revenue."

Source: www.findarticles.com

O - Rules of Thumb

Expenses as a percentage of annual sales

Cost of goods	35% to 45%
Payroll/labor Costs	10% to 15%
Occupancy	15% to 20%
Profit (estimated pretax)	25% to 30%

Industry Trend
- "More group practices and fewer single-doctor practices"
- "Perhaps stable. Surgery options will continue downslide."

Questions
- "Contact lens sales? Do they keep the profits from optician?"
- "Probability of staff retention. Number of active patient records."
- "Days they have exams. If only one or two, could be tough to generate sales."
- "What kind of equipment? Leased? Referral sources? Insurances accepted?"
- "Does he have a lab? How many lanes (exam room)? What type of finishing does he do? How many days is a doctor available for exams?"

Resources

Trade Publications
- Eyecare Business: www.eyecarebusiness.com

Optometry Practices (See also Optical Stores)

SIC 5999-04	NAICS 621320	Number of Businesses/Units 35,076

Rules of Thumb
- 50% to 65% percent of annual revenues includes inventory
- 2 to 2.5 times SDE includes inventory
- 2 to 2.5 times EBIT
- 2.5 to 3.5 times EBITDA

Pricing Tips
- "Practices with SDE below $100,000 are basically worth the value of equipment and inventory. Reduce price for outdated equipment and / or below benchmark inventory level."
- "Optometry professional fees are generally 40% of total sales if the office includes dispensary, 60% sales from eyewear and contacts. Cost of goods averages about 25%. Premises expense about 8%–12%."
- "Pricing based on % of sales and cash flow are more applicable at sales exceeding $500,000."
- "The inventory that's included in the selling price should be an average inventory amount. The selling price should be adjusted up or down if the figure is above or below that amount. The selling price should be adjusted downward if the practice has not installed an EHR system."
- "Increased value with more sophisticated instrumentation and conversion to electronic health records"

- "Pricing varies based on % of medical services and product sales. Also considerations in the percentage of private pay to insurance sourced revenue. (i.e., low-volume Medicaid practicev.s high-end cash patients."
- "Reduce price for lack of lease transferability."
- "Values vary depending on the percent of professional fees to material sales. Offices with higher professional-only fees as a percent of gross collections will have a lower multiple."
- "Smaller practices under $400K in gross revenue will have more emphasis on asset values. Large practices over $1MM gross revenue and those with multiple doctors may have different value methods."
- "Another benchmark is 1 x SDE, plus tangible assets."
- "Smaller offices are more asset based."
- "Offices without a dispensary typically have a lower multiple."
- "SDE + hard assets"
- "The intangible assets are difficult to value. Goodwill is 'the expectations of future profits under the ownership of someone other than the present owner.' According to the Internal Revenue Service, 'Goodwill is based upon earning capacity and its value, therefore it rests upon the excess of net earning over and above a fair return on net tangible assets...such factors as prestige and renown of successful operation over a prolonged period in a locality may be included in tangible value.' The American Medical Association simply defines goodwill as, 'the opportunity to take over the health care of a seller's patient base.'
- "There are 3 recognized formulas for determining the value of goodwill in an optometric practice. The first is simply calculating 25% of the last year's gross sales. The second method is calculating 25% of the average of the last 3 years' gross sales. The third method is a qualitative analysis. This is a series of value comparisons for the practice being appraised as it relates to the current market. [Such comparisons could include the factors listed below plus quality of records, office staff, etc.]."

Source: "Optometric Practice Appraisals" by Michael Bacigalupi, OD, Assistant Professor, www.optometry.nova.edu/opep/articles

Expert Comments

"Someone selling should develop an exit plan at least 3 to 5 years prior to the expected sale."

"A buyer should examine the practice momentum. Is the practice declining, stable, or growing—and what is the perceived reason."

"Replication is easy, however it requires a valid license for each respective state. Marketability is best in urban areas and can be poor in rural, less populated areas."

"Competition would be lower if not for increased pressure from the growth of chains and the impact of the Internet on retailing (eyewear sales)."

"While entry is rather easy (provided you are a doctor), it's customer service oriented and that takes years to build goodwill if you are starting from scratch. Other pressures include changes in

healthcare reimbursements and retail online and store eyewear and contact lens sales."

O - Rules of Thumb

"Offices that sell eyewear benefit from improved locations. Very customer driven service profession. Must be licensed OD in most states to own an optometry office"

"Online frame stores are becoming more competitive."

"The aging population will increase the demand for eyecare."

Benchmark Data

Statistics (Optometrists)

Number of Establishments	35,076
Average Profit Margin	15.0%
Revenue per Employee	$116,400
Average Number of Employees	3.8
Average Wages per Employee	$36,511

Products and Services Segmentation

Prescription eyewear	43.0%
Eye exams	22.0%
Medical eye care	17.0%
Contact lenses	16.0%
Other	2.0%

Industry Costs

Profit	15.0%
Wages	31.5%
Purchases	30.0%
Depreciation	2.8%
Marketing	1.5%
Rent & Utilities	6.2%
Other	13.0%

Source: IBISWorld, April 2015

- "43 annual complete exams per 100 active patients. Eyewear sales as 43% of gross revenue. $550,000 annual revenue per full-time OD."
- "25% profit is SDE before paying doctor wages. Net profit to owner after all doctor wages is around 10%. Must be optometrist or ophthalmologist to own a practice. Many states and opticians cannot hire a doctor to do exams."
- "$117 gross revenue per active patient.$530,000 gross revenue per OD."
- "Gross per exam: $260–$327, gross per OD hour: $197–$395, gross per sq. ft.: $227–$450, exams per OD hour: 0.76–1.15."
- "SDE percentage runs about 30% before debt service and before doctor production wages. Fixed costs play a large part because of the need for retail/visible setting. Therefore practice grossing under $500K might underperform."
- "Typical adjusted net before doctor/owner income is about 30% of collections. (10% profit after paying doctor wages)"
- "$63 average wholesale frames cost per pair. About $300 gross per exam. Office size about 2,000 square feet for solo practice, 3,000 for multiple OD practice."
- "Average optometry practice gross revenue nationwide is about $600K. Typically office shows 30% adjusted net (owner benefit) before any debt service."

- "Average revenue runs from $200 to $500 per patient. Offices focused on more retail high-end frames are higher."
- "Optometrists work mainly as solo practitioners or in small group practices. A typical group practice has less than $500,000 in annual revenue and four employees. About 1,000 practices have annual revenue over $1 million. Many optometrist practices include retail sales."

Source: www.findarticles.com

- "SDE is the biggest driver for buyers today."
- "Three to four staff per OD"

Expenses as a percentage of annual sales	
Cost of goods	25% to 35%
Payroll/labor Costs	10% to 20%
Occupancy	07% to 15%
Profit (estimated pretax)	20% to 30%

Industry Trend
- "The scope of optometry practice will continue to broaden as the supply of ophthalmologists fails to expand at the necessary pace."
- "Long term good, stable. Smaller offices shrinking in value. Larger offices stable (Over $1MM)."
- "The independent optometrist is operating in a highly dynamic retail environment, as online sales growth rapidly outpaces physical retail across categories. For example, nearly 20% of contact lenses sales are now moving online."
- "A certain amount of consolidation as larger independent practices purchase smaller ones. Increased competition for the retail sales of eyewear products from large, national chains and Internet-based companies."
- "A trend for solo practices to join alliances or merge with larger practices. Medical optometry will increase due to anticipated shortages of ophthalmologists and primary care physicians. Third-party reimbursements will account for a growing share of OD revenue."
- "Independent optometry faces a major challenge. Will the industry remain stable, with approximately 50% market share for overall vision care (including optometric services as well as materials like glasses and contact lenses), or will it be forever changed by the same market pressures that have disrupted other industries like books, consumer electronics and independent pharmacies?"

Seller Financing
- "Overwhelmingly outside financing due to a number of organizations that specialize in financing medical/professional practices at favorable terms."
- "The sale of well-run, profitable optometry practices are usually easy to bank finance. Many banks have separate practice acquisition financing departments that allow a qualified OD to purchase a practice with little or no money down."
- "Either 100% financing from specialty lenders or seller financing. Buyers don't have the funds."
- "Seller financing may be about 10-30% of sale price."
- 10 years
- "Partially seller financed with amortizations of 10 years and balloons in 3 to 5 years"

O - Rules of Thumb

Questions
- "Carefully check out the risks associated with the seller continuing to practice in an area or in a manner that would siphon past patients to him/her. The details of the Non-Compete Agreement are very important."
- "Review revenue by source. Fee schedules? List of insurance panels they are currently with?
- Determine what services are done and what could be added."
- "What is your rate of new patient generation? What have been the obstacles to growing your practice? Have you converted to electronic health records?"
- "Obtain fee schedules, review exam charts, review insurance panels (payor mix) and top billing codes. Also review frames and contact lens inventory"
- "Contact lens sales? Do they keep the profits from optician?"
- "Probability of staff retention.Number of active patient records?"
- "Days they have exams? If only one or two, could be tough to generate sales."
- "What kind of equipment? Leased? Referral sources? Insurances accepted?"
- "Who are your insurance providers? Amount of frame inventory? Frame suppliers? What are your recall procedures? Number of active patient records?Type of practice management software?"

Resources

Websites
- OptiBoard: www.optiboard.com

Trade Publications
- Optometric Management: www.optometricmanagement.com
- Optometry Times: optometrytimes.modernmedicine.com
- Review of Optometry: www.revoptom.com
- Vision Monday: www.visionmonday.com

Associations
- American Optometric Association: www.aoa.org
- American Academy of Optometry: www.aaopt.org
- American Optometric Society: www.optometricsociety.org

			Franchise
Orange Julius (See also Franchises)			
Approx. Total Investment			$345,000 to $375,000
	NAICS 722515		Number of Businesses/Units 465

Rules of Thumb
➢ 32 percent of annual sales plus inventory

Resources

Websites
- www.orangejulius.com

Rules of Thumb - **P**

Franchise
Original Italian Pie (See also Franchises, Pizza Shops)

Approx. Total Investment	$328,000 to $617,500
NAICS 722513	Number of Businesses/Units 14

Rules of Thumb

➢ 35 to 40 percent of annual sales plus inventory

Resources

Websites

- www.italianpie.com

Franchise
OXXO Care Cleaners (See also Dry Cleaners, Franchises)

Approx. Total Investment	$160,000 to $450,000
SIC 7212-01	NAICS 812320	Number of Businesses/Units 38

Rules of Thumb

➢ 60 percent of annual sales plus inventory

Resources

Websites

- OXXO Care Cleaners: www.oxxousa.com

Packaging (Industrial)	
NAICS 561910	Number of Businesses/Units 12,053

Rules of Thumb

➢ 5 to 6 times EBIT

➢ 60 to 70 percent of annual sales plus inventory

Benchmark Data

Statistics (Packaging & Labeling Services)

Number of Establishments	12,053
Average Profit Margin	7.9%
Revenue per Employee	$147,700
Average Number of Employees	4.2
Average Wages per Employee	$33,821

26th Edition   573

P - Rules of Thumb

Products and Services Segmentation

Other packaging and labeling service	45.1%
Packaging and labeling services for retail	45.1%
Other	7.6%
Resale of Merchandise	1.5%
Mailroom services and mailbox rentals	0.7%

Major Market Segmentation

Other retail product manufacturers	31%
Pharmaceutical companies	25%
Retail food and cosmetics manufacturers	22%
Other	15%
Government	7%

Industry Costs

Profit	7.9%
Wages	22.9%
Purchases	51.7%
Depreciation	2.1%
Marketing	1.2%
Rent & Utilities	6.2%
Other	8.0%

Market Share

Sonoco Products Company	20.5%

Source: IBISWorld, July 2015

Expenses as a percentage of annual sales

Cost of goods	60% to 65%
Payroll/labor Costs	08% to 10%
Occupancy	0
Profit (estimated pretax)	10% to 15%

Industry Trend

- "Global demand for flexible packaging is projected to reach $210 billion in 2015 according to a new market report by Smithers Pira.

  "The market is forecast to grow at an annual average rate of 3% reaching $248 billion in 2020. Flexible packaging has been one of the fastest growing packaging sectors over the past 10 years, thanks to increased consumer focus on convenience and sustainability, and this rapid development will continue to accelerate, the report has found.

  "The report shows that the global consumer flexible packaging market value is estimated at $91.7 billion for 2015 and is forecast to grow at an annual average rate of 4.4% during the period 2015–20 to reach $114 billion. The market tonnage of this segment is estimated at 26.2 million tons in 2015 and is forecast to grow on average by 3.8% during the period 2015–20 to reach 31.7 million tons."

  Source: http://www.smitherspira.com/news/2015/july/global-flexible-packaging-market-sees-rapid-growth

- "Consolidation will rule the packaging industry. Cheaper to buy than to grow market share in a mundane, non-innovative business, lacking pricing power and vulnerable to relocation of key accounts to offshore facilities."

Rules of Thumb - P

Questions
- "How stable is your customer base—what is your customer retention record? What % of total sales do your top 10 accounts represent? Is there really any real 'free cash flow' in the business?"

Paint & Decorating (Wallpaper) Retailers

SIC 5231-07	NAICS 444120	Number of Businesses/Units 8,626

Rules of Thumb
> ➢ 20 percent of annual sales plus inventory

Pricing Tips
- "They should have nationally known brand name plus 2 competitive paint lines. A wide variety of wallpaper from lesser priced to higher priced lines should be offered. National averages tell us these stores make from 16 to 17 percent plus reasonable wages for the owner/operators. The average markup is 40 percent. These stores are sold for fixtures, equipment plus inventory at cost."

Benchmark Data

Statistics (Paint Stores)
Number of Establishments	8,626
Average Profit Margin	11.1%
Revenue per Employee	$455,500
Average Number of Employees	3.2
Average Wages per Employee	$43,954

Products and Services Segmentation
Interior paint	43.0%
Exterior paint	24.8%
Painting equipment and supplies	18.6%
Stains, varnishes and other coatings	11.4%
Wallpaper and other flexible wall coverings	2.2%

Major Market Segmentation
Professional contractors	57.0%
Do-it-yourself customers	22.0%
Do-it-for-me customers	18.0%
Other	3.0%

Industry Costs
Profit	11.1%
Wages	10.4%
Purchases	57.3%
Depreciation	1.0%
Marketing	1.7%
Rent & Utilities	5.4%
Other	13.1%

26th Edition

P - Rules of Thumb

Market Share
The Sherwin-Williams Company 55.8%

Source: IBISWorld, April 2015

Industry Trend

Resources

Associations
- Paint and Decorating Retailers Association (PDRA): www.pdra.org

	Franchise
Pak Mail (See also Franchises, Mail and Parcel Centers)	
Approx. Total Investment	$186,000 to $180,215
NAICS 561431	Number of Businesses/Units 227

Rules of Thumb
➢ 50 percent of annual sales plus inventory

Resources

Websites
- www.pakmail.com

	Franchise
Panera Bread (See also Franchises)	
Approx. Total Investment	Net Worth of $7.5 million
Estimated Annual Sales/Unit	$2.5 million
NAICS 722513	Number of Businesses/Units 1,926

Rules of Thumb
➢ 35 to 40 percent of sales plus inventory

Industry Trend
- "As of June 30, 2015, there are 1,926 bakery-cafes in 46 states, the District of Columbia, and in Ontario, Canada, operating under the Panera Bread®, Saint Louis Bread Co.® and Paradise Bakery & Café® names, delivering fresh, authentic artisan bread served in a warm environment by engaging associates."

Resources

Websites
- www.panerabread.com

Papa John's Pizza (See also Franchises, Pizza Shops)

Franchise

Approx. Total Investment	$200,000 to $309,000
Estimated Annual Sales/Unit	$850,000
SIC 5812-22 NAICS 722513	Number of Businesses/Units 4,000

Rules of Thumb
➢ 38% to 40% of annual sales

Benchmark Data
- See Pizza Shops

Resources

Websites
- wwwpapajohns.com

Papa Murphy's Take 'N' Bake Pizza (See also Franchises, Pizza Shops)

Franchise

Approx. Total Investment	$216,430 to $381,220
Estimated Annual Sales/Unit	$550,000
NAICS 722513	Number of Businesses/Units 1,400

Rules of Thumb
➢ 35 to 40 percent of annual sales plus inventory

Benchmark Data
- See Pizza Shops

Resources

Websites
- www.papamurphys.com

Parcel Plus (See also Franchises, Mail and Parcel Centers)

Franchise

Approx. Total Investment	$206,720 to $245,795
NAICS 561431	Number of Businesses/Units 59

Rules of Thumb
➢ 25 percent of annual sales plus inventory

Resources

Websites
- Parcel Plus: www.parcelplus.com

P - Rules of Thumb

Parking Lots and Garages

| NAICS 812930 | Number of Businesses/Units 18,663 |

Rules of Thumb

> "[In some cities] they have been selling for 1.5 times their annual net before taxes, plus the value of fixtures, equipment and inventory at cost—plus real estate."

Benchmark Data

Statistics (Parking Lots and Garages)

Number of Establishments	18,663
Average Profit Margin	20.8%
Revenue per Employee	$70,600
Average Number of Employees	7.8
Average Wages per Employee	$19,213

Products and Services Segmentation

Off-street parking - hourly or daily	38.3%
Off-street parking in buildings - weekly or monthly	24.3%
Valet parking	12.7%
Off-street parking on lots - weekly or monthly	9.1%
Management fees for the operation of parking facilities	9.0%
Other	6.6%

Major Market Segmentation

Privately operated central business district	40.5%
College and university	14.2%
Off-premise airport	12.3%
On-premise airport	12.2%
Hotel	10.3%
Hospital	5.5%
Municipal central business district	5.0%

Industry Costs

Profit	20.8%
Wages	27.1%
Purchases	7.5%
Depreciation	4.3%
Marketing	0.8%
Rent & Utilities	28.3%
Other	11.2%

Market Share

SP Plus Corporation	16.1%
Vinci	9.4%
ABM Industries Inc.	6.4%

Source: IBISWorld, June 2015

- "Nearly four in 10 responding parking professionals are with organizations that currently contract with commercial operators for varying services. Contracted services include frontline attendants (39 percent), collections (36 percent), maintenance (36 percent), customer service (33 percent), transit/shuttle (31 percent), special events (30 percent), enforcement (29 percent), and security (29 percent). Of those surveyed, 18 percent outsource their entire operations to a commercial operator for turnkey services."

Source: 2015 Survey by the International Parking Institute

Industry Trend

- "Most respondents' programs also include a variety of elements beyond parking, such as improving conditions for bicyclists and pedestrians (47 percent) and bike/transit integration (43 percent), special event management (43 percent), shuttle services (40 percent), carsharing (40 percent), park and ride (33 percent), and ridesharing (33 percent). About one quarter of all those surveyed are also involved with shared parking, commuter trip reduction programs, traffic calming, bikeshare programs, and a wide range of programs that promote alternative transportation modes.

    "Among the top 10 emerging trends in parking, half relate directly to a range of different technologies that have revolutionized the parking sector in the past few years. Toppping the list are 'innovative technologies that improve access control and payment automation' (53 percent), the 'demand for electronic cashless payment' (44 percent), 'prevalence of mobile applications' (47 percent) and 'real-time communication of pricing and availability to mobile/smartphones' (41 percent), and 'wireless sensing devices for traffic management' (22 percent). Good news for parking professionals: A top trend remains greater 'collaboration between parking, transporation, and decision-makers,' which industry experts believe is a pathway to solving many problems."

    Source: 2015 Survey by the International Parking Institute

- "Factors Driving Parking Demand—Parking demand is a function of a number of factors, all working in tandem to affect demand and usage. When looking at macroeconomic, demographic, employment, and industry statistics, we see a picture of patterns that influence parking demand in North America.

    1. Population: Fundamental population growth of 9.6% from the 2000 U.S. Census to the 2010 U.S. Census is expected to continue into the future.
    2. Employment: In the U.S., 92% employment provides sustained parking demand, 6.2% unemployment as of August 2014.
    3. Baby Boomers: The Baby Boomer population will increase to 63 million by 2025, an 80% increase over 2000 levels.
    4. Colleges/Universities: College/University enrollment increased 30% from 2000–2009, from 15.3 million to 20.4 million.
    5. Municipalities: Public sector parking is beset by financial pressures; this pressure will accelerate automation and rate increases that will drive revenue.
    6. Pricing: Demand will be affected by demand pricing, mobile rate promotions, pre-paid parking and price increases both public/private, as well as price rates for peak parking periods.

    "However, while data suggests positive events on the horizon for the parking industry, there are a number of risk factors, such as increased taxes and increased government regulation."

    Source: "National Parking Association 2013–2015 Parking Demand Report"

P - Rules of Thumb

Resources

Associations
- International Parking Institute: www.parking.org
- National Parking Association: www.npapark.org

Parking Lot Sweeping

| SIC 1611-04 | NAICS 561790 | Number of Businesses/Units 12,000 |

Rules of Thumb
- 60 to 65% percent of annual sales includes inventory
- 2 to 2.5 times SDE includes inventory
- 5 to 5.5 times EBIT
- 5 to 6 times EBITDA

Pricing Tips

- "Some value factors are types of accounts, large box stores, nat'l shopping centers, small strips, construction, colleges, corporations. The stronger the account base with good contracts, the higher the value. Condition of equipment, quality of labor force and quality of service to the accounts separate the top companies from the rest."
- "Most of the time, prospective buyers for a sweeping company will primarily look at two factors, your sweeping equipment and your accounts. For the former, that's when you'll want to have preventative and scheduled maintenance documents on each piece of equipment available. If you know you're putting your business onto the market, you may even want to go through your sweepers and improve their cosmetics, installing items like seat covers and floor mats. These are low-cost items that provide a better overall impression to prospective buyers. It's best if you have all safety and normal operational items working, as well.

"When it comes to your contracts, savvy buyers will want to look at several areas of your accounts. Although quantity and margin are important, their perception of the quality of your accounts is perhaps even more so. This includes such factors as longevity on the books, ease of cancellation, whether or not escalation clauses are in the contract and more. For example, if all of your contracts allow for a 30-day, 'no reason required' cancellation by the customer, your business won't be worth as much when you want to sell it.

"In most buy/sell transactions, at least for sweeping businesses that have been operational for a number of years, 'goodwill' is also a factor. The seller typically wants money to compensate for having developed the business to its current state. As a buyer, your goal is to keep this amount to a minimum.

"'Everyone wants lots of money for the business they've put however many years of blood, sweat and tears into,' said Presutti. The reality, however, is often different. That will often become apparent when, as a buyer, you sit down with the owner and go through the actual current valuations of both contracts and depreciated equipment. This is central to the negotiation process.

Rules of Thumb - **P**

"Since most business owners plan ahead to sell, the machinery has typically not been replaced recently. Contracts usually have a 30-day cancellation clause where the customer can cancel for no reason. You have to ask yourself what that type of contract is really worth to you. 'In my view, giving more than 60 days of revenue to such an account is really a crapshoot.'"

Source: "Operate Your Business With a Resale in Mind" by Jay Presutti and Ranger Kidwell-Ross, October 2005, http://www.worldsweeper.com/ This is a very informative site and should be visited by anyone who has an interest in this business. Don't let the date fool you, still excellent information.

Expert Comments

"This industry has been unable to support national or regional consolidation. Mostly local, statewide, or small regional players."

Benchmark Data

- "$125K/employee or $150–$200K/driver"
- "Very generally speaking, using 2005 prices, it is not uncommon for a contractor with a smaller parking area sweeper, such as a three-yard-capacity sweeper on a 1-ton chassis, to be able to charge between $55 and $65 per hour, for a gross earnings of between $9,000 and $11,000 per month.

"For a larger sweeper, one which is suitable for performing a variety of duties other than parking lot cleanup, the same rule of thumb is a charge of between $65 and $75 per hour; this should net you a gross of between $11,000 and $14,000 per month. Street sweeping pricing should be about $90, since it is harder on your equipment, and the sweepers cost substantially more.

"Again, these are simply generalizations, and actual earnings are quite dependent upon work performed, charges in your area, etc. They are definitely, however, numbers which have been attained by many in the industry who have worked hard at developing their businesses."

Source: Schwarze Industries, Inc. Although this information is dated, it is still interesting.

Expenses as a percentage of annual sales

Cost of goods	20%
Payroll/labor Costs	15%
Occupancy	05%
Profit (estimated pretax)	10% to 12%

Questions

- "Must establish the quality of the accounts, condition of equipment, review contracts, examine labor force, etc. Is the owner tied to any special interests, people or other connections responsible for a significant portion of his company's business? If so how will this affect these accounts/sites? Future growth in a local area or region? Competition?"

Resources

Websites
- www.worldsweeper.com

Associations
- North American Power Sweeping Association (NAPSA): www.powersweeping.org

P - Rules of Thumb

Pawn Shops (See also Used Goods)		
SIC 5932-29	NAICS 522298	Number of Businesses/Units 12,026

Rules of Thumb

➢ 3 times SDE includes inventory

➢ 3 to 5 times EBIT

➢ 3.5 times EBITDA

➢ 40 to 70 percent of annual sales plus inventory. Since money is loaned using items of value belonging to the customer and said items serve as collateral for the loan, inventory against money loaned has to be taken into account.

Pricing Tips

- "Pricing pawnshops usually is far from the norm of a multiple of SDE, EBIT or EBITA. Typically the values that drive a pawnshop are the 'Money on the street' (value of the daily loans) and the inventory, with great interest in the MIX of all the items that have been taken and used as collateral and the type of inventory, i.e., if a certain shop has 80% Jewelry and 20% guns, tools, and electronics the inventory will be worth more than cost since gold and silver are extremely valuable. If the mix is 20% jewelry and 80% tools and electronics then it possibly could be worth less than cost due to depreciation. Not all shops handle guns but if they are a large percentage or even half of the inventory then it is a pretty safe bet it should be valued no less than cost. Today's buyers are typically corporate buyers and rely heavily on good records and computer systems. They will shy away from shops that are not computerized and the seller is telling them (wink wink) the shop makes more than it shows. Keep a close eye on the scrap gold sales and whether or not they are being recorded in the income for the shop. It is very common for those sales to not be recorded and will generally be $15,000–$25,000 per month for a shop doing $2 million in gross sales. This will drastically change the SDE for you."
- "Quality of inventory is very important. Stores with lots of unwanted 'junk' will not be of interest to educated pawn buyers. Need to understand pawn renewal rate, average loan, do they buy gold and at what rate."
- "A very large factor for selling pawn shops is what we call 'money on the street.' Some owners feel as though they should be able to collect 1–3 months' interest on this. It can be considered A/R, but keep in mind the national average is that 75% of this will be collected at anywhere from 200% to 300% APR. Yes, you read that right."

Expert Comments

"Let me take these one by one. The amount of competition is directly affected by the part of town and possibly the state you are in. Some states have very difficult pawn laws and others do not, so the competition is stiff in Detroit but none at all in San Francisco.

"Amount of risk is very little if you are somewhat educated in the pawn business; even a poorly run shop can be profitable if they know how to make educated loans. If you make poor loans your retail side will not be enough to sustain you for a long time.

"Location and facilities are key to your survival. You must be in the right location and contrary to popular belief that does not mean you want to be in a poor neighborhood. Areas with blue collar incomes are much more desirable than welfare or extremely poor neighborhoods. Marketability is very high for both small and large shops alike. The shops with at least $150,000 on the street are desirable to small to medium size chain buyers and anything smaller will be sought after by mom and pops. Any store with $400,000 or more on the street will be sold quickly. Remember that money on the street is the number one thing that all educated buyers of pawnshops look for. A high loan balance on good loans will eventually bring high revenue.

"Industry trend: with the boom in pawnshop reality shows pawnshops are getting some much needed positive spotlight from Hollywood and the TV world. This is driving the industry forward with both patrons and individuals wanting to try their hand at being a pawnshop owner.

"Ease of replication: the industry is growing and cities/municipalities are seeing the need for more ordinances to govern the business and practices of some of the owners. Therefore opening new shops is getting very difficult in some areas."

"Economic factors have created an environment where many individuals do not have access to credit other than pawn shops or other sub-prime lenders. This trend will continue for the next 1 to 3 years at a minimum."

"Risk is actually very low if you make educated loans on a daily basis. There are many factors that weigh in on this and typically 'education' in this field comes from 'learning the hard way,' but several large chains have been very successful in training personnel quickly to run shops successfully."

Benchmark Data

Statistics (Pawn Shops)

Number of Establishments	12,026
Average Profit Margin	9.6%
Revenue per Employee	$229,800
Average Number of Employees	2.4
Average Wages per Employee	$29,895

Products and Services Segmentation

Merchandise sales	58.1%
Secured loans for personal collateral	41.9%

Industry Costs

Profit	9.6%
Wages	13.1%
Purchases	48.1%
Depreciation	1.6%
Marketing	1.9%
Rent & Utilities	6.5%
Purchases	19.2%

P - Rules of Thumb

Market Share

Cash America International Inc. 14.4%
EZCorp Inc. 8.2%

Source: IBISWorld, November 2014

- "The average pawn customer:
    - ✓ Age: 36
    - ✓ Household Income: $29,000
    - ✓ 80% are employed
    - ✓ 82% have high school diploma or GED
    - ✓ 33% are homeowners
    - ✓ All ethnicities
    - ✓ National Average Loan Amount: $150"

  Source: http://pawnshopstoday.com/the-customer/

- "According to the National Pawnbrokers Association, 80 percent of all customers do end up reclaiming their items."

- "Finance charges. Interest rates can range from 3 to 25 percent of the cost of the loan, depending on the state. In Michigan, where Gold's (Leo Gold, a star on TV show "Hardcore Pawn") shops are located, the interest rate is 3 percent, and consumers are also charged $1 per month in storage fees. So if you took out a $100 loan, over three months, you'd pay $9 in interest and $3 in storage fees, says Gold.

  "How much money you'll likely get. Maybe not as much as you think. Gold says pawn stores will typically pay 60 percent of what the person paid for the item. So if you have a baseball collection that is determined to be worth $500, you'll probably get $300 for it."

  Source: "Pawn Shops Go Mainstream" by Geoff Williams, www.moneyusnews.com March 13, 2013

- "The National Pawnbrokers Association reports that there are over 30 million pawn store customers per year and they appreciate this unique form of credit and tend to borrow only what they need, as evidenced by the relatively low national average loan amount of $80. NPA President and pawn shop owner Dave Crume says, 'Pawn customers repay their loans and redeem their collateral at a correspondingly high average national redemption rate of 80 percent. These parameters appear to be holding constant, despite the current economy.

  "Most of the 13,000+ pawn stores in the U.S. are small, privately owned businesses and do not report their earnings publicly."

  Source: "Pawn Shops: Economic Barometer?" National Pawnbrokers Association, www.pawnshoptoday.com

- "Typically when a shop has $100,000 'on the street,' the shop becomes very very profitable and easier to sell."

- "As a rule of thumb, over 80% of a pawn shop loan base will come from within an 8 mile radius of the location. Therefore, in your business plan it is important to spell out your estimated default rate on your loan base (usually around 25%) and your estimated effective yield on your income producing loans. This makes it much easier to sell the idea to your investor on borrowing cash from him at 10% per year and loaning it out to your customers at a return of 10% per month."

  Source: Cloud Ten, Inc., a leading pawn shop consulting firm, www.startapawnshop.com, this appeared on the Web site of the National Pawnbrokers Association, a very informative site

- "The rise of the Internet allows employees to quickly determine what an item being pawned is worth—a skill that once took years to develop."

  Source:"Left Behind: Pawn Shop Franchise Has Right Economy" by Matt Bolch, *Franchise Times*

Rules of Thumb - P

- "A typical benchmark that several of my buyers are using is 3 times the money on the street (A/R) plus FFE plus inventory at cost. This is what I call a bottom feeders calculation and many sellers won't sell for that number especially if they are heavy in jewelry. Many times there will be a premium introduced if they have a high ticket number (number of tickets written per day (loans)) or if their inventory is very good or both."

Expenses as a percentage of annual sales	
Cost of goods	62%
Payroll/labor Costs	09%
Occupancy	04%
Profit (estimated pretax)	18%

Industry Trend

- "The National Pawnbrokers Association (NPA) today announced the results of the NPA 2015 Trend Survey that assesses how changes in the U.S. economy have affected the pawn industry since the beginning of 2014. Findings of the survey demonstrate conservative growth within the industry over the past year, as well as a dip in the number gold-based loans and gold-buying transactions. This decrease in gold-based transactions, according to industry experts, is due to consumers having released disposable gold during peak gold price periods. "While gold-based transactions may have leveled off, the majority of pawnbrokers surveyed reported a three to five percent increase in overall business. Collateral loans, also known as pawn loans, remain the core of pawnbrokers' businesses, with over 80 percent of pawnbrokers reporting that pawn loans are the most common transactions. According to the survey, the national average pawn loan amount remained at $150."

    Source: http://pawnshopstoday.com/trends/

- "The new wave of pawnbrokers, or collateralized lenders, as they like to be known, isn't just betting that people will pledge cars, planes, or, in the case of one ultrapawn customer, an earth mover. They are betting that as long as traditional bank lending remains tight for individuals, there will be repeat customers."

    Source: "Rich, too, find need for a good pawnshop," Paul Sullivan, *Boston Globe*, January 13, 2014

- "Trend is more competition and a steady customer base."

- "The pawn business model is diverse, including retail, jewelry sales and pawn loans. While one element of the pawn business may thrive in a slow economy, such as pawn loans, other elements such as retail sales, will decrease. Dave Crume notes, 'While many of our association members are making it through the dip in the economy, there are many pawn shops in the U.S. that are struggling and closing. Just like all sectors of the American economy, the pawn industry is challenged by the recent economy, the pawn industry is challenged by the recent economic trends."

    Source: www.pawnshopstoday.com

Seller Financing

- 2–3 years max

Questions

- "What type of software do you use to track pawn receivables and inventory? How do you value pawned items? What is the quality of your pawn receivable?

P - Rules of Thumb

- How do you measure and track bad inventory? What are the state laws regarding pawn shops, gun sales, and interest rates on loans?"
- "Do you have a good POS program and do you use it correctly? How is your accounting done? What type of software and is all income recorded?"

Resources

Websites
- Pawn Shops Today: www.pawnshopstoday.com

Associations
- National Pawnbrokers Association: www.nationalpawnbrokers.org

Payday Loans (See also Check Cashing Services)

NAICS 522291	Number of Businesses/Units 20,092

Rules of Thumb
➢ 70 percent of annual sales

Benchmark Data

Statistics (Payday Loans)
Number of Establishments	20,092
Average Profit Margin	13.7%
Revenue per Employee	$127,200
Average Number of Employees	4.5
Average Wages per Employee	$37,653

Products and Services Segmentation
Payday loans for recurring expenses	46.0%
Check cashing	33.3%
Payday loans for unexpected emergencies/expenses	10.7%
Payday loans for other reasons	10.0%

Industry Costs
Profit	13.7%
Wages	29.4%
Purchases	33.9%
Depreciation	1.6%
Marketing	2.2%
Rent & Utilities	2.8%
Other	16.4%

Market Share
AARC LLC	7.1%
Cash America International Inc.	5.6%

Source: IBISWorld, January 2015

- Payday Loan Borrowers Polled
    - ✓ "97 percent of borrowers agree that their payday lender clearly explained the terms of the loan to them, including nearly nine in 10 (88 percent) who strongly agree.
    - ✓ 68 percent prefer a payday loan over incurring a late fee of approximately $30 (4 percent) or an overdraft fee of $35 from their bank (3 percent) when faced with a short-term financial crisis and unable to pay a bill.
    - ✓ Fewer than one in 10 (8 percent) said that a payday loan was their only option and they had no other resources available.
    - ✓ 95 percent say payday loans can provide a safety net during unexpected financial difficulties.
    - ✓ 94 percent say they were able to repay their loan in the amount of time they had expected to.
    - ✓ 89 percent say they feel more in control of their financial situation because of this option when they need it.
    - ✓ 68 percent say they would be in worse financial condition than they are now without the option of taking out a payday loan."
        Source:"New Harris Poll: 9 in 10 Payday Loan Borrowers Felt Product Met Their Expectations,"
        http://cfsaa.com/our-resources/communications/recent-news/article-detail/newsid/77.aspx
- "Consequently, revenue for the Check Cashing and Payday Loan Services industry is expected to increase at an annualized rate of 2.0% from 2009 to 2014 to reach $11.1 billion; this growth includes a 2.2% rise in revenue expected in 2014 alone.
"According to The Pew Charitable Trusts, 5.5% of domestic adults have used a payday loan. In general, younger individuals that lack a college degree and generate less than $40,000 in annual income are the most likely to rely on payday loans. The average borrower takes out eight loans of $375 each and pays $520 in interest annually. Moreover, this average borrower is typically indebted for five months out of the year."
        Source: "Check Cashing & Payday Loans Services in the US Industry Market Research Report Now Available from IBISWorld," www.prweb.com, February 19, 2014
- "For the payday lending industry, and as previously discussed, smaller loans cost more to originate than larger ones on a cost-per-dollar basis. This is because lenders, regardless of their structure, incur fixed costs in originating a loan, whatever its size. In the case of payday lending, these costs include: defaults on extensions of unsecured credit to borrowers of moderate means; operating costs, such as salaries, facilities, processing applications, and collection of payments; taxes; and return on investment capital."
"Available data on defaults suggest that unpaid obligations to payday lenders amount to about 10 to 20 percent of the finance charges they levy over the course of a year.
"The operating costs, which represent the largest part by far, are fixed and are not affected by the loan amount. While the fixed costs of facilitating a $200 loan are not substantially different from those likely to be incurred to facilitate and place a $20,000 home equity loan or $5,000 cash advance on a credit card, actual labor costs associated with servicing payday loans are higher.
"Within the parameters of the marketing proposition — i.e., a quick, convenient loan, as an alternative to credit card borrowing — payday lenders can be expected to do as much as they can to ensure that the risk of default is low.
"For example, payday lenders require borrowers to produce proof of a checking account, identification and a pay-stub; some lenders screen for histories of bounced checks.

P - Rules of Thumb

"For payday loans—as for other unsecured, subprime loans—the costs relating to collection of payments is significant. Our reading of Prof. Caskey's analysis suggests that payday lenders are exceptionally close to their borrowers.
"Payday loans are generally originated and serviced by local loan offices."
Source: www.CIFA.net, Community Financial Services Association of America.
This is a very informative site.

Industry Trend

- "The agency (the Consumer Financial Protection Bureau) subsequently released a startling study of 12 million payday loans issued all across the country that thoroughly debunked the industry's claim that the loans were necessary to help people make it to the next payday—customarily two weeks away—at which point they could comfortably pay off what they owed. It turned out that only 15 percent of borrowers could find the money to repay the full debt without borrowing again within 14 days, which meant they were hit with more fees.
"One in five borrowers eventually defaulted on the loan; nearly two-thirds ended up renewing a loan, some more than 10 times, turning what began as a short-term loan into a long-term debt trap. The debt typically grew as the borrowers moved from one loan to the next, instead of being paid down, as happens with a traditional bank loan. In three-fifths of the cases studied, the fees ended up exceeding the original amount of the loan."
Source: "Progress on Payday Lending," *New York Times*, March 29, 2015

- "Each month, more than 200,000 needy US households take out what's advertised as a brief loan. The government is seeking to set standards for a multibillion-dollar industry that has historically been regulated only at the state level. The payday industry warns that if the rules are enacted, many impoverished Americans would lose access to any credit."
Source: Associated Press as reported in *Boston Globe*, March 27, 2015

- "Notably, borrowers almost unanimously agree that it should be their choice whether or not to use payday lending, not the government's choice (95 percent)."
Source:"New Harris Poll: 9 in 10 Payday Loan Borrowers Felt Product Met Their Expectations,"
http://cfsaa.com/our-resources/communications/recent-news/article-detail/newsid/77.aspx

- "According to IBISWorld Industry Analyst Stephen Hoopes, 'Given the industry's reliance on poorer consumers for revenue, regulatory agencies have sought to increase legislation surrounding industry operators, as they view payday loans and check cashing fees as exploitative.' As such, 15 states currently either ban payday loans or cap the annual percentage rate at 36.0% Furthermore, as national interest rate cap proposals are forecast to intensify, compliance costs are expected to increase, to the detriment of profit margins."
Source: "Check Cashing & Payday Loans Services in the US Industry Market Research Report
Now Available from IBISWorld," www.prweb.com, February 19, 2014

"Major banks have quickly become behind-the-scenes allies of Internet-based payday lenders that offer short-term loans with interest rates sometimes exceeding 500 percent.

- "With 15 states banning payday loans, a growing number of the lenders have set up online operations in more hospitable states or far-flung locales like Belize, Malta and the West Indies to more easily evade statewide caps on interest rates.
"While the banks, which include giants like JPMorgan Chase, Bank of America and Wells Fargo, do not make the loans, they are a critical link for the lenders, enabling the lenders to withdraw payments automatically from borrowers' bank

accounts, even in states where the loans are banned entirely. In some cases, the banks allow lenders to tap checking accounts even after the customers have begged them to stop the withdrawals.

"By 2016 Internet loans will make up roughly 60 percent of the total payday loans, up from about 35 percent in 2011, according to John Hecht, an analyst with the investment bank Stephens Inc. As of 2011, he said, the volume of online payday loans was $13 billion, up more than 120 percent from $5.8 billion in 2006."

Source: "Major Banks Aid Payday Loans Banned By States" by Jessica Silver-Greenberg, New York Times, February, 24, 2013

Resources

Associations
- Community Financial Services of America: www.cfsaa.com

Pest Control

SIC 7342-01	NAICS 561710	Number of Businesses/Units 26,871

Rules of Thumb
- ➢ 80 to 90 percent of annual sales plus inventory
- ➢ 2 to 3 times SDE plus inventory
- ➢ 3 to 4 times EBIT
- ➢ 3 to 4 times EBITDA

Pricing Tips
- "Pest Control Companies tend to be less based on a multiple of cash flow than other industries. The multiple is taken into account along with whether the customers are under contract, the longivity of the customer base, as well as whether they are serviced monthly, bi-monthly or quarterly and the cost per service."
- "Most buyers are looking for repetitive income. The buyer can reap the benefits of the purchase for multiple years but only pay once for the customers. A pest control company with contracts or year to year consistent sales and profits would be valued at a higher multiple than one with less consistent sales."
- "Profit x 4 to 6 plus or minus time in business as a %—plus or minus size of business in a %—plus or minus price of service as a %."
- "Length of time in business, methods used in treating, % of profit on total sales (higher=more value), annual contracts add value, increased sales each year adds value, no tax liens or other liens, good reputation with competitors and customers add value."
- "It is all about transferring profit from one company to the other. Profit being 10% to 45%, how much is transferable to the new owner? The more transferable, the higher the price."
- "It's not as easy as putting a percentage to a business or simply using a multiple of EBIT. Each business is different. It is more than likely a sum of the various positives and negatives of the business. A first class, growing, well-established business with good books, good cash flow, newer vehicles, and

P - Rules of Thumb

long-time employees will bring a better price than one without these attributes."

- "The following was asked by Frank Andorka, Editorial Director of PMP Buzz Online eNewsletter: 'What criteria do you use to determine whether a company is a good acquisition target?'
- "Stephen Good, Terminix International: 'We look at a high percentage of recurring revenues versus one-time revenues. We also look at a company's pricing relative to Terminix's pricing. Finally, we look at how a company may augment our geographic penetration and enhance our competitive position in a market or given region.'

"Kevin Burns, Arrow Exterminators: 'At Arrow, we typically consider the transaction more of a merger than an acquisition, as the integration phase is really a merger of employees and customers into the Arrow family. We pay particular attention to the owners and the culture of the company they have created over the years with their employees and the customer service they perform. We look at top-line revenue and revenue growth over the past three years, the mix of business, the service schedule, the mix of commercial vs. residential, detailed expenses and of course, net income. We consider the return on investment in the first year and each year thereafter based on typical revenue growth and net profit we've experienced at Arrow.'

"Victor Hamel, Rentokil North America: 'The most critical criteria for us is the cultural fit. This is most important for sellers as well. It is critically important that we share the same values.'

"Bob Hines, Orkin: 'The initial answers are reputation and length of time in the industry, size of the company and type of services rendered. There are times where we have left a company as a stand-alone, but had it assigned to one of our regions. We would do this with a large, well-run, multimillion dollar company that has a good reputation in an area. It wouldn't make sense to drop those key assets—the name and reputation.'"

Source: "Online Exclusive: Meet You on the Other Side," PMP Buzz Online eNewsletter

- "Range .60 to 1.15 times sales, as high as 1.5 annual sales for commercial pest control."
- "Pricing is based on recurring contractual revenue. Pest control companies generally sell for about 100% of recurring sales and between 20% and 50% of nonrecurring sales. SDE is generally not applicable to pest control companies, rather, use EBITDA. A company with a high degree of contractual recurring revenue will sell for the closer to 5 or 6 times EBITDA, whereas a company with a low proportion of contractual recurring revenue will sell for the low end of the range of 2 to 3 times EBITDA."
- "Profit on most pest control companies with 3 or more employees = 30%. $1 million to $5 million profit = 18 to 25%. One-man pest control ($100K volume) profit = 85%."
- "Normally no more than 1 year's gross sales for a good business. However, Terminix is paying in excess of 1.5 times gross on a pest control business (w/no termites). 1.5 times cash flow is another figure often used, based on monthly accounts with charges of $25 to $32 for average residential. Annual contracts might go for as high as 2 times cash flow."
- "$1 to $5 million in annual sales should make 18% to 22%."
- "Pest control with contracts—most valuable; termite renewals—2nd; lawn & ornamentals with contracts—3rd; fumigation value = equipment value only."
- "Price depends on profit, efficiency, category, location—volume is a big factor. Most buyers prefer to buy pest control as opposed to termite. Some companies in the South do exclusively lawn & ornamental."

Expert Comments

"Most states require licensing which makes it more difficult to get into the industry. It eliminates those wanting to get into the industry without proper training."

"Owner needs a pest control license; 4 categories—be sure you know the one you are working in. Possibly hire a certified operator. Use consultants often as possible. Get a good marketing manager because things are changing as fast as technology."

"There are more buyers than sellers. Have to train for three years in most productive states. Demand is extremely high and the supply is extremely low."

"Location and facilities are not important in this industry as long as they meet the needs of the business. Customers rarely visit the business."

Benchmark Data

Statistics (Pest Control)

Number of Establishments	26,871
Average Profit Margin	8.0%
Revenue per Employee	$106,100
Average Number of Employees	4.5
Average Wages per Employee	$39,004

Products and Services Segmentation

Insect control, including bed bugs, cockroaches and ants	55.1%
Termite control	17.0%
Other services, including bird-proofing and mosquito control	16.4%
Rodent extermination and control	11.5%

Major Market Segmentation

Residential homes	68.3%
Commercial establishments	29.4%
Government institutions	2.3%

Industry Costs

Profit	8.0%
Wages	36.8%
Purchases	18.6%
Depreciation	2.4%
Marketing	5.4%
Rent & Utilities	4.8%
Other	24.0%

Market Share

The ServiceMaster Company	11.6%
Rollins Inc.	11.1%

Source: IBISWorld, July 2015

- "$125k production per technician. Profit 20% or better."
- "Cost per hour to provide service + a reasonable amount of profit"
- "Companies over $1 million profit should be 18 to 24 percent of annual volume."

P - Rules of Thumb

Expenses as a percentage of annual sales

Cost of goods	08% to 15%
Payroll/labor Costs	25% to 30%
Occupancy	05%
Profit (estimated pretax)	20% to 30%

Industry Trend

- "In this industry there are always more buyers than sellers. I believe this should continue in the future."
- "The U.S. structural pest control industry generated an estimated $7.213 billion in total service revenue in 2013, a 5.9% increase from the $6.815 billion measured in 2012. The top four U.S. service providers, Orkin, Terminix, Ecolab, and Rentokil represented nearly 45% of the total industry revenue for the termite and general pest control market segments this past year."

  Source: Six percent growth for the U.S. structural pest control market, June 26, 2014, http://news.agropages.com/News/NewsDetail---12519.htm

- "Big boys buying everything they can. Always new start-ups. Good franchise potential."
- "With the increasing need to maintain a pest free environment, the sales of the pest control service providers has increased significantly, which in turn provides incentive for more players to enter into the market and establish themselves in the industry. The pest control services market is characterized by stiff competition within the industry, launch of eco-friendly products, offering of customized services and a number of mergers and acquisitions."

  Source: www.reuters.com, October 30, 2013

Seller Financing

- "Since this is not an inventory or equipment intensive business, the majority of buyers rely on Seller financing or pay cash for the business. Lender financing is frequently based on the profits of the business."
- "Typical financing is Seller financing. Banks don't loan money on service businesses."
- "Depends on the size of the business. Normally 3 to 5 years. A larger company would be eligible for an SBA loan or other lender financing and could be financed for up to 10 years."
- "Financing is directly related to the profits of the business. The buyer needs to feed his family and pay the debt service. When the seller is willing to finance a portion of the sale, it is normally between 3 and 7 years."
- "40% down financed 2 to 5 years depending on size."
- 3–5 years

Questions

- "Why are you selling? What are you going to do after the sale? How long will you be available for consulting?"
- "Any recent significant changes in your business such as the loss of a major account? What portion of your business is your largest customer?"
- "Why are you getting out of the business? What is your employee turnover rate? Have you paid all of your federal and state taxes and can you prove it?"
- "Like most businesses, a quality company sells for more. New equipment, good books and records, and a high profit margin make a business worth more. Repeat commercial accounts also affect the bottom line positively when pricing a business."

Rules of Thumb - P

- "Breakdown of services: commercial versus residential; general pest versus wood destroying."

Resources

Websites
- This is the Website of Al Woodward, a pest control brokerage specialist: www.servicebusinessconsulting.com/al-woodward-broker/

Trade Publications
- Pest Management Professional—an excellent site with lots of informative articles: www.mypmp.net
- PestWeb: www.pestweb.com

Associations
- Arizona Pest Control Professional Organization: www.azppo.org
- National Pest Management Association: www.pestworld.org

Pet Grooming (See also Dog Kennels)		
SIC 0752-04	NAICS 812910	Number of Businesses/Units 103,967

Rules of Thumb
- 40 to 45 percent of annual sales plus inventory
- 1.5 times SDE plus inventory

Benchmark Data

Statistics (Pet Grooming and Boarding)
Number of Establishments	103,967
Average Profit Margin	12.8%
Revenue per Employee	$37,200
Average Number of Employees	1.7
Average Wages per Employee	$14,580

Products and Services Segmentation
Pet boarding	41.2%
Pet grooming	31.8%
Other	19.0%
Pet training	8.0%

Industry Costs
Profit	12.8%
Wages	39.1%
Purchases	11.5%
Depreciation	3.6%
Marketing	2.5%
Rent & Utilities	12.2%
Other	18.3%

Source: IBISWorld, July 2015

P - Rules of Thumb

Industry Trend

- "The pet industry in the United States and many other countries is booming. Americans, for example, own more pets than ever before. Growth in the sector is derived both from increasing pet ownership as well as from increased spending per pet. Pet pampering is becoming the norm, as pet owner spending has moved far beyond simple food and grooming expenses to include innovative and specialized premium products. The bottom line: people increasingly view their pets as part of the family and are willing to spend even during difficult economic times.

  "A Golden Age for Pets and Pet Businesses—An overall rise in the number of pets in the U.S. and increased spending per pet are the main factors that will contribute to the pet industry's growth in the years ahead. Even with the overall economic recovery taking longer than expected, annual revenue growth in pet products and services is anticipated to clock in at some 4.4% through 2016 (one of the few industries that can say so). As the recovery takes hold, household disposable income will rise even faster, and spending on pets will pick up even more."

  Source: Pet Care Industry in 2015 at a Glance,
https://www.franchisehelp.com/industry-reports/pet-care-industry-report/

Resources

Websites
- PetGroomer—an amazing site, well worth visiting if you have any interest at all in the subject: www.petgroomer.com

Associations
- American Pet Products Association: www.americanpetproducts.org
- National Dog Groomers Association of America: www.nationaldoggroomers.com

Petland (See also Franchises, Pet Stores)	Franchise
Approx. Total Investment	$400,000 to $850,000
NAICS 453910	Number of Businesses/Units 150

Rules of Thumb
➢ 50 percent of annual sales plus inventory

Resources

Websites
- www.petland.com

Pet Stores		
SIC 5999-30	NAICS 453910	Number of Businesses/Units 18,242

Rules of Thumb
➢ 25 to 30 percent of annual sales plus inventory
➢ 2 times SDE plus inventory

Pricing Tips
- "Be sure to check inventory turnover rate to make sure inventory is saleable."
- "Dealing with reputable breeders increases value."
- "If they have an 'acceptable' system for acquiring pets for sale, increase the price by 5%."

Expert Comments

"This takes into consideration that the store would be privately owned and not a 'big box' store. Many of these privately owned businesses have been able to successfully compete on price against the big box stores. Stores in small towns tend to do well."

"Location is a key factor in pricing, as many people travel to pick out the 'right' dog. Location to major intersections is a definite plus. Although it is fairly easy to duplicate a pet or pet supply store, knowing the mechanics of the industry can be tricky. Risk is primarily associated with dealing with reputable breeders that stand by their product; diseases such as parvo and kennel cough can cost quite a bit."

"Unless there is a big box pet supply close by, a single ownership shop will do well in any dense residential area."

Benchmark Data

Statistics (Pet Stores)

Number of Establishments	18,242
Average Profit Margin	8.1%
Revenue per Employee	$146,900
Average Number of Employees	6.7
Average Wages per Employee	$19,918

Products and Services Segmentation

Pet food	52.0%
Pet supplies	29.0%
Pet services	13.0%
Live animals	6.0%

Industry Costs

Profit	8.1%
Wages	13.6%
Purchases	58.5%
Depreciation	1.1%
Marketing	1.9%
Rent & Utilities	10.1%
Other	6.7%

Market Share

PetSmart Inc.	38.6%
PETCO Animal Supplies Inc.	18.8%

Source: IBISWorld, August 2015

P - Rules of Thumb

Estimated 2015 Sales within the U.S. Market

For 2015, it estimated that $60.59 billion will be spent on our pets in the U.S.

Estimated Breakdown	2015 Estimate	% Growth (2015 vs. 2014)
Food	$23.04 billion	3.5
Supplies/OTC Medicine	$14.39 billion	4.7
Vet Care	$15.73 billion	4.6
Live animal purchases	$2.19 billion	1.9
Pet Services: grooming & boarding	$5.24 billion	8.3

Number of U.S. Households that Own a Pet (millions)

Bird	6.1
Cat	42.9
Dog	54.4
Horse	2.5
Freshwater Fish	12.3
Saltwater Fish	1.3
Reptile	4.9
Small Animal	5.4

- According to the 2015–2016 APPA National Pet Owners Survey, basic annual expenses for dog and cat owners in dog and cat owners in dollars include:

	Dogs	Cats
Surgical Vet Visits	$551	$398
Routine Vet	$235	$196
Food	$269	$246
Food Treats	$61	$51
Kennel Boarding	$333	$130
Vitamins	$62	$33
Groomer/Grooming Aids	$83	$43
Toys	$47	$28

Source: 2015–2016 APPA National Pet Owners Survey

- "The keys to success in this industry are low rent, knowledgeable and caring employees, spotlessly clean store, publicly accepted pet sales system, and competition in price against 'big box' stores."
- "Costs of goods should not exceed 75%."

Expenses as a percentage of annual sales

Cost of goods	50% to 60%
Payroll/labor Costs	08% to 10%
Occupancy	04% to 05%
Profit (estimated pretax)	20% to 25%

Industry Trend

- "The U.S. market for pet treats has a lot to bark about. Market research publisher Packaged Facts estimates that total U.S. retail sales of pet treats exceeded $5 billion in 2014, reflecting a compound annual growth rate (CAGR) of 6% during the 2010–2014 period. Sales growth in the treat market has consistently outpaced that of the more mature pet food market and pet supplies in general."

Source: "Packaged Facts: Pet Treat Market Grows 6%, Exceeds $5 Billion" 7/21/15
http://www.foodmanufacturing.com/news/2015/07/packaged-facts-pet-treat-market-grows-6-exceeds-5-billion

- "Thanks in part to the many calls from PAWS Chicago supporters, the Illinois

Rules of Thumb - **P**

state legislature unanimously passed a bill that strengthens disclosure requirements on all dogs or cats made available for adoption or sale by pet shop operators in Illinois pet stores, including adoptions or sales available over the Internet."

Source: "Pet Store Disclosure Bill Passes" www.pawschicago.org/news

Questions
- "Where do you get your puppies from and what is their guarantee?"
- "Do they have a publicly accepted way of selling pets?"
- "Do your customers have a desire to know about the food products? (This will give you an idea of the service the seller is providing.) How do you go about recruiting employees?"

Resources

Websites
- Pet Industry Joint Advisory Council: www.pijac.org

Associations
- American Pet Products Association: www.americanpetproducts.org
- World Pet Association: www.worldpetassociation.org

Pet Supply (Wholesale)

SIC 5199-32	NAICS 422990	Number of Businesses/Units 1,300

Pricing Tips
- "Treat like any other distribution company."

Pharmacies and Drug Stores

SIC 5912-05	NAICS 446110	Number of Businesses/Units 53,258

Rules of Thumb
➢ 18 to 42 percent of annual sales—depending on profits and includes inventory
➢ 70 times average daily sales (range 60 to 80 times) plus inventory
➢ 25 percent of annual sales (range 20% to 30%) plus inventory
➢ 6.5 times EBIT (range 5 to 8 times) plus inventory

Pricing Tips
- "Average total Rx filled daily, % new, % refills, & total Rx average price for year, % Rx third-party insurance & Medicaid & % cash sales, % charge sales. Inventory value in date & salable. Inventory turns per year; total cost of goods sold + inventory on hand (8 times); age analysis of all accounts receivable including welfare, Workers' Comp; hours open per day, per week, per month, # days per year open; lease."

P - Rules of Thumb

- "Good front business, e.g., gifts and greeting cards that improve profits. Look for niche business & profits."
- "Number of prescriptions filled daily, monthly, annually; divide by number of days open to arrive at number of prescriptions filled per day. Retail & cost of ingredients.In medical professional building—number of physicians in building. Does pharmacy do its own prescription compounding, & what percentage of business is third party; i.e., Medicare (welfare) & insurance company paid?"
- "Try 22% of [annual] sales. Net income, i.e., return on investment. Future income of business at least 5 years down the line. Demographics and customer review."

Benchmark Data

Statistics (Pharmacies and Drug Stores)

Number of Establishments	53,258
Average Profit Margin	3.9%
Revenue per Employee	$377,500
Average Number of Employees	13.5
Average Wages per Employee	$38,885

Products and Services Segmentation

Branded prescription drugs	52.3%
Other	13.0%
Generic drugs	10.0%
Branded generic drugs	9.3%
Nonprescription medicines	5.1%
Personal health supplies	4.8%
Groceries and food items	4.0%
Vitamins, minerals and dietary supplements	1.5%

Industry Costs

Profit	3.9%
Wages	10.1%
Purchases	75.0%
Depreciation	0.5%
Marketing	1.0%
Rent & Utilities	4.1%
Other	5.4%

Market Share

CVS Caremark	58.1%
Walgreen Co.	31.0%
Rite Aid Corporation	10.3%

Source: IBISWorld, September 2015

- "You might think of doctors, who have to go to medical school, as making six figures or more, but not pharmacists. In fact, the median salary for pharmacists in the U.S. is $113,000, according to Salary.com. It's not just filling out prescriptions, it's offering advice on dosage and side effects and interacting with doctors. Becoming a pharmacist requires a bachelor's degree and an advanced degree in pharmacy. The job prospects are expected to be good over the next decade—the number of pharmacist jobs is expected to jump 17 percent, according to the Labor Department."

Source: HTTP://www.salary.com

Rules of Thumb - **P**

- "Among multi-store owners, the average number of pharmacies owned is 2.8. For the independent sector as a whole, the average is 1.2 pharmacies."

Expenses as a percentage of annual sales	
Cost of goods	75%
Payroll/labor Costs	09%
Occupancy	02% to 03%
Profit (estimated pretax)	03% to 04%

Industry Trend

- "Over the years, pharmacy retailers have greatly accelerated their function in healthcare delivery. The pharmacy has evolved from a location where prescriptions are dispensed and a few necessities can be picked up, to a media channel powerhouse where a large and receptive audience can be reached. Here are some of the key trends for this booming platform.
    - ✓ Over 250 million people visit pharmacies each week; that's ¾ of the U.S. population.
    - ✓ 47% of OTC purchases are made in chain drug. Only 1% of consumers surveyed make an OTC purchase online.
    - ✓ 85% of prescription drugs are dispensed in retail pharmacy channels: independent—18%; supermarket—12%; chain—55%. Only 6% are dispensed via pharmacy mail order.
    - ✓ 70% of Americans are now taking at least one prescription drug; 50% of Americans take at least two prescription drugs; 20% of Americans are taking five or more prescription medications at the same time.
    - ✓ 94% of Americans plan to continue filling their prescriptions at their primary pharmacy.
    - ✓ Pharmacists are increasingly providing services to patients beyond drug dispensing.
    - ✓ The number of retail clinics is estimated to grow by 25%–30% annually; 73% of adults who have visited a retail clinic would go again."
  Source: http://www.pm360online.com/pharmacy-channel-trends-and-facts-2014/
- A Look at Overall Drug Trend
    - ✓ "The price gap between brand prices and generic drug prices, as depicted by our Prescription Price Index, continues to fluctuate as prices for brand and generic drugs change.
    - ✓ In the U.S., pharmacy-related waste adds up to almost $428 billion–$100 billion more than the amount the country spent for prescription drugs in 2012.
    - ✓ The trend forecast for the top traditional therapy classes reveals a stable, 2.0% climb year-over-year for the next three years, whereas specialty medications are expected to climb more than 16% annually in 2014, 2015 and 2016."
  Source: "A Look at Overall Drug Trend for 2013,"
  http://lab.express-scripts.com/drug-trend-report/introduction/year-in-review

Seller Financing

- "Mostly all cash sales. Owner finance 3 to 7 years with interest at prime +/- 1% or 2 %"
- 10 years

P - Rules of Thumb

Questions
- "Number of years on lease? Do you own the building?"

Resources

Associations
- National Community Pharmacists Association: www.ncpanet.org

---

Photographers & Photographic Studios (See also Camera Stores)

NAICS 541921	Number of Businesses/Units 178,843

Rules of Thumb
- 45 to 50 percent of SDE; add fixtures, equipment & inventory
- 2.5 to 3 times monthly sales; add inventory

Pricing Tips
- "They are usually sold for the new cost of fixtures and equipment, plus inventory, plus 30 percent of one year's net profit. National average states the gross profit usually runs about 62 percent, leaving a net profit of about 24 percent after expenses."

Benchmark Data

Statistics (Photography)

Number of Establishments	178,843
Average Profit Margin	5.9%
Revenue per Employee	$44,000
Average Number of Employees	1.3
Average Wages per Employee	$19,043

Products and Services Segmentation

Personal and group portrait photography	34.1%
Commercial and technical photography	23.8%
School portrait photography	15.9%
Weddings, holidays and other special occasions photography	14.7%
Other	11.5%

Industry Costs

Profit	5.9%
Wages	44.5%
Purchases	21.1%
Depreciation	2.8%
Marketing	2.4%
Rent & Utilities	7.7%
Other	15.6%

Market Share

Lifetouch Inc.	12.1%

Source: IBISWorld, May 2015

Rules of Thumb - **P**

Resources

Websites
- PhotoBizCoach: www.photobizcoach.com

Associations
- PhotoMarketing Association International - this contains valuable information on the photography business including the school market, the portrait business, etc.: www.pmai.org

Physical Therapy

	NAICS 621340	Number of Businesses/Units 115,845

Rules of Thumb
➤ 60 to 75 percent of annual sales
➤ 1.8 to 2.5 times SDE
➤ 1.5 to 2 times EBIT
➤ 1.5 to 3 times EBITDA

Pricing Tips
- "In an ACO, the family physician may be penalized, or prohibited, from referring patients to PTs not employed by the ACO. Many ACOs are building fully vertically integrated delivery systems that employ the PCPs, orthopaedists, and PTs, increasing risk of loss of business for independent PTs. ACOs should focus management efforts on reducing leakage to hospitals and specialists that are not part of the ACO. This will increase volume to ACO providers and help offset revenue loss due to improved utilization management. Hospitals are on an ACO practice-acquisition, and mergers binge. This is reducing the number of physicians available or interested in buying practices, and therefore limiting referrers to PTs. Even though patients can self-refer, many will follow their physician's referral. From the private practice perspective, the ACO question mark boils down to this: Will physical therapists participate as employees or as independent clinicians? Physicians have voted en masse to participate as employees. Record numbers of mergers and acquisitions, especially by large, publicly owned hospitals, have decreased independently owned physician practices to single digits in many regions of the country. Will 'integration,' in the name of health safety and cost-consciousness, destroy private enterprise in outpatient physical therapy?"
- "There is a national shortage of PTs, compensation for employment is increasing, so dividends to equity is decreasing. A full educational video on healthcare practice valuation is available at MedicalPracticeAppraisal.com homepage.
  "Most appraisers favor the Income Approach in valuing small, privately held professional services businesses, as it best reflects the impact of profit or dividends rather than just gross collections. It is the income above what the buyer could earn in employment that creates value in medical practices."
- "It's very important that when pricing a practice that is expected to go to market, calculating EBITDA is important. The first $70,000 to $95,000 in SDE

26th Edition

P - Rules of Thumb

is not important to buyers as many of them already earn this as a practicing PT. The income above that amount is one of the most important components of value. Also, diversification of referral sources increases value. When a practice has more than 25% of its referral sources coming from only one physician group, the structure of a transaction must be in the form of an earn-out and/or reduced value.

"Another important factor in value is location. Most buyers of physical therapy practices with less than $500,000 in SDE are physical therapists. Physical therapy practices located in livable areas sell for a higher multiple. The definition of livable means an attractive safe community, some physical beauty (mountains/oceans), good schools and additional employment opportunities for non-PT spouses. Practices in areas that are less desirable, even with very high SDEs, have a very limited market and are difficult to sell."

- "Industry is challenged with declining reimbursements. Pricing is dependent on whether practice is owner/operated or has DPT's on staff. Non-owner-operated will generate higher multiple. Lease is critical. Most practice sales need a minimum of 5 with a 5-year option to maximize value. Outside billing service preferred for control and highest revenue possible."

- "EBITDA is rarely appropriate due to low capital investment. Better ratio is multiple of dividends per IRS RR59-60."

- "Physical therapists depend on physician referrals, mostly primary care and orthopaedic. Those two specialties are top targets for inclusion in ACOs under the Accountable Care Act. PTs are typically insurance-reimbursement-dependent, so are at the mercy of insurance companies, similar to physicians. I find that sales have been at a cap rate of 65% on pretax dividends (per IRS RR59-60 definition) for most, at best (except for larger chains)."

- "Private Practice Physical Therapy Clinics: We have valued over 300 in the last 20 years. My valuation Rules of Thumb are based on this experience. Value is typically 60% to 100% of annual collected fees, 3–4 times amount available to owner (SDCF) and 2–3 times (SDCF less reasonable replacement salary for owner)."

Expert Comments

"A PT can learn how to start and run a practice in a day's consult with an expert. As a field of medicine, it is subject to most of the same hassle factors, like insurance and laws. Obamacare is causing ACOs to take over PT and control referrals. On the other hand, larger chains of PT practices are selling for a premium to private equity groups at up to 4–5x EBITDA, but I think it can't last due to PPACA laws and ACOs. "

"Owners of practices need to have a managing physical therapist. Many PTs are now incurring very high education expenses and the debt load on many of them may prevent them from owning practices in the future."

"The reductions in insurance reimbursements has affected buyer's interest level in owning a practice."

"Investment should include a gym and treatment area."

"Lots of employment available keeps sales difficult."

Rules of Thumb - **P**

Benchmark Data

Statistics (Physical Therapists)

Number of Establishments	115,845
Average Profit Margin	10.9%
Revenue per Employee	$71,400
Average Number of Employees	3.9
Average Wages per Employee	$42,076

Products and Services Segmentation

Diseases of the musculoskeletal system and connective tissue	59.3%
Other	17.6%
Symptoms, signs and ill-defined conditions	8.2%
Injury and poisoning	7.3%
Diseases of the nervous system and sense organs	4.4%
Mental disorders	3.2%

Industry Costs

Profit	10.9%
Wages	59.5%
Purchases	16.5%
Depreciation	1.5%
Marketing	1.0%
Rent & Utilities	8.5%
Other	2.1%

Source: IBISWorld, October 2015

- "At least a 2-week waiting list for new patient visits. No PPACA ACOs locally."
- "The best benchmark is revenue per employee. Revenue per full-time PT and patient visits by month are also helpful."
- "Need to have 3–4 patients per hour for high utilization. Each physical therapist should account for approximately $250,000 of billing."
- "Collected fees per full-time employed physical therapist should be $200,000 to $300,000 per year. Net profit after reasonable salary to owner should be 25%–35%. Collected fee per visit should be close to $100 and patient visits per PT should be 3,000–3,500."

Expenses as a percentage of annual sales

Cost of goods	27%
Payroll/labor Costs	15% to 25%
Occupancy	06% to 10%
Profit (estimated pretax)	12% to 25%

Industry Trend

- "7 Predictions for Physical Therapy in 2015
    - ✓ Consolidation will force independent PTs to be at the top of their 'referral management game.'
    - ✓ Small practices will become increasingly rare.
    - ✓ PQRS penalties will force more PTs to use an EMR.
    - ✓ ICD-10 will have less technical impact on physical therapy providers than FLR or PQRS—but will still impact cash flow.
    - ✓ Utilization management companies (i.e., ASH) will face a rebellion from PTs and patients (and maybe even employers).

P - Rules of Thumb

- ✓ PTs will feel pressure to adopt standardized functional outcomes from a growing number of payors.
- ✓ Billing and revenue cycle management (RCM) will only get more complex to manage."

Source: http://www.rehabpub.com/2015/01/7-predictions-pt-2015/

- "Integration into ACOs."
- "Declining reimbursements will force owners to increase patient time with aides and assistants, and reduce time with highly paid physical therapists."
- "Rollups and combination due to insurance issues. However, with the aging of the population and more joint replacements, there will be a demand for services."
- "Outpatient rehabilitation is a $29.6 billion industry that is expected to grow 7% annually through 2018. Physical therapy accounts for an estimated $26.6 billion, or approximately 90%, of all outpatient rehabilitation spending. It is a highly fragmented industry, with largest 50 competitors comprising less than 25% of the market. Numerous, positive factors are driving long-term growth:
  - ✓ Expanding patient population that provides favorable tailwinds
  - ✓ Aging U.S. population
  - ✓ Increasing penetration of physical therapy services
  - ✓ New government regulations (e.g., the PPACA) increasing patient access to physical therapy
  - ✓ Outpatient rehabilitation is significantly less costly than surgery or hospitalization, but with similar clinical effectiveness"

Source: "Physical Therapy Market Overview," www.harriswilliams.com February, 2014

Seller Financing
- "75% SBA guaranteed financing is generally available."
- "Seller financing is low especially if referral sources is widely diversified. 10–20% of a deal is seller financing with the remaining amount in the form of an SBA loan."
- "Financing is available through SBA guaranteed loans for those with good financial statements. Otherwise, they are seller financed. Banks generally approve of financing doctor practices although this has not been extended to physical therapists (unlike dentists and other medical and doctor practices)."
- 2 to 5 years

Questions
- "How long have they been practicing physical therapy? Have they managed people before? Why are they looking for a practice? What location is important to them and why?"
- "Patient visits per hour, per day, per week are critical. Trends in the revenue. Orthopedic referral sources and relationships. Hospital contacts. Length of lease and terms."
- "Many about state, federal and Medicare compliance, insurance contracts, ACO trends in market."

Resources

Websites
- Physical Therapy Practice Valuation: medicalpracticeappraisal.com

Rules of Thumb - P

Trade Publications
- ADVANCE for Physical Therapy & Rehab Medicine: physical-therapy. advanceweb.com

Associations
- American Physical Therapy Association: www.apta.org

Picture Framing		
SIC 5999-27	NAICS 442299	Number of Businesses/Units 7,946

Rules of Thumb
- ➢ 45 percent of annual sales plus inventory

Pricing Tips
- "Not a lot of activity to report in the framing industry. While there have been some transactions, most involve private sales where numbers aren't reported. I have valued a few businesses in the past year and found the same formulae apply as in the past. Values were less, but that is as a result of lower sales, inventories and other assets."
- "Perhaps most critical is the impact of a change in ownership. If the shop is small, that is the owner is the face of the business, rarely is the business worth any more than 10% of sales."

Expert Comments
"Location and co-tenancy is extremely important to value as long as lease is secure."

Benchmark Data

Statistics (Picture Framing Stores)
Number of Establishments	7,946
Average Profit Margin	3.7%
Revenue per Employee	$62,200
Average Number of Employees	4.4
Average Wages per Employee	$14,133

Products and Services Segmentation
Custom framing	60.0%
Photo Frames	16.0%
Other	14.9%
Ready-Mades	9.1%

Industry Costs
Profit	3.7%
Wages	22.9%
Purchases	62.4%
Depreciation	0.9%
Marketing	0.8%
Rent & Utilities	5.0%
Other	4.3%

P - Rules of Thumb

Market Share
Aaron Brothers Inc. 38.1%
Source: IBISWorld, September 2014

- "COGS (direct materials only) should be at or below 25% of sales."

Expenses as a percentage of annual sales
Cost of goods 25%
Payroll/labor Costs 12%
Occupancy 10%
Profit (estimated pretax) 14%

Industry Trend
- "With much competition eliminated from recession, we expect to see steady growth over the next 3 to 5 years."

Questions
- "In addition to the usual financial questions, you should conduct a market evaluation to determine the viability of the present pricing structure."

Resources

Associations
- Professional Picture Framers Association: www.pmai.org/ppfa/

		Franchise
Pillar to Post—Home Inspection (See also Franchises, Home Inspection)		
Approx. Total Investment		$61,000 to $107,900
	NAICS 541350	Number of Businesses/Units 455

Rules of Thumb
➢ 25 to 30 percent of annual sales plus inventory

Resources

Websites
- www.pillartopost.com

		Franchise
Pizza Factory (See also Franchises, Pizza Shops)		
Approx. Total Investment		$150,000 to $400,000
Estimated Annual Sales/Unit		$375,000
	NAICS 722513	Number of Businesses/Units 110

Rules of Thumb
➢ 30% to 35% of annual sales plus inventory

Rules of Thumb - **P**

	Franchise
Pizza Inn (See also Franchises, Pizza Shops)	
Approx. Total Investment	$80,000 to $764,000
Estimated Annual Sales/Unit	$450,000
NAICS 722513	Number of Businesses/Units 183

Rules of Thumb

➢ 45 percent of annual sales plus inventory

Resources

Websites
- www.pizzainn.com

Pizza Shops		
SIC 5812-22	NAICS 722513	Number of Businesses/Units 74,936

Rules of Thumb

➢ 35 percent of annual sales plus inventory for independent shops

➢ 38 percent of annual sales plus inventory for franchised or chain pizza shops

➢ 1.5 to 2 times SDE; plus fixtures, equipment and inventory

➢ 1.5 to 1.6 times EBIT

➢ 1.5 times EBITDA

➢ 4 times monthly sales plus inventory

Pricing Tips

- "Good books can help raise all of the pricing rule's of thumb. If there is substantial 'goodwill' being included in the sell price, positive online reviews will play an important part of the marketing of the pizza shop for sale."
- "Expect some business owners to purchase a fair amount of food in cash. Good employees are the most important part of this business. Large cash flow in and large cash flow out."
- "Typical pricing is 20 to 24 times weekly gross sales. Industry insiders and purchasers use this barometer consistently."
- "A 2x multiple is sometimes the best case scenario; often a 1.5x is the reality; of chief importance is the length of the lease, rent as well as location, and parking for customers and delivery persons. Lots of creative ways to understand cash flow, including pizza box purchases, cheese and tomato purchases as examples. An important part of due diligence should include on-site observation of the operation for several days."
- "Domino's Formula—45 percent of the first $400K in annual sales, 50 percent of the next $100K ($400 to $500K) in annual sales, then 55 percent of the next $250K of annual sales (from $500–$750k)"

P - Rules of Thumb

Pizza Franchise Rules of Thumb and Annual Sales—Quick Check

Blackjack's Pizza	40% of annual sales
Domino's Pizza	50% of annual sales —$800,000
Gatti's Pizza	30% of annual sales—$1,000,000
Godfather's Pizza	25% of annual sales—$380,000
Hungry Howie's Pizza	35% of annual sales—$550,000
Little Caesar's Pizza	50% of annual sales—$830,000
Mountain Mike's Pizza	30% of annual sales—$525,000
Mr. Jim's Pizza	35% of annual sales—$440,000
Papa Murphy's Take 'N' Bake	35% of annual sales—$550,000
Pizza Factory	30% of annual sales—$375.000
Pizza Inn	45% of annual sales—$450,000

October 2015

Note: Several of the businesses had a percentage multiple of, for example, 35% to 40%. The lower figure was the one used in tabulating an average. This produced an average rule of thumb of 38% of annual sales = the "ballpark" price. The above represent an average rule of thumb for franchised pizza restaurants. As you can see from the information above, independent pizza shops have an average rule of thumb of 35%. This slight difference may be due to more information being available for franchised units than independents.

Expert Comments

"Location is important, as most shopping centers have an existing pizza shop. It is important to get in on the ground floor."

"High profile locations are not as important if there is emphasis being put on delivery service. If that is the case, more rooftops in the area of the shop becomes the important factor."

"You must make the process as simple as possible if you are going to expand to multiple locations."

Benchmark Data

Statistics (Pizza Restaurants)

Number of Establishments	74,936
Average Profit Margin	7.6%
Revenue per Employee	$40,800
Average Number of Employees	13.1
Average Wages per Employee	$13,142

Products and Services Segmentation

Takeout and delivery	53.0%
Sit-down service	33.0%
Catering	14.0%

Industry Costs

Profit	7.6%
Wages	32.3%
Purchases	35.4%
Depreciation	2.5%
Marketing	4.7%
Rent & Utilities	6.8%
Other	10.7%

Rules of Thumb - **P**

Market Share

Pizza Hut Inc.	15.1%
Domino's Inc.	9.8%
Little Caesar's	8.3%
Papa John's International Inc.	6.5%

Source: IBISWorld, March 2015

- "Sales per employee should exceed $40,000. Food Costs can vary depending on what you are doing with the dough; scratch dough can bring the food cost to 30%, where buying a fully sheeted pie could bring food cost to 34%."

- U.S Pizza Sales—$38,524,732,336.00
  Year Ending September 2014

Independents	40.89%
Other Chains	20.16%
Pizza Hut	14.79%
Domino's	9.86%
Little Caesar's	7.85%
Papa John's	6.45%

- U.S. Pizza Stores 73,097
  Year Ending September 2014

Independents	54.25%
Other Chains	20.16%
Pizza Hut	8.65%
Domino's	6.82%
Little Caesar's	5.32%
Papa John's	4.38%

Source: Technomic - www.pmq.com, December- 2014/Pizza Power-The-2014 Pizza Power Report

- Top Ten U.S. chains according to number of units
  1. Pizza Hut
  2. Domino's Pizza
  3. Little Caesars
  4. Papa John's
  5. Papa Murphy's Pizza
  6. Godfather's Pizza
  7. Sbarro
  8. Hungry Howie's Pizza
  9. Chuck E. Cheese's
  10. CiCi's Pizza

Source: Technomic as reported in PMQ, December 2014

- Top 10 U.S. Chains (ranked by sales and based on 2013 sales)
  1. Pizza Hut
  2. Domino's Pizza
  3. Little Caesars
  4. Papa John's
  5. Papa Murphy's Pizza
  6. CiCi's Pizza
  7. Chuck E. Cheese's
  8. Round Table Pizza
  9. Sbarro
  10. Godfather's Pizza

Source: pmq.com, December 2014

P - Rules of Thumb

- "Independent pizza operations now account for 54.3% of all pizzerias in the country, up 1.1% from the 2013 figure of 53.2%. About 45.7% are chains, compared to 47% in the previous year. (For the record, we always define independents as pizzerias with fewer than 10 units; any company with more than 10 stores is considered a chain.) Even so, chains accounted for the majority of industry sales, th with $22,768,432,380 in 2014, compared to $21,425,686,281 the previous year,CHD Expert reports. Independent restaurants accounted for $15,756,299,956 this past yer, up from CHD Expert's estimate of $14,481,887,024 for 2013.

  "Technomic, meanwhile, reported data for the top 50 pizzeria chains in 2013 relative to 2012. Again, the numbers were up in 2013, totaling $21,546,298,000, with per-unit sales aveeraging $772,130 (among 27,905 units.). Compare that to 2012, when the top 50 chains' sales equaled $20,915,245,000 with per-unit averages of $721,995 (among 27,414 units). That means the top 50 experienced a total sales increase of $631,053,000 while store counts increased by a total of 491 units."

  Source: 2014 Pizza Power Report

- "Imperative to watch food costs for this business. Cannot be run absentee. Theft by employees sometimes a problem. Trend was seven days per week, seems to be changing in some areas to six. Expect 11AM to 11PM hours. Delivery is a must."

- "Nearly half (48%) of respondents this year own a stand-alone store, and the next biggest group (33.6%) own a strip-mall location. Almost half of the pizzeria operators in our survey also live in small towns. Meanwhile, nearly a third (31.6%) are newbies in the business, reporting that they've owned their store for less than five years."

- "58.6% of pizzeria operators don't serve any alcohol in their restaurants."

- "Independent pizzerias, on the other hand, are most often patronized by those who earn more than $75,000 per year, according to several studies, so a down economy might not hit them as hard."

- "Keep food costs below 30 percent, and labor, not counting manager's salary, below 20 percent."

Food Cost	28% to 30%
Payroll/Labor	25% to 30%
Occupancy	06% to 08%

  Expenses as a percentage of annual sales

Cost of goods	30% to 32%
Payroll/labor Costs	25% to 30%
Occupancy	07% to 10%
Profit (estimated pretax)	08% to 12%

Industry Trend

- "It's safe to say the pizza restaurant industry has entered the mature stage of its life cycle. Many towns and cities have reached the limit of pizza restaurants that their populations can support. That makes it harder for operators to open new stores and for new operators to get into the business. It also means that increasing sales-per-unit—rather than opening new stores—is a key driver of industry revenue.

  "Having said that, pizza sales in the States still rose over the past year, reaching $38,524,732,336 by the year ending September 30, 2014, according to data from CHD Expert. That's a 3.08% increase over PMQ's estimated sales figure of $37,375,108,000 for the industry in 2013. Meanwhile, total pizza store counts in the U.S. jumped by more than 2% over the past year, and the majority of that increase came from independent operators. For the year ending September 30, the total number of stores came to 73,097, a jump of 1,710 from last year's total store count of 71,387. Additionally, CHD Expert found that more new stores opened this year, with 4,107 new units compared to 2013's figure of 3,981 new stores. Meanwhile, far fewer pizza shops closed their doors—only 1,181 units shut down in 2014, while 2013 saw closure of 2,038 stores.

"Telephone orders are falling; just 55% of customers now typically order pizza by phone compared to 64% in 2012. More of them—especially Millennials and those aged 35 to 44—prefer online ordering.

"'Let's say your pizzeria employs 25 people,' Arena (John Arena, owner, Metro Pizza) says. 'Are you going to open a second store once you know it will put you over 50 employees and that each employee will cost you $3,000 more a year? For a company like mine that has 200 employees, that's $600,000. I don't have a spare $600,000 lying around at the end of the year.'"

Source: 2014 Pizza Power Report

- "A lot of the same as far as total numbers of establishments. Turnover of pizza shops is high because of competition. People are always interested in buying for the relatively low entry costs."

- "Meanwhile, total pizza store counts in the U.S. jumped by more than 2% over the past year, and the majority of that increase came from independent operators. For the year ending September 30, the total number of stores came to 73,097, a jump of 1,710 from last year's total store count of 71,387. Additionally, CHD Expert found that more new stores opened this year, with 4,107 new units compared to 2013's figure of 3,981 new stores. Meanwhile, far fewer pizza shops closed their doors—only 1,181 units shut down in 2014, while 2013 saw closure of 2,038 stores. Independent pizza operations now account for 54.3% of all pizzerias in the country.

"Over the next 10 years, the fastest restaurant job growth is projected to occur in Arizona with a rate of 15.6%, followed by Texas with 15.3% and Florida with 15%. Nevada (14.7%) and Georgia (14.4%) round out the top five states with the fastest restaurant job growth. Finally, there's social media. Younger customers also prefer to place their pizza orders digitally."

Source: pmq.com, December 2014

Seller Financing
- "Seller financing with 35-50% down with the balance being paid back in 3-5 years."
- "Five to seven years"

Questions
- "What is the reason for selling? Will you open another pizza shop and where? How long have you been in business and what were your sales trends?"
- "Why is the business for sale? Net Income? Unreported Income? Employees off the books? Number of employees? Amount of hours he or she personally works?"

P - Rules of Thumb

Resources

Trade Publications
- Guide to a Successful Pizza Business & Pizza Business Manual by Paul Shakarian: www.pizzabusiness.com
- National Restaurant News: www.nrn.com
- Pizza Magazine Quarterly: www.pmq.com
- Franchise Times: www.franchisetimes.com

	Franchise
Planet Beach (See also Franchises, Medical Spas, Tanning Salons)	
Approx. Total Investment	$140,800 to $281,000
NAICS 812199	Number of Businesses/Units 324
Rules of Thumb	
➢ 35 to 40 percent of annual sales	
➢ Planet Beach has day spa franchises in the U.S., Canada and Australia.	

Resources

Websites
- www.planetbeach.com

	Franchise
Play It Again Sports (See also Franchises)	
Approx. Total Investment	$240,500 to $390,700
NAICS 453310	Number of Businesses/Units 315
Rules of Thumb	
➢ 40 to 45% of annual sales plus paid-for inventory	

Resources

Websites
- www.playitagainsports.com

Podiatrists		
SIC 8043-01	NAICS 621391	Number of Businesses/Units 13,394
Rules of Thumb		
➢ 35 to 40 percent of annual sales plus inventory		
➢ 3 to 4 times SDE plus inventory		
➢ 1.5 times EBITDA		

Rules of Thumb - **P**

Pricing Tips

- "Doctors of Podiatric Medicine (DPMs) are podiatric physicians and surgeons, also known as podiatrists, qualified by their education and training to diagnose and treat conditions affecting the foot, ankle and related structures of the leg. Podiatrists are defined as physicians by the federal government and in most states. DPMs receive medical education and training comparable to medical doctors, including four years of undergraduate education, four years of graduate education at accredited podiatric medical colleges and two or three years of hospital residency training. Within the field of podiatry, practitioners can focus on many different specialty areas, including surgery, sports medicine, biomechanics, geriatrics, pediatrics, orthopedics or primary care.

  "Most podiatric practices are small. Most of the practices have only one or two doctors. The average partnership has 2 doctors and the typical podiatric medical group had 3 podiatrists, according to an APMA study. The median podiatrist has about $750,000 in annual collections, with a $180,000-$200,000 income, including benefits. Prescription foot orthoses are a foundation of non-surgical treatments utilized by podiatrists. The vast majority of orthotics dispensed by podiatrists are custom functional orthoses. The custom orthotic industry is headed into a crisis based upon a number of issues: ethics & accountability, verification of outcomes, coding & reimbursement, increased operational costs, and reduced profitability. As insurance companies look to reduce their services or payments, they have looked to orthotics as a way to cut costs, according to an article in *Podiatry Today*.

  "An American Podiatric Medical Association (APMA)-commissioned study of the podiatric workforce confirmed what many in the profession have suspected for years: the number of podiatrists practicing and graduating over the next 10 years will be insufficient to meet a projected surge in demand for foot-care services. The number of graduating podiatrists needs to triple by 2014 in order to meet the health needs of a population that is increasingly older, heavier, and diabetic. There is the possibility that an ongoing shortage also could force referring physicians to seek out other medical professionals to care for their patients. Many current podiatrists also will be nearing retirement age over the next decade. Only about 6.5 percent of podiatric physicians are younger than age 30, while about 56 percent are age 45 or older. Expansion of podiatry is facing strong opposition from various state physician orthopedic medical associations.

  "On March 21, 2010, the Democratic Congress passed Health System Reform Legislation (H.R. 3590), fulfilling President Obama's promise made in 2008 for the largest social legislation since the formation of the Social Security and Medicare programs. We now have a federal law applicable to ERISA plans that makes it against the law for insurance companies to discriminate against Doctors of Podiatry and other providers relative to their participation and coverage in health plans. The legislation establishes a National Health Care Workforce Commission to review needs in the healthcare workforce, and specifically includes podiatrists by defining them as part of the healthcare workforce, and includes them in the definition of health professionals. A number of states quickly filed lawsuits seeking to block it, the outcome of which will not be known for some time. The future of podiatric economics is still unclear."

- "Dividends are a better measure than EBITDA given the lack of need of capital assets."

P - Rules of Thumb

- "Inventory varies widely. Some podiatrists sell products and some don't. Product sales can be profitable, but surgical podiatry is usually the most profitable."

Expert Comments

"Easy for a podiatrist to learn how to do a startup in a day. Podiatry is a field of medicine accepting all the same insurances and Medicare, and subject to the same laws.

"The value of podiatric practices is generally at an all-time low. Decisions regarding what, where, when and how to practice are influenced by numerous factors, including: personal preferences, market forces, state and federal policies and programs, and institutions that constitute the health care system and podiatric education infrastructure. Increasing retirement, plus the trend toward shorter working hours, increases the supply of practices for sale, and decreases the available FTE workforce available as buyers. The increasing rate of boomer retirement and decreasing count of new physicians contribute to a reduction of value of practices for sale. A significant shortfall of physicians could develop over the next 15 or more years in the absence of increased output from U.S. podiatric schools, increased recruitment of foreign-trained physicians, or both. The American College of Physicians is concerned that the practice environment for those in medical practice has become so encumbered with regulation and practice hassles, at a time when reimbursement for care provided by physicians is declining, that physicians are finding it increasingly difficult to provide for their patients. Of particular concern when determining value of a podiatric practice is ensuring not only that the purchase price is Fair Market Value, but also that the valuation method does not take into account the volume or value of referrals that the selling physician has made or may make to the purchaser, such that the purchase price could be challenged as a kickback or inducement. The OIG has provided guidance on the question of how to value a physician practice or other healthcare provider. The ailing economy is leading many Americans to skip doctor visits, skimp on their medicine, and put off tests. Employment by hospitals is paying more, and insurance-reimbursement and gross income is often dropping, so the results of the Income Approach of valuation identifying 'dividends' [(SDE minus market rate compensation of one working owner) x 1.5 (i.e., 65% Cap rate)] is becoming more important for more specialties. 'Percentage of annual gross sales' or 'SDE multiplier' as valuation Rules of Thumb are obsolete, if ever valid. Growth rates are available through the Congressional Budget Office reports, rarely above 2% historically. Podiatric practice is riskier—and demands higher Cap rates—than other professional practices like accounting, law, architecture and engineering which are not subject to clinical malpractice risks, or subject to Medicare or insurance company changing reimbursement limitations or denials. Many practices can't even sell at the value of the liquidated assets, since jobs pay more without asset purchase. The impact of specialty and location is profound, as is the FTE work-schedule and leverage of employed licensed providers. Medicare is continually reducing reimbursement, which impacts other insurances which often base their payment on a percent of Medicare (i.e., 80–120% of Medicare), so dependence on insurance reimbursement is an important consideration in value. In addition, specific diagnosis and procedure ('ICD/CPT') billing-code reimbursement changes—like what has happened in dermatology, ophthalmology, allergy, cardiology, and other specialties—have further reduced reimbursement and profits during the past decade. Cash and cosmetic practices are usually worth more since there is a higher profit for less work, and often provide a better lifestyle, but even those can be difficult to sell. Many specialties are having trouble attracting new doctors no matter the income, so guaranteed wages are increasing, sales are becoming more difficult, and values are dropping. Make sure to read the white papers on supply and demand available on many specialty professional association websites. The best overhead statistics are usually available at http://www.NSCHBC.org. The best market rate compensation stats are usually available at http://www.MGMA.com. The Goodwill Registry on sale-data is helpful in some cases, but the often-quoted running-average 10-year median goodwill-value as a percentage of gross is irrelevant, as the average of many specialties reflects the midpoint of 10 years' steady decline. You need to acquire the full database and evaluate the underlying data to be useful; and look in particular at the Price:SDE data. The effect of the Medicare cuts which began in 2005 can distort the Registry summary statistics and need to be adjusted; and you need to remove results from court-valuations, divorces and other non-transactional data.

"Podiatric record charts are not a true asset of the practice since they can't be put on the balance sheet as an asset using the Asset Approach valuation methodology. Podiatric record valuation is only used to specifically allocate intangibles, assuming they exist at the time of the valuation. The physician has the physical chart but usually cannot legally sell or dispose of it without the patient's consent (per state statutes), only transfer custodianship. So the physician is basically a custodian of the record rather than an owner of an asset with independent value. When paper charts are involved, I have come to the opinion that the value of the chart is zero because of the attendant custodianship liability costs. With EMR, a digital record may need to be converted from one digital platform to another either by custodianship transfer or technology succession, in which case a printout and re-entry may be required, probably exceeding in labor costs any physical value to the original digital chart.

"The library in a smaller pediatric practice—as opposed to a university or a 'super-group'—is presumed to not include historical or rare publications, be organized with bibliographic cataloging, nor represent a complete or unique collection for the specialty. Materials are presumed to be of mixed currency and technological validity. No value is therefore assigned to the practice library.

"The billing process in a podiatric practice is very complex, both in generating the charges using appropriate diagnosis and treatment codes, and in recording the payment and adjustments for uncollectable amounts. Accounts Receivable represent past gross charges for services rendered and as yet uncollected or adjusted-off. These receivables must be discounted to reflect both insurance company reimbursement disallowances, plus the decreasing value over time due to difficulty in collections of past due accounts. In other words, the historic collection ratio of the practice does not yet include the "standing wave" of uncollectable

P - Rules of Thumb

accounts at practice end, or at a particular point in time, as in a valuation at a particular date."

"Serious shortages expected, plenty of jobs available, reduces need to buy business."

"Medicare and insurance dominated revenues and profits"

"An aging population will result in increased foot related issues. There will be increased growth in outpatient surgery."

"Competition in the primary markets is high, but low in rural markets. Risk is high due to medical malpractice issues, just like other specialties of surgery."

Benchmark Data

Statistics (Podiatrists)

Number of Establishments	13,394
Average Profit Margin	14.0%
Revenue per Employee	$94,600
Average Number of Employees	4.1
Average Wages per Employee	$42,485

Products and Services Segmentation

Footwear products, insoles and materials	41.0%
Equipment and therapeutic products	27.0%
Treatment and creams	18.0%
Hosiery, socks and other	14.0%

Industry Costs

Profit	14.0%
Wages	45.5%
Purchases	17.0%
Depreciation	1.5%
Marketing	1.5%
Rent & Utilities	6.5%
Other	14.0%

Source: IBISWorld, December 2014

- "At least a 2-week waiting list for patient appointments"
- "Most podiatrists see approximately 100 visits per 40-hour workweek"
- "A sole practitioner should generate around $250,000 in gross income. A doctor will treat over 94 patients per week."
- "3 to 4 staff per doctor"
- "Variables include whether 'midlevels' like nurse practitioners or P.A.'s are employed; orthotic sales or referral; surgical components."

Expenses as a percentage of annual sales

Cost of goods	05% to 06%
Payroll/labor Costs	20% to 23%
Occupancy	06% to 07%
Profit (estimated pretax)	40% to 43%

Rules of Thumb - **P**

Industry Trend
- "Poor due to Obamacare, or whatever replaces it"
- "Increasing demand by baby boomers"
- "There will be a trend to fewer solo practices and more group practices. There will be a trend toward group practices involving other health care disciplines."

Seller Financing
- "100% bank financing is usually available from specialty banks."
- "SBA will finance 75%."
- "Financing term of 5 to 7 years."
- 2 to 5 years

Questions
- "State and federal compliance"
- "Do you have nursing home contracts? Do you have Medicaid patients?"

Resources

Trade Publications
- Podiatry Today: www.podiatrytoday.com

Associations
- American Academy of Podiatric Practice Management: www.aappm.org
- American Podiatric Medical Association: www.apma.org

Pool Service (Swimming)		
SIC 7389-09	NAICS 561790	Number of Businesses/Units 53,821

Rules of Thumb
- ➢ 10 to 12 times the "Monthly Service Only Gross Income"— swimming pool routes throughout the country sell for this multiple.
- ➢ "Note: The monthly service gross income is just that. It does not include income from maintenance or repair. This is already considered in the multiple, because most pool service technicians agree that whatever your monthly service billing is, half of that again will translate into maintenance/repair income."
- ➢ 50 to 55 percent of annual sales plus inventory

Pricing Tips
- "These figures will vary based upon a solo business owner and one that has employees. A great estimate of profit without employees will be 80%; if employees are a factor you should anticipate 40% profit margins. Both of these issues will affect pricing of a business for sale, and will also affect sale price."
- "Pricing is going to vary depending on whether or not there are employees or a store involved. Typically an owner-operated pool route will have a 20% expense ratio, while a route operated with employees will have a 60% expense

26th Edition 617

ratio. This change in expenses can have a dramatic impact on sales price. Most routes in Florida are selling in the range of 10–12 months of annual gross income. If there is a store involved, this can have a dramatic impact on overall sale price due to multiple factors: expenses, employees, sales volume, etc."

- "As stated, there are two main sources of income, monthly service billing and maintenance/repair income. Throughout the United States the purchase price of a pool service route is based on a multiple times the Monthly Service Billing Only income. The multiple will vary from state to state and even within some states. However, it is an industry standard to use a multiple times the Monthly Service Billing Only income. In other words, the maintenance/repair income should not be included to arrive at a fair purchase price. Any other method of appraising the value of a pool route would be contrary to the industry standards. The maintenance and repair income is already considered in the multiple, because most pool service technicians agree that whatever your monthly service billing is, half of that again will translate into maintenance/repair income.

"We have been selling businesses for over 28 years. Pool routes are our specialty. We can tell that the most important step in purchasing a pool route is in verifying the monthly service billing. Financial statements, profit and loss statements, and balance sheets are usually not available, mainly because it is not necessary to keep an expensive bookkeeping system for one person operating out of their home. Therefore, there are not usually records available to satisfy a bank or financial institution to borrow the money to buy the route. Individual tax returns usually will not help either, because if you were buying 50 accounts of a route of 100, the tax returns would not be broken down that way. Also, if he is a pool builder or does a lot of business in major pool repairs or pool remodeling, again the tax returns would reflect all this income. What if he had 100 accounts and sold 50 accounts? His tax return would show an income for 100 accounts and you would have no way of knowing this.

"Pool routes are sold for cash and no terms are generally available. Therefore, you should have the funds available at the time of purchase, unless you are arranging for an equity loan, line of credit or other means to enable you to purchase a pool route.

"While most pool routes have the same expenses, they do not have the same income. Income is what you will be purchasing. One of the best ways to get a handle on the monthly service income, as well as what the owner is charging for repairs, is to look at his ledger cards. A ledger card is a monthly history for each account. A ledger card should show when an account was billed and when the account was paid. The payment history of the customer is one of the most important items to review during purchase. Who wants an account that does not pay his or her bill? The ledger card also shows what the account was billed for repairs. This part of the ledger card will show if the owner is charging for the proper extras. In addition, the ledger card will show how long the account has been on service. While this is very important to some, the length of time on service is not as important as the payment history. If the average age of the accounts is over a year and they have a good payment history that would be a good account.

"Another big question on the minds of most potential purchasers is the radius of the route and the quality of the neighborhoods. The overall radius of a pool route is not as important as the daily radius. Almost everyone has to drive to work or the office. Some people drive 30 minutes, some an hour, some

Rules of Thumb - P

much more. If you purchase a pool route that is within an overall radius of twenty miles but is under a five-mile daily radius, this would be considered a good route in the industry. Try to keep your pools clustered tight by service day. The neighborhood of your accounts is not as important as the way they pay their bills. There are several high-priced neighborhoods where collection is a problem. Most people in just average neighborhoods have a far better collection record than some so-called upper class neighborhoods."

Source: Contributed by Frank Passantino, Pool Route Brokers, Inc. Frank is a veteran business broker and the information provided has been taken from his Web site--www.poolroutebrokers.com. He is one of the country's leading pool route brokers. His firm is in California and the phone number is 800-772-6002

Expert Comments

"A business that has a strong long-term customer base should anticipate receiving a higher multiple of sales than someone who has a short-term history. If someone is willing to wait for the right buyer, expecting a 12-month multiple is realistic; however if someone is looking for a quick sale on a well-designed route, 10 times monthly income is realistic."

"Seller: Be sure to document your business income and expenses very well. Attempt to build a well- traveled route with limited drive time. Ensure customer record keeping so the buyer knows what they are receiving."

Benchmark Data

Statistics (Swimming Pool Cleaning Services)
Number of Establishments	53,821
Average Profit Margin	11.1%
Revenue per Employee	$50,500
Average Number of Employees	1.3
Average Wages per Employee	$16,424

Products and Services Segmentation
General cleaning services	41.1%
Equipment cleaning and maintenance	27.7%
Chemical adjustments	19.2%
Other	12.0%

Industry Costs
Profit	11.1%
Wages	32.4%
Purchases	25.2%
Depreciation	2.7%
Utilities	3.5%
Rent	4.5%
Other	20.6%

Source: IBISWorld, March 2015

- "On a well-designed route, each employee should generate $100k of gross sales based simply upon service; this figure should increase if repairs are included."
- "How many pools can I service in a day? A good question, but difficult to answer. The average pool service technician will service approximately 16 full-service pools a day, while some can service 25 to 30 in a day. It depends

26th Edition

P - Rules of Thumb

on the individual and what type of pools he or she is servicing. The average pool service technician will service two pools an hour including driving time. If the accounts are chemical only, he can do many more. If the accounts are commercial, he or she will do less.

"The average pool service technician, if running his route correctly, should be netting between $75,000.00 and $80,000.00 per year. If you have a monthly gross service billing income of $4,000.00 per month, that equates to $48,000.00 per year generated from weekly 'service only.' Your expenses should be approximately 2 months of your service income or in this example $8,000.00. This will cover your three major expenses, gas, insurance and chemical replacement. Therefore, your service income totaling $48,000.00 for the year, less estimated expense of $8,000.00, should produce a net profit of $40,000.00, assuming you are operating in a diligent manner. In addition to this profit, you will have a second income on the same accounts for maintenance (filter cleaning, algae, conditioner treatments and other preventive maintenance) charges that you will bill your account extra, plus repairs (motors, pumps, heaters, etc.). This second income should be fifty percent of your service net. If your net income from service is $40,000.00 then your net from maintenance and repairs should be $20,000.00. This is assuming that you are providing full service to your accounts."

Source: Contributed by Frank Passantino, Pool Route Brokers, Inc.

Expenses as a percentage of annual sales

Cost of goods	20%
Payroll/labor Costs	40%
Occupancy	0
Profit (estimated pretax)	40%

Industry Trend

- "On the franchising side, most of the attention has been given to the service-tech side of the industry. There's an important reason for that: It costs less. Return on investment is the major concern when starting a franchise, so prospects like the relatively low start-up costs of a service business. 'The ones that tend to grow fastest are the ones that have the lowest level of investment,' Siebert (Mark, CEO of iFranchise Group) says. 'So the service industry would probably be the one that would ultimately get the most franchisees.'

  "When Baron (Kevin, President of Probity Pools) wanted to expand his company, he chose the franchise model because he figured it best suited the kind of work done by service companies. To just grow a company organically removes the company owner farther and farther from the work itself as the organizational chart expands, he says, while franchising allows the owners to stay near those maintaining the pools.

  "While some professionals are quick to point out examples where these types of models did not work in the pool industry, others say the time for franchising and outside investment has come, and examples will only become more prevalent. But Porter (Paul, CEO of Premier Pools Management Corp.) doesn't see the transition going smoothly. 'It will happen ... kicking and screaming because we have a lot of people who are very resistant to change in our industry,' he says. But Baron expects it will be long-term. 'I think when the dust settles in 10 years, every city's probably going to have a half dozen or so major pool-maintenance brands,' he says."

  Source: http://www.poolspanews.com/business/coming-together_o.aspx?dfpzone=general

- "This industry should expand."
- "Competition getter stronger and more government enforcement of licensing."

Seller Financing
- "Seller financing is more typically used."

Questions
- "Find out how long they have had the clients. Determine the driving time of the route. Clearly understand what services are being delivered for what price."
- "How long have the pool service accounts been established? What is the average monthly service fee? How many times a week do they service the account? Do they charge extra for filter cleaning, conditioner and other treatments?"

Resources

Websites
- Pool and Spa News: http://www.poolspanews.com/
- Pool Pro: www.poolpro.com

Trade Publications
- SQUA Magazine: www.aquamagazine.com
- Pool and Spa News: www.poolspanews.com
- Service Industry News: www.serviceindustrynews.net

Associations
- Independent Pool and Spa Service Association: www.ipssa.com
- National Swimming Pool Foundation: www.nspf.org
- Florida Swimming Pool Association: www.floridapoolpro.com
- Association of Pool and Spa Professionals: www.apsp.org

Portable Toilet Companies		
SIC 7359-22	NAICS 562991	Number of Businesses/Units 9,126

Rules of Thumb
- $1,000 per unit
- 85 to 90 percent of annual revenues

Pricing Tips
- "An interesting statistic is that experienced purchasers anticipate the loss of customers when buying a company. The percentage, although not a scientific number, has been expressed as high as 25%. In terms of fast numbers, a business with gross sales of $500,000 along with a price conscious customer base could fall to $375,000 as fast as the ink dried on the check.
"In reality, it has been more common during the last three to five years for portable restroom businesses to sell for approximately 90.62% of annual sales.
"In revealing the percentage rate, it is important to note that the average percentage rate includes transactions where businesses sold for as little as 50% and as high as 150% of annual sales. Consideration for profitability is included with a highly profitable portable sanitation business demanding a

P - Rules of Thumb

higher price. Again, as an example, a business that does $500,000 in annual sales and is not a good fit or is not running profitably might fall into the lower percentage rate, while a company running the same numbers and showing an annual profit of $125,000 with good equipment and verifiable records might attract a buyer for 100% of annual sales."

Source: "What Is My Portable Restroom Business Worth?" *Sanitation Journal,* www.sanitationjournal.com

Benchmark Data

Statistics (Portable Toilet Rental & Septic Tank Cleaning)

Number of Establishments	9,126
Average Profit Margin	7.2%
Revenue per Employee	$139,600
Average Number of Employees	4.3
Average Wages per Employee	$42,001

Products and Services Segmentation

Portable toilet rentals	38.9%
Septic tank maintenance services	24.2%
Other services	20.9%
Drain and sewer services	16.0%

Major Market Segmentation

Businesses, farms and nonprofit organizations	54.0%
Individuals	31.2%
State and local governments	10.8%
Federal government	2.0%
Other	2.0%

Industry Costs

Profit	7.2%
Wages	30.2%
Purchases	22.3%
Depreciation	6.8%
Marketing	1.0%
Rent & Utilities	5.7%
Other	26.8%

Source: IBISWorld, October 2015

- "The portable sanitation industry has developed into a $4 billion-a-year business. There are an estimated 3 million portable restrooms in use, serviced by a fleet of over 10,000 trucks. The industry includes more than 3,600 businesses and 39,000 employees worldwide."

Source: Portable Sanitation Association International

Industry Trend
- "The toilet-rental business is up 25 percent in the past year or so."

Resources

Associations
- Portable Sanitation Association International: www.psai.org

Power/Pressure Washing

| | NAICS 561790 | |

Rules of Thumb
> 50 percent of annual revenues

		Franchise
Precision Tune Auto Care (See also Franchises)		
Approx. Total Investment		$123,000 to $208,075
	NAICS 811118	Number of Businesses/Units 411

Rules of Thumb
> 35 to 40 percent of annual sales plus inventory

Resources

Websites
- www.precisiontune.com

Printing/Flexographic

| | NAICS 323111 | |

Rules of Thumb
> 2 to 5 times EBITDA

> 3 times EBIT

> Note: "It is a different area—they print labels on Web presses using plates that are made of curved rubber. Web presses use rolls of material rather than sheets. Think newspaper printing. However, apparently the pricing multiples are similar."

Pricing Tips
- "Depending on size, EBITDA ranges from 2 to 4 unless special circumstances are present like exceptional profit or none."
- "Multiples range from 2 to 5 depending on size and sector."

Expert Comments

"It is probably the most stable section of the printing industry, but it is not growing."

"There is generally lots of competition but less than those of commercial printers. Profits have stabilized in recent years. Marketability is generally high. Replication is relatively easy, but can you get the business and can you keep going until you make a profit? This is a good sector of the printing industry."

P - Rules of Thumb

Benchmark Data
- "Look for stable customer base with no heavy concentration with one or two clients."
- "Sales $200,000 per employee"

Expenses as a percentage of annual sales
Cost of goods	43%
Payroll/labor Costs	43%
Occupancy	05%
Profit (estimated pretax)	05% to 09%

Industry Trend
- "Business should continue stable with not a big increase or decline."

Questions
- "Does the owner handle major customers personally and can they be transitioned to a new owner? Do they have contracts? What sets this company apart from others? Do you have non-compete agreements with your salesmen?"

Resources
Websites
- Greeneville Plate Services: www.greenevilleplateservices.com

---

Printing/Silk Screen
SIC 7336-09 | NAICS 323113

Rules of Thumb
- 40 to 45 percent of annual sales plus inventory
- 2.5 to 3 times SDE includes inventory
- 3.5 to 4 times EBITDA
- 3.5 to 4 times EBIT

Pricing Tips
- "SDE 2.5–3.0 range. Sales growth, market potential, age/quality of equipment, staffing, lease will determine which end of range to use."
- "Value affected by equipment, customer base, skilled labor, location and sales growth."
- "Value of any long-term contracts that are in place. Are contracts assignable?"
- "National/corporate accounts as customers increases value vs. small local accounts."

Expert Comments
"Can be high capital investment to start up."

"Anyone can open a small screen printing shop or store. Most companies do screen printed and embroidered products. They also sell small signs, graphics, etc. This industry can be capital intensive. High-speed equipment is necessary to produce larger volume and some companies add a second and third shift."

Benchmark Data
- "$60,000 to $90,000 sales per employee, depending upon area of country located, type of printing and products manufactured."
- "$100,000/employee. $175–$200 sq. ft."
- "Sales $75–$100K/employee"

Expenses as a percentage of annual sales	
Cost of goods	60%
Payroll/labor Costs	20% to 25%
Occupancy	05%
Profit (estimated pretax)	05% to 10%

Industry Trend
- "Economic downturn has lowered profitability."
- "Consolidation as weaker competitors are either sold or shut the doors."
- "Continued slow growth"
- "Increased competition & pressure on margins."
- "Growth due to U.S. society continuing to be more visually oriented"
- "Transition from traditional screen printing to digital printing output"

Questions
- "Sales & profit trend over past 3 years, and especially over most recent 12-month period."
- "Monthly revenue over past 3 years to gauge seasonality of business and to analyze competitive environment."
- "Provide concentration of customers. Any range, one-time orders in sales figures? Maintenance schedule for all equipment?"
- "How are sales generated? Competition?Breakdown of revenues?Condition of equipment?Maintenance records?Seasonality?Sales Structure?Website?"

Resources
Trade Publications
- Screen Printing Magazine: http://stmediagroupintl.com/brands/screen-printing/

Print Shops/Commercial Printers (See also Print Shops—General)

SIC 2752-02	NAICS 323111	Number of Businesses/Units 47,500

Rules of Thumb
- 50 to 55 percent of annual sales plus inventory
- 2 to 3 times SDE includes inventory
- 2.5 to 3 times recast EBITDA if sales under $2 million
- 2.5 to 3.5 times recast EBITDA if sales $2 to $5 million
- 3.5 times recast EBITDA if sales $5 to $25 million
- 4 times EBIT
- 1 to 1.5 SDE plus fair market value of assets (for smaller companies)
- 5 times EBITDA for Commercial Flexographic Printing (See also Printing/Flexographic)

P - Rules of Thumb

Pricing Tips

- "Smart sellers are well positioned and organized relative to qualitative and quantitative monitoring systems. Buyers buy on potential of the seller's enterprise."
- "RMA Benchmarks/Industry Ratios—EBITDA calculations"
- "Print for Pay is declining as volume users have purchased equipment and produce in-house. Walk-in trade is inconsistent, commercial accounts provide stability. Newer equipment is important to allow a greater range of products delivered in an efficient manner."
- "Be careful of long-term contracts that might go away if the business ownership changes."
- "Having current technology in computer to plate is a big plus."
- "There are two primary ways of valuing printing companies. Fair value of assets plus a half multiple of EBITDA for goodwill and customer lists. The other is 2–4 times EBITDA depending on size, profitability, equipment, sector, etc."
- "There are two common ways to value printing companies: a multiple of EBITDA and fair market value of assets plus 1 times EBITDA. In a perfect world they would come pretty close"
- "The bigger the printer, the higher the multiple."
- "Generally printing companies are sold as a multiple of EBITDA (less CAPEX) ranging from 2 times to 6 times. The multiple will depend on size, profitability, segment of the industry, growth factors, number and percentage of clients to total sales. For companies with few earnings you can use fair market value of assets plus 1 times seller's discretionary income."

Expert Comments

"Because of the various types and sizes of printing companies [e.g., large vs. small format equipment, digital vs. analog, screen vs. digital signage, etc.] the speed of technological changes makes the above factors inconsistent throughout this industry. More than any other industry I've seen through my 12 years in M&A, there is no greater challenge than selling a printing company."

"Market share, customer base, equipment capabilities, niche markets"

"Person-to-person relationships are still very important."

"The current regional market shows excess capacity and possibly short-term declines in sales. There is brisk competition, but capitalization costs are high to replicate these businesses. Consolidations are needed."

"Trend is toward large online providers. Level of technical knowledge is critical."

"Customer base important.Hard to steal customers from competition."

"There is a lot of over-capacity in this industry that is only growing slightly and that depends on the segment. For some segments the barrier to entry is low. A person can buy a small press and equipment for a few thousand dollars and he is in business in the lower end of the business. Web printers continue to face huge challenges."

"Printing is a mature industry that is growing at barely the growth in population."

Rules of Thumb - P

"Price competition from on-line providers. Short-run color work is being done on in-house printers and copiers. 'Pleasing quality' has become acceptable for the small-business owner."

Benchmark Data
- For additional Benchmark Data see Print Shops (General)
- "COGS, net profits, annual sales trend over $4 million"
- "Sales per employee should exceed $200K."
- "Revenue per employee should be at least $175,000."
- "Payroll less than 30% of sales"
- "No customer bigger than 10%, and direct-to-plate image making"
- "Profit (estimated) 0 to 17 percent depending on segment. Digital printing will be on high side, commercial printing will be much less."

Expenses as a percentage of annual sales	
Cost of goods	40% to 50%
Payroll/labor Costs	35% to 45%
Occupancy	03% to 10%
Profit (estimated pretax)	05% to 15%

Industry Trend
- "Because (1) new production equipment is becoming increasingly available and appropriate for the largest customers of printing companies; (2) traditional printing work is continuing to be replaced by digital media—for email and the Web; and (3) much of the printing equipment [digital & analog] remains in operation, long after they might be considered obsolete, there is an imbalance of supply (of services) and demand, so downward pressure on prices will continue for the foreseeable future."
- "Positive outlook—big players expanding with M&A strategies"
- "The industry is splitting into two distinct segments: specialty wholesale printers 'gang running' for the trade (other printers) and full-service B2B printers incorporating design, Web services, etc. as part of their offerings."
- "Greater competition from large online providers"

Seller Financing
- "More typical to be outside financing."
- 5 to 10 years

Questions
- "Do you have skilled & experienced people in place?"
- "1. Real estate options 2. IP advantages 3. Lean or sustainability programs 4. Owner financing options 5. Proforma forecasts 6. Management skill set 6. Supplier discounts"
- "Why are you leaving and are there any contracts still honored."
- "Commercial account base?Outside salespeople? What role(s) does owner fill? Product mix?Specialty vs. commodity."
- "Look for any niche they serve; client concentration is a risk; client contracts are rare and would be a premium multiple."
- "Is production equipment leased or owned?"

26th Edition

P - Rules of Thumb

- "How up-to-date is their equipment? Do they have a niche? Do they do digital printing? What is their salesperson(s) situation? Do they have non-compete agreements with salespeople?"
- "How tied to the customers is the owner, why do customers use this printer over others, does any customer account for more than 10% of revenue."
- "How has the business been trending over the past five years?"
- "Why would a customer do business with you, other than quality, price and turnaround time?"

Resources

Websites
- Printing Industries of America: www.printing.org
- Tag and Label Manufacturers Institute: www.tlmi.com

Trade Publications
- American Printer: www.americanprinter.com
- Printing Impressions, an online publication: www.piworld.com
- "Valuing Printing Businesses, Handbook of Business Valuation," West & Jones, 2nd Edition: www.wiley.com

Associations
- Specialty Graphic Imaging Association: www.sgia.org
- EPICOMM: http://epicomm.org/

Print Shops (General)		
SIC 2752-02	NAICS 323111	Number of Businesses/Units 45,321
Rules of Thumb		
➢ 30 to 45 percent of annual sales plus inventory		
➢ 2 to 3.5 times SDE plus inventory		
➢ 3.5 to 4 times EBITDA		

Pricing Tips

- "Pricing is based on EBITDA—multiples are determined by the buyers—buyers are strategic and financial."
- "EBIT, EBITDA, 3–5 years of financial statements, outsourced industry specific appraisal, best to have audited statements every 5 yrs."
- "In Southern California there is tremendous over-capacity in commercial sheet-fed printing firms. I separate them into two categories: 1) Profitable 2) Underperforming (unprofitable). The profitable firms transact as always although financing and underwriting is much tougher. The underperforming firms need to be liquidated. Selling equipment for cash and selling accounts with an earnout note tied to gross sales retained. Normally paid monthly for 2–3 years at 6–9% of gross."
- "Market share in region, quality of accounts, no more than 20% of annual revenues per key account. Profit margin vs. industry benchmarks"

Rules of Thumb - P

- "Owner benefit add-backs, IP protection, key account loyalty, key employees and non-compete agreements."
- "There are two primary methods of valuing printing companies. A multiple of EBITDA and fair market value of assets plus half times a multiple of EBITDA. If everything is equal, these two methods should come relatively close."
- "What is trend of business for the subject company?"

Expert Comments

"Focus on your niche; stay the course; be strategic and buy right; don't overpay on the short term."

"Leaders are in growing—M&A is a key strategy."

"Talent pool, key sales relationships, special capabilities, owner financing"

"Key accounts, brand awareness, strong sales force, experience of leadership, documented business plans and vision, funding and vendor relationships, diversity of markets, product mix."

"Some areas of printing are declining, which will cause support services to decline."

"Focus on specialty, lean operations, financial metrics, marketing/sales investment, growth strategies, cash flow and cash."

Benchmark Data

Statistics (Printing)

Number of Establishments	45,321
Average Profit Margin	2.7%
Revenue per Employee	$189,400
Average Number of Employees	22.7
Average Wages per Employee	$42,933

Products and Services Segmentation

Commercial lithographic printing	54.7%
Other printing	9.3%
Commercial screen printing	9.1%
Commercial flexographic printing	7.6%
Digital printing	6.6%
Book printing	5.3%
Commercial gravure printing	4.1%
Quick printing	3.3%

Major Market Segmentation

Advertisers	28.9%
Publishing	23.5%
Retailers	11.0%
Consumer goods manufacturers	8.9%
Other	8.4%
Exports	7.5%
Stationery and textile manufacturers	6.8%
Financial and legal firms	5.0%

P - Rules of Thumb

Industry Costs

Profit	2.7%
Wages	22.8%
Purchases	39.9%
Depreciation	3.9%
Marketing	0.4%
Rent & Utilities	3.7%
Other	26.6%

Market Share

RR Donnelley & Sons Co.	11.0%
Quad/Graphics Inc.	4.7%

Source: IBISWorld, October 2015

- "The average sales revenue is almost $3 million, although the median was $877,500."
- "$180,000 per employee for a profitable business."
- "$200,000.00 per employee—great target."
- "Having contracts and exclusive relationships"

Expenses as a percentage of annual sales

Cost of goods	35% to 45%
Payroll/labor Costs	25%
Occupancy	05%
Profit (estimated pretax)	20%

Industry Trend

- "Growth for print leaders; packaging, wide-format and labeling all growing. Babyboomers exiting; less family succession plans. Consolidation continues."
- "'Sales growth has been fairly constant over the past five years at somewhere between 3 and 5 percent,' said Sageworks analyst Jenna Weaver. 'In the year ended January 20, sales increased about 4 percent. That shows us this industry is still growing its revenue, even though the popular opinion is that this industry is dying or really struggling. Our data shows that's not the case, at least with these private companies.'
- "Weaver noted that net profit margin has increased to 5.2 percent from 1.4 percent four years ago. 'That's a real positive for the industry,' she said. Data on profit growth for the most recent period wasn't yet available, but Sageworks' preliminary results indicate another year of growth, which would follow four years in a row of double-digit percentage gains in pretax net profit. Weaver said the factors driving the sales increases and improved profitability are unclear, although outside reports have indicated some printing companies are diversifying, relying more on added services such as shipping, packing, signs, and graphic design."

Source: "Don't Print The Obituary For The Printing Industry Just Yet" by Mary Ellen Biery, January 25, 2015, Forbes.com

- "Growth 9% to 11%"
- "Higher capability and lower cost for in-house equipment to handle short-run requirements."

Rules of Thumb - **P**

Seller Financing
- "Outside financing is the standard; sellers want out. Cash is king."
- "Two years maximum or don't do it."
- 3 to 5 years

Questions
- "Competitive advantages? Retained talent pool for transitions? Last year of 3rd party valuation of business?Reasons for selling? Best identified and suited buyers of your business?"
- "What is the business plan? Vision of business? Key employees secured by non-compete? IP status? What do the next 3 years look like in contacts, sales revenues?"
- "Systems, controls, leadership team, competitive advantages, ideal clients."
- "Who are your largest customers and what percentage of the total do they account for? Are these relationships personal and can they be transitioned to a new owner? What has been done to grow the business? "
- "What is customer mix? What is age and type of equipment?"

Resources

Trade Publications
- Print Shop by John Stewart: www.quickconsultant.com

Associations
- EPICOMM: http://epicomm.org/

Print Shops/Quick Print (See also Print Shops/Commercial Printers)

SIC 2752-02	NAICS 323111	Number of Businesses/Units 13,094

Rules of Thumb
- ➤ 45 to 55 percent of annual sales plus inventory
- ➤ 2.5 to 3.5 times SDE plus inventory
- ➤ 2 to 5 times SDE plus inventory—SDE (Owner's compensation) treats depreciation as an expense and thus it is not included in SDE.
- ➤ 4 times EBIT
- ➤ 3 to 4 times EBITDA

Pricing Tips
- "Fair market salary adjustment required prior to calculating SDE or excess earnings."
- "Excess earnings should exclude a fair-market salary for a new owner/manager."
- "Quick printer valuations have been on the decline."
- "The terms of the leases on the digital equipment will affect the operating income and price."
- "2 to 4 times EBITDA but trends are on the low end."

P - Rules of Thumb

- "The business should be a solutions provider to their clients."
- "Competitive equipment is very important, including lease terms and click charges."
- "The condition of the equipment and whether or not it is up-to-date makes a big difference in the selling price. The buyers normally have industry experience and are knowledgeable about the equipment."
- "Review replacement cost of assets. Percentage of business with top ten clients. Receivable turn."

Expert Comments

"Printing customers today do not necessarily buy on price, but they are buying small quantities and cutting back . . . this favors smaller printers."

"Industry is equipment intensive and requires a high degree of marketing skills to succeed."

"Quick printers that don't adapt have been declining. The ease of publishing and printing with computers and various printing devices have taken business from the quick printers."

"These are marketable companies suitable for corporate dropouts or general business people."

"I'm not sure that 'Quick Printer' is a relevant category or that the answers to the questions relate to this as a classification. I recently sold a $3,000,000-per-year-sales digital printer that operates out of a retail location. Much of their printing is same day, about $800,000 is retail. I think of this business as 'digital.' I have a newspaper printer under agreement—over $4 million in sales. Within 6 hours of receiving files from the newspaper, the newspaper is printed, addressed, and at the post office. Is this a quick printer? I don't tend to think of it as a quick printer."

"The quick printer has been declining partly because of computers and a failure to adapt to a changing market."

"It is easy to obtain the equipment, but much harder to get people, since many need special skills. Customers are not easy to obtain; they have to be taken from the competition."

Benchmark Data

Statistics (Quick Printing)

Number of Establishments	13,094
Average Profit Margin	4.1%
Revenue per Employee	$149,900
Average Number of Employees	2.0
Average Wages per Employee	$28,423

Products and Services Segmentation

Printing	63.9%
Other services	14.8%
Bindery and finishing services	8.2%
Prepress services	7.1%
Mailing services	6.0%

Major Market Segmentation

In-store customers	47.0%
Small businesses	23.5%
Non-employing businesses	18.5%
Online customers	11.0%

Industry Costs

Profit	4.1%
Wages	19.1%
Purchases	40.4%
Depreciation	4.4%
Marketing	1.4%
Rent & Utilities	8.6%
Other	22.0%

Market Share

FedEx Corporation	13.9%

Source: IBISWorld, December 2014

- "Sales per employee highly indicative of potential success . . . $120,000 minimum and is calculated by dividing gross annual sales by total # of employees including working owners."
- "Sales per employee $200,000"
- "One that goes out and gets business instead of waiting for it to walk in the door; one that is more creative."
- "Owner's compensation 13%"
- "Sales per employee are more a measure of automation and type of work than a meaningful value. Net profit after allowance for equipment is the main factor."

Expenses as a percentage of annual sales

Cost of goods	30% to 40%
Payroll/labor Costs	25% to 30%
Occupancy	05% to 10%
Profit (estimated pretax)	10% to 20%

Industry Trend

- "Moderation of profits and growth"
- "Slight decline for companies unprepared to take necessary steps to modernize."
- "Very good for someone who is technically literate regarding computers and networks and has specific skills found in the printing industry."
- "Digital equipment is taking over this segment of the printing industry. Quick turns and high quality are important."
- "Sales and marketing skills important"
- "Continued decline as people do more with computers and advanced printers."
- "Large asset investment in equipment.Continued growth at 4%–6% annually."
- "More consolidation, declining number of printers"

Questions

- "Percent of sales represented by top 3–5 customers?"
- "How did the seller arrive at his initial asking price? What was the basis for this price, and what references did he refer to?"

P - Rules of Thumb

- "Describe competition, percentage of sales by category (products & customers)."
- "What percentage of customers makes up 80% of the business?"
- "Type of equipment, lease terms, click charges. What related services do they offer? How do they get and maintain sales?"
- "Top 10 client list to see what percentage of sales. Receivables turn. Type and age of equipment."
- "Sales per employee, how old is the equipment—and number of impressions. How long have the employees been with the business? How up-to date is the pre-press department?"

Resources

Trade Publications
- Quick Printing Magazine: www.myprintresource.com/

Associations
- EPICOMM: http://epicomm.org/

Process Serving
NAICS 541199

Rules of Thumb
➢ 35% to 40% sales includes inventory

Benchmark Data

Statistics (Conveyancing Services)

Number of Establishments	38,384
Average Profit Margin	11.7%
Revenue per Employee	$128,700
Average Number of Employees	2.9
Average Wages per Employee	$68,933

Products and Services Segmentation

Conveyancing and title abstract services	44.8%
Settlement and closing services	24.8%
Title search and other document filing services	14.5%
Other legal services	9.5%
Patent copyright and other intellectual property document services	3.3%
Process services	3.1%

Major Market Segmentation

Businesses	55.3%
Individuals	42.6%
Government and nonprofit organizations	2.1%

Industry Costs

Profit	11.7%
Wages	53.7%
Purchases	8.8%
Depreciation	1.1%
Marketing	2.4%
Rent & Utilities	5.2%
Other	17.1%

Market Share

Fidelity National Financial, Inc.	19.6%
First American Financial Corporation	9.4%
Stewart Information Services Corporation	3.5%

Source: IBISWorld, December 2014

Property Management Companies

SIC 6531-08	NAICS Residential Property 531311; Nonresidential 532312
	Number of Businesses/Units 243,947

Rules of Thumb

- 100 percent of annual revenues
- 6 to 7 months' revenues for firms selling under $500K
- 10 to 12 months' revenues for firms above $500K
- 2.5 to 5 times SDE based on a cash sale
- 3.5 to 6 times SDE with sales involving notes and/or contingencies
- 2.4 to 2.5 times EBIT
- 2.5 to 3 times EBITDA

Pricing Tips

- "These businesses have a tendency to sell between 2 and 2.6 times the owner benefit. In some cases individual contracts are sold, i.e., a seller may have 50 management contracts and sell off say 20, in which case they are sold on a contract basis according to the quality of the contract."
- "There are critical elements to valuation of these businesses that do not show in the financials. Booking sources for tenants, mortgage position of the property owners. In addition, the escrow monies must be measured and transferred at closing."
- "Length of time business owned, amount of work carried out by the seller, i.e., specifically in short-term rental homes owners can carry out lawn and pool care, as opposed to administration."
- "Occupancy is critical as is markup on services. Discovery of proximity of properties to attractions."
- "Specifically vacation rental PM: ask about billing to homeowner vs. service rate—also commission from booking companies vs. organic. Higher the commission the better compared to occupancy rate."
- "Key item is the longevity of accounts (i.e., any property managed for more than 3 years is good). Also, the transition period should have the owner (seller) remain visible for 2 to 3 months."

P - Rules of Thumb

Expert Comments

"We always make sure that the buyer has an independent accountant review the bookings and records of the business, preferably for three years. Should the buyer only be taking on contracts, as opposed to a full business, then have the accountant check the contracts thoroughly and if possible have a clause in the contract which allows for a replacement contract should one be lost during the first three months due to no fault of the buyer. For example a house is sold, then it should be replaced."

"After going through the recession, this industry has bounced back and it has been found that the demand for this type of business is still high but the supply has been lower."

"Home based generally, scalable, annuity revenue nature of some of the revenue streams"

"Not much competition. Expenses are low."

Benchmark Data

Statistics (Property Management)

Number of Establishments	243,947
Average Profit Margin	24.1%
Revenue per Employee	$83,700
Average Number of Employees	2.9
Average Wages per Employee	$44,694

Products and Services Segmentation

Residential property management	55.4%
Non-residential property management	24.7%
Other	14.2%
Real estate brokerage	2.8%
Land management	1.9%
Construction	1.0%

Major Market Segmentation

Residential properties	67.5%
Other non-residential properties	18.3%
Office buildings	5.2%
Industrial buildings	4.6%
Commercial	4.4%

Industry Costs

Profit	24.1%
Wages	54.3%
Purchases	6.6%
Deprecation	1.6%
Marketing	3.2%
Rent & Utilities	6.0%
Other	4.2%

Source: IBISWorld, October 2015

Rules of Thumb - **P**

- "It is difficult to give an average for occupancy, labor and cost of goods sold, due to the fact these businesses are so diverse and you have to determine according to the business being sold. Some businesses have a higher owner involvement, i.e., the owner may do some of the maintenance work, lawn and pool care as well as the administration; whereas in other businesses the owner simply handles the administration, including placing rentals into the properties, which creates a much higher income for the business."
- "2x owner benefit. Some value on a per house basis....not valid if property is not apple to apple comparison with other units."
- "This type of business allows an owner to do a variety of work within the business, which makes it attractive to a buyer. It is not too difficult to expand this type of business providing the owner is an organized person. Over the last 10 years or so I have seen contracts per house for short-term rental homes sell from $5,000 to $8,000 per unit, subject to the type of property and age."
- "$7,000 per home assuming right neighborhoods. 2 x cash flow for husband and wife (delta to normal modeling)."
- "$5,000 to $7,000 per home assuming all revenue streams are in place and homes have all amenities: pool, hot tub, game rooms, proximity to attractions"
- "Most property management firms earned 10 to 30 percent of their revenue from non-management activities, e.g., lease fees, maintenance contracts."

Expenses as a percentage of annual sales

Cost of goods	20%
Payroll/labor Costs	40% to 50%
Occupancy	05% to 10%
Profit (estimated pretax)	15% to 25%

Industry Trend

- "I believe this business will continue to thrive. It is extremely popular and one should note that no real estate license is required for the short-term rental property management, as it is governed in the state of Florida by the hotel and motel licensing and not the Florida Real Estate Commission."
- "Continued growth. Inventory of vacation homes has been stagnant and old inventory is aging out. New construction boom driving sales and need for this industry."

Seller Financing

- "I have been able to achieve all manner of financing. Many people have paid cash. I have also had success in SBA lending for a good solid business. Not much seller financing, the reason being, this is a very personal type of business and the sellers understand this. If a buyer does not have a good attitude, it could prevent the business expanding, and this is a fear for sellers, so they do not like to carry a large note "
- "Seller financing is less common for property management companies larger than $500,000 gross income, but for smaller companies it would be 3 to 5 years."
- "30% owner financing"
- "4 years. Note typically has fixed amortized payment, but may be contingent upon payments based on retention of accounts."

P - Rules of Thumb

Questions
- "Homeowner mortgage? How do you generate occupancy? What is the occupancy rate?"
- "What exactly do you do in the business? Do you hold escrow for the owners? Do you pay their bills without holding escrow? Can you show a contract for each of the owners you manage properties for?"
- "Insure that deposits and owner operating account funds transfer at closing."
- "How many homes? How many with pools? What are your service charges and corresponding costs for each? Your management fee? What is the homeowner's mortgage position? Occupancy rate seasonality?"
- "Why are you selling? Have there been any lawsuits or complaints?"

Resources

Websites
- Institute of Real Estate Management: www.irem.org

Associations
- Property Management Association: www.pma-dc.org
- National Property Management Association: www.npma.org
- Florida Vacation Rental Managers Association: https://fvrma.wildapricot.org/
- Central Florida Vacation Rental Managers Association: www.cfvrma.com
- Vacation Rental Managers Association: www.vrma.com

Publishers—Books (See also Publishers—In General)		
SIC 2731-01	NAICS 511130	Number of Businesses/Units 9,896

Rules of Thumb
- ➢ 70 percent of annual sales plus inventory
- ➢ 4 to 6 times EBIT
- ➢ 4 to 6 times EBITDA

Pricing Tips
- "Professional publishing is valued higher than educational publishing, and both are valued higher than consumer publishing. Proprietary and niche-specific publishing is most attractive."

Benchmark Data

Statistics (Book Publishing)
Number of Establishments	9,896
Average Profit Margin	7.8%
Revenue per Employee	$437,400
Average Number of Employees	17.6
Average Wages per Employee	$76,837

Rules of Thumb - **P**

Products and Services Segmentation

Textbooks	31.6%
Professional, technical and scholarly books	27.5%
Adult trade books	24.0%
Other books and services	10.3%
Children's books	6.6%

Industry Costs

Profit	7.8%
Wages	17.7%
Purchases	62.2%
Depreciation	1.6%
Marketing	3.2%
Rent & Utilities	0.5%
Other	7.0%

Market Share

Bertelsmann SE & Co. KGaA	13.2%
Pearson PLC	11.3%
Apollo Group Inc.	6.9%

Source: IBISWorld, September 2015

Industry Trend

- "Students are shouldering huge costs when it comes to the textbooks in their backpack, but companies are stepping in to lighten the load. Textbook prices increased 1,041% from January 1977 to June 2015, more than three times the rate of inflation, according to an NBC News analysis of Bureau of Labor Statistics data. As student loan debt continues to rise above the $1 trillion mark, the cost of a college education and all of its trappings is becoming increasingly unaffordable.

"He (Mark Perry, professor at the University of Michigan-Flint) added that the consolidation of the market into a few major publishers, such as Cengage, McGraw Hill and Pearson, allows for further price gouging."

Source: "How financial aid is driving up college textbook prices" by Kathleen Burke
August 6, 2015. marketwatch.com

Resources

Associations
- Association of American Publishers: www.publishers.org
- American Booksellers Association: www.bookweb.org
- Independent Book Publishers Association: www.ibpa-online.org

Publishers—In General

NAICS 511130

Rules of Thumb

➢ 75 to 100 percent of annual sales includes inventory
➢ 3.5 to 7 times SDE includes inventory
➢ 6 times EBIT
➢ 5 to 7 times EBITDA

26th Edition 639

P - Rules of Thumb

Pricing Tips
- "Pricing varies significantly by segment or niche, from a high of 1.5 times revenue and 8 to 10 times EBITDA for scientific technical publishing to 3 times EBITDA for trade book publishing."
- "Publishing is a diverse business. Electronic publications have higher multiples. Specialties such as scientific and technical publications have higher multiples. Books would have the lowest multiple. Magazines would be somewhere in the middle, with good trade magazines worth more than consumer magazines. City and local magazines are worth the least of the magazines with competition intense. Most print publications will have an electronic or digital component and if they do not, the value is negatively impacted. The publications of sufficient size and strategic interest to the major publishers such as Elsevier, Wiley or Wolters Kluwer are worth considerably more."
- "Publishing is quite diverse, making it difficult to generalize about a multiple. For example, business-to-business magazines are generally worth more than consumer magazines, due to low level of competition. On the other hand, the market share of a business-to-business magazine is critical in valuation. Scientific journals of reasonable size command very high multiples. Books, being very low margin, command low multiples."
- "Businesses are essentially goodwill, with little consideration of fixed assets. Strategic and financial buyers (PEGs) figure predominantly in valuation with considerably higher valuations, some as high as 8 to 10 times EBITDA, possible for a publisher of strategic interest. Size is also a critical factor in valuation, as most strategic buyers will not be attracted to a publishing business with gross revenue less than $3 to $4 million annually."

Expert Comments
"Publishing is a risky, competitive but profitable business for those who are successful. There are some declining segments which you should be aware of, such as general book publishing."

Benchmark Data
- "For magazines we use profit per page, cost per page and various other metrics of profitability and productivity."
- "Profit margins. Rank of the publication in its specific niche is very important. The number one publication in a category, such as construction, is worth far more than the number 2 or lower publication."
- "A general benchmark has been one-times sales but this is more difficult to measure now because of declining sales."

Expenses as a percentage of annual sales	
Cost of goods	25%
Payroll/labor Costs	10% to 25%
Occupancy	05% to 08%
Profit (estimated pretax)	15% to 20%

Industry Trend
- "Continued downward due to online competition and, for books, loss of bookstores."
- "The trend is clearly to digital and electronic products. Also, the valuable properties have a very highly defined niche and a leadership position in that niche."

Rules of Thumb - **P**

- "Internet will continue to negatively impact many segments of the publishing business."

Seller Financing
- "Outside financing"

Questions
- "The position of the publication in its niche is critical. Where would competition come from? How protected is the competitive position of the business?"
- "For magazines, what is the definition of your market segment and what is your rank in the segment? Number 1 can be worth considerably more than number 2 for a business-to-business magazine. Where do you print, who are your suppliers? Questions about subscribership are critical for consumer magazines. Newsstand distribution is difficult for consumer magazines—how do you do it? Is the magazine paid or free, and so on."

Resources

Websites
- Editor and Publisher: www.editorandpublisher.com

Trade Publications
- Booklist: www.booklistonline.com
- Publishers Weekly: www.publishersweekly.com
- Circulation Management: www.audiencedevelopment.com

Associations
- Magazine Publishers Association (MPA): www.magazine.org
- The Association of American Publishers: www.publishers.org
- International Association of Scientific, Technical & Medical Publishers: www.stm-assoc.org
- The Association of Business Information and Media Companies: www.abmassociation.com

Publishers—Internet (and Broadcasting)

NAICS 519130

Rules of Thumb
- ➢ 100 percent of annual revenue includes inventory
- ➢ 6 times SDE includes inventory
- ➢ 6 times EBIT
- ➢ 5 times EBITDA

Pricing Tips
- "Size matters. Multiples for larger companies >$5 million will be in the 10X range. Same goes for companies with a subscription base that represents recurring revenues."

P - Rules of Thumb

- "Faster growing companies will provide higher multiples. Higher multiples will also be paid for companies that can document recurring revenue streams, such as subscriptions or annual advertiser contracts. Publishers who provide original content or who own assets such as proprietary databases also can expect greater buyer interest."

Expert Comments

"Ease of replication; it really depends on the content provided. The best businesses have proprietary content and/or a market niche in which they operate."

"Online publishing is a popular business. The barriers to entry are low and the financial reward can be great. The key is developing something original that keeps users coming back to a site. Competition is growing, a factor that will make good sites more valuable while leading to the demise of weaker ones."

"The Web is the world's largest printing press. Everyone wants to be a publisher and competition for eyeballs, ad dollars, subscribers and market share is intense. Barriers to entry are low. On the flip side, publisher and broadcaster audiences tend to be loyal. If they like your site they will stay with you. This leads to lots of repeat business and higher profit margins."

"The ease of replication depends on the content being published. The more unique, the more valuable, the more timely—the better."

Benchmark Data

- "A successful Internet business will generate revenues at the rate of 2x employee costs."

Expenses as a percentage of annual sales
Cost of goods	10%
Payroll/labor Costs	65%
Occupancy	05% to 10%
Profit (estimated pretax)	20%

Industry Trend

- "Businesses will continue to grow as 'old' media ad dollars continue to migrate to Web-based 'new' media."
- "There will be significant consolidation as smaller operations are rolled into larger ones."

Questions

- "I would ask about stability of earnings, renewal rates, staff turnover, number of advertising contracts, and if there is any revenue/customer concentration."
- "1. How much of your revenue base is recurring? 2. What is your renewal rate? 3. How much do you spend on customer acquisition?"
- "I'd want to know about revenue growth, subscriber/advertiser diversification and renewal rates. Professional publications/broadcasts should be in the 80% range; consumer oriented services should be at 50%. These are rough metrics, but demonstrate 'stickiness.'"

Publishers—Magazines/Periodicals

(See also Publishers—In General)

| SIC 2721-02 | NAICS 511120 | Number of Businesses/Units 40,502 |

Rules of Thumb
- 7 times SDE includes inventory
- 2 to 5 times EBIT
- 2 to 5 times EBITDA

Pricing Tips
- "Publishers are generally selling for 2 to 5 times EBITDA, down from where they once were."
- "Publications generally sell for a multiple of EBITDA and have very little inventory. Depending on size, industry, if it is a consumer publication or business to business, profitability, etc. smaller ones will sell in the 2 to 5 times range, while the large companies will sell for as much as 12 times EBITDA."
- "Circulation questions are key, including various details of subscriptions and newsstand. Advertisers—number, new advertisers.Share of market in the specific specialty area such as log-home magazines, fishing — # of pages and revenue dollars."
- "Prices have been hurt due to low advertising and magazines not embracing an Internet strategy."
- "In magazine publishing, operating profits or EBITDA (earnings before interest, taxes, depreciation and amortization) of 15 to 20 percent are desired and frequently exceeded, while paid subscription renewals above 50 percent and newsstand 'sell-through' above 35 percent will support a higher selling price."

Expert Comments
"Publishing, especially trade publishing, is declining rapidly. People are looking to the Internet for trade information because it can be delivered daily and weekly and be received long before a magazine can even be produced."

Benchmark Data

Statistics (Magazine & Periodical Publishing)
Number of Establishments	40,502
Average Profit Margin	8.0%
Revenue per Employee	$346,800
Average Number of Employees	19.6
Average Wages per Employee	$67,813

Products and Services Segmentation
Entertainment magazines	30.6%
Academic and professional	28.8%
Home and living magazines	18.0%
General interest magazines	16.5%
Other periodicals	6.1%

26th Edition

P - Rules of Thumb

Industry Costs

Profit	8.0%
Wages	19.6%
Purchases	34.8%
Depreciation	1.5%
Marketing	2.8%
Rent & Utilities	3.2%
Other	30.1%

Market Share

Advance Publications Inc.	8.4%
Hearst Corporation Inc.	6.3%
Time Inc.	5.1%

Source: IBISWorld, September 2015

- "Publishing costs of goods sold will vary based on the type of publication as well as labor and occupancy costs. Profits have ranged from 10% to 30% based on type of publication but are declining. Publishing is undergoing a change. Successful publishing companies will be in a growth industry and will have an interactive presence."

Expenses as a percentage of annual sales

Cost of goods	50%
Payroll/labor Costs	35%
Occupancy	05%
Profit (estimated pretax)	10%

Industry Trend

- "95% of U.S. adults under 25 read print magazines. The percentage of U.S. adults who read digital edition magazines has more than quadrupled over the past 3 years."

Source: GfK MRI, Fall2014, Magazine Media Factbook

- "Publishing will continue to decline with the exception of the publishers that can embrace the Internet. Consumer magazines will fare better."

Questions

- "What are advertisers telling you? Look at circulation trends and costs."
- "What have you done to grow the company and how would you grow it in the future?"

Resources

Websites
- www.editorandpublisher.com

Associations
- The Association of Magazine Media: www.magazine.org

Publishers—Newsletters

NAICS 511120

Rules of Thumb

➢ 1 times revenues

Pricing Tips
- "High renewal rate (70 percent plus) increases value"

Publishers—Newspapers—Dailies		
(See also Publishers—Newspapers—Weeklies/Community Papers)		
SIC 2711-98	NAICS 511110	Number of Businesses/Units 6,995

Rules of Thumb
- 50% of annual sales includes inventory (only very large will get higher)
- 4 times EBITDA
- 4 times EBIT
- 5 times SDE includes inventory

Pricing Tips
- "EBITDA valuation multiples for mid and small market papers range from 3x to 6x. Publishing company values are currently in the 3x to 6x trailing EBITDA range with most transactions at 4x to 5x. Prices over 5x tend to be strategic acquisitions. Buyers typically look at the most recent performance, and the multiples indicated here are based on stable or improving performance. Companies with declining revenues and EBITDA tend to be valued at the lower end of the multiple scale."

  Source: www.cribb.com—An excellent site, full of valuable information on the publishing business, especially newspapers.
  "In today's market, most valuation methods for newspapers are out the window."

- "Multiples for newspapers can range from four to ten times EBITDA depending on size and type. Dailies can easily sell at 10 times while smaller weekly publications will be at the lower range."
- "5x EBITDA is a current average for newspaper properties with a history of stable earnings. Number may be considerably higher if publication is positioned for sale to a strategic buyer."
- "Key factors include: size of market, years in business. Is the newspaper geographically desirable by contiguous publishers or buyers looking to roll-up smaller publications into larger groups and take advantage of economies of scale? How active and dominant is the publication in its market and how dominant are its online activities?"

Expert Comments

"While the industry is certainly on a decline, there are still many strategic consolidation opportunities."

"Competition generally comes from other media such as TV and cable rather than other newspapers. As newspapers face new challenges, the risk will increase. Profits have historically been very high, reaching 30% EBITDA. Marketability is still strong but will probably decrease. Industry trend is down as circulation and advertising decline. You can replicate but you must sustain the losses for some time."

"Established newspapers with 10+ year track record tend to be extremely

P - Rules of Thumb

stable and low risk. Competition from Internet has not had a material impact on revenues or valuations . . . at least not yet."

"Subscriber acquisition and gaining solid market position takes many, many years for paid circulation newspapers, therefore time is the greatest barrier to entry."

Benchmark Data

Statistics (Newspaper Publishing)

Number of Establishments	6,995
Average Profit Margin	4.8%
Revenue per Employee	$145,600
Average Number of Employees	28.5
Average Wages per Employee	$41,506

Products and Services Segmentation

Print Advertising	49.8%
Sales and subscriptions	28.3%
Digital Advertising	11.0%
Other	7.3%
Printing services	3.6%

Industry Costs

Profit	4.8%
Wages	28.5%
Purchases	28.1%
Depreciation	3.4%
Marketing	1.8%
Rent & Utilities	4.0%
Other	29.4%

Market Share

Gannett Co. Inc.	10.1%
News Corp.	8.2%
Tribune Company	5.5%
The New York Times Company	5.2%

Source: IBISWorld, April 2015

- "Benchmarks vary greatly by type of publication. For instance, sellers of daily paid circulation newspapers may find that valuations based on subscriber base may be most advantageous. Publishers of free distribution publications are often tied to multiple of discretionary cash flow."
- "Generally multiple of EBITDA. Another is $50 to $400 per paid subscriber."
- "Sales per subscriber, number of subscribers, revenue per household reached (if free distribution publication)."

Expenses as a percentage of annual sales

Cost of goods	50% to 55%
Payroll/labor Costs	30%
Occupancy	05%
Profit (estimated pretax)	15%

Rules of Thumb - **P**

Industry Trend
- "Advertising in the traditional printed daily and Sunday newspaper decreased 8.6% in 2013 from the previous year. Retail advertising dropped 8%, with national advertising also declining by 8%. Classified advertising was off 10.5%."

  Source: "Newspaper Media Revenue 2013: Dollars Grow in Several Categories," www.naa.org

- "It's the year of the paywall: American newspapers have committed, for better or worse, to making readers pay for the news online, after years of giving away on the web what they charge a fortune for in print. Previously, Ebyline looked at statistics of paywall adoption and discovered that larger newspapers are building paywalls at significantly higher rates. But examining paywalls by newspaper size only tells part of the story.

  "The metered paywall approach (allowing readers to read, say, 5 or 10 articles before they have to pay for content) is the most popular, with 84% of the newspapers listed in NAA's database. It's also the paywall strategy used by the New York Times, which recently changed the number of free articles readers can access to 10, down from 20, earlier this year. On average, newspapers allow 11.2 free articles before readers encounter the paywall."

  Source: "Newspaper Paywalls Accelerating" by Susan Johnston, July 2012

Seller Financing
- 5 years

Questions
- "How effectively are you competing with online media? How are your renewal rates compared to your competitors'?"
- "How he would increase the circulation and advertising revenue and why he has not been successful if that is the case. Is the circulation audited?"

Resources

Websites
- Cribb, Greene and Associates—a newspaper appraisal and brokerage firm: www.cribb.com

Trade Publications
- Editor & Publisher: www.editorandpublisher.com

Associations
- National Newspaper Association: www.nnaweb.org
- Newspaper Association of America: www.naa.org

Publishers—Newspapers—Weeklies/Community Papers		
(See also Publishers/Newspapers—Dailies)		
	NAICS 511110	

Rules of Thumb
> "100 percent of annual sales"

P - Rules of Thumb

> ➤ "Some smaller weekly papers will have lower multiples in the 3 to 5 EBITDA area."
> ➤ "Community monthlies will sell for 3 x SDE if they produce at least $150,000 in SDE. Otherwise, multiple comes down to the 2 x SDE area."
> ➤ 3 times SDE
> ➤ 3 times EBIT
> ➤ 3 times EBITDA
> ➤ 1 times annual income for mid-sized weekly newspaper

Expert Comments

"Barriers to entry are low. This is a selling business. Getting good salespeople is very difficult. The buyers of this type of business should expect to spend half of their time selling."

Benchmark Data

- "The majority of community papers that answered the survey, however, still receive most of their ad income from grocery ads, 43.8 percent. The next two top earners are medical based (hospitals and urgent care clinics) 40.8 percent, and tied for third are new auto sales and banks or other financial institutions at 30.8 percent each."
  Source: "Survey: ad revenue showing improvement at community papers" by Stanley Schwartz, www.nnaweb.org July 3, 2013
- "Advertising to editorial should run 2/3rd to 1/3rd for maximum profitability."
- "Look for businesses where the owner does very little selling. You have to make a negative adjustment to SDE to account for sales commissions to replace an overactive seller."

Expenses as a percentage of annual sales

Cost of goods	25%
Payroll/labor Costs	25%
Occupancy	05%
Profit (estimated pretax)	20%

Industry Trend

- "Up. Local merchants are looking for a cost-effective way to reach their local customers. Major dailies are too expensive and provide too much reach for the local markets."
- "Community papers are following the rise in the housing market. New communities are receptive to local papers that educate them as to local restaurants, salons, etc. This trend will continue."

Questions

- "How many salespeople do you have?"

Resources

Websites
- Cribb, Greene & Associates—a newspaper appraisal and brokerage firm: www.cribb.com

Associations
- Association of Free Community Newspapers: www.afcp.org
- National Newspaper Publishers Association (NNPA): www.nnpa.org

Publishers—Software

NAICS 511210	Number of Businesses/Units 9,047

Rules of Thumb
> "Varies widely, particularly on multiple (revenue, earnings) of historical performance. Many acquisitions are strategic in nature."

Expert Comments
"Market momentum of software products can change quickly, both up and down. With specialized niche firms, buyers can be international companies. This is a trans-national market."

Benchmark Data

Statistics (Software Publishing)
Number of Establishments	9,047
Average Profit Margin	22.1%
Revenue per Employee	$461,300
Average Number of Employees	49.0
Average Wages per Employee	$149,613

Products and Services Segmentation
Application software publishing	36.3%
System software publishing	33.0%
All others	19.2%
Re-sale of computer hardware and software	3.8%
Information technology technical consulting services	3.4%
Custom application design and development	3.2%
Information Technology related training services	2.0%

Major Market Segmentation
Business	62.2%
Household consumers and individual users	30.3%
Government	7.5%

Industry Costs
Profit	22.1%
Wages	32.9%
Purchases	11.3%
Depreciation	2.1%
Marketing	3.3%
Rent & Utilities	5.6%
Other	22.6%

P - Rules of Thumb

Market Share

Microsoft Corporation	21.4%
Oracle Corporation	7.0%
International Business Machines Corporation	5.3%

Source: IBISWorld, August 2015

Industry Trend
- "Increasingly competitive"

Publishing—Monthly Community Magazines
NAICS 511120

Rules of Thumb
- 65–85 percent of annual sales includes inventory
- 3 times SDE includes inventory
- 3.5 EBIT
- 3.5 times EBITDA

Pricing Tips
- "The page count of the magazine and the size of the distribution is a key to attaining the higher number and the greater multiple suggested above. Most publications in this segment will be focused on an area or group within a geographical area, i.e., 'Lake Norman Woman,' 'Carolina Living,' or 'Iredell County Life' and will require that targeted readers identify themselves with the title implication and market. The attraction to a segment of the market creates a loyalty that should translate into long-time advertisers. Make sure the renewal rate is over 75% to confirm this loyalty is real & present."
- "If gross revenues exceed $500,000 then 1X sales is common. That usually equates to 3X SDE. A monthly that has the owner doing all of the sales is worth less than one with a good sales staff. Publications under $500,000 will sell closer to 2X SDE or 50% to 75% of sales."

Expert Comments

"The advertising industry as a whole is very competitive, which will show in the last 3 years' sales, but there is a strong opportunity for a great salesperson to make good money. Hiring great salespeople is very hard and a new owner should not count on a salesperson making a material difference in sales. This is the owner's primary responsibility."

"Monthlies are easy to start up and competition is great. Look for the thickest book (largest number of pages). Advertising should be around 70% of total pages. The thinner books will have the hardest time staying alive. Advertisers tend to stick with the publication they are in, so it's hard to be the new kid on the block."

Benchmark Data
- "The average cost is about $700 a page to print and distribute. The average sales commission should not exceed 25% of the sale. Most vanity magazines

Rules of Thumb - **P**

will operate out of a home or key-man office space with the occasional use of conference rooms for sales meetings. In any case, occupancy cost should not exceed 5% of sales."
- "Look for sales per salesperson of around $20,000 a month. That should pay a commission of $4,000 which is the minimum you need to keep good salespeople."

Expenses as a percentage of annual sales	
Cost of goods	25%
Payroll/labor Costs	25% to 30%
Occupancy	05%
Profit (estimated pretax)	20% to 30%

Industry Trend
- "The boutique magazine industry trend is positive as a larger number of people see this industry as attractive because it affords them the opportunity for a specific lifestyle in a targeted community setting without a significant liability and risk"

Questions
- "What are the top five advertisers? How long have they been with you? Could you grow the circulation? How long have you been with your current printer? Describe your 'layout' process."
- "How long have you been publishing and what are your historical trends? How many salespeople and how long have they worked for you? Who do you consider your competition?"

Publishing—Newspapers (In General)

SIC 2711-98	NAICS 511110	Number of Businesses/Units 5,400

Rules of Thumb
- 25 percent of annual sales includes inventory
- 3 times SDE plus inventory
- 3 to 5 times EBIT
- 3 to 5 times EBITDA

Pricing Tips
- "Depends on size and segment; for example, it would be very hard to sell a daily newspaper in today's environment."
- "Price can vary greatly depending on the size and frequency of publication, i.e., weekly, daily publication; if the company has its own printing plant; the value of printing equipment; and approximately 50% of gross revenue for recurring outside print work."
- "A stable weekly will sell for 5 to 7 times EBITDA. A strong weekly in a growth area can sell for as much as 9 to 11 times EBITDA. Variation in price is based upon age of property, market potential, competition, stability, growth history, community acceptance, reputation and market penetration. If printing equipment is owned, add value of equipment. If income is generated from

26th Edition

P - Rules of Thumb

outside printing, the profits for the printing portion of the business need to be separated and valued at 3 to 5 times EBITDA. "

- "Each newspaper is unique and its strengths and weaknesses must be analyzed in order to arrive at a Fair Market Value. There are industry rules-of-thumb that apply to Gross Revenues and EBITDA, which change according to the dictates of the market."

Expert Comments

"The growth of online advertising has significantly reduced profitability and gross revenues of newspapers."

"Amount of competition from all media in the market is important because there is a limited amount of advertising dollars to go around. Historic performance and competition will be large factors in determining the amount of risk. Location is of minor importance because the customer rarely goes to the business. Most publications with reasonable profits are marketable as there are sufficient buyers in the market for local community operations. While the trend in large metro dailies is declining revenue and profits, smaller community publications continue to do well. It is easy to start a new publication, but a lot more difficult to build a reader and advertising base."

"Competition generally comes from other media such as TV and cable rather than other newspapers. Profits have historically been very high, reaching 30% EBITDA, but have been falling recently. Marketability is decreasing."

"The industry is in a state of turmoil and transition. Large metro dailies are being hardest hit, while smaller community newspapers have been able to weather the perfect storm of Internet competition and a changing economic environment."

Benchmark Data

- For additional Benchmark Data see Publishers—Newspapers—Dailies
- "At one time $200 per daily newspaper subscriber, but not anymore. It is a matter of profitability. Some smaller newspapers in rural areas have a better chance because there are not as many advertising options."
- "The ratio of advertising space to editorial space has a lot to do with profitability. Ideally one should have two-thirds advertising, one-third profit."

Expenses as a percentage of annual sales

Cost of goods	35% to 45%
Payroll/labor Costs	25% to 35%
Occupancy	05% to 10%
Profit (estimated pretax)	15% to 25%

Industry Trend

- "After a year of slight gains, newspaper circulation fell again in 2014 (though tracking these data is becoming more complicated each year due to measurement changes). Revenue from circulation rose, but ad revenue continued to fall, with gains in digital ad revenue failing to make up for falls in print ad revenue. Despite widespread talk of a shift to digital, most newspaper readership continues to be in print. Online, more traffic to the top newspaper websites and associated apps comes from mobile than from desktop users, and the average visitor only stays on the site for three minutes per visit. And several larger media conglomerates spun off their newspaper divisions as separate companies in an attempt to prevent the newspaper industry's woes from affecting the health of their broadcast divisions."

- "Readership—Although the public conversation about newspapers focuses on the shift to digital, most newspaper reading still happens in print. According to readership data from Nielsen Scarborough's 2014 Newspaper Penetration Report, 56% of those who consume a newspaper read it exclusively in print, while 11% also read it on desktop or laptop computers; 5% also read it on mobile; and another 11% read it in print, on desktop and on mobile. In total, more than eight-in-ten of those who read a newspaper do so in print, at least sometimes. Only 5% read newspapers exclusively on mobile devices.
"For the past five years, newspaper ad revenue has maintained a consistent trajectory: Print ads have produced less revenue (down 5%), while digital ads have produced more revenue (up 3%) – but not enough to make up for the fall in print revenue. Overall ad revenue fell 4%, to just $19.9 billion."

Source: Newspapers: Fact Sheet by Michael Barthel, April 29, 2015, journalism.org

- "Fully 69% of Americans—or more than 164 million adults in the United States—access newspaper media content in print or online during a typical week or on mobile devices during a typical month, according to the survey of some 206,000 U.S. adults collected by Scarborough Research."

Source: Executive Summary, Newspaper Association of America, www.naa.org

- "Tough times will continue for this sector."

Seller Financing

- "About 50% of sales are financed. Larger papers generally sell for cash. Smaller papers will sell for as little as 30% down with terms averaging seven years."
- "Seller financing is typical with terms of five years or longer."

Questions

- "What is your online market position and share of market in each market that you serve?"
- "What are the reasons why you feel your media will continue to be relevant in the years to come?"
- "How would you increase the circulation and advertising? Why haven't you been successful in doing so?"
- "Revenue by category, cash flow, paid circulation and free circulation, average advertising percentage, competition, owner's duties, who sells the ads, number of ad contracts in place and dollar value?"
- "What contracts do you have; how are you handling the changes in the newspaper environment? Is it an all-cash sale or is the owner willing to carry some of the sale price?"
- "Subscription base, number of subscribers, subscriber retention, revenue trends, strength of online initiatives, years established"
- "Why they are selling; what their daily involvement is; what investment has been made to adapt to new technologies; how do they reach the individual reader and advertiser. Many more."

P - Rules of Thumb

- "How are you positioned in your market relative to competition in the online market? How are you protecting your employment and classified advertising base from online competition?"

Resources

Websites
- Cribb, Greene and Associates: www.cribb.com

Trade Publications
- Editor and Publisher Magazine: www.editorandpublisher.com

Associations
- Newspaper Association of America: www.naa.org

Pump It Up (See also Franchises)	Franchise
Approx. Total Investment	$500,000 to $1,250,000
NAICS 713990	Number of Businesses/Units 146

Rules of Thumb
➢ 30 percent of annual sales plus inventory
➢ (Provides children's parties with inflated/bouncy toys)

Resources

Websites
- www.pumpitupparty.com

Purrfect Auto (See also Franchises)	Franchise
NAICS 811118	Number of Businesses/Units 100

Rules of Thumb
➢ 45 percent of annual sales plus inventory
➢ Note: This franchise is on the West Coast—primarily California, Nevada and Arizona.

Resources

Websites
- http://purrfectauto.com/

Rules of Thumb - **Q/R**

	Franchise
Quaker Steak & Lube (See also Franchises)	
Approx. Total Investment	$1.2 million to $4.4 million
Estimated Annual Sales/Unit	$2,500,000
NAICS 722513	Number of Businesses/Units 60

Rules of Thumb

➢ 45 percent of annual sales

Resources

Websites
- www.thelube.com

	Franchise
Quiznos Classic Subs (See also Franchises, Sandwich Shops)	
Approx. Total Investment	$182,912 to $231,246
Estimated Annual Sales/Unit	$325,000
SIC 5812-19 NAICS 722513	Number of Businesses/Units 1,900

Rules of Thumb

➢ 20–25 percent of annual sales plus inventory

Benchmark Data
- For Benchmark Data see Sandwich Shops

Resources

Websites
- www.quiznos.com

Radio Communications, Equipment and Systems	
NAICS 443142	Number of Businesses/Units 3,700

Rules of Thumb

➢ 2 to 4 times SDE plus inventory

Pricing Tips

- "It is important to consider the revenue per customer and industry figures. A well-diversified company can weather downturns in business cycles that this industry may be subject to."

Expert Comments

"Not location dependent, but a well-trained staff and diversified product lines are important."

26th Edition

R - Rules of Thumb

Benchmark Data
- "GP of 40%, payroll 20%, advertising 4%"

Expenses as a percentage of annual sales
Cost of goods	60%
Payroll/labor Costs	20%
Occupancy	07%
Profit (estimated pretax)	10% to 12%

Industry Trend
- "FCC rule changes mandate replacement of older 2-way radio equipment being used."

Questions
- "Product line diversification? Service and installation capabilities? Employee tenure?"

Radio Stations (See also Television Stations)		
SIC 4832-01	NAICS 515112	Number of Businesses/Units 6,703

Rules of Thumb
- ➢ 8 to 10 times EBITDA
- ➢ 10 to 12 times cash flow in medium markets
- ➢ 15 times cash flow—large markets
- ➢ 1.5 to 6 times annual sales

Pricing Tips
- "Broadcast station 'stick' valuation or the conundrum of how to value a station that has never made any money...ever. Broadcast station valuation is usually done by using a multiple of the station's broadcast cash flow (BCF). Of course this assumes the station is producing a cash flow. Where there is no cash flow, it is the perceived value of what the license is worth plus any hard assets the station may have ... commonly referred to as the 'stick' or base value. There are several scholarly tomes on broadcast or radio station valuation (Search: broadcast station valuation). The problem here is that many stations have gone through a succession of owners and have never shown any positive cash flow or just enough to keep the power on until the next sale/transfer. What is a station like this worth? Many new construction permits (CP) are coming on the market as a result of the recent FM allocation auctions. What are these worth?

"In the case of a station that has never shown a positive cash flow you need to determine the reason. Is it an unfortunate combination of circumstances that has led to a succession of owners who had no clue as to what to do with the station? Poor market conditions? Improper format? Poor signal? Also, some stations can be artistic successes and commercial failures. Such a station might have a format that appeals to a significant audience but the station is unable to sell enough advertising to capitalize on the station's own success. This is frequently because the station has not developed a proper sales force.

Rules of Thumb - R

As any broadcast owner knows, the hardest positions to fill at a station are good sales representatives. I talk to would-be broadcasters all the time that have no clue as to what it takes to put together a sales staff.

"Back to how to evaluate a non-cash flowing station or a dark station ready to go back on the air. A common industry approach has been to factor the amount of revenue a particular facility may generate by looking at the amount of advertising revenue the station may be able to secure out of the total revenue available for radio in the market if it reaches a particular audience level ... whew ... got that? The problem here is there are many pieces of the puzzle that have to be put together to get an idea of what the numbers should be. What is the financial condition of the market? Power of the station? Is it AM or FM? Is the ownership/management talented? In today's market we have to contend with how much advertising revenue is going to other competitors on the Internet. This is where the question is asked... 'Is the Internet going to be a foe of the station or a tool to be used by it?' To stream or not to stream? Interactive Web site or not? Maybe even podcasts?

"Another major factor to look at in evaluating a start-up property is the technical condition of the station. Failure to conduct an engineering inspection can be a costly mistake. What looks like a cheap price for an AM property could be a pig in a poke with some nasty surprises. Questions that need to be answered: What is the condition of the AM ground system and tower? Do either need to be painted (tower), repaired or even replaced? Are the copper radials in the ground damaged or corroded away? If the AM station is a directional system, is the pattern still in compliance? Has there been lightning damage to the phasor system and other transmitter/audio processing components? What is the age of the transmitter? Will it need to be replaced? To get the answers, hire a competent broadcast engineering firm to do an evaluation. You will need to pay for this but it can save you big money and headaches later."

Source: David Garland, Media Brokerage, www.radiobroker.com.
Garland is one of the most successful radio brokers in the country.

- "Normally depends on historical (and projected) Broadcast Cash Flow, or EBITDA plus certain non-recurring charges and management-unique expenses. Value of the intangible rights to the license can vary widely with supply and demand.

"Some advice to sellers—you are not going to get 22 times cash flow on a small market station. Yes, I know that some stations recently, and one in particular in Texas, were reported as having sold for 22 times cash flow. This is only going to happen in probably the top 50 markets. Most banks will only (if you can get them to look at the deal) do 4 to 5 times cash flow. That means the buyer will have to put in the balance in cash unless you carry the paper yourself (and be in 2nd position behind the bank). The only way you are going to get a big premium is if your FM station has the potential to upgrade into a much larger market. My associate Burt Perrault has been in discussions with the owner of a small market combo, billing in the $150,000 range, about listing the stations for sale. The market has about 6,000 population, with 40,000 or so in the county. There are 3 other radio stations in the county also. He wants close to $1,000,000 for the combo. In a market this size, to bring $1 million he needs to cash flow $125K to bring 8 times cash flow (which is a realistic multiple) in a market this size. He also does not want to do the work to bring his station's cash flow, and, as a result, the value, up to where he wants it. That is to be left to the hoped-for buyer to do. Yes his combo may be worth $1 million one day but not on a present 'as is...where is' basis. There are lots of people wanting to get into the radio station ownership business, but pricing has got to be realistic in relation to market size. That's the way it is...deal with it."

Source: David Garland, Media Brokerage, www.radiobroker.com

R - Rules of Thumb

- "A multiple of broadcast cash flow (revenues minus operating expenses before interest, depreciation, taxes). Multiple varies by service (AM/FM/TV) & market size. All broadcasters need to own tower site. Consolidation opportunities within a market add value."
- "With rapid consolidation taking place in the radio industry sellers and buyers are happy with the multipliers they are achieving—buyers of multiple properties can reduce expenses. Ask about buyer's investment horizon. What expenses are in the business of the owner/operator that an investor may not have?"

Benchmark Data

Statistics (Radio Broadcasting)

Number of Establishments	6,703
Average Profit Margin	13.6%
Revenue per Employee	$197,300
Average Number of Employees	15.4
Average Wages per Employee	$58,804

Products and Services Segmentation

Other	39.1%
Country	14.2%
News/Talk	11.4%
Classic Rock	10.2%
Urban	8.8%
Top 40	8.2%
Adult Contemporary	8.1%

Industry Costs

Profit	13.6%
Wages	30.0%
Purchases	40.1%
Depreciation	4.6%
Marketing	4.5%
Rent & Utilities	6.7%
Other	0.5%

Market Share

Sirius XM Radio Inc.	21.8%
iHeartMedia Inc.	16.3%
Cumulus Media Inc.	6.8%
CBS Corporation	6.1%

Source: IBISWorld, April 2015

- "Profit (estimated)—25 percent for well-run stations"

Industry Trend

- "Radio today reaches more than 90 percent of people in the U.S. on a weekly basis; 236 million people listen to the radio each week; there are more than 13,500 radio stations across the United States, covering more than 40 different formats."

Source: Radio Facts and Figures,
http://www.newsgeneration.com/broadcast-resources/radio-facts-and-figures/

Rules of Thumb - **R**

Seller Financing
- "Rarely is there seller financing except for smallest of deals."

Questions
- "Can your signal be upgraded or moved to cover a larger market? How are you spending your revenue? How much do you do in trade? Can any barter be converted to cash? Do you really need to buy that new gadget, just because you have a few extra bucks this month? Spend the money to find out what can be done to expand or move that signal to more ears. Are you being a partner in your advertisers' business? The more you expand your advertisers' businesses, the more you expand yours and are therefore able to ask for more dollars on the selling market."

Source: www.buysellradio.com

Resources
Websites
- David Garland, Media Brokerage, also, a brokerage site, but well worth a visit.: www.radiobroker.com

---

Real Estate Offices

SIC Real Estate 6531-18 / Business Brokerage 7382-22	NAICS 531210
	Number of Businesses/Units 773,689

Rules of Thumb
➢ 2 times SDE; may require earnout
➢ 33 percent of annual sales (real estate offices) includes inventory

Pricing Tips
- "Price will depend on agent splits."
- "Time in the market and number of listings."
- "This industry has taken a huge hit. The multiples must be on SDE that is sustainable."
- "Must factor out owner's personal production. Smaller brokerages (under $1M in gross commissions) are about 1x SDE."

Benchmark Data

Statistics (Real Estate Agency Franchises)
Number of Establishments	26,756
Average Profit Margin	19.9%
Revenue per Employee	$105,000
Average Number of Employees	13.0
Average Wages per Employee	$42,393

Products and Services Segmentation
Residential real estate agency franchises	68.5%
Commercial real estate agency franchises	31.5%

26th Edition

R - Rules of Thumb

Major Market Segmentation

Sellers	45%
Lessors	30%
Buyers	25%

Industry Costs

Profit	19.9%
Wages	40.6%
Purchases	12.8%
Depreciation	2.0%
Marketing	1.6%
Rent and Utilities	7.1%
Other	16.0%

Market Share

Realogy Corporation	2.2%

Source: IBISWorld, September 2014

Statistics (Real Estate Sales and Brokerage)

Number of Establishments	746,933
Average Profit Margin	10.9%
Revenue per Employee	$127,900
Average Number of Employees	1.3
Average Wages per Employee	$44,702

Products and Services Segmentation

Residential sales	64.5%
Commercial rentals	11.4%
Other services	11.1%
Commercial sales	8.4%
Residential rentals	4.6%

Major Market Segmentation

Married or partnered residential homeowners and renters	46.3%
Single residential homeowners and renters	22.8%
Office and professional space	12.7%
Retail space	11.1%
Warehousing and other commercial space	4.4%
Manufacturing space	2.7%

Industry Costs

Profit	10.9%
Wages	35.3%
Purchases	9.0%
Depreciation	2.0%
Marketing	5.4%
Rent & Utilities	4.1%
Other	33.3%

Source: IBISWorld, September 2015

- "Should have 5 closings per agent annually"
- "Need to get to about $1 million in gross commissions."

Rules of Thumb - R

Expenses as a percentage of annual sales

Cost of goods	65% (commission payout)
Payroll/labor Costs	10%
Occupancy	05% to 10%
Profit (estimated pretax)	15%

Industry Trend

- "Now two of the leading real estate websites are merging—Zillow, the Seattle-based site known for assigning a "Zestimate" to home values, is buying San Francisco's Trulia for $3.5 billion in stock, the companies said today. Together they may finally get big enough to try to streamline the way homes are bought and sold.
  "What's remarkable about both sites is how little they've actually changed the selling and buying of homes. That's mostly by design. Both were founded nearly a decade ago with a healthy respect for the intractability of the real estate market, with its unique dual-agent process (one representing the buyer, and one the seller) and with its multiple listing services (MLS), which has a stranglehold on home listings."
  Source: "How a Zillow-Trulia Merger Could Finally Change the Business of Real Estate," by Brad Stone, www.businessweek.com July 28, 2014

Questions

- "Are you in production? What contract do you have for advertising and services? Where do you get your leads? Have you recently lost top-producing agents?"
- "Do you produce? What are your splits? Do you have non-competes?"
- "Will the owner be available?"

Records Management

	NAICS 541611	

Rules of Thumb
- ➢ 8 times SDE
- ➢ 200 percent of annual sales

Pricing Tips
- "Pricing [above] specifically for Records Management businesses"

Benchmark Data
- "Internal account growth of 5 to 7%. Sixty percent storage revenues with 40% service revenues."

Expenses as a percentage of annual sales

Cost of goods	0%
Payroll/labor Costs	35%
Occupancy	25%
Profit (estimated pretax)	30%

R - Rules of Thumb

Industry Trend
- "Continued industry growth with emphasis on document-destruction services"

Recruiting Agencies

SIC 7361-03	NAICS 56131	Number of Businesses/Units 23,976

Rules of Thumb
- 50 percent of annual revenues; may require earnout
- 1 to 1.5 times SDE; add fixtures equipment & inventory; may require earnout

Benchmark Data

Statistics (Employment and Recruiting Agencies)
Number of Establishments	23,976
Average Profit Margin	5.1%
Revenue per Employee	$91,200
Average Number of Employees	12.4
Average Wages per Employee	$38,625

Products and Services Segmentation
Permanent placement services	49.2%
Executive search services	32.8%
Temporary staffing services	8.6%
Independent contractor placement services	6.1%
Other	3.3%

Major Market Segmentation
Industrial	33.5%
Executive and managerial	32.0%
Administrative and clerical	16.0%
Technical	11.0%
Healthcare	7.5%

Industry Costs
Profit	5.1%
Wages	41.9%
Purchases	13.3%
Depreciation	0.3%
Marketing	2.1%
Rent & Utilities	3.9%
Other	33.4%

Market Share
Randstad Holding NV	4.8%
LinkedIn Corp.	4.1%

Source: IBISWorld, September 2015

Rules of Thumb - **R**

Recruiting Agencies (Online) (See also Recruiting Agencies)

	NAICS 56131	

Rules of Thumb
- 50% Annual Gross Sales including inventory
- 6 times SDE plus inventory
- 5 times EBITDA

Benchmark Data

Expenses as a percentage of annual sales

Cost of goods	50%
Payroll/labor Costs	20%
Occupancy	05%

Industry Trend
- "The online recruitment business is challenging. There are many new and free and very inexpensive competitors."

Seller Financing
- "Typically uses outside financing"

Questions
- "Where is the majority of traffic coming from: SEO, natural search, PPC, other?"

Resources

Associations
- International Association of Employment Websites: www.employmentwebsites.org

Recycling

	NAICS 562920	Number of Businesses/Units 1,589

Rules of Thumb
- 3 to 5 times SDE includes inventory
- 3 to 6 times EBIT
- 3 to 6 times EBITDA

Pricing Tips
- "Value is based on land and improvements, inventory (aged), earnings, and goodwill"
- "Once the EBITDA exceeds $1,000,000 most buyers will assume that normal levels of inventory, A/R, and FFE will be included in the transaction as working

26th Edition 663

R - Rules of Thumb

capital. The key is to understand how the buyer is structuring their offer and how they are accounting for these values."
- "Must consider if this is a commodity product that is sold. If so, consider the consistency of the source of the product as an important risk factor."

Benchmark Data

Statistics (Recycling Facilities)

Number of Establishments	1,589
Average Profit Margin	3.8%
Revenue per Employee	$233,300
Average Number of Employees	14.2
Average Wages per Employee	$38,194

Products and Services Segmentation

Recyclable material recovery and processing	54.7%
Sale of recycled materials	36.9%
Recyclables collection services	7.6%
Other	0.8%

Major Market Segmentation

Municipal governments	67.3%
Recyclable commodity wholesalers and manufacturers	17.6%
State governments, nonprofit organizations and individuals	15.1%

Industry Costs

Profit	3.8%
Wages	16.3%
Purchases	44.5%
Depreciation	5.4%
Marketing	0.5%
Rent & Utilities	5.1%
Other	24.4%

Market Share

Waste Management Inc.	21.2%
Republic Services Inc.	6.7%

Source: IBISWorld, September 2015

Expenses as a percentage of annual sales

Cost of goods	50%
Payroll/labor Costs	12%
Occupancy	10%
Profit (estimated pretax)	8%

Industry Trend

- "Companies associated with the waste management industry will continue to be attractive as they provide a 'green' business opportunity to both individual and strategic buyers."
- "Trend is overall growth in the recycling industry with a consolidation with middle to large sized companies seeking to purchase smaller competitors."

Rules of Thumb - R

Questions
- "What kind of contracts do you have with your paper suppliers? Are you contracted to sell your paper to certain mills or brokers? Who is your competition within 100 miles?"

Red Robin Gourmet Burgers (See also Franchises)	Franchise
Approx. Total Investment	$1,800,000 to $3,000,000
Estimated Annual Sales/Unit	$2,500,000
NAICS 722513	Number of Businesses/Units 500

Rules of Thumb
> 30 to 35 percent of annual sales

Resources
Websites
- www.redrobin.com

Registered Investment Advisors	
NAICS 523930	Number of Businesses/Units 62,222

Rules of Thumb
> 150 percent of annual sales
> 3 to 5 SDE

Pricing Tips
- "The structure of your deal will depend on the willingness of the seller to hold an earnout vs. a note and cash down payment at closing."

Expert Comments
"There will be continued major consolidation in the industry."

Benchmark Data

Statistics (Financial Planning and Advice)
Number of Establishments	62,222
Average Profit Margin	26.7%
Revenue per Employee	$276,300
Average Number of Employees	2.3
Average Wages per Employee	$97,426

Products and Services Segmentation
Business and government financial planning and management	41.3%
Personal financial planning and advice	33.0%
Other services	15.8%
Personal investment management	9.9%

26th Edition

R - Rules of Thumb

Major Market Segmentation

Individuals and households	42.9%
Businesses	27.7%
Other clients	15.8%
Governments	13.6%

Industry Costs

Profit	26.7%
Wages	36.5%
Purchases	4.3%
Depreciation	1.1%
Marketing	1.2%
Rent & Utilities	2.9%
Other	27.3%

Market Share

Morgan Stanley Wealth Management	19.9%
Wells Fargo & Company	18.5%
Bank of America Corporation	13.5%
Ameriprise Financial Inc.	13.3%

Source: IBISWorld, October 2015

- "Average account per client"

Expenses as a percentage of annual sales

Cost of goods	05% to 10%
Payroll/labor Costs	10% to 20%
Occupancy	05% to 15%
Profit (estimated pretax)	20% to 45%

Industry Trend
- "Continued major consolidation. Large players absorbing smaller operators for their higher margins. However, smaller players will have a disadvantage due to size."

Questions
- "Gross commissions? Net? Broker-dealer?Overhead?Fee-based or commission-based?Average fees? Average client investment, net worth?"

Remediation Services	
NAICS 562910	Number of Businesses/Units 8,487

Rules of Thumb
➢ 4 to 5 times EBITDA
➢ 40 percent of annual sales includes inventory
➢ 2 to 3 times SDE includes inventory

Pricing Tips
- "Union vs non-union work force. Private vs. public projects."
- "Contract and client direct relationships will be worth more than those performed as a subcontractor for a general contractor. Size makes a big difference in price—larger businesses with $1 million + EBITDA sell for higher multiples."
- "Value of future jobs under contract is a major factor in value and salability."

Expert Comments

"Industry has become increasingly competitive as more players are chasing fewer projects."

"Demand for remediation services is tied to the construction remodeling and improvement market. As demand for building modifications has decreased with the economic crisis, so too have remediation services."

"Competition varies based on union vs. non-union, and public vs. private market. Revenue varies with commercial real estate renovation and development."

Benchmark Data

Statistics (Remediation & Environmental Cleanup Services)

Number of Establishments	8,487
Average Profit Margin	6.0%
Revenue per Employee	$221,800
Average Number of Employees	26.4
Average Wages per Employee	$58,465

Products and Services Segmentation

Site remediation services	47.4%
Building remediation services	26.8%
Environmental emergency response services	13.1%
Other services	12.7%

Major Market Segmentation

Businesses	55.0%
Federal government	23.5%
State and local government	11.5%
Individuals	5.0%
Nonprofit organizations	5.0%

Industry Costs

Profit	6.0%
Wages	26.3%
Purchases	25.8%
Depreciation	7.6%
Marketing	0.8%
Rent & Utilities	4.5%
Other	29.0%

Market Share

CH2M Hill Inc.	8.8%
CB&I	5.2%

Source: IBISWorld, August 2015

R - Rules of Thumb

- "Owner compensation 3% of sales"
- "Flat management structure with an engaged owner will be much more profitable. Sales, estimating and production responsibility for each project should be with the same manager."
- "Gross margin should be 25%–30% and SDE 20% of revenue."

Expenses as a percentage of annual sales

Cost of goods	70%
Payroll/labor Costs	07%
Occupancy	04%
Profit (estimated pretax)	03% to 05%

Industry Trend
- "Project opportunities are a function of the overall commercial construction industry. Business will pick up when commercial renovation work picks up."

Questions
- "Have there been any DEP violations? Worker's comp claims?""Check for hidden liabilities. Union vs. non-union is important difference. Reputation is also important—how many jobs have they abandoned or not completed on time?"

	Franchise
Renaissance Executive Forums (See also Franchises)	
Approx. Total Investment	$61,500 to $150,000
NAICS 611430	Number of Businesses/Units 54

Rules of Thumb
➢ 70 percent of annual sales includes inventory

Resources

Websites
- www.executiveforums.com

Rental Centers (See also Rent-To-Own Stores)		
SIC 7359-59	NAICS 532310	Number of Businesses/Units 23,843

Rules of Thumb
➢ 95 to 100 percent of annual sales includes inventory

➢ 3 times SDE includes inventory

➢ 4 times EBITDA

➢ Depending on type of business (general, tool, construction, industrial, party) values will range from 3.0 to 5.5 EBITDA, $1.00 to $2.00 per annual revenues.

➢ 5 times SDE (party and tent rental)

Rules of Thumb - R

Pricing Tips

- "Age of equipment, depreciation expense. If equipment is old and depreciation expense getting lower each year, then examine equipment carefully. Equipment may be old and worn out requiring replacement with new."
- "A. Type of rental business: tool versus construction equipment versus party/event rental —earnings have a different set of criteria. B. Key ratios: rental equipment inventory; rental revenues; EBITDA percent of net revenues."
- "Percentage of rent to sales; capitalization versus expense policy for equipment purchases; age of rental fleet (inventory for rent); rental inventory is a fixed asset, not a current asset such as inventory for sale."
- "ROI—Return on Investment (annual rental revenues divided by original cost of equipment). Varies from $0.70:$1.00 to $2.00:$1.00, 1:1 depending on whether equipment is construction, general tool, or party. Values primarily based on multiple of EBITDA, net revenues, value of assets plus goodwill factor, customer base, organizational structure/employees & staff, physical plant facilities, including location and expansion area availability."
- "To be successful, a general equipment rental store should be doing a minimum of $800,000 gross sales per year."

Expert Comments

"Business location is very important relative to competition and accessibility for customers."

Benchmark Data

Statistics (Tool and Equipment Rental)

Number of Establishments	8,819
Average Profit Margin	12.0%
Revenue per Employee	$214,600
Average Number of Employees	2.8
Average Wages per Employee	$36,352

Products and Services Segmentation

Contractor equipment	46.9%
Home tools and DIY equipment rental	27.3%
Rental of other goods	11.6%
Consumer goods rental	8.7%
Delivery, repair and other services	5.5%

Major Market Segmentation

Construction firms	24.8%
Industrial firms	21.2%
Independent builders and contractors	19.6%
Private households	18.1%
Other	8.9%
Government	7.4%

R - Rules of Thumb

Industry Costs

Profit	12.0%
Wages	17.0%
Purchases	51.6%
Depreciation	3.9%
Marketing	1.3%
Rent & Utilities	5.0%
Other	9.2%

Market Share

United Rentals Inc.	46.2%
Sunbelt Rentals	7.9%
Hertz Global Holdings Inc.	5.3%

Source: IBISWorld, September 2015

Statistics (Party Supply Rental)

Number of Establishments	15,024
Average Profit Margin	11.2%
Revenue per Employee	$82,200
Average Number of Employees	3.9
Average Wages per Employee	$35,837

Products and Services Segmentation

Wedding rentals	34.8%
Corporate event rentals	31.3%
Other event rentals	18.7%
Birthday rentals	15.2%

Industry Costs

Profit	11.2%
Wages	43.4%
Purchases	21.7%
Depreciation	6.8%
Marketing	2.0%
Rent & Utilities	9.5%
Other	5.0%

Market Share

Classic Party Rentals	5.1%

Source: IBISWorld, January 2015

- "For tool and equipment, labor costs should be less than 25%. Party and tent rental less than 35%.$100.000 annual sales per employee."
- "Rental revenues should be $0.70 to $2.00 the value of inventory at cost and be in reasonable rental condition."

Expenses as a percentage of annual sales

Cost of goods	<10%
Payroll/labor Costs	<30%
Occupancy	<10%
Profit (estimated pretax)	05% to 15%

Industry Trend
- "Growing industry with growth areas. Dependent on construction cycle."

Seller Financing
- "Limited to 20 percent of the sales price"
- "7-year amortization"

Questions
- "Get a depreciation schedule and verify equipment age and condition. Do a thorough due diligence. If a stock sale, find out about lawsuits and environmental issues."
- "How does business account for equipment maintenance—expense or capitalize?"

Resources

Trade Publications
- Rental Management: www.rentalmanagementmag.com

Associations
- American Rental Association: www.ararental.org

Rent-To-Own Stores (See also Rental Centers)		
SIC 7359-30	NAICS 532310	Number of Businesses/Units 7,018

Rules of Thumb
> 55 percent of annual sales includes inventory

Pricing Tips
- "Eight (8) times monthly gross receipts (tops), includes lock, stock (inventory) and barrel. All underlying debts would be paid off by seller at this price. I think the multiple is now less because the industry has sustained a shakeout."

Benchmark Data

Statistics (Consumer Electronics & Appliances Rental)
Number of Establishments	7,018
Average Profit Margin	7.0%
Revenue per Employee	$214,300
Average Number of Employees	4.0
Average Wages per Employee	$28,852

Products and Services Segmentation
Electronics	48.3%
Appliances	27.7%
Computers	15.3%
Other	8.7%

26th Edition

R - Rules of Thumb

Industry Costs

Profit	7.0%
Wages	13.4%
Purchases	32.3%
Depreciation	25.8%
Marketing	2.5%
Rent & Utilities	8.3%
Other	10.7%

Market Share

Rent-A-Center Inc.	36.9%
Aaron's Inc.	31.5%

Source: IBISWorld, October 2015

- "The average store has annual revenue of $736,000 and serves 360 customers each year."
- "Operating costs for rent-to-own businesses are higher than traditional retail because of the ultimate return of merchandise, merchandise repair and replacement expenses, and the need to continually market the industry's services to a rotating customer base."

Product Breakdown

Furniture	36.7%
Appliances	18.6%
Electronics	24.9%
Computers	10.7%
Jewelry	.06%
Other	7.6%

Source: Association of Progressive Rental Organizations (APRO), www.rtohq.org, 2015

- The following data is a bit dated, but is the latest available.

  "Rental Revenue per Employee—Rent-A-Center 2007 Rental Revenue per employee rose to its highest level ever—$153,930.54, up from $121,209.57 in 2006.

  "Rental Revenue per Home Office Employee—After declining for four consecutive years, Rent-A-Center's Rental Revenue per Home Office Employee increased to $5,402,090.57 up from $4,843,475.71 in 2006.

  "Monthly Revenue per Location—Rent-A-Center's 2007 average monthly rental revenue per location reached its highest level ever at $77,439.90, up from $58,540.74 in 2006. Note: Based on store count at the end of 2007. If based on weighted average store count, average revenue per location for 2007 would have been $70,673.08. Rent-A-Center's lowest average monthly rental revenue per location ($29,797.00) was reported in 1998, the year Renters Choice acquired Rent-A-Center. For the entire 12-year period—1996 through 2007—Rent-A-Center's average monthly revenue per location is $58,701.53.

  "Rental Revenue per Square Ft.—Rent-A-Center's 2007 Rental Revenue per Square Ft., increased sharply to $202.02 up from $152.71 in 2006.

  "Average Store Size—Rent-A-Center's average store size remained at 4,600 square ft. in 2007. The company's average store size has grown from a low of 3,800 square ft. in 1998."

Source: Rent-to-Own Industry Statistics, www.rtoonline.com.

Industry Trend

- "Sears Holdings will launch a rent-to-own leasing program for CE, majaps (major appliances), mattresses and other big-ticket items this week, and has renewed efforts to sub-lease space in and around its stores. The rent-to-own program is managed by WhyNotLeaseIt, a national leasing service, and will be rolled out to all 900 U.S. Sears stores on Wednesday. The lease option will be offered on items priced $280 and more, and to customers 18 and older who earn at least $1,000 a month and have a Social Security or tax ID number. Customers can make payments for up to 18 months or pay off the balance after five months."

    Source: "Sears Launches Rent-To-Own Leasing Program" by Alan Wolfe, www.twice.com May 13, 2013

Resources

Associations

- Association of Progressive Rental Organizations (APRO)—a very good site: www.rtohq.org

Repair Services

Rules of Thumb

➢ "General type—When establishing a price for a repair business which caters to the general public, the selling price should be fixtures and equipment; inventory, which is usually rather small; plus two-thirds of one year's profit."

Repossession Services

| | NAICS 561491 | |

Rules of Thumb

➢ 85 to 95 percent of annual sales includes inventory

➢ 4 times SDE

➢ 2.5 to 3.5 times EBITDA

Pricing Tips

- "Some industry consolidation is happening by various large conglomerates."
- "Be careful of the depreciation associated with trucks. Towing is also a supplement of this industry."

Expert Comments

"There are barriers to entry in certain states which require licensing. The insurance costs are very high."

Benchmark Data

- "A successful company tracks on average how much fuel is consumed per recovery and also makes an allocation for insurance cost."
- "The average repo fee is $300.00 +."

R - Rules of Thumb

Expenses as a percentage of annual sales

Cost of goods	10% to 15%
Payroll/labor Costs	35% to 45%
Occupancy	10% to 15%
Profit (estimated pretax)	35% to 45%

Industry Trend

- "The business will grow as the economy continues to improve."

Resale Shops
(See also Clothing Stores—Used, Consignment Shops, Used Goods)

NAICS 453310	Number of Businesses/Units 30,000

Rules of Thumb

➢ 40 to 45 percent of annual sales plus paid-for inventory

Benchmark Data

- For additional Benchmark Data see Used Goods
- "According to America's Research Group, a consumer research firm, about 16–18% of Americans will shop at a thrift store during a given year. For consignment/resale shops, it's about 12–15%. To keep these figures in perspective, consider that during the same time frame, 11.4% of Americans shop in factory outlet malls, 19.6% in apparel stores and 21.3% in major department stores.

  "Resale is a multi-billion dollar a year industry. First Research estimates the resale industry in the U.S. to have annual revenues of approximately $16 billion including revenue from antique stores, which are 13% of their statistics."

  Source: "Industry Statistics & Trends," NARTS,The Association of Resale Professionals

Industry Trend

- "For the fifth year in a row, Plato's Closet and Once Upon A Child, both resale stores, made Entrepreneur Magazine's Franchise 500 List. In the 36th annual rankings, these two retailers nabbed the No. 108 and No. 140 spots overall, proving that the trend in growth of the resale industry is only growing."

  Source: "Two resale stores make top 150 franchise list" by Jacqueline Renfrow, February 3, 2015, http://www.fierceretail.com/story/two-resale-stores-make-top-150-franchise-list/2015-02-03
  February 3, 2015 | By Jacqueline Renfrow

- "While many businesses close their doors every day, resale remains healthy and continues to be one of the fastest growing segments of retail. With new stores entering the industry and current establishments opening additional locations, the industry has experienced a growth—in number of stores—of approximately 7% a year for the past two years. This percentage reflects the estimated number of new stores opening each year, minus the businesses that close."

  Source:Industry Statistics &Trends, http://www.narts.org/

- "Name Brand Exchange, another resale company based in Phoenix, also is doing well. 'Every hanger in the store is being used,' said Tamra Thomas, sales manager for the Mesa store. 'But we never turn it away, even though we have no room in the stores.' Thomas said the resale turnover and customer traffic at

Rules of Thumb - R

Name Brand are very high. 'It is crazy busy right at this time,' she said. 'People are selling clothes to get money for vacation, save up for college or for gas.' As a result, sales have increased at the two Name Brand locations. 'We make at least $10,000 to $15,000 more a month in sales than we did five years ago.' Traci Nelson, another manager at the Mesa location, said business depends on the economy. 'Everyone is trying to get something any way they can to get extra gas money,' she said."

Source: "Business is booming at used clothing, consignment shops during economic downturn" by Ashley Macha, www.bizjournals.com/phoenix/stories

- "The resale industry is one of the few recession-proof segments of retailing. Not only does it survive during economic slowdowns, but it grows and thrives. The appeal is twofold… consumers are attracted to buying quality merchandise at a fraction of the original cost, and there is a financial incentive to sell, consign, or donate their unused or unwanted items."

Source: www.narts.org

Restaurants—An Introduction

Restaurants-QUICK CHECK-2014

Bagels	30% of annual sales (Not as much interest today)
Bars	50% of annual sales (Very much in demand)
Bar & Grill	(50% liquor) 40% of annual sales (Very popular)
Barbecue	30% of annual sales (Limited pool of buyers)
Bistros	30% of annual sales (Typically chef owned)
Brew Pubs	40% of annual sales (A lot of interest in Craft Beer)
Billiard Parlors	40% of annual sales (Limited pool of buyers)
Cajun	30% of annual sales (Not big in New England)
Catering Businesses	30% to 40% of annual sales (Seller may have to stay for an earnout)
Caribbean	30% of annual sales
Chicken	30% of annual sales
Chinese	30% of annual sales (Of reported sales)
Coffee Houses	30% of annual sales
Continental	30% of annual sales (Heavy/rich menus not in vogue today)
Delis	30% to 40% of annual sales (Higher value if only 5/6 days)
Diners	30% of annual sales (Competing with Coffee Shops)
Fine Dining	30% of annual sales (Goodwill lost when Chef/Owner leaves)
Gourmet Shops	20% of annual sales (+ cost of inventory which can be expensive)
Hamburgers	30% to 40% of annual sales (Very popular today)
Ice Cream	30% to 40% of annual sales (Higher price in warmer climate)
Irish	40% of annual sales (If higher liquor sales)
Italian	30% of annual sales (Value down today)
Mexican	30% of annual sales (Popular concept today)
Night Clubs	30% of annual sales (High risk rate lowers value)
Pancake Houses	30% of annual sales
Pizza (if delivery)	30% of annual sales
Pizza (if no delivery)	40% of annual sales
Sandwiches	40% of annual sales (Not expensive to open)
Seafood	30% of annual sales (Very high food costs)
Sports Bars	40% of annual sales (Beverage sales over 40%)
Steakhouses	30% of annual sales (Higher food costs)

Source: Business Brokerage Press and the Boston Restaurant Group, September 2015

R - Rules of Thumb

VALUING A RESTAURANT

- **FAIR MARKET VALUE**

  "The asking price is what the seller wants. The selling price is what the seller receives. Fair Market Value is the highest price the buyer is willing to pay and the lowest price the seller is willing to accept."

  There is no formula for valuing a restaurant. Each business needs to be considered on an individual basis. There are, however, certain benchmarks and valuation approaches and methods that enable an experienced appraiser to determine the most probable price for which the business could be sold on the open market

- **INCOME STATEMENT ANALYSIS**

  The restaurant's operating expenses will be consolidated into four categories to more accurately reflect industry format and to allow for more meaningful comparisons with the industry averages:

SALES	$	%	COMMENTS
Cost of Goods			
Payroll/Benefits			
Other Expenses			
Occupancy Costs			
Income			

- **CASH FLOW ANALYSIS**

  When valuing a company it is customary to analyze the financial statements and make adjustments, where necessary, to better indicate the true earnings capacity of the business:

  ADJUSTMENTS
  1.
  2.
  3. etc.
  Total Adjustments

- **VALUATION ANALYSIS**

  The following approaches and methods should be considered in the valuation of any restaurant:

Approaches/Methods	Sales/Cash Flow		Multiple	Indicated Value
Multiple of Sale		X		
Multiple of Cash Flow		X		
Sales to Investment Ratio		%		
Appraisal Databases		X		
Industry Rules of Thumb		X		

  Source: Charles Perkins, The Boston Restaurant Group

- **WHY RESTAURANTS FAIL**

  A Cornell University study noted that the first year failure rate for restaurants is between 20 percent and 25 percent. Major contributors to a restaurant's failure in today's market: 1.The concept is not well defined – you know what you are going to get at Five Guys Burgers. 2. Poor management and lack of leadership skills. 3. Inconsistent customer service and product preparation. 4. The business being undercapitalized. 5. Ownership being unable or unwilling to react.

Source: Charles Perkins, The Boston Restaurant Group

Benchmark Data

- "In 1955, the restaurant industry's share of the food dollar was 25%. Today it is 47%."

Source: National Restaurant Association Pocket Factbook 2015

- "Facts at a Glance 2015
    - ✓ $709.2 billion: Restaurant industry sales.
    - ✓ 3.8%: Restaurant industry sales increase in nominal terms.
    - ✓ 1.5%: Restaurant industry sales increase in real (inflation-adjusted) terms.
    - ✓ 1 million: Restaurant locations in the United States.
    - ✓ 4%: Restaurant industry sales share of the U.S. gross domestic product.
    - ✓ $1.9 billion: Restaurant industry sales on a typical day.
    - ✓ 14 million: Restaurant industry employees.
    - ✓ 1.7 million: New restaurant jobs created by the year 2025.
    - ✓ 10%: Restaurant workforce as part of the overall U.S. workforce.
    - ✓ 47%: Restaurant industry share of the food dollar.
    - ✓ Nine in 10: Restaurant managers who started at entry level.
    - ✓ Eight in 10: Restaurant owners who started their industry careers in entry-level positions.
    - ✓ Nine in 10: Restaurants with fewer than 50 employees.
    - ✓ Seven in 10: Restaurants that are single-unit operations."

Source: www.restaurant.org/News-Research/Research/Facts-at-a-Glance

Industry Trend

- "The restaurant industry remains the nation's second-largest private-sector employer, with 13.5 million people working in the business. Restaurants are projected to add jobs at a national rate of 2.8% this year. Over the next 10 years, the fastest restaurant job growth is projected to occur in Arizona with a rate of 15.6%, followed by Texas with 15.3%, and Florida with 15%. Nevada (14.7%) and Georgia (14.4%) round out the top five states with the fastest restaurant job growth."

Source: 2015 Pizza Power Report, PMQ Pizza Magazine

- "According to Technomic, Americans now dine outside the home an average of 4.2 times per week. That practically makes it America's kitchen."

Source: "Top 10 trends in food service industry" by Jim Sullivan, for Post-Crescent Media, May 16, 2015

- "Sixty-one percent of the 1,000 people surveyed by the NRA said they eat Italian food at least once a month, and 26 percent said they eat it a few times a year. By comparison, the other two of the 'big three' ethnic cuisines in the United States, Mexican and Chinese, were eaten at least once a month by 50 percent and 36 percent of those surveyed, respectively, and a few times a year by 31 percent and 42 percent of respondents, respectively.

"The NRA defines 'ethnic' cuisine broadly as any cuisine originating in a different country or within a specific region of the United States. The recently

R - Rules of Thumb

released study was the first the NRA has conducted in 16 years."
_{Source: "Survey: Italian remains most popular ethnic cuisine" by Bret Thorn, August 28, 2015, nrn.com}

- "A three percent drop in independent restaurant unit counts compared to a year ago brought the total U.S. restaurant count down by one percent to 630,511 units, according to a census of U.S. commercial restaurant locations compiled in the spring and fall each year by industry tracker NPD Group. Full-service independent operators took the biggest hit, with a unit loss of three percent. Quick-service independent units held their ground, NPD says."
Source:www.restaurant-hospitality.com August 3, 2015

- "For the first time on record in December, monthly sales at restaurants exceeded grocery stores sales, according to data from the U.S Census Bureau.This development was hinted at through preliminary data releases in recent months, but was officially confirmed by today's annual benchmark of Census data.

  "The gap between monthly grocery store sales and restaurant sales started gradually shrinking in 2010—a trend that was partially due to the increase in consumers buying their groceries at big box stores. However, the most striking part of the chart is the dramatic shift toward restaurants that occurred in the last 10 months. In June 2014, grocery store sales exceeded restaurant sales by $1.6 billion. By April 2015, the gap had essentially reversed, with restaurant sales moving out in front by $1.5 billion. In fact, the $3.1 billion sales shift registered during the last 10 months is nearly as much as occurred during the previous 4.5 years."
_{Source: http://www.restaurant.org/News-Research/News/Restaurant-sales-surpass-grocery-store-sales-for-t}

- "Driven by an improving economy, restaurant industry sales are expected to hit a record high of $709.2 billion in 2015. Although this will represent the sixth consecutive year of real growth in restaurant sales, the gains remain below what would be expected during a normal post-recession period due to a range of challenges. However, the restaurant industry will remain the nation's second-largest private sector employer with a workforce of 14 million."
_{Source: http://www.restaurant.org/News-Research/Research/Forecast-2015}

Restaurants—Asian (See also Restaurants, Restaurants—Chinese)

NAICS Full Service—722511 / Limited Service—722513

Rules of Thumb

➢ 30 to 32 percent of annual sales plus inventory

Benchmark Data

Statistics (Sushi Restaurants)

Number of Establishments	4,323
Average Profit Margin	7.2%
Revenue per Employee	$86,000
Average Number of Employees	5.8
Average Wages per Employee	$29,478

Products and Services Segmentation

Full-service dining sushi sales	62.0%
Beverage sales	26.0%
Take-out sushi sales	12.0%

Industry Costs

Profit	7.2%
Wages	34.8%
Purchases	27.0%
Depreciation	2.4%
Marketing	3.2%
Rent/Utilities	5.5%
Other	19.9%

Source: IBISWorld, December 2014

Industry Trend
- "And Asian in general is one of the fastest growing categories in the U.S., though it's very fragmented."

Resources
Trade Publications
- Asian Restaurant News: www.a-r-n.net/

Restaurants—Barbecue (See also Restaurants)

NAICS 722513	Number of Businesses/Units 3,500

Rules of Thumb
- ➢ 30 percent of annual sales plus inventory

Benchmark Data
- Estimated Annual Sales: Sonny's Real Pit Bar-B-Q: $1.9 million; Smokey Bones Bar & Fire Grill: $2.6 million

Restaurants—Chinese (See also Restaurants, Restaurants—Asian)

NAICS full service—722511 / limited service—722513
Number of Businesses/Units 26,000

Rules of Thumb
- ➢ 30 percent of annual sales plus inventory

Restaurants—Full Service

(See also Restaurants—An Introduction, Limited Service)

SIC 5812-08	NAICS 722511	

Rules of Thumb
- ➢ 20 to 35 percent of annual sales includes inventory
- ➢ 1 to 3 times SDE includes inventory
- ➢ 2 to 3 times EBIT
- ➢ 2 to 3 times EBITDA

R - Rules of Thumb

> Note: California restaurants seem to be receiving higher multiples than the rest of the country with the possible exception of New York City. For example: 35 to 40 percent of annual sales and 2 to 5 times SDE.

Pricing Tips

- "Don't put a lot of weight for rule of thumb on annual sales, since the occupancy cost has increased significantly in the last 3 years. It's the same for the labor cost, therefore, it is very critical to multiply with SDE. The multiple of SDE goes up for the restaurants with $100,000 + SDE, and if the restaurant has a full liquor license type 47, B&W type 41 license, catering license type 58, entertainment license, etc."
- "Most restaurants with liquor sell for 70% multiple. Without liquor the ratio drops to 35-40% of sales. Light menu a big plus. Home cooking hard to duplicate for a buyer."
- "Price can vary with cash flow and, with leased properties, the quality and length of the lease."
- "Does the owner just manage the business or is he the chef or cook? Business is more valuable if owner just manages the business."
- "Ease of operation—five-day operation worth more than a seven-day. Always look at food to bar sales as to what percent."
- "Lease should be no more than six to eight percent of sales. Food cost and payroll costs are the key items to control after lease costs."
- "Much depends on the size of the revenues and earnings; the multiples increase above $500k in sales. Gross profit should be 70% or better."
- "We never use gross sales to determine a price. Only a multiple of SDE is used. For businesses that rent their space, the average is 2X SDE with 1.7-1.8X selling faster than 2X. For businesses that own their real estate, the formula becomes 1.4X SDE plus real estate--either appraised value or agreed.
- "The main factor that drives pricing from a sales perspective is if the restaurant has liquor or is just food. From an EBITDA or SDE provable figures drive the multiple as well as the condition of the equipment and decor in addition to the lease terms. The type of food served also will be a factor; the more ethnic, the more difficult to sell."
- "The more technical the business, the lower the percentage of gross sales. Another way to say that is the more difficult to operate the business and the more intense the management involvement, the lower the multiple. Fast food sells at higher multiples than a white tablecloth restaurant."
- "Lease terms and rent are a key factor. There is a great range of complexity within the industry that also contributes to determination within the range of 2.0–2.75."
- "Pricing based on cash flow can range from 2.0 to approx. 2.5 depending on several factors: lease terms, condition of FF&E, stability and years established, hours of operation, complexity of operations. Location is always a factor but is generally already reflected in the financials. Unprofitable restaurants are marketable based on location, infrastructure in place, ABC Licensing, quality of FF&E, and lease terms."
- "In suburban markets occupancy costs should not exceed 10%. Restaurants with revenue under $1 MM are less desirable and likely treated as startups from a lending standpoint unless significant cash flow can be shown."
- "Including real estate, the price can be up to gross sales and up to 35–40%

in leased space, but debt service should always be calculated to see if it makes sense for a buyer. This is going down as restaurants have become less desirable in recent years. The higher end restaurants are the toughest to sell, as the down payment needed is greater."

- "Each deal has a different set of circumstance depending on four factors I use: (1) strength of revenue—is it growing, flat, declining? (2) profitability—is it growing, flat decreasing? (3) lease and location—is it a high traffic location or a destination location? Are there plenty of years left on the lease? How's the rent compared to market and compared to the sales volume? And are there restrictions in the lease that could hurt a sale? (4) Finally, the condition of the restaurant and its equipment. Is the place in great shape or a bit worn? Is it clean or filthy? I score each of these factors to generate an average score and relate that to an estimated value."
- "Since 95% of all restaurant sales are seller-financed, the determined price is a direct function of 4 components: goodwill (sales), lease (7% of sales is ideal), equipment, seller financing…how is it structured."
- "Occupancy costs should be in line with industry averages of 6–8%."
- "90% of the restaurants in this market are sold as asset sales and have no verifiable cash flow or books and records. These are priced according to the market which is typically between $50K and $250K, depending on type of restaurant, and if the restaurant has a hood, grease trap, etc… Rent is a major factor in determining price. Restaurants with above market leases stay on the market a long time and are difficult to sell. The value of a full 4COP liquor license in Miami Dade is in the $175K range and this must be added to the price of the FF&E and Leasehold Improvements. Neighborhood is a huge factor in this market with restaurants in the top neighborhoods selling at higher levels. Restaurants for sale with good books and records and verifiable payroll records that are cash flowing are scarce in this market and when they are available they typically sell at a premium.(3X SDE all day) There are many buyers in this market looking to obtain their VISA's. The most common type of VISA buyer that we are seeing is for the E2 Investor Visa program where the purchase requirement seems to be in the $100K range. The story of the guy that needs to obtain his VISA and is willing to substantially over pay for a restaurant is a myth. Gross sales and rent are the best value indicators to me."
- "Proper use of the SDE formula is the most accurate way of valuing an independent restaurant with sales under $3 million per year."
- "Seasonal restaurants, 'takeout,' and 'to-go' style restaurants with strong cash flow are desirable and trade at a higher SDE multiple and gross sales multiple (40%). Year-round full-service restaurants with sales under $500k are less desirable and trade at (20–30% of sales) depending on profit."
- "The multiples increase as revenue and earnings increase due to economies of scale. Cost of goods should be at or below 30%. Must look for cash that is unaccounted for and non-operating assets and expenses."
- "Multiples are the highest possible. Need to look at prime costs to make sure they are within industry averages, must normalize owner's salary, and rent needs to be less than 8% as a ratio of sales (6% is ideal but not achievable in some markets)."
- "Twice the probable yearly seller's profit"
- "Key factors are the food cost, payroll cost and rent expense as a percentage of total revenue. Rent should be about 6% to 8% of total revenue. Food costs and payroll costs vary depending on the type of restaurant. Franchised units

R - Rules of Thumb

typically sell for more than mom and pop units."

- "You need to take into consideration the location, rent, any way to bring expenses down within reason and the concept."
- "Age of equipment and F&F very important and lease. Numerous leases are priced over market rents; it is important on a feasible rent structure ideal 6%-8% of sales volume. Equipment ages quickly in this industry key in that it is maintained on a regular basis."
- "We use Owner's Discretionary Benefit exclusively because a new owner wants to know what will be available for them. The cash component of a restaurant owner's owner benefit must be clearly proved; otherwise we refuse the listing."
- "100% of gross sales if the real estate is included and 30% if in leased space."
- "Rent ratio over 10% lowers the SDE, EBIT, EBITDA and the percent of annual sales. The percent of annual sales is reduced point for point on every point rent ratio above 10%."
- "% of annual gross needs to be supported by SDE so higher prices get higher % of sales and lower %'s may have no SDE and may be just the sale of the tangible and intangible assets. Lots of other factors to consider including comps for like businesses."
- "Obtain bank statements showing deposits to help verify income. Obtain check register to verify expenses. POS numbers will usually be higher as most of the cash will show on the POS (but maybe not the deposits). Taking a really good prospect to lunch or dinner almost always pays off! For businesses conveying real estate, our 13-year average of multiples for scores of restaurant sales shows a multiple of owner's discretionary income of 3.1X which includes real estate. These same sales show a multiple of 1.6X owner's discretionary income plus negotiated real estate value. I have averaged 98% of the asking price for 13 years using these formulas."
- "If long-term lease at under-market terms, could pay premium."
- "Every state is different; you need to understand the real estate impact with the lease or property ownership, licensing laws and food trends."
- "Whether franchise or independent restaurant, location, parking, rent, number of seats, any patios, equipment condition, compliance with the city and health dept. codes; any liquor license, entertainment license etc. will affect the multiple above; if the restaurant is located in A-plus location with all the above conditions, I would value as high as 3X SDE."
- "Make sure to adjust the pay for family members working in the restaurant to current market rates for equal skill level."
- "Home cooking lowers price. Number of seats.Food cost and menu prices."
- "Asset Sales Pricing: businesses doing between $200K and $500K in yearly sales are selling at an average of 32% of yearly sales; businesses doing between $501K and $999,999 in yearly sales are selling at an average of 29% of yearly sales; businesses doing between $1M and $1,999,999 in yearly sales are selling at an average of 21% of yearly sales; businesses doing $2M+ in yearly sales are selling at an average of 17% of yearly sales. Going Concern Pricing: selling at a multiple of 1.0 to 3.0 times adjusted cash flow depending on the degree of difficulty of the business, how long the business has been in operation, the quality of the location, the terms of the lease and upside for the business."
- "Compare COG to industry standards. Rent factor vs. sales. Extraneous cost

to generate sales, e.g., music, price deals, advertising, hours of operation."
- "1. Occupancy cost should not exceed 10% of annual gross sales. 2. Watch accounts-payable aging. Restaurant operators tend to drag vendors out to 60–90 days. 3. If cost of sales exceeds 35%, there is probably some skimming going on."
- "2 times EBITDA plus value of FFE + Liquor License + Inventory"
- "Most restaurants will sell for 30%–35% of gross sales, but the bigger the business the better. Over $2 million in annual sales normally needed to make real money."
- "Adjust for exceptionally low operating hours vs. extremely long hours."
- "Restaurants with small profits are worth more as an asset sale than based on sales or net cash flow. The cost of opening a new restaurant makes over 50% of the restaurants for sale only worth what the buyer feels he would have to spend to open a new one. The cost of permits and fees has driven the cost of new restaurants through the roof, and buyers should always consider taking over an existing one even if not profitable."
- "Non-franchise restaurants are worth 30%–40% of annual sales. Franchise sit-down have been selling for 50% of annual sales, if they make a profit big enough to justify the price. Johnny Rockets are now selling for around 1 year's gross income. Franchise food not making money; before debt service, they are worth the value of the assets in place."
- "The last 100 full-service restaurants sold were sold for an average of 2.2x Seller's Discretionary Cash Flow (SDCF), or cash flow available to a full-time working owner. The range was 0.0x (simply taking over a lease for a non-profitable venture) to 5.0x SDCF (well-established community icon with unique and non-duplicatable concept). Lease rate and term, and competitive environment are the most critical. In certain geographies, availability of liquor licenses may be even more critical."
- "Due to the high cost of creating a restaurant, we are seeing more conversion sales or asset sales. For unprofitable newer restaurants (with recent build-outs and newer equipment) having long-term leases in place, we can often recoup 1/3 to 1/2 of the total cost of creation."
- "5-day breakfast, lunch, or alcohol-only bar: 40% of sales. Large full-service over 6000-sf and $1 million in sales: 25% of sales. All others: between 30–35% of sales depending on profitability and condition of facility."
- "May require reverse gross margin proofing.EBITDA formulas typically larger restaurants."
- "Minimum length of lease: 10 years; consistent sales history over three years. Assumes no major renovations required. Pricing for going concern only with market rent."

Expert Comments

"Buyer should consider the minimum wage increase for the next 5 years and factor that into the labor expenses. Sales should be in the financial statement; today's buyers are very careful, and don't want to pay for just guessing. If the seller wants top dollar, then the seller has to show the top books. Gone are those days of buying a restaurant with observation only, with no books and records. If the restaurant doesn't have good books, then I value it based on sale of assets in place."

R - Rules of Thumb

"With liquor, hard to duplicate. Without liquor, much easier to open a restaurant."

"It's all about leasing and location in pricing and marketing."

"With the overreach of government regulation and the shrinking profit margins, success becomes a daunting task that is only attained with hard work, a competent staff, a good location, and hands-on management."

"A significant portion of the restaurant/bar business is from cash sales. A buyer should verify that sales reported by the owner are accurate."

"Depending on the type of food and menu price points the competition is high. There has been a squeeze on profits due to higher labor costs, fuel surcharges and possible impact of Obamacare."

"The restaurant business is a grueling one, and most sales are motivated by burnout of the owner after some period of years. Restaurants serving three meals, 7 days a week are most difficult to sell as they are burnout-prone operations. Primary traits of successful operators are drive, ability to multitask, human relations skills, ability to analyze a business and stay on top of costs. Everyone wants a restaurant because they think it is a dinner party every evening and don't realize the commitment a restaurant takes."

"Risk in the industry is always high but in today market it's worse. The industry trends are good because the good operations survive and many of the marginal businesses are disappearing. Customers are more selective today where they spend their limited disposable dollars."

"Costs of food and labor result in small profit margin. Very competitive, but industry overall has demand from consumers. Cost of entry can be very high relative to return on investment if doing a new build-out. Recommend second generation facility for this reason. Usually cost effective to buy an existing restaurant even if paying some goodwill and then changing the concept."

"Sellers need to understand that if they are the ones who made the initial capital investment, they may not recoup their investment. I try to make them understand that when they opened it was based on returning the investment in the form of operating profits over the course of ownership (years). Market value based on cash flow may not justify a price that would equal the high cost of investment. Normally the reason for sale is something other than, or in addition to, simply making money from the sale. Buyers should ask the typical questions about reason for sale and what the seller would do if he or she were to stay longer. The landlord relationship should be discussed. Competitive changes in the area should be researched."

"There is typically a very large capital investment to open a restaurant in compliance with building and health codes. Restaurants can usually be sold, whether profitable or not, mainly because of the high cost of build-out. Asset sales for conversion are common unless the restaurant is not viable, usually due to lease or location. Industry trend—there will always be a need for restaurants as people dine out for convenience or pleasure, but cost of goods, cost of labor, and regulatory environment continue to squeeze the profit margin which makes the business challenging and risky. Ease of replication—in relation to some other businesses I would say it is easy to create and open with the exception of the high cost of initial build-out and remodeling. It is not too difficult to open especially if the infrastructure is already in place, but it can be difficult to make a profit. Operational experience is important although many enter the business without the recommended experience, which then justifies the opinion that this is a high risk category."

"Experience is not required but preferred. Successful owners can run all aspects of their operation (including the kitchen); for restaurants performing $1MM or under this is a must, whereas larger operations (>$1MM) can allocate more payroll for specialists."

"Increased food costs have diminished profitability therefore showing an overall decline in historical profit trend. A general forecast that profits will be down in the New England markets based on this past winter having some of the worst weather on record."

"Make sure you have a busy location with a lease no more than 10% of the gross sales."

"The buyer should first sit down with an expert and let the expert explain to them the pluses and minuses of buying a restaurant. Too many buyers function strictly on an emotional level. With the help of someone who knows that type of business, ask for actual food and beverage purchases. Get a list of the suppliers and call them to verify."

"A profitable restaurant is easily marketable. Verification of sales and owner benefits is important, so a profitable restaurant with good financial records is very marketable."

"Historical profit seems to be trending upwards mainly due to the stability of the global economy. In seasonal locations like Cape Cod restaurant sales on average are trending upwards mainly due to consumer confidence and more vacationers dining out."

"This is a lifestyle, not a business, in most cases. Be prepared to put in long hours until systems, policies, procedures and a reliable staff (including managers) are in place. Restaurant experience is nearly always required to obtain financing due to the high risk and historical failure rate."

"Location, location, location. Also critically important, cleanliness, customer service and food quality."

"Normalize owner and/or manager salaries. Question how many hours the owner is working. Be very careful with lease options that are at market rent. If it is a triple net lease, check and see if the building is for sale. As an example; the current owner paid $800K 10 years ago. He wants to sell as an investment property. New landlord pays $1,600,000. Taxes that the tenant must pay just went from $15,000 annual to $30,000 or more. Nothing the buyer of the business can do but he should be prepared that it may happen in strong markets."

"I will advise the buyer to make sure that he watches the activity during the busy times, to be ready to spend enough time in the business in order to manage it correctly, that this type of business needs a full time owner operator to be successful and grow the business, and to make sure that he

R - Rules of Thumb

hires a due diligence expert that is familiar with restaurants. I will advise the seller to price the business in a realistic way since most of the businesses on the market for sale are restaurants. I will show the seller sold comps in his area, and also tell him to keep all his records in order to prove the numbers during due diligence."

"If the restaurant is leased, make sure that the lease is assumable and that renewal options exist so that similar rent going forward can be obtained."

"Understand the industry plan, budget, P&L weekly. Work hard to have the best service and food; understand the numbers and what they tell you."

"Develop a good business plan and make your changes slowly. Don't spend all your money on leasehold improvements! Buy the real estate if you can."

"Experience is very important in this field. Majority of restaurants close the door or sell within the first 5 years."

"Whereas a chain is a 'cookie cutter' build-out, an independent will usually have unique features that are not so simple to replicate. Restaurant profits appear to be higher than the past few years. More sellers of the really good restaurants want to sell."

"Salability is mostly dependent upon two factors; Profit to the owner and price. The 4X and 5X multiples will not sell. Neither will a business making less than $50,000. We don't accept an assignment for a business making under $75,000."

"Buyers have a much higher risk aversion in this market which slows the decision process and many deals are lost at the eleventh hour because of second guessing their decisions to buy. There are so many vacant, fully outfitted restaurant spaces available. The ease of replicating and consequently the lower cost of getting in business is attractive to first time restaurant owners. To experienced buyers it's still location, location, location, business trends and proven SDE history."

"Lease is key: at least 5 years with at least one 5-year option."

"Historical profit trend is less important than in some other industries, because many will buy the restaurant as a conversion opportunity, although the profit trend does impact the price. It is true that many restaurants and bars do not show a profit on the books or tax returns, but this is less of a factor today due to the dominance of debit and credit card revenues and POS systems."

"The rental rate per the lease agreement is very important. Watch out for percentage rent clauses as well. A below-market lease with years to go is a big benefit. A short lease or above-market rent is a problem."

"Barrier to entry can be restricted by number of pouring licenses in town or municipality."

"Competition in the surrounding area is not much of a factor because more restaurants together become a reason to visit a location (provided they are different concepts)."

"1. Competition is daunting. Big chains can & do kill independents. 2. Very risky business due in large part to competition but also changing customer attitudes and the media. 3. Profit trends are down due to increasing labor costs and competition. 4. Location, location, location! 5. Tough to sell due to all other factors. 6. The field is growing but is being diluted by grocery and big discount stores selling pre-packaged meals. 7. Most any concept can be fairly easily replicated in menu and design. The key is in quality, quantity and service."

"You never know why one concept works or doesn't, but location is key and you're only as good as your servers!"

"Competition and risk are both high because it's rather easy to enter the industry (getting harder) and too many novices attempt owning a restaurant. The economy is definitely affecting the bottom line. Due to the high cost of recent construction, the rent factors have increased and are cutting into the restaurant's profitability and also hindering the opening of new restaurants in prime locations. In the high-rent areas of Metro Orlando the costs have risen from $25.00/S.F. to as much as $60.00/ S.F. My office sales still constitute approx.. 45% food-related businesses. The industry is still growing although more difficult to replicate than in past years."

"The hard truth is that most restaurants fail. It is often the 2nd or 3rd restaurateur that makes a location work. Part of the reason is that that party has a lower initial cost than the original party that did the build-out, purchased new equipment, etc. Buyers benefit tremendously from seller's losses."

Benchmark Data

Statistics (Chain Restaurants)

Number of Establishments	32,576
Average Profit Margin	4.3%
Revenue per Employee	$59,000
Average Number of Employees	55.3
Average Wages per Employee	$18,789

Products and Services Segmentation

American food	51.0%
Breakfast foods	15.0%
Italian-American food	11.0%
Other food	9.0%
Seafood	6.0%
Asian cuisine	4.0%
Specialty burgers	4.0%

Industry Costs

Profit	4.3%
Wages	31.6%
Purchases	32.1%
Depreciation	2.4%
Marketing	2.2%
Rent & Utilities	12.9%
Other	14.5%

R - Rules of Thumb

Market Share

DineEquity Inc.	7.5%
Darden Restaurants Inc.	6.0%

Source: IBISWorld, July 2015

Statistics (Single Location Full-Service Restaurants)

Number of Establishments	263,710
Average Profit Margin	4.3%
Revenue per Employee	$52,600
Average Number of Employees	12.9
Average Wages per Employee	$18,089

Products and Services Segmentation

Asian restaurants	25.5%
American restaurants	20.2%
European restaurants	14.5%
Other	13.7%
Mexican restaurants	12.9%
Pizza restaurants	6.4%
Seafood restaurants	4.0%
Steakhouses	2.8%

Industry Costs

Profit	4.3%
Wages	34.4%
Purchases	38.9%
Depreciation	2.4%
Marketing	2.2%
Rent & Utilities	11.9%
Other	5.9%

Source: IBISWorld, June 2015

Statistics (Premium Steak Restaurants)

Number of Establishments	2,432
Average Profit Margin	6.2%
Revenue per Employee	$66,100
Average Number of Employees	45.5
Average Wages per Employee	$20,128

Products and Services Segmentation

Classic steak restaurants	35.0%
Steak and seafood restaurants	32.6%
Other premium steak restaurants	22.0%
Premium Brazilian steak restaurants	10.4%

Industry Costs

Profit	6.2%
Wages	30.1%
Purchases	33.5%
Depreciation	1.9%
Marketing	3.0%
Rent & Utilities	6.2%
Other	19.1%

Rules of Thumb - **R**

Market Share

Ruth's Hospitality Group, Inc.	9.2%
Darden Restaurants Inc.	6.4%

Source: IBISWorld, April 2015

- "Benchmark sales per square foot for a steakhouse are $400+. Food costs at a steakhouse typically average 40% +/-."
- "Must be able to keep food costs down. Spoilage kills lots of good restaurants."
- "Ideal prime cost is 50%."
- "$10,000 to $12,000 per seat per year."
- "Need to keep rent below 8% of gross sales to have a good chance of success."
- "Food costs vary according to the type of restaurant. Many fast food enterprises can be in the 28% to 33% range; full-service restaurants typically have a higher cost of sales in the 35% to 38% area. Controlling payroll costs while still covering shifts well requires good management."
- "The more alcohol in the sales mix the greater the profitability should be; requires inventory controls."
- "The major controllable expenses are FLP >> food goal 33–34%; labor goal, including employer payroll taxes, 25–27%; paper goal 1.5–2%. Occupancy cost should be between 6–8%; above 8% you have another partner, that being the landlord."
- "We look at margins as a common benchmark. Also income per hour opened per week."
- "Food costs range from about 25% to 35% depending on concept. Labor cost is about 22–25% for quick service and closer to 30% for full-service. Having owner replace general manager can save an average of 4–5% on labor depending on revenue. Therefore, most independent restaurants net between 10–15% with an owner manager. Franchises often net 10% or less depending on royalty and management cost."
- "Too often the RE has gotten too valuable for the sales level, thus the occupancy cost to the next buyer could go higher than industry averages, thus the seller is going to have to carry back more of the deal to make it work."
- "$300-$500 PSF sales yield, $50,000- $75,000 per employee per year. Casual category specific can go up to $75,000- $100,000. Food cost should average 32-40 % depending on type food (steaks & seafood) high vs. burgers and fries and southwestern (Mexican) low and competition in the market. Owner operators are more successful than absentee owners."
- "Occupancy cost (including all NNN/CAM charges) should not exceed 10% of annual revenue. This is a very difficult benchmark in high urban areas or sought-after vacation destinations, i.e., Nantucket; however, for one to be successful, reasonable occupancy cost is crucial."
- "COGS is a blend. With high protein costs I am finding food COGS are climbing to 34–36%;, liquor costs have been constant with a target of 19–21%. Payroll target is 30–35%. In theory if the prime costs are within industry averages, rent is 6–8%; a decent operator will drive 10% in EBITDA or more."
- "Prime cost needs to be 60%"
- "It's all over the board but a 6% lease in a hot location with a good assignment clause is like gold!"
- "$50 per sq. ft. in gross revenue per month should be expected. Food cost can range from 22% all the way up to 37% and payroll with a working owner can range from 23% to about 38%."

R - Rules of Thumb

Expenses as a percentage of annual sales

Cost of goods	25% to 35%
Payroll/labor Costs	25% to 35%
Occupancy	06% to 10%
Profit (estimated pretax)	08% to 20%

Industry Trend

- "Authentic restaurant in right location will do great, since people are looking for original and unique types of restaurants. People are tired of seeing the same franchise restaurant and will want something different. Of course the taste and the service is very critical, therefore, hiring a great chef is a must."
- "High-end steakhouses will continue to feel the pressure as more restaurants enter the market and the restaurant industry continues to become more promotionally driven."
- "Flat business growth.Economy a big factor."
- "A growing brand awareness among consumers = more chain and franchise units."
- "I see minimal growth with an increase in expenses creating a smaller profit for restaurants."
- "Business is getting better slowly after the recession."
- "Hopefully with a new president, repealing of a plethora of executive regulations, and a recovering economy, the well-funded, professionally managed operations will continue to thrive...those businesses that have been struggling will fall by the wayside and get picked up by the growing class of entrepreneurs that have a solid vision."
- "Expect things to remain very competitive—tough to compete against national chains, but it can be done if management is exceptional."
- "With the amount of new products emerging from the market with flavored wines, vodka, whisky...one has to stay up on what is in."
- "Restaurants and bars will continue to be a sought-after type of business. Turnovers will remain high. As rent will continue to rise, restaurant owners will be more creative in finding less popular locations and turn to social media for marketing and to promote their locations."
- "As the economy turns, if gas prices stay down thus putting more disposable income in consumers' hands, business should continue to improve for the restaurants with low to mid menu price points. The higher end restaurants will continue to have economic pressures."
- "Sole Proprietorship. Assuming the economy continues to improve I expect restaurant sales to increase marginally in the next few years. Generally, I think the trend will be to cover higher costs with moderate price increases. Once a new administration is in place and a new effort to lessen the impact of big government is functioning, a rapid improvement in sales and turnover will become evidenced. If we continue on this big government liberal approach, then the restaurant busines will limp along barely covering costs."
- "Much the same as we have seen over the last 3–5 years. Costs will rise. Limited disposable income will cause customers to be more selective. Owners will need to become more focused on limited menus and higher sales revenues on higher margins."
- "The demand for restaurants in general seems stable and strong, but it may become more difficult for the independently owned single operators to maintain

market share when dealing with costs and regulatory environment including minimum wage increases. California is more burdensome than many other states in this regard and some franchises and chain restaurants have avoided expansion to the area. People are more health conscious and particular with their food in general and there is an opportunity to cater to this market if the restaurant can provide a good value for the product. Bars and clubs including microbreweries and craft cocktail houses are doing well."

- "There will continue to be strong demand for restaurants in general, but it is challenging for the independent restaurants to compete with the franchises and chains. The independent owner must have a way of differentiating from the many choices available, in terms of the menu, or personal service. Ethnic and specialty restaurants (vegetarian for example) are increasing in popularity. However, in my experience, people say they are interested in healthy alternatives, but they are not willing to sacrifice taste or variety when dining out, so expectations are high."
- "Overall trends were positive in the Northeast with more disposable income with positive economic growth in the marketplace; however due to the brutal winter in 2015 for the Northeast, I anticipate first quarter profits to be substantially less than 2014."
- "These have been tougher to sell in recent years,less buyers interested."
- "Pricing trends up due to inflation and national pressure on minimum wage. A shift away casual dining and fast food to fast casual dining growing rapidly. National chains grabbing more market share from mom and pop operations. Continued sluggish growth."
- "Very good in terms of people going out to eat.Poor for independents opening new businesses due to gov't regulations and shrinking profit margins. Successful chains can sustain increased operating costs."
- "Pretty steady with more working spouses and our busy lifestyle(s). Take-out or pick-up should continue to grow."
- "Good service and good food priced fairly will always be popular."
- "Increased diversity of competition and the increase in independent restaurants."
- "I continue to see a very moderate sales increase in the independent restaurant business. Sales stagnant and expenses increasing lead to lower profits. That coupled with pressure on the salary and wage front leads me to think that sales will continue to be slow and financing very difficult."
- "Lots of downsizing and specialty food operations. Menu food types specific."
- "I see the trend in the restaurant business over the next few years as a large turnover of existing restaurants as people move in and out of the industry. A major push for the large chains will continue to move into city locations and squeeze the margins and business of the independent main street businesses."
- "As global economy improves, the U.S. will continue to flourish and families/individuals will have more disposable income which should help the industry. Massachusetts is a growing area and melting pot for restaurant entrepreneurs. Many multi-unit operators (with 5 or under locations) are now entering into high occupancy cost destinations such as new outdoor shopping center developments to compete with area chains. This trend is helping grow the restaurateur's concept organically without franchising their concept. These decisions are high risk/high reward for the multi-unit operator."

R - Rules of Thumb

- "Depends on the area—baby boomers will likely eat out more as long as they can. Tourist and sunbelt areas are expected to be hot markets."
- "In Denver extremely strong; Colorado in general strong. Other markets such as Texas are very strong but some markets are still struggling."
- "It has great potential for growth when an owner has industry experience and pays attention to the competition in his area. Giving great service and serving a quality product. Treating every customer like royalty and not letting a single patron leave his business unhappy. Satisfied customers are great advertising."
- "The industry is improving—highly competitive."
- "Will be turnover as it always has been; education and hard work will pay off"
- "Less independent sales, more franchised sales, more tenant reps for lease of both 2nd generation spaces and new startups! Landlords are paying big bucks to get credit worthy, experienced tenants!"
- "There should be a small increase."
- "Restaurant workers represent a whopping 10 percent of the workforce, and a vastly disproportionate share of low-wage workers.By changing a few policies and adjusting some industry practices, the nation could sharply reduce the number of families in poverty and enhance the middle class while actually saving taxpayer dollars."

Source: "For many restaurant workers, fair conditions not on the menu,"
Boston Sunday Globe Editorial, February 16, 2014

Seller Financing

- "Seller financing is typical, since SBA not excited to loan on restaurants, but the down payment should be large enough for restaurants with ABC liquor license, the liquor license has lot of value in case the restaurant fails."
- "Seeing many cash transactions on entry level businesses."
- "Smaller restaurants use seller financing. Bigger facilities can get institutional lending."
- "Outside financing is available only for national chains and franchises or for a few exceptional local restaurants with excellent long-term financials. Most local type restaurants require seller financing."
- "If the numbers can be substantiated on tax returns, bank financing is possible; if not, more seller financing will be needed."
- "Seller financing mainly because the typical restaurant lacks the sort of financials that a bank will loan against. The average amount of seller financing is 44% of the selling price."
- "Less than 20% fit the criteria for SBA guaranteed financing. Most sales are cash or have a component of seller financing."
- "Business with real estate outside financing is more common. Restaurant business with revenue under $1 MM seller financing."
- "Often a mix of traditional bank financing (SBA loan typically), some seller financing and maybe some outside investors."
- "In today's market it is mostly owner financing for small food service businesses because the financials are not typically good. This would apply for single owner businesses; in partnerships the businesses typically have better financials. Food service operations with over $1.5 million–$2.0 million sales are generally better managed and have better financial controls and frequent financial reporting. In those cases some outside financing is possible if the numbers are good and meet standard and theoretical costs."

Rules of Thumb - R

- "Bank financing is typical of the restaurant includes the real estate. Seller financing is common when the business owner is in a leasehold position. On average most deals have an element of seller financing, whether it's a portion of the acquisition price or the inventory."
- "In our market most are cash. SBA for very good businesses, owner carry for bars is not uncommon (40-50% down)."
- "Both seller financing and outside financing are typically available—the key factor is the quality of the financial statements."
- "Owner terms, but we're seeing more SBA driven loans."
- "Bank financing is always a challenge but with restaurants it is magnified. Banks will lend to restaurants that have good cash flow per tax returns however they may require some seller participation (seller carry some debt). Have done numerous seller financing deals as well as hybrid bank/seller financing."
- "Seller financing should always be done in conjunction with a lease assignment and the length of the seller financing should never exceed the current term of the lease."
- "Average time is 60 months. 78% of my sales over $200,000 are done with some owner financing. The average amount of owner financing is 44% of the selling price. Interest these days is 2 3/4% to 3%."
- "Because the payback here is short, up to 24 months for an independent and up to 36 months for a franchised restaurant, the finance portion won't be longer than that, invariable 6-12 months"
- "Less than 5% of our transactions are seller financed due to the high failure factor. Most sellers would rather have a smaller price and all cash. Those financed deals range in the 2 to 3 year range for payback always fully amortized."
- "It ranges from 3 to 7 years, with most industry experts reporting 5 years."

Questions

- "The buyers should find out the percentage of food vs. liquor when they perform due diligence. They also have to find out about key employees, especially the chef—if he/she will stay. The condition of equipment, grease trap, dishwasher hood if needed, and make sure it is current with city and health department codes."
- "How many hours owner works, if it's more than 40 to 45; I do adjust for employees."
- "What are the sales trends and respective profits. A buyer needs to dig into the financials and get a thorough understanding of all expenses. If they don't understand, they should ask an accountant for help. What are the terms of the lease. How is the landlord to deal with. Does he take care of his property and respond to your needs as a tenant. Is the seller current with payments to the landlord &vendors."
- "Staff loyal? Menu same for how long? Personal receipt? Age of kitchen equipment? Delivery?"
- "How much time is left on the lease; are renewal options fixed or at 'market.' How many hours a week does the owner spend in the restaurant."
- "Make sure the books are accurate—a lot of cash tends to pass through these businesses and sellers often cannot support claims with reliable data."
- "The business is not for the faint of heart but can be very fun to operate. Must

R - Rules of Thumb

ask the seller to prove the figures. Are all recipes written down? Is the kitchen staff trained, or is the owner required to do all the cooking?"
- "Buyer should review all sales tax payments and actual food and liquor receipts not just the P&L especially if there is a lot of unreported income."
- "Tell the seller that no one is going to buy their business unless they can answer three questions: 1. What does the business take in? 2. What are the necessary expenses to operate the business? 3. What is left over for the owner as profit (SDE)? We cover our document, What every seller should know, to school sellers on working with a business broker. In part it states that 'selling a business is nothing like selling a house where the seller doesn't even have to play a role in the sales process.' That cooperation is mandatory when questions are asked or documents are requested and an immediate response is required 'even to the occasional inconvenience' of the seller."
- "Are you willing to finance the sale? Buy what is on the financials."
- "Learn about the landlord. Understand the cost of goods. Know whether there are promos and discounts being used to generate revenue and what may be outstanding. Know who the key employees are in the kitchen and whether any are being paid outside of normal channels. Look into past health department reports and ABC conditions."
- "1.) Is the seller in good standing with the state Department of Revenue (DOR) and Department of Unemployment Assistance (DUA)? Failure to comply can result in delay of transfer and delay in transfer of liquor license. 2.) How old/how many tons are the heating/cooling units. I advise purchasers to inspect these, as this can be a large unforeseen cost."
- "How many hours have you been working? Are all sales recorded? Are there any employees being paid in cash? Do you know of any new competition coming to the area?"
- "How old is the air conditioning unit(s)? Inspect the A/C thoroughly. This is commonly overlooked by inexperienced buyers and can be a large unforeseen expense. Read your lease thoroughly and hire an attorney to review/negotiate it. Make sure to look at the gross sales to rent ratio"
- "How can I verify the sales number?"
- "What areas do you think you could grow your business? The seller should know where he sees room for instant growth and where they should 'trim.' What are the day to day roles of each employee? Many times employees can work additional jobs to save on labor. High labor cost can eat up your profit fast!"
- "Why did you buy or start this business and what do you think of it now?"
- "How many hours the owner works, food and beverage costs and payroll costs. How long is the lease—is there percentage rent, what are the escalations in the lease?"
- "Reason for selling, history of the business, what makes it special compared to competitors, any lawsuits pending, three years' P&Ls and tax returns, List of FF&E, Personnel info (duties, tenure, pay, hrs. worked weekly, any benefits, hours worked by owner, competitors' names and est. market shares, areas for growth of the business, catering done, monthly sales for past 3 years, published newspaper or magazine articles, names of professional advisers, zoning-license or EPA issues, inventory value, business hours, etc., etc., etc."
- "What are the food costs. Do you have trouble getting help. What type of marketing do you do."
- "How much are liabilities?"
- "What does the future look like for the location? Zoning, competition, lease rate, etc."

Rules of Thumb - R

- "Percentage of cash vs. credit. Is there reliance on a key chef?"
- "Is the price/sq. ft. of the lease within market?"
- "Which equipment is leased and which is paid, and the condition of the equipment. Is there a grease trap? What kind and what size? Any key employee, especially the cook, and whether he or she wants to stay."
- "Will the owner offer financing, training, non-compete (for how many miles); is the lease assignable; is all equipment approved by the NSF (many states do not allow domestic appliances in a commercial location); are trade name, Web site, recipes and training manuals included in the deal?"
- "It is useful to know if the owner has experimented with different hours (breakfast, lunch, dinner, weekend brunch, late night entertainment). Of course the reason for sale is good to know. Any expected modifications from health dept. or franchisor? Any liquor license violations or restrictions?"
- "Is there any competition coming to the area?"
- "Ask about cash payroll. May sellers pay all or part of their payroll in cash. Check if the POS computer is connected to the corporate headquarters or franchise. How long the seller has owned the business might be a good indication that after they bought it they decided that they made a mistake and want out."
- "Work histories of staff? Staffing resources? What vendors should I not deal with and why? Suggestions for growth or expansion?"
- "Do they have good and current tax returns; are the federal, state and payroll taxes current; and does the family have non-essential employees on the payroll? Are sales taxes and gratuities being included in the sales? Some accountants will permit the operator to do that, then remove them as an expense."
- "Which equipment do you own that is leased? Do you have any gift-card programs?"
- "Does a refurbishment need to occur? Why are you selling now?"
- "What is your strongest area in your business? What part of your business needs the most improvement?"

Resources

Websites
- Today's Restaurant News: www.trnusa.com
- Muradian Business Opportunities: http://muradianbusiness.com
- We Sell Restaurants Blog: blog.wesellrestaurants.com
- ServSafe: www.servsafe.com

Trade Publications
- Restaurant Hospitality: www.restaurant-hospitality.com
- Restaurant Start-up and Growth: www.rsgmag.com
- Restaurant Business Magazine: http://www.restaurantbusinessonline.com/
- "Appetite for Acquisition": www.wesellrestaurants.com
- Restaurant Finance Monitor: www.restfinance.com
- Nation's Restaurant News: www.nrn.com

Associations
- National Restaurant Association: www.restaurant.org
- Massachusetts Restaurant Association (MRA): http://www.themassrest.org/
- Ohio Restaurant Association: www.ohiorestaurant.org

R - Rules of Thumb

Restaurants—Limited Service

(See also Franchises, Restaurants—Full Service, Restaurants—An Introduction)

| SIC 5812-08 | NAICS 722513 | Number of Businesses/Units 363,24 |

Rules of Thumb

➢ 30 to 4 percent of annual sales for independents; 45 to 60 percent for many franchises—plus inventory

➢ 1.5 to 2.5 times SDE plus inventory

➢ 2 to 3 times EBIT

➢ 2.5 to 3.5 times EBITDA

➢ For a rule of thumb for many limited-service franchises see Franchised Food Businesses, Franchises, and the specific franchise listing, if available.

Pricing Tips

- "Location and lease will affect the sale price directly"
- "Add liquor license cost & value of FF&E"
- "Food and labor costs are value drivers."
- "Not all restaurants are valued the same—each segment has their own value."
- "Analyze food costs—ideally, they should be less than 30%. Industry average ranges from 30–40%. Look for non-operating assets and unreported cash."
- "5-day breakfast/lunch: 40% annual sales; alcohol only (no food) bar: 40% annual sales; national franchises: 50% sales (if profitable also); full service over $1 million sales or facility >6,000 sq ft.: 25% sales"
- "Location and history are important. Independents are less attractive but often more profitable than franchises. The key is low overhead, and most franchises have high overhead. Considering owner financing is a must."
- "Limited-service may be lower volume than a full-service restaurant allowing for some higher rent as a % of sales. Make sure that true profitability is over 20% (near 25%)."
- "Independent restaurants priced to sell should be around 1.5 to 2.0 times EBITDA (real estate not included) and owner must be willing to consider some sort of owner financing. Franchised limited-service restaurants may go for as high as 3 times EBITDA but be prepared to go through the franchise-transfer process. You will need patience."
- "Price: twice the yearly net income"
- "3.0 x SDE and 75% of sales assumes that the owner operator can make a 25% cash to owner."
- "You arrive at two sets of figures, based on profit and sales. Price tends to move towards higher figure when a new store, has length of lease, volume increasing, and favorable market placement. Price tends to go lower if short lease, declining volume, no franchise term, equipment old, store tired, dropping profitability."
- "Gross revenue is the key, but if the SDE doesn't support the debt service requirements and a reasonable salary, then the % of gross will have to come down."
- "35 percent of annual sales for independents and 50 percent for franchises"
- "Sales are a much better indicator of value than bottom-line numbers. Different

Rules of Thumb - **R**

operators can have a huge impact on food and labor costs running the same business."
- "Limited menu a bonus; delivery and length of lease major considerations."
- "Location, lease, concept, operating manuals, recipes"
- "Normal situation—I would take last year's net plus any adjustments such as cars, insurance for owner, depreciation and interest, and make it a multiple of .72 to 2 times that number depending upon location, growth or decline of sales, age of fixtures and condition of building, then add value of FF&E, liquor license and other assets for a good value number."
- "Increase in upcoming rental amount; ease of menu; delivery and competition in the market"

Expert Comments

"Fast casual with concentrating on one item is the hottest trend; it provides a full-service meal at almost a fast-food price, and if the owner or manager ran it efficiently, will be more profitable than full service; examples: Chipotle, Schnitzel and Things, etc. This kind of operation has lower food and labor cost."

"Operations closing, which will help the ones left as long as consumers keep spending. Expensive to equip and furnish without knowing if the concept will go. Takes a lot of money to find out. Controlling overhead is key."

"Established independents often are better deals than the franchises as far as net cash flow."

"Tough to compete against national chains and big franchises"

"Most models project labor as a percentage of total sales, but I find this method highly inaccurate. I view the majority of labor as a fixed expense. A restaurant needs the majority of its staff whether or not any customers are served. As a result, unpredictable sales generate high labor cost as a percentage of sales. Sending an hourly employee home can reduce labor only slightly. Therefore I recommend treating labor as a fixed expense."

Source: "The New Restaurant Entrepreneur" by Kep Sweeney

"Highly competitive; tied to economic outlook"

"Large capital investment in equipment required. Makes resales a bargain!"

"Increasing food costs squeezing profits"

"Low-price menus helps during difficult economic times."

"Restaurants are tough work. They are usually profitable but owners tend to burn out very quickly. Too many owners have a good thing, try to expand, and then spread themselves too thin and end up failing at both locations. One good location does not assure you the 2nd one will be as profitable. Keep your overhead under control."

"Any food service is risky, however, there are always people looking to buy these types of businesses."

"By limited service, one would think of something like a smoothie shop. With limited offerings, however, keep in mind sales may hit a peak. Must keep an eye on food cost and labor cost as well as fixed costs."

R - Rules of Thumb

"Easy to open, hard to master. Very difficult to run absentee; owner must be present."

"Fast food is here to stay. People like the fast route, and fast food is it. There is a ready work force always coming up with the next generation of young people and first-time workers."

"Lots of competition. Risk factor: must give consistent product, with good quality. Catering a plus for today's business environment. Many sandwich shops add catering. Some catering-only locations with delivery, in low-rent areas with little highway exposure."

Benchmark Data

Statistics (Fast Food Restaurants)

Number of Establishments	292,273
Average Profit Margin	5.1%
Revenue per Employee	$55,500
Average Number of Employees	14.1
Average Wages per Employee	13,589

Products and Services Segmentation

Burgers	42.0%
Sandwiches	14.0%
Asian	10.0%
Chicken	10.0%
Pizza and Pasta	9.0%
Mexican	8.0%
Other	7.0%

Industry costs

Profit	5.1%
Wages	24.6%
Purchases	36.4%
Depreciation	2.9%
Marketing	2.8%
Rent & Utilities	13.1%
Other	15.1%

Market Share

McDonald's Corp.	15.4%
Yum! Brands Inc.	8.7%
Subway	6.2%
Wendy's Company	4.1%

Source: IBISWorld, July 2015

Statistics (Coffee & Snack Shops)

Number of Establishments	70,974
Average Profit Margin	6.7%
Revenue per Employee	$60,800
Average Number of Employees	9.1
Average Wages per Employee	$15,417

Rules of Thumb - R

Products and Services Segmentation

Coffee beverages	51.0%
Food	36.0%
Other beverages	9.0%
Other	4.0%

Industry Costs

Profit	6.7%
Wages	25.2%
Purchases	39.0%
Depreciation	3.8%
Marketing	3.5%
Rent & Utilities	11.9%
Other	9.9%

Market Share

Starbucks Corporation	38.0%
Dunkin' Brands Inc.	21.4%

Source: IBISWorld, September 2015

- "Prime cost (cost of goods plus payroll costs divided by sales) must remain below 60%"
- "Food costs—sub shops < 30%, fine dining 35% +, breakfast/lunch < 30%, pizza & pasta 29%–32%."
- "Food costs under 33% are critical, and labor costs under 30% are important."
- "Restaurants (non-franchise) should net 15% with professional operator."
- "2 times EBITDA plus real estate is most often used."
- "An owner-operated place should keep labor costs below 15%. Food cost should never go over 32%, the lower the better. Rent can be 10%–12% of sales."
- "Food costs should be in 28% to 30% range."
- "Again sales must be at a point that there is enough margin to cover fixed costs and then some."
- "Lower quartile per seat is $5,115, median is $7,510, and $14,293 is upper. $10,000 per seat is a benchmark for a successful quick-service restaurant."
- "Food usually maximum of 35%. Sandwich shops very popular today. Catering a plus, hard to prove without good reliable records."
- "I look for a 20% plus EBIT and 'Prime Costs' (Cost of Sales & Labor) combined below 50%."
- "Good menu can add to success. Location, visibility, and parking key ingredients for profitable business."
- "Mall fast food should be $1,000+ per square foot."
- "Ownership of real estate very desirable. Franchise stores more marketable than independents. Franchise presence in marketplace very important."

Expenses as a percentage of annual sales

Cost of goods	28% to 32%
Payroll/labor Costs	25% to 35%
Occupancy	08% to 12%
Profit (estimated pretax)	15% to 20%

R - Rules of Thumb

Industry Trend

- "Fast-casual restaurants and new quick-service chains are entering the market with narrower, more specialized menus. 'Fast casual and new QSRs have very focused menus,' said Jana Mann, senior director of menu trends at Datassential. 'They might be smaller in size. They focus on one item. If you want the best taco, or you want the best burger, do you go to someone that specializes in them, or one that has a general menu?'

   "Existing quick-service restaurants are responding by cutting menus or limiting menu additions to focus more on quality, speed and service. 'QSRs' game is being upped,' Mann said. 'They now know there is competition with these places and the whole industry is being elevated.'

   "Chick-fil-a, the Atlanta-based chicken sandwich chain, has all three dayparts, a menu that is half the size of McDonald's, and unit volumes over $3 million per location. Plus, it's not open on Sundays. In-N-Out, headquartered in Irvine, Calif., likewise has high unit volumes and a narrow menu. Raising Cane's Chicken Fingers' systemwide sales have grown 52 percent over the past two years, according to Nation's Restaurant News Top 100 data. The chain, based in Baton Rouge, LA, sells chicken fingers—and that's about it."
   Source: "Quick-service restaurants take a bite out of menus" by Jonathan Maze, August 7, 2015, nrn.com

- "When challenged on their low wages and lack of benefits, fast-food chains tend to depict their workers as teenagers saving for college, for whom the hourly receipts are a step toward a better future rather than a way to make ends meet now. Apparently, all those smiling kids wear their brightly colored smocks and golf visors with the same pride as Marines donning their colors, and are just as happy to serve. But those workers, if they exist, are a distinct minority."
   Source: "For $1 per Big Mac, a truly livable salary for millions," *Boston Globe* Editorial, February 18, 2014

- "Prepared food purchases from supermarkets, drug stores and other retail outlets will grow 10% by 2022 compared to a 4% increase in restaurant visits, according to a new forecast by The NPS Group."
   Source: "NPD Prepared Food Growth to Outpace Restaurant Visits"
   (The NPD Group does consumer market research) www.supermarketnews.com July 16, 2013

- "Slow sales, higher expenses"
- "Lots of turnover"
- "Many units with expensive leases are likely to close."
- "Less upscale dining, more family-oriented businesses"

Seller Financing

- "Five years—8 percent"
- 3 to 4 years
- "7 to 10 years with a 3 to 5 year stop"
- "Average of 5 years and prime plus 2 percent"
- "Depends on size and cash flow; 8 years is an average of our last 20 restaurant transactions."

Questions

- "This kind of operation that requires low supervision, why are you selling?"
- "What can be done to improve the business that you are not doing?"
- "Sales, purchase invoices, detail of expenses"
- "Food costs & payroll costs"
- "Who are your key people? How many hours per week do you work? How long

Rules of Thumb - R

have you been in business?"
- "Tax issues.Relationship with franchisor if applicable.Any mandatory remodeling in near future. Lease terms and length. CAM charges."
- "When was the last time you had a menu change or price change?"

Restaurants—Mexican	
	NAICS full service—722511 / limited service—722513
	Number of Businesses/Units 46,691

Expert Comments

"Chains that specialize in Mexican food do well, but not at the expense of independent competitors that serve authentic fare and outnumber them by a wide margin."

Source: "Mom-and-pop model endures in the Mexican segment," by Brad Bloom, restaurant-hospitality.com, June 23, 2015

Benchmark Data

Statistics (Mexican Restaurants)
Number of Establishments	46,691
Average Profit Margin	5.6%
Revenue per Employee	$43,300
Average Number of Employees	19.4
Average Wages per Employee	$13,473

Products and Services Segmentation
On-premises limited-service restaurants	32.0%
Drive-thru limited-service restaurants	27.0%
Full-service restaurants	22.0%
Off-premises (take out) limited-service restaurants	15.0%
Cafeterias and buffets	4.0%

Industry Costs
Profit	5.6%
Wages	31.2%
Purchases	31.5%
Depreciation	3.6%
Marketing	2.6%
Rent & Utilities	6.9%
Other	18.6%

Market Share
Taco Bell Corp. 23.0%	
Chipotle Mexican Grill	12.2%

Source: IBISWorld, April 2015

- "According to CHD FIND there are approximately 57,000 Mexican restaurants in the U.S., of which approximately 15,000 are classified as chain restaurants. As the third most popular menu type, Mexican accounts for eight percent of all

R - Rules of Thumb

restaurants in the U.S. Texas tops the list for states with the largest share of Mexican restaurants at 17 percent. California and New Mexico follow with 14 percent each. Arizona and Colorado come in with 13 percent and 12 percent, respectively.

"The average Mexican restaurant, whether chain or independent, grosses $735,000 per year. According to CHD FIND, 58 percent of independent Mexican restaurants gross between $500,000 and $1,000,000. Surprisingly, just 33 independent Mexican restaurants make up the top tier of this menu type by grossing more than $5 million in annual sales."

Source: "Mom-and-pop model endures in the Mexican segment," by Brad Bloom, restaurant-hospitality.com, June 23, 2015

Industry Trend

- "While prominent chains like Chipotle, Qdoba, and Taco Bell maintain their place in the media with hip add-ons like tofu, innovative breakfast meals and efforts to use fresh local ingredients, it's the smaller independent Mexican restaurants that are using this market to their advantage.

"In order to accurately evaluate the current Mexican restaurant landscape in the U.S., we pulled Mexican Menu Type data from CHD Expert's Foodservice Industry National Database (FIND). CHD collects, manages and analyzes data for the away-from-home global foodservice market, with information on more than five million foodservice operators around the world."

Source: "Mom-and-pop model endures in the Mexican segment," by Brad Bloom, restaurant-hospitality.com, June 23, 2015

Retail Businesses (In General)

Rules of Thumb

- 30 to 35 percent of annual sales plus inventory
- 1.5 to 3 times SDE plus inventory
- 10 times EBIT
- 12 times EBITDA

Pricing Tips

- "Excess Inventory or slow moving inventory may have to be included in normal level of inventory."
- "Occupancy—lease terms"

Benchmark Data

- "Location is a critical factor in retail and business needs to be attractive."
- "Most independent retails average around $240 per square foot but this can vary dramatically based on product lines carried and store concept, i.e., big box, boutique, etc."
- "No business lends itself more to benchmarking than retailing. Two important benchmarks for retail operations that may measure profitability, or just how a particular business may stack up against its peers, are sales per square foot and sales per employee."
- "Pat O'Rourke, the creator of BizStats, has written a very interesting—and

informative—article titled "Why Sales per Foot Is the Critical Benchmark for Retailers." Here are a few excerpts—a bit dated, but still of interest.

- "Think of sales per foot in terms of sun protection factor—SPF—a healthy SPF will help prevent you from getting burned in a retail business. SPF is one of many retail benchmarks, but I believe it's the best gauge of a retailer's efficiency, and, ultimately, its profitability. It's also easy to compute—just divide sales by the store's gross square feet. Some retailers calculate SPF based on selling feet (excluding in-store administrative, storage and other space), but this can be subjective and impair meaningful comparisons.

"SPF differs among industries. For example, a big box discounter with high inventory turnover (such as Costco) is going to have a much higher SPF than a clothing chain or sports equipment outlet. Another key element is location, SPF is typically much higher for merchants in a destination mall, than for similar stores in a local shopping center—of course you pay much higher rent in the big mall.

"An upward trend in SPF is almost always a positive sign of a retailer's health, whereas a downward trend in SPF is often a warning sign that business performance is suffering—even if the company's total sales are increasing.

"There can be many reasons for a low SPF. The first reason is obvious—the retailer simply has too much space. By having excessive space, a retailer will be adversely impacted by high fixed costs:

  ✓ Rent costs are excessive
  ✓ Labor costs are excessive, since additional floor space requires additional personnel
  ✓ Flooring costs are excessive, since additional space requires additional merchandise
  ✓ Insurance utilities and theft costs all increase with additional floor space
  ✓ "Assuming the store size is reasonable, there are many reasons for a poor SPF relative to competitors. Here are 10 primary reasons for a low SPF—these are considerations for retailers of all sizes:
  ✓ Poor product/merchandising mix
  ✓ Insufficient floor inventory (e.g., empty shelves, missing sizes)
  ✓ Un-competitive pricing
  ✓ Poor location
  ✓ Poor sales and customer service personnel
  ✓ Non-optimal store hours
  ✓ Poor store layout and design
  ✓ Cannibalization of nearby owned stores
  ✓ Insufficient/poor marketing
  ✓ Fixed consumer perception"

Expenses as a percentage of annual sales

Cost of goods	25%
Payroll/labor Costs	20% to 25%
Occupancy	15% to 18%
Profit (estimated pretax)	28% to 30%

Industry Trend

- "Always competing with 'big retailers'"

R - Rules of Thumb

- "According to GE Capital, the key trends in retail include the following:
  - ✓ Channel shift to continue: Consumers' focus on value and convenience will continue to shift discretionary spending away from traditional retail channels in favor of e-commerce and discount venues.
  - ✓ Margin pressure from accelerated growth in e-commerce: The accelerated growth and shift to e-commerce/m-commerce has diminished the pricing power of most retailers. This trend has increased margin pressure, given increased competition on free shipping and negative leverage of in-store fixed costs due to declining traffic.
  - ✓ Retail square footage rationalizing: Mall traffic will remain difficult, exacerbated by accelerated growth of the online channel on top of the encroachment by the discounters for many years.
  - ✓ Contrarily, the secularly pressured sectors, such as office products, consumer electronics, teen apparel retailers and department stores will continue to rationalize their retail locations."

  Source: "GE Capital: 2015 retail industry trends" by Marianne Wilson, February 5, 2015, http://www.chainstoreage.com/article/ge-capital-2015-retail-industry-trends

- "Retail will continue to shift to the Internet and any retail concept must contain a fully functional retail shopping site that must be managed like it is a completely separate facility. The value and business the Internet will bring is very dependent on the product line with commodity type goods being very vulnerable."

Seller Financing

- "Seller financing unless the property is also being sold."
- "Typically there is a large amount of seller financing. This doesn't mean you can get a partial loan for the purchase price but collateralization is a big issue in buying a retail operation. Most retail transactions also involve some nature of outside collateral to make a lender comfortable enough to deal with the large amount of good will involved with retail companies."

Questions

- "How long in business; trend of sales; expected new competition; why selling, product mix and industry changes, industry trade shows. Will the seller help the new owner in buying?"
- "A buyer needs to look at more than just the P&L and balance sheet. Look hard at the inventory. Do they have excessive amounts of merchandise that haven't moved? Are the racks empty? Are the payables up to date? A retail company can be showing a profit and still go out of business because of poor cash management. Does the P&L have any shrinkage? All retail companies are subject to significant amount of theft. If they don't show any losses on the P&L, then they aren't properly inventorying the store and the inventory on the balance sheet can be way off. Don't buy inventory without going in and doing a physical count at cost. If the inventory is out of line with the balance sheet, be sure the selling price is adjusted at close to reflect the proper amount."

Resources

Trade Publications

- Stores Magazine: https://nrf.com/connect-us/stores-magazine

Rules of Thumb - **R**

Retail Stores (Small Specialty)

		Number of Businesses/Units 134,420

Rules of Thumb

➢ 15 to 20 percent of annual sales plus inventory

➢ 1.8 to 2.2 times SDE plus inventory

➢ Miscellaneous Small Retail Stores:
    Tobacco Stores .... 15 percent of annual sales plus inventory
    Bridal Shops .... 10 to 15 percent of annual sales plus inventory
        (see also Bridal Shops entry)
    Souvenir Shops .... 15 to 20 percent of annual sales plus inventory
    Collectable Stores............................... 15 to 20 percent of annual sales plus inventory
        (see also Collectibles entry)
    Coin/Stamp Shops .... 5 to 10 percent of annual sales plus inventory
    Religious Goods (not books) .... 5 to 10 percent of annual sales plus inventory
    Process Serving.. 35–40 percent of annual sales

Pricing Tips

- IBISWorld includes such businesses in this category as tobacco stores, artists' materials, souvenirs & collectibles, coin & stamp shops, religious goods (not books), occupational supplies and other similar type businesses. Approximately 85 percent of them are single-owner/small family businesses. Eighty-eight percent of these businesses have 9 or fewer employees.

Benchmark Data

Statistics (Small Specialty Retail Stores)

Number of Establishments...	134,420
Average Profit Margin	3.6%
Revenue per Employee	$190,200
Average Number of Employees..	1.6
Average Wages per Employee	$14,562

Products and Services Segmentation

Tobacco product and smokers' accessories	31.3%
Other..	21.2%
Pools, pool chemicals, pool supplies and accessories	19.2%
Precious metals, coins, medals, and other numismatic items	14.3%
Monuments, grave markers, caskets and urns..	4.3%
Artists' materials and supplies	3.4%
Kitchenware and home furnishings..	3.4%
Collectibles	2.9%

Industry Costs

Profit	3.6%
Wages...	8.2%
Purchases...	53.1%
Depreciation...	0.9%
Marketing	2.1%
Rent & utilities..	6.9%
Other...	25.2%

Source: IBISWorld, May 2015

R - Rules of Thumb

Retirement Homes (See also Assisted Living, Nursing Homes)

	NAICS Retirement homes with nursing care 623110
	NAICS Retirement homes without nursing care 623312

Rules of Thumb

> "Selling price is quite varied, from $2,000 to $3,000 + per bed, depending upon the number of beds. There is no hard and fast rule of thumb which will apply because of the condition of the real estate, whether or not there are quarters for the owner/operator, and the size of the home."

Rita's Italian Ice (See also Franchises, Ice Cream/Yogurt Shops) — Franchise

Approx. Total Investment		$167,700
Estimated Annual Sales/Unit		$230,000
	NAICS 722515	Number of Businesses/Units 560

Rules of Thumb

> 80 to 100% times annual sales plus inventory

Resources

Websites
- www.ritasice.com

Rocky Mountain Chocolate Factory — Franchise

(See also Candy Stores, Franchises)

Approx. Total Investment		$126,300 to $421,400
Estimated Annual Sales/Unit		$350,000
	NAICS 311352	Number of Businesses/Units 235

Rules of Thumb

> 50 to 55 percent of annual sales plus inventory

Resources

Websites
- www.sweetfranchise.com

Rules of Thumb - R

Franchise
Roly Poly Sandwiches (See also Franchises, Sandwich Shops)
Approx. Total Investment $101,050 to $220,200
NAICS 722211 — Number of Businesses/Units 125

Rules of Thumb
> 35 percent of annual sales plus inventory

Benchmark Data
- For Benchmark Data see Sandwich Shops

Resources

Websites
- www.rolypoly.com

Route Distribution Businesses

Rules of Thumb
> 50 percent of annual sales plus inventory
> 1 to 4 times SDE plus inventory
> 3 times SDE plus inventory—3 to 4 times for name brands; 1 to 2 times for no-name brands
> 1 to 4 times EBIT
> 10 to 20 times weekly gross plus inventory

Pricing Tips
- "The larger transactions involve a multiple of sales. The multiple range is 1–2 x sales. 1x sales—sometimes even less, depending on a number of factors—is common for the smaller transactions. The larger ones are clearly in the M & A field, as these can be $5 million to $50 million also involving land, bottling plants, spring sources and truck fleets.
  "The sales that are in our ranges of $50,000 to about $2 million are in the multiple range of .75 to 1.5 x sales and usually include assets that are needed to run the business (office, warehouse, inventory, and trucks). The .75 range or even less is for the smallest of these under $200,000 with owners that are very anxious to sell. The higher multiple is generated when buyers are very anxious to buy for strategic regions and the sellers are not forced to sell.
  "Profitability, EBITDA, etc. are not factors, because the buyer rolls the accounts into his own operation inheriting none of the overhead. Often there is not even an increase in the cost of delivery. This depends on how large an operation the buyer has and the size of the business he is buying. Therefore the sales less COGS drops to the bottom line and is extremely profitable for the buyer. COGS in the water industry is only 10%–20% of sales. In coffee, it would be 33%–50%."
- "The name of product one distributes, area of operation, hours expended &

R - Rules of Thumb

weight/shelf life of product are all equally strong variables that affect the price value of a given route/distribution business."
- "The going rate on most franchised routes is about 2.5–3 times a year's net income, while non-franchised routes sell for 1-2 times a year's net income."
- "Major factors involved in pricing a route include: (1) Where the route is located; (2) What is the year & condition of the vehicle included? (3) Is the truck owned or leased? (4) How many years the route is established; (5) Is the route protected stops territory or is it an unprotected route? (6) What is the brand of the product that the route is distributing? (7) How close to the depot is the route?"
- "Franchised Routes: Approximately 2 times SDE. Note that franchised routes, which usually exist on the more consumer-recognized products, have 'Distribution Agreements' in force between wholesales and distributor."
- "Non-Franchised Routes: Approximately 1 times SDE. Non-franchised routes have no such contracts [Distribution Agreements] and they usually distribute staple items and/or non-consumer recognized products."

Expert Comments

"Easy to check out business, learn business, operate business and grow business."

Benchmark Data

- "The route must net a minimum of $175 per day after all expenses. What are categorized as 'A' routes are the most common in the market. They are one-man routes that operate out of a truck that does not require a CDL license; operate 4–5 days per week & net an income between $700–$1400 per week. The next larger category of routes is classified as 'B' routes. They may require a helper; may operate out of a CDL truck & net a weekly income of $1400–$2500 per week. The largest routes are classified as 'C' routes. They require the use of helper(s), operate out of CDL trucks & net a weekly income of more than $2500 per week."
- "Most routes sell at a multiple of 'weekly sales' from 12 to as high as 50:1 on each dollar of sales."
- "Cost of goods should never be more than 35 percent."

Expenses as a percentage of annual sales	
Cost of goods	35%
Payroll/labor Costs	08% to 15%
Occupancy	10%
Profit (estimated pretax)	10% to 20%

Industry Trend

- "Questions are on the minds of industry professionals about whether to switch from a DSD (Direct Store Delivery) to centralized distribution model, or a combination of both. The steady growth of online purchases (led by Amazon with almost $70b of sales in 2013alone) is showing no signs of slowing down. Aside from worrying brick-and-mortar retailers and emptying malls, it's also creating more awareness of the expansive array of products available to consumers. It's not just the long-haul sector that is having difficulty replacing a workforce that is beginning to age out – distribution in general is suffering from a lack of visibility for new job-seekers.

Rules of Thumb - R

"The DOT seems to modify the HOS (Hours of Service) rules for commercial drivers on a fairly consistent basis, creating both confusion and uncertainty for some carriers and their drivers. These HOS mandates are even more onerous for short-haul delivery drivers, besieged by a frenetic workday (with an average of 14 stops a day) they generally have little time for keeping HOS logbooks up-to-date. Add to this the new ELD rules coming into effect during 2015 and the high probability of more compliance changes to come, and it's not surprising that 2015 will be the year that a lot of fleets will be eager to adopt automated solutions to make sure drivers (and route planners) stay HOS compliant."

Source: http://www.telogis.com/blog/3-big-trends-distribution-2015-telogis-industry-forecast

- "Over the years there has been much consolidation within the industry, with larger regional firms buying smaller regionals, the smaller regionals buying larger local firms, and the larger locals buying smaller (under $500,000) companies. Today super-large national companies such as Nestle (which controls 50% of the US market and is worldwide) bought most of the regional brands, and DS Waters, another national water company, bought the rest. So virtually all of the mega-consolidation has already taken place. However there is still plenty of consolidation being done on a smaller basis, with transactions ranging from $50,000 to $5,000,000. There are still a number of smaller regional bottlers and distributors buying companies in this range."
- "If the economy keeps tightening, many companies will be combining with other companies, therefore reducing the overall number of routes available in the market place. A recent example of such a change was when one of the oldest pretzel companies, Bachman Pretzels, was taken over by one of the four largest chip companies, Utz. Bottom line, Bachman had 20+ routes in the metro area...they have been combined with ongoing Utz routes."
- "One difficult issue facing vending is the shrinking customer base at locations. During the past 10 years there has been a lot of consolidation in the business sector. This has left vendors with a high percentage of B&I accounts in a delicate position. They have been forced to reevaluate the machines at locations. Sometimes the drop in sales is the only notice vendors get that now there are fewer employees at a location. Despite the recovering economy there are areas where employee levels haven't returned to normal. This makes the issue of evaluating if you have the right number of machines and types of products at a location even more important to profitability."

Source: "Location Intel—How do you know who is really there?" by Emily Refermat, VendingMarketWatch.com, March 19, 2015

- "Since this business is not linked to 'high rent' real estate market, it can still flourish even though 'per store' sales are down."
- "Has been growing for the past 75 years and the trend is definitely up."

Seller Financing

- "90% may be seller financed, with the exception of some companies (like Bimbo & Pepperidge Farm) that provide financing to Buyers looking to come into their company with a route purchase."
- "Sellers often tend to be more apprehensive in offering financing in these businesses for 2 reasons: it is a low asset business with little to attach & it is very dependent upon the Seller's relationship with his customer base. Thus many Sellers (most of the time incorrectly) believe that the Buyer coming in cannot be as successful in taking care of his customer base as he has been."
- 3-10 years

26th Edition

R - Rules of Thumb

Questions
- "Look for verification of his last year's purchase history, a representation of % profit worked on, & then do a random sampling of customer invoices to confirm the % profit margin."
- "Where is route operated? Is it franchised? Hours of operation? Type/year truck included?"
- "Ask the Seller to point out problem customers & carefully check the route's receivables & parables policies."

Resources

Websites
- www.routebrokers.com

RV Dealerships

SIC 5561-03	NAICS 441210	Number of Businesses/Units 7,022

Rules of Thumb
➢ 15 percent of annual sales plus RV inventory & parts, etc.

Benchmark Data

Statistics (Recreational Vehicle Dealers)

Number of Establishments	7,022
Average Profit Margin	2.4%
Revenue per Employee	$476,500
Average Number of Employees	6.0
Average Wages per Employee	$41,390

Products and Services Segmentation

Travel trailers	58.9%
Fifth-wheel trailers	21.9%
Class A	5.9%
Class C	5.3%
Folding trailers	3.5%
Parts and services	2.6%
Truck campers	1.2%
Class B	0.7%

Industry Costs

Profit	2.4%
Wages	8.7%
Purchases	84.0%
Depreciation	0.4%
Marketing	3.0%
Rent & Utilities	0.3%
Other	1.2%

Source: IBISWorld, June 2015

Rules of Thumb - **R**

- "By the Numbers:
    - ✓ 8.9 million US households own an RV
    - ✓ There are 460 RV rental outlets across the country
    - ✓ The RV rental business is $350 million annual industry"

    Source: Cruise America, Recreation Vehicle Industry Association, www.gorving.com

Industry Trend

- "General Electric one of the RV industry's largest lenders, expects the trend to continue. "What we have seen since 2015 has begun is very strong attendance at retail shows," said Tim Hyland, president of the RV group at Commercial Distribution Finance for GE. The growth in attendance has been consistent nationwide, and it speaks to current consumer interest.
    "In a survey conducted by GE at the annual RVIA trade show in Louisville, Kentucky, in December, 41 percent of survey respondents—the majority of which were RV dealers—said they expected sales to rise 5 percent to 10 percent next year, and 26 percent expected a 10 to 15 percent growth."

    Source: "The RV industry, thriving, is getting younger," by Rebecca Ungarino, cnbc.com 3/28/15

- "The RV market continued to track upward in the first half of 2015 with total RV wholesale shipments reaching 202,653 units through June, an increase of 5.5% over the 192,065 units shipped during the same time frame in 2014 according to RVIA's June 2015 survey of manufacturers."

    Source: "RV Shipments Climb Through First Half of 2015,"
http://www.rvia.org/?ESID=preleases&PRID=1710&SR=1 8/6/15

Resources

Associations
- Recreational Vehicle Industry Association, (RVIA)—a very informative site: www.rvia.org

RV Parks (See also Campgrounds)		
SIC 7033-02	NAICS 721211	Number of Businesses/Units 6,954

Rules of Thumb

> 3.3 percent of annual sales plus inventory

> 8.5 times SDE plus inventory

Pricing Tips

- "4.2 times gross profit. I would use the same guidelines as 'Campgrounds.' The more important differences would be if the park is a 'resort,' 'overnight park' or a 'monthly park.' Do not use cap rates that are intended for a real estate investment property. Most RV Parks and Campgrounds are run as a mom and pop business until they reach maybe $600,000 in revenue and have full time managers. Also, the number of sites is not a good indicator of value or income."
- "The industry is getting more sophisticated at marketing and pricing. Many hotel/motel pricing strategies are starting to work for campgrounds."
- "Too variable for Rules of Thumb. Cap rates of 9 to 15 percent. Urban parks at

low end of cap rate spectrums. Destination parks are at higher end. Number of ancillary revenue sources will affect cap rates on destination parks—more revenue sources, lower cap rates. Parks with fewer than 100 sites are very inefficient, and value tends to be exclusively in the real estate, with little or no intrinsic value."

Expert Comments

"It is difficult to build new facilities due to permitting."

Benchmark Data

Expenses as a percentage of sales:

Marketing	10%
Utilities	14%
Payroll	25%
G&A	05%

- "Below 5,000 camper nights per year is difficult to operate the business and make a profit."
- "Expenses should run between 40 and 60% of gross profit"
- Note: See Campgrounds for additional Benchmark Data

Expenses as a percentage of annual sales

Cost of goods	10%
Payroll/labor Costs	10%
Occupancy	40%
Profit (estimated pretax)	40%

Industry Trend

- "Gradually better "
- "Affordable travel that should grow. Retired baby boomers should keep the business strong for several years."

Seller Financing

- 20 years
- 50% of all sales

Resources

Trade Publications

- Guide to Appraising Recreational Vehicle Parks published by the Appraisal Institute: www.appraisalinstitute.org
- RV Life—an industry publication: www.rvlife.com

Associations

- National Association of RV Parks and Campgrounds: www.arvc.org

Rules of Thumb - **S**

Safe Ship (See also Franchises)	Franchise
Approx. Total Investment	$39,900 to $94,800
NAICS 488991	Number of Businesses/Units 40

Rules of Thumb
➢ 40 percent of annual sales

Resources
Websites
- www.safeship.com

Sales Businesses (In General)	
	Number of Businesses/Units 750,000

Rules of Thumb
➢ 1 to 2 times SDE plus inventory

Pricing Tips
- "In this industry, there is an abundance of owner benefits such as: high-end automobiles that are not necessary to conduct business, but are definitely a benefit, extensive travel throughout the world, dining out at five-star restaurants, etc."

Benchmark Data
- "40% of your gross commission should equate to your owner's benefit"

Seller Financing
- "36 months"

Questions
- "Are all of your lines paying 5% or more? How long have you had each line? How many of your lines are industry leaders?"

Sales Consulting		
SIC 8748-08	NAICS 541613	

Rules of Thumb
➢ 33 percent of annual sales includes inventory

Pricing Tips
- "Price paid should be affected by current accounts surviving the exit of the owner."

S - Rules of Thumb

Franchise
Samurai Sam's Teriyaki Grill (See also Franchises, Restaurants—Asian)

Approx. Total Investment		$125,350 to $506,300
	NAICS 722513	Number of Businesses/Units 30

Rules of Thumb
➢ 45 percent of annual sales
➢ 1.5 times SDE

Resources

Websites
- www.samuraisams.net

Sand and Gravel Mining		
SIC 5032-11	NAICS 212321	Number of Businesses/Units 2,348

Rules of Thumb
➢ 100 percent of annual sales plus inventory
➢ 5 times EBITDA

Benchmark Data

Statistics (Sand and Gravel Mining)
Number of Establishments	2,348
Average Profit Margin	11.1%
Revenue per Employee	$470,500
Average Number of Employees	12.9
Average Wages per Employee	$61,691

Products and Services Segmentation
Construction sand and gravel	54.2%
Industrial (silica) sand	32.5%
Kaolin	6.8%
Other clays and ceramic minerals	4.2%
Common clay	2.3%

Industry Costs
Profit	11.1%
Wages	13.3%
Purchases	12.9%
Depreciation	7.8%
Marketing	0.1%
Rent & Utilities	11.2%
Other	43.6%

Market Share
CRH PLC	7.1%
HeidelbergCement	AG 5.6%
Martin Marietta Materials, Inc.	5.4%

Source: IBISWorld, September 2015

Rules of Thumb - **S**

- "At least 150,000 tons/year is the minimum usually necessary for a profitable site."

Sandwich Shops (See also Individual Franchised Sandwich Shops)

SIC 5812-19	NAICS 722513	Number of Businesses/Units 38,124

Rules of Thumb
➢ 40 to 50 percent of annual sales plus inventory
➢ 2 times SDE plus inventory
➢ 3 times EBIT
➢ Franchised Sandwich Shops
  Blimpie .... 45% to 50% of annual sales
  Li'l Dino .... 50% of annual sales
  Quiznos .... 25% to 30% of annual sales
  Roly Poly .... 35% of annual sales
  Jimmy John's .... 60% to 65% of annual sales
  Jersey Mike's .... 50% of annual sales
  Subway .... 60% to 65% of annual sales

All above Rules of Thumb are plus inventory

Average Rule of Thumb for above franchises is 46% of annual sales plus inventory

Note: In averaging the Rules of Thumb for some of the larger franchised sandwich shops, it turns out that it is just about the same as sandwich shops in general—independent or franchised. However, they seem to be more saleable than independents.

Benchmark Data

Statistics (Sandwich & Sub Store Franchises)
Number of Establishments 38,124
Average Profit Margin 4.6%
Revenue per Employee $42,000
Average Number of Employees 14.0
Average Wages per Employee $10,198

Products and Services Segmentation
Limited-service restaurants 46.8%
Cafeteria restaurants 33.5%
Takeout restaurants 19.7%

Industry Costs
Profit 4.6%
Wages 24.3%
Purchases 36.9%
Depreciation 3.1%
Marketing 2.9%
Rent & Utilities 11.9%
Other 16.3%

Market Share
Subway 65.8%
Jimmy John's 9.7%

Source: IBISWorld, February 2015

S - Rules of Thumb

Expenses as a percentage of annual sales

Cost of goods	28%
Payroll/labor Costs	22%
Occupancy	10%
Profit (estimated pretax)	20%

Industry Trend

"Although most of these sandwiches are made at home, restaurant sandwiches rank a very strong second place, such that the sandwich strides proudly on menus across restaurant sectors. On the high side, Datassential MenuTrends tracking shows that 74% of quick-service restaurants feature sandwiches on the menu. Even on the (relatively) low side, in the fine dining sector, 62% serve sandwiches on their white tablecloths or polished wood. Across the board, sandwiches are more prevalently featured than portable, sandwich-like competition such as burgers, hot dogs, and pizza (which arguably is an open-faced hot sandwich)."

Source: "Let Them Eat Brioche! Sandwich Trends Impacting the Food Industry," Posted by David Sprinkle, marketresearch.com June 18, 2015

		Franchise
Sarpino's Pizzeria (See also Franchises, Pizza Shops, etc.)		
Approx. Total Investment $246,995 to $333,795		
SIC 5812-22	NAICS 722513	Number of Businesses/Units 46

Rules of Thumb

➢ 50 percent of annual sales plus inventory

Resources

Websites
- www.sarpinosfranchise.com

Schools—Educational & Non-Vocational	
NAICS 61	Number of Businesses/Units 13,031

Rules of Thumb

➢ 40% to 50% of Annual Gross Sales
➢ 2.5 to 3 times SDE includes inventory
➢ 1.5 times EBIT
➢ 4.5 times EBITDA

Pricing Tips

- "Simple rule for schools:preschools 20% rent or bank loan, 20% other expenses, 40 to 45% staff, balance is yours.As for private schools up to 12th grade, staff is 50 to 55%."
- "Sales can be based on the number of students in the school. Today's range is from $5,000 to $12,000 per student."
- "For small schools (revenues < $5M 3 to 4 X Adjusted EBITDA. For medium schools (revenues between $5M and $20M) 4 to 5 X Adjusted EBITDA. For

large schools (revenues > $20M) 5 to 6 X Adjusted EBITDA. Accreditation adds to value. Good regulatory metrics add to value."
- "Use cash flow to determine price and what the lenders will do with that figure."

Expert Comments

"Look at books, enrollment numbers, staff expense. You do not have to go back far; look at more current data. You're buying today not 3 years ago."

"High school and college type schools are in big demand and there is a limited number of schools on the market. Trade school is a new area that is in demand."

"Both school buyers and sellers should work with M&A Intermediaries who are extremely knowledgeable in the industry. Because of the challenging regulatory environment, logic alone cannot be relied upon. Buyers and sellers need to know the right questions to ask and what information to request. Most importantly, they need to clearly understand the answers that are provided. Additionally, every transaction requires an industry-experienced attorney. There are many nuances in today's regulatory environment that require the knowledge that only experience can provide."

"Overall there are more childcare centers in the country than private schools, adult ed schools, and other types of schools. There is a market for schools."

"There are no physical barriers to entry, but creating a quality school or day care takes more than a facility. It takes quality teachers and leaders. Finding these is the real barrier to entry."

Benchmark Data

Statistics (Business Certification & IT Schools)

Number of Establishments	13,031
Average Profit Margin	3.9%
Revenue per Employee	$93,700
Average Number of Employees	2.2
Average Wages per Employee	$29,591

Products and Services Segmentation

General computer and IT courses	45.0%
Product-specific computer and IT certification courses	30.0%
Other	10.0%
General administrative training	7.5%
Specialized administrative training	7.5%

Industry Costs

Profit	3.9%
Wages	31.5%
Purchases	19.2%
Depreciation	2.5%
Marketing	9.8%
Rent & Utilities	6.5%
Other	26.6%

Source: IBISWorld, June 2015

S - Rules of Thumb

- "Student roster and valuation per student enrolled"
- "Cash flow of the school will determine price. It's hard to use per employee, per student, or per foot."
- "Some people use a crude measure to value of between $1,500 and $2,500 per student enrolled for childcare facilities in leased space."

Expenses as a percentage of annual sales	
Cost of goods	10% to 20%
Payroll/labor Costs	40% to 50%
Occupancy	15% to 20%
Profit (estimated pretax)	10% to 20%

Industry Trend
- "As the population grows so does the business. Parents need care in preschool, and education leads to better jobs."
- "The sale of schools is coming back. Buyers are looking for good investments that have a good track record."
- "There are many trends that affect transactions:
  - ✓ Currently baby-boomer school owners are ready for retirement. They have built great schools and want to divest to help support their retirement.
  - ✓ Increased regulations are forcing some good as well as bad schools to sell. This creates opportunities for qualified and knowledgeable buyers.
  - ✓ The international market is growing. International schools and investors are seeking U.S. acquisitions in international-friendly cities."
- "There is plenty of growth as the population increases. Franchises and corporate-owned schools are increasingly popular."
- "Always students who need help fall behind, need passing grades to pass"

Seller Financing
- "Smaller schools—seller financing; larger schools—outside financing"
- 5 years

Questions
- "Look at the books, look at staff cost, look at student income and make sure your debit if you get a loan can service the loan and give you a profit."
- "Do you have program kids? How is the establishment record with community care licensing? Do you provide snacks, lunch? What curriculum is being utilized and what is the average experience of the teachers? Do you have a director? What are his or her responsibilities?"
- "A buyer of a career school should ask all the questions that would be asked during any business transaction. In addition, of great importance for a career school acquisition, are:
  - ✓ Names and contact information of all regulatory bodies.
  - ✓ Updates on past and current regulatory issues.
  - ✓ Status of all approvals and dates of upcoming renewals.
  - ✓ Enrollment trends.
  - ✓ Job saturation for programs and community served.
  - ✓ How long the owners will stay on."
- "What is your market area?"

Rules of Thumb - S

Resources

Websites
- U.S. Department of Education: www.ed.gov

Associations
- Association of Private Sector Colleges and Universities (APSCU): www.apscu.org
- Middle States Association of Colleges and Schools: www.middlestates.org
- New England Association of Schools and Colleges (NEASC): www.neasc.org
- Northwest Commission on Colleges and Universities (NWCCU): www.nwccu.org
- The Southern Association of Colleges and Schools Commission on Colleges: www.sacscoc.org
- Accrediting Bureau of Health Education Schools (ABHES): www.abhes.org
- Accrediting Commission of Career Schools and Colleges (ACCSC): www.accsc.org
- Accrediting Council for Continuing Education and Training (ACCET): www.accet.org
- Accrediting Council for Independent Colleges and Schools (ACICS): www.acics.org
- The Higher Learning Commission: https://www.hlcommission.org/
- Distance Education Accrediting Commission: http://www.deac.org/

Schools—Tutoring & Driving Schools

(See also Schools/Educational, Vocational)

		NAICS tutoring 611691 / driving schools 611692
		Number of Businesses/Units 142,836

Rules of Thumb
➤ Driving Schools/Instruction
➤ 1 times SDE + fair market value of fixed assets
➤ 40 to 45 percent of annual sales + fair market value of fixed assets

Pricing Tips
- Driving Schools/Instruction
  "High barrier to entry due to increasingly higher and stricter state regulations and standards."
  The rule of thumb above applies to "learn-to-drive schools" that primarily teach teenagers to drive and pass a state driving test. It is mandatory in many states. However, there are many other types of driving schools such as: winter driving, commercial driving (trucks, etc.), race driving, etc.

S - Rules of Thumb

Benchmark Data

Statistics (Tutoring & Driving Schools)
Number of Establishments	142,836
Average Profit Margin	6.5%
Revenue per Employee	$32,800
Average Number of Employees	2.0
Average Wages per Employee	$13,414

Products and Services Segmentation
Other schools	46.2%
Exam preparation and tutoring	45.5%
Driving schools	8.3%

Industry Costs
Profit	6.5%
Wages	40.4%
Purchases	14.8%
Depreciation	3.0%
Marketing	6.7%
Rent & Utilities	9.3%
Other	19.3%

Source: IBISWorld, December 2014

Schools—Vocational & Training

(See also Schools—Educational/Non-Vocational)

NAICS 611210

Rules of Thumb

➢ 75 to 100 percent of annual sales plus inventory
➢ 2 to 4 times SDE plus inventory
➢ 1.5 times EBIT
➢ 3 to 5 times EBITDA

Pricing Tips

- "Home based franchise sells for much higher multiple of 4 or above, if it's generating $300K+ in revenue. Educational franchise that allows office location contributes to higher SDE. Customer base of 4–14 years is highly preferred due to high demand."
- "Accreditation and Title IV funding provides for higher pricing."
- "Pricing is all over the board because of the size of a facility. The larger the school, the more the owners profit."
- "Value is driven by type of program (longer, more expensive programs are more valuable), enrollment, and enrollment growth."

Expert Comments

"Great industry with room to grow. The childcare, private school and adult education industry is on the move."

Rules of Thumb - S

Benchmark Data

Statistics (Trade and Technical Schools)
Number of Establishments	8,282
Average Profit Margin	9.4%
Revenue per Employee	$98,000
Average Number of Employees	16.2
Average Wages per Employee	$38,673

Products and Services Segmentation
Other professional development programs	57.6%
Flight training programs	18.5%
Cosmetology and barber schools	14.5%
Apprenticeship training programs	9.4%

Industry Costs
Profit	9.4%
Wages	39.1%
Purchases	13.3%
Depreciation	3.2%
Marketing	3.4%
Rent & Utilities	10.8%
Other	20.8%

Source: IBISWorld, March 2015

- "Sales per license cap can range from $6,000 to $ 14,000. An example: a 100-student licensed school could sell for as much as $1.4 million. Most schools sell based on Cash Flow."

Expenses as a percentage of annual sales
Cost of goods	10% to 20%
Payroll/labor Costs	35% to 40%
Occupancy	05%
Profit (estimated pretax)	20% to 30%

Industry Trend
- "Trend is going up in terms of new type of businesses. Trend is going down if the franchise does not innovate and provide new services."
- "Generally increasing revenues"

Seller Financing
- "Most of the time seller finance due to lack of tangible assets"
- 10 years

Questions
- "Customer retention rate; method of new customer acquisition; employee qualifications, turnaround and hiring process."
- "Is the school accredited and what is the status?"

S - Rules of Thumb

Resources

Websites
- RWM provides a database of private post-secondary vocational schools in all 50 states: www.schoolsforsale.com

Sears Carpet and Upholstery Care & Home Services *Franchise*
(See also Carpet Cleaning, Franchises)

Approx. Total Investment		$25,960 to $191,550
	NAICS 561740	Number of Businesses/Units 295

Rules of Thumb
➢ 35 percent of annual sales plus inventory

➢ Note: Sears offers three home service franchises to choose from: Carpet & Upholstery Cleaning; Air Duct Cleaning & Indoor Air Quality; Garage Solutions (Doors, Repairs, Repairs, etc.). We believe that the rule of thumb above would apply to any of the three franchises.

Resources

Websites
- www.searsclean.com
- www.ownasearsfranchise.com

Secretarial Services

	NAICS 561410	

Rules of Thumb
➢ 50 percent of annual revenues includes inventory

Security Services/Systems (See also Guard Services)

SIC 7382-02	NAICS 561621	Number of Businesses/Units 78,869

Rules of Thumb
➢ 50 percent of annual sales includes inventory

➢ 2 times SDE includes inventory

➢ 3 times EBIT

➢ 4 times EBITDA

➢ 24 to 28 times monthly revenue based on an average $25 mo. per account plus inventory

Rules of Thumb - S

Pricing Tips

- "Typically, an alarm company sells for a multiple of Recurring Monthly Revenue (RMR), plus any additional assets the company may own. In addition, the multiple of RMR may vary for contract vs non-contracted customers. Typically, contracted customers generate between 33x–36x RMR and non-contracted will get between 10x–25x RMR."
- "Weighted monthly billing times 4"

Expert Comments

"An alarm company can be run from any location because all work is completed at a customer's home or business. They are very marketable and are not easy to replicate. The hurdle is that a new owner needs to hold a Class C & D license for low-voltage wiring, which is a 3–5 year process to obtain."

Benchmark Data

Statistics (Security Alarm Services)

Number of Establishments	62,358
Average Profit Margin	4.6%
Revenue per Employee	$127,800
Average Number of Employees	2.8
Average Wages per Employee	$35,574

Products and Services Segmentation

Residential security alarm system services with monitoring	48.0%
Nonresidential security alarm system services with monitoring	26.6%
Nonresidential security system and lock installation without monitoring	16.2%
Residential security system and lock installation without monitoring	9.2%

Major Market Segmentation

Residential clients	47.9%
Business and commercial clients	40.1%
Government clients	12.0%

Industry Costs

Profit	4.6%
Wages	27.8%
Purchases	35.1%
Depreciation	1.5%
Marketing	2.0%
Rent & Utilities	4.5%
Other	24.5%

Market Share

ADT Security Services Inc.	15.6%

26th Edition

S - Rules of Thumb

Number of Employees | Share

Number of Employees	Share
1–4	61.6%
10–19	10.9%
20–99	7.1%
100–499	1.1%

Source: IBISWorld, June 2015

Statistics (Security Services)

Number of Establishments	16,511
Average Profit Margin	4.3%
Revenue per Employee	$39,900
Average Number of Employees	47.8
Average Wages per Employee	$26,122

Products and Services Segmentation

Security guard services for buildings and grounds	67.0%
Investigation services	16.3%
Armored vehicle services	6.9%
Other services	6.2%
Security guard services for special events	3.6%

Major Market Segmentation

Corporations	29.3%
Financial institutions	19.2%
Government clients	18.5%
Residential and other	17.8%
Retail and leisure	15.2%

Industry Costs

Profit	4.3%
Wages	65.8%
Purchases	8.6%
Depreciation	0.6%
Marketing	1.3%
Rent & Utilities	3.8%
Other	15.6%

Market Share

Securitas AB	11.1%
G4S PLC	7.8%
AlliedBarton Security Services LLC	6.0%

Source: IBISWorld, September 2015

Dealers' Revenue Segmented by Business Services

Monitoring	49%
Sales/Installation	30%
Service contracts	9%
Non-contracted service	5%
Test & inspection	3%
Other	2%
Hosted & managed services	1%

Source: "Performance Remains Solid" by Laura Stepanek, sdmmag.com, May 8, 2015

Rules of Thumb - S

Expenses as a percentage of annual sales

Cost of goods	40%
Payroll/labor Costs	40%
Occupancy	10%
Profit (estimated pretax)	10%

Industry Trend

- "ASIS International and the Institute of Finance and Management (IOFM) jointly released an extensive benchmark study of the private security industry's expansion over the past decade and its projected future growth. 'The United States Security Industry: Size and Scope, Insights, Trends, and Data' presents an analysis of the security products and services market, as well as the industry's personnel market.

  "Key highlights and top line results of the report are:
    - ✓ The $350 billion market breaks out to $282 billion in private sector spending and $69 billion in federal government spending on homeland security.
    - ✓ Operational (non-IT) private security spending is estimated to be $202 billion with expected growth of 5.5 percent in 2013; IT-related private security market is estimated at $80 billion with growth of 9 percent projected in 2013.
    - ✓ Number of full-time security workers is estimated to be between 1.9 million and 2.1 million.
    - ✓ Private detective/investigator is one of the fastest-growing occupations, with anticipated growth of 23 percent projected through 2020; several IT positions are anticipated to grow 22 percent through 2020."

    Source: "Groundbreaking Study Finds U.S. Security Industry to be $350 Billion Market Integrators Vital to End User's Decision-Making" www.sdmag.com, August 20, 2013

Seller Financing

- "There are industry specific financing companies that will hold contracted accounts as collateral. Also the SBA has gone 10 years because of the RMR."
- "3 to 5 years and an average of 20 to 50 percent of transaction value financed by seller"

Questions

- "1. Do they own the central station? 2. If not, do they own the phone lines that connect to central station? 3. What % of their customers are contracted?"
- "What are the contract terms? How long have you had this account? Buyers do not like government contracts."
- "Type of guard services and customer list. Most guard companies have one major client."

Resources

Websites
- The American Society for Industrial Security (ASIS): www.asisonline.org

Trade Publications
- www.sdmmag.com

S - Rules of Thumb

Associations
- National Burglar & Fire Alarm Association: www.alarm.org
- Security Industry Association (SIA): www.siaonline.org

Self Storage (Mini Storage)

	NAICS 531130	Number of Businesses/Units 54,419

Rules of Thumb
> 1 times EBITDA

Pricing Tips
- "Very few buyers or appraisers will count revenues in excess of 90% of potential rents, except in very unusual circumstances.
  "What are We Selling—Dirt, Bricks or Income? The reality is that while the dirt and bricks will be transferred by the deed, it is the income stream that creates the value in self-storage properties.
  "Operating Expenses: It is considered a rule of thumb that operating expenses generally run between 35%–45% with many in the range of 40%. However, this is just a rule of thumb, and if your project falls out of this range further analysis may be required.
  Typical Operating Expense Categories:
  - ✓ Real estate taxes
  - ✓ On-site salaries & benefits
  - ✓ Property insurance
  - ✓ Utilities
  - ✓ Repairs and maintenance
  - ✓ Off-site management fees
  - ✓ Marketing & advertising
  - ✓ Office expenses
  - ✓ Capital reserves

  Source: "Market Monitor," June 2015 by Ben Vestal, President of the Argus Self Storage Sales Network
- "These are difficult because they are often a means of holding land until it reaches the point where it is more profitable to redevelop it for another use. Most buyers look for a cash on cash return of about 20% on the amount they must invest to purchase the property compared to the purchase price/financing that can be obtained."
- "Key factors are vacancy and turnover of units. Buyers want to get at least a 20% cash-on-cash return."
- "Most involve the real estate"
- "Pricing is driven by capitalization rates and expense ratios."

Cap Rate Adjustments
The little chart that follows is about the best thing we have seen in pricing a business. It outlines specific business issues and assigns them an adjustment to the cap rate. What is so good about this chart is the specific areas it covers and that it essentially assigns a rating to each one that impacts the valuation or pricing of each business.

Rules of Thumb - **S**

Item	9.50 - 10.00	10.00 - 11.00	11.00 - 11.50
Occupancy (last 2 years)	95%-100%	90%-95%	<90%
Rates (last 2 years)	Continuous Rise	Steady	Falling
Size	>45,000	30,000-45,0000	<30,000
Competition (3 mile radius)	None	One	More than One
Competition's Vacancy	95%-100%	90%-95%	<90%
Surrounding Area	Growing Metro	Large City	Rural
Density (5 mile radius)	>200,000	100,000-200,000	<100,000
Median Household Income	Above Average	Average	Below Average
Manager	Full-time	Full-time	Other
Records (last 3 years)	Computerized & Professionally Audited	Computerized	Other
Computer System	Computers & SS Accounting Software	Computers	None
Construction	Concrete or Brick	Combination Brick & Metal	Metal
Maintenance	Pristine	Little Deferred Maintenance	Modest Deferred Maintenance
Security	Full Gate & Card Access	Full Gate	Other
Access	Very Direct	Clear, but Not Direct	Difficult
Visibility	Can see Sign & Facility	Can see Sign & Entrance	Can see Sign only
Drives	Concrete	Paved	Gravel

Source: Argus Real Estate, Inc., Denver, CO

Note: This is from an excellent article by Michael L. McCune, Cap Rates and Sales Prices. For more information visit www.selfstorage.com—an excellent site. The above is a bit dated but still of interest.

- "You can look at it a couple of different ways. It depends on your location; but here in southern Indiana, mini-storage facilities are being appraised based upon the number of units. Age, condition and income are also looked at. Our appraiser just today told us that they are ranging from $3,000 to $3,500 per unit. So your 131-unit facility would appraise for around $393,000 if it were located here.

  "Another way to figure out what your potential income will be: if you are totally full, then multiply that number by 60 to 75 percent, because of the reality of occupancy. Use those numbers to figure out what your income/expense ratio will be. Your income should be at least 1.25 over your debt service (if it's not, then you're paying too much for the property). That extra 25 percent will help cover vacancies, utilities, labor, etc."

  Source: www.autocareforum.com

- "We sold a 195-unit mini-storage in Idaho last year. It had annual gross receipts of $105,000 and an annual net cash flow of $80,000. It sold for $640,000 with $235,000 cash down payment and the balance at 8.3 percent over 15 years.

  "We have another mini-storage in the process of being sold. It looks like it will go for $500,000 with $150,000 cash down payment, the balance over 20 years at 8.5 percent. It has annual gross income of $70,000 and cash flow debt

S - Rules of Thumb

service of $61,000.

"I believe that a cash-on-cash return of 15 percent to 20 percent is required to sell one of these mini-storage projects. A minimum of 15 percent seems to be required."

Expert Comments

"Storage units are a great way to warehouse land until the highest and best use changes."

"This is a real-estate purchase with a business element attached to it. The value of the underlying real estate controls a large part of the value of the property. Management is more important than most people realize."

Benchmark Data

Statistics (Storage and Warehouse Leasing)

Number of Establishments	54,419
Average Profit Margin	36.8%
Revenue per Employee	$214,400
Average Number of Employees	2.5
Average Wages per Employee	$21,520

Products and services Segmentation

10-by-10-foot storage spaces	16.0%
10-by-15-foot storage spaces	15.3%
Other	15.3%
10-by-20-foot storage spaces	13.7%
10-by-30-foot storage spaces	11.3%
20-by-40-foot storage spaces	10.5%
Five-by-10-foot storage spaces	9.1%
Five-by-15-foot storage spaces	8.8%

Major Market Segmentation

Long-term residential customers	41.1%
Short-term residential customers	32.0%
Commercial firms	17.1%
Students	4.7%
Military	4.0%
Seasonal Visitors	1.1%

Industry Costs

Profit	36.8%
Wages	12.9%
Purchases	4.5%
Depreciation	14.7%
Marketing	2.7%
Rent & Utilities	13.0%
Other	15.4%

Market Share

Public Storage Inc.	8.6%

Source: IBISWorld, April 2015

Rules of Thumb - **S**

- Self Storage Industry Fact Sheet
    - ✓ "The self storage industry has been one of the fastest-growing sectors of the United States commercial real estate industry over the period of the last 40 years.
    - ✓ There are now over 48,500 "primary" self storage facilities in the United States as of year-end 2014; another 4,000 are 'secondary' facilities ('primary' means that self storage is the 'primary' source of business revenue—U.S. Census Bureau).
    - ✓ Total self storage rentable space in the US is roughly 2.5 billion square feet [more than 210 million square meters]. That figure represents more than 78 square miles of rentable self storage space, under roof—or an area well more than 3 times the size of Manhattan Island (NY).
    - ✓ The distribution of U.S. self storage facilities (Q2-2015) is as follows: 32% urban, 52% suburban and 16% rural.
    - ✓ The average revenue per square foot varies from facility to facility; however, here are the data for Q2 2015: $1.25 PSF for a non-climate controlled 10 x 10 unit and $1.60 PSF for a climate controlled 10 x 10 unit.
    - ✓ U.S. self storage facilities employed more than 170,000 persons, or an average of 3.5 employees per facility.
    - ✓ The average (mean) size of a 'primary' self storage facility in the US is approximately 56,900 square feet.
    - ✓ Occupancy rates for self storage facilities as of Q2 2015 were 90% (percentage of units rented per facility) up from 86.8% at year-end 2013.
    - ✓ Of over 10,000 facilities surveyed, the mean facility size is 546 units and the median facility size is 517 units.
    - ✓ About 13% of all self storage renters say they will rent for less than 3 months; 18% for 3-6 months; 18% for 7–12 months; 22% for 1–2 years; and 30% for more than 2 years.
    - ✓ Some 47% of all self storage renters have an annual household income of less than $50,000 per year; 63% have an annual household income of less than $75,000 per year.
    - ✓ The top-5 self storage companies, including 4 real estate investment trusts (Public Storage, Extra Space, Sovran and CubeSmart) plus U-Haul (a public company/non-REIT), own, operate and/or manage some 5,600 self storage facilities, or about 11.5% of all U.S. facilities. Several public companies are now offering third-party management of facilities owned by other investors. Hundreds of facilities are now being managed by the three public companies that have moved into this service area.
    - ✓ In addition to the public companies in the industry (above), there are more than 150 privately held firms that own and operate 10 or more self storage facilities. In addition, there are some 4,000 firms that own and operate from 2–9 self storage facilities. Lastly, there are more than 26,000 firms that own and operate just one facility."

Source: 2015–2016 Self Storage Industry Fact Sheet, 7/1/2015

S - Rules of Thumb

Sample facility

"Size	40,000 SF
Average Rent	$71/month
Rent/SF	$8.52/yr.
Current Occupancy	88%
Market Occupancy	70%
Potential Rent	$341,000
Rents Collected @ 88%	$300,000/yr.
Expenses	$100,000
Net Operating Income	$200,000/yr.
Value @ 9.5	$2,100,000
Loan Amount @ 75%	$1,575,000
Debt Service @ 6.5%	$128,000/yr."

Source: "The State of Self Storage Real Estate" by Michael L. McCune, Argus Self-Storage Sales Network

Expenses as a percentage of annual sales

Cost of goods	0
Payroll/labor Costs	0
Occupancy	0
Profit (estimated pretax)	05%

Industry Trend

- "This is more apparent today than ever before as we are seeing large operators winning business away from smaller operators whether by pricing, advertising or property amenities. I would also note that in general, the large operators are able to get a rent premium over the small operators that have similar properties in the same market. This leads me to believe that the self-storage industry has reached a crossroads and operators need to make the necessary adjustments in order to compete as the industry continues to mature.

"The effects of the continuing low interest rate environment have had a very dramatic impact on self-storage investments over the last six to nine months. The most obvious and positive result is that owners are able to sell their properties at close to historically high prices once again (reflecting back on 2006–2007) or refinance and keep a larger share of their hard-earned income by paying less to the lenders."

Source: "Extraordinary Times—How Long Will They Last?" by Ben Vestal, www.argusselfstorage.com

Seller Financing

- 10 to 15 years

Questions

- "Who manages the site and are they willing to stay on. Can existing financing be assumed."
- "Occupancy and waiting list"
- "Management turnover"

Resources

Websites

- Argus Self-Storage Sales Network: www.argusselfstorage.com

Rules of Thumb - **S**

Trade Publications
- Mini Storage Messenger—excellent resources: www.selfstoragenow.com

Associations
- Self Storage Association—an excellent site with lots of information: www.selfstorage.org

		Franchise
Senior Helpers (See also Franchises, Home Health Care—Care Giving)		
Approx. Total Investment		$81,300 to $117,300
	NAICS 621610	Number of Businesses/Units 265

Rules of Thumb
> ➤ 40 to 45 percent

Resources

Websites
- www.seniorhelpers.com

Service Businesses (In General)

Rules of Thumb
> ➤ 35 percent to 50 percent of annual revenues [sales] plus inventory; however it is not unusual for service businesses to sell for a much higher figure
> ➤ 72 percent of annual sales plus inventory
> ➤ 2 times SDE

Pricing Tips
- "One of the most important factors is determining how replaceable the owner is, and how much of the revenue the owner generates him/herself."
- "Consider the last 3 to 5 years—is it an up or down trend? Is the business expandable or is it at its peak?"
- Valuation Issues for Service Companies
  "On the plus side, almost all service companies have recurring revenue. Some, like funeral homes, have very little, while others, like Paychex (payroll service), Cintas (uniform rental) and Dun & Bradstreet (credit reports) have a lot of recurring revenue with each customer. Another plus is that service companies usually have modest capital equipment requirements resulting in a high return on assets. Expansion and geographic roll-outs like retail and restaurant chains can be readily expedited. Additionally, service companies are less impacted by foreign competition. From a macro-economic view, the U.S. had a $65 billion service trade surplus in 2002 while the U.S. had a large manufactured goods deficit in 2002. And, from a competitive point of view, large service companies can source services off-shore just as manufacturing companies have done in order to reduce costs. For example, the annual cost for a computer-related employee in the U.S. is $61,600 compared to India at $5,800.

S - Rules of Thumb

"On the minus side, service companies are largely dependent on their management team and employees. They are, by and large, the assets of the company... so imagine what would happen to the value of an architectural firm or a law firm if the people walked off their job. Since labor is the major expense of service companies, they are more difficult to substantially increase sales (or scale-up) compared to manufacturing companies where labor might only represent 20% of sales.

"From a service owner's perspective, rarely can they fully cash-out at closing or rarely can they walk away from the business at closing, as service companies are highly relationship driven... not only with the customers but with the employees. Further, unlike some small niche manufacturers, many service companies need to reach a higher revenue threshold of $10+ million to prove the company's viability of not being dependent on just a few key people or a few key customers.

"The valuation multiples vary widely across the various sectors and equally divergent are the various structures of the transactions. Of course, the critical issues in the valuation of service companies include the extent of their profitability, relative size, proprietary nature of the service firm's capabilities and the potential growth. Conventional wisdom dictates that service firms are valued between .5 x to 1.0 x revenues, but a closer look at the following sectors shows a wide differential of valuation metrics based on Last Twelve Months (LTM) of revenues and EBITDA."

Expert Comments

"Competition and the industry trends (growing or constant) are important for calculating the ROI on the intangible part."

ServiceMaster Clean — Franchise
(See also Franchises, Janitorial Services, Maid Services, etc.)

Approx. Total Investment		$48,610 to $176,335
	NAICS 561720	Number of Businesses/Units 3,000

Rules of Thumb
➢ 55 to 60 percent of annual sales plus inventory

Resources

Websites
- www.ownafranchise.com

Servpro — Franchise
(See also Franchises, Janitorial Services, Maid Services, etc.)

NAICS 561720	Number of Businesses/Units 1,000

Rules of Thumb
➢ 90 to 95 percent of annual sales plus inventory

Resources

Websites
- www.servpro.com

Shoe Stores

SIC 5661-01	NAICS 451110	Number of Businesses/Units 31,652

Rules of Thumb
> 15 to 20 percent of annual sales plus inventory

Benchmark Data

Statistics (Shoe Stores)
Number of Establishments	31,652
Average Profit Margin	4.1%
Revenue per Employee	$167,500
Average Number of Employees	6.9
Average Wages per Employee	$18,774

Products and Services Segmentation
Women's shoes (not including athletic)	32.3%
Men's athletic shoes	22.5%
Children's shoes	15.0%
Men's shoes (not including athletic)	14.8%
Women's athletic shoes	11.1%
Slippers and other shoes	4.3%

Industry Costs
Profit	4.1%
Wages	11.2%
Purchases	55.4%
Depreciation	0.9%
Marketing	2.3%
Rent & Utilities	10.4%
Other	15.7%

Market Share
Foot Locker Inc.	14.5%
Designer Shoe Warehouse Inc.	7.3%
Payless ShoeSource	5.8%
Brown Shoe Company Inc.	5.5%

Source: IBISWorld, July 2015

Industry Trend
- "The U.S. market for athletic shoes is one of the strongest of the global markets. However, U.S.-based companies and their competitors have long been multi-national firms operating in diverse overseas markets selling footwear and also athletic apparel in increasingly competitive markets. The athletic footwear is highly dependent on fashion trends, customer preferences

S - Rules of Thumb

and other fashion-related factors. Many of the industry's highest-margin products are sold to young males between the ages of 12 and 25 and are subject to frequent shifts in fashion trends."

Source: "Athletic Shoe Industry Analysis" by Robert Shaftoe, Demand Media
http://smallbusiness.chron.com/athletic-shoe-industry-analysis-74098.html

Resources

Associations
- National Shoe Retailers Association: www.nsra.org

Short Line Railroads
NAICS 482112

Pricing Tips
- "These are highly regulated businesses that, as businesses, tend to be basically real estate businesses. Many buyers tend to be hobby buyers. Historically, buyers have grossly overpaid to purchase these businesses, then not exploited the potential of the real estate business. Buyers are almost always industry related in some way. Sellers are mainly large operating corporations who cannot operate these units economically."
- "Buyers are quoting 1.6 to 1.85 times gross revenues and in most cases it is a seller's market."
- "If it's for sale, that pretty much guarantees that someone with expertise has determined that they cannot operate it profitably and/or make the capital investments required. Sellers have usually deferred capital investment and maintenance to an extreme degree prior to sale."

Industry Trend
- "The U.S. economy continues to grow, and strong demand for rail service demonstrates that the freight rail industry is integral to this growth. By providing cost-effective transportation of goods, from lumber to oil to auto parts, freight rail is playing a central role in positive economic trends—including rising gross domestic product, improving employment statistics and low gasoline prices.

  "Freight rail is ready for this and more. In 2015, the nation's major freight railroads plan to spend an estimated $29 billion—which would set an annual record—to build, maintain and grow the rail network. This private spending will go to expenditures like new equipment and locomotives, installation of new track and bridges, the raising of tunnels and new technology used to keep America's rail network the best in the world.

  "With the right federal policies in place, measures that support market pricing and do not stifle railroad investment, the world's best rail network is on track to be even better."

  Source:"For 2015, Freight Rail Will Carry the Economy,"
https://www.aar.org/policy/2015-outlook

- "America's short line railroads provide fuel savings and environmentally friendly shipping for small businesses and communities around the country. One freight rail car can carry a ton of cargo 436 miles on just one gallon of fuel. Short line railroads take the equivalent of nearly 33 million truck loads off the

Rules of Thumb - **S**

highways, saving the country over $1.4 billion annually in highway repair costs and improving highway safety and congestion."

Source: American Short Line and Regional Railroad System (ASLRRA)

Shuttle Services & Special Needs Transportation

NAICS shuttle services 485999 / special needs transportation 485991

Rules of Thumb
➢ 3 times EBITDA plus the value of the vehicles

Benchmark Data

Statistics (Airport Shuttle Operators)
Number of Establishments	4,022
Average Profit Margin	7.7%
Revenue per Employee	$61,900
Average Number of Employees	2.6
Average Wages per Employee	$24,944

Products and Services Segmentation
Local shuttle services for business	53.5%
Local shuttle services for leisure	41.6%
Long-distance shuttle services	3.2%
Other	1.7%

Industry Costs
Profit	7.7%
Wages	40.1%
Purchases	29.1%
Depreciation	4.5%
Marketing	1.1%
Rent & Utilities	4.6%
Other	12.9%

Source: IBISWorld, April 2015

Signarama (See also Franchises, Manufacturing—Signs, Sign Companies) — Franchise

Approx. Total Investment		$168,000–$172,000
	NAICS 339950	Number of Businesses/Units 875

Rules of Thumb
➢ 55 to 60 percent of annual sales plus inventory

Resources

Websites
- www.signarama.com

26th Edition

S - Rules of Thumb

Sign Companies (See also Manufacturing—Signs)

NAICS 339950

Rules of Thumb
- 48 percent to 50 percent of annual sales includes inventory
- 2.5 times SDE includes inventory
- 3.5 to 5 times EBITDA

Pricing Tips
- "Relative to annual revenue—critical to have a 3rd party certified valuation of the business & commercial real estate when optional."
- "Businesses with gross sales of over $1M typically will get slightly higher #'s than the rule of thumb. Technology can have an impact on the sales price. Large format printers and flatbed printers have become more commonplace and are expected to be in house by many buyers."
- "Margins do vary significantly in this industry. The product is custom made, and there are a variety of products that can be produced, with margins varying within the product ranges. So, one company that is producing one product 'niche' within the category may be more profitable than another company focusing on a different product 'niche.'"
- "Most sign companies are small independents—SDE is a better calculation than EBIT or EBITDA. Inventory is not usually an excessive number, and usually included as part of a 2.5–3 x multiple of SDE."

Expert Comments

"Difficulty in selling operations—real estate is usually more valuable than the business."

"There are many segments/areas of specialization within the industry that can affect margins and equipment needed. Additionally, some buyers will view the location as a critical element and others do not. The industry is a B2B service, so there are varying points of view on the issue of 'location.'"

"Make sure that customer base is diverse—both in terms of types of industries served as well that one or two key customers aren't a huge percentage of the total revenue."

Benchmark Data

Statistics (Sign & Banner Manufacturing Franchises)
Number of Establishments	2,025
Average Profit Margin	4.9%
Revenue per Employee	$196,300
Average Number of Employees	1.9
Average Wages per Employee	$46,260

Products and Services Segmentation
Traditional signs and displays, including trade shows exhibits	31.8%
Electric signs and displays, including trade show exhibits	27.7%
Other sign manufacturing	20.9%
Miscellaneous receipts	14.8%
Other products	4.8%

Rules of Thumb - S

Major Market Segmentation

Others	23.7%
Entertainment and miscellaneous services	20.0%
Restaurants and bars	15.0%
Financial services, insurance and real estate	13.8%
Media and advertising agencies	10.5%
Miscellaneous retailers	8.8%
Public transportation, hotels and resorts	8.2%

Industry Costs

Profit	4.9%
Wages	23.1%
Purchases	48.0%
Depreciation	3.5%
Marketing	1.5%
Rent & Utilities	2.5%
Other	16.5%

Market Share

Fastsigns International Inc.	35.3%
Signarama	31.6%
Signs By Tomorrow	8.2%
Signs Now	8.0%

Source: IBISWorld, April 2015

- "Sales per employee—$150,000 to $180,000"

Expenses as a percentage of annual sales

Cost of goods	25% to 28%
Payroll/labor Costs	20% to 25%
Occupancy	15% to 20%
Profit (estimated pretax)	20% to 25%

Industry Trend

- "Big transitions: outdoor signage going to digital wide-format printing, installation, even car wraps. Promotional, fragmented, small players, local. Very few regional, national players interested in operations; focus is on project management."
- "The ascendency of large format digital printing has changed the picture of the sign industry considerably. Franchise companies like Fast Signswith the ability to invest and manage large scale printing equipment have grown tremendously and are now penetrating wayfinding and rebrand markets.
"Specialty printing companies in non-sign markets like exhibition and retail have also begun to move into sign markets. On the other hand, traditional sign companies have been using large format printing to move into wider areas including exhibition and placemaking.
"Wendy's alone is spending up to $750,000 per restaurant, or over a half billion dollars, to renovate its company-owned restaurants with a large part of that going to signs and graphics. Competitive pressures have made rebranding a necessity, and constant corporate mergers have forced airlines and banks to change frequently.
"Lately, though, there has been a bit of a backlash identified by sign fabricators. Mark Andreasson of DCL states, 'Customers want to see products that are durable and work long term, and not just be a momentary fad. This includes durable paint and materials.'

S - Rules of Thumb

"This skepticism on the benefits of sustainable products and services could benefit companies that take a more holistic view. Sustainability, though, will remain an important feature of sign companies with approaches like lifecycle management where sustainability is part of the entire fabrication process, becomes part of the maturing of the field."

Source: Mike Santos, October 1, 2014
http://www.novapolymers.com/5-leading-trends-impacting-sign-companies-in-2015/

- "Embracing new technology continues to be critical to long-term success in the industry. Technological advancements continue to improve labor efficiency."

Seller Financing
- "Cash; very few sellers have options to offer financing. Buyers are offering bargain prices."
- "Outside financing is usually available, although we have seen some seller finance deals over the last few years."
- "Typically use outside financing"
- 3 to 5 years

Questions
- "Ensure that the customer database is diverse and that no one customer dominates the sales."
- "How do they secure customers? What kind of repeat customer base do they have? How much of the business/sales depends on their personal relationship with customers?"

Resources

Trade Publications
- Signs of the Times Magazine: www.stmediagroupintl.com
- Sign & Digital Graphics Magazine: www.sdgmag.com

Associations
- International Sign Association: www.signs.org
- Specialty Graphic Imaging Association: www.sgia.org

	Franchise
Sir Speedy Printing (See also Franchises, Print Shops)	
Approx. Total Investment	$275,000 to $350,000
NAICS 323111	Number of Businesses/Units 480

Rules of Thumb
> 55 to 60 percent of annual sales plus inventory

Resources

Websites
- www.sirspeedy.com

Rules of Thumb - **S**

Ski Shops

SIC 7011-10	NAICS 532292	Number of Businesses/Units 385

Rules of Thumb

- 1.8 to 2.5 times EBIT; very rare 3.0 times (plus inventory), unless store is very exclusive with no competition in area.
- 40 percent of gross annual sales plus inventory
- 2.5 to 3.5 times SDE plus inventory

Pricing Tips

- "It depends if the business is retail, service, rental, or some combination of all of these offerings. We find we are able to get good multiples because of the desirability of the businesses."
- "Key is long-term lease, since location is so important in resort retail sales. If lease is less than 3 years, a heavy discount in percentage of gross sales is appropriate. The price goes down the higher the inventory—which is always in addition to price [calculated on Rules of Thumb]. Every store is different. Be careful—the trend is for ski companies to get into the retail business and compete with independent shops."
- "In resort businesses, location is key. Businesses must be in the tourist foot traffic areas. A strong lease securing such a location is the key in determining the multiple of cash flow. Since most areas have limited real estate, competition plays a large factor in determining price; e.g., how many ski shops are in your immediate area?"

Expert Comments

"Our market tends to be competitive and the bar is set high. The businesses are expected to be very knowledgeable and have a lot of inventory in stock. We have seen a trend in retailers having difficulty in maintaining margins in order to keep or increase market share. In certain industries, having the right brands or product lines is very important."

Benchmark Data

Statistics (Ski & Snow Board Resorts)

Number of Establishments	385
Average Profit Margin	9.6%
Revenue per Employee	$34,800
Average Number of Employees	232.9
Average Wages per Employee	$9,126

Products and Services Segmentation

Skiing facilities	53.7%
Equipment Rental	12.6%
Ski schools	12.5%
Food and beverages	8.3%
Merchandise	7.2%
Other	5.7%

26th Edition

S - Rules of Thumb

Major Market Segmentation
Destination visitors	58.7%
Local visitors	41.3%

Industry Costs
Profit	9.6%
Wages	26.2%
Purchases	19.4%
Depreciation	10.7%
Utilities	8.0%
Rent	8.3%
Other	17.8%

Market Share
Vail Resorts Inc.	33.6%
Intrawest Corporation	8.5%
Boyne Resorts	7.5%
POWDR Corporation	4.9%

Source: IBISWorld, December 2014

- "Gross profit is the single biggest benchmark for success. After that it's sales per square foot and inventory turns that matter."

Expenses as a percentage of annual sales
Cost of goods	45% to 50%
Payroll/labor Costs	22% to 28% (rising due to labor shortages)
Occupancy	08% to 12% (seeing some 18% to 20%)
Profit (estimated pretax)	0

Industry Trend

- "According to National Ski Areas Association, the total number of snowsports visits in the US for the 2014/15 season was 53.6 million—more than three times as many as the number of people who attended NFL games in 2014. This winter was 5% behind the season prior, which recorded 56.5 million snowsports visits, but up 5% from the record low season of 51 million in 2011-12.

"Despite the drop in visits, it is encouraging that season pass sales were up an average of 6%. Ski areas have become increasingly creative with season passes and other multi-day products like the Mountain Collective, giving skiers and riders more flexibility and greater value than ever before."

"Total Number of Snow Sports Participants

Season	Alpine	Snowboarding	Cross Country
2013/2014	9,004,000	7,339,000	4,291,000
2012/2013	8,243,000	7,351,000	3,307,000

Gender of Skiers and Snowboarders—2013/14 Season

Gender	Alpine	Snowboarding	Cross Country
Male	59%	63%	56%
Female	41%	37%	44%

Products Purchased at Snow Sports Specialty Stores

Season	Apparel	Equipment	Accessories
2013/14	$615,978,266	$618,874,381	$736,434,172
2012/13	$603,392,631	$565,042,091	$615,337,671"

Source: 2015 SIA Snow Sports Fact Sheet,
http://www.snowsports.org/research-surveys/snow-sports-fact-sheet/

- "Positive, based upon an improving economy and increased discretionary income. Recreation is a perceived need rather than perceived want. "

Seller Financing
- "3 years maximum"

Resources

Websites
- Snowsports Industries America: www.snowsports.org

Smartbox Portable Storage & Moving
Franchise

(See also Franchises, Self Storage)

Approx. Total Investment	$365,900 to $849,300
NAICS 484210	Number of Businesses/Units 25

Rules of Thumb
➢ 45 to 50 percent of annual sales includes inventory

Resources

Websites
- http://smartboxmovingandstorage.com/

Smoothie King (See also Franchises)
Franchise

Approx. Total Investment	$176,300 to $403,550
NAICS 722515	Number of Businesses/Units 730

Rules of Thumb
➢ 40 to 45 percent of annual sales

Resources

Websites
- www.smoothieking.com

S - Rules of Thumb

	Franchise
Snap Fitness (See also Fitness Centers, Franchises)	
Approx. Total Investment	$107,257 to $258,140
NAICS 713940	Number of Businesses/Units 1,350
Rules of Thumb	
➢ 40 percent of annual sales plus inventory	

Resources

Websites
- www.snapfitness.com

Soft Drink Bottlers	
NAICS 312111	Number of Businesses/Units 227
Rules of Thumb	
➢ $10/case sold annually	

Benchmark Data

Statistics (Soda Production)
Number of Establishments	227
Average Profit Margin	5.5%
Revenue per Employee	$945,000
Average Number of Employees	94.4
Average Wages per Employee	$60,228

Products and Services Segmentation
Regular carbonated soft drinks	53.0%
Diet carbonated soft drinks and sparkling water	24.3%
Energy and sports drinks	22.7%

Major Market Segmentation
Grocery Stores	34.1%
Warehouse clubs and supercenters	19.2%
Gas stations and convenience stores	18.7%
Other	17.0%
Vending machines	11.0%

Industry Costs
Profit	5.5%
Wages	6.1%
Purchases	64.8%
Depreciation	2.8%
Marketing	0.1%
Rent & Utilities	1.1%
Other	19.6%

Rules of Thumb - S

Market Share

The Coca-Cola Company	26.8%
PepsiCo Inc.	16.4%
Dr. Pepper Snapple Group Inc.	10.7%
Red Bull	7.3%
Monster Beverage Corp.	5.7%

Source: IBISWorld, April 2015

Software Companies
NAICS 511210

Rules of Thumb

- 1 to 3 times revenue (trailing 12 months) plus inventory
- 7.5 times SDE
- 5 to 7 times EBITDA
- 4 to 6 times EBIT

Pricing Tips

- "Enterprise value is a factor of:
    1. Recurring maintenance revenue (stable and adds more value)
    2. Recurring subscription revenue (increasing and adds more value)
    3. Legacy system license revenue (lessening and adds less value)
    4. Percentage of products engineered/re-engineered for SaaS
    5. Industry (stable)
    6. Client type (B2B, B2C, combo- value higher for B2B due to stickness of base)
    7. Foundation (i.e., size of base and ability to influence demand of product type)
    8. Competitive inhibitors (can influence value dramatically, mostly to the negative)
    9. Organization (particularly engineering base—higher value for core engineering component and reasonable access to professionals, offshore use)
    10. Architecture (engineering platform—more generally accepted/current technology gets better value)"
- "SDE, EBIT, & EBITDA ratios are meaningless in this industry because of the great differences in product, market, and development stage from company to company. Businesses even without profits or negative net worth can command multiples of gross revenue. Values are more focused on revenues trending upward, consistency and sustainability of the existing customer base, and potential for growth."
- "Software companies are guided by two major factors: new/existing product sales and most important, continuing maintenance dollars. A look under the covers to truly understand the sales pattern, not just the GL account sales are posted to, will greatly influence the value attached to any organization. Less sophisticated and entrepreneurial software companies tend to forget that the delineation of how they earn their income can drive their value, and

S - Rules of Thumb

in many cases will not breakdown or record their income correctly, thereby limiting potential value and possibly buyers and investors. If revenue is broken down correctly, you will place a larger multiple on maintenance (particularly maintenance for mission critical and higher cost software), than you would new sales. Additionally, companies that lack a SaaS (Software as a Service) model, tend to have lower multiples unless they service industries that have heavy data security requirements that diminish that need."

- "Pricing is determined by the type of software and customers a tech company seeks. Two major areas are Web-based/consumer centric vs mission-critical/commercial based. Web-based has pre-determined value based upon subscriber base, whereas mission-critical based gain value from growing maintenance (recurring) revenue that organically grows over time."
- "Usually no bank financing involved, companies can be unprofitable or have negative net worth and still sell. Average deal is 50 percent liquid, 2 year employment agreement—3 to 4 year non-compete. Most buyers are public and hi tech in order to leverage the purchase—35 percent international buyers."

Expert Comments

"Software development and sales requires different cultures than typical brick, manufacturing, or other service based companies. They tend to be younger, have complex requirements that cannot be easily learned, and have changing requirements that outpace many other industries.

"Because the products are people-centric in use, the ability to generate demand is based upon functionality, usability, and fitness for a particular purpose. Cost issues place demands on companies such that without traction, it's not cost effective to create competitive offerings against well-established companies. Personnel costs for qualified engineers, business analysts, designers, and QA/QC professionals is, per capita, expensive. As the Internet of Things (IoT) becomes more prevalent, the need for technology solutions that incorporate more complex solutions is growing geometrically."

"Software development is very difficult. The programming must be completed in view of superior user interface design, process modeling, and speed (response times). Because of the low cost as a barrier to entry, many individuals who gain education and skills don't fully understand that programming is not, in and of itself, a business. Getting product to market (i.e., in this case, deploying the software) is complex and costly, such as it is in many other industries.

"Many companies with 'great software products' never succeed because they lack first mover status, or the marketing prowess to gain mass customer adoption. Those are key to an enterprise value since the likelihood of continuous revenue when a customer has been acquired is high. The change from one software platform/program/application is difficult and costly. Cost-of-ownership models have been around for a long time, but the key metrics still exist and many companies will not make changes in their software very often accordingly."

"Software companies must attract highly qualified individuals who work both in teams and on their own. Their experience is difficult to replicate, as software can be developed in many different platforms and require

Rules of Thumb - S

knowledge in a wide array of languages and development methodologies. Accordingly, companies that are valuable tend to have very liberal benefits and workplace accommodations to keep their staff. Employee acquisition costs are high."

"Success in this business requires both technical talent and business acumen. One without the other is a recipe for disaster."

"Software, by its unique nature and protections through patents (algorithms), copyright, trade secret, and 'stealth' processes, is very difficult to replicate without extensive reverse engineering and creative paths around the legal boundaries."

"Software is unique. A company that has a product that is used in commerce, in a reasonably large deployment, has a lot of value since the cost to replace and deploy new systems is prohibitive. No two software systems are the same, although they may work to achieve a similar objective. Keep in mind, valuation is different in a B2B vs. B2C type software company. B2C will require a market plan that provides continuous R&D and product justification since loyalty, as well as replacement costs, are low. The better the history of product development and strength of the developers, the higher the multiple. In B2B it is different, and the higher multiple will come with large scale adoption, difficulty in system transition, and continuous development cycles that lock in long-term association with the product."

Benchmark Data

- "Typical models for rev/employee is difficult unless you split pre-revenue/emerging companies from established ones. Also, in the software space, different types of software garner different KPI's. So ERP software development is different than consumer versus HR versus vertical software platforms."
- "Gross profit is very high on software. Typically companies will sell software and related services. Software typically 70% of revenues, services 30% for B2B companies. For B2C, Support contracts help to define continued customer contracts assist in customer relations, marketing, social media comments, etc."
- "Actual and replication costs per source code line is a significant measurement used by potential acquirers."
- "For B2B look at average length of maintenance agreement—not the length of the contract, but the length of time the average client stays with the vendor. For B2C software companies, its more sales focused, so gauge their development life cycle, and their ability to keep innovating, and remain ahead of the marketplace. Remaining ahead of the marketplace also includes ability to provide products that consumers need and want. In a larger scale B2B, with mission-critical type systems, look for average length of contracts in excess of 5 years to achieve a higher multiple. In a B2C, look for scheduled and periodic releases, their contribution to revenue, and their future development lifecycle. B2C companies have had pressure to drop prices over the years, as the model for less expensive 'throw away' software becomes more mainstream. Brand effectiveness is key. SaaS offerings are required in most cases to be considered 'current', but legacy systems will be around for a long time."
- "Quality companies who are already earning a return on investment for an

S - Rules of Thumb

established time should have a greater than 75%–80%+ gross margin. Typical R&D allocation can/should be up to 25% allowing for future growth of product line, as well as maintenance substantiation. Number of salespeople should be relative to the marketplace being addressed."

Expenses as a percentage of annual sales

Cost of goods	05% to 10%
Payroll/labor Costs	60% to 65%
Occupancy	10% to 15%
Profit (estimated pretax)	25%

Industry Trend

- "The Internet of Things (IoT) promises to enhance the need for sophisticated technology in all aspects of life. From wearable tech like the Apple Watch, Fitbit, refrigerators, automotive, to clothing like Ralph Lauren shirts that measure various health factors through integrated threads that transmit wireless data, the confluence of everyday life and software systems to control them will give rise to many new companies. The key is to see who can generate an accepted marketplace and monetize it. Software companies will be continually looking to new extensions of areas that in the past would never have been considered digitally connected."
- "Accordingly, and in an attempt to gain traction, more companies specialize in segments they believe will become more commonplace in the future. Some companies develop software that are integral to future plans and offerings of larger entities and become competitive targets for acquisitions. That is where the true value is at."
- "As the industry continues its rise from the recession ashes, sales and profits will trend upward"

"Growth Drivers (percent answering 'important' or 'most important')

Developing New Upgraded Products & Services	87.4%
New Distribution Channels/Key Partnerships	76.4%
Acquisition of Companies	35.4%"

Source: Spencer Stuart/Software & Information Association

Seller Financing

- "It varies. There is no average, as many software companies are sold with equity participation vs. seller notes in order to value the upside of the future software adoption."
- "Given the competitive landscape for this type of business, sales typically have significant cash or stock components. Sellers are requested to hold notes that vary in scale based upon the maturity of the product and customer base. When there is a large base of existing customers with a high probability of continuous maintenance or upgrade revenue to continue, the valuation will likely exceed normal/median valuation for an average company and have limited seller financing. If acquired by a public company, leverage using the company's public stock offering is used to sweeten the deal and lessen the need for outside or seller financing."

Questions

- "Some key questions: a) Define the marketplace served by your software products. b) What is the life cycle for product development (SDLC). c) What percentage of your clients is on maintenance? (B2B). d) What percentage of your clients on maintenance has been on contracts for over 5 years? (B2B). e) What percentage of your total product income comes from maintenance? Over the last three years? (B2B). f) What do you sell your products for (MSRP)? (B2C). g) What is your policy for product updates (time and cost to consumer)? (B2C). h) Who is your competition? i) Explain your distribution model (B2B and B2C). j) Critique your development personnel, average longevity, and income patterns. (k) Do you deploy a high percentage of your development or support offshore? l) Do you have an SaaS model? If not why not? If planned, when will it be released and what competition do you see in that marketplace? m) What is your revenue per employee over the last three years, and what has been your average tenure for engineers in your company? n) What is your average employee longevity? o) Explain in-house technical skill set. p) Explain benefit package and cost (remember, it will be different than average, and that is to be expected). q) What is unique about your business plan? r) Do you have a customer retention plan? s) How do you formulate your product/service pricing plan? t) Are you subject to any regulatory issues, especially if paving new ground with product introduction?"
- "Ask for a pro-forma income statement to maintain business. Industry trends. Competition and how the business/software compares. Similar questions as you would ask any business owner."
- "1. Explain the product(s) you have, and the benefits to the end users. 2. Who are the end users? 3. What R&D do you allow for? What percentage of the company's revenue or investment dollars are allocated to R&D? 4. How long has your product been available? 5. How many releases have you had? How often do you provide updates to your products? Explain your development cycle. 6. What percentage do you charge for maintenance? 7. What monthly/yearly fee do you charge for online access? 8. Do you offer your products on a SaaS (Software as a Service) basis? If not, what will it take to re-engineer to do this? 9. Describe your staff. How many? What positions? Areas of technical expertise? Domain experience? Average age of technicians? 10. What software platforms do you use? 11. What does your business plan call for in terms of monetizing the product, revenue growth, and personnel needs to achieve this, over time? 12. What impediments do you currently need to overcome in developing/selling the product? 13. What competition do you have, do you see coming down the pike which could jeopardize any investment in the company or allocation of income to future R&D?"
- "Calculations of net cash flow, consistently applied, are good for historical analysis. Discounted cash flow models vary widely, but commonly use higher rates because of risk and uncertainty. Premiums for control, discounts for illiquidity are usually magnified from more 'stable' industries. The broker/intermediary should inquire about capitalization policies of the software 'asset.' Many companies will not capitalize their product; others will be based on cost accumulation. 'Niche' software with an established client base will attract buyers because of the ongoing service revenues."

S - Rules of Thumb

Resources

Websites
- Industry/Company Analysis and Trends (fee based): www.factset.com

Trade Publications
- How to evaluate a Software Company:
  http://www.essensys.ro/whitepapers/How-to-Evaluate-a-Software-Company.pdf

Associations
- Software & Information Industry Association: www.siia.net
- Association for Computing Machinery: www.acm.org
- Association of Information Technology Professionals: www.aitp.org
- Association of Software Professionals: www.asp-software.org

---

Sound Contractors		
SIC 5065-07	NAICS 238210	

Rules of Thumb
- 75 percent of annual sales includes inventory
- 2 to 3 times SDE and/or 30 to 60 times monthly contract billing for music services includes inventory
- 5 times EBIT
- 3 times EBITDA

Pricing Tips
- "Most contractors in this industry supply some type of music service; if it is a recurring base and the contractors are on their paperwork, then this company will have more value to a buyer."
- "Any inventory over 24 months is dead inventory and should not be part of sale."

Expert Comments
- "If company is a commercial contractor, the economy does not have much effect on industry. If they give good service and have experience in technical support, business will be stable."
- "There are few good sound contractors with a great customer list."

Benchmark Data
- "Recurring services are a key in value to this industry."
- "One tech per $400K in revenue"

Expenses as a percentage of annual sales

Cost of goods	35%
Payroll/labor Costs	35%
Occupancy	10%
Profit (estimated pretax)	20%

Industry Trend
- "5% to 10% growth each year"
- "Business is stable."

Seller Financing
- 5 to 8 years

Questions
- "Inventory, how much is dead and on the books?"
- "Relationship to customers"

Soup Man (The Original)		Franchise
(See also Franchises, Restaurants—Limited Service)		
	NAICS 722513	Number of Businesses/Units 14

Rules of Thumb
> ➢ 30 percent of annual sales includes inventory

Resources

Websites
- www.originalsoupman.com

Sporting Goods Stores		
SIC 5941-13	NAICS 451110	Number of Businesses/Units 44,970

Rules of Thumb
> ➢ 25 percent of annual sales plus inventory
> ➢ 4 times EBIT

Pricing Tips
- "Add or subtract based on nearby competition"
- "Inventory should be excluded due to rapid obsolescence."

Expert Comments
"Increasing competition from on-line retailers"

"Declining profitability due to ability of customers to comparison shop online"

Benchmark Data

Statistics (Sporting Goods Stores)
Number of Establishments	44,970
Average Profit Margin	3.4%
Revenue per Employee	$180,700
Average Number of Employees	6.2
Average Wages per Employee	$20,323

S - Rules of Thumb

Products and Services Segmentation

Sporting equipment	61.8%
Athletic apparel	18.2%
Athletic footwear	10.8%
Other	9.2%

Major Market Segmentation

Households with children	55.0%
Other households	30.0%
Sports teams	10.0%
Professional athletes	5.0%

Industry Costs

Profit	3.4%
Wages	11.3%
Purchases	63.6%
Depreciation	0.8%
Marketing	2.2%
Rent & Utilities	6.2%
Other	12.5%

Market Share

Dick's Sporting Goods Inc.	15.0%
Academy Sports & Outdoor	8.7%
Cabela's Inc.	8.0%
The Sports Authority Inc.	7.8%

Source: IBISWorld, August 2015

- "Cost of goods sold should be no more than 55%."

Expenses as a percentage of annual sales

Cost of goods	45% to 55%
Payroll/labor Costs	17%
Occupancy	15% to 20%
Profit (estimated pretax)	08%

Industry Trend
- "Dick's Sporting Goods has put its thumb to the wind and judged that shoppers want less golf and more athletic apparel."

  Source: "Dick's Sporting Goods Follows the Trends to Earnings Beat" by Samantha Sharf, forbes.com, August 19, 2014

- "Short term declining due to economic climate, longer term return to moderate growth due to increased interest in sports/leisure activities."

Questions
- "Are the sales personnel knowledgeable in their specific areas?"

Resources

Associations
- National Sporting Goods Association: www.nsga.org

Rules of Thumb - S

Staffing Services (See also Office Staffing, Temporary Agencies)

SIC 7361-03 | NAICS temporary positions 561320 / permanent positions 561311

Rules of Thumb
- 35% of Annual Gross Sales
- 2 to 5 times SDE
- 2 to 5 times EBITDA
- 3 to 4 times EBIT

Pricing Tips
- "Multiples based on SDE vary with segment, annual revenues, and growth. Location also influences multiple. Some examples:
    Light Industrial
    - ✓ $5 million minimum 2.5–3.2X
    - ✓ $10 million 3–4 X
    - ✓ $10–$19 million 3.5–4.25 X
    - ✓ $20 million plus (especially if multiple office locations) 4–5X
    IT
    - ✓ $5 million minimum 3.5–4X
    - ✓ $10 million 3.6–4.5X
    - ✓ $20 million 4–5 X (higher if strong gross profit and if in major metro market)
    - ✓ $50 million or higher 5–7X"
- "Pricing depends on industry sector, gross margin, client concentration, and size."
- "Light industrial $250,000 EBIT, valued at 2 to 3X EBIT + owner's earnings. IT staffing @2.5X to 4X EBIT based on specialty served and sales volume. PEO firms @2 to 4X EBIT based on sales volume, HR services offered, etc."
- "Staffing valuations vary by segment. Light industrial staffing businesses with a minimum gross profit of 16% have been valued at 2.5-4 X SDE with companies with revenues of $10 million or higher commanding higher multiples. Wild card is working capital base provided as many companies factor A/R (sixty days max is typical). Light industrial often requires locations on a 'bus line' and many such companies provide transportation. Obamacare looms as a management challenge for such business if, or when, they have to provide health care to temporary workers."

Expert Comments

"Gross profit and A/R performance influence the multiple selection as does strength of locations (near bus lines). Factoring is common in this industry and net factoring expenses can impact profitability. Customer concentration issues require analysis with balanced weighting across several segments supporting higher valuations."

"Workers' comp., risk management, and mod factors affect light industrial staffing\PEO firms substantially."

"Profits are up in past two years as the general economy upticks but companies are reluctant to add overheads. Temp workers are utilized as a response to increased demand."

S - Rules of Thumb

"Entry into the industry is relatively easy. Competition can be tough but the market is big. The industry has been on a strong upswing over the last couple of years but is very susceptible to economic conditions."

Benchmark Data
- For additional Benchmark Data see Employment Agencies
- "16% minimum gross profit for light industrial and clerical. IT, healthcare, and professional can average ten points higher on gross profit line—25–28%"
- "Hours billed per branch. Recruiting cost per employee. Workers Comp mod factor."
- "A key is the gross margin %. Buyers will look at that very closely. Here again, margin and markups will vary based upon the specialty area."
- "Multiple of SDE: 2 to 5; Gross Profit: 22% to 30%"

Expenses as a percentage of annual sales
Cost of goods	0%
Payroll/labor Costs	70% to 75%
Occupancy	05%
Profit (estimated pretax)	9% to 15%

Industry Trend
- "According to Teresa Carroll, senior VP and general manager, Global Talent Solutions for Kelly Services, these are the five types of free agents that exist today and the percentage of the global free agent population they represent; free agents may be represented in multiple categories:
    - ✓ Independent contractors (workers who perform independent work on a project-to-project basis): 64%
    - ✓ Freelance business owners (business owners with up to five employees who identify as both a freelancer and a business owner): 28%
    - ✓ Temporary workers (workers typically hired for a fixed duration, often through an agency): 24%
    - ✓ Moonlighters (workers who hold a primary, traditional job and also participate in free agency work on the side): 13%
    - ✓ Diversified workers (workers with multiple sources of income, derived from a mix of traditional and freelance work with the majority of their income derived from freelance work): 4%"

    Source: "Third of workers globally are 'free agents,' Kelly survey finds"
    staffingindustry.com, September 3, 2015

- "The U.S. temporary staffing industry is projected to grow 6% in 2015 to reach $115 billion and expand another 5% in 2016 to reach an all-time high of $121 billion, according to the U.S. Staffing Industry Forecast, a semi-annual report released recently by Staffing Industry Analysts. The report, based on staffing company revenues, serves as a benchmark for the staffing industry, charting the size and growth of temporary staffing skill segments.

    "Skill Segment Trends—The U.S. Staffing Industry Forecast is comprised of 10 different skill segments and all are forecasted for growth in 2015. Education, a relatively small and emerging segment, has the highest growth forecast at 15% as education continues to experience a surge in demand from K-12 school districts turning to staffing firms to hire substitute teachers. Engineering has the lowest growth forecast at 3% due to the lack of recovery in employment since the recession and a downturn in oil and gas exploration and production. Healthcare, IT, finance/accounting and marketing/creative all show 7% increases. The remaining segments of office/clerical, industrial, legal and clinical/scientific segments are also expected to grow.

"While the likelihood of a recession occurring in 2015 or 2016 is low, an unexpected downturn in the overall economy remains the most severe risk to the forecasted growth rates of the industry, according to the report."

Source: http://www.staffingindustry.com/About/Media-Center/Press-Releases/Staffing-Industry-Analysts-Projects-U.S.-Temporary-Staffing-Industry-Will-Reach-115-Billion-in-2015

- "Staffing is a leading economic indicator and moves early in the economic cycle. Reluctance by companies to add to overheads has directly benefited staffing business models. Watch Obamacare initiatives and their impact on the Staffing Industry."
- "These businesses will continue to consolidate and there will be continued gross margin pressures over the coming years. Businesses that can service multiple locations will attract higher multiples."
- "The industry is expected to grow significantly through 2024. This isn't a skill intensive business and many types of buyers are qualified to be owners."
- "Demand should remain strong as employers respond to rebounding economy and Obamacare uncertainties by hiring temps and avoiding adding to their overhead."
- "Growing industry in medical staffing and some IT areas. Heavy competition in the home care workers segment."

Seller Financing

- "50% or more owner financing common on transactions with less than $2 million in consideration. Owner financing declines to 20% level as transaction values climb over $5 million."
- "Outside financing is very common. Owner financing can be expected if there are client concentration issues."
- "This industry has an above average requirement for seller financing. Not uncommon for sellers to provide up to 50-70% financing."
- "25–35% down, balance over 2–3 years with variable performance-based component often added."

Questions

- "Length of service by account. Gross Profit by account. Bad debt experience."
- "Who in the organization has the relationships with the clients? What is the gross margin? Which clients have vendor management systems in place? How frequently do they put these out to bid? What is the turnover of the recruiting and sales staff?"
- "Need to understand working capital requirements. Will sellers include some accounts receivable in seller price?Review client hiring patterns for past three years and match against their payment history."
- "What is concentration of sales for top five accounts? How long have you serviced these accounts? How many recruiters do you have? What is your bad debt experience for past two years?"
- "Closeness of relationships to clients; length of transition; recent changes to business or competition; staff retention."

S - Rules of Thumb

Resources

Trade Publications
- Staffing Industry Analysts: www.staffingindustry.com

Associations
- American Staffing Association: www.americanstaffing.net
- National Association of Personnel Services: www.naps360.org

Staffing Services (Health Care)
(See also Employment Agencies, Staffing Services)

Rules of Thumb
> "Barry Asin, chief analyst at Staffing Industry Analysts, in Los Altos, California, says that most health care staffing firms sell for four to five times EBITDA."

Source: "Businesses For Sale" by Elaine Appleton Grant, *Inc. Magazine*, January 2008

Industry Trend
- "Thirty-four staffing firms each generated at least $50 million in healthcare temporary staffing revenue in 2014; combined, they generated $6.5 billion and comprised 61% of the market. AMN and CHG each garnered 9% market share. "The report also provides four rankings of the largest firms in each healthcare sub-segment: travel nurse, per diem nurse, locum tenens and allied healthcare. This year's report ranks 21 travel nurse firms that generated in total $2.1 billion, 12 per diem nurse staffing firms that generated $1.0 billion, 10 locum tenens firms that generated $1.9 billion, and 21 allied healthcare staffing firms that generated $1.5 billion."

Source: "Healthcare Staffing Report: Sept. 3, 2015" staffingindustry.com

Resources

Websites
- Staffing Industry Analysts: www.staffingindustry.com

Subway (See also Franchises, Sandwich Shops) — Franchise

Approx. Total Investment	$116,000 to $263,000
Estimated Annual Sales/Unit	$470,000
SIC 5812-06 NAICS 722513	Number of Businesses/Units 44,000

Rules of Thumb
> 50 percent to 60 percent of annual sales includes inventory
> 3.3 to 3.8 times SDE includes inventory
> 3.5 times EBIT
> 3.5 times EBITDA
> 35 to 40 times weekly sales

Pricing Tips

- "Discount value for sales less than national average of $8,500 a week but compare with local average. Discount for remodeling required. Discount for short lease. Discount for rent over 10% of sales. Discount if SDE less than $50,000."
- "Factor in costs of high rent(>12%), remodel costs, short lease, new store coming nearby"
- "70% of asking price minus remodel cost if any."
- "Deduct for remodel expense; deduct for high rent; deduct for less than 7 yrs. on lease. C-Store and Walmart locations need an adjustment too."
- "If sales less than $400,000, price is less than 50% of sales. If sales over $400,000 and closer to $500,000 and above, can get 60%. Subject to lease term over 7 yrs., and remodel done, rent 10–12% of sales."
- "Influx of many Subway restaurants and similar competitors has caused a decline in the attractiveness of this franchise. Franchises grossing over $8,000 per week are attractive and profitable. The business is very dependent on location, many of which have been compromised in an effort to add additional units."
- "60–70% of sales. I have seen higher and lower, depends on lease, compliance issues, remodel issues and proximity to other stores or impending new store construction."
- "Lease of less than 8 years diminishes the value. This is typical valuation for Subway type store."

Expert Comments

"60 hours a week to start, then 40. Must be hands-on owner operator for efficiencies. Buy a store with $350k plus price tag if you can find one, and sales about $550k plus. Always keep rent below 10%, mall stores not recommended."

"Subway has matured as a brand and I am starting to see cracks in their marketwide growth. Many owners leaving system now, and marginal stores closing rather than relocating. Cannibalization of sales by overexpansion is now showing its ugly face. We told them so several years ago....!! Many taking a haircut from previous values, but overall they did OK."

"Quiznos is a non-entity for the most part, some new names are appearing in the market as people experiment or get tired of Subway, but Subway is still the segment leader and the juggernaut."

"Very high demand, low number of opportunities"

"Good franchise, happy owners"

Benchmark Data

- For additional Benchmark Data see Sandwich Shops
- "29% food, 18% labor with owner working 40 hours and rents below 8%. That is a winner."
- "True cost of goods is 30% in a well-run, owner-operated store. Rent should be less than 10% for real profitability. Valuation/pricing does range from 25% to 85% of sales, depending on the numbers and region."

S - Rules of Thumb

- "Most stores are 1,000 s/f, have approximately 20 seats and are owner operated. Food cost is controllable."
- "Food costs—30% or below, rent 10% or below, average sales per store per week over $10,000 makes a good store. Subway average nationwide is about $7300 per week in store sales."

Expenses as a percentage of annual sales
Cost of goods	30% to 31%
Payroll/labor Costs	20% to 21%
Occupancy	10%
Profit (estimated pretax)	15% to 25%

Industry Trend
- "Maturing, losing out market share gradually to new sandwich concepts, but that is not catastrophic as they command such presence and are market leaders. New generation are opting for more exotic fare and fancy chains to be hip. I was too once upon a time!!!"
- "More competition from other Subway stores opening near existing ones, cannibalization of sales but that is nothing new. New menu items and flavors."
- "Steady sales increase"

Seller Financing
- "Seller financing best option, but financing not very difficult as the brand is favoured."
- "Rarely seller financed"
- 5 years

Questions
- "Are they going to open a new store nearby? Does it need a remodel?"
- "Is the DA support good?"
- "Lease length and terms, trend of gross sales, years established"
- "Remodel due? Rent and CAM? Combo report?"

Resources

Websites
- Subway: www.subway.com
- Mr. FranchiseMan: mrfranchiseman.com/mm/view/subfranchise

Sun Room and Awning Installation

SIC 1521-22	NAICS 326199	Number of Businesses/Units 5,000

Rules of Thumb
> ➢ 35 percent of annual sales plus inventory

Pricing Tips
- "Strong, knowledgeable managers who have been with this specialty business for a long time can add a lot of value to the company. This would also increase the buyer pool greatly. A buyer with no knowledge or experience in this business could purchase it and be successful."

Rules of Thumb - **S**

Expert Comments

"Competition—this is a specialty business; risk—there is an abundance of work in this field; profit trend—sales have shown steady increases; location—a shop and a central location is all you need; marketability—there is a high demand for this type of work; industry trend—new housing boom and damages from hurricane have this business booked for years; replication—this being a specialty business, most construction workers don't have the necessary knowledge to do these jobs."

Benchmark Data

- "30%+ net income based on gross sales"

Expenses as a percentage of annual sales
Cost of goods	15%
Payroll/labor Costs	25% to 30%
Occupancy	15%
Profit (estimated pretax)	30%

Industry Trend

- "Growing due to housing boom in area"

Questions

- "What contracts do you have with whom?"

Resources

Websites
- National Sunroom: www.nationalsunroom.org

Franchise

SuperCoups (See also Coupon Books, Franchises, Valpak)

Approx. Total Investment		$22,400 to $28,000
	NAICS 541870	Number of Businesses/Units 21

Rules of Thumb

➢ 40 to 45 percent of annual sales plus inventory

➢ "If a cooperative direct mail business, such as Money Mailer or SuperCoups is making $100,000, it could be sold for $150,000 to $225,000, and $250,000 if it was a perfect situation. Now, on the other hand, if it is a Valpak, I believe you could get up to 3 times what it is making because Valpak is the undisputed leader. They are owned by COX Publishing and they are within 50 franchises of being sold out."

Resources

Websites
- www.supercoups.com

S - Rules of Thumb

Supermarkets/Grocery Stores

| SIC 5411-05 | NAICS 445110 | Number of Businesses/Units 67,075 |

Rules of Thumb

- 10 to 22 percent of annual sales plus inventory
- 2 to 3 times SDE; add fixtures, equipment plus inventory
- 3 times EBIT
- 3 to 3.5 times EBITDA

Pricing Tips

- "There are different departments within a supermarket, with some departments having a gross profit of 30% or more and others having lower than 10% and even negative gross profit on sale items; so depending on the store customers' buying habits and how these departments are managed, the selling price will be adjusted."
- "3 times yearly net income"
- "When we benchmarked the typical hard-discounter P&L versus traditional grocers, we found that the discounters turn a 12 percentage-point disadvantage in gross margin into a 3.5 percentage-point advantage in EBITDA. They do this with carefully designed operations that leverage deep sourcing expertise, massive sales intensity per SKU on a small number of 'bull's eye' lines, low-labor merchandising and very small-footprint stores. The result is a store that can be profitable with prices up to 20 percent below Walmart's, and in locations that are too densely populated to support a Walmart Supercenter."
- "Since traditional grocers today run with 2 percent earnings before interest and tax (EBIT) and a 20 percent volume variable margin, a 10 percent market share to online would erase their aggregate profitability at current footprint."
- "Gas & lottery sales should not be included in gross sales."
- "3 times annual cash flow is a good rule of thumb, assuming no new competition is entering the market."
- "EBITDA is most reliable. Gross sales are fairly irrelevant for smaller stores (sales under $5M)."
- "Location, demographics, and competition are the 3 biggest factors in pricing."
- "Rent above 3% of sales, or a short-term lease will reduce value of business."

Expert Comments

"Competition from chain stores is very high. The biggest threat to an existing store is new competition. Competition has kept profits from growing. Projection for future growth is low. Demand for grocery/convenience stores is high. This is a desirable business for owner/operators and there are many multi-location owners looking to grow."

"A good location is difficult to secure, but once you have established a strong business it can be very lucrative. The food business is a low margin business with nice cash flow but there is always new competition coming aboard. Walmart, drug stores, dollar stores, and convenience stores require store operators to constantly run a tight ship."

Rules of Thumb - S

"We see a high demand for established retail food stores. New or threatened competition can decrease value greatly and diminish buyer interest. Stores in smaller, rural areas have a reduced threat of larger operators and are in good demand."

"Competition, employee costs, and the economy in general have decreased profitability."

Benchmark Data

Statistics (Supermarkets and Grocery Stores)

Number of Establishments	67,075
Average Profit Margin	1.7%
Revenue per Employee	$234,700
Average Number of Employees	37.6
Average Wages per Employee	$22,906

Products and Services Segmentation

Other food items	31.7%
Beverages (Including alcohol)	16.1%
Dairy Products	14.2%
Other non-food items	10.5%
Fresh and frozen meat	10.1%
Frozen foods	8.4%
Drugs and health products	6.1%
Fruit and vegetables	2.9%

Industry Costs

Profit	1.7%
Wages	9.8%
Purchases	73.4%
Depreciation	1.0%
Marketing	0.7%
Rent & Utilities	4.8%
Other	8.6%

Market Share

The Kroger Co.	15.4%
Safeway Inc.	6.2%
Publix Super Markets Inc.	5.5%

Source: IBISWorld, October 2015

- "As consumers adopt more healthy eating habits, organic and locally sourced products grow in importance. The study found that 48 percent prefer to buy organic products, when given a choice. Produce is by far the most popular organic item—90 percent said they had purchased it in the previous 30 days. Meat wasn't far behind with 55 percent, dairy was a close third with 54 percent, and packaged canned (soups, sauces, etc.) and dry products (cereal, pasta, etc.) were each cited by 29 percent to tie for fourth. On the flip side, only 6 percent of shoppers reported purchasing organic baby products."

Source: http://www.progressivegrocer.com/industry-news-trends/trader-joes-leads-market-force-ranking-favorite-grocers

S - Rules of Thumb

- "The typical U.S. grocery store now stocks up to 50,000 products, up from 15,000 in 1991, but a quarter of those products sell less than one unit a month, according to a report last year from Accenture PLC."
  Source: "McDonald's Menu Problem: It's Supersized" by Julie Jargon,
  Wall Street Journal, December 4, 2014

- "The average square footage of supermarkets in the U.S. has been falling since 2006, and is now roughly 46,000 square feet, according to Packaged Facts. 'The pendulum definitely is swinging back to smaller store formats,' analysts wrote, noting that Wal-Mart is expanding its smaller-format stores. Kroger also has a small-format store called Turkey Hill Market, which averages about 6,800 square feet."
  Source: "Consumers Want More Personalized Shopping Experiences: PwC Report," from www.progressivegrocer.com, 6/10/14

Supermarket Facts

Total supermarket sales—2014	$638,338 billion
Number of supermarkets—2014 ($2 million or more in annual sales)	37,716

Source: Progressive Grocer Magazine

Net profit after taxes—2014	1.5%
Median Total Store Size in Square Feet—2014	46,000
Median weekly sales per supermarket—2014	$516.727

Source: Food Marketing Institute

Percentage of disposable income spent on food--USDA figure for 2013
food-at-home	5.6%
food away-from-home	4.3%

Source: USDA

Weekly sales per square foot of selling area—2014	$11.98
Sales per customer transaction—2014	$29.90
Sales per labor hour (median, unweighted)—2014	$148.00
Average number of trips per week consumers make to the supermarket—2015	1.5
Average number items carried in a supermarket in 2014	42.214

Source: Food Marketing Institute
Source: http://www.fmi.org/research-resources/supermarket-facts

Expenses as a percentage of annual sales

Cost of goods	70% to 75%
Payroll/labor Costs	05% to 14%
Occupancy	05% to 05%
Profit (estimated pretax)	02% to 15%

Industry Trend

- "Independent grocery store owners are worried about their livelihoods as big supermarket chains such as Wegmans and BJ's Wholesale Club open more locations in Greater Boston neighborhoods. The arrival of new competition is particularly troubling for small grocers already struggling to gain market share in an industry dominated by large companies."
  Source: "Fiercely Independent—Neighborhood grocery stores brace themselves for intense competition as big supermarket chains move onto their turf" by Taryn Luna, *Boston Globe*, April 18, 2014

- "Trader Joe's took the No. 1 spot out of the 14 grocery chains studied, with a score of 78 percent, and was closely followed by Publix with 74 percent. Aldi, Hy-Vee and H-E-B rounded out the top five. Brands such as WinCo Foods, Albertsons and Sam's Club made this year's list, after failing to garner enough mentions in 2014."
  Source: http://www.progressivegrocer.com/industry-news-trends/trader-joes-leads-market-force-ranking-favorite-grocers

Rules of Thumb - S

- "Grocers need to provide more targeted shopping experiences tailored to specific consumer needs and changing demographics, a new report from PricewaterhouseCoopers (PwC) suggests. The report, 'Front of the Line: How Grocers Can Get Ahead for the Future,' is based on a survey of more than 1,000 shoppers.

  "Grocers can no longer rely on providing a one-size-fits-all customer experience. The next wave of millennial consumers is likely to demand individualized attention and a shopping experience that meets their specific wants and needs," said Steven Barr, PwC's U.S. retail and consumer practice leader. According to the London-based global professional services firm, 83 percent of survey respondents prefer to shop at traditional grocery stores.

  "More than half of the shoppers surveyed complained of long lines and crowded stores. Grocers that provide a smoother in-store experience by taming congestion are likely to earn repeated shopper visits. Furthermore, shoppers will increasingly look to store employees as shopping advisers, whether for additional product information, new recipe tips or purchase recommendations, as consumers will want increased service and assistance with decision-making.

  "Although online shopping is seeing exponential growth in the retail industry, the grocery segment has not shown the same levels of engagement. Only 1 percent of survey respondents consider online shopping their primary way of purchasing groceries, though 92 percent reported having the option to shop for groceries online.

  "'While online channels may not become a common way to buy groceries in the near future, technology will still play a major role in the evolving grocery experience,' said Sabina Saksena, managing director in PwC's U.S. retail and consumer practice. 'Shoppers expect information at their fingertips, and, according to our survey, more than half of respondents want to integrate their mobile devices into their future grocery experience. Grocers that innovate and build on their digital channels to meet this demand will be most successful.'

  "PwC's report provides five tips for grocery retailers to prepare for the future and stay ahead of the curve as demographics shift and consumer needs evolve:
  - ✓ Tailor your brick-and-mortar stores
  - ✓ Personalize your marketing strategies
  - ✓ Empower your staff
  - ✓ Transform your technology
  - ✓ Reinvent your loyalty programs"

  Source: "Consumers Want More Personalized Shopping Experiences: PwC Report," www.progressivegrocer.com, June 10, 2014

- "Here are some of the top trends that are changing the grocery shopping landscape.
  1. Consumers are shopping for food and beverages across multiple channels
  2. Private label is gaining popularity
  3. Shoppers want more product curation
  4. Fresh produce is a main driver for consumers in deciding where to shop

  Source: "4 Ways American Grocery Shopping Is Changing Forever," by Hayley Peterson, www.businessinsider.com April 15, 2014

S - Rules of Thumb

Seller Financing
- 5 years
- "Most larger stores are sold with outside financing. Smaller stores that do not include real estate usually require seller financing."
- "Generally, we are seeing sellers financing a small portion, along with a primary lender."
- 7–10 yrs.

Questions
- "Why are you selling? Check the store order history to determine what kind of clients are shopping the store. A store with high add ordering and low everyday items ordering is not a good store, and you have to examine the P&L very carefully."
- "What additional incentives do your suppliers provide that may not show on the financial statements?"
- "Consider the possibility of a new competitor coming into the market and what effect it will have on the store location. It is also important to have effective security measures in place to minimize employee theft. Look at the ability to expand the square footage of the store in order to offer more variety and departments within the business."

Resources

Websites
- Food Marketing Institute (FMI): www.fmi.org

Trade Publications
- Supermarket News: www.supermarketnews.com
- Progressive Grocer: www.progressivegrocer.com

Associations
- New Hampshire Grocers Association (NHGA): www.grocers.org
- Grocery Manufacturers of America (GMA): www.gmaonline.org
- National Grocers Association (NGA): www.nationalgrocers.org

	Franchise
Swisher (Restroom Hygiene Service) (See also Franchises)	
Approx. Total Investment	$100,000 to $150,000
NAICS 561720	Number of Businesses/Units 110

Rules of Thumb
➢ 50% of annual sales plus inventory

	Franchise
Sylvan Learning Center (See also Children's Educational Franchises)	
Approx. Total Investment	$159,291 to $282,213
NAICS 611691	Number of Businesses/Units 700

Rules of Thumb
➢ 1.7 times SDE plus inventory

Rules of Thumb - T

Pricing Tips
- "The multiples of SDE vary depending on the owner benefit. Higher owner benefits drive higher multiples."

Expert Comments
"With the advent of SylvanSync, Sylvan has brought technology to the forefront and no other competitor has such a product to offer."

Seller Financing
- 2 years

Questions
- "How much in prepaid revenues as of today?"

Resources

Websites
- http://franchise.sylvanlearning.com/brand-strength

Synergy HomeCare		Franchise
(See also Franchises, Home Health Care—Care-Giving)		
Approx. Total Investment		$59,000 to $156,000
	NAICS 621610	Number of Businesses/Units 259

Rules of Thumb
- ➢ 30 to 35 percent of annual sales includes inventory

Resources

Websites
- www.synergyhomecare.com

Taco John's (See also Franchises)		Franchise
Approx. Total Investment		$336,000 to $1,094,000
Estimated Annual Sales/Unit		$850,000
	NAICS 722513	Number of Businesses/Units 430

Rules of Thumb
- ➢ 30 percent of annual sales plus inventory

Resources

Websites
- www.tacojohns.com

26th Edition

T - Rules of Thumb

Tanning Salons

| SIC 7299-44 | NAICS 812199 | Number of Businesses/Units 11,096 |

Rules of Thumb
- 2 to 2.5 times SDE includes inventory
- 50 to 60 percent of annual sales plus inventory
- 2 times EBIT
- 2 times EBITDA

Pricing Tips
- "Age of the equipment. Age of the tanning lamps. High pressure tanning beds & tanning booths vs low pressure ones. High pressure equipment has more value and brings in more revenue, but the lamp replacements cost more. They tend to be newer equipment. Variety & diversity of the equipment adds value, for example, having equipment that provides red light therapy for skin rejuvenation, equipment that senses skin sensitivity to prevent burning, having equipment with mostly UVA rays for very light skin or sensitive skin, having stand up booths & lay down beds, providing body wrap services, tooth whitening services."
- "Salons with standup beds and spray tanning have higher gross margins and levels of profitability. This type salon can command a multiple of 3.0."
- "The recently imposed federal 10% surtax on tanning will most likely reduce the demand for services and thus impact cash flow."
- "How To Value A Tanning Salon—As a general rule, tanning beds that are 3 years old and are properly maintained will have a value of about $.15 to $.20 on the dollar. For example: if the purchase price of the bed was $10,000 new, then the value of that bed is around $1500, $2000 after 3 years provided it is in an average condition."
- "The value of a tanning salon business is sometimes determined by multiplying its net profit by 2.5, plus the depreciated value of its assets. So if a tanning salon earned $40,000 net profit last year, and has $50,000 in depreciated assets, the estimated value of that business is $150,000."
- "The Main Valuation Drivers:
    - ✓ Equipment: Tanning beds can run to $30,000 apiece and require significant maintenance.
    - ✓ Utilities: While newer models are more energy efficient, utility costs can still be a large part of operating costs.
    - ✓ Taxes: As part of President Obama's massive health care bill, there is now a 10% tax on tanning services.
    - ✓ Health Concerns: There are concerns that tanning can lead to skin cancer. Some states even have laws that place age limits on who can go to a tanning salon.
    - ✓ Seasonality: Business tends to ramp up from January through June, given the weather.
    - ✓ Competition: Barriers to entry are small and there are a variety of alternatives, such as gyms, spas, and apartment complexes."
- "How many outstanding tans have yet to be delivered to both active and

inactive clients? This is probably the most overlooked element when negotiating the purchase of a tanning salon. If a decision is made to buy the salon and a large number of outstanding tans exist, the previous owner will have had the benefit of depositing the money of those sales into their account while the new owner will have the burden of delivering the service and paying for the overhead associated with it. The buyer should always negotiate the value of outstanding tans out of the purchase price of the salon."

Source: www.insun.us/negotiate-salon-purchase.php

- "If equipment is very new, calculate FMV less debt outstanding."
- "Pricing may vary based on the time of year the salon is sold, due to seasonality. Higher multiples will be achieved in the December to February time frames, as peak season is March until June. Buyers will seek to get in and implement changes prior to the busy season. Salon values are then depressed from June until November, as the salons are far less lucrative (or even operating in the red) during these months."

Expert Comments

"Good equipment is very expensive, thus it is not easy to replicate. It will cost a minimum of $100,000.00 in equipment alone to set up a new & modern salon. All new equipment can go up much higher."

"According to the American Academy of Dermatology and the World Health Organization, indoor tanning heightens the risk of developing melanoma by 59 percent, and the risk goes up with each use. Despite these risks, according to the American Cancer Society (ACS), thousands of Americans will opt for an indoor tan. The ACS estimates that nearly 13,000 people die each year from skin cancers—approximately 9,700 of which are from melanoma. The ACS predicts that in 2014, melanoma will account for 76,100 cases of skin cancer."

Source: www.fda.gov 5/29/14

- "Concern with skin cancer has dampened public interest. Also parents are controlling their teenage daughters from going to salons."
- "Gyms, nail salons and beauty shops continue to add single tanning beds, so perceived competition or threat of new entrants is high due to the low cost in doing so. Such novice entrants are rarely successful in tanning, however, the perception may differ."
- "While the industry is growing overall, competition has created saturation in many markets, especially high-growth areas that experienced a recent housing boom. New commercial development has enticed many new operators to enter the market. The older 'mom and pop' site locations are being overtaken by more upscale, higher end facilities."
- "Locations are often difficult to replicate, but they are one of the most important factors in valuation. Adjacent anchor tenants, nearby gyms, or complementary neighbors such as hair and nail salons or day spas also influence value and provide a business a sustainable competitive advantage."
- "Tanning salons can vary greatly. People prefer the most modern beds and/or stand-up booths. Also spray-on is very popular. An ideal location would be next to or near a health club like LA Fitness and/or a massage facility like Massage Envy."
- "Local competition is key in determining a location's competitive environment. A competitor cannot replicate an ideal location next to a gym or next to a grocery store."

T - Rules of Thumb

- "In a highly competitive industry like tanning, the ability to market to your target market is your business's life blood. The client base can be very fickle, so customer service is of the utmost importance."
- "Competition varies greatly by location. California, Nevada, Arizona, Texas, and Florida are highly competitive in most areas. Some college towns (i.e., Ann Arbor, Michigan) also see a great deal of competition."

Benchmark Data

Statistics (Tanning Salons)

Number of Establishments	11,096
Average Profit Margin	8.4%
Revenue Per Employee	$47,800
Average Number of Employees	5.7
Average Wages per Employee	$15,217

Products and Services Segmentation

UV tanning	57.2%
Sunless tanning	23.3%
Merchandise sales	17.1%
Other	2.4%

Industry Costs

Profit	8.4%
Wages	31.9%
Purchases	29.5%
Depreciation	4.1%
Marketing	3.1%
Rent & Utilities	12.7%
Other	10.3%

Market Share

Palm Beach Tan	3.6%

Source: IBISWorld, September 2015

- "Average sales per Tanner/client should be around $15 in addition to the membership fees."
- "Rent, payroll, COGS, and utilities should account for approximately 90% of total expenses."
- "One general manager and two (rotated) employees per store. If multi-unit, also include a regional manager."
- "It will be worthwhile to determine bed utilization, electrical power capacity utilization, sales per square foot, and percentage of sale percentages from monthly electronic fund transfers, recurring memberships or single sessions."
- "There are few industry benchmarks, as the industry has a broad spectrum of competitors."
- "Roughly 20% of sales should be derived from retail sales. Retail sales levels are a good indicator of how aggressively a seller is incentivizing employees to maximize profits. Rent, payroll, utilities and COGS should account for 90% of an operation's expenses."
- "Annual sales of $250,000 should lead to a successful salon. Payroll should be heavily weighted on bonus and incentive programs, versus salaries and fixed wages."

Rules of Thumb - T

Expenses as a percentage of annual sales

Cost of goods	10%
Payroll/labor Costs	20% to 25%
Occupancy	25%
Profit (estimated pretax)	30%

Industry Trend

- "More consolidation & better profit margin"
- "For decades, researchers saw indoor tanning as little more than a curiosity. But a review of the scientific evidence published last year estimated that tanning beds account for as many as 400,000 cases of skin cancer in the United States each year, including 6,000 cases of melanoma, the deadliest form.
- "There were about 14,000 salons across the country as of early 2014, according to John Overstreet, executive director of the Indoor Tanning Association. That does not count tanning beds in gyms and beauty parlors. The number is down by about a fifth in recent years, he said, as the recession eroded young women's disposable income and the tax imposed under the new health care law squeezed salons' profits."
  Source: "Warning: That Tan Could Be Hazardous" by Sabrina Tavernise, *New York Times*, January 11, 2015
- "Using sunlamp products such as tanning beds or tanning booths increases the risk of skin damage, skin cancer and eye injury, according to the Food and Drug Administration (FDA) and numerous other health organizations. A particularly dangerous result is melanoma, the deadliest type of skin cancer.

"To help protect consumers and inform them about the risks of indoor tanning, FDA is changing its regulation of sunlamp products and UV lamps intended for use in sunlamp products. The changes strengthen the oversight of these devices, and require that sunlamp products carry a visible, black-box warning stating that they should not be used on people under the age of 18.

"FDA is also requiring that certain user instructions and promotional materials for sunlamp products and UV lamps intended for use in sunlamp products include the following warnings and contraindications (a contraindication means that the risk outweighs the benefit):

  ✓ the product is committed for use on persons under the age of 18 years;
  ✓ the product must not be used if skin lesions or open wounds are present;
  ✓ the product should not be used on people who have had skin cancer or a family history of skin cancer; and
  ✓ people repeatedly exposed to UV radiation should be regularly evaluated for skin cancer."
  Source: "Indoor Tanning Raises Risk of Melanoma: FDA Strengthens Warnings for Sunlamp Products," FDA Consumer Updates, 5/29/14

Questions

- "Seller to keep good books and records where the computer sales reports match the tax returns. Buyer should ask & verify the age of the equipment and age of the bulbs in each equipment. The good thing for a buyer is that a lot of information can be analysed, verified through the salon computer in terms of sales breakdown by demographics, age & gender of the clients, amount spent by each client, busy time of the day or busy time of the year and much more."
- "Have any of your competitors gone out of business within the last 12 months? Who has opened up within the last 12 months? How old are each of the beds?

T - Rules of Thumb

How old are the bulbs in each bed?"
- "How many hours are truly worked by owner? Are there any new competitors?"
- "Revenue trends"
- "How many members have you lost in the last 12 months? What is your retention percentage? How old is each piece of equipment? Do you have every bed metered? How do you check on your employees to make sure they are not giving away free time?"
- "How old is the equipment? How often is maintenance performed? Is there an EFT system in place?"

Resources

Trade Publications
- Smart Tan Magazine: www.smarttan.com
- ist Magazine: www.istmagazine.com

Associations
- The National Tanning Training Institute (NTTI): www.tanningtraining.com

Tattoo Parlors

SIC 7299-43	NAICS 812199	Number of Businesses/Units 38,333

Rules of Thumb
➢ 50 percent of annual sales includes inventory

Benchmark Data

Statistics (Tattoo Artists)
Number of Establishments	38,333
Average Profit Margin	14.5%
Revenue per Employee	$13,600
Average Number of Employees	1.5
Average Wages per Employee	$9,646

Products and Services Segmentation
Custom tattoos	69.0%
Body piercing	15.0%
Predesigned tattoos	12.0%
Aftercare tattoo services	4.0%

Industry Costs
Profit	14.5%
Wages	70.9%
Purchases	5.3%
Depreciation	2.8%
Marketing	1.5%
Rent & Utilities	4.0%
Other	1.0%

Source: IBISWorld, March 2015

Rules of Thumb - T

Industry Trend

- "With a quarter of Americans sporting at least one tattoo, it's become impossible to walk down the street in summertime without navigating a virtual museum of color on skin."

    Source: The hand that held the needle" by Luke O'Neil, *Boston Globe*, May 25, 2014

- "'Tattoos,' she (Elizabeth Schlessinger) said, 'can be an unwanted reminder of an impulsive decision made over spring break.' It typically takes about 10 sessions at a cost of several hundred dollars or more per treatment. The lighter the color, the harder it is to take off. 'Some stats say half of all people with tattoos eventually want them removed.....'"

    Source: "Erasing the Signs of Youth for Whims" by Cindy Atoji Keene, *Globe* Correspondent, *Boston Sunday Globe*, July, 2013

Taxicab Businesses (See also Ground Transportation, Limousine Services)		
SIC 4121-01	NAICS 485310	Number of Businesses/Units 249,328

Rules of Thumb

> ➢ 4 times EBITDA plus value of vehicles

Pricing Tips

- "Selling price should be between 1 year and 2 years' net profit, depending upon the number of cabs and their respective ages."

Benchmark Data

Statistics (Taxi & Limousine Services)

Number of Establishments	249,328
Average Profit Margin	13.6%
Revenue per Employee	$52,100
Average Number of Employees	1.3
Average Wages per Employee	$34,556

Products and Services Segmentation

Taxi services	55.1%
Leasing to taxi operators	23.7%
Luxury and corporate sedan services	7.2%
Stretch limousine services	5.8%
Other	5.7%
Special needs transportation services	2.5%

Major Market Segmentation

Private consumers	54.5%
Corporations	29.5%
Tourists	13.2%
Other	2.8%

26th Edition

T - Rules of Thumb

Industry Costs

Profit	13.6%
Wages	66.9%
Purchases	8.3%
Depreciation	4.9%
Marketing	0.8%
Rent & Utilities	4.0%
Other	1.5%

Source: IBISWorld, August 2015

Industry Trend

- "As Transportation Network Companies (TNCs) continue to disrupt the transportation industry, there are a growing number of taxi drivers who are banding together in a unique way to compete with the likes of Uber and Lyft. Drivers in Denver, Portland, San Jose, New Jersey, and other areas are now teaming up to create cooperatives, a type of business in which each employee owns a share of the company and is able to participate in decision making. While cooperatives exist in many industries, including banking, retail, and manufacturing, there is a particular appeal for workers in the transportation industry who are often subject to long working hours and steep operating fees. Better working conditions and ownership of the business are two of the primary benefits of working for a cooperative business."

    Source: "Cooperatives a Growing Trend in the Taxi Industry" researchunderwriters.com, March 19, 2015

- "Taxis are losing business travelers to ride-hailing services like Uber, a survey shows. In the three months ended in June, Uber overtook taxis as the most expensed form of ground transportation, according to Certify, a provider of expense management systems. Uber accounted for 55 percent of ground transportation receipts, versus taxis at 43 percent. That's a big jump from just the beginning of the year. In the first quarter, Uber Technologies had 46 percent of receipts tracked by Certify, compared with 53 percent for taxis. Certify based its finding on the 28 million trip receipts its North American clients submit each year. Business travelers whose companies use other services to track expenses are not included in the results."

    Source: Associated Press as reported in *Boston Globe*, 7/17/15

- "To drive a cab in Boston, drivers need access to one of the city's 1,825 taxi permits, generally known as medallions. Fatefully, the city long ago let medallions trade on the open market, and only a minority of Boston cab drivers have scraped together enough money to buy their own.

    "Instead, most Boston cabbies are independent contractors driving taxis owned by someone else. Just to work, they have to pay a medallion owner a fee that can top $100 for a single 12-hour period, and on slow nights only the driver suffers. For the medallion owner, meanwhile, the arrangement has been rather cushy: Shift after shift, week after week, drivers' fees far exceed the cost of buying and maintaining cabs.

    "Inevitably, the going rate for a medallion shot up over time, reaching $700,000 last spring. Because drivers need to cover the fees they pay to medallion owners, the inequity in this system filters down to street level in the form of some of the country's highest cab rates.

    "The system was sustainable as long as passengers had no alternative. But with passengers—and even some drivers—defecting to the likes of Uber, Lyft, and Sidecar, the value of taxi medallions is in free fall. In October, a medallion changed hands for $561,000. In the last month, a medallion sold for $350,000 in a foreclosure auction. Lenders are abandoning the market, and sales have slowed to a trickle."

Source: "The $700,000 taxi medallion is doomed," *Boston Sunday Globe*, March 15, 2015

	Franchise
TCBY (See also Franchises, Ice Cream/Yogurt Shops)	
Approx. Total Investment	$215,000 to $420,000
NAICS 722515	Number of Businesses/Units 880

Rules of Thumb
➤ 40 to 45 percent of annual sales plus inventory

Resources

Websites
- www.tcby.com

Technology Companies—Information

Rules of Thumb
➤ 100 percent of annual sales plus inventory
➤ 3 times SDE plus inventory
➤ 3 times EBIT
➤ 3 times EBITDA

Pricing Tips
- "Renewal rates are paramount, whether the business is advertiser supported or subscription supported."

Benchmark Data
- "The sales ratio to employee expense should exceed 1.5 to 1."

Expenses as a percentage of annual sales	
Cost of goods	40%
Payroll/labor Costs	25%
Occupancy	05%
Profit (estimated pretax)	20%

Industry Trend
- "I see continued consolidation as smaller providers are rolled into larger companies. It is easier for larger companies to buy than to build."

Seller Financing
- 5 years

T - Rules of Thumb

Technology Companies—Manufacturing		
	NAICS 334111	

Rules of Thumb
- Niche market—4.25 to 4.75 adjusted net plus inventory
- PCB—4.65 to 5.0 plus inventory
- Software—4.50 to 6.0 plus inventory
- Non-niche—4.35 to 5.5 plus inventory

Pricing Tips
- "Adjusted net times [EBIT] 4 to 5.5 (depending on prior growth curves)"
- "Additions: location, 1st impression on walk-through, how competitive is marketplace, how clear P&L is. High tech or low tech? How much is straightforward in P&L & how much has to be recast?"

Technology Companies—Service		
	NAICS 541	

Rules of Thumb
- Temporary Agencies—1.25 to 3.5 EBITDA
- Test Services—2.75 to 3.35 EBITDA
- Design Services—2.5 to 3.5 EBITDA
- 3 to 7 times EBITDA
  (Adjusted net for large companies is EBITDA, for smaller ones SDE is used as adjusted net)

Pricing Tips
- "Growth is very important; stagnating companies tend to be closer to 3xSDE or 4-5x EBITDA. Growth companies can get 4–5x SDE and 5–8x EBITDA"
- "There is usually no rule of thumb. Right combination of technology and customers can push deal prices up significantly. Typically financed by cash, stock and earnouts."
- "Usually goes for multiple of revenues—especially when the company is not highly profitable but has valuable technology."

Expert Comments

"Most companies in the industry have been around a while and have their own niche—a lot of long-term customers—usually good down-side protection."

"Software services are typically very sticky and highly valued. At the same time technology changes rapidly and risk of obsolescence is high. Customer concentration tends to be high."

Benchmark Data
- "Good businesses tend to have above $100K per employee in revenue; margins should almost always be more than 50%."

Rules of Thumb - T

Expenses as a percentage of annual sales

Cost of goods	40%
Payroll/labor Costs	20%
Occupancy	05%
Profit (estimated pretax)	15%

Industry Trend
- "Stable segment—most of the high growth was in the past—still growing faster than overall economy."

Seller Financing
- "Combination of cash and seller financing—buyer may tap into existing lines of credit—typically no new SBA financing."
- "Typically sellers get a good parity of value on earnouts, non-competes, etc."

Questions
- "Focus should be on strategic value of the business because most of the time the value has very little to do with current financials."

Tee Shirt Shops		
SIC 5699-17	NAICS 448190	Number of Businesses/Units 11,500

Rules of Thumb
- ➢ 30 percent of annual sales plus inventory

Telecommunication Carriers (Wired)		
	NAICS 517110	

Rules of Thumb
- ➢ 2.5 times SDE includes inventory

Pricing Tips
- "Need to understand how the carrier commission structure will impact the current client base and future sales. Trained, knowledgeable and professional sales staff is critical—this is not an order-taking environment."

Expert Comments
"Very robust, competitive landscape, but a savvy operator can carve out a healthy market share."

Benchmark Data
- "Sales per employee"

T - Rules of Thumb

Expenses as a percentage of annual sales
Cost of goods 40%
Payroll/labor Costs 24%
Occupancy 12%
Profit (estimated pretax) 17%

Industry Trend
- "Continued growth, especially in smart phones and data services"

Questions
- "Trends for client counts. Cancellation rates and velocity."

Telecommunications		
	NAICS 517110	

Rules of Thumb
➢ $700 to $1,400 per line
➢ 3 times SDE includes inventory
➢ 5 times EBITDA

Pricing Tips
- "Depends on the amount of equipment involved as well as the quality. Differentiate from fiber optic splicers and diggers."
- "Three variables—$1,000 to $2,000 per installed port; 20 to 40 percent of annual revenues, depending upon sales mix & earnings; earnings impact selling price, but on a case by case basis relating to the first two variables plus cash flow analysis. This industry is far from exact, as market share, client base revenues, product line exclusivity, market potential (saturation) and earnings all impact market value. The old adage 'beauty is in the eye of the beholder' definitely applies to the telecom industry. Client (installed) base revenue mix and profit margin? New system sales product mix? Competition? Service reputation? Customer retention rate? Inventory obsolescence factor? Overall pretax profit?"

Industry Trend
- "These businesses are growing exponentially as the demand is starting to catch up with the amount of fiber in the ground"

Seller Financing
- 3–5 years

Questions
- "Point of differentiation. Where do your customers come from?"
- "Are there any Competitive Local Exchange Carriers (CLECs) operational in market area? Do they have their own facilities or are they reselling?"

Resources

Trade Publications
- Telephony Magazine: www.tmcnet.com

Rules of Thumb - T

Telephone Companies/Independent

| | NAICS 517110 | |

Rules of Thumb

➤ "Sales price throughout the nation has been established at between $800 and $1,200 per subscriber."

Television Sales & Service (See also Appliance Repair, Appliance Stores)

| | NAICS 443142 | |

Rules of Thumb

➤ 2 times monthly sales plus inventory

Television Stations (See also Radio Stations)

| SIC 4833-01 | NAICS 515120 | Number of Businesses/Units 4,000 |

Rules of Thumb

➤ 9 to 12 times EBITDA

Industry Trend

- "Many of the 290 TV station purchases in 2013 occurred as group acquisitions by some of the largest owners, building their portfolios of stations even more. The Tribune Co. emerged from bankruptcy to make the richest single deal, spending $2.73 billion to acquire 19 stations from Local TV Holdings. Gannett completed a $2.2 billion transaction to buy 17 stations from Belo Corp., almost doubling Gannett's TV holdings and giving it national reach. Twelve stations changed hands when Media General merged with New Young Broadcasting."

    Source: "A Surge in Local TV Acquisitions Puts More Stations in the Hands of a Few," by Deborah Potter and Katerina Eva Matsa, www.journalism.org March 26, 2014

Temporary Agencies (See also Office Staffing)

| SIC 7363-04 | NAICS 561320 | Number of Businesses/Units 11,000 |

Rules of Thumb

➤ 1 to 2 times annual sales plus inventory

➤ 3 times SDE plus inventory

➤ 2 to 5 times EBIT (smaller deals under $25 million)

➤ 5 to 7.5 times EBIT (larger deals over $25 million)

➤ 6 to 9 times EBIT (Information Technology)

➤ 3 to 6 times EBITDA—Depending on revenues

T - Rules of Thumb

Pricing Tips
- "The price depends on the industry served."
- "Multiple depends on size of company."

Expert Comments
"Very nice business for financial buyer"

"Easy to start, and smart owners can really grow these quickly."

Benchmark Data
- For Benchmark Data see Office Staffing

Expenses as a percentage of annual sales	
Cost of goods	10%
Payroll/labor Costs	70%
Occupancy	10%
Profit (estimated pretax)	10%

Seller Financing
- "3-year earnouts are most typical"
- 2 to 5 years

Questions
- "What industry do you serve?"
- "Who does the sales?"

Resources

Associations
- American Staffing Association: www.americanstaffing.net

The Maids (See also Franchises, Janitorial Services, Maid Brigade, Molly Maid) — Franchise

Approx. Total Investment	$93,000 to $125,000
NAICS 561720	Number of Businesses/Units 1,100

Rules of Thumb
➢ 40 to 45 percent of annual sales plus inventory

Resources

Websites
- www.maids.com

Ticket Services

| SIC 7999-73 | NAICS 561599 | Number of Businesses/Units 1,600 |

Rules of Thumb
- 2 times SDE
- 4 times EBITDA for small to midsize operations; 5 times EBITDA for larger companies

Pricing Tips
- "Due to StubHub, RazorGator and private equity shops, multiple has increased."
- "Number of corporate clients?"
- "Length of time in business? Stability of earnings? How do they get tickets? Average markup? Repeat business?"

Industry Trend
- "Wall Street has its trading floor. Ticket sales have StubHub. StubHub.com, the San Francisco-based online marketplace, has become the ticket scalper of the digital age, the ultimate middleman to shake up the way people interact to buy and sell tickets to almost any concert, theater performance or sporting event."

Source: StubHub, Revolutionizing the Modern-Day Ticker Scalper," www.abcnews.go.com, February 6, 2013

Resources

Associations
- National Association of Ticket Brokers: www.natb.org

Tire Stores

| SIC 5531-23 | NAICS 441320 | Number of Businesses/Units 54,218 |

Rules of Thumb
- 25% of Annual Gross Sales
- 1 to 3 times SDE plus inventory
- 3 to 4 times EBIT
- 2.5 to 3 times EBITDA

Pricing Tips
- "Tire stores grossing over $1 million are very desirable, despite low margins, and are fetching a 3–3.5 multiple."
- "The buyer needs to know what percentage of the revenues are tires vs. auto repair. A good mix is 50/50, tires to auto repair."
- "This business has shown some growth but has been affected by the price of oil per barrel. Tire prices have gone up as well as the other normal business expenses, i.e., rent, utilities, parts and labor costs have increased and these are four main variables. As such the owner needs to increase his hourly labor rate and product costs to offset these increases."

T - Rules of Thumb

- "A product name identity on the business as shown above does generate a greater multiple as shown. If the business does not have a name identity or management in place, you will need to reduce the multiple by 10%. The above multiples do not include inventory, at cost; the multiples do include equipment, FF&E."

Expert Comments

"The tire industry has seen a higher number of new tire lines coming into the marketplace, mostly from Japan, China, and Korea. The gross profit on tire sales is not as high compared to auto service repair, so you prefer at least a 70/30 mix, tiresto auto repair services."

Benchmark Data

Statistics (Tire Dealers)

Number of Establishments	54,218
Average Profit Margin	3.3%
Revenue per Employee	$186,600
Average Number of Employees	4.0
Average Wages per Employee	$32,864

Products and Services Segmentation

Automotive services	49.8%
Passenger car and light-truck tires	38.3%
Medium- and heavy-duty truck tires	9.4%
Farm tires	1.4%
Off-road tires	1.1%

Industry Costs

Profit	3.3%
Wages	17.6%
Purchases	70.1%
Depreciation	1.2%
Marketing	1.3%
Rent & Utilities	3.6%
Other	2.9%

Market Share

Sumitomo Corporation	10.1%
Discount Tire Co.	6.0%
Les Schwab Tire Centers	5.6%

Source: IBISWorld, September 2015

U.S. Consumer Tire Retail Market Share (based on retail sales)

Distribution channel	2014
Independent tire dealers	60.5%
Mass merchandisers	13.0%
Warehouse clubs	9.0%
Auto dealerships	8.0%
Tire company-owned stores	7.5%
Miscellaneous outlets	2.0%

Source: Modern Tire Dealer, January 2015

Rules of Thumb - T

- "Benchmark in this industry is determined by daily car count vs. the average price per invoice per vehicle. This is an integral factor on each customer who walks through the door."

Expenses as a percentage of annual sales
Cost of goods	36% to 43%
Payroll/labor Costs	24% to 28%
Occupancy	09% to 15%
Profit (estimated pretax)	13% to 20%

Industry Trend

- "Although it is 6,000 miles away, the People's Republic of China is the center of the universe to the U.S. tire industry. In 2014, China exported a record 60.5 million passenger and light truck tires to the United States, representing one-quarter of all domestic replacement consumer tire shipments.
- "U.S. Consumer Tire Imports by country (units, in parentheses, are in millions)

2014 rank/country	% change vs. 2013
1. China (60.5)	+17.9%
2. Canada (19.6)	-4.8%
3. South Korea (18.0)	-9.0%
4. Thailand (12.2)	+10.9%
5. Indonesia (11.1)	-0.9%
6. Mexico (10.8)	-0.9%
7. Japan (10.1)	-2.9%
8. Taiwan (7.3)	+1.4%
9. Chile (6.8)	+13.3%
10. Germany (3.7)	+5.7%

Source: *Modern Tire Dealer*, January 2015

- "The trend on tire centers is stability, and the industry should hold its own for the next five years. The competition is stronger than, let's say, 10 years ago, with discount tire companies and major big box companies selling tire brands."
- "Half of dealers expect tire sales to improve in the next six months, according to industry analyst Nick Mitchell, senior vice president research for Northcoast Research in Cleveland, Ohio, and author of Modern Tire Dealer's Your Marketplace column. The other half expects sales to remain level.
"Truck tire dealers likewise are evenly split, with 50% seeing business improving and 50% believing it will stay level. None of the respondents to Modern Tire Dealer's exclusive 'Your Marketplace' survey feel business levels will drop."
Source: http://www.moderntiredealer.com/news/story/2015/03/half-of-dealers-expect-to-sell-more-tires.aspx
3/24/15

Seller Financing
- "Normally five years, note of 30 to 35% of the total price, at 6% interest."
- "5 to 7 years, on average"

Questions
- "Reason for selling. What he/she does on a daily basis. Worker's comp mode rate. Upside potential."
- "Key employees, their duties and positions. Will mgr. stay, will key techs stay? Term of the lease? Any major changes in the industry?"

T - Rules of Thumb

Resources

Trade Publications
- Modern Tire Dealer—a great Website, one of the best: www.moderntiredealer.com
- Tire Business: www.tirebusiness.com

Title Abstract and Settlement Offices		
SIC 6541-02	NAICS 541191	
Rules of Thumb		
➢ 60 percent of annual sales		
➢ 3 times SDE		
➢ 5 times EBIT		
➢ 4.5 times EBITDA		

Pricing Tips
- "'Affiliated Business Arrangements' (ABAs) are in vogue. Make sure the ABA is transferable upon sale. Title agencies will command higher prices in states with higher filed premiums."
- "Criteria include the sales history and trends. Title companies' revenues are affected by interest rates, but the stronger ones will maintain profits through the ups and downs by adjustments of variable expenses."

Expert Comments

"Although there is significant competition, this is a highly profitable industry with relatively low barriers to entry."

"Buyers for title agencies have increased due to legislative changes."

Benchmark Data

Statistics (Conveyancing Services)
Number of Establishments	38,384
Average Profit Margin	11.7%
Revenue per Employee	$128,700
Average Number of Employees	2.9
Average Wages per Employee	$68,933

Products and Services Segmentation
Conveyancing and title abstract services	44.8%
Settlement and closing services	24.8%
Title search and other document filing services	14.5%
Other legal services	9.5%
Patent copyright and other intellectual property document services	3.3%
Process services	3.1%

Major Market Segmentations

Businesses	55.3%
Individuals	42.6%
Government and nonprofit organizations	2.1%

Industry Costs

Profit	11.7%
Wages	53.7%
Purchases	8.8%
Depreciation	1.1%
Marketing	2.4%
Rent & Utilities	5.2%
Other	17.1%

Market Share

Fidelity National Financial, Inc.	19.6%
First American Financial Corporation	9.4%
Stewart Information Services Corporation	3.5%

Source: IBISWorld, December 2014

- "Title companies typically retain 70% of the premium on title insurance policies issued, with remaining 30% going to the underwriter."
- "Labor/Gross Revenues = <35% for metropolitan markets; Labor/Gross Revenues = <30% for rural markets"

Expenses as a percentage of annual sales

Cost of goods	30%
Payroll/labor Costs	20%
Occupancy	07%
Profit (estimated pretax)	35%

Questions
- "How many referral sources does the company have solid relationships with?"

Tobacco Stores (See also Retail Stores—Small Specialty)

SIC 5993-01	NAICS 453991	Number of Businesses/Units 10,000

Rules of Thumb
> 15 to 20 percent of annual sales plus inventory

Resources

Associations
- Tobacco Merchants Association (TMA): www.tma.org

T - Rules of Thumb

Franchise
Togo's Eatery (See also Franchises, Sandwich Shops)

Approx. Total Investment	$257,813 to $419,796
Estimated Annual Sales/Unit	$595,000
NAICS 722513	Number of Businesses/Units 250

Rules of Thumb
- ➢ 60 percent plus inventory

Resources

Websites
- www.togos.com

Tour Operators		
SIC 4725-01	NAICS 561520	Number of Businesses/Units 2,539

Rules of Thumb
- ➢ 2 to 4 times SDE
- ➢ 2 times SDE for small companies
- ➢ 3 to 5 times EBITDA—multiple expands as profits go up

Pricing Tips
- "Upscale or mid-grade?"
- "Average mark up? Wholesale or direct?"
- "Length of time in business? Single destination operators warrant a bit higher; type of travel (golf, ski, scuba, etc.)—specialist vs. generalist. Wholesale via agents or direct business? Inbound or outbound?"

Expert Comments

"Travel & tourism is universal. World is shrinking. Huge inheritance in USA to fuel 20-year boom."

Benchmark Data

Statistics (Tour Operators)
Number of Establishments	2,539
Average Profit Margin	5.2%
Revenue per Employee	$301,700
Average Number of Employees	9.2
Average Wages per Employee	$52,193

Products and Services Segmentation
International packaged tours	51.6%
Domestic packaged tours	41.0%
Reservation services	5.0%
Reselling packaged tours	1.4%
Other	1.0%

Rules of Thumb - T

Major Market Segmentation

Travel agents	65.0%
Tour wholesalers	28.9%
Consumers	6.1%

Industry Costs

Profit	5.2%
Wages	17.7%
Purchases	46.8%
Depreciation	1.2%
Utilities	3.0%
Rent	6.0%
Other	20.1%

Market Share

Flight Centre Ltd.	13.5%
The Travel Corporation	9.4%
The Mark Travel Corporation	6.6%

Source: IBISWorld, January 2015

Expenses as a percentage of annual sales

Cost of goods	80%
Payroll/labor Costs	55% (after COG)
Occupancy	15% (after COG)
Profit (estimated pretax)	20%

Industry Trend
- "Moderate—economy is not robust."

Questions
- "Which key employees stay post-sale? Are wholesale contracts transferable?"

Resources

Associations
- National Tour Association: www.ntaonline.com

Towing Companies

SIC 7549-01	NAICS 488410	Number of Businesses/Units 8,913

Rules of Thumb
- 70 percent of annual revenues plus inventory
- 2.75 times EBITDA

Pricing Tips
- "Extreme care with adding back depreciation, and/or allowance to replace trucks. Define which segment of industry, and check to see if the insurance premium is fair market value. Small companies and those in non-consent business are hard to sell."

T - Rules of Thumb

- "The last of the consolidators has liquidated its acquisitions at a loss. The implication is that there are negative economies of scale at both ends of the scale, large and small, i.e., above some size these businesses based on revenue, etc. have a declining value, and that optimal values are found within the span of control of one person. Ease of entry has been increasing, so going-concern values have been declining."

Expert Comments

"These businesses vary widely. Hands-on management is almost always a critical element. Control of operating real estate is usually a major element in profitability."

Benchmark Data

Statistics (Automobile Towing)

Number of Establishments	8,913
Average Profit Margin	6.7%
Revenue per Employee	$110,200
Average Number of Employees	6.2
Average Wages per Employee	$33,788

Products and Services Segmentation

Passenger car towing services	41.2%
Light duty truck towing services	40.5%
Roadside assistance services	18.3%

Major Market Segmentation

Individuals	42.5%
Local and state governments	34.8%
Commercial customers	22.7%

Industry Costs

Profit	6.7%
Wages	30.6%
Purchases	25.0%
Depreciation	5.0%
Marketing	1.2%
Rent & Utilities	6.7%
Other	24.8%

Source: IBISWorld, October 2015

Expenses as a percentage of annual sales

Cost of goods	30%
Payroll/labor Costs	30%
Occupancy	08%
Profit (estimated pretax)	20%

Industry Trend

- "Trend is positive, but competition is fierce. Many companies come and go."
- "More than 85 percent of all tows in the U.S. involve passenger cars and light trucks. The majority of these tows are provided by small, family-owned towing businesses."

Source: Towing and Recovery Association of America (TRAA)

Seller Financing
- 5 years

Resources

Trade Publications
- Tow Times Magazine: www.towtimes.com

Toy Stores (See also Hobby Shops)

SIC 5945-17	NAICS 451120	Number of Businesses/Units 6,500

Rules of Thumb
- ➢ 20 to 25 percent of annual sales plus inventory

Benchmark Data
- For more Benchmark Data see Hobby Shops

Annual Sales Data

Categories	Annual 2013
Total Traditional Toy Categories	$22.09 billion
Action Figure/Accessories/Role Play	$1.41 billion
Arts & Crafts	$1.16 billion
Building Sets	$2.00 billion
Dolls	$2.70 billion
Games/Puzzles	$1.86 billion
Infant/Preschool	$3.62 billion
Youth Electronics	$565 million
Outdoor & Sports Toys	$4.37 billion
Plush	$1.39 billion
Vehicles	$1.51 billion
All Other Toys	$1.51 billion

- "The toy industry's annual total economic impact in the U.S. is nearly $75.03 billion.
    - ✓ The average price of a toy is less than $8, but the estimated 3 billion units sold across the nation each year generate approximately $22 billion in direct toy sales.
    - ✓ From toy inventors to store clerks in every state from Alabama to Wyoming, the toy industry supports an estimated 607,020 jobs (FTE) generating $26.69 billion in wages for U.S. workers.
    - ✓ The toy industry also generates $11.54 billion in tax revenue each year (combined State taxes of $5.27 billion; combined Federal taxes of $6.26 billion)."

Source: www.toyassociation.org

Industry Trend
- "Since the launch of Skylanders in 2011, toys-to-life have been one of the fastest-growing product categories in toys and games. With the launch of LEGO Dimensions in late 2015 the market is poised for dynamic growth in 2015 and 2016. However, the product's limited appeal in emerging markets and competition from emerging technologies such as smart toys and virtual

T - Rules of Thumb

reality gaming mean that the market will saturate very quickly and growth will slow significantly in 2017.

"LEGO Dimensions is expected to be a major growth driver over the second half of 2015 and 2016. The product brings together a large array of popular licensed characters and settings with significant cross-generational appeal and real world playability that is not matched by rival offers."

Source: "The Future of Toys-to-Life: Prospects and Forecasts" euromonitor.com, September 2015

- "With limited appeal in emerging markets and growing competition from emerging gaming and entertainment technologies such as virtual and augmented reality gaming demand for toys-to-life will start to stagnate by 2018."

Source: "Key Global and Regional Trends Shaping Toys Licensing" euromonitor.com, September 2015

- "The holiday season is a crucial time for many specialty toy-store owners. The period from Black Friday to Christmas can account for as much as 50% of a small toy shop's yearly sales, and the season can make up for losses during the rest of the year.

"The number of small toy stores plummeted 40%, to 1,500 from 2,500, over the past 10 to 15 years, estimates Kathleen McHugh, the president of the American Specialty Toy Retailing Association. 'Toys are being sold now in a lot of different places, like bookstores, gift shops and educational supply stores,' she adds."

Source: "Peruse the Puzzles, Have Some Wine" by Adam Janofsky, *Wall Street Journal*, December 4, 2014

Resources

Associations
- Toy Industry Association—good site: www.toyassociation.org

Translation and Interpretation Services

SIC 7389-20	NAICS 541930	Number of Businesses/Units 56,447

Rules of Thumb
➢ 40 to 45 percent of annual sales plus inventory

Benchmark Data

Statistics (Translation Services)
Number of Establishments	56,447
Average Profit Margin	25.1%
Revenue per Employee	$79,400
Average Number of Employees	1.3
Average Wages per Employee	$20,823

Products and Services Segmentation
Interpretation services	54.6%
Written translation services	41.7%
Other	3.7%

Major Market Segmentation

Technology, finance, and retail	42.5%
State and local governments	30.4%
Marketing and advertising	14.7%
Medicine, engineering and natural sciences	7.0%
Other	5.4%

Industry Costs

Profit	25.1%
Wages	26.0%
Purchases	12.1%
Depreciation	1.8%
Marketing	1.2%
Rent & Utilities	4.2%
Other	29.6%

Market Share

LanguageLine Solutions	6.0%
Lionbridge Technologies Inc.	5.2%

Source: IBISWorld, April 2015

- "It's all about supply and demand and since the U.S. became involved in Afghanistan after the Sept. 11 attacks, there has been demand for linguists or interpreters of the two main Afghan languages, Dari and Pashto. The average salary for a linguist or interpreter who speaks Dari is $187,000 and it's $193,000 for those who speak Pashto, according to Indeed.com. The jobs range from an interpreter for military personnel to a media desk officer who would translate Afghan news stories and communicate with Afghan media."

Source: http://www.salary.com

Travel Agencies

SIC 4724-02	NAICS 561510	Number of Businesses/Units 18,782

Rules of Thumb

- 45 percent of annual gross profit
- 1.8 to 3 times SDE plus inventory
- 2 to 3 times EBIT for small to mid-size agencies
- 3 to 5 times EBITDA for larger agencies
- "Small operations, $1 to $3 million—35 percent of annual commissions and fees; $4 to $8 million—40 percent; $9 to $20 million—45 percent; 3.5 times EBITDA above $20 million in volume; 5 times EBITDA for shops earning over $1 million net profit."
- "For agencies with $1 to $4 million in sales, 1.5 to 2.0 SDE is customary. If $5 to $10 million, then 2.0 to 2.5 SDE"

Pricing Tips

- "For both SDE and EBITDA, the multiple expands as profits go higher. SDE is 2–3x and EBITDA is 3–5x."

T - Rules of Thumb

- "Top importance is: 1. The gross income not gross sales 2. In-house income not independent agent income. Income verification is easy in this business as there is a paper trail for all transactions."
- "Profitability? Agency more than 3 years old? Agency does not depend on more than one account for more than 10 percent of gross? Agency does not rebate? Manager stays on?"
- "Would need last 18 months' financials to spot any trends"
- "Today a common formula for the pricing of travel agencies is paid via earnout with a minimal down payment applied to the overall earnout. 25% of revenue over two years is a common multiplier. For example if gross sales were $5,000,000 and gross commission income were $500,000, it would be calculated as follows, assuming the sales remain stable over the two year earnout: 25% of $500,000=$125,000 multiplied by 2 for two years, give a total purchase price of $250,000. With the current economic situation, we are seeing multipliers of 20% the first year and 15% the second year applied to this formula in some cases."
- "The market is soft, however business volume is growing. Travel industry is the biggest industry in the world, and people love to be in it for the lifestyle it provides. Profits are slimmer; however the bigger volume brings overrides & incentives."
- "Buyers simply need to receive what they pay for. With zero tangible assets, all transactions now include performance-laden contracts."
- "Always include service charges, fees and markups to the gross sales. These are becoming a more and more important part of agencies' income."
- "Several factors. Most important staff, goodwill. Airline contracts for net rates, specialty clients, etc."
- "Look at commission and fee income; both are important."
- "Most important are long-term good employees, long-term goodwill, owner's covenant not to compete, high volume and special contracts net or override with the vendors. It's important to count all service fees as well as commissions from suppliers when calculating SDE. Also overrides and CRS money."
- "One-quarter down, balance earned out over 24 months"
- "Earnouts are very common, with a percentage of the income generated from the selling agency's customer list paid over a 2-year period—maximum."

Expert Comments

"Good financials are important and a good spread of business, i.e., not one big client."

"With the aging of the baby boomers more and more demand will be put on agents for leisure travel and tours."

"Must have continued growth with various client bases, groups, incentives, meeting & conventions, constant marketing, stable staff, industry trend is upwards."

"The small travel agency's income has declined due to commission cuts & Internet, however the industry is growing due to more people traveling and many people willing to pay service fees for good travel agents. It is good to have corporate & leisure mix to weather all possibilities. The bigger the volume, the bigger the ratio of income."

Rules of Thumb - T

"Service is most important, ARC & IATAN appointments transfer require 2 years' experienced manager. Better to purchase an agency with goodwill."

"Competition is high as it is an easy business to learn. Fully licensed agencies are more difficult due to their financial requirements. Location is not important; services & cost are more important."

"Agents are vanishing—no new blood is entering the industry."

"The travel industry's volume is higher as more people are traveling; however, with commission cuts and direct Internet sales from the airlines, revenue has shifted. Major sources of revenue are service fees, commissions paid by cruise, hotels, car and other vendors. Belonging to a good consortium is important for higher revenue."

Benchmark Data

Statistics (Travel Agencies)

Number of Establishments	18,782
Average Profit Margin	2.6%
Revenue per Employee	$190,500
Average Number of Employees	10.1
Average Wages per Employee	$59,757

Products and Services Segmentation

Tours and packaged travel bookings	32.0%
Cruise bookings	26.0%
International and domestic airline bookings	23.0%
Accommodation bookings	11.0%
Other services	5.0%
Car rental	3.0%

Major Market Segmentation

Leisure—international travel	52.0%
Leisure—domestic travel	25.0%
Corporate—unmanaged	11.0%
Corporate—managed	8.0%
Other	4.0%

Industry Costs

Profit	2.6%
Wages	32.1%
Purchases	20.0%
Depreciation	0.6%
Marketing	7.5%
Rent & Utilities	10.8%
Other	26.4%

Market Share

Expedia Inc.	9.5%
Priceline.com LLC	5.4%

Source: IBISWorld, October 2015

26th Edition

T - Rules of Thumb

- "Each agent should produce 2.5x their salary."
- "Gross sales of $1 million per agent, appraisal or evaluation should be done carefully as there are many factors in the successful profitable agency."
- "Corporate agents should book $1M in volume per year; leisure agents should book $700K volume per year."
- "Sales per employee should be high. Most important factor the ratio between inside(salary) or outside(independent contractor) employees. On sale of the business independent employees can leave & goodwill will be lost."
- "SDE should equal 20% of Gross Commissions in a well-run agency."
- "$1 million sales per employee; specialty groups, corporate accounts and low rent."
- "Higher net commissions due to special contracts. Service fee income. Overall control on expenses."
- "Look for preferred supplier and override agreements, written contractual agreements with corporate customers, relationships with wholesalers on airline tickets. GDS (airline computer system) contract situation is a key factor."

Expenses as a percentage of annual sales
Cost of goods	10% to 20%
Payroll/labor Costs	50% to 60%
Occupancy	15% to 20%
Profit (estimated pretax)	05% to 15%

Industry Trend

- "Meanwhile, from 2003 to 2014, the number of independent agents working primarily from their homes rose 434%, and as of 2013, they now eclipse the number of U.S. retail location agents. However, even though 40,000 independent agents have entered the marketplace in the 21st century, their combined sales are relatively small compared to storefront and corporate agencies.

  "'Consumers are increasingly using travel advisors and I think the data bears that out,' says Kerby (Zane Kerby, president/CEO of ASTA). 'Average sales are on the rise, and agencies are thriving with 84% of our members in the first three quarters of 2014 reporting that their revenues were better than the year before. I think the reason behind that is there is so much information available now to people on the Internet that you need a professional guide to make sense of it all.'"

  Source: "Travel Agent Industry Executives Argue That Agents Are Coming Back" by Greg Oates, skift.com, February 3, 2015

- "Good and getting better with baby boomers retiring"
- "Good if geopolitical factors stay in calm state"
- "Expedia said Thursday that it will buy online booking rival Orbitz Worldwide for roughly $1.6 billion, cementing its place as the No. 1 digital travel provider while potentially disrupting the hotel and airline industries. With the acquisition, the largest online travel agency in the U.S., will be incorporating the sector's third-largest player. Together, Expedia and Orbitz had 29.4 million unique visitors in the U.S. in December, according to comScore.

  "Airlines get 10% to 15% of their bookings through online travel agencies, but they don't have to haggle with those portals as much since they generally don't pay them commissions. Hotels may be the travel sector with the most concern. Online travel agencies are responsible for roughly 19% of their sales, Harteveldt (Henry Harteveldt, a travel industry analyst) says. And hotels pay

fees, on average of 15%, to online sites for bookings that are steered their way, Cole (Robert Cole, a travel industry analyst and consultant) says.
Source: "Traveling together: Expedia to buy rival Orbitz" by Charisse Jones, http://www.usatoday.com/story/money/business/2015/02/12/expedia-is-buying-orbitz-worldwide-for-12-per-share/23283797/ 2/13/15

- "Supply is dwindling, demand is there."

Seller Financing
- 2 to 5 years

Questions
- "Buyer should check ARC reports right up to closing. Any big accounts up for bid?"
- "What is the client base stability? What is the mix of in-house vs. outside independent agent business? What is the promotion budget? Reason for sale?"
- "The breakdown of revenue for salary & independent employees. Covenant not to compete clause."
- "Who stays on post-sale? Any client over 10% of biz? How long have your key accounts and employees been on board? Are you 100% credit card? Willing to do earnout on performance basis?"
- "What are your GDS and override contracts?"
- "Ask about who controls the business, is it under contract? Length of GDS contract, location, lease expiration date? Any net pricing? Do customers have written contracts to use the agency? Is there a database of past leisure customers? How often is this database contacted? The net commissions earned, service price charged, special override commission contracts from the vendors. Employees' goodwill, inside or independent contractors, all licenses, covenant not to compete."

Resources

Trade Publications
- Travel Agent Magazine: www.travelagentcentral.com
- Travel Weekly: www.travelweekly.com
- TravelAge West: www.travelagewest.com

Associations
- U.S. Travel Association: www.ustravel.org
- American Society of Travel Agents (ASTA): www.asta.org
- National Tour Association: www.ntaonline.com

Travel Wholesalers/Consolidators		
	NAICS 561520	

Rules of Thumb
- ➢ 3 to 5 times EBITDA
- ➢ "3 times EBITDA for small to midsize companies; 4 times EBITDA when profits exceed $350,000"

T - Rules of Thumb

Pricing Tips
- "Airlines not giving out as many contracts as they have in the past due to 90 percent of all airline seats being filled as number of aircraft has decreased. Airlines pushing more direct channels to their own Websites. Value of wholesaler is under some pressure."

Questions
- "Are the contracts owned or are they subcontracted?"
- "Length of time in business? Salary vs. commission? Who controls the business? How long are contracts valid?"

Trophy Studios	
NAICS 453998	Number of Businesses/Units 7,000

Rules of Thumb
- ➢ 40 to 45 percent of annual sales plus inventory

Industry Trend
- "Should be about the same as it has been, but technology is changing the business."

Tropical Smoothie Café (See also Franchises)	Franchise
Approx. Total Investment	$166,750 to $424,200
Estimated Annual Sales/Unit	Approximately $490,000
NAICS 722515	Number of Businesses/Units 340

Rules of Thumb
- ➢ 50 to 55 percent of annual sales plus inventory

Trucking Companies	
NAICS 484230	Number of Businesses/Units 588,163

Rules of Thumb
- ➢ 50 percent of annual sales
- ➢ 5 times EBIT
- ➢ 2 to 3 times EBITDA
- ➢ 1 to 2 times SDE + market value of assets
- ➢ $4,000 to $6,000 per driver

Rules of Thumb - T

Pricing Tips

Operating Ratio (EBIT divided by gross sales)
Excellent	85% or less
Good	86% to 92%
Fair	93% to 96%
Poor	97% or greater

Revenues per Mile
Excellent	1.40 or more
Good	1.35 to 1.39
Fair	1.30 to 1.34
Poor	1.29 or less

- "Focus should be on strategic value of the business because most of the times the value has very little to do with current financials"
- "Gross Sales important of course; understand all costs involved from licensing, broker (trucking brokers) fees, fuel surcharges, trailer and truck parking and driver salaries; all are important to understand. Understand the length of contracts; some contracts are not for actual work, but allow for bids to do the work/deliveries."
- "Special Equipment +15 percent; special services +5 to 25 percent; routes & relationships +10 to 25 percent."

Expert Comments

"This is difficult because of the variations in different types of motor carriers."

Benchmark Data

Statistics (Long-Distance Freight Trucking)
Number of Establishments	381,984
Average Profit Margin	5.4%
Revenue per Employee	$160,200
Average Number of Employees	3.0
Average Wages per Employee	$41,841

Products and Services Segmentation
Truckload carriers	58.8%
Less-than-truckload carriers	24.5%
Other transportation services	16.7%

Major Market Segmentation
Manufacturing sector	38.2%
Wholesale sector	19.9%
Other	16.4%
Retail sector	11.9%
Oil refiners	6.8%
Chemical companies	4.2%
Agricultural sector	2.6%

T - Rules of Thumb

Industry Costs

Profit	5.4%
Wages	26.4%
Purchases	27.6%
Depreciation	4.5%
Marketing	3.7%
Rent & Utilities	10.6%
Other	21.8%

Source: IBISWorld, October 2015

Statistics (Local Freight Trucking)

Number of Establishments	206,179
Average Profit Margin	5.8%
Revenue per Employee	$111,700
Average Number of Employees	1.8
Average Wages per Employee	$34,838

Products and Services Segmentation

Truckload transportation	44.4%
Less-than-truckload transportation	23.1%
Other Services	15.4%
Intermodal transportation	10.3%
Dry bulk transportation	6.8%

Major Market Segmentation

Retail and wholesale sectors	53.7%
Manufacturing sector	46.3%

Industry Costs

Profit	5.8%
Wages	31.1%
Purchases	30.7%
Depreciation	3.7%
Marketing	0.8%
Rent & Utilities	7.2%
Other	20.7%

Source: IBISWorld, October 2015

- "The average pay for a long-haul trucker is just shy of $50,000, according to the A.T.A., and an experienced trucker with a good safety record can make significantly more than that. The work typically offers lavish benefits that are increasingly rare for nonunion blue-collar employees.
  "An average long-haul truck can now cover 8,000 miles a month, down from almost 11,000 in 2007, according to the trade association. This helps account for downward wage pressure."
  Source: "Where have all the truckers gone?" by Neil Irwin, *New York Times*, Sunday August 10, 2014

Expenses as a percentage of annual sales

Cost of goods	0
Payroll/labor Costs	40% to 60%
Occupancy	0
Profit (estimated pretax)	08% to 15%

Rules of Thumb - T

Industry Trend
- "Trucking is becoming even more important as Internet sales and the need for packages to be moved from place to place increase."
- "In the 1980's there were approximately 300,000 trucking companies. That number has ballooned to over 675,000 carriers currently operating in the U.S. Additionally the miles driven and the trucks on the road at these carriers have increased. Freight volume shipped by trucks in the US is expected to grow 50% over the next 20 years, and the country's infrastructure will not even come close to keeping up."

Source: www.truckinjurylawyerblog.com

Seller Financing
- "2 years, up to 50%. Earnouts can work in this industry."

Questions
- "How old are the trucks, who owns the trailers? Where do you park and do you offer warehousing?"

Resources

Associations
- America's Independent Truckers Association: www.aitaonline.com

---

Truck Stops (See also Gas Stations)		
SIC 5541-03	NAICS 447190	Number of Businesses/Units 3,000

Rules of Thumb
- ➢ 75 percent of annual sales
- ➢ 5 times SDE plus inventory, may deduct cost of cosmetic update.
- ➢ 5 times EBITDA

Pricing Tips
- "The rule of thumb for truck stops is going to be 5–6 times EBITDA with the factors coming into play like the quality of the assets, and are there any environmental issues that will need to be deducted from the value of the truck stop. However, to arrive at an EBITDA one must add up all of the different profit centers that comprise the truck stop such as: income from the scales, truck wash, video games, gift shop, restaurant income or restaurant lease income if the unit is leased out, and sometimes there are other ancillary forms of income that will all need to be added together to get to the EBITDA of the truck stop."
- "A lot of people will try to pump up the value of a truck stop by stating how much property is comprised by the truck stop, because it takes several acres to make a truck stop, but anything beyond the basic amount of property needed that is being used to support the business should not be included as additional value. For example there may be a truck stop that sits on a 10-acre tract of ground and the seller has another 5 acres that he thinks add additional value to the truck stop, but it doesn't. Only the property that is being used at the present time."

T - Rules of Thumb

- "Be sure to check to see if they have any additional profit centers such as scales and if the scales are leased or owned. Other profit centers such as gambling machines (video poker etc.) sometimes are not included in the P & L's due to skimming."
- "Due to the multiple streams at one location the goodwill can go for a premium."
- "Limited buyers who buy this kind of business, due to the large number of employees and size of operation."
- "Business Only 2.5 to 3.5 times the Net/EBITDA; Real Estate + Business 7 to 10 times Net/EBITDA."
- "I only do cash deals. Environmental risk can turn into a nightmare on contract sales."

Expert Comments

"The truck stop industry has taken a severe beating lately due to the increased diesel fuel prices. Plus added to that the fact that the major truck stop operators such as Love's, Petro, Flying J, and Pilot are ruthless on their competition and have decreased the fuel margins considerably. Plus the majors that I just mentioned have made it a point to have fueling agreements with most of the major truck carriers across the country leaving only the independent truckers who will stop at the independent truck stops."

"Very expensive to replicate and build, few buyers, due to the heavy labor involvement and the 24X365 days business, yet very profitable."

"The truck stop/travel plaza industry is in turmoil as is the convenience store industry. High fuel prices, credit card fees, low margins and increased competition are taking their toll. Many convenience store operators have thought they would try their hand at a truck stop thinking that they are the same thing only larger with more volume. Not so. A truck stop is a different animal with a completely different customer base, nothing like that of a convenience store. In a truck stop the main seller is diesel fuel and the wants and needs of the customers are totally different. A convenience store deals mostly with local people and is really a little grocery store with gas, whereby a truck stop is a small city having to furnish more complete services to individuals that are going to be staying for an extended period of time, unless the truck stop/travel plaza, as they are known now, is something like a Love's that has formed an alliance with McDonalds and is selling their fuel at rock bottom prices because of their volume discounts and agreements made with national carriers."

"Even though the travel plazas are profitable, the size of operation and management acumen required can be daunting. Also the upfront monies required are pretty hefty as compared to most small businesses."

"The average return on investment for a truck stop is 6 to 8 percent. The high profit return on investment for a truck stop is 16 to 17 percent. In order for a buyer to determine a good deal—12 to 15 percent ROI for a truck stop should provide a good rule of thumb."

"Replication is difficult because 5 to 25 acres of prime real estate is required, and the cost can be between $5 million and $10 million to build one. Truck stops/travel plazas have been steady, but also the older or small mom/pops are being eliminated due to competition."

Benchmark Data
- "To be a profitable truck stop it seems inevitable that there is a restaurant connected to the facility. Many of the truck stops are now partnering with Hardee's, Wendy's, McDonald's, Arby's etc., while the others have a sit-down restaurant."
- "Convenience/Retail combined is approx. $500 per sq. ft."
- "Per employee sales annually: $135,000; Gross Profit Margins: 24%; Net Profit Margins: 1.8%"
- "Average annual sales are nearly $7 million with the larger, high-profit centers doing in excess of $20 million annually with a net of 6% of sales."
- "Typical Full-Service Travel Plaza Statistics
  At a typical full-service travel plaza you will find:
  - ✓ Convenience or retail stores (97%)
  - ✓ Check cashing (98%)
  - ✓ Private showers (89%)
  - ✓ Free parking (93%)
  - ✓ Buses welcome (82%)
  - ✓ Public fax machines (81%)
  - ✓ Restaurants or delis (77%)
  - ✓ Platform scales (59%)
  - ✓ Laundry facilities (58%)
  - ✓ Truck repair (50%)
  - ✓ Emergency road service (63%)
  - ✓ ATM machines (91%)
  - ✓ Security/local police patrol (54%)
  - ✓ Load boards (75%)
  - ✓ Postal service (53%)
  - ✓ Truck washes (28%)
  - ✓ Hotels or motels (28%)
  - ✓ Driver lounges (48%)
  - ✓ Recreational vehicle facilities (23%)
  - ✓ On-site fast food (51%)
  - ✓ Church services (38%)
  - ✓ Food court (15%)
  - ✓ Internet services (39%)"

Expenses as a percentage of annual sales

Cost of goods	63%
Payroll/labor Costs	08%
Occupancy	02% to 03%
Profit (estimated pretax)	04%

Industry Trend
- "There are not many independent truck stops left in the country with Pilot acquiring Flying J and making deals with other operators like Road Ranger to sell their Pilot fuel. It has been said that Pilot alone controls almost 60% of the diesel fuel sales in the United States."
- "The trend has been going down due to increased competition and reduced

margins. The independents are dropping out because they cannot compete with the major players who are expanding. Many of the independents have overbuilt and cannot compete."
- "Large chains will survive and mom and pops will have to specialize or get out."
- "Very slow growth due to the nature of the business. Large lots of 10+ acres required, and investments upwards of $10+ million per site make the field of players very limited."

Seller Financing
- "Property and land included: 10 to 15 years (8% to 11%); business only: 3 to 8 years (8% to 10%)"

Questions
- "Do they own the restaurant or lease it out? What is the environmental situation?"
- "Does he have any fuel agreements with any trucking lines? Does he have Fuel Man or similar fuel agreements that would be in place to draw regional or national trucking companies to him? Any hidden income, i.e., video machines, laundry, showers etc.?"
- "As much paperwork as possible including tax returns."
- "When valuing the business be sure to question the Seller about all of the sources of income. Most units have income from video games which is very lucrative, but that doesn't make it to the P & L; scale income and do they own the scales or lease them, any contracts with carriers, do they have Mr. Fuel or other recognized fuel discount programs, shower income etc.? The money is still made on the inside so the higher the fuel volume, the more people that visit the facility, the more money they will spend inside. Is the unit branded with Shell, BO, TA etc.? If so how much time is left on the contract with them and what are their costs to them? Who do they buy their fuel from? To purchase fuel you must have a fuel purchase agreement with your supplier and what is the length of the term and the charge for the fuel? Most agreements are for 7–10 years and if it is a branded unit you will be required to pay them back if you do not fulfill the length of the agreement, and this can be very costly. Are there any rebates coming back from the fuel supplier? How much over rack are they charging you? Very important that you know what the cost to buy fuel is. If you are doing 400,000 gallons of fuel per month and you are paying 1 cent over the posted rack price, that is $4,000 per month plus freight to bring it to your facility. The seller will know this and the buyer should know it too."

Resources

Websites
- www.npnweb.com
- America's Independent Truckers' Association, Inc.: www.aitaonline.com

Associations
- National Association of Truck Stop Operators—an excellent site: www.natso.com

Rules of Thumb - U

Franchise
Two Men and a Truck (See also Franchises, Trucking Companies)

Approx. Total Investment	$173,000 to $578,500
NAICS long distance 48412 / local 48411	Number of Businesses/Units 225

Rules of Thumb
> 40 to 45 percent of annual sales plus inventory

Benchmark Data
- "The first year, the franchise generated $835,000 in gross revenue. This year, he expects that figure to reach $1.8 million. Crain started with two trucks, added a third that November and two more in March 2008. He currently owns nine trucks and leases a 10th during the busy summer season. Three more are on order."

Source: "Young entrepreneur moves up with franchise" by Susan Jacobson, *Orlando Sentinel*, August 31, 2014

Resources
Websites
- www.twomenandatruck.com

Uniform Rental (See also Hospital Laundry)	
NAICS 812331	Number of Businesses/Units 4,454

Rules of Thumb
> 40 to 45 times weekly sales plus inventory

Pricing Tips
- An industry expert says that if there are contracts with the accounts serviced, the rule of thumb will be 70 percent of gross annual sales.

Benchmark Data

Statistics (Industrial Laundry & Linen Supply)
Number of Establishments	4,454
Average Profit Margin	6.8%
Revenue per Employee	$123,600
Average Number of Employees	26.3
Average Wages per Employee	$40,033

Products and Services Segmentation
Work uniform rental and cleaning	31.2%
Flat linens rental and cleaning	21.2%
Linen garments rental and cleaning	16.3%
Other	14.1%
Industrial mats rental and cleaning	12.2%
Industrial wiping cloths rental and cleaning	5.0%

26th Edition

U - Rules of Thumb

Major Market Segmentation
Healthcare	24.0%
Food service	19.3%
Retail and service	19.0%
Hospitality and lodging	15.8%
Manufacturing and distribution	12.7%
Other	9.2%

Industry Costs
Profit	6.8%
Wages	31.7%
Purchases	29.9%
Depreciation	4.0%
Marketing	1.0%
Rent & Utilities	8.6%
Other	18.0%

Market Share
Cintas Corporation	25.9%
Aramark Corporation	10.9%
UniFirst Corporation	9.3%
G&K Services Inc.	5.5%

Source: IBISWorld, September 2015

UPS Store (See also Franchises, Mail & Parcel Centers) — Franchise

Approx. Total Investment	$50,152 to $420,299
NAICS 561431	Number of Businesses/Units 4,590

Rules of Thumb
- 35 to 40 percent of annual sales plus inventory
- 2 to 3 times SDE plus inventory
- "Franchises will sell for higher % of Annual Gross Sales. High volume UPS stores sell for over 1 times annual sales (STR—Subject to Royalty)."

Resources
Websites
- www.theupsstore.com

U Save Car and Truck Rental (See also Auto Rental, Franchises) — Franchise

Approx. Total Investment	$60,000 to $681,300
NAICS 532111	Number of Businesses/Units 170

Rules of Thumb
- "10 percent of annual sales (price does not include cost of vehicles, and revenues do not include auto & truck sales)"

Rules of Thumb - **U**

Resources

Websites
- www.usave.net

Used Goods

(See also Clothing Stores—Used, Consignment Shops, Resale Shops)

NAICS 45331	Number of Businesses/Units 77,865

Rules of Thumb
➢ 20 to 25 percent of annual sales plus inventory unless it is on consignment

Benchmark Data

Statistics (Used Goods Stores)
Number of Establishments	77,865
Average Profit Margin	4.2%
Revenue per Employee	$63,400
Average Number of Employees	3.0
Average Wages per Employee	$18,568

Products and Services Segmentation
Other	43.1%
Women's, juniors' and misses' wear	14.9%
Furniture, including outdoor furniture, and sleep equipment	9.3%
Books	7.3%
Kitchenware and home furnishings	7.3%
Jewelry, including watches	7.2%
Children's wear	5.6%
Menswear	5.3%

Industry Costs
Profit	4.2%
Wages	29.2%
Purchases	51.2%
Depreciation	1.0%
Marketing	2.2%
Rent & Utilities	4.0%
Other	8.2%

Market Share
Goodwill Industries International Inc.	24.6%
Savers Inc.	6.9%
Winmark Corporation	5.8%

Source: IBISWorld, May 2015

V - Rules of Thumb

Valpak Direct Marketing Systems — Franchise
(See also Coupon Books, Franchises, SuperCoups)

Approx. Total Investment	$32,500 to $2,000,000
NAICS 541870	Number of Businesses/Units 170

Rules of Thumb
- 40 to 45 percent of annual sales plus inventory
- 2 times SDE plus inventory
- "If a cooperative direct mail business, such as Money Mailer or SuperCoups is making $100,000, it could be sold for $150,000 to $225,000, and $250,000 if it was a perfect situation. Now, on the other hand if it is a Valpak, I believe you could get up to 3 times what it is making because Valpak is the undisputed leader. They are owned by COX Publishing."

Resources

Websites
- www.valpak.com

Valvoline Instant Oil Change — Franchise
(See also Auto Lube/Oil Change, Franchises)

Approx. Total Investment	$200,000 to $2,000,000
NAICS 811191	Number of Businesses/Units 900

Rules of Thumb
- 50 percent of annual sales

Resources

Websites
- www.viocfranchise.com

Vending Machine Industry
(See also Route Distribution Businesses)

SIC 2599-02	NAICS 454210	Number of Businesses/Units 24,251

Rules of Thumb
- SDE is from 2–3 times depending on gross sales. Under $500k in sales usually 2 timesSDE; over $500k gross 2.5–3 times SDE.
- 65 to 75 percent of annual sales plus inventory
- 2 to 3 times SDE plus inventory
- 3 to 4 times EBIT
- 2 to 4 times EBITDA

Rules of Thumb - V

- "Smaller, one-man operations sell for less than one year's gross sales. Larger vending businesses are based on cash flow and asset value. A common rule of thumb would be 1 to 2 times SDE plus assets. Again, companies with new assets would be closer to 2 times SDE plus hard assets."
- "Listing price should be less than 1 year's gross. Some vending businesses are heavy in assets, so assets plus 1 to 1½ times cash flow. Highly profitable may sell for 2 to 3 times cash flow."

Pricing Tips

- "Inventory in machines on location & coins in coin machines are included in the price—estimate at $100 per machine. Inventory in trucks and warehouse is not included. Most machines should be MDB capable—this allows machines to be fitted for credit cards and inventory control software."
- "Are machines owned and/or financed? Head count in the accounts; commissions paid out? Time access/restriction to servicing each account."
- "2x owner's benefit for gross sales under $500k. Near 3x owner's benefit for gross sales over $500k."
- "Type of vending (bulk vs. full line vs. crane, etc.) >0; are machines owned; age of equipment; commissions paid to customers."
- "Price could be 70 to 80 percent of last year's sales if business is well established."
- "Take a pricing survey of what is sold...soda selling for less than $1 or candy selling for less than .75 is not good."
- "Major factors involved in pricing a route include: (1) Where the route is located; (2) What is the year & condition of the vehicle included? (3) Is the truck owned or leased? (4) How many years the route is established; (5) Is the route protected stops, territory or is it an unprotected route? (6) What is the brand of the product that the route is distributing? (7) How close to the depot is the route? (8) Value of equipment included (vending machines, validators, step-climbing hand trucks, coin & bill counters)?"
- "How much does a route cost? The net profit of the route is the main factor in determining its value. Other significant factors include the type of route, the gross, the area, days and hours, and the vehicle. A general rule to keep in mind for the purchase of a route is 'double net.' The amount that you net in one year will be the approximate down payment amount, and double that figure will be the total purchase price. (Example: route netting $1,000/wk would cost approximately $100,000 with $50,000 down.) As a rule of thumb, the bigger the name a brand route is, the more the route will cost. Independent routes and service routes, on the other hand, cost usually 1 to 1 ½ year's net as opposed to 2 years' net (double net)."

    Source: Mr. Route, www.mrrouteinc.com—a very informative Web site

- "These factors will also influence price determination: ownership status of the machines coming with the sale; are they leased, owned, financed; the type of machines that the route consists of and the service schedule that they would need to have the machines produce income (sandwiches need daily servicing … soda/snacks many need weekly servicing); the locale of the machines … inside, outside, 24-hour access, limited access; is the commission paid to accounts above the normal 10% to 15%?"
- "Ratios of investment dollars (borrowed or asset) and estimated length of return"

V - Rules of Thumb

Expert Comments

"'The vending industry and atmosphere is not the same as it was ten, or even five years ago,' said Rosset (Marc Rosset, CEO of Professional Vending Consultants). 'It is a different industry in many ways, and that includes buying and selling.' According to Rosset, there are four things every operator should consider when thinking about selling.

"One: The region your company serves—'Within the last few years there has been so much consolidation in the industry that there are only a handful of vending operations in each state that are looking to buy,' said Rosset.

"Two: Technology investment history—When it comes to investing to make a vending company look more desirable, many operators look towards technology. Rosset says this is a good idea for some, but not all. 'Sometimes it is not appropriate to invest in technology,' he said.

"Three: Life outside of the industry—Rosset recommends that operators think about life outside of vending. 'For many, the vending company has been their life. It's an emotional process and once it's sold, you don't get it back. It's life changing, so really be sure that you're ready to let go.'

"Four: Obtain professional help—Obtaining professional help, such as that of an acquisitions consultant, may also ease the process."

Source: "4 Things to Consider When Selling Your Vending Business," Marc Rosset, contributor www.vendingmarketwatch.com

"The industry is experiencing consolidation as baby boomer owners are retiring. Further, the implementation of technology is narrowing the ranks as less sophisticated owners are leaving the industry."

"It is a relatively easy business to enter...even for a novice. The problem is finding decent to good income generating accounts...ones that will make it worthy of investing in the costly equipment to operate in this type business."

"Oftentimes cost of replication exceeds value based on SDE. Vending is easy for novice to learn. Risk usually is spread out over many customers."

"Risk is low as machines can be relocated to more profitable locations. Replication difficult due to high cost of equipment and marketing to secure good locations. Industry trend will parallel the economy—as the economy improves, companies hire more people increasing the number of breakroom customers for the machines. Opposite is true as well."

"De-industrialization, c-store competition are factors"

"It is a relatively easy business to enter, but its potential for growth is limited (mostly due to increasing product costs versus consumer resistance to higher vending prices)."

"The vending industry (at least in the metro New York area) is dominated by several large companies. However, the market usually views this business as being a 'good part-time,' making it generally a highly desirable business opportunity."

Rules of Thumb - V

Benchmark Data

Statistics (Vending Machine Operators)

Number of Establishments	24,251
Average Profit Margin	3.7%
Revenue per Employee	$116,700
Average Number of Employees	2.7
Average Wages per Employee	$20,225

Products and Services Segmentation

Movies and games	31.9%
Food	30.2%
Soft drinks and cold beverages	21.0%
Other products	10.6%
Office coffee service	6.3%

Major Market Segmentation

Manufacturing sites	27.3%
Schools and colleges	16.0%
Other	15.0%
Offices	14.7%
Hospitals and nursing homes	12.2%
Retail sites	8.0%
Military bases	6.8%

Industry Costs

Profit	3.7%
Wages	17.7%
Purchases	52.1%
Depreciation	3.4%
Marketing	1.0%
Rent & Utilities	5.1%
Other	17.0%

Market Share

Outerwall Inc.	24.6%
Compass Group PLC	12.0%
Aramark Corporation	10.2%

Source: IBISWorld, September 2015

- "Vending has experienced another growth year. The aggregate industry revenue rose 2.4 percent in 2014 to $20.2 billion, exceeding the revenues for the past 5 years."

Operator Sales

Size	Revenue Range	% of 2014 operators	Projected 2014 sales	% of 2014 sales
Small	under $1M	51%	$1.82B	9%
Medium	$1M–$4.9M	23%	$4.24B	21%
Large	$5M–$9.9M	8%	$4.44B	22%
Extra large	$10M+	18%	$9.68B	48%

26th Edition 805

V - Rules of Thumb

Machines by Location

Manufacturing	22%
Offices	22%
Hotels/motels	6.6%
Restaurants, bars, clubs	2.8%
Retail sites	7.8%
Hospitals, nursing homes	8.2%
Universities, colleges	7.4%
Elementary, middle, high schools	6.8%
Military bases	3%
Correctional facilities	3.3%
Other	10.1%

Share of Sales by Category

Candy/snacks/confections	35.9%
OCS	1%
Ice cream	2.9%
Vended food	6.5%
Cold beverages	37.7%
Hot beverages	5.2%
Milk	1.9%
Cigarettes	1.2%
Other	7.7%

Projected Sales by Category (in billions)

Candy/snacks/confections	$7.24B
Ice cream/frozen	$0.59
Sundries/Toiletries	$.20
Milk	$.39
Vend food	$1.30
Hot beverages	$1.05
Cigarettes	$.25
Cold beverages	$7.61
Other	$1.55
OCS	$2.68
Manual foodservice	$1.53
Micro Markets	$1.79"

Source: *Automatic Merchandiser* 2015 State of the Vending Industry Report

- "1. Cost of goods at or below 48%
  2. Labor costs below 20%
  3. Customer commissions below 7%"
- "The higher the 'head count' in that particular location (minimum of 20), the more potential that account should have in generating income. For a small independent vending operator, the rule of thumb in account volume is usually a modest $75–$100 per week in sales...as the vending company gets bigger this desired sale goes up as it costs that vendor more (payroll, etc.) to service each account."
- "One route driver should do about $350k per year gross sales. COGS should be less than 50% of gross sales. Labor cost no more than 10% of gross sales."
- "Route average $8,000 to $10,000 per week"
- "Bulk machines should sell at least $100 per month/per location to be considered viable; soda machines should vend at least four cases per week to be considered viable, and snack machines should produce a minimum of $50 per week/per location to be viable."

Rules of Thumb - **V**

- "Gross sales in vending businesses are directly related to the number of employees per location. A few locations with 100 or more employees normally make for a good business."
- "Profit depends on volume and percentage paid to customer providing space & power."

Industry Profitability

Item	<$1M	$1–$3M	$3–$5M	$5–$10M	>$10M
Sales	100%	100%	100%	100%	100%
Product Cost	50%	49.9%	47.4%	47.5%	44.5%
Gross Margin	50%	50.1%	52.6%	52.5%	55.5%
Labor Costs	22.6%	22.6%	21.8%	23.8%	21.7%
Commissions	5.2%	6.4%	8.0%	7.6%	10.1%
Other Costs	24.7%	19.9%	19.2%	18.1%	18.4%
Op. Profit	(2.5%)	1.2%	3.6%	3.0%	5.3%

Expenses as a percentage of annual sales

Cost of goods	35% to 50%
Payroll/labor Costs	25% to 30%
Occupancy	02% to 10%
Profit (estimated pretax)	15% to 20%

Industry Trend

- "The vending industry has witnessed rapid transformations in the past few decades. From the conventional coin-operated vending machines to today's advanced touch screen unattended coinless vending machines; this industry has successfully implemented dynamism in all the aspects. Vending has always been a profitable customer oriented business approach that offers convenient public food and beverages at a pocket-friendly price—anywhere, anytime.

  "Now, when it comes to identifying the latest growth trends that will hit this industry in 2015, several experts agree on a common point that this industry will evolve substantially on the basis of customer preferences and requirements. The determinants of the growth will undeniably depend upon the wants of the customers including value, quality and convenienc . . . the most striking growth trends that will take this industry to a new level in the coming years: preference for commodities that are healthy, upgraded machines, cashless vending."

  Source: "Latest Growth Trends that will Shape Vending Industry in 2015" by Simon Hopes, http://www.wamda.com/simonhopes2013/2014/12/latest-growth-trends-that-will-shape-vending-industry-in-2015, December 9, 2014

- "A majority, 82.7 percent, of operators report having locations request healthier products be placed in the machines. This is a trend that is not receding.

  "In 2014, 16.1 percent of operators report making an acquisition, compared to 17.7 percent the year before. However, there was a small increase,1.4 percent, to the number of vendors who sold off parts of their businesses.

  "There are five factors really pulling at today's vending operation. Those factors are rising product costs from manufacturers; technology adoption in operators management and at the vending machine; regulations that changed the face of school vending; changing consumer preferences; and, most importantly, taking advantage of new product and service opportunities."

  Source: Automatic Merchandiser 2015 State of the Vending Industry Report

V - Rules of Thumb

- "Both margins and operating results should steadily improve as technology makes the operators more efficient and able to better manage their businesses."
- "Growing in popularity as more people look for secondary sources of income."
- "Disappearing 'middle class'; gross sales more than $300k and less than $2MM; big operators getting bigger and going into smaller locations; there will always be the mom & pops. Micro markets for larger locations. Credit card reader technology coming down in price—will see more machines taking credit cards"
- "Profits are up due to price increases by operators. Replication difficult as purchase price is usually near asset value which does not take into account the marketing and effort to locate the machines."

Seller Financing

- "We see both outside and seller financing. The recent trend has been for an increased willingness of the banking/lending sector to loan into the industry reducing the need for seller financing."
- "Mostly seller financing...but the fact that it is a hard asset business, there are many finance companies that would lend experienced vendors $$ based on the value of their equipment."
- "50% financed for 3–5 years."
- "3 to 5 years. A seller will need to carry for a longer period if the cash flow is low and assets high. Could carry for 5 to 7 years—10 percent interest."

Questions

- "Seller: 1) Get your books and records in order, 2) Make sure you have clean financial statements, 3) Have a professional valuation completed. Buyer: 1) Fully grasp the capital requirements for both new business and the maintenance of existing business, 2) Be prepared to invest in technology."
- "Are machines owned or leased? How old is equipment? Is any equipment supplied with E-Ports? Commissions paid? How geographically far apart are the accounts located? Access to machines? 24/7?"
- "Sellers, clean up your books. Are your machines MDB capable? Geographically, how tight is your route? Do you fill the machines yourself? Are you doing OCS?"
- "Are your machines DEX capable? What controls do you have on the cash in the machines? Is all the money going into the bank? If no, they have to hold paper."
- "Head count at the particular location & permissible servicing time for each account."
- "Do you have contracts?"
- "How many people work at a location? How close are accounts? Are commissions paid to all or some customers? Do you pay commissions to accounts; do machines carry perishable food stuffs?"
- "Will seller finance the deal? Lenders do not want to own a lot of vending machines in case the loan would go bad."

Resources

Websites
- www.vendingmarketwatch.com

Rules of Thumb - **V**

Trade Publications
- Vending Times: www.vendingtimes.com
- Automatic Merchandiser: www.vendingmarketwatch.com/magazine/

Associations
- Amusement & Music Operators Association (AMOA): www.amoa.com
- National Automatic Merchandising Association (NAMA)—good site with lots of educational information: www.vending.org

Veterinary Hospitals

	NAICS 541940	

Rules of Thumb
➢ 65 to 70 percent of annual revenues plus inventory

Veterinary Practices

SIC 0742-01	NAICS 541940	Number of Businesses/Units 51,681

Rules of Thumb
➢ 70 to 75 percent of annual sales includes inventory
➢ 2 to 3 times SDE for small-animal practices includes inventory
➢ 2 to 5.2 times EBIT
➢ 3 to 5 times EBITDA
➢ "Usually 70 to 80 percent of past 12 months' gross revenues [sales] (includes tangible and intangible assets)"

Pricing Tips
- "Pricing is strongly associated with a multiple of EBITDA, after adjustments for non-operating, non-recurring and discretionary expenses. The largest factors affecting the size of the selected multiple are location, local demographics, local competition, curb appeal and growth or decline in earnings.Multiples of gross sales have declined over the past 20 years because of increased costs of labor and supplies. The major factors affecting profitability are COGS, staff wages and rent expense. Poor management of these expenses leads to poor profitability and decreased value."
- "In regard to financial analysis, the gross multiple has declined over the past 30 years because of increased cost for labor, outside services and products. It should not be relied upon for a sales valuation, but can be used as a test for reasonableness of pricing. The most reliable multiples are for SDE (solo doctor practice, only) and EBITDA (solo and multi-doctor practice), both based on a normalized income statement or tax return. Fundamental factors, such as location, curb appeal, practice growth, quality of equipment, average transaction fee and competition are all very important to buyers. Large animal practices will have lower multiples. Rural and remote small animal practices are difficult sales."

V - Rules of Thumb

- "Average sales price is about 70% of annual gross. Average for practices grossing over $750K is a little higher at around 75%, though sales price range is very wide, often 45%–100% of gross. Many factors apply: profit margin, hours worked by owner, support staff ratio, amount and condition of equipment, drug/retail inventory, services provided, type of practice. Small-animal practices tend to sell well. Equine only practices and mobile practice often have much lower value and can be hard to sell. Profit margins are different for services. It is important to understand the service mix of professional services, boarding, grooming, drug wholesaling, retail sales, etc. Practices grossing under $400K are often unprofitable and hard to sell. Income, expenses, and doctor compensation varies with practice type."
- "The price will be skewed downward for mixed-animal and large-animal practices. The absence of a nearby emergency clinic would have a depressing effect on the sale price of a practice. A practice generating a profit lower than a competitive full-time veterinarian salary will be valued downward."
- "Type of vet practice is important. Small-animal (dog/cat) sell well as do ER practices. Large- or mixed-animal practice can be tougher to sell. Mobile practices, and racetrack equine practices have little to no transferable goodwill value. Examine profit centers other than professional services; many practices have boarding/kennels, grooming, drug wholesaling, retail, pet food, or acupuncture/chiropractic components. These have lower profit margins than profession vet med services. Must adjust for this."
- "Sale price ratios very wide above/below average. Common range is 40%–100% of gross."
- "Rural and small offices have lower values"
- "Average is 72% of gross. Wide variance of plus/minus 35%. Higher grossing practices & multi-doctor practices tend to sell for more than solo practice. Practices grossing under $350K difficult to sell (not enough cash flow). Large-animal, mixed, and equine-only practices may have little transferable goodwill."
- "Small-animal practices sell for 1.5 to 3.0 SDE. Other types of veterinary practices sell for varying amounts, and market demand varies."
- "Inventory included in the sale is usually a working level or 30-day supply. Most sales are asset sales and include equipment, furniture, removable fixtures, working levels of consumable inventory, and intangibles (goodwill)."

Expert Comments

"Competition can be quite variable, tending to moderate to heavy in desirable places to live. The risk is low, as evidenced by the ease of lender financing up to 100% of the acquisition price. Trends in historical profit have been variable through the economic downturn. High fee practices have suffered declines in revenues, while moderate fee practices have actually grown during the past few years. Location and facilities are variable. Most practices are located in accessible sites within a community, but some communities, mainly rural locations, have a limited number of potential buyers making sales difficult. Marketability is good because there is currently strong demand for practices by potential buyers. Trends are good because pet-owning clients will take care of their animals, even in difficult economic times. Replication is hard because of the extensive education, training and licensing requirements."

"The practice transition process is so complex that both seller and buyer should utilize consultants who are knowledgeable in veterinary practice sales transactions."

"Competition has been growing because of many new veterinary colleges that have opened in the past 20 years, producing more graduates. Risk is low because lenders have a very low default rate with licensed veterinarians, indicating most acquisitions are successful. Profitability has been difficult to maintain because of the economic downturn, competition from human and online pharmacies, animal shelters providing vaccinations and spays and neuters. Small animal practices are giving up lower cost margin income sources because many procedures and treatments are referred to specialty centers. Facilities are generally good because practice clients expect a clean and presentable clinic/hospital. Urban/suburban locations are the best. Marketability has been good because there are many buyers and few sellers. Many Boomers, who should retire, are holding on to their practices because their revenues have declined, and their real estate holdings and retirement accounts took a big hit during the recession. Industry trends are positive because animal owners will still spend money on their pets and sacrifice discretionary income for other types spending. Ease of replication is very dependent on the buyer's ability to replace the seller's skill level and communication abilities (bedside manner). Most buyers are quite competent in the practice of veterinary medicine, but the change in the practice's culture and perceived quality of care, whether better or worse, can be a challenge to a new owner. Typically, it is best for a new buyer to change the acquired practice's culture and the fees gradually."

"Competition varies by region. The typical small-animal vet needs about 1,500 active clients to make a decent living. Small-animal fixed base practices sell best. Mobile practices usually have little value other than asset value."

"Doctors are able to obtain 100% financing to buy or start up an office. A DVM license is required, but the hospital can be owned by a non-licensed professional in most states. However, offices are not suited for investment/absentee ownership unless the gross is well above $1 million."

"Long-term growth industry. For small-animal practices fairly low risk. Practices in metro areas sell well. Hard to sell in many rural locations. Good financing up to 100% if px cash flows."

"Many practices owned by baby boomers are being transferred to recent graduates; usually with a buyout."

"Competition is keen in most urban areas with significant investment required for facilities, equipment, drugs and supplies needed. Profitability is trending lower due to increased costs of care and decreasing revenues in a challenging economic environment. Facilities vary by location. There are fewer buyers today wanting to purchase veterinary practices and this is due to changes in attitudes regarding business ownership and greater emphasis on quality-of-life issues. Great opportunities exist in many rural areas for those desiring large-animal and mixed-animal practice opportunities."

"Female veterinarians numbered close to 45,000, while male veterinarians numbered just over 43,000. In another trend, more veterinarians are becoming specialists."

V - Rules of Thumb

"Fairly good market for profitable small-animal practices"

"Fewer young veterinarians desire their own business. The costs of veterinary practice are increasing."

"Stable pet care market but more competition for the discretionary dollars used to underwrite the cost of care. Costs to provide services are increasing."

"Risk is low. Loan default rates very low. Can get up to 100% financing. Cost of entry for vet practice is higher than for human medical practice."

"Some states now allow non-vets to own vet practices, providing that the licensed vet runs the medical practice."

Benchmark Data

Statistics (Veterinary Services)

Number of Establishments	51,681
Average Profit Margin	10.8%
Revenue per Employee	$98,200
Average Number of Employees	6.8
Average Wages per Employee	$34,655

Products and Services Segmentation

Surgical procedures	34.3%
Other	28.1%
Pet food	18.6%
Routine visits	15.6%
Pet vitamins	3.4%

Major Market Segmentation

Cats and dogs	65.0%
Production animals	21.0%
Exotic animals	7.0%
Birds	4.6%
Horses	2.4%

Industry Costs

Profit	10.8%
Wages	35.1%
Purchases	22.0%
Depreciation	1.1%
Marketing	1.3%
Rent & Utilities	8.1%
Other	21.6%

Market Share

VCA Antech Inc.	5.5%

Source: IBISWorld, September 2015

- "Support staff costs with payroll taxes, Workers Comp and employee benefits under 25% of gross sales. Productivity of support staff between $150,000 to $200,000 each, annually. Employed veterinarians being paid between 20% and

Rules of Thumb - V

23% of actual W-2 wages."
- "The expenses above are the most common benchmarks used for expenses. Revenues per full-time veterinarian= $525,000 to $600,000. Revenues per full-time employee (non-veterinarian)=$130,000 to $170,000 (median about $150,000). Ancillary income (grooming, boarding, diet food and retail sales) of 14% to 16% of revenues is desirable because higher ancillary income tends to increase the productivity of the doctors."
- "Average annual gross income per DVM is about $500K, of which about $450K is professional services (as opposed to retail, prescription refills, grooming, etc). Average transaction charge is $114. Income per square foot is $338. Should have about 4 support staff for every full-time veterinarian."
- "Major expenses: Rent: 6%–12% depending on city and area. Labor (excluding doctors): 15%–22%. Medical supplies/costs of goods: 20%. Profit (before doctor salaries): 20%–30%. Profit after doctor salaries: 10% (provided office has sufficient gross revenue)."
- "Good Benchmark Data from AVMA and AAHA. Can be purchased for $100–$200. Staff, drugs, and rent expense are 3 biggest expenses."
- "Profit after accounting for a reasonable return on professional labor or reasonable salary for the doctor's efforts should be 10%–20%."
- "Practice should gross about $400K–$545K per FTE DVM."
- "Today, the practice is devoted 100 percent to small animals, mostly dogs and cats, Tucker [Robert Tucker, veterinarian, co-owner of Concord Animal Hospital, Concord, MA] said. 'Many of the families we see have several pets.' Some 2,500 dogs and 2,500 cats are treated every year, he said.
- "Because many clients don't have animal health insurance, 'we try to charge what's reasonable,' he said, pointing out that fees range from less than $50 for a routine office visit to more than $1,000 for a major procedure."
- "3.4 employees per FTE veterinarian"
- "Vet wages should be approximately 23% of gross vet professional fees generated."

Expenses as a percentage of annual sales

Cost of goods	15% to 20%
Payroll/labor Costs	20% to 30%
Occupancy	05% to 10%
Profit (estimated pretax)	20% to 30%

Industry Trend
- "For practice acquisitions, there may be a change in supply and demand. Boomers, who have been holding on to their practices, may be forced to sell because of age and health reasons. As the economy rebounds, the aging Boomers may feel more comfortable retiring because their real estate holdings and investment accounts have returned to pre-recession levels. Many veterinary practice analysts expect far more practices to become available in the coming years."
- "Will continue to grow"
- "The trend will continue toward larger practices with more upscale facilities."
- "Positive. Some slowdown with economy but now holding their own"
- "Boomers selling, younger vets seem to prefer working for another owner rather than taking on the burden of debt to start or buy a practice."
- "Good stable revenue. Smaller offices exhibit downward pressure on values."
- "An increase in consumer demand for better access, convenience, technology, diagnosis, and feedback will continue to shape veterinary practices."

V - Rules of Thumb

Seller Financing
- "Many lenders, both conventional and SBA, are ready to lend 100% of the acquisition price. Seller financing tends to be minimal."
- "For qualified buyers, greater than 90% of practices sold are completed with outside financing. Sellers typically receive all cash or contribute minimally (<20%) to buyer financing."
- "Specialty lenders off 100% financing. Sellers may carry up to 20% usually for 10 yrs. Real estate portion may be 25 years"
- "Financing can be 100% (no down payment) with 7- to 10-year notes if credit is good."
- 10 years

Questions
- "Practice type; hours worked; gross; support staff ratio; how are after hours emergencies handled?"
- "Gross hours worked, type of patients seen, and percentage mix; ancillary profit centers support staff info; number active clients in last 2 years"
- "What is the turnover rate, large vs. small animal, surgery vs. treatment, retail sales, inventory size, payroll costs?"
- "Ask what medical services they do not provide that could be added."
- "Review cash flow. Check conditional use permits. Fees schedule and list of procedures."
- "What percentages of revenues are from: vaccines, surgery, boarding, retail sales and grooming?"
- "Are they willing to sign a covenant not to compete? Can they work in the practice after the sale? How was price arrived at and justified? What is the value of the real estate and how was the price arrived at? What is being sold for the asked price? How many hours per week are worked by the owner/doctor? How are emergencies calls covered?"
- "At least 5 years of financial statements and tax returns, current detailed depreciation schedule, practice management and production reports, and payroll and staffing information to begin analysis. Then follow up information and details. Site visit is extremely informative!"
- "# hours worked/week; ancillary profit centers (grooming, boarding); non-Western therapy procedures (i.e., acupuncture, chiropractic, holistic); type of practice (small, mixed, large, equine, ER, referral, mobile)?"
- "Be sure to understand how the price was determined and be sure cash flows allow for a reasonable salary after debt. Be sure the seller agrees to a covenant not to compete where legal."
- "Standard recasting info for sellers. Types of surgery performed? 1 or 3 vaccination schedule? Relationship with local shelters/humane societies? How are emergencies handled?"

Resources

Websites
- Vet Quest Classifieds : www.vetquest.com
- Veterinary Information Network: www.vin.com
- VetPartners: www.vetpartners.org

Rules of Thumb - **V**

Trade Publications
- Veterinary Practice News: www.veterinarypracticenews.com/
- Veterinary Economics: www.veterinarynews.dvm360.com/
- DVM360: www.dvm360.com

Associations
- American Veterinary Medical Association: www.avma.org
- American Animal Hospital Association: www.aahanet.org

Video Stores

SIC 7841-02	NAICS 532230	Number of Businesses/Units 7,796

Rules of Thumb

➢ "Most buyers want to recover their investment within 24 months, so 2 times SDE is a safe bet, including inventory."

➢ "It used to be one year's SDE plus the fair market value of the tapes and games, but inventory drops in value too dramatically after the 'new release' prime period (90 days) has passed."

➢ "1 to 2 times SDE to a working owner plus fair market value for videos, games & DVDs"

➢ .65 to 1.0 annual revenues plus inventory

Pricing Tips

- "The inventory price of the videos and games drops drastically from its original retail. Unit prices can be as low as $5.00 or less."
- "If the current owner can computer-generate a video rental report that shows you how many times each video in inventory has been rented and the income associated with it, you will see how much 'dead inventory' could be replaced to increase revenues. Special- interest videos and games like Nintendo and PlayStation 2, etc. would be good profit generators."

Expert Comments

"The industry has changed with the switch to games."

Benchmark Data

Statistics (DVD, Game & Video Rental)

Number of Establishments	7,796
Average Profit Margin	2.6%
Revenue per Employee	$78,900
Average Number of Employees	5.0
Average Wages per Employee	$14,717

Products and Services Segmentation

DVD and video tape rental	68.4%
DVD, video tape and game sales	18.6%
Other merchandise sales	6.8%
Game rental	6.2%

26th Edition

V - Rules of Thumb

Industry Costs

Profit	2.6%
Wages	18.5%
Purchases	34.6%
Depreciation	8.0%
Marketing	5.4%
Rent & Utilities	11.9%
Other	19.0%

Source: IBISWorld, November 2014

- "Stores should have well-stocked concession areas including popcorn, candy, soft drinks. They should be close to cash registers."

Expenses as a percentage of annual sales

Cost of goods	33%
Payroll/labor Costs	27%
Occupancy	15%
Profit (estimated pretax)	25%

Industry Trend

- "Over 70% of video consumption takes place on the television. Younger viewers are selecting other screens as their primary entertainment platforms. The laptop is ranked ahead of the television for those ages 18–34. Household penetration of set-top and portable streaming devices reached 25% at the end of 2014. 51% of U.S. households own a dedicated game console. 53% of video gamers say they prefer to buy the physical game over the digital version."

  Source: "EMA's 2015 D2 Report: Discs and Digital—The Business of Home Entertainment Retailing"

- "Almost half of all U.S. households subscribe to Amazon Prime, Hulu Plus, Netflix or a combination of these services. UltraViolet has over 21 million users with 110 million movies and TV shows in their libraries."

  Source: http://entmerch.org/industry/facts-home-video-mkt.html

Seller Financing

- 12 to 24 months
- 3 years

Resources

Associations

- Entertainment Merchants Association: www.entmerch.org/

Visa/Passport Companies

Rules of Thumb

➢ 3 to 5 times EBITDA

➢ 3 times EBITDA for small to midsized operations, 4.5 times EBITDA for larger ones.

Pricing Tips
- "Immigration is rising."
- "Total number of applications processed year over year (up or down?)"
- "Due to new U.S. Government requirements, this industry multiple has increased."

Expert Comments
"This industry deals as expeditors of government travel documents."

Questions
- "How do they execute quick turnaround? How long does it take them to fulfill applications?"

Waste Collection (See also Garbage/Trash Collection)

NAICS 56211	Number of Businesses/Units 11,707

Rules of Thumb
- ➢ 95 percent of annual sales
- ➢ 3 times SDE
- ➢ 5 times EBIT
- ➢ 4 times EBITDA

Pricing Tips
- "For a company with predictable repeat earnings with service contracts, eleven times the last twelve months' revenue. For a company involved in the construction industry, there may be a holdback of an amount multiple to adjust for homebuilder risk. The most valued are ongoing commercial accounts, which might have an adjustment or an earnout up or down. The best buyers are the 'big boys' in waste management."

Expert Comments
"This has been a very difficult business dominated by a few large companies."

Benchmark Data

Statistics (Waste Collection Services)
Number of Establishments	11,707
Average Profit Margin	8.8%
Revenue per Employee	$230,700
Average Number of Employees	17.8
Average Wages per Employee	$46,420

W - Rules of Thumb

Products and Services Segmentation

Residential waste collection services	35.3%
Nonresidential waste collection services	25.2%
Other	18.3%
Transfer and storage facility services	8.2%
Hazardous waste collection services	5.2%
Recyclable material collection services	4.3%
Construction and demolition site waste collection services	3.5%

Major Market Segmentation

Individuals and households	38.7%
Retail and office businesses	29.6%
Industrial companies	15.4%
Government and not-for-profit organizations	10.1%
Construction and demolition companies	6.2%

Industry Costs

Profit	8.8%
Wages	20.4%
Purchases	21.9%
Depreciation	7.4%
Marketing	1.0%
Rent & Utilities	7.2%
Other	33.3%

Market Share

Waste Management Inc.	27.9%
Republic Services Inc.	19.3%

Source: IBISWorld, June 2015

Expenses as a percentage of annual sales

Cost of goods	20%
Payroll/labor Costs	50%
Occupancy	05%
Profit (estimated pretax)	25%

Industry Trend

- "The top two companies, Waste Management and Republic Services accounted for 39 percent of total industry revenue. All of the publicly traded companies together comprised 61 percent of total revenues. All told, the private sector represents 78 percent of the industry while the municipal sector controls the remaining 22 percent. This is a sharp contrast to 1992 when municipalities controlled 35 percent of industry revenue.

  "Recent mergers, including that of Veolia's U.S. waste business by Advanced Disposal, promise a reshaped industry much further along its path of privatization. The companies understand that one way to deal with turbulent economic times amidst rising fuel, labor and equipment costs is to streamline operations and vertically integrate their markets.

  "Rising costs have focused company managers on disciplined price increases especially now that the industry is more consolidated, more attentive to return on invested capital, more rational about valuing existing landfill capacity and mindful of lessons in the past when pricing was sacrificed."

  Source: "New Report Details the $55 Billion U.S. Waste Industry,"
  http://www.wastebusinessjournal.com/overview.htm

Rules of Thumb - **W**

- "Growing by leaps with no bounds"

Resources
Websites
- Waste 360: www.waste360.com

Water Companies

	NAICS 22131	Number of Businesses/Units 53,000

Rules of Thumb
➢ "The market price varies greatly, between $75 and $150 per metered customer. The normal meter hookup charge is approximately $100. These are not saleable unless they have a minimum of 250 customers with growth potential."

Web-Based Companies

Rules of Thumb
➢ "Right now it's 2 times SDE maximum or asset liquidation value. ISP's are being sold for 3–6 times monthly gross sales."

Pricing Tips
- "It depends on if there is any profit. If there is, about 2 times SDE."

Seller Financing
- "Very short—2 to 4 years"

Weight Loss Services/Centers

SIC 7299-34	NAICS 812191	Number of Businesses/Units 136,712

Rules of Thumb
➢ 50 to 55 percent of annual sales

Benchmark Data

Statistics (Weight Loss Services)
Number of Establishments	136,712
Average Profit Margin	14.8%
Revenue per Employee	$32,500
Average Number of Employees	1.5
Average Wages per Employee	$9,898

Products and Services Segmentation
Meeting fees	48.5%
Internet fees	32.4%
In meeting product sales	13.2%
Other	5.9%

26th Edition

W - Rules of Thumb

Industry Costs

Profit	14.8%
Wages	30.5%
Purchases	30.0%
Depreciation	2.6%
Marketing	1.9%
Rent & Utilities	12.8%
Other	7.4%

Market Share

Weight Watchers International Inc.	11.8%
Nutrisystem Inc.	7.1%

Source: IBISWorld, July 2015

Industry Trend

- "To grasp the plight of the diet industry these days, consider these two statistics: 77% of Americans are actively trying to eat healthier, according to a poll conducted this month for *Fortune* by SurveyMonkey—but only 19% say they're on a diet.

  "It's not that Americans have slimmed down; more than a third of U.S. adults are still considered obese. It's the fact that more and more people are focused on health first—and calories second. The percentage of women reporting they are on a diet has dropped 13 points over the past two decades, according to research firm NPD Group.

  "The result: crimped revenues for companies in the business of helping people lose weight. Market leader Weight Watchers has reported sales declines for two consecutive years and is projecting a weak 2015. Revenues have also shriveled at Jenny Craig and meal provider Medifast. Another meal provider, Nutrisystem, whose revenues were soaring a few years ago, has seen sales tumble 21% compared to four years ago."

  Source: "Lean times for the diet industry" by John Kell, fortune.com, 5/22/15

			Franchise
Wienerschnitzel (See also Franchises)			
Approx. Total Investment			$350,000 to $500,000
Estimated Annual Sales/Unit			$650,000
	NAICS 722513	Number of Businesses/Units	325

Rules of Thumb

> ➢ 30 to 35 percent of annual sales plus inventory

Wild Bird Shops		
	NAICS 453910	

Rules of Thumb

> ➢ 30 percent of annual sales plus inventory

Wild Birds Unlimited (See also Franchises) — Franchise

Approx. Total Investment		$96,997 to $165,295
	NAICS 453910	Number of Businesses/Units 288

Rules of Thumb
➤ 30 to 35 percent of annual sales plus inventory

Resources

Websites
- www.wbu.com

Wind Farms (Energy)

	NAICS 333611	Number of Businesses/Units 300

Rules of Thumb
➤ 10 times EBITDA

Pricing Tips
- "Use a cap rate, similar to pricing commercial real estate."

Expert Comments
"This industry is, for a number of reasons, going to grow dramatically over the next decade. The economic model is very similar to that of commercial real estate—high upfront capital costs followed by extremely consistent cash flows, with upside appreciation potential. The smart money will get in early and ride the wave."

Benchmark Data
- "Revenue per kilowatt hour, capacity factor, PPA rate"

Industry Trend
- "Low-cost, zero-emission wind energy will become even more valuable as states and utilities develop plans to cost-effectively reduce carbon pollution to comply with EPA's Clean Power Plan, according to new economic analysis from the Energy Information Administration (EIA), a nonpartisan branch of the Department of Energy (DOE). EIA's analysis modeled a range of options for complying with EPA's proposed rule across a variety of scenarios, and wind energy consistently emerged as the lowest cost option for reducing emissions. "EIA's analysis saw a large role for wind across more than a dozen different scenarios. As shown below, EIA saw a large amount of wind deployment in all scenarios it examined, even with low gas prices, more use of energy efficiency, and greater use of nuclear energy. As a result, states and utilities should look to wind energy as a 'no-regrets' option that will be valuable under any scenario for unexpected market changes, creating further impetus for states and grid

W - Rules of Thumb

operators to begin planning now for infrastructure to connect cost-effective wind."

<small>Source: "EIA finds wind energy will have largest role in cost-effectively meeting Clean Power Plan" by Michael Goggin, http://www.aweablog.org/eia-finds-wind-energy-will-have-largest-role-in-cost-effectively-meeting-clean-power-plan/ May 27, 2015</small>

- "Driven by record low costs and high demand from power purchasers, the U.S. wind industry was at its busiest ever in the third quarter while completing the record number of wind projects that were under construction at the start of the quarter.

"So far, 19 wind projects have been completed in America this year, with as much wind generating capacity as in all of 2013, according to Third Quarter results released today. The American Wind Energy Association expects a strong finish to the year and stepped-up installations in 2015, CEO Tom Kiernan said Monday at the industry's annual gathering for Wall Street investors at the Roosevelt Hotel in New York. . . America as of Sept. 30 had 46,400 wind turbines operating, with a total generating capacity of 62,300 MW."

<small>Source: "Record low costs drive opportunities in U.S. wind energy" http://www.awea.org/MediaCenter/pressrelease.aspx?ItemNumber=6904 October 20, 2014</small>

Resources

Trade Publications
- Windpower Monthly: www.windpowermonthly.com

Associations
- American Wind Energy Association: www.awea.org/

Window Cleaning

| | NAICS 561720 | |

Rules of Thumb
➢ 60 percent of annual sales

Resources

Associations
- International Window Cleaning Association—a site with a lot of valuable information: www.iwca.org

Window Treatment/Draperies

| | NAICS 442291 | |

Rules of Thumb
➢ 35 to 40 percent of annual sales plus inventory

Resources

Trade Publications
- Draperies and Window Coverings: www.dwconline.com

Rules of Thumb - W

	Franchise
Wine Kitz (Canada) (See also Franchises)	
Approx. Total Investment	$106,000 to $135,000 (See Rule of Thumb)
NAICS 312130	Number of Businesses/Units 95

Rules of Thumb

> 55 percent of annual sales plus inventory
> Note: The investment above is for a retail store with an in-store winery. The investment for a retail only is approximately $73,000 to $100,000.

Wineries	
SIC 2084-01	NAICS 312130	Number of Businesses/Units 6,481

Rules of Thumb

> 25 percent of annual sales (does include real estate)
> 10 times SDE
> 60 times EBIT (does include real estate)
> 89 times EBITDA (does include real estate)

Expert Comments

"Wineries take 1–2 years to sell if they are priced well."

Benchmark Data

Statistics (Wineries)
Number of Establishments	6,481
Average Profit Margin	7.6%
Revenue per Employee	$403,600
Average Number of Employees	7.5
Average Wages per Employee	$49,546

Products and Services Segmentation
Chardonnay	27.0%
Cabernet Sauvignon	20.0%
Zinfandel, Riesling and other blends	17.0%
Merlot	11.0%
Pinot Grigio	11.0%
Pinot Noir	8.0%
Sauvignon Blanc	6.0%

Industry Costs
Profit	7.6%
Wages	12.2%
Purchases	42.7%
Depreciation	5.1%
Marketing	4.2%
Rent & Utilities	5.5%
Other	22.7%

W - Rules of Thumb

Market Share

E. & J. Gallo Winery	20.5%
Constellation Brands Inc.	11.9%
The Wine Group, Inc.	7.8%

Source: IBISWorld, August 2015

- "California Wine Profile 2013
    - ✓ America's top wine producer—California makes 90% of all U.S. wine and is the world's 4th leading wine producer after France, Italy and Spain.
    - ✓ 4,100 bonded wineries—up 119% from 1,870 wineries in 2003; nearly all family owned businesses.
    - ✓ 214.6 million cases—California wine sales volume in the U.S. market, with shipments growing 22% since 2003's 175.4 million cases.
    - ✓ $23.1 billion retail value—estimated retail value of California wine sales in the U.S.
    - ✓ 57% share of U.S. market by volume—three of every five bottles sold in the U.S. is a California wine.
    - ✓ $1.55 billion in export revenue—U. S. wine exports, 90% from California, reached a record high, growing 16.4% in value from 2012; up 150% from $621 million in 2003."

Source: http://www.discovercaliforniawines.com/media-trade/statistics/

Expenses as a percentage of annual sales

Cost of goods	59%
Payroll/labor Costs	20%
Occupancy	20%
Profit (estimated pretax)	10%

Industry Trend

- "Economist says wages and lack of housing will force Napa wineries and vineyards to get competitive."
    Source: "Labor Trends May Challenge Wine Industry by Paul Franson," www.winesandvines.com
- "Greater divide between small family business and global corporations is increasing."

Questions

- "Will you [the seller] stay on as a consultant?"

Resources

Websites
- California Wineland: www.winesandvines.com

Trade Publications
- Wine Business Monthly: www.winebusiness.com

Associations
- Family Winemakers of California: www.familywinemakers.org
- American Society for Enology and Viticulture: www.asev.org

Rules of Thumb - W

	Franchise
Wingstop Restaurants (See also Franchises)	
Approx. Total Investment	$242,787 to $569,528
Estimated Annual Sales/Unit	$1,480,000
NAICS 722513	Number of Businesses/Units 550
Rules of Thumb	
➢ 30 to 35 percent of annual sales plus inventory	

Resources

Websites
- www.wingstop.com

Wireless Communications		
(Carriers, dealers & resellers of cellular, PCs, & paging)		
SIC 5999-02	NAICS 517210	Number of Businesses/Units 14,000
Rules of Thumb		
➢ 30 percent of annual gross sales		
➢ 2 to 3 times SDE plus inventory		
➢ 2.5 to 5 times EBITDA includes inventory		
➢ $50 to $130 per pop for operational market—less if naked license		

Pricing Tips
- "It is important to consider revenue per customer."
- "Strong employee technical base/tenure desirable along with non-competes for key personnel"
- "Trend upward in volume and downward in service income is not abnormal"
- "Subscribers, physical plant capacity, client retention and gross margins"
- "Calculating furniture, fixtures and equipment value along with any real estate involved"

Expert Comments

"Multi-store operators with strong sales and net earnings are in demand."

"Difficult to replicate due to technical nature of business as well as myriad supplier relationships required"

"Expanding into synergistic product lines is becoming the norm."

"This is a fairly mature market, however, the advent of the Internet and Voice over Internet Protocol are changing the landscape of the wired telecommunications market. While core services (long distance and data) have become a commodity, there is plenty of opportunity to differentiate with platform applications and custom architecture."

W - Rules of Thumb

Benchmark Data
- "3x SDE is a good place to begin. Inventory/chargebacks and deactivations can be an issue if not clearly discussed."
- "35%–40% percent gross profit"
- "COGS 25%, payroll 20%, profit 28%, occupancy cost 18%"
- "Sales per employee"
- "Number of years owner has operated the business, along with how long they will stay and train. Are the employees staying or leaving? Location of the business and any customer lists they may have are all similar factors."

Expenses as a percentage of annual sales
Cost of goods	60%
Payroll/labor Costs	20%
Occupancy	05% to 10%
Profit (estimated pretax)	10%

Industry Trend
- "Trend toward commodity-based marketing and addition of synergistic product lines in an effort to offset eroding equipment profits"
- "There will be large consolidations of operators, and wireless penetration in U.S. will continue to increase. More use of data."
- "Increasing competition, need for international services, data and cell services will see dramatic increases."
- "Continued growth in wireless communications and launch of new products increases."

Seller Financing
- 1–2 years
- "Depends on size and complexity of transaction."

Questions
- "Seller Financing? Lease issues? Any problems with the carrier transferring the business to a buyer and what are those exact requirements? Timing."
- "Ask if market is built out (to what percentage of population and geography) and if it is operational (how long)."
- "Number of activations per month currently doing? How many deactivations per month? What is advertising budget? How long at this location? Are employees on commission or salary or both? Number of locations?"
- "Pricing strategy and debt owed"
- "How will inventory be paid for and when? Period of time post-close that seller will be responsible for chargebacks and de-activations for pre-sale customers."

Resources

Trade Publications
- Wireless Dealer Magazine: www.wirelessdealermag.com
- Wireless Week: www.wirelessweek.com
- RCR Wireless News: www.rcrwireless.com

Rules of Thumb - W

Franchise
Wireless Toyz (See also Cellular Telephone Stores, Franchises)

Approx. Total Investment	$219,000 to $648,000
Estimated Annual Sales/Unit	$650,000
NAICS 443142	Number of Businesses/Units 187

Rules of Thumb
> 45 to 50 percent of annual sales plus inventory

Resources
Websites
- www.wirelesstoyz.com

Women's Clothing

SIC 5621-01	NAICS 448120	Number of Businesses/Units 60,322

Rules of Thumb
> 20 percent of annual sales plus inventory

> 2 times monthly sales plus inventory

Benchmark Data

Statistics (Women's Clothing Stores)
Number of Establishments	60,322
Average Profit Margin	4.9%
Revenue per Employee	$111,700
Average Number of Employees	7.4
Average Wages per Employee	$15,447

Products and Services Segmentation
T-shirts, knit and woven shirts, blouses and sweaters	32.0%
Pants, jeans, shorts and skirts	24.0%
Dresses	18.0%
Coats, jackets and suits	17.0%
Sports apparel (including swimwear and sweatshirts)	6.0%
Other apparel (including fur and custom garments)	3.0%

Industry Costs
Profit	4.9%
Wages	13.8%
Purchases	35.0%
Depreciation	1.1%
Marketing	20.0%
Rent & Utilities	11.1%
Other	14.1%

Y - Rules of Thumb

Market Share
Ascena Retail Group Inc. 6.8%
Chico's FAS Inc. 5.5%

Source: IBISWorld, October 2015

	Franchise
World Wide Express (See also Delivery Services, Franchises)	
Approx. Total Investment	$25,000 to $150,000
NAICS 561431	

Rules of Thumb
➢ 50 to 55 percent of annual sales plus inventory

Resources

Websites
- www.wwex.com

	Franchise
Your Office USA (See also Franchises)	
Approx. Total Investment	$200,000 to $500,000+
NAICS 531120	Number of Businesses/Units 7

Rules of Thumb
➢ 60 percent of annual sales plus inventory

Resources

Websites
- www.youroffice.com

		Franchise
You've Got Maids (See also Franchises, Janitorial Services, Molly Maid, etc.)		
Approx. Total Investment		$45,000 to $123,000
SIC 7349-23	NAICS 561720	Number of Businesses/Units 40

Rules of Thumb
➢ 60 percent of annual sales plus inventory

Resources

Websites
- You 've Got Maids: www.youvegotmaids.com

Rules of Thumb - Z

	Franchise
Ziebart International (**Auto Services**) (See also Franchises)	
Approx. Total Investment	$75,000 to $250,000
NAICS 8111	Number of Businesses/Units 400

Rules of Thumb
➢ 42 percent of annual sales plus inventory

Resources

Websites
- www.ziebart.com

	Franchise
Zoo Health Club (See also Fitness Centers, Franchises)	
Approx. Total Investment	$73,899 to $278,499 (equipment purchased)
	$48,399 to $189,249 (equipment leased)
NAICS 713940	Number of Businesses/Units 25

Rules of Thumb
➢ 20 percent of annual sales

Resources

Websites
- www.zoogym.com